READINGS IN WESTERN
RELIGIOUS THOUGHT

READINGS IN WESTERN RELIGIOUS THOUGHT

THE ANCIENT WORLD

EDITED BY
PATRICK V. REID

PAULIST PRESS
New York/Mahwah

Library of Congress Cataloging-in-Publication Data

Reid, Patrick, 1944–
    Readings in Western religious thought.

    Includes bibliographies.
    1. Mediterranean Region—Religion. 2. Judaism—
History—To 70 A.D. 3. Bible—Text-books. 4. Church
history—Primitive and early church, ca. 30-600.
I. Title.
BL687.R45   1986   291.8   86-25152
ISBN 0-8091-2850-0 (pbk.)

Published by Paulist Press
997 Macarthur Boulevard
Mahwah, New Jersey 07430

Printed and bound in the United States of America

CONTENTS

v

Acknowledgements are due to the following for permission to reproduce copyright translations.

The Bible text used in this anthology is from the *Revised Standard Version Bible* copyrighted 1946, 1952, © 1971, 1973 by the Division of Christian Education of the National Council of Churches of Christ in the U.S.A., and used by permission.

Hackett Publishing Company, Inc. from *The Essential Plotinus,* translated by Elmer O'Brien, S.J., excerpts from the *Enneads.* Copyright, 1964, by Elmer O'Brien, S.J.

Harvard University Press from *The Loeb Classical Library:* Cicero: *De Legibus,* translated by Clinton Walker Keyes in *Cicero: De Republica, De Legibus,* Vol XVI. Copyright, 1928, by Harvard University Press.

Macmillan Publishing Company from *Ancient Roman Religion* translated by Frederick C. Grant, "The Dream of Scipio." Copyright © 1957 by Macmillan Publishing Company.

Macmillan Publishing Company from *Hellenistic Religions: The Age of Syncretism* translated by Frederick C. Grant, "On Isis and Osiris," "The Praises of Isis," "Isis Restores Lucius," "Hymn of Zeus," "Epicurus on Human Happiness and the Gods." Copyright 1953 by Macmillan Publishing Company, copyright renewed 1981.

W.W. Norton and Company from *Homer/The Odyssey* translated by Albert Cook. Copyright, 1967, by Albert Cook.

Princeton University Press from James B. Pritchard, ed., *Ancient Near Eastern Texts: Relating to the Old Testament,* 3rd edn. with Supplement: E.A. Speiser, *The Creation Epic; The Gilgamesh Epic; The Descent of Ishtar to the Nether World;* T. Meeks, *The Code of Hammurabi;* John A. Wilson, *The Theology of Memphis; The Protestation of Guiltlessness; The Instruction for Meri-Ka-Re; The Hymn to the Aton.* Copyright © 1969 by Princeton University Press.

Scholars Press from *Sources for the Study of Greek Religion* translated by David G. Rice and John E. Stambaugh, *Bacchae, The Homeric Hymn to Demeter.* Copyright © 1979 by the Society of Biblical Literature.

The University of Chicago Press from *The Iliad of Homer* translated by Richmond Lattimore. Copyright, 1951, by the University of Chicago.

The University of Michigan Press from *Hesiod: The Works and Days, Theogony, The Shield of Herakles* translated by Richmond Lattimore, Copyright, 1965, University of Michigan Press.

PREFACE

This book has been prepared with the conviction that the best introduction for the college student to the Western religious heritage is to read the primary texts which have shaped the Western religious consciousness. This volume provides selections from the primary religious writings of the ancient Western world from the beginnings of civilization in Mesopotamia and Egypt (c. 3000 B.C.E.) to the collapse of the Roman Empire (c. 450 C.E.). The text may be used in an interdisciplinary program in Western Civilization or in a course in the history of Western religious thought. Because the Judaeo-Christian tradition has had the greatest impact on the religious consciousness of the West, this book should be used in conjunction with the Hebrew Scriptures and the Christian New Testament in one of the critical modern translations. For purposes of completeness and comparison with other ancient cultures, I have provided introductions and recommended readings for the biblical material.

This volume includes sections on ancient Near Eastern religion, ancient and classical Greek religion, Hellenistic and Roman religion, the New Testament and the early Christian fathers and councils. In the selection of texts I have tried to choose those documents which best reflect the basic religious values of the culture or movement and their adaptation during the course of history. I have attempted to make the selections long enough to give the flavor of the work, and, at the same time, varied enough to give the instructor an opportunity to introduce the student to a wide variety of religious texts. This volume includes a general introduction to each section and introductions to the individual works within the section. A minimal bibliography is provided as part of the introductory sections.

I am pleased to acknowledge the help I have received in preparing this collection: Providence College for granting me a half-year sabbatical to work on this volume, the Development of Western Civilization faculty at Providence College for their inspiration and shared insights in eight years of teaching in the program, the typing of preliminary drafts by Sylvia White, secretary of Development of Western Civilization, the copying of various stages of the manuscript by Mary Garvey and her student assistants in the Religious Studies Department. A special debt of thanks is owed to my colleague Edward McCrorie who spent countless hours in proofreading the manuscript, editorial sugges-

1

tions, and typing. Portions of Dr. McCrorie's fine poetic translation of Virgil's *Aeneid* appear in this volume for the first time. He is Professor of English at Providence College and author of *After Cremation,* a book of poems (Thorp Springs Press, Berkeley, Calif., 1975). He has published poems and reviews in a variety of periodicals and his second book of poems, *Needle Man,* is now looking for a publisher.

1

ANCIENT NEAR EASTERN RELIGIONS: MESOPOTAMIA AND EGYPT

Although the Near East is not part of the area in which Western civilization developed, early Mesopotamian and Egyptian civilizations had a profound impact on subsequent cultural and religious development in the Western Mediterranean world. Long before the ancient Israelite, Greek and Roman civilizations emerged, these Near Eastern civilizations had produced flourishing cultures with distinct social and political organizations, writing systems, architectural and artistic styles, and religious beliefs—all of which were to influence cultural development in the West. Our selections in this section will illustrate the characteristic religious beliefs of these two cultures by sampling their mythologies, epic traditions, and behavioral codes. For a fine anthology of ancient Near Eastern religious thought the reader should consult James B. Pritchard (ed.), **Ancient Near Eastern Texts** (Princeton: Princeton University Press, 1969). An excellent discussion of the mythopoeic thought of the ancient Near East can be found in Henri Frankfort and others, **Before Philosophy** (Chicago: The University of Chicago Press, 1966).

MESOPOTAMIA

When recorded history began in Mesopotamia (c. 3000 B.C.E.), the Tigris-Euphrates valley was inhabited by two distinct peoples: the Sumerians, a non-Semitic people, living in the south, and the Akkadians, Semites who were settled in the north. Mesopotamia in the early third millennium B.C.E. had a series of autonomous walled city-states, ruled by a king or priest-king and a council of elders. Each city had its patron deity and often a multi-storied mudbrick temple or *ziggurat*. The city-state was regarded as the property of the god or goddess and the king was the steward of the estate. Thus Mesopotamian civilization was from the beginning permeated by religion; the whole of life found its meaning in the service of the gods who dwelt in the heavens and in maintaining order and unity by absolute obedience to the king in whom the will of heaven had become concentrated and embodied.

The creativity of the Mesopotamians, especially the Sumerians, was truly astounding. They developed the first writing system, a cuneiform script inscribed on clay tablets

3

and stone monuments, and had monumental architecture, sculpture, relief art, a rich literature, a body of scientific knowledge, and public law codes.

Our sources for Mesopotamian religious thought are the archaeological discoveries in the region over the past century and a half. These come from various sites, the most important of which is the ancient city of Nineveh which contained the library of the seventh century Assyrian king Ashurbanipal. We now have a great variety of ancient Mesopotamian religious texts: mythologies, epics, incantations, rituals, hymns, prayers, as well as law codes, proverbs, and other wisdom compositions.

THE ENUMA ELISH

Our first selection is the Babylonian myth of creation which is written in Akkadian and is entitled **Enuma Elish,** "When on high," from the opening words of the poem. Although the tablets utilized in this translation only go back to the first millennium B.C.E., scholars assign the myth to the Old Babylonian period, the early part of the second millennium B.C.E.

A myth, in the sense in which it will be used in this book, is an explanation for profound religious, psychological, cosmological and even political realities in the form of a story that features gods and goddesses who represent natural or psychological forces which deeply influence humanity but which cannot be controlled. The **Enuma Elish** fulfills these functions. It accounts for various deities worshiped in Mesopotamia by relating their births in successive generations. This theogony, or generation of the gods, contains within itself the memory of an evolution of gods from the primordial parents, the chaotic waters, to the latter gods of the Mesopotamian religious tradition. The myth is cosmological in that it gives an explanation of how the universe comes to be a cosmos, or ordered place. Its political function is to explain the supremacy of Babylon over the other city-states of Mesopotamia. This is done by casting Marduk, a relative newcomer in Mesopotamian religion and the god of Babylon, in the role of the hero who defeats the forces of chaos and is rewarded by being made king in the pantheon, or assembly of gods. The myth even has a psychological function in that it explains humanity's lowly position in the Mesopotamian view as the fearful servants of the gods and caretakers of their earthly estates.

The **Enuma Elish** was an enacted myth which was performed on the fourth day of the twelve-day New Year festival in the spring of the year in order to guarantee the cosmic order against the forces of chaos which were always threatening life in the Tigris-Euphrates valley. The Mesopotamians believed that sea and water surrounded the universe on all sides and were the engendering sources of the cosmos, and, therefore, the myth opens with the generation of the gods from the primordial waters: the sweet waters of the rivers and the salt waters of the seas. These powerful and life-giving waters are deified as the primeval father and mother: the god Apsu and his consort Tiamat. As the myth proceeds, a generational conflict develops between Apsu who, in a very human fashion, only wants peace and quiet, and the vigorous and noisy younger gods of the cosmos: Anu, the sky-god, Enlil, the god of the wind and atmosphere, and the benevolent Ea, the god of the earth and waters. Significantly, the mother goddess Tiamat opposes her husband who wants to destroy the younger gods. In the first round of battle, Ea, with the help of a magical spell, defeats and slays the tyrannical father, Apsu. In the second encounter Marduk, the son of Ea and the god of Babylon, in a skillful political fashion succeeds in getting himself designated by the assembly of gods to oppose the now vengeful mother, Tiamat, and her forces. Marduk defeats her in a titanic struggle and proceeds to create an ordered universe out of her body. Marduk's last creative act is to form man for the service of the gods from the blood of Tiamat's henchman, Kingu. The myth concludes with the lesser deities participating in the construction of Marduk's temple-shrine, the *Esagila* in Babylon, and the celebration of a banquet in which Marduk is lauded as the king of the pantheon. This basic mythic sequence is also found in the Greek tradition in Hesiod's **Theogony.** The Israelite creation story in Genesis, with its account of one God creating simply by his word of command, stands in sharp contrast to these polytheistic traditions.

The translation is by E.A. Speiser in **Ancient Near Eastern Texts** (Princeton: Princeton University Press, 1969) 60–72.

THE CREATION MYTH

TABLET I

The birth of the gods
When on high the heaven had not been named,
Firm ground below had not been called by name,
Naught but primordial Apsu,[1] their begetter,
(And) Mummu[2]—Tiamat,[3] she who bore them all,
Their[4] waters commingling as a single body;
No reed hut had been matted, no marsh land had appeared,
When no gods whatever had been brought into being,
Uncalled by name, their destinies undetermined—
Then it was that the gods were formed within them.[5]
Lahmu and Lahamu[6] were brought forth, by name
    they were called.
For aeons they grew in age and stature.
Anshar and Kishar[7] were formed, surpassing the others.

They prolonged the days, added on the years.
Anu[8] was their son, of his father the rival;
Yea, Anshar's first-born Anu, was his equal.
Anu begot in his image Nudimmud.[9]
This Nudimmud was of his fathers the master;
Of broad wisdom, understanding, mighty in strength,
Mightier by far than his grandfather, Anshar.
He had no rival among the gods, his brothers.
(At this point the younger gods disturb their parents with their revelry, and Apsu announces his intention to destroy his offspring. The remainder of Tablets I-III recounts Ea's victory over his tyrannical father, the birth of Marduk, and Tiamat's preparations to avenge Apsu's death. When Tablet IV opens Marduk is skillfully acquiring kingship among the younger gods by having himself designated as the champion who will oppose the vengeful Tiamat.)

TABLET IV

Marduk is proclaimed king
They erected for him a princely throne.
Facing his fathers, he sat down, presiding.

"Thou art the most honored of the great gods,
Thy decree is unrivaled, thy command is Anu.[10]
Thou, Marduk, art the most honored of the great gods,
Thy decree is unrivaled, thy word is Anu.
From this day unchangeable shall be thy pronouncement.
To raise or bring low—these shall be (in) thy hand.
Thy utterance shall come true, thy command shall not be doubted.
No one among the gods, shall transgress thy bounds!
Adornment being wanted for the seats of the gods,
Let the place of their shrines ever be in thy place.
O Marduk, thou art indeed our avenger.
We have granted thee kinship over the universe entire.
When in Assembly thou sittest, thy word shall be supreme.
Thy weapons shall not fail; they shall smash thy foes!
O lord, spare the life of him who trusts thee,
But pour out the life of the god who seized evil."
Having placed in their midst a piece of cloth,
They addressed themselves to Marduk, their first-born:
"Lord, truly thy decree is first among gods,
Say but to wreck or create; it shall be.
Open thy mouth: the cloth will vanish!
Speak again, and the cloth shall be whole!"
At the word of his mouth the cloth vanished.
He spoke again, and the cloth was restored.
When the gods, his fathers, saw the fruit of his word,
Joyfully they did homage: "Marduk is king!"
They conferred on him scepter, throne, and *palu*;
They gave him matchless weapons that ward off the foes:
"Go and cut off the life of Tiamat.
May the winds bear her blood to places undisclosed."

Bel's[11] destiny thus fixed, the gods, his fathers,
Caused him to go the way of success and attainment.
He constructed a bow, marked it as his weapon,
Attached thereto the arrow, fixed its bow-cord.
He raised the mace, made his right hand grasp it;
Bow and quiver he hung at his side.
In front of him he set the lightning,
With a blazing flame he filled his body.
He then made a net to enfold Tiamat therein.
The four winds he stationed that nothing of her might escape.
The South Wind, the North Wind, the East Wind, the West Wind.
Close to his side he held the net, the gift of his father Anu.
He brought forth Imhullu, "the Evil Wind," the Whirlwind, the Hurricane,
The Fourfold Wind, the Sevenfold Wind, the Cyclone, the Matchless Wind;
Then he sent forth the winds he had brought forth, the seven of them.
To stir up the inside of Tiamat they rose up behind him.
Then the lord raised up the flood-storm, his mighty weapon.
He mounted the storm-chariot irresistible (and) terrifying. . . .

The battle between Marduk and Tiamat
The lord approached to scan the inside of Tiamat,
(And) of Kingu, her consort, the scheme to perceive.
As he looks on, his[12] course becomes upset,
His will is distracted and his doings are confused.
And when the gods, his helpers, who marched at his side,
Saw the valiant hero, blurred became their vision.
Tiamat emitted (a cry), without turning her neck,
Framing savage defiance in her lips:

"Too (imp)ortant art thou (for) the lord of the gods to rise up against thee!
Is it in their place that they have gathered, (or) in thy place?"
Thereupon the lord, having (raised) the flood-storm, his mighty weapon,
(To) enraged (Tiamat) he sent word as follows:
"(Mightily) art thou risen, art haughtily exalted;
(Thou hast) charged thine own heart to stir up conflict,
(So that) sons reject their own fathers,
(And thou), who has born them, dost hate ..(.)!
Thou hast aggrandized Kingu to be (thy) consort;
(A rule), not rightfully his, thou has substituted for the rule of Anu.
Against Anshar, king of the gods, thou seekest evil;
(Against) the gods, my fathers, thou hast confirmed thy wickedness.
(Though) drawn up be thy forces, girded on thy weapons,
Stand thou up, that I and thou meet in single combat!"
When Tiamat heard this,
She was like one possessed; she took leave of her senses.
In fury Tiamat cried out aloud.
To the roots her legs shook both together.
She recites a charm, keeps casting her spell,
While the gods of battle sharpen their weapons.
Then joined issue Tiamat and Marduk, wisest of gods.
They swayed in single combat, locked in battle.
The lord spread out his net to enfold her,
The Evil Wind, which followed behind, he let loose in her face.
When Tiamat opened her mouth to consume him,
He drove in the Evil Wind that she close not her lips.
As the fierce winds charged her belly,
Her body was distended and her mouth was wide-open.

He released the arrow, it tore her belly,
It cut through her inside, splitting the heart.
Having thus subdued her, he extinguished her life.
He cast down her carcass to stand upon it.
After he had slain Tiamat, the leader,
Her band was shattered, her troupe broken up;
And the gods, her helpers who marched at her side,
Trembling with terror, turned their backs about,
In order to save and preserve their lives.
Tightly encircled, they could not escape.
He made them captives, and he smashed their weapons.
Thrown into the net, they found themselves ensnared;
Placed in cells, they were filled with wailing;
Bearing his wrath, they were held imprisoned
. . .

Marduk constructs the heavens and
the earth from Tiamat's slain body
And turned back to Tiamat whom he had bound.
The lord trod on the legs of Tiamat,
With his unsparing mace he crushed her skull.
When the arteries of her blood he had severed,
The North Wind bore (it) to places undisclosed.
On seeing this, his fathers were joyful and jubilant,
They brought gifts of homage, they to him.
Then the lord paused to view her dead body,
That he might divide the monster and do artful works.
He split her like a shellfish into two parts:
Half of her he set up and ceiled it as sky,
pulled down the bar and posted guards.
He bade them to allow not her waters to escape.
He crossed the heavens and surveyed (its) regions.
He squared Apsu's quarter, the abode of Nudimmud,
As the lord measured the dimensions of Apsu.
The Great Abode, its likeness, he fixed as Esharra,

The Great Abode, Esharra, which he made as
the firmament.
Anu, Enlil,[13] and Ea he made occupy their
places.

TABLET V

He constructed stations for the great gods,
Fixing their astral likenesses as constella-
tions.
He determined the year by designating the
zones;
He set up three constellations for each of the
twelve months.
After defining the days of the year (by means)
of (heavenly) figures,
He founded the station of Nebiru[14] to deter-
mine their (heavenly) bands,
That none might transgress or fall short,
Alongside it he set up the stations of Enlil and
Ea.
Having opened up the gates on both sides,
He strengthened the locks to the left and the
right.
In her[15] belly he established the zenith.
The Moon he caused to shine, the night (to him)
entrusting.
He appointed him a creature of the night to sig-
nify the days:
"Monthly, without cease, form designs with a
crown.
At the month's very start, rising over the land,
Thou shalt have luminous horns to signify six
days.
On the seventh day be thou a (half)-crown.
At full moon stand in opposition[16] in mid-
month.
When the sun (overtakes) thee at the base of
heaven,
Diminish (thy crown) and retrogress in light.
(At the time of disappearance) approach thou
the course of the sun,
And (on the twenty-ninth) thou shalt again
stand in opposition to the sun."
(The remainder of this tablet is broken away or
too fragmentary for translation.)

TABLET VI

The creation of man
(The text at the end of Tablet V is fragmentary,
but to judge from what follows, the lesser gods
are afraid that they will be compelled to pro-
vide unending service for the great gods in the
maintenance of their temples and so they ap-
peal their case to Marduk.)
When Marduk hears the words of the gods,
His heart prompts (him) to fashion artful
works.
Opening his mouth, he addresses Ea
To impart the plan he had conceived in his
heart:
"Blood I will mass and cause bones to be.
I will establish a savage, "man" shall be his
name.
Verily, savage-man I will create.
He shall be charged with the service of the gods
That they might be at ease!
The ways of the gods I will artfully alter.
Though alike revered, into two (groups) they
shall be divided."
Ea answered him, speaking a word to him,
To relate to him a scheme for the relief of the
gods:
"Let but one of their brothers be handed over;
He alone shall perish that mankind may be
fashioned.[17]
Let the great gods be here in Assembly,
Let the guilty be handed over that they may
endure."
Marduk summoned the great gods to Assem-
bly;
Presiding graciously, he issued instructions.
To his utterance the gods pay heed.
The king addresses a word to the Anunnaki:
"If your former statement was true,
Do (now) the truth on oath by me declare!
Who was it that contrived the uprising,
And made Tiamat rebel, and joined battle?
Let him be handed over who contrived the up-
rising.
His guilt I will make him bear that you may
dwell in peace!"

The Igigi, the great gods, replied to him,
To Lugaldimmerankia,[18] counselor of the gods,
   their lord:
"It was Kingu who contrived the uprising,
And made Tiamat rebel, and joined battle."
They bound him, holding him before Ea.
They imposed on him his guilt and severed his
   blood (vessels).
Out of his blood they fashioned mankind.
He[19] imposed the service and let free the gods.
After Ea, the wise, had created mankind,
Had imposed upon it the service of the gods—

(At this point the rebel gods are assigned to new and responsible tasks in heaven and the underworld. Then the gods propose to build Marduk a temple, the *Esagila* in Babylon which becomes a great religious center for the other gods and men. The final scene of the myth takes place in Marduk's temple. The "destinies"—the eternal, unchangeable states of things—are determined, and in a long ceremony, which ends with the reciting of his fifty names, the destiny or status of Marduk himself is established.)

NOTES

[1]God of subterranean waters; the primeval sweet-water ocean.

[2]Not to be confused with the vizier Mummu for grammatical reasons. Perhaps an epithet in the sense of "mother."

[3]A watery deity; the primeval salt-water ocean.

[4]I.e., the fresh waters of Apsu and the marine waters of Tiamat.

[5]The waters of Apsu and Tiamat.

[6]The first generation of the gods.

[7]Gods.

[8]The sky-god.

[9]One of the names of Ea, the earth- and water-god.

[10]I.e., it has the authority of the sky-god Anu.

[11]I.e., Marduk's destiny.

[12]I.e., Kingu's course.

[13]The god of the wind, i.e., of the earth.

[14]I.e., the planet Jupiter.

[15]Tiamat's.

[16]I.e., with regard to the sun.

[17]Out of his blood.

[18]Meaning "The King of the gods of heaven and earth."

[19]Ea.

THE GILGAMESH EPIC

The greatest literary product of ancient Mesopotamian culture is **The Gilgamesh Epic** whose hero is the legendary king of the ancient city-state of Uruk. It is written in Akkadian on twelve clay tablets, and although the primary extant texts come from the seventh century B.C.E., the earliest episodes are attested in Sumerian texts from the third millennium. In its present form, the epic is a composite that grew over the course of centuries much as the biblical material in Genesis and Exodus.

Gilgamesh is the earliest of several epics written in the ancient world. In this book the term epic will be used to refer to a long narrative poem centered around one character who engages in an heroic struggle to fulfill his destiny. Epic usually has a strong cultural interest in that it expresses the values of the civilization and often treats the foundational events of the nation's/city's history. Common epic motifs include warfare, conquest, journey, and return to or founding of the homeland. The gods and goddesses of the culture have an integral role in the ancient epic. They enter the human world and participate in the action to either hinder or aid the hero in his quest.

Despite its composite character, **Gilgamesh** in its present form is a skillfully composed epic centered around one character and the theme of the human struggle against the inevitability of death. As such, it reflects the profound pessimism that permeated Mesopotamian culture. Although they had created the first urban culture, the Mesopotamians never developed any deep sense of security. The movement of the rivers was always uncertain; floods and droughts were frequent, and Mesopotamia was surrounded by fierce nomadic neighbors who invaded the vulnerable valley from the Arabian desert or the mountains to the north and east. As a consequence, fear was a predominant feature of the Mesopotamian psyche. The gods could not be wholly trusted, and the unseen world was populated with demons who had to be manipulated by magical rites. Hopes were concentrated on this life. The advice of the divine barmaid, Siduri, to Gilgamesh was the common wisdom:

> "Gilgamesh, wither rovest thou?
> The life thou pursuest thou shalt not find.
> When the gods created mankind,
> Death for mankind they set aside,
> Life in their own hands retaining.
> Thou, Gilgamesh, let full be thy belly,
> Make thou merry by day and by night.
> Of each day make thou a feast of rejoicing,
> Day and night dance thou and play!
> Let thy garments be sparkling fresh,
> Thy head be washed; bathe thou in water.
> Pay heed to the little one that holds on to thy hand,
> Let thy spouse delight in thy bosom!
> For this is the task of (mankind)!"

Against this stark backdrop, Gilgamesh defies the gods and strives for everlasting fame, undying friendship, permanent health and immortality. Although he inevitably fails in his search for these things, Gilgamesh is profoundly changed, in the course of his quest, from a tyrannical despot to a truly human hero who has loved his friend Enkidu and has come to accept the limited joys of human achievement in the creation of a civilized culture. The story ends with Gilgamesh, having lost the plant that was to give him immortality, returning to the city of Uruk and proudly pointing out the walls which he had built to Urshanabi, the boatman, and saying:

"Go up, Urshanabi, walk on the ramparts of Uruk.
Inspect the base terrace, examine its brickwork,
If its brickwork is not of burnt brick,
And if the Seven Wise Ones laid not its foundation . . . "

The Gilgamesh Epic explores in a moving way what it meant to be human in ancient Mesopotamia. Various non-human options are vividly portrayed in the course of the epic. To live the innocent and carefree life of Enkidu when he roams with the animals in the steppe is to be less than human, without knowledge of sexuality, culture and friendship. On the other hand, the cruel and tryannical Gilgamesh in the opening of the epic is equally inhuman. The paradisal life of Utnapishtim, the immortal hero of the flood, is also not an option for Gilgamesh or other humans. Rather, to be human is to live in the walled city with its culture and laws which humanity has created in defiance of a hostile environment and in the face of the inevitability of death.

The Gilgamesh story finds several echoes in the early chapters of Genesis. The creation and humanization of Enkidu treats many of the same themes as Genesis 2–3: creation from the clay of the earth, the differences between animals and humans, the power of sexual attraction, the gaining of wisdom like the gods, the wearing of clothing, etc. Gilgamesh's loss of the plant of immortality to a serpent is at least evocative of the serpent's role in the Garden story in Genesis 3. Perhaps the most striking parallel is the detailed similarity between the flood story in Tablet XI and Genesis 6–9. These similarities have led scholars to conclude that the biblical version is in some way dependent upon the older Mesopotamian tradition. There are, of course, significant differences in the way that the biblical God is portrayed in the Genesis flood account and the capricious and argumentative gods of the Gilgamesh version. A final noteworthy comparison is the contrasting attitude toward the significance of the human achievement in building a city. Gilgamesh takes understandable pride in the walls and temples of Uruk, but in the comparable biblical story, the Tower of Babel is seen simply as a monument to human pride and rebelliousness against God (cf. Gen 11:1–9). [The translation is by E.A. Speiser in **Ancient Near Eastern Texts,** 72–99. For a moving verse narrative version of Gilgamesh see H. Mason, **Gilgamesh: A Verse Narrative** (New York: New American Library, Inc., 1970)].

SUMMARY OF GILGAMESH'S DEEDS

TABLET I

He who saw everything [to the end]s of the land,
[Who all thing]s experienced, [consider]ed all!
. . .
The [hi]dden he saw, [laid bare] the undisclosed.

He brought report of before the Flood.
Achieved a long journey, weary and [w]orn.
All his toil he engraved on a stone stela.
Of ramparted Uruk the wall he built,
Of holy Eanna,[1] the pure sanctuary.
Behold its outer wall, whose cornice is like copper,
Peer at the inner wall, which none can equal!
Draw near to Eanna, the dwelling of Ishtar,
Which no future king, no man, can equal.
Go up and walk on the walls of Uruk,

Inspect the base terrace, examine the brickwork:
Is not its brickwork of burnt brick?
Did not the Seven [Sages] lay its foundation?
(The remainder is broken. We gather from
fragments that several gods had a hand in
fashioning Gilgamesh, whom they endowed
with superhuman dimensions. At length, Gilgamesh arrives in Uruk.)

Gilgamesh's despotic rule
Two-thirds of him is god, [one-third of him is
human].
(mutilated or missing)
The onslaught of his weapons verily has no
equal.
By the drum are aroused [his] companions.
The nobles of Uruk are gloo[my] in [their
chamb]ers:
"Gilgamesh leaves not the son to [his] father;
[Day] and [night] is unbridled his arro[gance].
[Yet] th[is is Gil]gamesh, [the shepherd of
Uruk].
He should be [our] shepherd: [strong, stately,
(and) wise]!
[Gilgamesh] leaves not [the maid to her
mother],
The warrior's daughter, [the noble's spouse]!"
The [gods hearkened] to their plaint,
The gods of heaven, Uruk's lord(s) [. . .]:
"Did not [Aruru]² bring forth this strong wild
ox?
[The onslaught of his weapons] verily has no
equal.
By the drum are aroused his [companions].
Gilgamesh leaves not the son to his father;
    Day and night [is unbridled his arro-
gance]. . . .
When [Anu] had heard out their plaint,
The great Aruru they called:
    "Thou, Aruru, didst create [Gilgamesh];
Create now his double;
    His stormy heart let him match.
Let them contend, that Uruk may have peace!
When Aruru heard this,
    A double of Anu she conceived within her.

Aruru washed her hands,
    Pinched off clay and cast it on the steppe.
[On the step]pe she created valiant Enkidu,
    Offspring of . . . , liegeman of Ninurta.³
[Sha]ggy with hair is his whole body,
    He is endowed with headhair like a
woman.
The locks of his hair sprout like Nisaba.⁴
He knows neither people nor land;
    Garbed is he like Sumuqan.⁵
With the gazelles he feeds on grass,
With the wild beasts he jostles at the watering-
place,
With the teeming creatures his heart delights
in water.
(At this point a trapper/hunter discovers
Enkidu who fills in his pits and releases his
trapped animals. The hunter's father suggests
that his son go to Uruk and have Gilgamesh
send a harlot to seduce Enkidu who will then
be rejected by the beasts of the steppe. In the
meantime Gilgamesh learns of Enkidu's existence through dreams. As the text begins the
hunter is leading the harlot to Enkidu.)

The seduction of Enkidu
Forth went the hunter, taking with him a har-
lot-lass.
They took the road, going straight on (their)
way.
On the third day at the appointed spot they ar-
rived.
The hunter and the harlot sat down in their
places.
One day, a second day, they sat by the water-
ing-place.
The wild beasts came to the watering-place to
drink.
The creeping creatures came, their heart de-
lighting in water.
But as for him, Enkidu, born in the hills—
With the gazelles he feeds on grass,
With the wild beasts he drinks at the watering-
place,
With the creeping creatures his heart delights
in water—

The lass beheld him, the savage-man,
The barbarous fellow from the depths of the
steppe:
"There he is, O lass! Free thy breasts,
Bare thy bosom that he may possess thy ripe-
ness!
Be not bashful! Welcome his ardor!
As soon as he sees thee, he will draw near to
thee.
Lay aside thy cloth that he may rest upon
thee.
Treat him, the savage, to a woman's task!
Reject him will his wild beasts that grew up on
his steppe,
As his love is drawn unto thee."
The lass freed her breasts, bared her bosom,
    And he possessed her ripeness.
She was not bashful as she welcomed his ardor.
She laid aside her cloth and he rested upon her.
She treated him, the savage, to a woman's task,
As his love was drawn unto her.
For six days and seven nights Enkidu comes
forth,
    Mating with the lass.
After he had had (his) fill of her charms,
He set his face toward his wild beasts.
On seeing him, Enkidu, the gazelles ran off,
The wild beasts of the steppe drew away from
his body.
Startled was Enkidu, as his body became taut,
His knees were motionless—for his wild beasts
had gone.
Enkidu had to slacken his pace—it was not as
before;
But he now had [wi]sdom, [br]oader under-
standing.
Returning, he sits at the feet of the harlot.
He looks up at the face of the harlot,
His ears attentive, as the harlot speaks;
[The harlot] says to him, to Enkidu:
"Thou art [wi]se, Enkidu, art become like a
god!
Why with the wild creatures dost thou roam
over the steppe?
Come, let me lead thee [to] ramparted Uruk,
To the holy temple, abode of Anu and Ishtar,

Where lives Gilgamesh, accomplished in
strength,
And like a wild ox lords it over the folk."
As she speaks to him, her words find favor,
His heart enlightened, he yearns for a friend.
Enkidu says to her, to the harlot:
"Up, lass, escort thou me,
To the pure sacred temple, abode of Anu and
Ishtar,
Where lives Gilgamesh, accomplished in
strength,
And like a wild ox lords it over the folk.
I will challenge him [and will bo]ldly address
him,
[I will] shout in Uruk: 'I am he who is mighty!
[I am the] one who can alter destinies,
[(He) who] was born on the steppe is mighty;
strength he has.' "
"[Up then, let us go, that he may see] thy face.
[I will show thee Gilgamesh; where] he is I
know well.
Come then, O Enkidu, to ramparted [Uruk],
Where people are re[splend]ent in festal attire,
(Where) each day is made a holiday, . . . "

TABLET II

(In the beginning of the tablet, which only exists in an Old Babylonian version, Gilgamesh
has a series of dreams foreshadowing the arrival of Enkidu. The actual encounter between
the two heroes results in a fierce battle which
occurs in a rather broken section. The two heroes "Grappled each other,/Butting like bulls."
Their fight ends in a draw, and Enkidu recognizes Gilgamesh's right to kingship over the
people of Uruk.)

TABLET III

(Gilgamesh has decided on an expedition
against Huwawa/Humbaba, a terrible ogre
whom Enlil has appointed to guard the cedar
forest. Enkidu tries to dissuade him, but is un-
successful, as may be gathered from the following verses.)

"[In the forest resides] fierce Huwawa.
[Let us, me and thee, s]lay [him].
[That all evil from the land may ban]ish!
(too fragmentary for translation)
Enkidu opened his mouth,
Saying to Gilgamesh:
"I found it out, my friend, in the hills,
As I was roaming with the wild beasts.
For ten thousand leagues extends the forest.
[Who is there] that would go down into it?
[Huwa]wa—his roaring is the flood-storm,
His mouth is fire,
His breath is death!
Why dost thou desire
To do this thing?
An unequal struggle
Is tangling with Huwawa."
Gilgamesh opened his mouth,
Saying to [Enkidu]:
"Who, my friend, is superior to de[ath]?
Only the gods [live] forever under the sun.
As for mankind, numbered are their days;
Whatever they achieve is but the wind!
Even here thou art afraid of death.
What of thy heroic might?
Let me go then before thee,
Let thy mouth call to me, 'Advance, fear not!'
Should I fall, I shall have made me a name:
'Gilgamesh'—they will say—'against fierce
   Huwawa
Has fallen!' (Long) after
My offspring has been born in my house," . . .
(In Tablets IV and V, Gilgamesh and Enkidu,
with the aid of Ninsun and Shamash, the sun-
god, succeed in entering the cedar forest and
slaying Huwawa. Upon his victorious return to
Uruk, the triumphant Gilgamesh attracts the
attention of Ishtar, the goddess of fertility and
love.)

TABLET VI

Ishtar's proposal
He (Gilgamesh) washed his grimy hair, polished his weapons,

The braid of his hair he shook out against his
   back.
He cast off his soiled (things), put on his clean
   things,
Wrapped a fringed cloak about and fastened a
   sash.
When Gilgamesh had put on his tiara,
Glorious Ishtar raised an eye at the beauty of
   Gilgamesh:
"Come, Gilgamesh, be thou (my) lover!
Do but grant me of thy fruit.
Thou shalt be my husband I will be thy wife.
I will harness for thee a chariot of lapis and
   gold,
Whose wheels are gold and whose horns are
   electrum.
Thou shalt have storm-demons to hitch on for
   mighty mules.
Under the fragrance of cedars thou shalt enter
   our house.
When our house thou enterest,
Threshold (and dais) shall kiss thy feet!
Humbled before thee shall be kings, lords, and
   princes!
The yield of hills and plain they shall bring
   thee as tribute.
Thy goats shall cast triplets, thy sheep twins,
Thy he-ass in lading shall surpass thy mule.
Thy chariot horses shall be famed for racing,
[Thine ox] under the yoke shall not have a ri-
   val!"

Gilgamesh's refusal
[Gilgamesh] opened his mouth to speak,
[Saying] to glorious Ishtar:
["What am I to give] thee, but that I may take
   thee in marriage?
[Should I give oil] for the body, and clothing?
[Should I give] bread and victuals?
[. . .] food fit for divinity.
[. . .] drink fit for royalty.
   (mutilated)
[. . . if I] take thee in marriage?
[Thou art but a brazier which goes out] in the
   cold;

A back door [which does not] keep out blast and
   windstorm;
A palace which crushes the valiant [. . .];
A turban whose cover [. . .];
Pitch which [soils] its bearers;
A waterskin which [soaks through] its bearer;
Limestone which [springs] the stone rampart;
Jasper [which . . .] enemy land;
A shoe which [pinches the foot] of its owner!
Which lover didst thou love forever?
Which of thy shepherds pleased [thee for all
   time]?
Come, and I will na[me for thee] thy lovers: . . .
   For Tammuz,[6] the lover of thy youth,
Thou hast ordained wailing year after year.
Having loved the dappled shepherd-bird,
Thou smotest him, breaking his wing.
In the groves he sits, crying 'My wing!'
Then thou lovedst a lion, perfect in strength;
Seven pits and seven thou didst dig for him.
Then a stallion thou lovedst, famed in battle;
The whip, the spur, and the lash thou or-
   dainedst for him.
Thou decreedst for him to gallop seven leagues,
Thou decreedst for him the muddied to drink;
(Gilgamesh continues to recount how Ishtar
   emasculates all her lovers.)

Ishtar's complaint to her father, Anu
When Ishtar heard this,
Ishtar was enraged and [mounted] to heaven.
Forth went Ishtar before Anu, her father,
To Antum, her mother, she went and [said]:
"My father, Gilgamesh has heaped insults
   upon me!
Gilgamesh has recounted my offenses,
My offenses and my curses."
Anu opened his mouth to speak,
Saying to glorious Ishtar:
"But surely, thou didst invite .[. . .],
And so Gilgamesh has recounted thy offenses,
Thy offenses and thy cu[rses]."
Ishtar opened her mouth to speak,
Saying to [Anu, her father]:

"My father, make me the Bull of Heaven [that
   he smite Gilgamesh],
[And] fill Gil[gamesh . . .]!
If thou [dost not make] me [the Bull of Heaven],
I will smash [the doors of the nether world],
I will [. . .],
I will [raise up the dead eating (and) alive],
So that the dead shall outnumber the living!"
(After considerable hesitation Anu consents.
The bull is sent down on Uruk, and a whole
army of men fail to kill him. Finally, Enkidu
and Gilgamesh succeed in catching him and
running him through with a sword.)
When they had slain the Bull, they tore out his
   heart,
Placing it before Shamash.
They drew back and did homage before Sha-
   mash.
The two brothers sat down.
Then Ishtar mounted the wall of ramparted
   Uruk,
Sprang on the battlements, uttering a curse:
"Woe unto Gilgamesh because he insulted me
   By slaying the Bull of Heaven!"
When Enkidu heard this speech of Ishtar,
He tore loose the right thigh of the Bull of
   Heaven
   And tossed it in her face:
"Could I but get thee, like unto him
I would do unto thee.
His entrails I would hang at thy side!"
[Thereupon] Ishtar assembled the votaries,
The [pleasure-]lasses and the [temple-]harlots.
Over the right thigh of the Bull of Heaven she
   set up a wail.
(Gilgamesh then dedicates the bull's horns to
his tutelary god, Lugalbanda. The two heroes
proceed to wash their hands in the Euphrates
and lead a triumphant procession though the
streets of Uruk, as Gilgamesh calls out in ex-
ultant gladness: "Who is most splendid among
the heroes?/ Who is most glorious among
men?" The citizens respond: "Gilgamesh is
most splendid among the heroes,/ Gilgamesh is
most glorious among men.")

TABLET VII

(That night Enkidu has a dream foreboding his own end. He sees the gods assembled together as they deliberate which of the two heroes must die for killing Huwawa and the Bull of Heaven and learns that he is fated to die. When Gilgamesh sees his comrade becoming ill, he weeps "O my brother, my dear brother! Me they would/ Clear at the expense of my brother!" In a deathbed review of his life, Enkidu seems to bemoan the events that led up to this sorry state, cursing the successive steps in his fated life. Later Shamash chides Enkidu and reminds him of the joys he has found through his discovery of his humanity and his friendship with Gilgamesh.)

When Shamash heard [these words] of his mouth,
Forthwith he called down to him [from] heaven:
"Why, O Enkidu, cursest thou the harlot-lass,
Who made thee eat food fit for divinity,
And gave thee to drink wine fit for royalty,
Who clothed thee with noble garments,
And made thee have fair Gilgamesh for a comrade?
And has (not) now Gilgamesh, thy bosom friend,
Made thee lie on a noble couch?
He has made thee lie on a couch of honor,
Has placed thee on the seat of ease, the seat at the left,
That [the prin]ces of the earth may kiss thy feet!
He will make Uruk's people weep over thee (and) lament,
Will fill [joyful] people with woe over thee.
And, when thou art gone,
    He will his body with uncut hair invest,
Will don a lion skin and roam over the steppe."
[When] Enkidu [heard] the words of valiant Shamash,
[. . .] his vexed heart grew quiet.
(After a short break, the text recounts how Enkidu changed his curse into a blessing.)

TABLET VIII

(When Tablet VIII first becomes legible, Gilgamesh is addressing the elders of Uruk at the deathbed of Enkidu:)

Gilgamesh's lament over Enkidu
"Hear me, O elders, [and give ear] unto me!
It is for Enkidu, my [friend], that I weep,
Moaning bitterly like a wailing woman.
The axe at my side, the [bow] in my hand,
The dirk in my belt, [the shield] in front of me,
My festal robe, my [greatest] joy—
An evil [demon] rose up and [robbed] me!
[O my younger friend], thou chasedst
The wild ass of the hills, the panther of the steppe!
Enkidu, my younger friend, thou who chasedst
The wild ass of the hills, the panther of the steppe!
We who [have conquered] all things, scaled [the mountains],
Who seized the Bull [and slew him],
Brought affliction on Hubaba, who [dwelled in the Cedar Forest]!
What, now, is this sleep that has laid hold [thee]?
Thou art benighted and canst not hear [me]!"
But he lifts not up [his eyes];
When he touches his heart, it does not beat.
Then he veiled (his) friend like a bride [. . .]
Like a lion he raises up [his voice]
Like a lioness deprived of [her] whelps.
He paces back and forth before [the couch],
Pulling out [his hair] and strewing [it forth],
Tearing off and flinging down his finery [. . .]

TABLET IX

(Steeped in sorrow at the death of his friend, Gilgamesh leaves Uruk and roams over the steppe in search of Utnapishtim, the hero of the Flood.)

Gilgamesh's journey to Utnapishtim
For Enkidu, his friend, Gilgamesh
Weeps bitterly, as he ranges over the steppe:

"When I die, shall I not be like Enkidu?
Woe has entered my belly.
Fearing death, I roam over the steppe.
To Utnapishtim, Ubar-Tutu's son,
I have taken the road to proceed in all haste.
When arriving by night at mountain passes,
I saw lions and grew afraid.
I lifted my head to Sin[7] to pray.
To [. . .] of the gods went out my orisons.
[. . .] preserve thou me!"
[As at night] he lay, awoke from a dream.
[There were . . .], rejoicing in life.
He raised his axe in his hand,
He drew [the dirk] from his belt.
Like an ar[row] he descended among them.
He smote [them] and hacked away at them.
(The remainder of the column is broken away.
The rest of Tablet IX recounts Gilgamesh's
harrowing journey through the Mashu moun-
tain range. When he comes out on the other
side of the mountain range, Gilgamesh stands
before a beautiful garden of precious stones,
beautiful trees, shrubs, fruit and vines. In the
distance at the edge of the sea, dwells Siduri,
the divine barmaid.)

TABLET X

Gilgamesh's meeting with Siduri
(Beginning lost. Gilgamesh is addressing Si-
duri, the divine barmaid:)
"He who with me underwent all hard[ships]—
Enkidu, whom I loved dearly,
Who with me underwent all hardships—
Has now gone to the fate of mankind!
Day and night I have wept over him.
I would not give him up for burial—
In case my friend should rise at my plaint—
Seven days and seven nights,
Until a worm fell out of his nose.
Since his passing I have not found life,
I have roamed like a hunter in the midst of the
    steppe.
O ale-wife, now that I have seen thy face,
Let me not see the death which I ever dread."
The ale-wife said to him, to Gilgamesh:

"Gilgamesh, whither rovest thou?
The life thou pursuest thou shalt not find.
When the gods created mankind,
Death for mankind they set aside,
Life in their own hands retaining.
Thou, Gilgamesh, let full be thy belly,
Make thou merry by day and by night.
Of each day make thou a feast of rejoicing,
Day and night dance thou and play!
Let thy garments be sparkling fresh,
Thy head be washed; bathe thou in water.
Pay heed to the little one that holds on to thy
    hand,
Let thy spouse delight in thy bosom!
For this is the task of [mankind]!"
(The remainder of the column is broken away.)
(Despite Siduri's discouragement, Gilgamesh
persists in his plan, and at last she directs him
to Urshanabi, Utnapishtim's boatman, who
has come across from the other side of the sea
where Utnapishtim dwells. With much difficulty the two cross the sea and the waters of
death and finally arrive at the shores of the
land of the blessed Utnapishtim. The concluding part of their meeting follows:)

Gilgamesh meets Utnapishtim
Gilgamesh also said to him, to Utnapishtim:
"That now I might come and behold Utnapish-
    tim,
    Whom they call the Faraway,
I ranged and wandered over all the lands,
I traversed difficult mountains,
I crossed all the seas!
My face was not sated with sweet sleep,
I fretted myself with wakefulness;
    I filled my joints with aches.
I had not reached the ale-wife's house,
    When my clothing was used up
[I sl]ew bear, hyena, lion, panther,
    Tiger, stag, (and) ibex—
The wild beasts and creeping things of the
    steppe.
Their [flesh] I ate and their skins I wr[apped
    about me]."
(The remainder of this column is too mutilated

for translation. The beginning of the last column is broken away, except for the conclusion of Utnapishtim's observations:)
"Do we build houses for ever?
    Do we seal (contracts) for ever?
Do brothers divide shares for ever?
Does hatred persist for ever in [the land]?
Does the river for ever rise (and) bring on floods,
The dragon-fly [leaves] (its) shell
That its face might (but) glance at the face of the sun?
Since the days of yore there has been no [permanence];
The resting and the dead, how alike [they are]!
Do they not compose a picture of death,
The commander and the noble,
    Once they are near to [their fate]?
The Anunnaki, the great gods, foregather;
Mammetum, maker of fate, with them the fate decrees:
Death and life they determine.
(But) of death, its days are not revealed."

TABLET XI

Utnapishtim narrates the story of the Flood
Gilgamesh said to him, to Utnapishtim the Faraway:
"As I look upon thee, Utnapishtim,
Thy features are not strange; even as I art thou.
My heart had regarded thee as resolved to do battle,
[Yet] thou liest indolent upon thy back!
[Tell me,] how joinedst thou the Assembly of the gods,
    In thy quest of life?"
Utnapishtim said to him, to Gilgamesh:
"I will reveal to thee, Gilgamesh, a hidden matter
And a secret of the gods will I tell thee:
Shurippak—a city which thou knowest,
(And) which on Euphrates' [banks] is set—
That city was ancient, (as were) the gods within it,

When their heart led the great gods to produce the flood.
[There] were Anu, their father,
Valiant Enlil, their counselor,
Ninurta, their herald,
Ennuge, their irrigator.
Ninigiku-Ea was also present with them;
Their words he repeats to the reed-hut:[8]
'Reed-hut, reed-hut! Wall! wall!
Reed-hut, hearken! Wall, reflect!
Man of Shuruppak,[9] son of Ubar-Tutu,
Tear down (this) house, build a ship!
Give up possessions, seek thou life.
Despise property and keep the soul alive!
Aboard the ship take thou the seed of all living things.
The ship that thou shalt build,
Her dimensions shall be to measure.
Equal shall be her width and her length.
Like the Apsu[10] thou shalt ceil her.'
I understood, and I said to Ea, my lord:
'[Behold], my lord, what thou hast thus ordered,
I shall be honored to carry out.
[But what] shall I answer the city, the people and elders?'
Ea opened his mouth to speak,
Saying to me, his servant:
'Thou shalt then thus speak unto them:
"I have learned that Enlil is hostile to me,
So that I cannot reside in your city,
Nor set my f[oo]t in Enlil's territory.
To the Deep I will therefore go down,
    To dwell with my lord Ea.
[But upon] you he will shower down abundance,
[The choicest] birds, the rarest fishes.
[The land shall have its fill] of harvest riches.
[He who at dusk orders] the husk-greens,
Will shower down upon you a rain of wheat."[11]
With the first glow of dawn,
The land was gathered [about me].
    (too fragmentary for translation)
The little ones [carr]ied bitumen,
While the grown ones brought [all else] that was needful.

On the fifth day I laid her framework.
One (whole) acre was her floor space,
Ten dozen cubits the height of each of her walls,
Ten dozen cubits each edge of the square deck.
I laid out the shape of her sides and joined her together.
I provided her with six decks,
Dividing her (thus) into seven parts.
Her floor plan I divided into nine parts.
I hammered water-plugs into her.
I saw to the punting-poles and laid in supplies.
Six 'sar' (measures)[12] of bitumen I poured into the furnace,
Three sar of asphalt [I also] poured inside.
Three sar of oil the basket-bearers transferred,
Aside from the one sar of oil which the calking consumed,
And the two sar of oil [which] the boatman stored away.
Bullocks I slaughtered for the [people],
And I killed sheep every day.
Must, red wine, oil, and white wine
[I gave the] workmen [to drink], as though river water,
That they might feast as on New Year's Day.
I op[ened . . .] ointment, applying (it) to my hand.
[On the sev]enth [day] the ship was completed.
[The launching] was very difficult,
So that they had to shift the floor planks above and below,
[Until] two-thirds of [the structure] [had g]one [into the water].
[Whatever I had] I laded upon her:
Whatever I had of silver I laded upon her;
Whatever I [had] of gold I laded upon her;
Whatever I had of all living beings I [laded] upon her.
All my family and kin I made go aboard the ship.
The beasts of the field, the wild creatures of field,
    All the craftsmen I made go aboard.
Shamash had set for me a stated time:

'When he who orders unease at night
    Will shower down a rain of blight,
Board thou the ship and batten up the gate!'
That stated time had arrived:
'He who orders unease at night showers down a rain of blight.'
I watched the appearance of the weather.
The weather was awesome to behold.
I boarded the ship and battened up the gate.
To batten up the (whole) ship, to Puzur-Amurri, the boatman,
I handed over the structure together with its contents.
With the first glow of dawn,
A black cloud rose up from the horizon.
Inside it Adad[13] thunders,
While Shallat and Hanish[14] go in front,
Moving as heralds over hill and plain.
Erragal[15] tears out the posts;[16]
Forth comes Ninurta and causes the dikes to follow.
The Anunnaki lift up the torches,
Setting the land ablaze with their glare.
Consternation over Adad reaches to the heavens,
Turning to blackness all that had been light.
[The wide] land was shattered like [a pot]!
For one day the south-storm [blew],
Gathering speed as it blew, [submerging the mountains],
Overtaking the [people] like a battle.
No one can see his fellow,
Nor can the people be recognized from heaven.
The gods were frightened by the deluge,
And, shrinking back, they ascended to the heaven of Anu.
The gods cowered like dogs
    Crouched against the outer wall.
Ishtar cried out like a woman in travail,
The sweet-voiced mistress of the [gods] moans aloud:
The olden days are alas turned to clay,
Because I bespoke evil in the Assembly of the gods.
How could I bespeak evil in the Assembly of the gods,

Ordering battle for the destruction of my people,

When it is I myself who give birth to my people!

Like the spawn of the fishes they fill the sea!'

The Anunnaki gods weep with her,

The gods, all humbled, sit and weep,

Their lips drawn tight, [. . .] one and all.

Six days and [six] nights

Blows the flood wind, as the south-storm sweeps the land.

When the seventh day arrived,

The flood[-carrying] south-storm subsided in the battle,

Which it had fought like an army.

The sea grew quiet, the tempest was still, the flood ceased.

I looked at the weather: stillness had set in,

And all of mankind had returned to clay.

The landscape was as level as a flat roof.

I opened a hatch, and light fell upon my face.

Bowing low, I sat and wept,

Tears running down on my face.

I looked about for coast lines in the expanse of the sea:

In each of fourteen (regions)

There emerged a region (-mountain).

On Mount Nisir the ship came to a halt.

Mount Nisir held the ship fast,

Allowing no motion.

One day, a second day, Mount Nisir held the ship fast,

Allowing no motion . . .

When the seventh day arrived,

I sent forth and set free a dove.

The dove went forth, but came back;

There was no resting-place for it and she turned round.

Then I sent forth and set free a swallow.

The swallow went forth, but came back;

There was no resting-place for it and she turned around.

Then I sent forth and set free a raven.

The raven went forth and, seeing that the waters had diminished,

He eats, circles, caws, and turns not round.

Then I let out (all) to the four winds

And offered a sacrifice.

I poured out a libation on the top of the mountain.

Seven and seven cult-vessels I set up,

Upon their plate-stands I heaped cane, cedar-wood, and myrtle.

The gods smelled the savor,

The gods smelled the sweet savor,

The gods crowded like flies about the sacrificer.

As soon as the great goddess[17] arrived,

She lifted up the great jewels which Anu had fashioned to her liking:

'Ye gods here, as surely as this lapis

Upon my neck I shall not forget,

I shall be mindful of these days, forgetting (them) never.

Let the gods come to the offering;

(But) let not Enlil come to the offering,

For he, unreasoning, brought on the deluge

And my people consigned to destruction.'

As soon as Enlil arrived,

And saw the ship, Enlil was wroth,

He was filled with wrath against the Igigi gods:[18]

'Has some living soul escaped?

No man was to survive the destruction!'

Ninurta opened his mouth to speak,

Saying to valiant Enlil:

'Who other than Ea can devise plans?

It is Ea alone who knows every matter.'

Ea opened his mouth to speak,

Saying to valiant Enlil:

'Thou wisest of gods, thou hero,

How couldst thou, unreasoning, bring on the deluge?

On the sinner impose his sin,

On the transgressor impose his transgression!

(Yet) be lenient, lest he be cut off,

Be patient, lest he be dis[lodged]!

Instead of thy bringing on the deluge,

Would that a lion had risen up to diminish mankind!

Instead of thy bringing on the deluge,

Would that a wolf had risen up to diminish mankind!
Instead of thy bringing on the deluge,
Would that a famine had risen up to l[ay low] mankind!
Instead of thy bringing on the deluge,
Would that pestilence had risen up to smi[ite down] mankind!
It was not I who disclosed the secret of the great gods.
I let Atrahasis[19] see a dream
    And he perceived the secret of the gods.
Now then take counsel in regard to him!'
Thereupon Enlil went aboard the ship.
Holding me by the hand, he took me aboard.
He took my wife aboard and made (her) kneel by my side.
Standing between us, he touched our foreheads to bless us:
'Hitherto Utnapishtim has been but human.
Henceforth Utnapishtim and his wife shall be like unto us gods.
Utnapishtim shall reside far away, at the mouth of the rivers.'

Gilgamesh attempts to defeat sleep
But now, who will for thy sake call the gods to Assembly
That the life which thou seekest thou mayest find?
Up, lie not down to sleep
    For six days and seven nights."
As he sits there on his haunches,
Sleep fans him like a mist.
Utnapishtim says to her, to his spouse:
"Behold this hero who seeks life!
Sleep fans him like a mist."
His spouse says to him, to Utnapishtim the Faraway:
"Touch him that the man may awake,
That he may return safe on the way whence he came,
That through the gate by which he left he may return to his land."
Utnapishtim says to her, to his spouse:

"Since to deceive is human, he will seek to deceive thee.[20]
Up, bake for him wafers, put (them) at his head."
And she marked on the wall the days he slept. . . .
And just as he touched the seventh, the man awoke.
Gilgamesh says to him, to Utnapishtim the Faraway:
"Scarcely had sleep surged over me,
When straightway thou dost touch and rouse me!"
Utnapishtim [says to him], to Gilgamesh:
"[Go], Gilgamesh, count thy wafers,
[That the days thou hast slept] may become known to thee:
Thy [first] wafer is dried out,
[The second is leathe]ry, the third is soggy;
    The crust of the fourth has turned white;
The fifth has a moldy cast,
    The sixth (still) is fresh-colored.
[As for the seventh], at this instant thou hast awakened."
Gilgamesh says to him, to Utnapishtim the Faraway:
"[What then] shall I do, Utnapishtim,
    Whither shall I go,
[Now] that the Bereaver has laid hold on my [members]?
In my bedchamber lurks death,
And wherever I se[t my foot], there is death!"

Gilgamesh loses the plant of immortality
Utnapishtim [says to him], to Urshanabi, the boatman:
"Urshanabi, may the landing-pl[ace not rejoice in thee],
    May the place of the crossing despise thee!
To him who wanders on its shore, deny thou its shore!
The man thou hast led (hither), whose body is covered with grime,
The grace of whose members skins have distorted,

Take him, Urshanabi, and bring him to the
    washing-place.
Let him wash off his grime in water clean as
    snow,
Let him cast off his skins, let the sea carry
    (them) away,
That the fairness of his body may be seen.
Let him renew the band round his head,
Let him put on a cloak to clothe his naked-
    ness,
That he may arrive in his city,
That he may achieve his journey.
Let not (his) cloak have a moldy cast,
    Let it be wholly new."
Urshanabi took him and brought him to the
    washing-place.
He washed off his grime in water clean as
    snow.
He cast off his skins, the sea carried (them)
    away,
That the fairness of his body might be seen.
He renewed [the band] round his head,
He put on a cloak to clothe his nakedness,
That he might ar[rive in his city],
That he might achieve his journey.
[The cloak had not a moldy cast, but] was
    wholly new.
Gilgamesh and Urshanabi boarded the boat,
[They launch]ed the boat on the waves (and)
    they sailed away.
His spouse says to him, to Utnapishtim the
    Faraway:
"Gilgamesh has come hither, toiling and
    straining.
What wilt thou give (him) that he may return
    to his land?"
At that he, Gilgamesh, raised up (his) pole,
To bring the boat nigh to the shore.
Utnapishtim [says] to him, [to] Gilgamesh:
"Gilgamesh, thou hast come hither, toiling and
    straining,
What shall I give thee that thou mayest return
    to thy land?
I will disclose, O Gilgamesh, a hidden thing,
And [. . . about a plant I will] tell thee:
This plant, like the buckthorn is [its . . .].

Its thorns will pr[ick thy hands] just as does the
    rose.
If thy hands obtain the plant, [thou wilt attain
    life]."
No sooner had Gilgamesh heard this,
    Than he opened the wa[ter-pipe],
He tied heavy stones [to his feet].
They pulled him down into the deep [and he
    saw the plant].
He took the plant, though it pr[icked his
    hands].
He cut the heavy stones [from his feet].
The [s]ea cast him up upon its shore.
Gilgamesh says to him, to Urshanabi, the boat-
    man:
"Urshanabi, this plant is a plant apart,
Whereby a man may regain his life's breath.
I will take it to ramparted Uruk,
    Will cause [. . .] to eat the plant . . . !
Its name shall be 'Man Becomes Young in Old
    Age.'
I myself shall eat (it)
    And thus return to the state of my youth."
After twenty leagues they broke off a morsel,
After thirty (further) leagues they prepared for
    the night.
Gilgamesh saw a well whose water was cool.
He went down into it to bathe in the water.
A serpent snuffed the fragrance of the plant;
It came up [from the water] and carried off the
    plant.
Going back it shed [its] slough.

The return to Uruk
Thereupon Gilgamesh sits down and weeps,
His tears running down over his face.
[He took the hand] of Urshanabi, the boatman:
"[For] whom, Urshanabi, have my hands
    toiled?
For whom is being spent the blood of my heart?
I have not obtained a boon for myself.
For the earth-lion[21] have I effected a boon!
And now the tide will bear (it) twenty leagues
    away!
When I opened the water-pipe and spilled the
    gear,

I found that which has been placed as a sign for
me:
    I shall withdraw,
And leave the boat on the shore!"
After twenty leagues they broke off a morsel,
After thirty (further) leagues they prepared for
the night.
When they arrived in ramparted Uruk,
Gilgamesh says to him, to Urshanabi, the boat-
man:
"Go up, Urshanabi, walk on the ramparts of
Uruk.

Inspect the base terrace, examine its brickwork,
    If its brickwork is not of burnt brick,
And if the Seven Wise Ones laid not its foundation!
One 'sar' is city, one sar orchards,
One sar margin land; (further) the precinct of
the Temple of Ishtar.
Three sar and the precinct comprise Uruk."
(Tablet XII has been omitted from this abridgement since it is apparently an inorganic appen-
dage.)

NOTES

[1]The temple of Anu and Ishtar in Uruk.
[2]A goddess.
[3]War-god.
[4]Goddess of grain.
[5]God of cattle.
[6]The god of vegetation.
[7]The moon-god.
[8]Probably the dwelling of Utnapishtim. The god Ea addresses him (through the barrier of the wall), telling him about the decision of the gods to bring on the flood and advising him to build a ship.
[9]Utnapishtim.
[10]The subterranean waters.
[11]The purpose is to deceive the inhabitants of Shurupak as to the real intent of the rain.
[12]A 'sar' is about 8,000 gallons.
[13]God of storm and rain.
[14]Heralds of Hadad.
[15]I.e., Nergal, the god of the nether world.
[16]Of the world dam.
[17]Ishtar.
[18]The heavenly gods.
[19]"Exceeding wise," an epithet of Utnapishtim.
[20]By asserting that he had not slept at all.
[21]The serpent.

THE DESCENT OF ISHTAR INTO THE NETHER WORLD

Besides the cosmogonic myth, the **Enuma Elish,** which recounted the origins of the cosmos, the Mesopotamians also celebrated ancient fertility myths which were concerned with the productive forces of nature. The fertility goddess in Mesopotamia was Inanna (Sumerian) or Ishtar (Akkadian). She had various features as the goddess of earth, love, fertility, war, as well as the mother of humankind. We have already encountered Ishtar in **The Gilgamesh Epic** where she appears as the spiteful goddess of love and fertility who weakens or kills her lovers and who sends the Bull of Heaven against Gilgamesh when he refuses her advances. **The Descent of Ishtar into the Nether World** is the Akkadian version of the recurrent mythic theme of the death and rebirth of nature each year. Ishtar decides to visit the nether world, the realm of her sister Ereshkigal, the goddess of death and sterility. Apparently, her reason for the journey is to rescue her lover, the shepherd-god Tammuz. Ishtar's arrival at the entrance to the nether world threatens Ereshkigal who seems to believe that her sister has come to take away her place as ruler in the realm of the dead. Therefore, as she forces her way into the nether world and descends through its seven gates, Ishtar is progressively stripped of her robes and finery, until she finally meets Ereshkigal who orders that she be put to death. The consequences of Ishtar's descent are catastrophic for nature; all animal and human reproduction comes to a halt. Papsukkal, the vizier of the gods, then implores the great gods to revive Ishtar and bring her back to the land of the living. Ea creates a eunuch Asushunamir who descends to the nether world and forces Ereshkigal to revive her sister by sprinkling her with "the water of life." In the end Ishtar seems to return successfully with her lover Tammuz who is playing "on a flute of lapis."

Variants of the fertility myth are found throughout the Near East and the Mediterranean world: in Egypt the Osiris-Isis cycle, in Canaan the Baal-Anat poems, and in Greece the Demeter-Persephone myth celebrated in the Eleusian mysteries. Israel is the one culture that does not have a fertility myth as a part of its official religion. When the Israelites settled in the land of Canaan, they were constantly tempted toward the fertility cult of Baal, but the great prophets resisted any identification of the god Yahweh with the reproductive forces of nature. (The translation is by E.A. Speiser in **Ancient Near Eastern Texts**, 106–109.)

Ishtar's decision to descend to the netherworld
To the Land of no Return, the realm of (Eresh-
    kigal),
Ishtar, the daughter of Sin, (set) her mind,
Yea, the daughter of Sin set (her) mind
To the dark house, the abode of Irkal[la],[1]
To the house which none leave who have en-
    tered it,
To the road from which there is no way back,
To the house wherein the dwellers are bereft of
    li[ght],
Where dust is their fare and clay their food,
[Where] they are clothed like birds, with wings
    for garments,
[And where] over door and bolt is spread dust.

Ishtar forces her way into the Underworld
When Ishtar reached the gate of the Land of no
    Return,
She said (these) words to the gatekeeper:
"O gatekeeper, open thy gate,
Open thy gate that I may enter!
If thou openest not the gate so that I cannot en-
    ter,
I will smash the door, I will shatter the bolt,
I will smash the doorpost, I will move the doors,
I will raise up the dead, eating the living,
So that the dead will outnumber the living."
The gatekeeper opened his mouth to speak,
Saying to exalted Ishtar:
"Stop, my lady, do not throw it[2] down!

I will go to announce thy name to Queen E[reshk]igal."

The gatekeeper entered, saying (to) Er-esh[kigal]:

"Behold, thy sister Ishtar is waiting at [the gate],

She who upholds the great festivals,

Who stirs up the deep before Ea, the k[ing]."

When Ereshkigal heard this,

Her face turned pale like a cut-down tamarisk,

While her lips turned dark like a bruised ku-ninu-reed.

"What drove her heart to me? What impelled her spirit hither?

Lo, should I drink water with Annunaki?

Should I eat clay for bread, drink muddied water for beer?

Should I bemoan the men who left their wives behind?

Should I bemoan the maidens who were wrenched from the laps of their lovers?

(Or) should I bemoan the tender little one who was sent off before his time?[3]

Go, gatekeeper, open the gate for her,

Treat her in accordance with the ancient rules."

Ishtar is forced to strip away her finery

Forth went the gatekeeper (to) open the door for her:

"Enter, my lady, that Cutha[4] may rejoice over thee,

That the palace of the Land of no Return may be glad at thy presence."

When the first door he had made her enter,

He stripped and took away the great crown on her head.

"Why O gatekeeper, didst thou take the great crown on my head?"

"Enter, my lady, thus are the rules of the Mistress of the Nether World."

When the second gate he made her enter,

He stripped and took away the pendants on her ears.

"Why, O gatekeeper, didst thou take the pendants on my ears?"

"Enter, my lady, thus are the rules of the Mistress of the Nether World."

When the third gate he had made her enter,

He stripped and took away the chains round her neck.

"Why, O gatekeeper, didst thou take the chains round my neck?"

"Enter, my lady, thus are the rules of the Mistress of the Nether World."

When the fourth gate he had made her enter,

He stripped and took away the ornaments on her breasts.

"Why, O gatekeeper, didst thou take the ornaments on my breasts?"

"Enter, my lady, thus are the rules of the Mistress of the Nether World."

When the fifth gate he had made her enter,

He stripped and took away the girdle of birth-stones on her hips.

"Why, O gatekeeper, didst thou take the girdle of birthstones on my hips?"

"Enter, my lady, thus are the rules of the Mistress of the Nether World."

When the sixth gate he had made her enter,

He stripped and took away the clasps round her hands and feet.

"Why, O gatekeeper, didst thou take the clasps round my hands and feet?"

"Enter, my lady, thus are the rules of the Mistress of the Nether World."

When the seventh gate he had made her enter,

He stripped and took away the clasps round her body.

"Why, O gatekeeper, didst thou take the breachcloth on my body?"

"Enter, my lady, thus are the rules of the Mistress of the Nether World."

The consequences of Ishtar's descent

As soon as Ishtar had descended to the Land of No Return,

Ereshkigal saw her and was enraged at her presence.

Ishtar, unreasoning, flew at her.
Ereshkigal opened her mouth to speak,
Saying (these) words to Namtar, her vizier:
"Go, Namtar, lock [her] up [in] my [palace]!
Release against her, [against] Ishtar, the sixty
    mis[eries]: . . .
Against every part of her, against [her whole
    body]!"
After Lady Ishtar [had descended to the Land
    of no Return],
The bull springs not upon the cow, [the ass im-
    pregnates not the jenny],
In the street [the man impregnates] not the
    maiden.

The man lay [in his (own) chamber, the maiden
    lay on her side], [. . . l]ay[. . .].
(At this point Papsukkal the vizier of the gods
implores the gods to revive Ishtar and bring
her back to earth. Ea creates the eunuch Aš-
sushunamir who descends to the nether world
and forces Ereshkigal to revive her sister by
sprinkling her with "the water of life." Ishtar
reascends through the seven gates of the Under World and receives again her ornaments.
Tammuz, "the lover of her youth," is apparently with her as he is washed with pure water,
anointed with sweet oil, and playing "on a flute
of lapis.")

NOTES

[1]Another name for Ereshkigal.
[2]The door.
[3]Ereshkigal would weep if all occupants of the nether world should be liberated by Ishtar.
[4]A name of the nether world.

THE CODE OF HAMMURABI

Of all the original contributions made by the Sumero-Akkadian civilization to the development of Western civilization, the greatest and most enduring was the enactment of public laws. Four ancient Mesopotamian legal codes have been discovered, the most famous of which is the Code of the Babylonian king Hammurabi (c. 1728–1686 B.C.E.). The code is written on a diorite stele, topped by a bas-relief showing Hammurabi in the act of receiving the commission to write the lawbook from the god of justice, the sun-god Shamash. Our excerpts from the prologue and epilogue illustrate the Mesopotamian con-cept of the king as the agent established by the gods from the foundation of the cosmos as the one responsible for the justice of the land. This understanding of the king's role will influence the latter Israelite view of kingship (see Psalm 72) and even the Messianic vi-sion of the prophets (see Isaiah 9 and 11). The actual laws themselves regulate the rela-tions between humans on the basis of the principle that the punishment should fit the crime. The laws are stated in the conditional form of case laws and make a sharp distinc-tion between the various social classes. The content and form of the laws have a general similarity to the Israelite collection in Exodus 21–23. (The translation is by T. Meeks in **Ancient Near Eastern Texts,** 163–180.)

The prologue

When lofty Anum,[1] king of the Anunnaki,[2]
(and) Enlil,[3] lord of heaven and earth,
determined for Marduk,[4] the first-born of
    Enki,[5]

the Enlil functions over all mankind,
made him great among the Igigi,[6]
called Babylon by its exalted name,
made it supreme in the world,

established for him in its midst an enduring kingship,

whose foundations are as firm as heaven and earth—

at that time Anum and Enlil named me

to promote the welfare of the people,[7]

me, Hammurabi, the devout, god-fearing prince,

to cause justice to prevail in the land,

to destroy the wicked and the evil,

that the strong might not oppress the weak,

to rise like the sun over the black-headed (people),[8]

and to light up the land.

Hammurabi, the shepherd, called by Enlil, am I;

the one who makes affluence and plenty abound;

who provides in abundance all sorts of things for Nippur-Duranki;[9]

the devout patron of Ekur;

the efficient king, who restored Eridu to its place . . . [10]

the ancient seed of royalty, the powerful king, sun of Babylon,

who causes light to go forth over the lands of Sumer and Akkad;[11]

the king who has made the four quarters of the world subservient;

the favorite of Inanna[12] am I.

When Marduk commissioned me to guide the people aright,

to direct the land,

I established law and justice in the language of the land,

thereby promoting the welfare of the people.

At that time (I decreed):

The laws

1: If a seignior[13] accused a[nother] seignior and brought a charge of murder against him, but has not proved it, his accuser shall be put to death.[14]

2: If a seignior brought a charge of sorcery against a[nother] seignior, but has not proved it, the one against whom the charge of sorcery was brought, upon going to the river,[15] shall throw himself into the river, and if the river has then overpowered him, his accuser shall take over his estate; if the river has shown that seignior to be innocent and he has accordingly come forth safe, the one who brought the charge of sorcery against him shall be put to death, while the one who threw himself into the river shall take over the estate of the accuser.

3: If a seignior came forward with false testimony in a case, and has not proved the word which he spoke, if that case was a case involving life, that seignior shall be put to death.

4: If he came forward with false testimony concerning grain or money, he shall bear the penalty of that case. . . .

8: If a seignior stole either an ox or a sheep or an ass or a pig or a boat, if it belonged to the church[16] (or) if it belonged to the state, he shall make thirtyfold restitution; if it belonged to a private citizen,[17] he shall make good tenfold. If the thief does not have sufficient to make restitution, he shall be put to death.[18] . . .

195: If a son has struck his father, they shall cut off his hand.[19]

196: If a seignior has destroyed the eye of a member of the aristocracy, they shall destroy his eye.[20]

197: If he has broken a[nother] seignior's bone, they shall break his bone.

198: If he has destroyed the eye of a commoner or broken the bone of a commoner, he shall pay one mina of silver. . . .

200: If a seignior has knocked out a tooth of a seignior of his own rank, they shall knock out his tooth.

201: If he has knocked out a commoner's tooth, he shall pay one-third mina of silver. . . .

Epilogue

I, Hammurabi, the perfect king,

was not careless (or) neglectful of the black-headed (people),

whom Enlil had presented to me,

(and) whose shepherding Marduk had committed to me;
I sought out peaceful regions for them;
I overcame grievous difficulties . . .
With the mighty weapon which Zababa[21] and Inanna entrusted to me,
with the insight that Enki[22] allotted to me,
with the ability that Marduk gave me,

I rooted out the enemy above and below;
I made an end of war;
I promoted the welfare of the land;
I made the peoples rest in friendly habitations
    . . .
The great gods called me,
so I became the beneficient shepherd whose scepter is righteous . . . [23]

NOTES

[1]The sky-god, the leader of the pantheon.
[2]The lesser gods attendant upon Anum.
[3]The storm-god, the chief executive of the pantheon.
[4]The son of Enki and consort of Sarpanit; the god of Babylon.
[5]Lord of the earth and the mass of life-giving waters within it; the father of Marduk and the god of wisdom.
[6]The lesser gods attendant on Enlil.
[7]Lit., "to make good the flesh of the people."
[8]The late-Sumerian expression for men in general.
[9]Duranki "bond of heaven and earth," was a time-honored Sumerian name of Nippur, the cult-center of Enlil, whose temple was Ekur.
[10]Hammurabi's accomplishments are eulogized for another 210 lines.
[11]Sumer was the ancient name of southern Babylonian and Akkad of northern Babylonia, the two together constituting a common name of the whole country.
[12]The queen of heaven; the Sumerian name for Ishtar.
[13]The word in Akkadian is *awelum* which here means any free man of standing.
[14]With this law and the three following cf. Deut 5:20; 19:16ff; Exod 23:1–3.
[15]The word "river" in this section has the divine determinative, indicating that the river (the Euphrates) as a judge in the case was regarded as a god.
[16]Literally "the property of the god," i.e. the temple.
[17]As distinct from the temple or state personel.
[18]The laws on theft in the Code do not agree among themselves; in some laws theft was punished by death, but in others severalfold restitution or fine is substituted for the death penalty. This variance indicates a development in the history of Mesopotamian legal practice.
[19]Cf. Exod 21:15.
[20]Cf. Exod 21:23–25; Lev 24:19f; Deut 19:21.
[21]The war-god.
[22]Renowned for his wisdom.
[23]The text continues in this vein for several more columns.

EGYPT

Egyptian civilization, like the Sumero-Akkadian civilization, grew up in a great river valley. The Nile divides Egypt into two lands: Upper Egypt, the long narrow valley from the first cataract in the south to the Memphis district in the north, and Lower Egypt, the delta region. Rainfall is virtually non-existent in Egypt; the country is, as the ancient Greek historian Herodotus said, "the gift of the Nile." The annual inundation of the river deposits fresh silt in the narrow valley of Upper Egypt, and the swampy delta region is composed entirely of river-borne alluvium.

The unique geographical features of Egypt produced a civilization with distinct differences from its contemporary in Mesopotamia. The Nile river valley, unlike the Tigris-Euphrates, is isolated and defended by the desert to the west, the Mediterranean to the north, the Red Sea to the east, and the cataracts in the south. Until the invasion of the Hyksos in the seventeenth century B.C.E., Egypt experienced no threat from without. The navigability of the Nile in the 750 mile stretch from the first cataract to the Mediterranean also enabled a strong sovereign to govern the whole valley by a centralized administration. In contrast to the autonomous walled cities of Mesopotamia, Egypt was from the beginning of its recorded history a rural mass ruled by an incarnate god, the king, who was later known as pharaoh.

Egypt enjoyed its greatest prosperity when the country was united and irrigation centrally controlled. The Early Dynastic Period (c. 3100–2700 B.C.E.), the Old Kingdom (c. 2700–2200 B.C.E.), the Middle Kingdom (c. 2052–1786 B.C.E.), and the New Kingdom (c. 1575–1087 B.C.E.) were times when Egypt was unified. They were separated by so-called "intermediate" periods when the kings/pharaohs did not control the land, or outside invaders (the Hyksos), gained temporary political control.

Most of the important socio-political and cultural-religious creations of Egypt took place in the Early Dynastic and Old Kingdom periods. Egyptian civilization remained throughout its history extremely conservative, honoring the traditions and monuments of the beginning of history which was closely linked with the beginning of creation. According to tradition, the unification and founding of the state were the work of Menes, a native of Upper Egypt, who built the new capital of the kingdom in Lower Egypt at Memphis. The founding of the state was an event of extreme importance; it established a new world, a civilization infinitely more complex and richer than the preceding Neolithic culture, and it is immortalized on the famous Narmer tablet.

THE THEOLOGY OF MEMPHIS

The creation of a unified Egypt was an event of religious and cosmologial significance. In the mythology of Memphis, the two events—the creation of the state and the creation of the cosmos—were inextricably interwined. Our first text is from an inscription, the Shabaka Stone which was composed c. 700 B.C.E., but it derives from an original written in the early third millennium B.C.E., not long after Upper and Lower Egypt were united at the capital city of Memphis. In the text one enters the mysterious world of Egyptian religion which was highly polytheistic and never a unified whole. There were always local gods up and down the land, among whom were Ptah, the artificer-god of Memphis, who is the leading deity in this myth. Other cities had their gods and their mythic accounts of the beginning; Hermopolis had Thoth, the god of learning and the moon; Thebes had

Amun, "the hidden," who became the state god in the second millennium. There were also cosmic gods: Re or Atum, the sun-god, whose daughter *Ma'at* personified Truth, Justice, and cosmic order; Nut the sky-goddess and Shu, Geb and Ne, the gods of air, earth and the primordial waters. In this text, the unification of Egypt is presented as the accomplishment of Geb, the earth god, attended by the Ennead, or council of nine gods. Geb first reconciled a quarrel between his grandsons, Horus of Lower Egypt and Seth of Upper Egypt, and made each of them king of his respective part. Later Geb revised this first verdict and gave Horus, the son of Osiris, the entire earth, especially the two Great Sorceresses, the crowns of Upper and Lower Egypt. Horus resided at the Wall of the Nome, i.e., Memphis, and the god of Memphis, Ptah, with mind ("heart") and speech ("tongue") brought forth Atum, the creator-god. Ptah is the "mighty Great One" who gave life to all the gods and to their *kas,* or vital forces. The cosmological, religious and political orders are thus linked in a single mythological account as in the **Enuma Elish.** However, in the Egyptian myth the mode of creation is through Ptah's thinking and commanding which gives order to the whole cosmos as a body, rather than through a victory over the forces of chaos represented by Tiamat. This significant difference reflects the more orderly and confident perspective of the Egyptian experience. The idea of creation by the command of the god is reminiscent of the mode of creation in the biblical creation myth (Gen 1:1–2:4a), although the Genesis story does not have the polytheism of the Egyptian account. [The translation is by John A. Wilson in **Ancient Near Eastern Texts,** 4ff.]

THE THEOLOGY OF MEMPHIS

Geb appoints Seth and Horus to their respective lands

The Ennead, gathered themselves to him (Geb), and he judged Horus and Seth.[1] He prevented them from quarreling further, and he made Seth the King of Upper Egypt, at the place where he was born, Su. Then Geb made Horus the King of Lower Egypt in the land of Lower Egypt, at the place where his father[2] was drowned, Pezhet-Tawi. Thus Horus stood in one place, and Seth stood in another place, and they were reconciled about the Two Lands. . . .[3]

Words spoken by Geb to Seth: "To the place in which thou wert born." Seth—Upper Egypt.

Words spoken by Geb to Horus: "Go to the place in which thy father was drowned." Horus—Lower Egypt.

Words spoken by Geb to Horus and Seth: "I have judged you." Lower and Upper Egypt.

Geb changes his mind and appoints Horus over all Egypt

But then it became ill in the heart of Geb that the portion of Horus was only equal to the portion of Seth. So Geb gave his entire inheritance to Horus, that is, the son of his son, his first born.[4] . . . Thus Horus stood over the entire land. Thus this land was united, proclaimed with the great name: "Ta-tenen, South-of-His Wall, the Lord of Eternity."[5] The two Great Sorceresses grew upon his head.[6] So it was that Horus appeared as King of Upper and Lower Egypt, who united the Two Lands in Wall Nome,[7] in the place in which the Two Lands are united.

The conclusion of the quarrel

It happened that reed and papyrus were set at the great double door of the House of Ptah.[8] That means Horus and Seth, who were reconciled and united, so that they associated and their quarreling ceased in the place which they reached, being joined in the House of Ptah, "the Balance of the Two Lands," in which Upper and Lower Egypt have been weighed....

Ptah creates the divine order

The gods who came into being as Ptah:—[9] Ptah who is upon the Great Throne...; Ptah-Nun, the father who begot Atum; Ptah-Naunet, the mother who bore Atum; Ptah the Great, that is, the heart and tongue of the Ennead...[10]

There came into being as the heart and there came into being as the tongue something in the form of Atum. The mighty Great One is Ptah, who transmitted life to all gods, as well as to their *kas,* through this tongue by which Thoth became Ptah.[11]

Thus it happened that the heart and tongue gained control over every other member of the body, by teaching that he[12] is in everybody and in every mouth of all gods, all men, all cattle, all creeping things, and everything that lives, by thinking and commanding everything that he wishes....

Summary and conclusion

And so Ptah was satisfied,[13] after he had made everything, as well as all the divine order. He had formed the gods, he had made cities, he had founded nomes, he put the gods in their shrines, he had made their bodies like that with which their hearts were satisfied. So the gods entered into their bodies of every kind of wood, of every kind of stone, of every kind of clay, or anything which might grow upon him,[14] in which they had taken form. So all the gods, as well as their *kas* gathered themselves to him, content and associated with the Lord of the Two Lands....

NOTES

[1]The nine great gods attended Geb, the earth-god, for his judicial ruling on the contest between Horus and Seth for the rule of Egypt.

[2]Osiris.

[3]Here the text exhibits its form for dramatic purposes. A notation is used for speakers and stage directions.

[4]Geb revises his decision and gives all to Horus.

[5]A form of Ptah was Ta-tenen, "the land arising" (out of the primordial waters), so that creation may take place.

[6]The crowns of Upper and Lower Egypt.

[7]The province of Memphis was named "White Wall."

[8]The intertwining plants symbolize the reconciliation of the two parts of Egypt and their gods.

[9]Or, "who have (their) form in Ptah."

[10]Three other forms of Ptah appear in badly broken context. Nun was the abysmal waters, and Naunet was his consort. In these capacities Ptah brought forth Atum, the creator-god of Heliopolitan theology.

[11]Ptah thought of and created by speech the creator-god Atum ("Totality"), thus transmitting the divine power of Ptah to all other gods.

[12]Ptah as heart and tongue.

[13]Or, "so Ptah rested." Cf. Gen 2:1–4.

[14]Upon Ptah, in his form of the "rising land." Note that divine images are not the gods themselves, but only the places in which they might assume appearance.

THE OSIRIS MYTH

The nearest thing to a truly national religion in Egypt was the Osiris cycle. The story is not extant in a full epic version but must be pieced together from several ancient and classical sources: **The Pyramid Texts** of the Old Kingdom, **The Coffin Texts** of the Middle Kingdom, the **Book of the Dead** from the New Kingdom, a ribald text entitled **The Contest of Horus and Seth for the Rule** from the Twentieth Dynasty, and the summary of Plutarch in **Concerning Isis and Osiris** from the second century C.E.

When all of these sources are considered, it is apparent that the Osiris myth had a wide range of functions in the fluid world of Egyptian mythology. Osiris was a legendary king responsible for introducing civilization to Egypt. According to Plutarch, "he made the Egyptians give up their destitute and brutish mode of life, showing them the fruits produced by cultivation, and giving them laws, and teaching them how to worship the gods." After doing this he travelled the whole earth and introduced civilization by means of persuasion, reasoning and music, rather than weapons.

The Osiris cycle was also the Egyptian fertility myth in which Osiris as the god of vegetation died and was reborn in connection with the annual rise of the Nile and consequent rebirth of Egypt. This myth contains the familiar motif of the conflict between brothers (cf. the Cain and Abel story in Genesis 4). Osiris is murdered by his brother Seth who tricks him into entering a beautiful coffin prepared especially for him, but he eventually triumphs over death through the persistent and faithful love of his spouse-sister Isis and his son Horus. The fullest version of this story is Plutarch's **Concerning Isis and Osiris** which was written in the second century C.E. and contains at times Greek equivalents to the Egyptian gods. Throughout this text the Greek god Typhon is cast in the role of Seth. The translation is by Frederick Grant in **Hellenistic Religions: The Age of Syncretism** (New York: The Liberal Arts Press, 1953) 83–88.

ON ISIS AND OSIRIS

Osiris: the patron of civilization

As soon as Osiris became king, he made the Egyptians give up their destitute and brutish mode of life, showing them the fruits produced by cultivation, and giving them laws, and teaching them how to worship the gods. After doing this he traveled over the whole earth, civilizing it; instead of using weapons, he won over the masses by persuasion and reasoning, combined with song and with all kinds of music which he introduced . . .

The death of Osiris

During his absence Typhon[1] made no attempt at revolution, because Isis was on her guard and was able to keep vigilant watch of him. But after Osiris returned home, Typhon devised a plot against him, taking seventy-two men into the conspiracy and having as a helper a queen who came from Ethiopia, whom they call Aso. He secretly measured the body of Osiris and made to proper size a beautiful and highly ornamented chest, which he carried into the banquet hall. Everyone was delighted with its appearance and admired it greatly, and Typhon promised in jest that whoever should lie down inside it, and fit it exactly, him would he make a present of it. After the others had tried it, one after another, and no one had fit it, Osiris got in and lay down; at this the conspirators rushed up, slammed down the lid, and fastened it with nails on the outside, pouring melted lead over them. Then they carried the chest to the river, and let it drift down the Tanitic mouth into the sea . . .

Isis' search for Osiris

When she heard the news, Isis sheared off one of her tresses and put on a garment of mourning, . . . She wandered about everywhere, not knowing what to do, she met no one without speaking to him; even when she met some little children she asked them about the chest. And they, it so happened, had seen it, and they told her the mouth of the river (the Nile) through which Typhon's accomplices had let the chest drift into the sea . . .

Soon thereafter she learned by inquiry that the chest had been washed up by the sea at a place called Byblus,[2] and that the surf had gently lodged it in a patch of heather. This heather is a most lovely plant, growing up very large in a short time, and it had enfolded, embraced, and concealed the chest within itself. The king of the country was astonished at the size of the plant, and having cut away the clump that concealed the chest, he set it up as a pillar to support his roof . . . Sitting down at the side of a spring, dejected and weeping, she spoke not a word to anyone, except that she welcomed and made friends with the maidservants of the queen, plaiting their hair for them and infusing into their bodies a wonderful fragrance which came from herself. When the queen saw her maids again, a longing came over her to see the stranger whose hair and whose body breathed of ambrosial perfume, and so she (Isis) was sent for and became so intimate with the queen that she was made nurse of her infant . . .

Isis is said to have nursed the child by giving it her finger to suck, instead of her breast, and at night she burned away the mortal parts of his body. She turned herself into a swallow and flew around the pillar with a wailing cry until the queen, who was watching her, cried out when she saw her child all afire, and so took away the boy's immortality. Then the goddess, manifesting herself, asked for the pillar of the roof, and having removed it with the greatest ease, she cut away the heather that surrounded it. This plant she wrapped up in a linen cloth, pouring perfume over it, and entrusted it to the care of the kings; and to this day the people of Byblus venerate the wood, which is preserved in the temple of Isis. She then threw herself down upon the chest and wailed so loudly that the younger of the king's sons died of fright; the elder son she took with her, and placing the chest on board a ship, put to sea; . . .

As soon as she found privacy and was left to herself, she opened the chest and laid her face upon the face of the corpse, caressing it and weeping . . .

The dismemberment and recovery of Osiris

But when Isis had gone to see her son Horus[3] (who was being brought up in the city Buto) and had put the chest away, Typhon, being out hunting by moonlight, came upon it and, recognizing the corpse, tore it into fourteen pieces and scattered them about. Isis heard of this and went looking for the fragments, sailing through the swamps in a papyrus boat . . .

The consequence of Osiris' dismemberment is that there are many places all over Egypt called tombs of Osiris; for whenever Isis came upon a fragment of his body, she celebrated a funeral there . . .

Of the parts of Osiris' body the only one Isis was unable to find was the genital member, for this had at once been thrown into the river; and the lepidotus, the phagrus, and the oxyrhynchus had fed upon it, which kinds of fish the natives strictly refuse to eat. Instead,

Isis made a model of the organ and consecrated it, namely the phallus, in honor of which the Egyptians even at the present day hold a festival.

Horus avenges his father's death

Afterward Osiris came to Horus from the other world and trained and exercised him for war, and then asked him what he thought to be the finest thing possible. When Horus replied, "To avenge one's father and mother when they are ill-treated," he asked him secondly what he considered to be the most useful thing to anyone going into battle; and when Horus answered, "A horse," Osiris was surprised and asked why he had said a horse instead of a lion. But Horus explained that a lion is indeed useful (to guard) anyone needing help, but that a horse can both cut off the flight of the enemy and also destroy him. On hearing this Osiris was greatly pleased, supposing that Horus was adequately provided (with horses). And as many persons were coming over from time to time to the side of Horus . . .

The battle lasted for many days, and Horus was victorious; but Isis, after receiving from him Typhon bound in chains, did not destroy him, but on the contrary released him and let him go free. Horus could not endure this with patience, and so laid hands on his mother and tore the royal diadem from her head; whereupon Hermes[4] gave her a cow's head for a helmet.

Horus succeeds his father

When Typhon brought a charge of illegitimacy against Horus, Hermes acted as his counsel and Horus was pronounced legitimate by the gods . . .

NOTES

[1]Plutarch identifies Seth with the Greek giant, Typhon, who is Greek mythology attacked Zeus, cut the sinews of his hands and feet, and imprisoned him in a cave where a dragon guarded him until he was rescued by Hermes and Pan. Eventually, Zeus conquered Typhon with his thunderbolts and buried him under Mt. Aetna.

[2]An ancient city in Phoenicia, which some accounts say is the oldest city in the world.

[3]The son of Isis and Osiris.

[4]The Greek messenger-god.

THE BOOK OF THE DEAD

The story of Osiris also functioned as a dynastic myth which guaranteed the succession of a god-king on the Egyptian throne. From the Early Dynastic Period the succession from one king to his son was viewed as a realization of this myth. The deceased king (identified with Osiris) was succeeded by his son (identified with Horus). The Osiris cycle was also closely connected with the Egyptian understanding of death and the afterlife. First the king, and eventually the individual Egyptian, could be identified with Osiris revivified in his kingdom hereafter. The so-called **Pyramid Texts** which are inscriptions carved on the inside of pyramids from the Old Kingdom period insist upon the triumph of the king/pharaoh over death. The mythological device used is to identify the deceased king with the immortal gods, particularly Osiris who triumphed over death by being made ruler and judge in the underworld. Originally used for the king only, the texts were extended to queens by the end of the Sixth Dynasty and to worthy non-royal persons by the Eleventh and Twelfth Dynasties (21st century B.C.E. and after). The Egyptian belief in an afterlife and judgment on the basis of one's actions in this life stands in sharp contrast to the beliefs of ancient Mesopotamia and Israel—both of whom viewed the afterlife as a shadowy and unfulfilling mode of existence. Among the literary remains from ancient Egypt, a large number of texts seek to secure eternal happiness for the deceased individual. In the New Kingdom and later, such mortuary texts were normally on papyrus and have been gathered together by modern scholars under the title, **The Book of the Dead.** These texts frequently envision the deceased testifying before a posthumous court and denying any quilt in various crimes and short-comings. Such testimonies, along with the rich Egyptian wisdom literature, are our major sources for Egyptian ethical thought. In the following text, entitled "The Protestation of Guiltlessness," we discover a very high moral code which despite the polytheism is reminiscent of the Biblical Decalogue or Holiness Code (see Exodus 20; Leviticus 18–23). Throughout the text there is an interesting combination of high ethical standards and a belief in magic. The deceased professes to have lived according to the standards of "truth" (*ma'at*), but also assures the 42 divine jurors that he knows their names. The conclusion contains instructions for the use of the spell. The translation is by John A. Wilson in **Ancient Near Eastern Texts**, 34–36.

THE PROTESTATION OF GUILTLESSNESS

What is said on reaching the Broad-Hall of the Two Justices,[1] absolving X[2] of every sin which he has committed, and seeing the faces of the gods:

Hail to thee, O great god, lord of the Two Justices![3] I have come to thee, my lord, I have been brought that I might see thy beauty, I know thee; I know thy name and the names of the forty-two gods who are with thee in the Broad-Hall of the Two Justices,[4] who live on them who preserve evil and who drink their blood on that day of reckoning up character in the presence of Wennofer.[5] Behold, "Sati-mertifi, Lord of Justice," is thy name.[6] I have come to thee; I have brought thee justice; I have expelled deceit for thee.

(A1) I have not committed evil against men.
(A2) I have not mistreated cattle.
(A3) I have not committed sin in the place of truth.[7]
(A4) I have not known that which is not.[8]
(A5) I have not seen evil. . . .[9]

(A7) My name has not reached the Master of the Barque.[10]
(A8) I have not blasphemed a god.
(A9) I have not done violence to a poor man.
(A10) I have not done that which the gods abominate.
(A11) I have not defamed a slave to his superior.
(A12) I have not made (anyone) sick.
(A13) I have not made (anyone) weep.
(A14) I have not killed.
(A15) I have given no order to a killer.
(A16) I have not caused anyone suffering.
(A17) I have not cut down on the food-(income) in the temples.
(A18) I have not damaged the bread of the gods.
(A19) I have not taken the loaves of the blessed (dead).
(A20) I have not had sexual relations with a boy.
(A21) I have not defiled myself.
(A22) I have neither increased nor diminished the grain measure.
(A23) I have not diminished the aroura.[11]

(A24)   I have not falsified a half-aroura of land.

(A25)   I have not added to the weight of the the balance.

(A26)   I have not weakened the plummet of the scales.

(A27)   I have not taken milk from the mouths of children.

(A28)   I have not driven cattle away from their pasturage.

(A29)   I have not snared the birds of the gods.

(A30)   I have not caught fish in their marshes.

(A31)   I have not held up the water in its season.[12]

(A32)   I have not built a dam against running water.

(A33)   I have not quenched a fire at its (proper) time.

(A34)   I have not neglected the (appointed) times and their meat-offerings.[13]

(A35)   I have not driven away the cattle of the god's property.

(A36)   I have not stopped a god on his procession.

Words to be spoken by X:[14]

Hail to you, ye gods who are in this Broad-Hall of the Two Justices! I know you; I know your names. I shall not fall for dread of you. Ye have not reported guilt of mine up to this god in whose retinue ye are; no deed of mine has come from you. Ye have spoken truth about me in the presence of the All-Lord, because I acted justly in Egypt. I have not been abusive to a god. No deed of mine has come from a king who is in his day.

Hail to you who are in the Broad-Hall of the Two Justices,[15] who have no deceit in your bodies, who live on truth and who eat of truth

in the presence of Horus, who is in his sun disc. May ye rescue me from Babi, who lives on the entrails of elders on that day of the great reckoning.[16] Behold me—I have come to you without sin, without guilt, without evil, without a witness (against me), without one against whom I have taken action. I live on truth, and I eat of truth. I have done that which men said and that with which gods are content. I have satisfied a god with that which he desires. I have given bread to the hungry, water to the thirsty, clothing to the naked, and a ferry-boat to him who was marooned.[17] I have provided a divine offering for the gods and mortuary offerings for the dead. (So) rescue me, you; protect me, you. Ye will not make report against me in the presence (of the great god). I am one pure of mouth and pure of hands, one to whom "Welcome, welcome, in peace!" is said by those who see him, because I have heard those great words which the ass discussed with the cat in the house of the hippopotamus, when the witness was His-Face-Behind-Him and gave out a cry.[18] I have seen the splitting of the ished-tree in Rostau.[19] I am one who has a concern for the gods, who knows the nature of their bodies. I have come here to testify to justice and to bring the scales[20] to their (proper) position in the cemetery.

O thou who art high upon his standard, Lord of the Atef-Crown, whose name has been made "Lord of Breath,"[21] mayest thou rescue me from thy messengers who give forth uncleanliness and create destruction, who have no covering up of their faces,[22] because I have effected justice for the Lord of Justice, being pure—my front is pure, my rear is clean, my middle is in the flowing water of justice; there is no part of me free of justice. . . . .[23]

NOTES

[1]The place of the next-world judgment.
[2]The name and title of the deceased.
[3]Osiris, the judge of the dead.
[4]The knowledge of a name was an important force for control or influence.
[5]Wennofer is Osiris.. The 42 jurors are also avengers of guilt.

[6]Sati-mertifi means "The Two Daughters, His Two Eyes," but its application to Osiris is inexplicable.

[7]The temple or the necropolis.

[8]See the tree of knowledge of good and evil in Genesis.

[9]A6 is untranslatable.

[10]The sun barque, but the application is not clear.

[11]A measure of land area.

[12]Denying the inundation waters to others.

[13]The offerings at the regular feasts.

[14]X stands for the name and title of deceased.

[15]The 42 jurors and other gods attendant in court.

[16]Babi is the devourer of the condemned dead.

[17]These sentiments are common in mortuary texts.

[18]The episode is unknown.

[19]Also found in the 17th chapter of the **Book of the Dead.** The meaning is not perfectly clear.

[20]In which the character of the deceased was weighed.

[21]Osiris.

[22]Have not compassion?

[23]The translation omits three magical examinations.

THE INSTRUCTION FOR MERI-KA-RE

The Egyptians delighted in compilations of wise sayings, which were directive for a successful and happy life. During the Old Kingdom, a time of stability and prosperity, these wisdom collections reflect the optimistic outlook that a person can advance and increase in material well-being by the pursuit of a practical life of wisdom. The collapse of political and social order in the First Intermediate Period (2200–2052 B.C.E.) caused people to think more deeply and ponder moral issues as never before. **The Instruction for King Meri-Ka-Re** presents the advice which one of the many competing rulers of that time gives to his son and successor. The text illustrates the high moral plane that the Egyptians attained long before the Israelites would have entered Egypt. The first paragraph exhorts the king to act justly and kindly in this life in a way reminiscent of the Israelite prophets of the eighth and seventh centuries B.C.E. The second paragraph links the fate of a person in the afterlife to his good deeds upon earth. This is one of the loftiest expressions of the Egyptian belief in the continued existence of the individual after death. It is noteworthy that the Israelites did not come to such an understanding until the second century B.C.E. The final paragraph included in this abridgement refers to an Egyptian tradition in which men are referred to as "images" of the hidden god who has given them plants, animals, fowl, and fish to feed them and who disciplines them as a father does his children. There is also an oblique reference to the Egyptian flood tradition which is understood as coming as a result of the rebellion of the god's children. On the whole the sentiments are very close to those in the Israelite tradition in Genesis 1–11 and stand in sharp contrast to the more arbitrary actions of the gods of the Mesopotamian flood tradition. The translation is by John A. Wilson in **Ancient Near Eastern Texts**, 414–418.

Do justice whilst thou endurest upon earth. Quiet the weeper; do not oppress the widow; supplant no man in the property of his father; and impair no officials at their posts. Be on thy guard against punishing wrongfully. Do not slaughter: it is not of advantage to thee. (But) thou shouldst punish with beatings and with arrests; this land will be (firmly) grounded thereby—except (for) the rebel, when his plans are discovered, for the god knows the treacherous of heart, and the god condemns his sins in blood.[1]. . . . Do not kill a man when thou knowest his good qualities, one with whom thou once didst sing the writings.[2] He who reads in the sipu-book[3] . . . god, free-moving of foot in difficult places, (his) soul comes to the place which it knows. It does not miss the ways of yesterday. No magic can oppose it, (but) it reaches those who will give it water.[4]

The council which judges the deficient, thou knowest that they are not lenient on that day of judging the miserable, the hour of doing (their) duty.[5] It is woe when the accuser is not of knowledge. Do not trust in length of years, for they regard a lifetime as (but) an hour.[6] A man remains over after death, and his deeds are placed beside him in heaps.[7] However, existence yonder is for eternity, and he who complains of it is a fool. (But) as for him who reaches it without wrongdoing, he shall exist yonder like a god, stepping out freely like the lords of eternity. . . .

Generation passes generation among men, and the god, who knows (men's) characters, has hidden himself. (But) there is none who can withstand the Lord of the Hand: he is the one who attacks what the eyes can see.[8] Revere the god upon his way, made of costly stones and fashioned (of) metal, like a flood replaced by (another) flood. There is no river that permits itself to be concealed; that is, it breaks the (dam) by which it was hidden.[9] (So) also the soul goes to the place which it knows, and deviates not from its way of yesterday. Enrich thy house of the West; embellish thy place of the necropolis, as an upright man and as one who executes the justice upon which (men's) hearts rely. More acceptable is the character of one upright of heart than the ox of the evildoer.[10] Act for the god, that he may act similarly for thee, with oblations which make the offering-table flourish and with a carved inscription—that is what bears witness to thy name. The god is aware of him who acts for him.

Well directed are men, the cattle of the god. He made heaven and earth according to their desire, and he repelled the water-monster.[11] He made the breath of life (for) their nostrils. They who have issued from his body are his images. He arises in heaven according to their desire. He made for them plants, animals, fowl, and fish to feed them. He slew his enemies and injured (even) his (own) children because they thought of making rebellion.[12] He makes the light of day according to their desire, and he sails by in order to see them. He has erected a shrine around about them, and when they weep he hears.[13] He made for them rulers (even) in the egg,[14] a supporter to support the back of the disabled. He made for them magic as weapons to ward off what might happen or dreams by night as well as day. He has slain the treacherous of heart among them, as a man beats his son for his brother's sake.[15] For the god knows every name. . . .

NOTES

[1]Treason against the state was the one capital crime. Yet the Egyptian did not wish to lay the responsibility for capital punishment upon the pharaoh and stated that the punishment was divine vengeance.

[2]A former schoolmate.

[3]An otherwise unknown book, perhaps an "inventory," helpful in attaining eternal happiness in the next world.

[4]The soul of the rightly instructed will attain eternal happiness.

[5]The reference is to judgment after death by a tribunal of gods, at this time under the presidency of the sun-god, later with Osiris as judge.

[6]The judges of the dead remember all sins no matter how long the time may be.

[7]As legal exhibits.

[8]God, "Lord of the (creative) Hand," remains unseen from age to age, but he must be respected. Invisible, he controls the visible.

[9]The creator god, a sun disc of stone and metal, goes his daily way like the annual, irresistible inundation.

[10]See 1 Sam 15:22; Prov 15:17.

[11]"The submerger (determined with a crocodile) of the water." Reminiscent of Tiamat in the Mesopotamian tradition and Rahab or Leviathan in the biblical traditions.

[12]The most complete version of the Egyptian flood story is contained in a text entitled **The Deliverance of Mankind from Destruction.**

[13]The unseen god is still close to men through his shrine in the temple.

[14]A reference to the primordial egg of creation.

[15]The god's punishments are for man's good, like a father's discipline.

THE HYMN TO THE ATON

One of the most intriguing developments in Egyptian religion was the advancement of Aton, the solar disc, as the sole supreme deity by the young and nearly physically deformed Pharaoh Amen-hotep IV (c. 1369–1353 B.C.E.). Early in the New Kingdom period, Egypt, in reaction to the Hyksos invasion, had developed a world empire by conquering Palestine-Syria and setting up the national boundary as far from Egypt as possible. This move was rooted in a certain xenophobia, but it paradoxically opened Egypt to influences from the rest of the Near East and to a certain universalism in thinking. The chief god of the empire was Amon-Re, a combination of Amon ("the hidden one") and Re (the sun-god) whose hymns describe him as the universal creator and ruler of the universe. The temples to Amon-Re in Thebes were enlarged and their revenues increased, and the priesthood of Amon-Re gained considerable power in Egypt. The religious revolution of Amen-hotep IV was partly due to his attempt to free himself from the domination of the priesthood of Amon-Re. Soon after his enthronement, the young pharaoh deprived the high priest of Amon of the administration of the god's properties which in effect took away the source of his power. Then, he changed his name from Amen-hotep ("Amon is satisfied") to Akhen-aton (probably "He who is servicable to Aton"). He moved the capital from Thebes to a newly built city 500 kilometers to the north, which he named Akhet-Aton (now Tell el-Amarna) where he built palaces and temples to Aton. Part of the so-called Amarna revolution was an artistic style which encouraged "naturalism" in the figurative arts and the use of popular language in royal inscriptions and official decrees.

The Hymn to the Aton reflects the spiritual significance of the natural order and the rhythms of life for Akh-en-aton. The Aton is described as the creative source of all life and the distant, but providential, ruler of the physical cosmos. The "living Aton" is addressed as "the beginning of life" which "hast filled every land with thy beauty." Darkness or night is a time of terror and death for all creation when "he who made them rests in his horizon." But daybreak brings the providential rays of Aton to all creation: the Two. Lands of Egypt, the beasts, trees, plants, birds and fishes. Everything from "the seed in women" to "the chick in the egg" are created and sustained by the Sun. The general similarities between these sentiments and Psalm 104 have led scholars to suggest a possible connection between the Hebrew psalm and this hymn.

Aton's reign is not limited to Egypt. The countries of Syria and Nubia (part of Egypt's empire) are included. The distinctions of speech, race and color are determined by Aton. A bit of Egyptian chauvinism is evident in the images of the way Egypt and the other lands receive their water. Egypt is given the superior gift of a "Nile in the underworld" to maintain "the people" as opposed to the "Nile in heaven" which waters the "distant foreign countries."

Despite the universalism in the hymn, only Akh-en-aton and his immediate family worshiped the Aton. His courtiers worshiped the pharaoh himself, and most Egyptians were ignorant of, or hostile to, the new faith which was largely obliterated after the pharaoh's early death. The translation is by John A. Wilson in **Ancient Near Eastern Texts,** 369–371.

Thou appearest beautifully on the horizon of heaven,
Thou living Aton, the beginning of life!
When thou art risen on the eastern horizon,
Thou hast filled every land with thy beauty.
Thou art gracious, great, glistening, and high over every land;
Thy rays encompass the lands to the limit of all that thou has made:
As thou art Re, thou reaches to the end of them.[1]
(Thou) subduest them (for) thy beloved son.[2]
Though thou art far away, thy rays are on earth;
Though thou art in their faces, no one knows thy going.
When thou settest in the western horizon,
The land is in darkness, in the manner of death.
They sleep in a room, with heads wrapped up,
Nor sees one eye the other.
All their goods which are under their heads might be stolen,

(But) they would not perceive (it).
Every lion is come forth from his den;
All creeping things, they sting.
Darkness is a shroud, and the earth is in stillness.
For he who made them rests in his horizon.
At daybreak, when thou arisest on the horizon,
When thou shinest as the Aton by day,
Thou drivest away the darkness and givest thy rays.
The Two Lands are in festivity every day,
Awake and standing upon (their) feet,
For thou has raised them up.
Washing their bodies, taking (their) clothing,
Their arms are (raised) in praise at thy appearance.
All the world, they do their work.
All beasts are content with their pasturage;
Trees and plants are flourishing.
The birds which fly from their nests,
Their wings are (stretched out) in praise to thy ka.
All beasts spring upon (their) feet.

Whatever flies and alights,
They live when thou hast risen (for) them.
The ships are sailing north and south as well,
For every way is open at thy appearance.
The fish in the river dart before thy face;
Thy rays are in the midst of the great green sea.
Creator of seed in women,
Thou who makest fluid into man,
Who maintainest the son in the womb of his mother,
Who soothest him with that which stills his weeping,
Thou nurse (even) in the womb,
Who givest breath to sustain all that he has made!
When he descends from the womb to breathe
On the day when he is born,
Thou openest his mouth completely,
Thou suppliest his necessities.
When the chick in the egg speaks within the shell,
Thou givest him breath within it to maintain him.
When thou hast made him his fulfillment within the egg, to break it,
He comes forth from the egg to speak at his completed (time);
He walks upon his legs when he comes forth from it.
How manifold it is, what thou hast made!
They are hidden from the face (of man).
O sole god, like whom there is not other!
Thou didst create the world according to thy desire,
Whilst thou wert alone:
All men, cattle, and wild beasts,
Whatever is on earth, going upon (its) feet,
And what is on high, flying with its wings.
The countries of Syria and Nubia, the land of Egypt,
Thou settest every man in his place,
Thou suppliest their necessities:
Everyone has his food, and his time of life is reckoned.
Their tongues are separate in speech,

And their nature as well;
Their skins are distinguished,
As thou distinguishest the foreign peoples.
Thou makest a Nile in the underworld,
Thou bringest it forth as thou desirest
To maintain the people (of Egypt)[3]
According as thou madest them for thyself,
The lord of all them wearying (himself) with them,
The lord of every land, rising for them,
The Aton of the day, great of majesty.
All distant foreign countries, thou makest their life (also),
For thou hast set a Nile in heaven,
That it may descend for them and make waves upon the mountains,
Like the great green sea,
To water their fields in their towns.[4]
How effective they are, thy plans, O lord of eternity!
The Nile in heaven, it is for the foreign peoples
And for the beasts of every desert that go upon (their) feet;
(While the true) Nile comes from the underworld for Egypt.
Thy rays suckle every meadow.
When thou risest, they live, they grow for thee.
Thou makest the seasons in order to rear all that thou hast made,
The winter to cool them,
And the heat that they may taste thee.
Thou hast made the distant sky in order to rise therein,
In order to see all that thou dost make.
Whilst thou wert alone,
Rising in thy form as the living Aton,
Appearing, shining, withdrawing or approaching,
Thou madest millions of forms of thyself alone.
Cities, towns, fields, road, and river—
Every eye beholds thee over against them,
For thou art the Aton of the day over the earth
. . .
Thou art in my heart,
And there is no other that knows thee
Save thy son Nefer-kheperu-Re Wa-en-Re,[5]

For thou hast made him well-versed in thy plans and in thy strength.[6]
The world came into being by thy hand,
According as thou hast made them.
When thou hast risen they live,
When thou settest they die.
Thou art lifetime thy own self,
For one lives (only) through thee.
Eyes are (fixed) on beauty until thou settest.
All work is laid aside when thou settest in the west.

(But) when (thou) risest (again),
Everything is made to flourish for the king, . . .
Since thou didst found the earth
And raise them up for thy son,
Who came forth from thy body:
The King of Upper and Lower Egypt, . . . Akh-en-Aton, . . . and the
Chief Wife of the King . . . Nerfert-iti, living and youthful forever and ever.

NOTES

[1]Pun: *Ra* "Re," and *er-ra* "to the end."

[2]Akh-en-Aton.

[3]The Egyptians believed that their Nile came from the waters under the earth, called by them Nun.

[4]The rain of foreign countries is like the Nile of rainless Egypt.

[5]Even though the hymn was recited by the official Eye, he states that Akh-en-Aton alone knows the Aton.

[6]The pharaoh was the official intermediary between the Egyptians and their gods. The Amarna religion did not change that dogma.

2

ISRAEL AND THE HEBREW SCRIPTURES

Although politically and materially inferior to the great civilizations of Mesopatamia and Egypt and often a pawn in their political power games, the ancient Israelites had a much greater religious influence on Western civilization. The three great religious traditions of the West—Judaism, Christianity, and Islam—are rooted in the events and beliefs recorded in the Hebrew Scriptures of ancient Israel. All three in some way understand these writings as the inspired revelation of the one Creator God who has entered history to save his chosen people and reveal his moral will to them. Ancient Israel shared with Mesopotamia and Egypt certain cosmological, ethical and even religious conceptions. However, its religion is distinguished from the polytheistic naturalism of its neighbors by a consistent emphasis on moral behavior, the worship of only one God who is not identified with the forces of nature or the human psyche, but who is revealed through the events of history and guides them for saving purposes.

The following introductions to the most important books of the Hebrew Scriptures are meant for the student who is studying the Bible in the context of an interdisciplinary course in Western civilization or ancient Western religious thought. For a more complete introduction to the Hebrew Scriptures, the student can refer to Lawrence Boadt's **Reading the Old Testament: An Introduction** (New York, N.Y./Mahwah, N.J.: Paulist Press, 1984). For commentaries on individual books, the student can consult the commentary series entitled **Old Testament Message: A Biblical-Theological Commentary** (Wilmington, Del.: Michael Glazier, 1982–1984). All quotations in the following introduction are from the **Revised Standard Version Bible** copyrighted 1946, 1952 © 1971, 1973 by the Division of Christian Education of the National Council of Churches of Christ in the U.S.A., and used by permission.

THE TORAH

The most sacred portion of the Hebrew Scriptures is the Torah or "Revelation" which is composed of the first five scrolls (Pentateuch): the Books of Genesis, Exodus, Leviticus, Numbers, and Deuteronomy. It narrates the foundational events in the Israelite tradition: the creation of heavens and the earth and the primeval history of human rebellion against God (Genesis 1–11); the revelation to the Israelite patriarchs which promises that they would be the source of blessing for the nations of the earth through becoming a numerous people in the land of Canaan (Genesis 12–50); the exodus from slavery in Egypt (Exodus 1–18); the giving of the law in connection with the covenant at Sinai (Exodus 19–40; Leviticus); God's guidance of the people through the wilderness toward the promised land of Canaan (Numbers); and Moses' farewell address to the Israelites on the eastern border of the promised land (Deuteronomy).

In its present form the Torah is the product of a long period of oral and literary development from the time of the patriarchs and Moses in the second millennium B.C.E. to its final editing after the exile in Babylon, probably sometime in the late fifth century B.C.E. Scholars are able to distinguish at least four distinct literary strands in the present text of the Pentateuch on the basis of duplicate narratives, inconsistencies, variations in divine names, vocabulary, literary style and theology. Despite its antiquity and literary complexity, the Torah is stamped with a religious unity which has made it the source of religious and artistic inspiration throughout the history of the West.

GENESIS

The Book of Genesis or "Beginning" is the Israelite story of origins from the time of creation to the sojourn of the family of Jacob/Israel in Egypt. The book naturally divides into two sections: the primeval history (Genesis 1–11) and the patriarchal history (Genesis 12–50) which treats of the Israelite forefathers (Abram/Abraham, Isaac, Jacob/Israel, and Joseph).

The material in the primeval history, although written in prose, shares much in common with the poetic mythic and epic traditions of the ancient Near East, especially Mesopotamia, the land from which the Israelite ancestors migrated (cf. Genesis 11–12) sometime in the first half of the second millennium B.C.E. We find, for example, a myth of the creation of an ordered world from chaos (Gen 1:1–2:4a), an account of the marring or loss of the gifts of fertility and immortality in the Garden of Eden story (Gen 2:4b–3:24), a cosmic flood which destroys most of the human race (Genesis 6–9), and the story of the building of the city of Babylon (Babel) (Gen 11:1–9). However, in place of Mesopotamian polytheism, the Israelite accounts are monotheistic, with only rare hints of an earlier polytheism (cf. Gen 1:26; 3:22; 6:1–4; 11:1–9). The Israelite God is not a personification of the forces or processes of nature, nor does he have a female consort; he is the Creator of the cosmic order through his word of command (Genesis 1). Although he is responsible for the gifts of the earth's fertility, human life and sexuality (Genesis 2), these are not to be maintained by fertility rites, but by obedience to his moral will (Gen 2:15–17). Despite the fact that the details of the flood story in Genesis 6–9 are remarkably similar to the account in **The Gilgamesh Epic,** the motive for sending the flood in the biblical version is consistent with the moral character of Israel's God. Throughout the primeval history he acts to judge and punish sin, but also to make provision for the maintenance of his creation and the human family.

The biblical portrayal of the human condition makes an interesting contrast with that in the **Enuma Elish.** The creation myth in Genesis 1:1–2:4a has an exalted view of the position of humans in the cosmos. In contrast to the **Enuma Elish** where man is an afterthought created to relieve the lesser gods of the burden of caring for the earth, the Genesis account sees humans as the climactic pinnacle of God's orderly plan, created in the "image" and "likeness" of God and commissioned to rule by having dominion over the whole created order (Gen 1:26–30). The succeeding stories in Genesis 2–11 balance this exalted view of humanity's capabilities with a series of sin-punishment narratives which portray the actual condition of the human family. According to the Garden of Eden story (Gen 2:4b–3:24), humans were intended to be happy farmers, enjoying the gifts of a fertile earth, sexuality, and even immortality which is symbolized by the "tree of life" in the midst of the garden (2:1–24). However, the actual character of human existence is something quite different. Humans are rebels who strive to be like the gods, knowing good and evil, i.e., experiencing everything (Gen 3:1–7). They fall victim to jealousy and commit the most callous fratricide, so that Cain's defiant "Am I my brother's keeper?" can lead to the unlimited vengeance of Lamech who sings:

> "I have slain a man for wounding me,
> a young man for striking me.
> If Cain is avenged sevenfold,
> truly Lamech seventy-sevenfold." (Gen 4:23–24)

In contrast to the Mesopotamian view in which the vicissitudes of human existence were determined by the capricious will of the gods, in the biblical view the difficulties and enigmas of the actual human condition are seen as largely the consequence of humanity's rebellious character. The immediate consequences of sin are portrayed as a retreat from the highest potentials of humanity into shame, fear, hiding, and refusal to take responsibility before God for one's action (Gen 3:8–13). The long range results of sin are multiple and strike at the very heart of human existence: domination of women by men and pain in childbirth (3:16); a never-ending struggle with the earth for man the farmer until he returns in death to the ground from which he was taken (3:17–19); alienation and confusion in the communication between the peoples of the earth who in their arrogant dedication to their own projects no longer can speak to one another (Gen 11:1–9).

The turning point in the Genesis narrative is the call of Abram/Abraham in Genesis 12. God's creation has been marred by humanity's persistent wickedness which not even the flood has erased. Israel's understanding of its special role in the divine plan is personified in the story of Abram/Abraham. Out of the curse-ridden human family God separates one man to whom he promises the destiny of being the instrument of blessing for all the dispersed families of the earth. In his journey in Genesis 12, Abram, in contrast to the disobedient man in Genesis 3, fulfills God's command by obediently leaving his country, kindred and father's house for the land and destiny that God has promised him. Enormous obstacles block the fulfillment of the promise. Sarai, Abram's wife, is barren, and Abram himself is seventy-five years of age. When he arrives in Canaan, Abram discovers that the land is already occupied by the Canaanites. Even the patriarch himself endangers the promise by not always being a model of faith. In the story of his sojourn in Egypt in the time of famine (Gen 12:9–20), he jeopardizes the ancestress out of fear and fraility when he pretends that his beautiful wife Sarai is his sister and allows her to be taken into Pharaoh's harem.

In Genesis 15 and again in Genesis 17 the divine promises are sealed in solemn covenants in which God unconditionally binds himself on oath to give the childless Abram/Abraham an heir, offspring as numerous as the stars, and the land of promise. As recipient of these promises, Abraham is in a position to mediate God's blessing for sinful humanity in the memorable story of Sodom and Gomorrah in which his persistent and wily intercession saves the innocent Lot and his two daughters from the destruction of the cities of the plain (Genesis 18–19). Finally, in the terrifying story of his testing in Genesis 22, Abraham proves his worthiness to be the recipient of the divine promises by his willingness to undertake the journey to sacrifice his long-awaited and beloved son, Isaac.

Although the stories of the Israelite patriarchs are based on a long oral tradition, much like the Homeric epics, they do reflect something of the background of the Near East in the second millennium B.C.E. Such things as the pastoral way of life, marriage and inheritance customs, personal names, divine names, and religious customs have been documented by extra-biblical sources from the second millennium. In their present form, however, the narratives reflect the mature faith of post-exilic Israel. In fact, the power of these narratives does not rest on their exact historicity, but on their vision of God and his purpose in human affairs.

The recommended reading is Genesis 1–22.

EXODUS

After tracing the story of the promise through the generations of Isaac and Jacob (Genesis 25–35), Genesis ends with the magnificent story of Joseph and his brothers (Genesis 37–50), the forefathers of the twelve tribes of Israel. Joseph, the favored of Jacob's twelve sons, is sold by his jealous brothers into slavery in Egypt only to rise providentially to a position of responsibility under the Pharaoh because of his God-given ability to interpret dreams. When the family of Jacob is forced to come to Egypt in time of famine, Joseph is in a position to test his brothers and arrange a family reconciliation and reunion in Egypt. Genesis concludes on the happy note of the settling of the family of Jacob/Israel in Egypt under the protection of Joseph. However, although the descendants of Abraham have begun to grow numerous, the promise of the land still awaits fulfillment as the Israelites are living as aliens in the land of Egypt.

Exodus opens with the oppression of the Israelites under an unnamed Egyptian king "who did not know Joseph." It goes on to narrate the most crucial events in Israelite history: the miraculous deliverance of Israel from Egyptian bondage (Exodus 1–15), the journey to Mount Sinai/Horeb (Exodus 16–18), and the formation of a covenant community under the Lord's law (Exodus 19–40). From the time of the exodus, Israel's God will be identified, not in a abstract or mythical way, but as the one who brought his people out of Egypt and led them to the promised land. In the words of the cultic credo in Deuteronomy 26:5ff:

> "A wandering Aramean was my father; and he went down into Egypt and sojourned there, few in number; and there he became a nation, great, mighty, and populous. And the Egyptians treated us harshly, and afflicted us, and laid upon us hard bondage. Then we cried to the Lord, the God of our fathers, and the Lord heard our voice, and saw our affliction, and our toil, and our oppression; and the Lord brought us out of Egypt with a mighty hand and an outstretched arm, with great terror, with signs and wonders; and he brought us into this place and gave us this land, a land flowing with milk and honey . . . "

The exodus story is patterned after the mythic battle to control chaos in the **Enuma Elish** in Mesopotamian culture. The hero of the account is the Lord, the God of the enslaved Israelites, who like Marduk fights against a tyrant who is bent on destruction. There are of course significant differences between the Israelite version and the Mesopotamian myth. The time of the action is within the historical memory of the people of Israel and not in the prehistoric time of the creation myth. And the opponent is not the vengeful divine mother Tiamat, the personification of the primordial salt waters, but the Pharaoh whose tyrannical policies are designed to oppress and even destroy the Israelite slaves.

The exodus narrative is designed to glorify the Lord, the God of Israel. It begins by painting the bleakest possible situation. The Israelites are under the threat of genocide, and their only would-be leader is living as an exile in the wilderness of Midian (Exodus 1–2). Against this stark backdrop we are told:

> In the course of those many days the king of Egypt died. And the people of Israel groaned under their bondage, and cried out for help, and their cry under bondage came up to God. And God heard their groaning, and God remembered his covenant with Abraham, with Isaac, and with Jacob. And God saw the people of Israel, and God knew their condition. (Ex 2:23–25)

Exodus 3–15 narrates in dramatic fashion the Lord's actions to liberate his people. He calls Moses as his agent to deliver the Israelites from oppression and lead them to the land of promise (Exodus 3–6). In the plague traditions (Exodus 7–11), the Passover (Exodus 12–13) and the defeat of Pharaoh and his army at the Red Sea (Exodus 14) the Lord is a divine warrior who defeats the agent of chaos, the sinful and proud Pharaoh, for his cruel and unjust enslavement of the Israelites. The identification of God with the rights of the oppressed and the overthrow of political despotism is a persistent feature of the Israelite religion, especially in the preaching of the prophets. Fittingly, the exodus story ends with the triumphant Song of Moses in which the Lord is lauded as the victorious warrior and king (Ex 15:1–18).

"I will sing to the Lord, for he has
    triumphed gloriously;
the horse and his rider he has
    thrown into the sea.
The Lord is my strength and my song,
    and he has become my salvation;
this is my God, and I will praise him,
    my father's God, and I will exalt him.
The Lord is a man of war;
    the Lord is his name . . ." (Ex 15:1–3)

The story of Israel's journey from Egypt through the wilderness to Mount Sinai (Exodus 15:22–18:27) is an archetypal story of danger and testing, comparable to Gilgamesh's journey in search of Utnapishtim and the secret of immortality. The Israelites encounter danger and obstacles as they move from one camping place to another: bitter water (15:22–27), lack of food (16:1–36), lack of water (17:1–7), and the attack of fierce enemies (17:8–16). In most cases the Israelites are fearful and complaining, unprepared for the freedom of the wilderness and longing for the security of slavery in Egypt. At Elim, for example, they murmur against Moses and Aaron and say:

"Would that we had died by the hand of the Lord in the land of Egypt, when we sat by the fleshpots and ate bread to the full; for you have brought us out into this wilderness to kill this whole assembly with hunger." (Ex 16:3)

They are pictured as putting the Lord to the test by wondering: "Is the Lord among us or not?" (Ex 17:7). In contrast to the complaining Israelites, the Lord is portrayed as providing for the sustenance of his people in the midst of the dangers of the wilderness. He makes the bitter water sweet (15:25), gives manna and quail to eat (16:13–15), brings forth water from the rock (17:6), and enables them to defeat the Amalekites (17:13).

The account of Israel's stay at Sinai also reflects basic Israelite values. The transcendent nature of the Lord as the God who chose Israel and now makes challenging moral and religious demands is evident in the terrifying theophany at Sinai and the stipulations of the so-called decalogue, or ten commandments (Exodus 19–20). The covenant ceremony in Exodus 24 demonstrates that Israel was a unique community in the ancient world in that the basis of its unity was not a common political overlord, but the choice to serve the Lord by identifying with his gracious deliverance and pledging to obey his will. Finally, the golden calf incident (Exodus 32) illustrates that Israel itself was not immune to the allurement of sin that enticed the other nations (cf. Genesis 3–11, 19) and that it too is in need of intercession and forgiveness.

The human hero of the exodus, and the remainder of the Torah, is Moses. He is so central to the narrative that in some ways the rest of the Torah is the story of Moses' life. It begins with his birth in Egypt during a time of oppression (Exodus 2) and ends with his death at the age of one hundred and twenty years in the plains of Transjordan in sight of the promised land (Deuteronomy 34). Moses combines in his person all of the leadership roles that will later be differentiated into several offices in Israel's community. He is the Lord's agent in delivering Israel from slavery and leading them to the promised land, the interpreter of his saving deeds, and the mediator of the covenant. Each of the literary strands in the Pentateuch portrays him in a slightly different light, but all agree that he was the one who laid the spiritual foundations of Israel's faith. In the words of Deuteronomy:

> And there has not arisen a prophet since in Israel like Moses, whom the Lord knew face to face, none like him for all the signs and wonders which the Lord sent him to do in the land of Egypt, to Pharaoh and to all his servants and to all his land, and for all the mighty power and all the great and terrible deeds which Moses wrought in the sight of all Israel. (Deut 34:10–12)

Unlike the Mesopotamian hero, Gilgamesh, who is highly individualistic in his quest for friendship, fame, adventure and immortality, Moses is a communal hero who finds his purpose in a God-given mission for his people and their destiny in God's plan. Gilgamesh was a semi-divine figure whose mother was the goddess. He was endowed with superhuman gifts of strength and courage, but in the beginning of the epic he is an oppressor of his own people. Moses, on the other hand, is the son of an Israelite slave who providentially escapes death in time of oppression (Exodus 2). Although raised in the Egyptian court, he is sensitive to his people's plight, and even feebly attempts to remedy it by killing an Egyptian overseer who is beating one of the Hebrews (Ex 2:11–12). But Moses is totally inadequate for leadership of his people. When he tries to stop the two Hebrew slaves from fighting, one of them rejects his efforts with the retort,

> "Who made you a prince and judge over us? Do you mean to kill me as you killed the Egyptian?" (Ex 2:14)

This rude confrontation with his human limitations in a situation of oppression forces Moses to flee into the wilderness of Midian (Ex 2:15–22). If Moses is to liberate his people, he must be divinely equipped for his task which is the point of the burning bush story in Exodus 3–4. Even in the call story the emphasis is on Moses' reluctance and sense of human inadequacy. His initial response to his commission to lead his people forth from Egypt is to say, "Who am I that I should go to Pharaoh, and bring the sons of Israel out of Egypt?" (Ex 3:11). The numerous miraculous powers and aids given to Moses in Exodus 4:1–17 are designed to convince the incredulous Israelites that the Lord has indeed appeared to Moses.

Once Moses undertakes his task, he is challenged to be obedient to it in the midst of the greatest adversity, but he is also ever aware that the source of power comes from the Lord. When faced with the angry Israelite foremen after they are have been forced to gather their own straw and maintain their quota of bricks (Ex 5:1–23), Moses turns to the Lord and says,

> "O Lord, why hast thou done evil to this people? Why didst thou ever send me? For since I came to Pharaoh to speak in thy name, he has done evil to this people, and thou hast not delivered thy people."

Also with the approach of Pharaoh's army at the Red Sea, Moses quiets the terrified Israelites with the words:

> "Fear not, stand firm, and see the salvation of the Lord, which he will work for you today; for the Egyptians whom you see today, you shall never see again. The Lord will fight for you, and you have only to be still." (Ex 14:13–14)

When the Israelites break the covenant in the golden calf incident, Moses assumes the role of an heroic intercessor who literally stands between his angry Lord and the people. In a manner reminiscent of the flood account, the Lord announces his intentions to destroy the Israelites and begin again with the innocent Moses (Ex 32:7–10). At this point Moses is able to calm the Lord's anger by reminding him of the deliverance from Egypt and the promises made concerning his people to the patriarchs.

> "O Lord, why does thy wrath burn hot against thy people, whom thou hast brought forth out of the land of Egypt with great power and with a mighty hand? . . . Turn from thy fierce wrath, and repent of this evil against thy people. Remember Abraham, Isaac, and Israel, thy servants, to whom thou didst swear by thine own self, and didst say to them, 'I will multiply your descendants as the stars of heaven, and all this land that I have promised I will give to your descendants, and they shall inherit it for ever.' " (Ex 32:11–13)

This heroic plea successfully turns the Lord from his intention to destroy the whole people (Ex 32:14).

Although Egyptian records do not mention the exodus, there is little doubt that Israel's faith rests upon actual historical events. The evidence from Exodus points to the 19th dynasty in Egypt (c. 1350–1200 B.C.E.) as the historical setting for the Israelite departure from Egypt and eventual entrance into the land of Canaan.

The recommended reading is Exodus 1–20, 24, 32–34.

THE FORMER PROPHETS

The second portion of the Hebrew Scriptures is the so-called Former Prophets which contains the books of Joshua, Judges, 1–2 Samuel and 1–2 Kings. This collection is a lengthy theological history tracing the story of Israel in the land of promise from the time of the conquest of the land under Joshua (c. 1250 B.C.E.) to the tragic loss of the land and exile into Babylon (c. 586 B.C.E.). The history is divided into distinct periods by the editors who put the work together in its final form during the exile (c. 550 B.C.E.), and each period is evaluated in terms of its fidelity to the law of Moses as expressed in the Book of Deuteronomy. For this reason scholars refer to the work as the Deuteronomic History.

1–2 SAMUEL

The most interesting section of this history, from both a literary and theological standpoint, is 1–2 Samuel which recounts the origin of the Israelite monarchy and the careers of Samuel and the first two kings, Saul and David (c. 1020–960 B.C.E.). The background for these events is the struggle with the heavily armed Philistines for control of the land of Canaan. This was Israel's heroic age in which she was led by valiant men of arms, and, as such, 1–2 Samuel makes an interesting comparison and contrast to the Homeric epics in the Greek tradition.

Although in its present form 1–2 Samuel comes from the time of the exile (c. 550 B.C.E.), the material that the exilic editors used comes from a time much closer to the events narrated. Most scholars think that the account of David's rise and his kingship was written during the reign of his son and successor Solomon and that it represents the earliest example of true historiography (history writing) in Western civilization. It predates Herodotus, the father of Greek historiography, by five hundred years.

Characterization is much more fully developed than in earlier Hebrew narative. Samuel is a colossal figure who stands at the end of one era, the tribal federation, and the beginning of another, the monarchy. He combines in himself the offices of priesthood, judge and prophet (1 Samuel 1–7). In the beginning he was bitterly opposed to the monarchy (1 Samuel 8), but then, under the Lord's direction, anoints first Saul and then David to lead the people (1 Samuel 9–10, 16). He also announces to Saul the Lord's displeasure and rejection when his commands are violated (1 Samuel 13, 15).

Saul is a classic tragic figure. He begins his career with great expectations and auspicious success. When he first appears, Saul is a tall, handsome young farm boy who is a reluctant leader (1 Samuel 9). Nevertheless, Samuel anoints and commissions him with the words:

> "Has not the Lord anointed you to be prince over his people Israel? And you shall reign over the people of the Lord and you will save them from the hand of their enemies round about." (1 Sam 10:1)

In his initial battle Saul delivers the people of Jabesh-Gilead from oppression by successfully rallying the twelve tribes and defeating Nahash the king of the Ammonites (1 Samuel 11). Although this is the one of the few times a successful battle is actually narrated, we can gather from a summary text that Saul was a valiant and frequently victorious warrior.

When Saul had taken over Israel, he fought against all his enemies on every side, against Moab, against the Ammonites, against Edom, against the kings of Zobah, and against the Philistines; wherever he turned he put them to the worse. And he did valiantly, and smote the Amalekites, and delivered Israel out of the hands of those who plundered them. (1 Sam 14:47–48)

However, after beginning so well, Saul quickly loses the favor of Samuel and the Lord when he fails to obey the Lord's commands in time of crisis. For example, rather than waiting for Samuel to offer sacrifice before a battle with the Philistines, Saul panics when he sees his men slipping away and offers the sacrifice himself (1 Sam 13:2–10). Immediately Samuel is on the scene to confront Saul with his deed and announce that he has lost favor with the Lord.

"You have done foolishly; you have not kept the commandment of the Lord your God, which he commanded you; for now the Lord would have established your kingdom over Israel for ever. But now your kingdom shall not continue; the Lord has sought out a man after his own heart; and the Lord has appointed him to be prince over his people, because you have not kept what the Lord commanded you." (1 Sam 13:13–14)

Obedience to the Lord's commands is the highest of Israelite values. As Samuel says to Saul after yet another failure to obey his command to put the Amalekites to the ban:

"Behold, to obey is better than sacrifice and to hearken than the fat of rams . . . " (1 Sam 15:22)

Saul's loss of divine favor is manifested in severe fits of depression which the text describes as "an evil spirit from the Lord" (1 Sam 16:14). Even though David's skillful lyre playing is able to temporarily sooth Saul's spirit, this is not a permanent solution to his malaise. In fact, Saul soon becomes insanely jealous of David's considerable success as a warrior and repeatedly tries to kill the very man who could have helped him personally and aided him militarily. Saul's paranoia makes him suspicious of his own children and isolates him from his once loyal troops (1 Samuel 18–22). The tragic result of Saul's insecurity is his senseless slaughter of the priests at Nob whom he incorrectly suspects of having willingly aided David (1 Sam 22:6–23). The final picture of Saul is extremely pathetic. Unable to consult the Lord by any of the traditional means, he is forced to violate his own law and consult with a woman medium to bring up the ghost of the dead Samuel in order to receive an oracle before entering battle with the Philistines (1 Sam 28:1–25). Samuel's shade reiterates Saul's previous rejections and announces that he and his sons will die in battle with the Philistines.

Saul recaptures a measure of heroism in his death. He does not run from his fate, but enters the fateful battle. In the end he is forced to take his own life when his armor bearer refuses to slay him after he has been wounded by the Philistines (1 Sam 31:1–7). Saul is actually more honored by the narrative after his death than during his life. The loyal people of Jabesh-Gilead rescue his corpse from the Philistines and give it a proper burial (1 Sam 31:8–13), and David eulogizes both Saul and his beloved Jonathan in his memorable elegy.

> "Thy glory, O Israel, is slain upon thy high places!
> How are the mighty fallen! . . .
> From the blood of the slain,
> from the fate of the mighty,
> the bow of Jonathan turned not back,
> and the sword of Saul returned not empty.
> Saul and Jonathan, beloved and lovely!
> In life and in death they were not divided;
> they were swifter than eagles,
> they were stronger than lions.
> Ye daughters of Israel, weep over Saul,
> who clothed you daintily in scarlet,
> who put ornaments of gold upon your apparel." (2 Sam 1:19–27)

David is perhaps the most fully developed character in the Hebrew Scriptures. Beginning his career as a young shepherd boy, who with the help of the Lord slays the Philistine giant Goliath, David rises to become the king of both Judah and Israel. His considerable personal gifts are evident throughout the narrative: prowess as a warrior, diplomatic skill and cunning, sensitivity as a composer and musician, steadfast loyalty to Saul and his covenant friend, Jonathan, and religious leadership in bringing the ark to Jerusalem (1 Samuel 16–2 Samuel 6).

Despite this obviously favorable portrait, 1–2 Samuel is not a piece of political propaganda for David which glorifies the king to the point of ignoring his faults. The narrative is consistently theological throughout, tracing the providential rise of the young king, but also chronicling his nearly tragic degeneration because of his sin in later years (2 Samuel 11–20, 1 Kings 1–2). After receiving from Nathan the prophet the glorious promise that his dynasty would last for ever (2 Samuel 7), David, in typical despotic fashion, commits adultery with Bathsheba and orchestrates the murder of her husband Uriah (2 Samuel 11). Israel's persistent sense of the Lord's covenant demands is evident when Nathan reappears to confront David with his sin in the unforgettable parable of the ewe lamb (2 Samuel 12:1–6) and to announce the Lord's inevitable punishments (2 Samuel 12:7–15).

> "Why have you despised the word of the Lord, to do what is evil in his sight? You have smitten Uriah the Hittite with the sword, and have taken his wife to be your wife, and have slain him with the sword of the Ammonites. Now therefore the sword shall never depart from your house, because you have despised me . . . " (2 Sam 12:9–10).

David was the Lord's anointed, but, unlike the semi-divine kings of Egypt and Babylon, he was a man who was also under the judgment of Israel's covenant Lord.

2 Samuel 13–20 and 1 Kings 1–2 goes on to narrate the tragic fulfillment of Nathan's prophecies. The sword truly devours the house of David who displays a fatal weakness for indulging his sons. Amnon, David's eldest son, rapes his half-sister Tamar and David fails to take action in punishing him (2 Sam 13:1–22). Then, Absalom, Tamar's full brother avenges the deed by murdering Amnon his brother (13:23–33). This drives Absalom from Jerusalem, and when he finally returns, he is hopelessly alienated from his father (13:34–14:33). The ambitious Absalom then leads a revolution against his father who abandons the city of Jerusalem as a chastened and penitent sinner (2 Sam 15:1–16:23). When Absalom enters the city, his first act is to sleep with David's concubines to show his break with his father and in fulfillment of Nathan's earlier prophecy (16:20–23; cf. 12:11–12). David's forces eventually defeat Absalom, but the king is all but immobilized by grief over his son's death (2 Samuel 17–18). David has to be brought to his senses by the ruthless, but practical, Joab who convinces him to greet his victorious troops and begin the process of restoring order to a divided kingdom (2 Samuel 19–20). The sins of David have had near disastrous effects not only on his own family but on the entire nation.

When we last see David, he is a pathetic old king who has still not made provision for succession and has to be forced into action by the ambition and palace intrigue around him (1 Kings 1). The succession of Bathsheba's son Solomon is marked by violence and needless bloodshed—indicating that the sword has still not left the house of David. Solomon consolidates his power by executing his rival and elder brother Adonijah and either murdering or exiling those who did not support his claim to the throne (1 Kings 2).

The portrayal of Israel's God in the Books of Samuel, especially in the David story, is quite different from that in the Books of Genesis and Exodus. The story is still concerned with the Lord's involvement in events, but no longer are there spectacular divine interventions through plague or miracle. Rather, the Lord is active through the words of the prophet Nathan and in the consequences of the king's own actions and decisions. The Lord is still pictured as a moral God who makes covenant demands, confronts and punishes sin, but the divine presence is not seen as an intervention from outside the normal course of historical events. The Lord is also understood as continuing to make provision for the sustenance of his chosen people. Despite David's sin and its near disastrous consequences, the nation and the Davidic line continues.

The recommended reading is 1 Sam 1:1–2 Sam 20:22; 1 Kgs 1:1–2:46.

THE PROPHETS

The prophetic books in the Hebrew Bible represent the collection of the oracles, largely in poetry, of the so-called classical prophets of Israel and Judah who were active in the period from c. 750–400 B.C.E. Their message is in the judgment of many the high point of Israelite religious consciousness. The prophetic conception of God as a personal, yet universal, force who guides all human history according to moral purposes and their vision of a future universal kingdom of God in which the human family will live under

God's law in lasting peace have had a permanent impact on the religious outlook of Western civilization.

The historical books of Samuel and Kings record the oracles and actions of such prophetic figures as Nathan, Ahijah, Elijah and Elisha, but not until the eighth century did Israel produce prophets whose words were written down and collected in separate volumes. By this time the united kingdom of David and his son Solomon (c. 1000–922 B.C.E.) was divided into two distinct nations: the larger, but more unstable, kingdom of Israel in the north with its capital at Samaria, and the smaller kingdom of Judah in the south with its capital and temple in Jerusalem. Judah was still ruled by the Davidic line, but Israel was governed by a succession of dynasties that were never able to maintain power for more than three or four generations.

The outburst of prophetic activity in the eighth century was occasioned by a combination of religious, economic and political factors. Both nations were susceptible to the allurements of the indigenous fertility cult of Canaan: the worship of the storm and fertility god Baal and his female consort. The syncretistic confusion between this fertility religion, with its rites of sacred prostitution, and the worship of the Lord was widespread. Toleration of the fertility cult was accompanied by a neglect of the ethical and social demands of the Mosaic covenant. A wealthy aristocracy exploited peasants and perverted the system of justice through bribery. In the face of these practices, the prophets insisted upon the continued relevance of the Mosaic legislation. Finally, in the eighth century the Assyrians, the most militaristic of all Mesopotamian peoples, began to expand to the West in order to build an empire in competition with the decadent power of Egypt. Against this background the prophets appear as reformers and messengers of Israel's covenant Lord who will chastise Israel and Judah for their violations of the covenant through the agency of Assyria.

AMOS

The first of the eighth century prophets is Amos, a herdsman and dresser of fruit trees from the hill country of Judah who surprisingly spoke as a prophet in the northern kingdom of Israel (1:1). Amos was not one of the professional prophets who earned their living by giving advice to the king in military and political matters; in fact he was thought by the religious establishment to be a threat to the political order. When Amaziah the priest of Bethel hears Amos' prophecy he sends the following message to Jeroboam II the king of Israel:

> "Amos has conspired against you in the midst of the house of Israel; the land is not able to bear all his words. For thus Amos has said,
> 'Jeroboam shall die by the sword,
> and Israel must go into exile
> away from his land.'" (Amos 7:10–11)

Like the other great classical prophets, Amos attributed his message to the experience of a personal call to prophesy in behalf of the Lord against the nation and its religious and social practices which violated the demands of the Mosaic covenant. When Amaziah tries to send him back to Judah to "prophesy there," Amos replies,

> "I am no prophet, nor a prophet's son; but I am a herdsman, and a dresser of sycamore trees, and the Lord said to me, 'Go, prophesy to my people Israel.' " (Amos 7:14–15)

He did not limit his message to Israel. In the opening oracles of his book (1:3–2:5), the prophet announces the punishment of Israel's neighbors for their crimes of violence against other nations. This represents the earliest written expression of an ethical universalism in Israel. It is an universalism rooted in Israel's covenant theology as opposed to the rational universalism that will be developed by the Greek philosophers. For Amos, the Lord, the God of Israel, is operative in the history of all nations. Israel herself, though, is particularly chastised for her social injustice and empty worship because of her covenant relationship with the Lord.

> Hear this word that the Lord has spoken against you, O people of Israel, against the whole family which I brought up out of the land of Egypt:
> "You only have I known
> of all the families of the earth;
> therefore I will punish you
> for all your iniquities." (3:1–2)

Amos is particularly concerned with the breakdown of social justice in the land of Israel, and he sees the inevitable destruction of the nation directly linked to this fact.

> "They do not know now to do right," says the Lord,
> "those who store up violence and robbery in their strongholds."
> Therefore thus says the Lord God:
> "An adversary shall surround the land,
> and bring down your defenses from you,
> and your strongholds shall be plundered." (Amos 3:10–11)

In Amos' eyes the cult and priesthood of Israel has become hopelessly corrupt, and the nation's purpose as a covenant community really has nothing to do with its worship.

> "I hate, I despise your feasts,
> and I take no delight in your solemn assemblies. . . .
> Take away from me the noise of your songs;
> to the melody of your harps I will not listen.
> But let justice roll down like waters, and righteousness like an
> ever-flowing stream." (Amos 5:21–24)

Although there may have been a time when Amos held out some hope that the nation of Israel would repent (cf. 5:4–15), throughout most of his prophecy the destruction of the nation appears inevitable. A hopeful oracle has been added at the end of the book (9:11–15), but most scholars attribute this to a later scribe.

The recommended reading is Amos 1–9.

HOSEA

The other great prophet who was active in Israel during the eighth century B.C.E. was Hosea. He repeated Amos' denunciations of ritualistic observances, but went further in expressing the positive ideal of true religion as an attitude of mind and heart. Hosea conveyed this message by using a daring marital metaphor, similar to that used in the fertility cult of Baal, to express the relation between Yahweh and his people. Rather than use the metaphor to express the relationship between the deity and the fertility of the earth, Hosea used it to express the historical relationship between the Lord and his people. Israel had originally been married to Yahweh in covenant, but now she had prostituted herself with the gods of Canaan in the false belief that Baal produced good harvests. Israel has played the harlot.

> "For their mother has played the harlot;
> she that conceived them has acted shamefully.
> For she said, 'I will go after my lovers,
> who give me my bread and my water, my wool and my
> flax, my oil, and my drink.' " (Hos 2:5)

Hosea seems to have given parabolic expression to his message by actually marrying a harlot named Gomer. When the Lord first spoke through Hosea, the Lord said to Hosea,

> "Go, take to yourself a wife of harlotry and have children of harlotry, for the land commits
> great harlotry by forsaking the Lord." So he went and took Gomer the daughter of Diblaim,
> and she conceived and bore him a son. (Hos 1:2–3)

The prophet goes on to give Gomer's children names symbolic of the broken covenant relationship (Hos 1:4–9).

In contrast to Amos, Hosea sees the judgment that awaits the nation as potentially redemptive. Israel will learn from her punishment to turn from the fertility cults and return to her covenant Lord.

> "Therefore I will hedge up her way with thorns,
> and I will build a wall against her,
> so that she cannot find her paths.
> She shall pursue her lovers,

> but not overtake them;
> and she shall seek them,
> but shall not find them.
> Then she shall say, 'I will go
> and return to my first husband,
> for it was better with me then than now.' " (Hos 2:6–7)

Continuing his marital metaphor, the prophet looks beyond the day of punishment to a remarriage between the Lord and Israel and a restored paradisal relationship with nature.

"And in that day, says the Lord, you will call me, 'My husband,' and no longer will you call me, 'My Baal.' . . . And I will make for you a covenant on that day with the beasts of the field, the birds of the air, and the creeping things of the ground; and I will abolish the bow, the sword, and war from the land; and I will make you lie down in safety. And I will betroth you to me for ever; I will betroth you to me in righteousness and in justice, in steadfast love, and in mercy. I will betroth you to me in faithfulness; and you shall know the Lord." (Hos 2:16–20)

Hosea lived through the chaotic final years of Israel's existence when the nation was under constant threat from Assyria and living in virtual anarchy. Four Israelite kings were assassinated in the short space of fourteen years after the death of Jeroboam II. The prophet has left us vivid pictures of the court intrigue and the ultimate futility of trying to save the nation by political means rather than internal spiritual reformation.

> They are all adulterers;
> they are like a heated oven,
> whose baker ceases to stir the fire,
> from the kneading of the dough
> until it is leavened.
> On the day of our king the princes
> became sick with the heat of wine;
> he stretched out his hand with mockers.
> For like an oven their hearts burn with intrigue;
> all night their anger smolders;
> in the morning it blazes like a flaming fire.
> All of them are hot as an oven
> and they devour their rulers.
> All their kings have fallen;
> and none of them calls upon me. (Hos 7:4–7)

The prophet was also critical of trying to save the nation by making various political alliances with the superpowers of the day.

Ephraim is like a dove,
silly and without sense,
calling to Egypt, going to Assyria.
As they go, I will spread over them my net;
I will bring them down like birds of the air;
I will chastise them for their wicked deeds. (Hos 7:11–12)

The oracles of punishment announced by Amos and Hosea were fulfilled in 722/721 B.C.E. when the Assyrian armies conquered the northern kingdom of Israel and deported nearly thirty thousand of its leading citizens (cf. 2 Kgs 17:1–41). The brutal realization of these prophets' predictions undoubtedly contributed greatly to the fact that their oracles came to be treasured as "the word of the Lord" in subsequent generations.

The recommended reading is Hosea 1–3; 5–7; 11–14.

ISAIAH

The greatest of the eighth century prophets in Judah was Isaiah whose prophetic message reflects the religious traditions associated with the Jerusalem temple and the Davidic dynasty that reigned in Judah as opposed to the Mosaic traditions found in Amos and Hosea.

The passage in which Isaiah describes his call in the Jerusalem temple is a masterpiece of religious mysticism. The prophet becomes aware at once of the aweful holiness of God and the uncleanness of both himself and his people.

In the year that King Uzziah died I saw the Lord sitting upon a throne, high and lifted up; and his train filled the temple. Above him stood the seraphim; each had six wings. . . . And one called to another and said:
"Holy, holy, holy is the Lord of hosts;
the whole earth is full of his glory."
And the foundations of the thresholds shook at the voice of him who called, and the house was filled with smoke. And I said: "Woe is me! For I am lost; for I am a man of unclean lips, and I dwell in the midst of a people of unclean lips; for my eyes have seen the King, the Lord of hosts!" (Is 6:1–5)

Despite his sense of unworthiness, the prophet is purified and commissioned to go as the Lord's messenger to a recalcitrant people (Is 6:6–13).

The main theme of Isaiah's preaching is that the holiness of the Lord requires justice and not ritual, and in this respect his message resembles Amos'.

"When you spread forth your hands,
I will hide my eyes from you;
even though you make many prayers,

> I will not listen;
> your hands are full of blood.
> Wash yourselves; make yourselves clean;
> remove the evil of your doings
> from before my eyes;
> cease to do evil,
> learn to do good;
> seek justice, correct oppression;
> defend the fatherless, plead for the widow." (Is 1:15–17)

Throughout his long career Isaiah, like Hosea, was opposed to foreign alliances as a basis of security for his nation. No doubt the prophet feared religious contamination, but he also was convinced that the nation's hope lay in a faithful relationship with "the Holy One of Israel."

> Woe to those who go down to Egypt for help
> and rely on horses,
> who trust in chariots because they are many
> and in horsemen because they are very strong,
> but do not look to the Holy One of Israel
> or consult the Lord! (Is 31:1)

For Isaiah, as for Hosea, Assyria was "the rod" of the Lord's "anger" sent to punish "a godless nation" (Is 10:5ff), but the prophet also expressed the conviction that Assyrian pride and wanton destruction would in turn be punished (Is 10:12–19).

Judah's judgment came in 701 B.C.E. when the Assyrian king Sennacherib swept down from the north, cut off communication with Egypt, and laid siege to Jerusalem as Isaiah had predicted (Is 29:1–4). In a famous Assyrian inscription Sennacherib boasts of sealing up Hezekiah, the king of Judah, "like a bird in a cage" and of extorting enormous sums of gold and silver, as well as skilled artisans and royal children, as payment for ending the siege. Although Jerusalem escaped destruction, the surrounding Judean countryside was devastated, and relegated to political dependence.

Chapters 36 and 37 of Isaiah, as well as 2 Kings 18:13–19:37, present a strikingly different account of the events. In this version, Hezekiah is pictured as showing absolute faith in the Lord's power to rescue Judah from the Assyrian forces, and his trust is rewarded by a miracle. The Assyrian forces are devasted by a plague and forced to withdraw. Whether the Isaiah-Kings version represents a second Assyrian siege, or whether both the Assyrian and biblical accounts are exaggerated versions of the same event is not known. In any case, Jerusalem did not suffer the same destruction visited upon Israel, and its unexpected escape contributed dramatically to the belief that David's holy city was specially protected by the hand of Israel's God (cf. Jeremiah 7 and 26).

Like Hosea, Isaiah looked beyond the period of punishment to a hopeful future. He believed that a small remnant would preserve authentic faith and become the basis for the Lord's restoration of a universal kingdom of peace centered in Jerusalem and ruled by an ideal king in the Davidic line (cf. Is 2:1–5; 9:1–7; 11:1–16). Isaiah's vision of the nations coming to Zion to learn the Lord's law and turn their weapons into instruments of productive agriculture is one of the most memorable in the Western religious heritage.

> It shall come to pass in the latter days
> that the mountain of the house of the Lord
> shall be established as the highest of the mountains,
> and shall be raised above the hills;
> and all the nations shall flow to it,
> and many peoples shall come and say:
> "Come, let us go up to the mountain of the Lord,
> to the house of the God of Jacob;
> that he may teach us his ways
> and that we may walk in his paths."
> For out of Zion shall go forth the law,
> and the word of the Lord from Jerusalem.
> He shall judge between the nations,
> and shall decide for many peoples;
> and they shall beat their swords into plowshares,
> and their spears into pruning hooks;
> nation shall not lift up sword against nation,
> neither shall they learn war any more. (Isa 2:1–4; cf. Mic 4:1–4)

The recommended reading is Isaiah 1–12; 36–37.

JEREMIAH

The prophet Jeremiah lived through the tragedy of Judah's defeat and the destruction of Jerusalem and its temple at the hands of the Babylonian armies in the beginning of the sixth century B.C.E. He was a descendant of a priestly family from the village of Anathoth near Jerusalem (Jer 1:1). In his early years the prophet witnessed the zealous reforms of King Josiah (c. 640–609 B.C.E.) who attempted to dedicate the nation of Judah to a pure form of Mosaic religion after the blatant idolatry of his grandfather Manasseh (cf. 2 Kings 21–23). The reform was given impetus by the discovery of the book of the law (probably some form of our present Deuteronomy) during the course of repairs on the temple. Josiah's program was also abetted by the collapse of Assyrian power which had terrorized the Near East for two centuries. However, after the premature and tragic death of Josiah in 609 B.C.E., his successors and the people of Jerusalem did not heed Jeremiah's repeated warnings that a return to the idolatry and social injustices of the recent past would result in the destruction of the nation and its temple. In his famous temple sermon at the beginning of the reign of Jehoiakim, Jeremiah warned:

"Thus says the Lord of hosts, the God of Israel, Amend your ways and your doings, and I will let you dwell in this place. Do not trust in these deceptive words: 'This is the temple of the Lord, the temple of the Lord, the temple of the Lord.'" (Jer 7:3–4)

He reminded the people of Jerusalem that the former temple at Shiloh had been destroyed by the Philistines in the time of Eli because of the wickedness of the people and that the Lord could do the same to the Jerusalem temple (Jer 7:8–15).

When Judah joined a pro-Egyptian alliance and refused to pay tribute to Babylon, the emperor Nebuchadnezzar invaded and laid siege to Jerusalem, and, in 597 B.C.E., looted the temple and deported the young King Jehoiachin and ten thousand of the leading citizens of Judah to Babylon (2 Kgs 24:10–15). Nebuchadnezzar appointed Zedekiah as a puppet king (2 Kgs 24:16), but unfortunately he made the same foolish mistake as his predecessors and also rebelled against Babylon (2 Kgs 24:20). During this period Jeremiah urged submission to the yoke of Babylon as the only way to preserve the nation (cf. Jeremiah 27). He was opposed in this policy by nationalistic prophets like Hananiah (Jeremiah 28) who announced that the exile would be brief and the deportees would soon be returning home. Jeremiah, on the other hand, exhorted the exiles in a letter to settle in Babylon for a long stay (Jeremiah 29). His message seemed to many of his contemporaries as treason, and the prophet was publicly rejected, imprisoned and nearly assassinated (cf. Jeremiah 37–39). The agony of his personal suffering during his unpopular prophetic ministry is vividly reflected in the so-called "Confessions"—laments in which he struggles with his Lord about his task.

Woe is me, my mother, for you have borne me to be a man of strife and of dissension for all the land. I neither lend nor borrow, yet all of them curse me. (Jer 15:10; cf. Jer 11:18–12:6; 15:10–21; 17:14–18; 18:18–23; 20:7–13; 20:14–18).

Jeremiah's advice was not heeded, and, when Zedekiah rebelled, the Babylonian armies again laid siege to Judah and this time destroyed Jerusalem and its beloved temple. In the darkest hour of Judah's tragedy, when the Babylonian armies were besieging the city, Jeremiah's message suddenly became hopeful. He bought a plot of land that he had the right to purchase in the tribal system of family land inheritance in order to indicate that "homes and fields and vineyards shall again be bought in this land" (32:15). During this period he probably spoke his hopeful oracles which look forward to a return to the land of promise (Jeremiah 30–31). The most famous of these is his description of the new covenant in which he anticipates the time when the demands of the covenant will be interiorized and written upon the hearts of the Lord's people.

"But this is the covenant which I will make with the house of Israel after those days, says the Lord: I will put my law within them, and I will write it upon their hearts; and I will be their God, and they shall be my people . . ." (Jer 31:31–34)

Jeremiah did not witness the fulfillment of his hopes for the restoration of Judah. He was spared by the invading Babylonian armies, but, after the assassination of the governor appointed by Babylon, Jeremiah was taken into Egypt by the rebels (Jeremiah 39–43). Our last information about the prophet is his continued critique of his fellow Jews in Egypt who lapse into the worship of the queen of heaven (Jeremiah 43–45).

The recommended reading is Jeremiah 1–2; 7–8; 11; 15; 21–23; 26–33; 36–39; 52.

ISAIAH 40–55

The fall of Jerusalem (587/86 B.C.E.) was a tragedy of almost inconceivable proportions for the little kingdom of Judah. The religion and life of the nation had been built around the land of promise, the city of Jerusalem, its temple and sacrifices, and the dynasty of David. Now all of these were lost. The Book of Lamentations poignantly expresses the desolation and despair in Zion after its collapse.

> How lonely sits the city
> that was full of people!
> How like a widow has she become,
> she that was great among the nations!
> She that was a princess among the cities
> has become a vassal.
> She weeps bitterly in the night,
> tears on her cheeks;
> among her lovers
> she has none to comfort her;
> all her friends have dealt
> treacherously with her,
> they have become her enemies. (Lam 1:1–2)

The future of the people lay, as Jeremiah had indicated, with the exiles in Babylon, but they were challenged to adapt the institutions and beliefs of their religion to the changed circumstances of living as aliens in a foreign land. Psalm 137 graphically expresses the sense of loss, estrangement and anger felt by the exiles.

> By the waters of Babylon,
> there we sat down and wept,
> when we remembered Zion.
> On the willows there
> we hung up our lyres.
> For there our captors
> required of us songs,
> and our tormentors, mirth, saying,
> "Sing us one of the songs of Zion!" (Ps 137:1–3)

By all logic the Jews should have disappeared from the pages of history, but their faith proved equal to the challenge. The exile was a time of enormously creative religious activity. The prophet Ezekiel, a priest deported in 597 B.C.E., announced in a highly visionary message that Judah would be punished for its cultic corruption but would eventually repent, be restored and rebuild the temple in Jerusalem. In the meantime the exiles followed the pragmatic advice of Jeremiah and made a new life for themselves in Babylon while they awaited their distant redemption. The faithful avoided assimilation by zealously following religious laws that could be maintained independently from the temple: circumcision, sabbath observance, and the food laws. Scribes began the important process of setting down the Torah and the pre-exilic prophets in a more definitive form. Historians edited the history of the nation while in the land (Joshua–Kings) in an effort to explain the tragedy of the exile as a consequence of the failure of both Israel and Judah to obey the law of Moses as expressed in the Book of Deuteronomy.

The greatest prophet during the exile was the anonymous poet who produced the lyrical oracles in Isaiah 40–55, the so-called Second Isaiah. His message differs from that of the previous prophets in that it is made up almost exclusively of oracles of salvation which offer glad tidings to the disillusioned exiles.

> Comfort, comfort my people,
> says your God.
> Speak tenderly to Jerusalem,
> and cry to her,
> that her warfare is ended,
> that her iniquity is pardoned,
> that she has received from the Lord's hands
> double for all her sins. (Is 40:1–2)

In hymns and oracles of assurance which describe a new exodus, a second journey through the wilderness, and a restored city of Zion the prophet fired the imagination and hopes of his fellow Jews for a return to their homeland.

> "In the wilderness prepare the way of the Lord,
> make straight in the desert a highway for our God.
> Every valley shall be lifted up,
> and every mountain and hill be made low;
> the uneven ground shall become level,
> and the rough places a plain.
> And the glory of the Lord shall be revealed,
> and all flesh shall see it together,
> for the mouth of the Lord has spoken." (40:3–5)

The agent for this act of liberation, according to the prophet, is to be the Persian king, Cyrus the Great (c. 600–530 B.C.E.) whom he daringly designates as the Lord's "shepherd" and "anointed" (Is 44:24–45:13)—titles formerly reserved for the Davidic kings. The prophet's conviction that the God of Israel can use foreign kings as his agents for both punishing and saving his people leads him to repeatedly announce in dramatic fashion that the Lord, the God of Israel alone is the God of the universe and that the gods of the other nations are simply idols.

> "You (the exiles) are my witnesses," says the Lord,
> "and my servant whom I have chosen,
> that you may know and believe me
> and understand that I am he.
> Before me no god was formed,
> nor shall there be any after me.
> I, I am the Lord,
> and besides me there is no savior.
> I declared and saved and proclaimed,
> when there was no strange god among you;
> and you are my witness,"
> says the Lord.
> "I am God, and also henceforth I am he;
> there is none who can deliver from my hand;
> I work and who can hinder it?" (Is 43:10–13)

This prophet's oracles represent the most unequivocal statement of monotheism in the Hebrew Scriptures.

Second Isaiah also radically transforms the understanding of Israel's role in the Lord's plan of salvation. Rather than nationalistic visions of a Davidic world empire, the prophet describes Israel as a people called to walk in righteousness and thus be a "covenant to the people" and "a light to the nations" (Is 42:5–9). Closely related to this purified role for Israel is the mysterious figure of the servant of God described in the so-called Servant Songs (Is 42:1–6; 49:1–6; 50:4–11; 52:13–53:12). This servant, whose portrait has undoubtedly been influenced by suffering prophets like Jeremiah and possibly Second Isaiah himself, brings salvation for others by voluntarily offering his suffering and prophetic mission as a sacrifice to atone for the nation's sin. He does not come in power and pomp but in suffering and meekness. He dies rejected and despised and yet makes atonement for sin. His life in retrospect brings those who witnessed it to a new understanding of God and his purpose.

> Surely he has borne our griefs
> and carried our sorrows;
> yet we esteemed him stricken,
> smitten by God and afflicted.
> But he was wounded for our transgressions,
> he was bruised for our iniquities;

upon him was the chastisement that made us whole,
and with his stripes we are healed. (Is 53:4–6)

The figure of the suffering servant implies a complete rejection of all worldly standards and represents the highest expression of the Israelite religious tradition. Christians
will later see the embodiment of the suffering servant in the person of Jesus (cf. Acts 9:32–
40).
The recommended reading is Isaiah 40–55.

EZRA AND NEHEMIAH

Second Isaiah's dream of a return to the promised land came true. In 539 B.C.E. Cyrus' armies peacefully entered a non-resistant Babylon and put an end to the Babylonian
empire. This enlightened monarch conceived of his Persian empire as a commonwealth of
provinces enjoying a large degree of autonomy under the control of viceroys or satraps. As
part of a general policy of relocation of "displaced persons," he authorized the Jewish exiles to return to their country which became the Persian province of Judea and to rebuild
the temple (Ezr 1:1–4; 6:1–5). A small minority of Jews made the trek back to their homeland, led by Sheshbazzar, a prince of Judah. Others remained in Babylon, and became a
part of the so-called diaspora or "dispersion" of the Jews through out the Near Eastern
and Mediterranean world. The returning exiles found a ruined Jerusalem which needed
to be totally rebuilt. Only by 515 B.C.E. were they able to complete the rebuilding of the
second temple under the urging of the prophets Haggai and Zechariah and the leadership
of Zerubbabel, another prince of Judah, and Joshua, a priest (cf. Haggai 1–2; Zechariah
1–8; Ezra 1–6). Although both Haggai and Zechariah entertained messianic expectations
for Zerubbabel, Judea was not destined to be led by a Davidic prince. He mysteriously
disappears from the accounts of the post-exilic community; possibly he was removed by
the Persians who may have feared a revival of the Davidic dynasty. Judea was to remain
a Persian province until the time of Alexander's conquests, and leadership during this
period belonged to the priesthood which was no doubt less of a political threat to Persian
hegemony.
Our chief sources of information for the restoration during the Persian period are the
Books of Ezra and Nehemiah which along with 1 and 2 Chronicles are part of a single
historical work written from a priestly and cultic perspective about 350 B.C.E. Although
the sequence and chronology of the events they relate cause serious problems, the historical substance of these books is sound. Ezra was a Jewish priest and scribe who returned
to Jerusalem from Babylon during the reign of the Persian emperor Artaxeres I (c. 465–
423 B.C.E.) to promulgate the Mosaic Torah and to supervise a reformation of the Jewish
religion (Ezra 7–10). The book that bears his name is made up partially of his memoirs
(cf. 7:27–28; 8:1–31; 9:1–15). Ezra's influence on later Judaism was so great that he is
sometimes called "the father of Judaism" which is the term properly used for the religion
of the people of Judea after the return from the Babylonian exile.

Nehemiah was a Jewish court official at the court of Artaxerxes in Susa who persuaded the emperor to commission him to go to Judea and rebuild Jerusalem's walls (Neh 1:1–2:20). Although he encountered resistance from Judah's jealous neighbors, Nehemiah rapidly finished the rebuilding (Neh 3:33–6:19), and, with the help of Ezra, effected numerous social and religious reforms among the returned exiles (Neh 8:1–9:3; 11:1–3; 12:27–13:3).

The spirit of these reforms was understandably conservative. The openness of Second Isaiah's vision was replaced by a more narrow outlook based on the need to preserve the Jewish people and their religious identity in a pagan environment. Mixed marriages were halted; those who had taken foreign wives were forced to divorce them. Strict sabbath observance was enforced. Circumcision and dietary laws were emphasized. The second temple had an elaborate ritual for "sin offerings" and "guilt offerings" (see Leviticus 1–7). Judaism was now consolidated into a religion with a universally accepted written authority (the Torah) and permanent institutions, especially the temple which was the rallying point for Jews who lived in Judea. They visited the temple for three great annual festivals: Passover in April–May which commemorated the exodus from Egypt; Weeks (or Pentecost), the feast of the spring harvest, celebrated fifty days after Passover; and Tabernacles (or Booths), an autumn agricultural festival of thanksgiving during which the celebrants lived in booths reminiscent of the wilderness encampments used during Israel's journey from Egypt to Canaan.

The recommended reading is Ezra 1–10 and Nehemiah 1–2; 4–6; 8–9; 10–13.

THE WRITINGS

Religious leadership in the post-exilic period of consolidation was the province of the priest, the scribe, and the sage, as opposed to the king and prophet. During this time "the Writings," the third major portion of the Hebrew Scriptures, took shape and was written. This collection is the most diverse of all the sections of the Hebrew Bible. It contains a wide variety of literary genres: religious and secular songs (Psalms, Lamentations, and the Song of Songs), wisdom writings (Proverbs, Job, Qoheleth), historical novels (Ruth, Esther), historical chronicles (Ezra, Nehemiah and 1–2 Chronicles), and apocalyptic visions (Daniel).

THE PSALMS

The best expression of the living spirituality of a people is in its prayer, the lyrics of its inspired poets. This is supremely true of the Jews who, in the psalms, have given to Western civilization the most influential body of psalmody ever written. The present collection of one hundred and fifty psalms developed over the course of approximately a thousand years. The various types of psalms (hymns, laments, songs of thanksgiving and trust, etc.) are also found in ancient Mesopotamia, Egypt and Canaan, and in fact some psalms like Psalm 29 or 104 may have actually been partially borrowed from neighboring cultures. Many of the psalms were used in the liturgy of Solomon's temple (c. 950–587 B.C.E.), and, in something like their present form, the psalms made up the hymnal of the second temple (c. 515 B.C.E.–70 C.E.). Today the psalms continue to play a vital part in the liturgy of the Jewish synagogue and the various Christian churches.

The poetry of the Psalter vividly reflects the faith and culture of its composers. Its lyric is concentrated totally on God in his relation to the world of nature, to the people of Israel, and to the individual in all the joys and vicissitudes of life. The imagery of the psalms is extremely concrete and drawn from the everyday life in the land. The God-fearing person is "like a tree planted by streams of water"; the wicked "are like chaff which the wind drives away" (Ps 1:3–4). God is described with human and emotion-charged images. He is a shepherd who "makes me lie down in green pastures" and "leads me beside still waters" (Ps 23:2–3). The heavens are "the works of his fingers" (Ps 8:3).

The psalms also give graphic expression to the entire range of human spiritual emotion. Psalm 104, for example, expresses the lyrical joy at the wonder of God's presence in nature as the one "who stretches out the heavens like a tent" (Ps 104:2). The memory of how God "opened the rock, and water gushed forth" in the wilderness inspires the psalmist to invite the congregation to "give thanks to the Lord, call on his name, make known his deeds among the peoples" (Ps 105:1, 41). The sense of being forsaken by God is being "poured out like water" or "dried up like a potsherd" (Ps 22:14–15). Attack by malicious mockers is described as having "dogs . . . round about me" or "many bulls encompassing me" (Ps 22:12,16). The heartfelt need for removal of guilt leads to the cry "wash me thoroughly from my iniquity and cleanse me from my sin" (Ps 51:2).

The primary characteristics of the poetry of the psalms, and of all ancient Hebrew poetry, are rhythmic beat and parallelism. The commonest verse form is two, but sometimes three or four, lines of two to four stressed syllables. Parallelism is essentially "thought rhyme" in which the second half of a verse either repeats the thought of the first in different words, or completes the first, or expresses the same idea by way of contrast.

The recommended reading is to sample the major types of psalms: hymns of praise, trust, or thanksgiving (Pss 8, 19, 23, 24, 46, 103, 104, 114, 115, 118, 131, 136, 139, 150); enthronement, royal or messianic psalms (Pss 2, 21, 45, 72, 110); psalms of lament, petition, penitence, and indebtedness (Pss 22, 44, 51, 74, 79, 80, 105, 106, 130); psalms of blessing and cursing (1, 109, 137); psalms of wisdom, meditation and instruction (1, 32, 37, 49, 52, 73, 90, 112, 119, 128).

PROVERBS

Israel like her neighbors in Egypt, Mesopotamia, Edom and Phoenicia had a wisdom literature which aimed at giving maxims for conduct based on the observation of nature and human experience. The Book of Proverbs is a thirty-one chapter compendium of proverbs from the long Israelite wisdom tradition. One section (Prov 22:17–24:22) even appears to be modeled upon the Egyptian instruction entitled "The Instruction of Amen-em-ope." The superscription (Prov 1:1) ascribes the proverbs to "Solomon, son of David, king of Israel." This attribution is probably not totally historical and is due to the tradition that Solomon composed more than three thousand proverbs (1 Kgs 4:29–33). In fact Solomon became the patron of the wisdom tradition in much the same way as Moses was for the Torah and David for the Psalms.

The style of Proverbs stands in sharp contrast to that of the prophets. Instead of the prophet messenger formula and judgment speech which is usually addressed to the entire nation, Proverbs uses the form of a personal appeal to the individual, usually the young man:

> Hear, my son, your father's instruction,
> and reject not your mother's teaching . . . (Prov 1:8)

There are also no appeals to Israel's unique historical traditions and covenant theology. Rather, the young man is addressed simply as a human being who can be won over to the path of wisdom as opposed to folly. This makes Proverbs one of the more universalistic books in the Hebrew Scriptures. Much of its advice is non-religious and pragmatic in tone and equally applicable in other societies. For example, the following proverb about the value of diligent hard work has its equivalent in almost any culture.

> Go to the ant, O sluggard;
> consider her ways, and be wise.
> Without having any chief, officer or ruler,
> she prepares her food in summer,
> and gathers her sustenance in harvest.
> How long will you lie there, O sluggard?
> When will you arise from your sleep?
> A little sleep, a little slumber,
> a little folding of the hands to rest,
> and poverty will come upon you like a vagabond,
> and want like an armed man. (Prov 5:6–11)

This is not to say that Proverbs is unethical. In fact the tone throughout is highly moral, didactic, and even dogmatic. But the foundation for morality tends to be conformity to the laws of God's creation—to the order put in the cosmos by the wise Creator (Proverbs 8) which the sage has discovered and expressed in proverbs. Wisdom is to know this divine Wisdom and attune one's life to it. The first step in this process is to acknowledge God as the primary reality:

> The fear of the Lord is the beginning of knowledge;
> fools despise wisdom and instruction. (Prov 1:7)

Wisdom, *hokmah* in Hebrew, is, as in most languages, a feminine noun and fittingly is personfied as a woman throughout Proverbs (cf. 1:20–33; 8:1–36; 9:1–6). Lady Wisdom is like a hawker in the street who invites the simple and foolish to follow her admonitions and forsake their foolish ways before their complacency destroys them (Prov 1:20–33). In a surprising development for monotheistic Israel, Lady Wisdom is portrayed like a goddess who exists with the Lord before creation, working beside him, delighting and rejoicing before him:

> The Lord created me at the beginning of his work,
> the first of his acts of old.
> Ages ago I was set up,
> at the first, before the beginning of the earth. . . .
> I was beside him, like a master workman;
> and I was daily his delight,
> rejoicing before him always,
> rejoicing in his inhabited world
> and delighting in the sons of men. (Prov 8:22–23, 30–31)

This passage, which shows the Lord creating the world through a mediator, Wisdom, was used by later Jewish thinkers who were interested in finding connections between Greek philosophy and Hebrew revelation. Philo Judaeus, who lived in Alexandria in Egypt during the first century C.E., linked the Stoic notion of *logos,* "word" or "divine reason" with this Hebrew concept of pre-existent Wisdom. The hymn to the Logos in John's gospel (John 1:1–18) is also related to Philo's concept and ultimately to Proverbs 8.

Finally, the allegory in Chapter 9 contrasts Wisdom and Folly as two women who invite the simple to their respective banquets. Lady Wisdom says:

> "Whoever is simple, let him turn in here!"
> To him who is without sense she says,
> "Come, eat of my bread
> and drink of the wine I have mixed.
> Leave simpleness, and live,
> and walk in the way of insight." (Prov 9:4–6)

On the other hand, Folly, personified as a wanton harlot, says:

> "Whoever is simple, let him turn in here!"
> And to him who is without sense she says,
> "Stolen water is sweet,
> and bread eaten in secret is pleasant."

Unfortunately the fool "does not know that the dead are there, that her guests are in the depths of Sheol" (Prov 9:18).

The recommended reading is Proverbs 1–9; 12; 13; 22; 31.

THE BOOK OF JOB

The maxims in the Book of Proverbs represent the traditional wisdom of Israel's sages. They are highly moral, but also pragmatic, conservative and conventional. Although the Israelite wise man was, like the Greek ethical philosopher, concerned with the search for happiness and the good life, he is not ordinarily probing and speculative in the way a Socrates was. Conventional Hebrew wisdom was built on the conviction that God in his wisdom and justice is the ultimate reality and that the ways of God in the world can be adequately captured in the proverb of the sage so as to be a successful guide for living a virtuous and happy life. Such wisdom simply ignores, for the most part, certain data of human experience, like the incidents in which virtuous and wise persons may suffer inexplicable personal tragedy, because they do not conform to its maxims and view of God as a just and wise Creator. The Book of Job, arguably the greatest masterpiece of ancient Hebrew literature, is a dramatic protest against traditional wisdom in the name of a more probing approach to human experience and a more mysterious understanding of God and his ways in governing the cosmos.

In the prologue (1–2) the author sets the scene for his dramatic dialogue (3:1–42:6) with a traditional prose folktale in which a righteous Job patiently endures incredible personal tragedy and suffering when God allows Satan, "the adversary," to test his commitment to being God-fearing. In a single day the patriarch hears the news of the loss of all his livestock and then the tragic death of his children (1:13–19). In a second test Job himself is afflicted "with loathsome sores from the sole of his foot to the crown of his head." Through both tests "Job did not sin with his lips." The original folktale probably ended much as the epilogue (42:10–17) does with the restoration of Job who had faithfully endured his test. Such a view was quite traditional, as Hebrew tradition recognized that the Lord may discipline or test his faithful ones only to eventually restore them (cf. the story of Abraham's test in Genesis 22).

In the cycle of poetic speeches in 3:1–42:6, the author explodes the traditional view of both the character of the patient Job and the understanding of God's justice as humanly comprehensible. In the prologue Job had responded to the loss of his children and possessions with almost incredible resignation to God's will:

> "Naked I came from my mother's womb
> and naked I shall return;
> the Lord gave and the Lord has taken away;
> blessed be the name of the Lord." (1:21)

But now he vehemently protests his treatment by God. In his opening lament Job is in the depths of depression as he longs for death as a release from his suffering and God's apparent injustice.

> "Why did I not die at birth,
> come forth from the womb and expire? . . .

> There (in the realm of the dead) the wicked cease from troubling,
> and there the weary are at rest.
> There prisoners are at ease together;
> they hear not the voice of the taskmaster." (3:11,17–18)

The author uses the three friends of Job—Eliphaz, Bildad, and Zophar—as foils who represent the various theories of the conventional wisdom. In the prologue they had come to comfort Job and sat in silence when they saw his great suffering (2:11–13). But in the dialogue they become incredibly callous, "objective" observers who, from the perspective of traditional wisdom, presume to argue with and lecture Job about the reasons for his personal tragedy. Eliphaz, for example, implies that Job himself must somehow be guilty.

> "Think now, who that was innocent ever perished?
> Or where were the upright cut off?
> As I have seen, those who plow iniquity
> and sow trouble reap the same." (4:7–8)

Bildad goes so far as to suggest that Job's children's sin may have caused their death.

> "If your children have sinned against him,
> he has delivered them into the power of their transgression." (8:4)

Zophar, irritated at Job's presumption in demanding from God an explanation for his suffering, accuses him of blasphemy (11:4–6).

The friends' advice is that Job repent, for surely he has committed some iniquity.

> "If you set your heart aright,
> you will stretch out your hands toward him.
> If iniquity is in your hand put it far away,
> and let not wickedness dwell in your tents.
> Surely then you will lift up your face without blemish;
> you will be secure, and will not fear." (11:13–15)

The reader, of course, has an ironic perspective on the whole dialogue and knows from the prologue that Job is innocent and that the friends' presumptions and advice are totally unfounded.

Job, on the other hand, is forced to struggle in his suffering for an explanation in the face of his friends' "ashy maxims," and without their sympathy. In his speeches he longs for justice and blames God directly for his suffering.

> "O that my vexation were weighed,
>   and my calamity laid in the balances!
> For then it would be heavier than the sand of the sea;
>   therefore my words have been rash.

> For the arrows of the Almighty are in me;
>   my spirit drinks their poison;
> the terrors of God are arrayed against me." (6:2–4)

He chides his friends for their failure to have compassion.

> "He who witholds kindness from a friend
> forsakes the fear of the Almighty.
> My brethren are treacherous as a torrent-bed,
> as freshets that pass away,
> Which are dark with ice,
> and where the snow hides itself.
> In the time of heat they disappear;
> when it is hot, they vanish from their place." (6:14–17)

He accuses them of spiritual dishonesty, of lying in the name of God.

> "As for you, you whitewash with lies;
> worthless physicians are you all.
> O that you would keep silent,
> and it would be your wisdom. . . .
> Will you speak falsely for God,
> and speak deceitfully for him?
> Will you show partiality toward him,
> will you plead the case for God?
> Will it be well with you when he searches you out?
> Or can you deceive him, as one deceives a man?" (13:4–9)

Increasingly in the course of the dialogue Job is driven to begin to speak to God directly and to explore how he might prove his innocence in God's court. At first this is a terrifying prospect (9:1–35), but, as he speaks, Job seems to grow in courage and conviction. His suffering and demand for justice move him well beyond the traditional wisdom of his friends. He begins to question whether God's norms of justice are the same as those of humans.

> "Does it seem good to thee to
> oppress,
> to despise the work of thy hands
> and favor the designs of the wicked?
> Have thou eyes of flesh?
> Dost thou see as man sees?" (10:3–4)

Periodically Job calls for an umpire or mediator who will arbitrate between God and him (9:33–35; 16:19–21), and he eventually expresses his faith that such a redeemer or vindicator will stand on his side (19:23–27). By Job's last speeches in chapters 29–31, he has reached a catharsis. In a final summary of his case, he reviews his past blessings (29), recounts his present loss of all dignity and respect (30), and in an elaborate oath insists that he has lived up to the highest of ethical standards (31). He ends by stating:

> "Oh, that I had one to hear me! . . .
> Oh, that I had the indictment
> written by my adversary!
> Surely I would carry it on my shoulder;
> I would bind it on me as a crown;
> I would give him an account of all my steps;
> like a prince I would approach him . . . " (31:35–37)

The Lord's reply to Job in the dramatic speeches from the whirlwind (39–42) does not provide Job with a written indictment, nor do they answer his questions. In fact the speeches take the form of further questions which confront Job with the limits of his understanding and power and which point to the divine order in the universe which does not apparently revolve around human concerns.

> "Gird up your loins like a man,
> I will question you,
> and you shall declare to me.
> Where were you when I laid the foundations of the earth?
> Tell me, if you have understanding.
> Who determined its measurements
> —surely you know!" (39:3–5)

Job's response to this personal encounter with God in majesty and mystery is to humbly repent.

> "I know that thou canst do all things,
> and that no purpose of thine can be thwarted. . . .
> Therefore I have uttered what I did not understand,
> things too wonderful for me, which I did not know . . .
> I had heard of thee by the hearing of the ear,
> but now my eye sees thee;
> therefore I despise myself,
> and repent in dust and ashes." (42:2–6)

In the beginning of the epilogue the author provides an evaluation of the speeches of Job and his friends.

> After the Lord had spoken these words to Job, the Lord said to Eliphaz, the Temanite: "My wrath is kindled against you and against your friends; for you have not spoken of me what is right, as my servant Job has . . . " (42:7)

Job's courageous and forthright demand for justice is the more correct way to speak of God than the facile and unfeeling "wisdom" of the friends. This righteous Job, who has suffered into a deeper experience of God, can now make intercession for his friends so that God does not deal with them according to their folly (42:8–9).

The restoration of Job in 42:10–17 is extremely anticlimactic and goes against the insights of the whole of the dialogue. Some scholars have suggested that it may have been attached by pious editors who could not allow the work to end without a material vindication of Job.

The recommended reading is Job 1–19; 29–31; 38–42.

THE BOOK OF DANIEL

The latest book in the Hebrew Scriptures and the fullest example of Jewish apocalyptic writing in the canonical Bible is the Book of Daniel. The background necessary for understanding Daniel is the invasion of Hellenism in the Near East in the wake of Alexander's conquests of the Persian Empire and the East (334–323 B.C.E.) and the subsequent struggle between Judaism and Hellenistic culture which eventually led to the Maccabean revolt (175–135 B.C.E.). The conquests of Alexander introduced sweeping changes in the ancient Near Eastern world. The invading Greeks brought with them their culture, and many of the peoples of the East assimilated it. The Greek language came to be spoken and written throughout the East. Greek cities with Greek temples, theaters, gymnasia, and race tracks were constructed in places like Egypt and Syria. The wealthy aristocracy adopted Greek names, dress and customs.

Judaism was not exempt from the influences of Hellenism. In Alexandria in Egypt the Hebrew Scriptures were translated into Greek in the version called the Septuagint from the tradition that seventy or seventy-two Palestinian scholars made the translation during the reign of Ptolemy II (285–246 B.C.E.). In the first century C.E. the Alexandrian Jewish philosopher Philo will explore what he considers the common truth shared by Greek philosophy and Jewish revelation.

Hellenization even reached Judea itself where the aristocratic high priesthood was especially enamored of the Greek culture. Here it met with resistance, as some Jews, the *Hasidim* ("Pious"), saw Hellenism as a rejection of everything Judaism stood for. Our sources for this period are the Books of Maccabees (c. 100 B.C.E.) and the writings of the Jewish historian Josephus Flavius (c. 37–100 C.E.). 1 Maccabees describes the policy of Hellenization in Judea in the following way:

> In those days lawless men came forth from in Israel, and misled many, saying, "Let us go and make a covenant with the Gentiles round about us, for since we separated from them many evils have come upon us." This proposal pleased them, and some of the people eagerly went to the king (Antiochus IV). He authorized them to observe the ordinances of the Gentiles. So they built a gymnasium in Jerusalem according to Gentile custom, and removed the marks of circumcision, and abandoned the holy covenant. They joined with the Gentiles and sold themselves to do evil (1 Mac 1:11–15).

The conflict between Judaism and Hellenism came to a head in 168 B.C.E. during the reign of Antiochus IV Epiphanes who was ruler of the Syrian part of Alexander's legacy. For rather complicated political reasons, he determined on a policy of imposing Hellenistic culture on his subjects and wiping out the Jewish religion. Judea had been under Syrian control since c. 200 B.C.E. after a century of more benevolent rule by the Ptolemies. 1 Maccabees 1:41–64 describes Antiochus' program in detail.

> And the king sent letters by messengers to Jerusalem and the cities of Judah; he directed them to follow customs strange to the land, to forbid burnt offerings and sacrifices and drink offerings in the sanctuary, to profane sabbaths and feasts, to defile the sanctuary and the priests, to build altars and sacred precincts and shrines for idols, to sacrifice swine and unclean animals, and to leave their sons uncircumcised. They were to make themselves abominable by everything unclean and profane, so that they should forget the law and change all the ordinances. "And whoever does not obey the command of the king shall die." (1 Mac 1:44–50)

The culmination of the program was the construction of an altar to Zeus Olympios, "the abomination," in the temple (1 Mac 1:54; Dan 9:27; 11:31; 12:11).

Antiochus' policies divided the people of Judea. 1 Maccabees tells us, "Many even from Israel gladly adopted his (Antiochus') religion; they sacrificed to idols and profaned the sabbath" (1 Mac 1:43). Others however resisted to the point of martrydom. We read of how the soldiers of Antiochus "put to death the women who had their children circumcised, and their families and those who circumcised them; and they hung the infants from their mothers' necks" (1 Mac 1:60). Despite the violent persecution, "many in Israel stood firm and resolved in their hearts not to eat unclean food. They chose to die rather than to be defiled by food or to profane the holy covenant; and they did die" (1 Mac 1:62–63).

The Book of Daniel was written during the midst of this persecution to give hope to the faithful that their God was with them and would ultimately overthrow their cruel oppressors. The unknown author of Daniel was facing a very different situation than the pre-exilic prophets. He was not addressing a sinful nation and warning them of punishment for violation of the covenant. His audience was the faithful who were undergoing persecution precisely because of their loyalty to the Torah.

The author of Daniel believed that his faithful community was living in the midst the final crisis in history which would lead to the definitive establishment of God's kingdom. He did not look forward to God's action in ordinary human history as the prophets had, but rather to the complete overthrow of the historical and cosmic order. In the meantime he advocated a patient and faithful endurance on the part of the people. The literary devices he used to convey his message were: (1) folktales about the legendary figure of Daniel who proved faithful to God's law in similar situations of persecution (Daniel 1–6) and (2) apocalyptic visions which in cryptic language and symbolic imagery announced the ultimate triumph of God's kingdom over the demonic forces of evil represented by the nations who had oppressed Israel over the past four-hundred and fifty years, particularly the figure of Antiochus (Daniel 7–12). This apocalyptic genre will become extremely popular in Judaism and early Christianity for the next two centuries.

Although Daniel was written in the crisis of the second century B.C.E., the purported setting for the tales and visions of Daniel is the Babylonian captivity of the sixth century B.C.E. when the hero and visionary was a courtier in the Babylonian, Median and Persian courts. The first six chapters recount in an episodic and folktale fashion the adventures of Daniel who remains a faithful Jew while living in an hostile pagan environment. These stories have a repeated theme and pattern. Daniel and/or his friends are threatened precisely because of their fidelity to Jewish religious practices: refusal to violate the dietary laws (1:8–21), refusal to worship idols (3:1–12), or refusal to pray to any god but the God of the Jews (6:6–13). In each case Daniel and his comrades remain faithful to their Judaism, and they are rewarded or delivered by their God. Because of their fidelity to the Jewish dietary laws, Daniel and his companions are given "learning and skill in all letters and wisdom," and Daniel is given "understanding in all visions and dreams" (1:17). For refusing to obey Nebuchadnezzar's command to worship his golden image, Daniel's three companions are thrown in the fiery furnace, but they are miraculously preserved from harm (3:13–23). Later Daniel himself is thrown in the lions' den for failing to pray in the name of Darius, but again he is saved from the lions' mouths. Finally each of the stories culminates with the foreign king being forced to recognize that Daniel's God is in control of history and has the power to save his faithful ones. After Daniel has successfully made known and interpreted Nebuchadnezzar's dream about the colossal statue of various metals, the king says to Daniel, "Truly, your God is God of gods and Lord of kings, and a revealer of mysteries, for you have been able to reveal this mystery" (2:47). When Nebuchadnezzar sees how Shadrach, Meshach, and Abednego have been delivered from the fiery furnace, he says,

> "Blessed be the God of Shadrach, Meshach, and Abednego, who has sent his angel and delivered his servants, who trusted in him, and set at nought the king's command, and yielded up their bodies rather than worship any god except their own God . . . " (3:28)

Finally, after Daniel was saved in the lions' den, King Darius wrote:

> "I make a decree, that in all my royal
> dominion men tremble and fear
> before the God of Daniel,
> for he is the living God,
> enduring for ever;
> his kingdom shall never be destroyed,
> and his dominion shall be to the end.
> He delivers and rescues,
> he works signs and wonders
> in heaven and on earth,
> he who has saved Daniel
> from the power of the lions." (6:26–27)

These statements of faith in the power of "the God of Daniel" are meant to give confidence to the suffering Jews of the second century B.C.E., and they prepare the reader for the visions in the second half of the book.

The apocalyptic visions of Daniel in chapters 7–12 likewise have a similar pattern. For our purposes the first and most famous of the visions in chapter 7 will serve to illustrate the pattern. In this section of the book, Daniel is no longer the one interpreting others' dreams and visions as he was in chapters 3 and 5, but now he is the visionary who must have his own dreams explained by an angelic interpreter who is a part of his vision.

The imagery and outlook of Daniel's visions are reminiscent of the creation myths of the ancient Near East. They contain beasts who represent the forces of chaos, now identified with historical nations who have oppressed the Jewish people and controlled the history of the Near East in the period between 600–168 B.C.E. The visions also have the element of conflict between these evil forces of chaos and the good God of Israel who defeats their power and reorders the cosmos according to his intentions. In Daniel's first vision he sees four beasts coming out of the sea which disguise the Babylonian, Median, Persian, and Greek empires: a lion with eagles' wings (Babylon), a bear with ribs in its mouth (Media), a winged leopard with four heads (Persia), and a ferocious ogre with iron teeth and ten horns (the Greeks and their successors, the Ptolemies of Egypt and the Seleucids of Syria). Last of all there is a boastful "little horn" who is a symbol of Antiochus (7:1–8).

In contrast to this parade of beasts, Daniel next sees the heavenly throne room of "the Ancient of Days," i.e., the God of Jews (7:9–10). Daniel then witnesses the destruction of the fourth beast and the removal of the dominion of the rest of the beasts (7:11–12). This is followed by another vision in which "one like a son of man" ascends "with the clouds of heaven" into the heavenly court and receives from the Ancient of Days everlasting "dominion and glory and kingdom" (7:13–14). At this point an anxious Daniel asks "one of those who stood there" for an interpretation of the visions, and he learns that the four beasts are four kings who will arise out of the earth and that the son of man is "the saints of the Most High" who will receive the kingdom and possess it forever. This section continues with more veiled remarks about the length of time that the "little horn" (Antiochus IV) will make war on the "saints" (the faithful Jews). The vision closes with the assurance, meant of course for the readers of Daniel, that:

> "The court shall sit in judgment,
> and his (Antiochus') dominion shall be taken away,
> to be consumed and destroyed to the end.
> And the kingdom and the dominion
> and the greatness of the kingdoms under the whole heaven
> shall be given to the people of the saints
> of the Most High;
> their kingdom shall be an everlasting kingdom,
> and all dominions shall serve and obey them."

The Book of Daniel also represents the earliest and only unequivocal expression in the Hebrew Scriptures of a belief in resurrection from the dead. The author regarded the persecutions of Antiochus as inaugurating the sufferings of the "end time," and he expressed the belief that those Jews who had died defending their faith against the wicked Syrian king would be vindicated by a bodily resurrection as a part of the triumph of God's kingdom. In chapter 12 the angel Gabriel tells Daniel that when history draws to its predetermined climax in the pagan nations' assault on the righteous, Michael (the guardian spirit of Israel) will "stand up" for his people and decisively defeat their enemies. At that point a resurrection of "many" just and unjust persons who had been "sleeping in the dust" will occur.

> "At that time shall arise Michael, the great prince who has the charge of your people. And there shall be a time of trouble, such as never has been since there was a nation till that time; but at that time your people shall be delivered, every one whose name shall be found written in the book. And many of those who sleep in the dust of the earth shall awake, some to everlasting life, and some to shame and everlasting contempt." (12:1–2)

The context for Israel's first expression of a belief in an afterlife is very significant. Recall that in Egyptian culture as early as the Old Kingdom period there had been a belief in the immortality of the pharaoh, and eventually worthy ordinary persons were thought to receive a favorable judgment in the court of Osiris. Israel, on the other hand, comes to a belief in the afterlife relatively late (mid second century B.C.E.), and in the context of the martyrdom of righteous persons for their faith. The only way the author of Daniel can reconcile the justice of the kingdom of God with the present reality of the martyrdom of the faithful is to postulate a resurrection of the just and their subsequent participation in God's kingdom.

> "And those who are wise shall shine
> like the brightness of the firmament;
> and those who turn many to righteousness,
> like the stars forever." (Dan 12:3)

The crisis caused by Antiochus IV's Hellenization did not end in the definitive establishment of the kingdom of God as the author of Daniel had envisioned. Rather, loyal Jews responded actively to the threat by an armed revolution against the Syrian king and his forces. The leaders of the revolt were the sons of a pious priest from Modein named Mattathias of the Hasmonean family who refused to capitulate to the demands to give up their religion and were sooned joined by a group called the Hasideans, "the pious," who were zealous for obedience to the law of Moses (1 Maccabees 2). One of the sons, Judas Maccabeus, led a guerilla war against the Syrian forces, and against tremendous odds he defeated the Syrian armies in several decisive battles, then marched into Jerusalem where he cleansed the ransacked temple and rebuilt its altar. He then instituted the joyous festival of rededication (Hanukkah) which according to the tradition occurred three years to the day after Antiochus had defiled the temple (1 Mac 4:36–61).

What had begun as a resistance movement flared up into a full-scale war against the Syrians. Judas succeeded in gaining a treaty with the Romans, and gradually, under the leadership of his brothers, Jonathan and Simon, the Jews threw off Syrian domination. Unfortunately the Maccabees themselves established the so-called Hasmonean dynasty and claimed for themselves the titles of high priest and king. They became increasingly ambitious and Hellenized themselves, and were extremely unpopular with their people.

The recommended reading is Daniel 1–3; 7; 12.

3

ANCIENT AND CLASSICAL GREEK RELIGION

The impact of Greek culture on Western civilization cannot be overestimated. It is primarily because of the Greeks that the West has its unique humanistic orientation. In contrast to the ancient Near Eastern civilizations in Mesopotamia, Egypt and Israel which developed various theocratic forms of government, the Greeks eventually created a civilization in which the basic political unit was the *polis,* or small city-state, governed by all its male citizens. And, unlike Israelite culture, where the individual found meaning through submission to the will of the Lord their God expressed in the teachings of the law and the prophets, the Greeks became increasingly human-centered with an emphasis on heroic achievement and virtue, individual excellence (*arete,*) intellectual speculation, rule by rational laws believed to be imbedded in nature, and love of the beautiful which was discoverable by the human person and expressible in art. Although the religion of the ancient Greeks was not destined to become the foundation of the great monotheisms of the West, the literary artistry and profound insight of their myths have continued to influence Western culture in literature, drama, art and psychology. For a classic treatment of the Greek experience in the ancient and classical ages the student should consult Werner Jaeger's **Paideia: The Ideals of Greek Culture** (New York: Oxford University Press, 1939–1944).

Greek civilization did not develop as early as the Near Eastern river civilizations nor the luxurious culture of the island of Crete to its south. Greek-speaking peoples probably began arriving in the Greek mainland during the Bronze Age in the first centuries of the second millennium B.C.E. They intermingled with the indigenous population which seems to have had a form of an agricultural religion expressed in the worship of various forms of the mother goddess as is attested throughout the Near East and the eastern Mediterranean. By c. 1500 B.C.E. this so-called Mycenaean culture had reached its pinnacle in the royal fortresses of southern Greece at such sites as Mycenae, Tiryn and Pylos. The warrior monarchs of these palaces possessed powerful bronze weapons, built large defensive walls, and buried their dead in impressive beehive tombs cut into the hillsides. These tombs contained wealthy stores of jewelry and gold which were apparently acquired from trade with Crete and the Near East and from plundering expeditions. The most famous of these was the raid on Troy, which the Mycenaeans probably sacked about 1250 B.C.E., roughly the same time as the Israelites were coming out of slavery in Egypt. And, just as the exodus from Egypt was the formative event in the religious experience of ancient Israel, so the Trojan War became the source and subject matter of ancient Greek epic poetry in the immortal poems of Homer which continued to influence Greek religion and values into the classical age. This Mycenaean civilization collapsed sometime between 1200 and 1100 B.C.E. The cause was apparently a series of invasions by Greek speakers from the North, the so-called Dorians. Most of the Mycenaean cities were abandoned and its way of life forgotten, except for the tradition of oral epic poetry which had grown up around the events of the Trojan War.

The major literary sources for ancient Greek religion are the poems of Homer and Hesiod. According to Herodotus, the fifth century Greek historian, "It was Homer and Hesiod who first compiled genealogies of the gods for the Greeks, gave the gods their titles, defined their honors and skills and described their appearances" (Histories II. 53). Both poets are usually dated to the eighth century B.C.E., as Greece was coming out of the so-called Dark Ages which followed the Dorian invasion and entering the age of the *polis*. Although Homer and Hesiod generally agree on the names and functions of the gods, they represent quite distinct strata of society and value systems. Homer's epics, **The Iliad** and **The Odyssey,** celebrate the heroic age, the events of the Trojan War and the values of the warrior aristocracy; Hesiod's **Works and Days** and **Theogony,** on the other hand, represent a poetic tradition which comes from the farming class in Boeotia in central Greece.

HOMER

For the Greeks Homer was the supreme poet and also a spiritual and moral guide whose poems were listened to almost as reverently as the Torah among the Jews. His epics played a decisive role in stabilizing and popularizing the religion of the Greeks and establishing the aristocratic value system which continued into the classical age (fifth and fourth centuries B.C.E.). **The Iliad** and **The Odyssey** immortalize events of the Trojan War and the return of the Greek heroes from the war. They represent the culmination in a written form of a long oral epic tradition which had been kept alive for five centuries by minstrels like Demodocos who in Book VIII of **The Odyssey** sings of "the fate of the Achaians, all they acted and endured, all the Achaians suffered . . . " Although Homer is the heir to this long oral tradition, his poems bear the mark of the shaping hand of a single poetic genius.

THE ILIAD

Our first selections are taken from Books I and XXIV of **The Iliad,** the first and last books of Homer's great war poem. Homer does not recount the whole of the Trojan War but focuses on the events of a few weeks in the ninth year of the ten-year siege of Ilium or Troy by the Achaians (the allied Greek forces). The theme of the poem, as the invocation of the Muse announces, is "the anger of Peleus' son Achilleus," the greatest of the Greek warriors who by his decision to withdraw from battle over an offense to his honor brought "devastation" and "pains thousandfold upon the Achaians." Homer's concern with human heroes and their action is similar to the spirit of **The Gilgamesh Epic** and characteristic of Greek thought throughout the ancient and classical periods. This interest in the human hero for his own sake stands in sharp contrast to the Israelite tradition which is consistently theocentric in its orientation.

Achilleus, like Gilgamesh, and unlike the biblical warrior David, is a highly individualistic hero. He is the greatest of the Achaian warriors, and he fights for personal honor and glory, rather than for the glory of "the living God of Israel," as in the case of the young David (cf. 1 Samuel 17). Public honor before one's fellow warriors is the highest value for Achilleus, and therefore he withdraws from battle and brings disaster on the Greek troops over an offense to his personal honor.

Achilleus' heroic struggle is not against the gods and the inevitability of death, as was Gilgamesh's. Rather, Achilleus' greatest battle is with his fellow warriors and himself. He is driven by the Greek code of personal honor which Agamemnon has offended, and he cannot be brought back to the battle, even when Agamemnon offers innumerable gifts (Book IX). When Achilleus does return to war, he does so out of a sense of honor and loyalty to his friend Patroklos who has died at Hektor's hands while wearing his armor. Achilleus knows that in returning to the battle he is choosing a short life with a heroic death on the battlefield, as opposed to a long but uneventful life at home in Phthia (Book XVIII). In contrast to Gilgamesh after the death of his friend Enkidu, the thought of death seems to arouse no fear in Achilleus. In Homer there is no thought of personal fulfillment in an afterlife, but this does not drive his heroes to rebel against such a fate; rather the Homeric hero is compelled to seek immortality by achieving excellence in this life. Achilleus knows that he has no fulfillment apart from war where he can win his immortality through glory and honor. When he withdraws from the war, we are told he "missed the cries of battle," and as he returns, he is described as "avid again for war." Achilleus' individual excellence, *arete*, is as a man of heroic action in battle. Homer's poetic genius, in typical Greek fashion, is able to use the events surrounding Achilleus' anger to explore realistically and unforgettably issues of universal significance for humanity: the underlying causes of human conflicts and the dispositions necessary for their resolution, the nature of cowardice and bravery, the glories and terrors of war, the beauty of compassion and peace, the limits of human freedom and the nature of fate, the various human virtues and the destructive capacities of human folly. Homer's greatness is such that he anticipates many of the major philosophical problems which later concerned Socrates, Plato and Aristotle.

The literary artistry of Homer is evident in the contrast and parallelism between Book I and Book XXIV. In Book I Homer uses the unique and particular dispute between Achilleus and Agamemnon to portray the universal causes of war and strife. Agamemnon's heartless disregard for Chryses' request for the return of his daughter shows an inability to sympathize with the plight of another, and the quarrel between Agamemnon and Achilleus brilliantly illustrates a stubborn commitment to personal honor at all costs.

Book XXIV, on the other hand, gives a poignant picture of what is required if humanity is to find peace. Achilleus' acceptance of Priam's request for Hector's body comes only when he can sympathize with the aged Trojan king as a father who has lost a son. This experience of compassion moves Achilleus to give up his insane rage which is rooted in his offended honor over the death of his beloved Patroklos at the hands of Hektor. Homer's war epic ends with a brief and fragile moment of peace as the Trojans are given time to perform the funeral rites for Hector, the defender of their soon to be destroyed city.

Although Homer's primary interest throughout **The Iliad** is with the human characters, the Greek gods have an integral, and not easily categorized, role in the action. In his portrayal of the gods Homer is both the heir to long and complicated religious tradition and the creator of a conception of the gods which would have lasting influence after him. Originally many of the gods were typical nature gods who had quite distinct origins and cults. Zeus, "the gatherer of the cloud," was originally a storm god like Baal Hadad in the Canaanite mythology or Enlil and Marduk in the Mesopotamian myths. Hera, his wife, was probably originally an agricultural fertility goddess. In Homer, as in **The Gilgamesh Epic,** all the gods are organized into a family council; they live on Mount Olympus and from there intervene in the action of the war for their favorite hero or people. They are portrayed in a strikingly human and at times even playfully humorous fashion with distinct personalities that are motivated by the same honor code as the human characters in the epic; they are sensitive to whether or not humans honor them by the appropriate sacrifices and offerings. Unlike humans, however, they are immortal, and, because they do not have to face death, they are not capable of heroism, and therefore are not really admirable.

The situation in Homer is very similar to that in **The Gilgamesh Epic**; the gods, who represent the powers and forces beyond human control, form the backdrop against which the human heroes struggle for honor and glory. The gods of course are not all opposed to or unconcerned with the fate of the heroes. They have their favorites. Both Gilgamesh and Achilleus are superhuman in their gifts and therefore enjoy special divine favor. Each has his divine mother who aids him in his heroic struggle. Ninsun, Gilgamesh's mother, assists him and his friend Enkidu in their battle against the monster Huwawa. Achilleus' mother Thetis is able to get Zeus to favor the Trojan side when her son withdraws from battle, and later, when he returns to combat, she can provide him with special armor constructed by Hephaistos the divine smithy.

In contrast to Israel where one God is above the natural world and yet can manifest himself in historical events which run counter to normal expectations, like the liberation of slaves from tyranny in Egypt, the many gods of the Greeks are often infused in the natural and human world. For example, in Book I of **The Iliad** when the passionate Achilleus wishes to kill the arrogant Agamemnon but then thinks better of it, his impulse to self-control is attributed to Pallas Athene, the goddess of wisdom, who says:

"I have come to stay your anger—but will you obey me?—
from the sky; and the goddess of white arms Hera sent me,

who loves both of you equally in her heart and cares for you.
Come then, do not take your sword in your hand, keep clear of fighting,
though indeed with words you may abuse him, and it will be that way.
And this also will I tell you and it will be a thing accomplished.
Some day three times over such shining gifts shall be given you by reason of this outrage.
Hold your hand then, and obey us."

Athene's intervention is what philosophers will later call wisdom or reason controlling the passion of anger. For Homer, Achilleus' decision to control his anger is a manifestation of divinity. This gives a certain universality and depth to Achilleus' particular action. For Homer, when humans nobly struggle to control their instinct to anger for a higher purpose, the goddess Athene is operative in human affairs.

At times the Homeric gods represent ethical values somewhat like the Lord in the biblical tradition. These ethical values are not expressed in a written covenant law or revelation, however. The moral code in the Homeric epics seems to be rooted in the intuitive feeling, akin to an aesthetic sense, that certain actions are honorable and others shameful. The virtues of the warrior are courage, courtesy, hospitality to travelers, generosity, pursuit of personal glory, personal honor and integrity. Shameful actions are to violate an oath, to take advantage of the weakness of a traveler or suppliant, to deny a corpse the proper funeral rites, to have excessive pride (*hubris*) which does not accept the limits placed on all humans. Failure to abide by this code will inevitably lead to tragic consequences.

In the **Iliad** Apollo the Archer god represents the values of the warrior's honor code. In Book I he initiates the action which brings on the quarrel between Agamemnon and Achilleus by plaguing the Achaian army because Agamemnon has brutally despised the request of his priest, Chryses, for the return of his daughter who had been taken as a war prize. Agamemnon's action violates a basic tenet of the honor code; he has rejected a suppliant father's request, an action which even his soldiers recognize as exceeding the limits of decency. Apollo's plague comes as a direct consequence of the tearful prayer of the brutalized priest, and the Achaians learn this in the the midst of the plague when the seer Kalchas informs them:

> "No, it is not for the sake of some vow or hecatomb he blames us,
> but for the sake of his priest whom Agamemnon dishonoured
> and would not give him back his daughter nor accept the ransom.
> Therefore the archer sent griefs against us and will send them
> still, nor sooner thrust back the shameful plague from the Danaans
> until we give the glancing-eyed girl back to her father
> without price, without ransom, and lead also a blessed hecatomb
> to Chryses; thus we might propitiate and persuade him."

Likewise in Book XXIV, Apollo initiates the process to end Achilleus' defilement of Hektor's corpse. He preserves the body from disfigurement during the eleven days of Achilleus' insane rage, and on the twelfth day, speaks to the divided Olympian gods:

> "You are hard, you gods, and destructive. Now did not Hektor
> burn thigh pieces of oxen and unblemished goats in your honour?
> Now you cannot bring yourselves to save him, though he is only
> a corpse, for his wife to look upon, his child and his mother
> and Priam his father, and his people, who presently thereafter
> would burn his body in the fire and give him his rites of burial.
> No, you gods; your desire is to help this cursed Achilleus
> within whose breast there are no feelings of justice, nor can
> his mind be bent, but his purposes are fierce, like a lion
> who when he has given way to his own great strength and his haughty
> spirit, goes among the flocks of men, to devour them.
> So Achilleus has destroyed pity, and there is not in him any shame,
> which does much harm to men but profits them also."

Apollo stands for the instinct which separates humanity from animals: the capacity for decency, temperance, and the awareness of limits which are not to be exceeded. He ends his speech to the gods by saying:

> "Great as he is, let him take care not make us angry;
> for see, he does dishonour to the dumb earth in his fury."

Not all of the gods are motivated by such nobility of purpose. Zeus' wife Hera, for example, is jealous and petty. She is on the side of the Greeks even when she witnesses the indignities that Achilleus inflicts upon Hektor's body. Hera and Athene have an implacable hatred toward the Trojans since the day of the divine beauty contest in which the Trojan prince, Paris (Alexandros), chose Aphrodite, the goddess of love, over them. Aphrodite had offered Paris Helen, the wife of Menelaus, and the most beautiful woman in the whole world; Paris chose Helen over Hera's offer of power and Athene's promise of wisdom. Now Hera will use any expediency to further her cause. In Book I she nags Zeus to find out why Thetis, the sea-nymph and mother of Achilleus, has come to speak to him because she suspects that Thetis has asked Zeus to favor the Trojan side now that her son has withdrawn from the battle, and in Book XIV she seduces her husband and causes him to fall to sleep so that her beloved Greek forces may win a temporary victory in Achilleus' absence. Even in Book XXIV she angrily tries to defeat Apollo's plea to save Hektor's corpse by arguing that Achilleus is more worthy of honor than Hektor because he is the first-born of a goddess.

The foil to Hera is Zeus, the supreme head of the Olympian pantheon, "the father of gods and men" whose will is ultimately accomplished in **The Iliad.** Zeus is clearly the most powerful figure among the Olympian gods. He is open to persuasion from the other deities, but once he has made a decision, the other gods are expected to obey his wishes.

Zeus also seems to operate according to the honor code of the Greek warrior. In Book I Thetis is able to persuade him to favor the Trojans while her son Achilleus withdraws from battle over his offended honor. Likewise in Book XXIV, Zeus is persuaded by Apollo's argument that the defilement of Hektor's corpse must cease, and he wisely gives orders that the body not be stolen away but that Achilleus be commanded to accept the gifts that Priam will bring when he requests his son's body. Zeus literally stages the moving scene of tenderness and compassion between Achilleus and Priam. He sends Thetis to tell her son to give up his insane rage and return Hector's body because he has now offended the gods with his behavior. Zeus also informs Priam that the gods pity him and will protect him as he goes with gifts to ransom his son's body. He even provides an omen so that the old king has the assurance of divine assistance as he undertakes his perilous journey. Homer is using Zeus' involvement in this episode to convey the divine nobility of Achilleus' turning from the emptiness of senseless rage to compassion and at the same time Priam's incredible courage in entering the Achaian camp to request the body of his son. Priam's courageous request stirs in Achilleus memories of his own father and moves him to compassion. For Homer this is a moment of divine grace.

> So he spoke, and stirred in the other a passion of grieving
> for his own father. He took the old man's hand and pushed him
> gently away, and the two remembered, as Priam sat huddled
> at the feet of Achilleus and wept close for manslaughtering Hektor
> and Achilleus wept now for his own father, now again
> for Patroklos. The sound of their mourning moved in the house.

Homer is not rigidly logical in the roles that he assigns to the gods. Although their functions are set within certain parameters, his treatment of the gods is subordinated to his literary purpose. This can be seen in the relationship between Zeus and fate or destiny. At times Zeus' will seems to be identical with fate. The poem opens with an identification of Zeus' will with the fact that Achilleus' anger caused "pains thousandfold upon the Achaians." This is a mythic way of saying that the angry withdrawal of the Greeks' greatest warrior necessarily had diastrous consequences for their side. Zeus also seems to be the one who dispassionately determines the fates of individuals. In Achilleus' tender speech to Priam in Book XXIV, he speaks of the difficult destiny given to humans by Zeus.

> Such is the way the gods spun life for unfortunate mortals,
> that we live in unhappiness, but the gods themselves have no sorrows.
> There are two urns that stand on the door-sill of Zeus. They are unlike
> for the gifts they bestow: an urn of evils, an urn of blessings.
> If Zeus who delights in thunder mingles these and bestows them
> on man, he sifts, and moves now in evil, again in good fortune,
> But when Zeus bestows from the urn of sorrows, he makes a failure
> of man, and the evil hunger drives him over the shining
> earth, and he wanders respected neither by the gods nor mortals.

At other places in **The Iliad** Zeus himself must comply with Fate. In Book VIII Zeus is described as measuring the fates of the Greek and Trojan sides in golden scales in order to find out which is ordained to be victorious, and in Book XVI, although he wishes to rescue his son Sarpedon, whose death has been decreed, Hera reminds him that if he attempts to thwart the decisions of the fates, his own authority over the gods and men will be underminded.

For Homer the ultimate authority over the universe is Fate. The fates determine the broad outlines of human life; they bring sorrow and death to all. The wills of the gods and humans are only effective within a limited sphere. Humans can incur suffering beyond their fates if they act foolishly or criminally. In Book I of **The Odyssey,** for example, Zeus reflects on the death of Aigisthos who had stolen Agamemnon's wife Klytaimnestra while he was away at war and then murdered him on his return home:

> "Well now, how indeed mortal men do blame the gods!
> They say it is from us evils come, yet they themselves
> By their own recklessness have pains beyond their lot.
> So this Aigisthos married beyond his lot the lawful
> Wife of the son of Atreus, and killed him on his return;
> Knowing he would be destroyed, since we told him beforehand:
> We had sent sharp-eyed Hermes, the slayer of Argos,
> To tell him not to kill the man and not to woo his wife,
> Or payment would come through Orestes, descendant of Atreus.
> As soon as he came of age and longed for his own land.
> So Hermes told him; but though for good mind himself, he did not
> Change Aigisthos' mind. And now he has paid for it all."

This clear-headed acceptance of both the reality of Fate and responsibility for one's own actions is a part of Homer's immeasurable legacy to Western civilization. It will become an important aspect of Stoical philosophy and eventually lead to the Western idea of a natural law.

The translation is by Richmond Lattimore, **THE ILIAD OF HOMER** (Chicago: University of Chicago Press, 1951).

BOOK I

The invocation of the Muse

Sing, goddess,[1] the anger of Peleus' son Achilleus[2]
and its devastation, which put pains thousandfold upon the Achaians,
hurled in their multitudes to the house of
Hades strong souls
of heroes, but gave their bodies to be the delicate feasting—
of dogs, of all birds, and the will of Zeus was accomplished
since that time when first there stood in divi-
son of conflict
Atreus' son the lord of men[3] and brilliant
Achilleus.

Agamemnon rejects Chryses' request
What god was it then set them together in
bitter collision?

Zeus' son and Leto's, Apollo,[4] who in anger at the king drove

the foul pestilence along the host, and the people perished,

since Atreus' son had dishonoured Chryses,[5] priest of Apollo,

when he came beside the fast ships to the Achaians to ransom

back his daughter, carrying gifts beyond count and holding

in his hands wound on a staff of gold the ribbons of Apollo

who strikes from afar, and supplicated all the Achaians,

but above all Atreus' two sons, the marshals of the people:

'Sons of Atreus and you other strong-greaved Achaians,

to you may the gods grant who have their homes on Olympos

Priam's[6] city to be plundered and a fair homecoming thereafter,

but may you give me back my own daughter and take the ransom,

giving honour to Zeus' son who strikes from afar, Apollo.'

Then all the rest of the Achaians cried out in favour

that the priest be respected and the shining ransom be taken;

yet this pleased not the heart of Atreus' son Agamemnon,

but harshly he drove him away with a strong order upon him:

'Never let me find you again, old sir, near our hollow

ships, neither lingering now nor coming again hereafter,

for fear your staff and the god's ribbons help you no longer.

The girl I will not give back; sooner will old age come upon her

in my own house, in Argos,[7] far from her own land, going

up and down by the loom and being in my bed as my companion,

so go now, do not make me angry; so you will be safer.'

Apollo's plague

So he spoke, and the old man in terror obeyed him

and went silently away beside the murmuring sea beach.

Over and over the old man prayed as he walked in solitude

to King Apollo, who Leto of the lovely hair bore: 'Hear me,

lord of the silver bow who set your power about Chryse

and Killa[8] the sacrosanct, who are lord in strength over Tenedos,[9]

Smintheus,[10] if ever it pleased your heart that I built your temple,

if ever it pleased you that I burned all the rich thigh pieces

of bulls, of goats, then bring to pass this wish I pray for:

let your arrows make the Danaans[11] pay for my tears shed.'

So he spoke in prayer, and Phoibos Apollo heard him,

and strode down along the pinnacles of Olympos, angered

in his heart, carrying across his shoulders the bow and the hooded

quiver; and the shafts clashed on the shoulders of the god walking

angrily. He came as night comes down and knelt then

apart and opposite the ships and let go an arrow.

Terrible was the clash that rose from the bow of silver.

First he went after the mules and the circling hounds, then let go

a tearing arrow against the men themselves and struck them.

The corpse fires burned everywhere and did not stop burning.

Nine days up and down the host ranged the god's arrows,

but on the tenth Achilleus called the people to assembly;

a thing put into his mind by the goddess of the white arms, Hera,[12]

who had pity upon the Danaans when she saw them dying.

Now when they were all assembled in one place together,

Achilleus of the swift feet stood up among them and spoke forth:

'Son of Atreus, I believe now that straggling backwards

we must make our way home if we can escape death,

if fighting now must crush the Achaians and the plague likewise.

No, come, let us ask some holy man, some prophet,

even an interpreter of dreams, since a dream also

comes from Zeus, who can tell why Phoibos Apollo is so angry,

if for the sake of some vow, some hecatomb[13] he blames us,

if given the fragrant smoke of lambs, of he goats, somehow

he can be made willing to beat the bane aside from us.'

   He spoke thus and sat down again, and among them stood up

Kalchas, Thestor's son, far the best of the bird interpreters,

who knew all things that were, the things to come and the things past,

who guided into the land of Ilion the ships of the Achaians

through that seercraft of his own that Phoibos Apollo gave him.

He in kind intention toward all stood forth and addressed them:

'You have bidden me, Achilleus beloved of Zeus, to explain to

you this anger of Apollo the lord who strikes from afar. Then

I will speak; yet make me a promise and swear before me

readily by word and work of your hands to defend me,

since I believe I shall make a man angry who holds great kingship

over the men of Argos, and all the Achaians obey him.

For a king when he is angry with a man beneath him is too strong,

and suppose even for the day itself he swallow down his anger,

he still keeps bitterness that remains until its fulfilment

deep in his chest. Speak forth then, tell me if you will protect me.'

   Then in answer again spoke Achilleus of the swift feet:

'Speak, interpreting whatever you know, and fear nothing.

In the name of Apollo beloved of Zeus to whom you, Kalchas,

make your prayers when you interpret the gods' will to the Danaans,

no man so long as I am alive above earth and see daylight

shall lay the weight of his hands on you beside the hollow ships,

not one of all the Danaans, even if you mean Agamemnon,

who now claims to be far the greatest of all the Achaians.'

   At this the blameless seer took courage again and spoke forth:

'No, it is not for the sake of some vow or hecatomb he blames us,

but for the sake of his priest whom Agamemnon dishonoured

and would not give him back his daughter nor accept the ransom.

Therefore the archer sent griefs against us and will send them

still, nor sooner thrust back the shameful plague from the Danaans

until we give the glancing-eyed girl back to her father

without price, without ransom, and lead also a blessed hecatomb to Chryse; thus we might propitiate and persuade him.'

(After a long quarrel, Agamemnon returns Chryses, but then sends his men to seize Achilleus' prize, Briseis. We resume the text as Achillues cries to Thetis his goddess mother to right the wrong done to his honor.)

Achilleus and his mother Thetis
Many times stretching forth his hands he called on his mother:

'Since, my mother, you bore me to be a man with a short life,

therefore Zeus of the loud thunder on Olympos should grant me

honour at least. But now he has given me not even a little.

Now the son of Atreus, powerful Agamemnon,

has dishonoured me, since he has taken away my prize and keeps it.'

So he spoke in tears and the lady his mother heard him

as she sat in the depths of the sea at the side of her aged father,

and lightly she emerged like a mist from the grey water.

She came and sat beside him as he wept, and stroked him

with her hand and called him by name and spoke to him: 'Why then,

child, do you lament? What sorrow has come to your heart now?

Tell me, do not hide it in your mind, and thus we shall both know.'

(At this point Achilleus recounts for his mother the story of the plague and his dispute with Agamemnon. We resume with Achilleus' request to his mother.)

'You then, if you have power to, protect your own son, going

to Olympos and supplicating Zeus, if ever before now

either by word you comforted Zeus' heart or by action.

Since it is many times in my father's halls I have heard you

making claims, when you said you only among the immortals

beat aside shameful destruction from Kronos' son the dark-misted,

that time when all the other Olympians sought to bind him,

Hera and Poseidon[14] and Pallas Athene. Then you,

goddess, went and set him free from his shackles, summoning

in speed the creature of the hundred hands to tall Olympos,

that creature the gods name Briareus, but all men

Aigaios' son, but he is far greater in strength than his father.

He rejoicing in the glory of it sat down by Kronion,[15]

and the rest of the blessed gods were frightened and gave up binding him.

Sit beside him and take his knees and remind him of these things

now, if perhaps he might be willing to help the Trojans,

and pin the Achaians back against the ships and the water,

dying, so that thus they may all have profit of their own king,

that Atreus' son wide-ruling Agamemnon may recognize

his madness, that he did no honour to the best of the Achaians.'

Thetis answered him then letting the tears fall: 'Ah me,

my child. Your birth was bitterness. Why did I raise you?

If only you could sit by your ships untroubled, not weeping,

since indeed your lifetime is to be short, of no length.

Now it has befallen that your life must be brief and bitter

beyond all men's. To a bad destiny I bore you in my chambers.

But I will go to cloud-dark Olympos and ask this

thing of Zeus who delights in the thunder. Perhaps he will do it.

Do you therefore continuing to sit by your swift
ships

be angry at the Achaians and stay away from
all fighting.

For Zeus went to the blameless Aithiopians at
the Ocean[16]

yesterday to feast, and the rest of the gods went
with him.

On the twelfth day he will be coming back to
Olympos,

and then I will go for your sake to the house of
Zeus, bronze-founded,

and take him by the knees and I think I can
persuade him.'

(At this point Homer completes the account of
Chryses' return. We resume the text as Thetis
approaches Zeus to adopt Achilleus' cause.)

Thetis gets Zeus to adopt Achilleus' cause

She found Kronos' broad-browed son apart
from the others

sitting upon the highest peak of rugged Olympos.

She came and sat beside him with her left hand
embracing

his knees, but took him underneath the chin
with her right hand

and spoke in supplication to lord Zeus son of
Kronos:

'Father Zeus, if ever before in word or action

I did you favour among the immortals, now
grant what I ask for.

Now give honour to my son short-lived beyond
all other

mortals. Since even now the lord of men Agamemnon

dishonours him, who has taken away his prize
and keeps it.

Zeus of the counsels, lord of Olympos, now do
him honour.

So long put strength into the Trojans, until the
Achaians

give my son his rights, and his honour is increased among them.'

She spoke thus. But Zeus who gathers the
clouds made no answer

but sat in silence a long time. And Thetis, as
she had taken

his knees, clung fast to them and urged once
more her question:

'Bend your head and promise me to accomplish
this thing,

or else refuse it, you have nothing to fear, that
I may know

by how much I am the most dishonoured of all
gods.'

Deeply disturbed Zeus who gathers the
clouds answered her:

'This is a disastrous matter when you set me in
conflict

with Hera, and she troubles me with recrimi-
nations.

Since even as things are, forever among the immortals

she is at me and speaks of how I help the Trojans in battle.

Even so, go back again now, go away, for fear
she

see us. I will look to these things that they be
accomplished.

For this among the immortal gods is the mightiest witness

I can give, and nothing I do shall be vain nor
revocable

nor a thing unfulfilled when I bend my head in
assent to it.'

He spoke, the son of Kronos, and nodded
his head with the dark brows,

and the immortally anointed hair of the great
god

swept from his divine head, and all Olympos
was shaken.

So these two who had made their plans
separated, and Thetis

leapt down again from shining Olympos into
the sea's depth,

but Zeus went back to his own house, and all
the gods rose up

from their chairs to greet the coming of their
father, not one had courage

to keep his place as the father advanced, but
stood up to greet him.
Thus he took his place on the throne; yet Hera
was not
ignorant, having seen how he had been plotting counsels
with Thetis the silver-footed, the daughter of
the sea's ancient,
and at once she spoke revilingly to Zeus son of
Kronos:
'Treacherous one, what god has been plotting
counsels with you?
Always it is dear to your heart in my absence
to think of
secret things and decide upon them. Never
have you patience
frankly to speak forth to me the thing that you
purpose.'
    Then to her the father of gods and men
made answer:
'Hera, do not go on hoping that you will hear
all my
thoughts, since these will be too hard for you,
though you are my wife.
Any thought that it is right for you to listen to,
no one
neither man nor any immortal shall hear it before you.
But anything that apart from the rest of the
gods I wish to
plan, do not always question each detail nor
probe me.'
    Then the goddess the ox-eyed lady Hera
answered:
'Majesty, son of Kronos, what sort of thing have
you spoken?
Truly too much in time past I have not questioned nor probed you,
but you are entirely free to think out whatever
pleases you.
Now, though, I am terribly afraid you were
won over
by Thetis the silver-footed, the daughter of the
sea's ancient.
For early in the morning she sat beside you and
took your

knees, and I think you bowed your head is assent to do honour
to Achilleus, and to destroy many beside the
ships of the Achaians.'
    Then in return Zeus who gathers the
clouds made answer:
'Dear lady, I never escape you, you are always
full of suspicion.
Yet thus you can accomplish nothing surely,
but be more
distant from my heart than ever, and it will be
the worse for you.
If what you say is true, then that is the way I
wish it.
But go then, sit down in silence, and do as I tell
you,
for fear all the gods, as many as are on Olympos, can do nothing
if I come close and lay my unconquerable hands
upon you.'
    He spoke, and the goddess the ox-eyed lady
Hera was frightened
and went and sat down in silence wrenching
her heart to obedience,
and all the Uranian[17] gods in the house of Zeus
were troubled.
(Book I concludes with a humorous incident in
which Hephaistos, the lame smithy god, begs
Hera his mother to stop quarreling with Zeus.)

BOOK XXIV

(When Book XXIV opens the games for Patroklos' funeral have just ended, but Achilleus'
rage has not. For eleven days he fastens Hektor's body to his chariot and drags it around Patroklos' tomb.)

*The quarrel among the gods over Achilleus'
defilement of Hektor's corpse*
And the games broke up, and the people scattered to go away, each man
to his fast-running ship, and the rest of them
took thought of their dinner
and of sweet sleep and its enjoyment; only
Achilleus

wept still as he remembered his beloved companion, nor did sleep
who subdues all come over him, but he tossed from one side to the other
in longing for Patroklos, for his manhood and his great strength
and all the actions he had seen to the end with him, and the hardships
he had suffered; the wars of men; hard crossing of the big waters.
Remembering all these things he let fall the swelling tears, lying
sometimes along his side, sometimes on his back, and now again
prone on his face; then he would stand upright, and pace turning
in distraction along the beach of the sea, nor did dawn rising
escape him as she brightened across the sea and the beaches.
Then, when he had yoked running horses under the chariot
he would fasten Hektor behind the chariot, so as to drag him,
and draw him three times around the tomb of Menoitios' fallen
son, then rest again in his shelter, and throw down the dead man
and leave him to lie sprawled on his face in the dust. But Apollo
had pity on him, though he was only a dead man, and guarded
the body from all ugliness, and hid all of it under the golden
aegis, so that it might not be torn when Achillues dragged it.
    So Achilleus in his standing fury outraged great Hektor.
The blessed gods as they looked upon him were filled with compassion
and kept urging clear-sighted Argeiphontes[18] to steal the body.
There this was pleasing to all the others, but never to Hera
nor Poseidon, nor the girl of the grey eyes, who kept still

their hatred for sacred Ilion as in the beginning,
and for Priam and his people, because of the delusion of Paris[19]
who insulted the goddesses when they came to him in his courtyard
and favoured her who supplied the lust that led to disaster.
But now, as it was the twelfth dawn after the death of Hektor,
Phoibos Apollo spoke his word out among the immortals:
'You are hard, you gods, and destructive. Now did not Hektor
burn thigh pieces of oxen and unblemished goats in your honour?
Now you cannot bring yourselves to save him, though he is only
a corpse, for his wife to look upon, his child and his mother
and Priam his father, and his people, who presently thereafter
would burn his body in the fire and give him his rites of burial.
No, you gods; your desire is to help this cursed Achilleus
within whose breast there are no feelings of justice, nor can
his mind be bent, but his purposes are fierce, like a lion
who when he has given way to his own great strength and his haughty
spirit, goes among the flocks of men, to devour them.
So Achilleus has destroyed pity, and there is not in him
any shame; which does much harm to men but profits them also.
For a man must some day lose one who was even closer
than this; a brother from the same womb, or a son. And yet
he weeps for him, and sorrows for him, and then it is over,
for the Destinies put in mortal men the heart of endurance.

But this man, now he has torn the heart of life from great Hektor,

ties him to his horses and drags him around his beloved companion's

tomb; and nothing is gained thereby for his good, or his honour.

Great as he is, let him take care not to make us angry;

for see, he does dishonour to the dumb earth in his fury.'

Then bitterly Hera of the white arms answered him, saying:

'What you have said could be true, lord of the silver bow, only

if you give Hektor such pride of place as you give to Achilleus.

But Hektor was mortal, and suckled at the breast of a woman,

while Achilleus is the child of a goddess, one whom I myself

nourished and brought up and gave her as bride to her husband

Peleus, one dear to the hearts of the immortals, for you all

went, you gods, to the wedding; and you too feasted among them

and held your lyre, o friend of the evil, faithless forever.'

In turn Zeus who gathers the clouds spoke to her in answer:

'Hera, be not utterly angry with the gods, for there shall not

be the same pride of place given both. Yet Hektor also

was loved by the gods, best of all the mortals in Ilion.

I loved him too. He never failed of gifts to my liking.

Never yet was my altar gone without fair sacrifice,

the smoke and the savour of it, since that is our portion of honour.

The stealing of him we will dismiss, for it is not possible

to take bold Hektor secretly from Achilleus, since always

his mother is near him night and day; but it would be better

if one of the gods would summon Thetis here to my presence

so that I can say a close word to her, and see that Achilleus

is given gifts by Priam and gives back the body of Hektor.'

(Thetis now learns of Zeus' will for Achilleus and instructs her son about the gods' decree. Zeus then sends Iris to Priam and orders him to take the ransom for Hektor's corpse to the Greek camp. Led by Hermes, Priam makes his way through the Greek lines. We resume the text as Priam comes into the presence of Achilleus.)

The meeting between Priam and Achilleus

The old man made straight for the dwelling

where Achilleus the beloved of Zeus was sitting. He found him

inside, and his companions were sitting apart, as two only,

Automedon the hero and Alkimos, scion of Ares,[20]

were busy beside him. He had just now got through his dinner,

with eating and drinking, and the table still stood by. Tall Priam

came in unseen by the other men and stood close beside him

and caught the knees of Achilleus in his arms, and kissed the hands

that were dangerous and manslaughtering and had killed so many

of his sons. As when dense disaster closes on one who had murdered

a man in his own land, and he comes to the country of others,

to a man of substance, and wonder seizes on those who behold him,

So Achilleus wondered as he looked on Priam, a godlike

man, and the rest of them wondered also, and looked at each other.

But now Priam spoke to him in the words of a suppliant:

'Achilleus like the gods, remember your father, one who

is of years like mine, and on the door-sill of sorrowful old age.

And they who dwell nearby encompass him and afflict him,

nor is there any to defend him against the wrath, the destruction.

Yet surely he, when he hears of you and that you are still living,

is gladdened within his heart and all his days he is hopeful

that he will see his beloved son come home from the Troad.

But for me, my destiny was evil. I have had the noblest

of sons in Troy, but I say not one of them is left to me.

Fifty were my sons, when the sons of the Achaians came here.

Nineteen were born to me from the womb of a single mother,

and other women bore the rest in my palace; and of these

violent Ares broke the strength in the knees of most of the,

but one was left me who guarded my city and people, that one

you killed a few days since he fought in defence of his country,

Hektor; for whose sake I come now to the ships of the Achaians

to win him back from you, and I bring you gifts beyond number.

Honour then the gods, Achilleus, and take pity upon me

remembering your father, yet I am still more pitiful;

I have gone through what no other mortal on earth has gone through;

I put my lips to the hands of the man who has killed my children.'

So he spoke, and stirred in the other a passion of grieving

for his own father. He took the old man's hand and pushed him

gently away, and the two remembered, as Priam sat huddled

at the feet of Achilleus and wept close for manslaughtering Hektor

and Achilleus wept now for his own father, now again

for Patroklos. The sound of their mourning moved in the house.

Then

when great Achilleus had taken full satisfaction in sorrow

and the passion for it had gone from his mind and body, thereafter

he rose from his chair, and took the old man by the hand, and set him

on his feet again, in pity for the grey head and the grey beard,

and spoke to him and addressed him winged words: 'An, unlucky,

surely you have had much evil to endure in your spirit.

How could you dare to come alone to the ships of the Achaians

and before my eyes, when I am one who have killed in such numbers

such brave sons of yours? The heart in you is iron. Come, then,

and sit down upon this chair, and you and I will even let

our sorrows lie still in the heart for all our grieving. There is not

any advantage to be won from grim lamentation.

Such is the way the gods spun life for unfortunate mortals,

that we live in unhappiness, but the gods themselves have no sorrows.

There are two urns that stand on the door-sill of Zeus. They are unlike

for the gifts they bestow: an urn of evils, an urn of blessings.

If Zeus who delights in thunder mingles these and bestows them

on man, he shifts, and moves now in evil, again

in good fortune.
But when Zeus bestows from the urn of sorrows, he makes a failure
of man, and the evil hunger drives him over the shining
earth, and he wanders respected neither of gods nor mortals.
Such were the shining gifts given by the gods to Peleus
from his birth, who outshone all men beside for his riches
and pride of possession, and was lord over the Myrmidons.
          Thereto
the gods bestowed an immortal wife on him, who was mortal.
But even on him the god piled evil also. There was not
any generation of strong sons born to him in his great house
but a single all-untimely child he had, and I give him
no care as he grows old, since far from the land of my fathers
I sit here in Troy, and bring nothing but sorrow to you and your children.
But now the Uranian gods brought us, an affliction upon you,
forever there is fighting about your city, and men killed.
But bear up, nor mourn endlessly in your heart, for there is not
anything to be gained from grief for your son; you will never
bring him back; sooner you must go through yet another sorrow.'
          In answer to him again spoke aged Priam the godlike:
'Do not, beloved of Zeus, make me sit on a chair while Hektor
lies yet forlorn among the shelters; rather with all speed
give him back, so my eyes may behold him, and accept the ransom
we bring you, which is great. You may have joy of it, and go back

to the land of your own fathers, since one you have permitted me
to go on living myself and continue to look on the sunlight.'
          Then looking darkly at him spoke swift-footed Achilleus:
'No longer stir me up, old sir. I myself am minded
to give Hektor back to you. A messenger came to me from Zeus,
my mother, she who bore me, the daughter of the sea's ancient.
I know you Priam, in my heart, and it does not escape me
that some god led you to the running ships of the Achaians.
For no mortal would dare come to our encampment, not even
one strong in youth. He could not get by the pickets, he could not
lightly unbar the bolt that secure our gateway. Therefore
you must not further make my spirit move in my sorrows,
for fear, old sir, I might not let you alone in my shelter,
suppliant as you are; and be guilty before the god's orders.'
          He spoke, and the old man was frightened and did as he told him.
The son of Peleus bounded to the door of the house like a lion,
nor went alone, but the two henchmen followed attending,
the hero Automedon and Alkimos, those who Achilleus
honoured beyond all companions after Patroklos dead. These two
now set free from the yoke the mules and the horses,
and led inside the herald, the old king's crier, and gave him
a chair to sit in, then from the smooth-polished mule wagon
lifted out the innumerable spoils for the head of Hektor,

but left inside it two great cloaks and a fine-spun tunic
to shroud the corpse in when they carried him home. Then Achilleus
called out to his serving-maids to wash the body and anoint it
all over; but take it first aside, since otherwise Priam
might see his son and in the heart's sorrow not hold in his anger
at the sight, and the deep heart in Achilleus be shaken to anger;
that he might not kill Priam and be guilty before the god's orders.
Then when the serving-maids had washed the corpse and anointed it
with olive oil, they threw a fair great cloak and a tunic
about him, and Achilleus himself lifted him

and laid him on a litter, and his friends helped him lift it to the smooth-polished
mule wagon. He groaned then, and called by name on his beloved companion:
'Be not angry with me, Patroklos, if you discover,
though you be in the house of Hades, that I gave back great Hektor
to his loved father, for the ransom he gave me was not unworthy.
I will give you your share of the spoils, as such as is fitting.'
(That evening Achilleus and Priam eat together, and Priam sleeps in the forecourt. During the course of the night, Hermes awakens Priam and safely escorts him back to the Xanthos river. **The Iliad** ends with the funeral of Hektor, the defender of Troy.)

NOTES

[1]The Muse who inspires epic poetry.

[2]Achilleus, the son of Peleus and the sea-goddess Thetis, is the greatest Greek warrior in the Trojan War.

[3]Atreus' two sons were Agamemnon and Menelaus who were married to Klytaimnestra and Helen respectively. Helen's elopement with Paris was the cause of the Trojan War.

[4]Apollo the Archer is the god of prophecy, music, medicine and music. He is the son of Zeus by Leto, one of the many goddesses he loved. Apollo is on the Trojan side in the war. Later he will be identified with Helios the sun-god. His oracular shrine at Delphi will be the most important in all Greece.

[5]The priest of Apollo from Chryse whose daughter Chryses has been taken as a prize by Agamemnon.

[6]King of Troy.

[7]The name of the principal town in Argolis in Greece.

[8]Towns near Troy.

[9]An island off the Trojan coast.

[10]A cult title of Apollo.

[11]Another name, along with Achaians and Argives, for the Greek army.

[12]Wife and sister of Zeus. She was bitterly hostile to the Trojan side and favorable to the Greeks.

[13]Literally a sacrifice of one hundred animals.

[14]Brother of Zeus, god of earth-quake and sea.

[15]Son of Kronos, a title of Zeus.

[16]The Ethiopians who were thought to live at the end of the earth.

[17]"Heavenly," Uranus was "Father Sky," the most ancient of the gods.

[18]Hermes, the messenger of the gods.

[19]He was asked to judge which goddess was most beautiful: Hera, Athena or Aphrodite. All offered him bribes, but Aphrodite offered him the love of Helen, and he chose her.

[20]Automedon and Alkimos are two warrior companions of Achilleus. Ares is the god of war.

THE ODYSSEY

The other great Homeric epic is **The Odyssey** whose hero, Odysseus, struggles for ten years to make his return journey from Troy to his island home on rocky Ithaca. The two Homeric poems and their respective heroes share a similar mythological background and reflect the same heroic code, but they also make an interesting contrast. **The Iliad** is a war poem and its hero, Achilleus, is highly individualistic. He is destined for a short and glorious life on the battlefield, and has no identity or fulfillment apart from war where he wins undying honor and glory. **The Odyssey,** on the other hand, is a journey story whose hero is a survivor. Odysseus is "the man of many turns," "who many ways wandered," who longs "for his wife and return." Odysseus is a capable warrior, but he strives "for his life and his companions' return." Although his men perish because of their rashness in eating the cattle of Helios, the sun-god, Odysseus himself succeeds in his journey to re-establish his identity by returning home. He finds honor through his relationship to his home and family. When alone, separated from them on the island of the lovely goddess Kalypso, he desires "merely to see the hearthsmoke leaping upward from his own island." And, although Kalypso offers him immortality, Odysseus, in contrast to Gilgamesh, has no interest in this gift; he "longs to die" if he cannot return home to Ithaca. Odysseus finds his fulfillment not in immortality nor in battle, but in his homecoming in which as a disguised beggar he fights to regain his proper place in his homeland and family with his son Telemachus, his faithful wife Penelope and his father Laertes.

Our selection is taken from Book XXIV, the concluding book in which Odysseus is reunited with his father, and they, with Telemachus and their loyal servants, put an end to the blood feud that threatens to break out in Ithaca over the death of Penelope's suitors whom Odysseus has killed to avenge their abusive treatment of his family and estates in his absence.

The opening scene has the ghosts of the slain suitors being led into the dark underworld by Hermes. Homer's picture of the underworld and the afterlife here, and in Odysseus' journey there in Book XI, is one in which the dead are portrayed as weak ephemeral shades who find no fulfillment in the afterlife. In the meeting between Achilleus and Odysseus in Book XI, the former tells the living Odysseus,

> "I would rather serve on the land of another man
> Who had no portion and not a great livelihood
> Than to rule over all the shades of those who are dead."

The speeches of the various shades in the beginning of Book XXIV of **The Odyssey** show that for the ancient Greek the character of one's life and death and the reputation or honor that these leave among the living are the source of personal fulfillment, rather than a fulfilling afterlife in Hades. Agamemnon says to Achilles "Blessed are you . . . god-like Achilles" because he died honorably in battle at Troy and received the proper honors of a warrior in funeral rites and games arranged by Zeus, his mother Thetis and his fellow warriors. Agamemnon concludes by saying,

> "So you did not lose your name even when you died, Achilles.
> There shall be noble renown for you always among all men."

In contrast Agamemnon's own death was shameful. At his homecoming he was killed by his adulterous wife, Klytaimnestra, and her lover Aigisthos. Instead of a hero's welcome, Agamemnon was received by a traitorous wife who had exiled his son and taken his own cousin as her lover.

Homer contrasts Odysseus' return to that of Agamemnon throughout **The Odyssey.** He comes home to a situation that was potentially as dangerous as the one Agamemnon faced. His wife's suitors have devoured his estates and dishonored his wife, son and father. Given the opportunity, they would have killed Odysseus and taken his place as king of Ithaca. However, in contrast to Agamemnon, Odysseus returns to a faithful family. When Agamemnon hears from the shades of the suitors the story of how Odysseus' son, Telemachus, and his faithful wife, Penelope, had aided him in defeating the suitors, he exclaims:

> "Blessed son of Laertes, Odysseus of many wiles,
> Truly you have won a wife of great excellence.
> How good was the mind of blameless Penelope,
> Daughter of Icarios, who remembered Odysseus well,
> Her wedded husband! And so the fame of her excellence
> Shall never die. The immortals shall make for men on the earth
> A delightful song about constant Penelope."

In the last half of Book XXIV Homer points out the limits of the warrior's honor code and looks beyond it to a vision of compassion and peace in a way reminiscent of the conclusion of **The Iliad.** Odysseus is reunited with his father Laertes in a tender and moving scene, but they face the prospect of having to fight the families of the suitors who are bent on avenging the honor of their sons and brothers, although the wise Halithese Mastorides had reminded them that these men had died for their shameful behavior in raiding Odysseus' flocks and dishonoring his queen. At this point the scene switches to Olympos where Athene, Odysseus' protectoress, asks Zeus,

> "Our father, son of Cronos, highest of all rulers
> Tell me when I ask, what plan of yours is concealed here?
> Will you fashion further an evil war and dread battle,
> Or will you establish friendship between both sides?"

If the battle between the two factions goes forward, Ithaca will be destroyed in an endless blood feud. Zeus tells Athena to conclude the matter as she will, but he suggests:

"Do as you wish, but I will tell you what seems fitting.
Since godly Odysseus has done vengeance on the
suitors,
Let them solemnize an oath, that he may always
reign.
And let us bring about oblivion for the murder
Of their sons and kinsmen. Let them love one another
As before, and let there be abundant wealth and
peace."

Here Homer puts the Olympian gods on the side of peace and reason which transcends a blind commitment to family honor. In the midst of the ensuing battle Athene intervenes by crying, "Ithacans, hold off from war, which is disastrous,/So you may separate without bloodshed as soon as you can." Odysseus has to be stopped from pursuing the fleeing townspeople by Zeus' thunderbolt, and then Athena can command him:

"Zeus-born son of Laertes, Odysseus of many wiles,
Hold off and cease from the strife of impartial war,
Lest Zeus, the broad-seeing son of Cronos, in some way get angry."

Odysseus yields, and his heart is glad as both parties come to peace terms set by Athena.

Both of Homer's great poems end with the gods bringing the two great warriors to an experience of compassion and peace which transcends a pursuit of personal honor and blood revenge. This ending anticipates the conclusion of the **Oresteia,** the great dramatic trilogy of Aeschylus in the fifth-century B.C.E.

The translation is by Albert Cook, **The Odyssey** (New York: W.W. Norton & Company, 1967).

BOOK XXIV

A meeting of the shades of the heroes of the Trojan War

And Hermes of Cyllene[1] summoned forth the souls
Of the suitors, and he held in his hand the lovely gold wand
With which he enchants the eyes of those men he wishes,
And others he wakens even when they are asleep.

He stirred them with it and drove them. They followed squeaking,
As when bats in the corner of a prodigious cave
Squeak as they fly when one of them falls away
From the cluster on the rock where they cling to one another;
So they squeaked as they went together. And Hermes,
The deliverer, led them on along the dank ways.
They went past the streams of Oceanos, past the White Rock;

Past the gates of the Sun also, and the district of dreams

Did they go. And at once they reached the asphodel meadow[2]

Where the souls dwell, phantoms of those who are worn out.

They came upon the soul of Achilles, son of Peleus,[3]

The soul of Patroklos[4] and of excellent Antilochos,[5]

And of Ajax,[6] who was the finest in body and form

Of all the Danaans, after the excellent son of Peleus.

So they thronged around that man, and right close to them

The soul of Agamemnon came on, the son of Atreus,[7]

Grieving. And the others drew in together, all those

Who had died with him and met their fate in Agisthos'[8] house.

The soul of the son of Peleus[9] spoke out to him first:

"Son of Atreus,[10] we thought you were dear beyond other heroes

To Zeus who hurls the thunderbolt, for all your days,

Because you were lord over many valiant men

In the land of the Trojans where we Achaians[11] suffered pains.

And yet the destructive fate that no one who is born

Can avoid was destined to come early upon you as well.

Would that when you were enjoying the honor of which you were the master

In the land of the Trojans, you had met death and destiny!

Then all the Achaians would have made you a funeral mound

And you would have won great glory for your son hereafter.

As it is, you were fated to be caught in a grievous death."

Then the soul of the son of Atreus spoke to him:

"Blessed are you, son of Peleus, godlike Achilles,

You who died in Troy far from Argos.[12] Around you, others,

The best sons of the Achaians and of the Trojans were killed

Contending over you. You in a whirling cloud of dust

Lay great and greatly fallen, having forgotten horsemanship.

And we contended the whole day. Nor would we at all

Have stopped the battle if Zeus had not stopped it with a storm.

But when we had brought you up on the ships out of battle,

We set you down upon a bier and cleaned off your lovely skin

With warm water and oil, and the Danaans shed

Many hot tears over you and sheared off their hair.

Your mother[13] came from the sea with the deathless girls of the sea[14]

When she heard the report. A prodigious cry arose

Over the ocean, and a trembling seized all the Achaians,

And they would have sprung up and gone to the hollow ships

If a man had not restrained them who knew many ancient matters,

Nestor,[15] whose advice had also before seemed best.

With good intent he spoke out to them and addressed them:

'Hold back, Argives; do not flee, young Achaians. His mother

This is, here from the sea with the deathless girls of the sea;

She has come to be beside her son who has died.'

So he said, and the great-hearted Achaians were held back from flight.

About them stood the daughters of the old man of the sea,

Wailing piteously; they clothed you in ambrosial garments.

All the nine Muses,[16] changing off with lovely voice, sang a dirge. There you would have seen none of the Argives[17]

Who did not weep, so stirring was the clear Muses' song.

Seventeen days for you, and also the nights alike,

Did we lament, both immortal gods and mortal men.

On the eighteenth we gave you to the fire and about you

Killed many fat sheep and cattle with crumpled horns.

You were burned in the clothes of the gods and with much oil

And with sweet honey. Many of the Achaian warriors

Marched around the fire in armor while you were being burned,

Foot soldiers and horsemen, and a great din arose.

But when the flame of Hephaistos[18] had made an end of you,

At the dawn, Achilles, we gathered your white bones

In unmixed wine and in oil. And your mother gave

A golden two-handled jar.[19] She said it was a gift

Of Dionysos,[20] the work of highly renowned Hephaistos.

So in it, glorious Achilles, your white bones lie,

Mingled with those of dead Patroklos, Menoitios' son;

Apart are those of Antilochus, whom you honored

Above all your other companions after the dead Patroklos.

And then we, the sacred army of Argive spearmen, heaped

A great and excellent funeral mound up over them

On a strand jutting forward on the broad Hellespont,[21]

So that it might be seen far over the ocean by men,

Both those who are born now and those who shall be hereafter.

And your mother asked the gods for beautiful prizes

And set them up for a contest amid the best of the Achaians.

Already you have been present at the burial of many men,

Of warriors; when, because a king has passed away,

The young men gird themselves and prepare for the prizes.

But you would have marveled in your heart most to see those,

The beautiful prizes that the goddess set up for you,

Thetis of the silver foot. You were very dear to the gods.

So you did not lose your name even when you died, Achilles.

There shall be noble renown for you always among all men.

But what pleasure did I have, when I had wound up the war?

For Zeus planned woeful destruction for me on my return

At the hands of Aigisthos and my accursed wife."

The shades of the suitors tell their story

And so they said such things to one another.

The Runner, the slayer of Argos,[22] came up close to them,

Leading the souls of the suitors subdued by Odysseus.

The two, marveling, went straight up when they saw them.

The soul of Agamemnon, son of Atreus, recognized

The dear son of Melaneos, renowned Amphimedon,[23]

For he was a guest of his who dwelt in Ithaca.

The soul of the son of Atreus spoke out to him first:

"Amphimedon, what did you suffer to go under
   the gloomy earth,
All you chosen men of the same age? Not otherwise
Would someone pick out and gather the best
   men in a city.
Was it that Poseidon[24] overcame you in your
   ships
By raising up oppressive winds and giant
   waves,
Or did hostile men ravage you upon the main-
   land
As you were cutting off their cattle and fine
   flocks of sheep,
Or as they were fighting on behalf of their city
   and women?
Tell me what I ask—I declare I am your guest
   friend.
Do you not remember when I came there to
   your house,
Urging Odysseus on to come along to Ilion
With godlike Menelaos[25] upon the well-tim-
   bered ships?
An entire month we spent crossing the whole
   broad ocean
Since we could scarcely persuade Odysseus, the
   sacker of cities."
And then the soul of Amphimedon addressed
   him:
"Glorious son of Atreus, Zeus-nourished Aga-
   memnon,
Lord of men, I do remember all the things you
   say,
And I shall tell you everything truthfully and
   well,
The evil end of our death, the way it came
   about.
We wooed the wife of Odysseus, who was gone
   so long;
She neither refused the hateful wedding nor
   carried it out,
Contriving for us death and black destiny;
And she devised in her mind this other deceit:
She set a great loom in the halls, and on it she
   wove

A large and delicate fabric. She told us at once:
'Young men, my suitors, since godlike Odys-
   seus is dead,
Wait, though you are eager for this marriage
   of mine, till I finish
This robe, so that the yarn will not waste in
   vain,
The burial sheet for the hero Laertes[26] for the
   time
When the ruinous fate of long-sorrowful death
   seizes him,
Lest one of the Achaian women in the district
   blame me
If he who had won so much lay without cover-
   ing.'
So she said, and the bold heart was persuaded
   within us.
Then every day she kept weaving there on the
   great loom,
And in the nights she undid it when she had
   the torches set up.
So three years she fooled the Achaians and persuaded them.
But when the fourth year came and the seasons
   came on
Of the waning months and many days came to
   an end,
Right then one of the women who perceived it
   clearly told it.
And we happened upon her undoing the shiny
   fabric.
Then she finished it, though unwilling and under duress.
And when, having woven the great fabric and
   washed it,
She showed forth the robe that resembled the
   sun or the moon,
Just then some evil god led Odysseus from
   someplace
To the verge of the field where the swineherd
   had his home.
There, too, the beloved son of Odysseus had
   come
When he went from sandy Pylos[27] in his black
   ship.

The two of them, contriving an evil death for
the suitors,
Had arrived at the city of great renown. Odys-
seus
Was last, and Telemachus[28] led the way ahead
of them.
The swineherd brought the man, who wore vile
clothes on his skin
And resembled a wretched beggar who was an
old man
Walking with a staff. He had sorry clothes on
his skin.
None of us could recognize that it was he
When he appeared suddenly, not even those
who were older,
But we rebuked him with missiles and evil
speeches.
Still, he held out all the while with enduring
heart
When he was being beaten and rebuked in his
own walls.
But when the purpose of aegis-bearing Zeus
aroused him
He took up the beautiful weapons with Tele-
machos
And placed them in the chamber and locked
the fastenings,
And resourcefully he gave the order to his wife
To set before the suitors the bow and the gray
iron,
A contest and start of slaughter for us in our
dread fate.
None of us was able to stretch out the string
        Of the mighty bow, for we were too weak
by far.
But when the great bow came into Odysseus'
hands,
Then all of us made a common outcry with
speeches,
Not to give him the bow, however much he
might say.
Telemachos alone urged him on and gave him
the order.
Then godly Odysseus, who had endured much,
took it in his hand,

Easily strung the bow and shot through the
iron.
He went and stood on the threshold, poured the
swift arrows out,
Peering round terribly, and hit King Anti-
noos.[29]
And then on the others he let the groan-car-
rying darts fly,
Taking aim straight across. And they fell thick
and fast.
It was known then that one of the gods was
their helper for them.
For at once they went on through the house in
their rage
And killed them one after another. A sad
groaning
Rose as their heads were struck. The whole
ground ran with blood.
Agamemnon, this is the way we perished, we
whose bodies
Are still lying uncared for now in the halls of
Odysseus.
For the dear ones in the home of each man do
not know it yet,
Those who, when they have washed the black
gore from the wounds,
May lay us out weeping. For that is the prize of
the dead."
Then the soul of the son of Atreus spoke out to
him:
"Blessed son of Laertes, Odysseus of many
wiles,
Truly you have won a wife of great excellence.
How good was the mind of blameless Penelope,
Daughter of Icarios, who remembered Odys-
seus well,
Her wedded husband! And so the fame of her
excellence
Shall never die. The immortals shall make for
men on the earth
A delightful song about constant Penelope.
Not so did the daughter of Tyndareus[30] devise
her evil deeds,
Who killed her wedded husband; and a hateful
song shall there be

Among men, and she will bestow a harsh reputation

On womankind, even on one who is good in
what she does."

And so they said such things to one another,

Standing in the halls of Hades under the
depths of the earth.

(On the next day Odysseus went to visit his father Laertes whom he found on his estate
weeding his garden. While they were having a
tender reunion, Eupeithes, the father of Anti-
noos, organized an attack upon them. We resume the text as Athene speaks to Zeus of the
impending battle.)

The plan of Athene and Zeus

Then Athene spoke out to Zeus, the son of
Cronos:

"Our father, son of Cronos, highest of all rulers,

Tell me what I ask, what plan of yours is concealed here?

Will you fashion further an evil war and dread
battle,

Or will you establish friendship between both
sides?"

And cloud-gathering Zeus addressed her in answer:

"My child, why do you ask me and question me
about this?

Why did you not think out this idea by yourself,

That Odysseus might indeed take vengeance
on them when he came?

Do as you wish, but I will tell you what seems
fitting.

Since godly Odysseus has done vengeance on
the suitors,

Let them solemnize an oath, that he may always reign.

And let us bring about oblivion for the murder

Of their sons and kinsmen. Let them love one
another

As before, and let there be abundant wealth
and peace."

The battle

When he said this, he aroused Athene, who was
eager before.

She went down in a rush from the summit of
Olympos.

And when the men had taken their fill of mind-
honeying food,

Godly Odysseus, who had suffered much, began speaking to them:

"Let someone go out and see lest they are coming close."

So he said, and the son of Dolios went out as he
bid.

He went and stood on the threshold and saw
them all close.

Right away he addressed winged words to
Odysseus:

"Here they are nearby. Let us quickly arm ourselves!"

So he said. They rose up and got their armor
on,

Four including Odysseus, and the six sons of
Dolios,

And among them Laertes and Dolios put armor
on,

Gray though they were, warriors by necessity.

And when they had put the glittering bronze
round their skin,

They opened the doors and went out; Odysseus
led.

Athene, daughter of Zeus, came up close to
them,

Likening herself to Mentor[31] in form and in
voice.

Godly Odysseus, who had endured much, rejoiced to see her;

At once he spoke out to his dear son Telemachos:

"Telemachos, you will soon learn, now you
have come yourself to where men are fighting and the best ones are judged,

Not to disgrace the family of your fathers, who
before

Were distinguished for strength and prowess
on the whole earth."

Then sound-minded Telemachos said to him in
answer:

"In my present spirit, dear father, you will see,
if you wish,

That, as you say, I shall not at all disgrace your family."

So he said, and Laertes rejoiced and spoke a word:

"What a day is this for me, dear gods! I greatly rejoice

That my son and my grandson contend over excellence."

Bright-eyed Athene stood beside him and addressed him:

"Son of Arkesios, dearest by far of all my companions,

When you have prayed to the bright-eyed maid and to father Zeus,

Brandish your long-shadowy spear at once and hurl it forth."

So she said, and Pallas Athene breathed great strength into him.

Then he prayed to the daughter of the mighty Zeus

And brandished his long-shadowy spear at once and shot it forth.

He hit Eupeithes through the bronze cheek piece of his helmet.

This did not keep the spear back; the bronze went right through.

He made a crash as he fell, and his armor clattered upon him.

Odysseus and his glorious son fell upon the fighters in the front

And struck at them with their swords and their two-edged spears.

The making of peace

Now they would have destroyed all and made them without return,

If Athene, the daughter of Aegis-bearing Zeus, had not

Shouted with her voice and restrained the whole host:

"Ithacans, hold off from war, which is disastrous,

So you may separate without bloodshed as soon as you can."

So did Athene say. And sallow fear got hold of them.

As they were afraid, all their arms flew out of their hands

And fell on the ground, as the goddess uttered her voice.

They turned back toward the city, longing for life.

Godly Odysseus, who had endured much, shouted dreadfully.

He bunched himself up and swooped down like a high-flying eagle.

Then the son of Cronos shot a smoldering thunderbolt.

It fell before the bright-eyed daughter of the mighty father.

Then bright-eyed Athene spoke out to Odysseus:

"Zeus-born son of Laertes, Odysseus of many wiles,

Hold off and cease from the strife of impartial war,

Lest Zeus, the broad-seeing son of Cronos, in some way get angry."

So Athene said. He obeyed, and rejoiced in his heart.

Then Pallas Athene, daughter of aegis-bearing Zeus,

Established oaths for the future between both sides,

Likening herself to Mentor in form and voice.

NOTES

[1]One of Hermes' duties as messenger-god was conducting the shades of the dead to Hades.
[2]The meadow of the dead.
[3]The great Greek warrior who died at Troy from Paris' arrow.
[4]The friend of Achilles who, while wearing Achilles' armor, was killed by Hektor of Troy.
[5]Eldest son of Nestor and friend of Achilles. Died at Troy and was buried in the same grave as Achilles and Patroklos.

[6]Bravest Greek warrior after Achilles.
[7]Killed by his wife Klytaimnestra and her lover Aigisthos upon his return from Troy.
[8]Son of Thyestes and lover of Klytaimnestra who killed Agamemnon upon his return.
[9]Achilles
[10]Agamemnon.
[11]The Greek forces at Troy.
[12]Chief town of Argolis in the eastern Peloponnessus.
[13]Thetis, a sea nymph and mother of Achilles by Peleus.
[14]Nereids, fifty sea nymphs who were attendant upon Poseidon, the god of the sea.
[15]King of Pylos, noted for his eloquence and wisdom.
[16]Goddesses responsible for song and epic poetry.
[17]Another term for the Greeks.
[18]The craftsman god.
[19]An amphora.
[20]God of wine and revelry.
[21]Helle, the daughter of Athamus and Nephele, with her brother Phrixus rode away on a ram with golden fleece, but then fell into the body of water which now bears her name (Hellespont), and drowned.
[22]Hermes.
[23]A suitor of Penelope.
[24]God of earthquakes and the sea.
[25]Brother of Agamemnon and son of Atreus. His wife Helen was taken by Paris and this occasioned the Trojan War. 'Ilion' was another name for Troy.
[26]Odysseus' father.
[27]Town in Messenia in the Peloponnesus in southern Greece and home of Nestor which Telemachos had visited in search of news of his father.
[28]Odysseus' son.
[29]The most brutal, cruel and insolent suitor for Penelope.
[30]Klytaimnestra.
[31]Mentor was an Ithacan friend of Odysseus in whose guise Athene aided him.

HESIOD

The gods of Homer became the gods of the various *poleis* in the eighth and seventh centuries B.C.E.; each city adopted one member of the Olympian pantheon as its special patron. But the Homeric gods remained closely associated with the aristocratic families, who often claimed to be descendants from the gods and mortal women. With the rise of the *polis,* the demand for more democratic institutions and for the rights of classes below the aristocracy became increasingly important. The old Olympian religion was not adequate to the task. Zeus had shown no concern for the rights of the lower classes in the Homeric epics.

The earliest known attempt to transform the Olympian gods into defenders of popular rights is the work of Hesiod, a Boeotian shepherd poet, who probably lived at the end of the eighth century B.C.E. Hesiod, like his contemporaries the Hebrew prophets, was convinced that the world was steadily deteriorating because of human wickedness. His poetry seems to deliberately counteract the Homeric emphasis on war, military glory, and individual excellence by celebrating hard work, honesty, and sobriety. In contrast to Homer whose epics are centered on the exploits of the great heroes in the Trojan War, Hesiod's poems record aspects of life not otherwise represented in Greek literature: the life of the peasant farmer and his equally heroic struggle to make a living from the mountainous and rocky land of Greece.

THE WORKS AND DAYS

Hesiod's **Works and Days** is a highly didactic and moralistic poem which celebrates the values and ethic of the hardworking Greek farmer and attacks the injustice of aristocratic landlords to their peasants in a manner reminiscent of contemporary Hebrew prophets like Amos and Isaiah. The occasion for this work was Hesiod's dispute with his brother Perses who had bribed the local gentry and gained a larger share of their deceased father's inheritance. The poem is addressed to Perses in order to win him to a life of justice and hard work.

In his invocation of the Muses, we learn that Hesiod's song will praise Zeus through whose inscrutable will "men are renowned or remain unsung . . ." But the Zeus of Hesiod's poetry is not the one who favors the powerful warrior; in fact, he is the protector of the oppressed, a figure who:

> lightly brings strength to confusion
> lightly diminishes the great man,
> uplifts the obscure one,
> lightly the crooked man straightens,
> withers the proud man.

Hesiod seems closer in spirit to the author of the Song of Hannah (1 Sam 2:1–10) in the Israelite tradition who describes the Lord as the one by whom "the bows of the mighty are broken, but the feeble gird on strength."

In the beginning of his exhortation Hesiod displays the Greek capacity for analysis by distinguishing universal concepts. He describes the two types of Strife: the harsh one which leads to war and slaughter and the kindly one which Zeus sets among men to push them to work and healthy competition. Hesiod urges Perses to "put all this firmly away in your heart," to follow the one Strife by working hard, but to give up the other and not try to best others in unjust lawsuits as he has done in the division of their father's inheritance.

In the next section Hesiod accounts for the facts of human misery, laborious work and evil by using traditional Greek myths in a way comparable to the sin-punishment stories in Genesis 3–11 in the Israelite tradition. Hesiod's version of the Prometheus story makes an interesting comparison and contrast to the Garden of Eden story in Genesis 2–3. Both traditions view the present condition of the human race as a fallen state from a lost paradise. Hesiod mentions a time when a single day's work sufficed for the full year and when "the races of men" were "free from all evils, free from laborious work and free from all wearing sickness . . . " This paradisal existence did not include immortality, however, as Hesiod refers to this all-male race as "mortals."

Both stories blame the loss of paradise on a primeval offense which involved a successful, but catastrophic, attempt at making humans share in a divine secret of knowledge which the divinity jealously protected. In the Genesis story the sin is committed by the woman and man themselves, who, influenced by the serpent's temptation, eat of the forbidden tree of knowledge of good and evil in an attempt to become like God in wisdom (Gen 3: 1–7). They are in some sense successful as is indicated by the speech of the Lord God before expelling them from Eden and the tree of life—"Behold, the man has become like one of us knowing good and evil . . . " In Hesiod's myth the offense is committed by "devious-minded" Prometheus ("Forethought"), a divine Titan, the son of Iapetos and Klymene, who attempts to help mortal humans by stealing "fire" (a symbol of technological knowledge) from Zeus, who had jealously hidden it.

The divine punishments for these bold offenses are severe, and they reflect the prejudices of the patriarchal societies which produced these stories. In Genesis women are doomed to a subordinate position in a male-dominated society and to the pains of childbirth; men are condemned to eke out a living from the recalcitrant earth; and the "tree of life," which would have given immortality, is lost. In **Works and Days** Zeus' punishment is to give the previously all-male race an evil in the form of woman. He instructs the gods to create the irresistible, but treacherous, Pandora ("all gifts"). When Epimetheus ("Afterthought"), the hapless brother of Prometheus, forgets his brother's warning and receives this gift from Zeus, Pandora opens a mysterious jar and unleashes "sad troubles for mankind." Hope is the only spirit that stays within the jar.

The contrast in the view of women in the two traditions is worth noting. Both accounts are highly patriarchal and reflect the subordinate role of women in their respective societies. In the biblical account, however, woman is intended to be a divine gift to man, and she completes his person in a way in which the animals cannot. When the woman is brought to the man, he exclaims: "This one at last is bone of my bones and flesh of my flesh . . . " (Gen 2:23). In Hesiod's story, however, Pandora is a deceptive gift who is actually a punishment, an evil given to mankind.

Hesiod's myth of the Five Ages of Humanity has the same purpose as the Prometheus story: to illustrate the deterioration of human existence from a paradisal to a curse-ridden state. Hesiod gives a description of each generation, its demise, and an account of its present state. The Golden Age was a race of godlike creatures whose "hearts were free from sorrow." They spent their time in festivals, enjoying the bounty of the earth, and without fear of aging. They were on intimate terms with the gods, and "when they died, it was as if they had fallen asleep." Now members of this generation are the pure and blessed spirits under the earth who "watch over mortal men and defend them from evil." The Silver Age was inferior to its predecessor in every respect, and it reminds us of the generations leading up to the flood in the biblical tradition. No longer were humans ageless. Children had a prolonged, hundred year childhood, and, when they became adults, their "foolishness brought trouble," and they committed "reckless crimes against one another." They failed to honor the gods, and finally Zeus in his anger "engulfed" them. They too are now called "blessed spirits," but they are secondary to their predecessors. The Bronze Age was the age of violence in which men with their bronze weapons destroyed each other. They are now "nameless," having gone "down into the moldering domain of cold Hades." Before describing his own Iron Age, Hesiod inserts a fourth generation, the Heroic Age which Homer had eulogized. This age interrupts the gradual deterioration of the race, as Hesiod recognized that "these were better and nobler . . . " Some of this generation were taken by "evil war and terrible carnage" at Thebes and Troy, but on others Zeus "settled a living and a country of their own apart from humankind at the end of the world." There they enjoy a carefree existence in the islands of the blessed, like Utnapishtim in **The Gilgamesh Epic**. The last of the ages is Hesiod's own Iron Age. He describes it very briefly as having no end to hard work, pain and anxiety, "yet with some good things mixed with evils." In a prophetic manner, he predicts the destruction of his own age when all familial, social and moral order has collapsed.

Hesiod's solution to the blatant injustice of his age, described vividly in the fable of the hawk and the nightingale, is to exhort his brother and others to "listen to justice; do not try to practice violence." He personifies Justice (*Dike*) as the maiden daughter of Zeus who curses the city which violates her and blesses the city where she is revered. Hesiod's picture of the city of justice is comparable to Isaiah's messianic visions (cf. Is 2:1–7; 9:1–7; 11:1–9).

According to Hesiod, Justice is Zeus' gift to humans, and the capacity for justice is what separates them from the violent animal world where "they feed on one another." Hesiod's belief in Zeus as the guardian of justice anticipates Solon, an early sixth century Athenian statesman and poet, and Aeschylus, the great fifth century Athenian dramatist, who also associates the Olympian gods with the establishment of enlightened human justice, as opposed to barbarous blood revenge or class conflict.

The latter sections of the poem, which are not in our selection, are a catalogue like a farmer's almanac which urges Perses to enjoy the pleasures and virtues of the farmer's life. The translation is by Richmond Lattimore in **Hesiod: The Works and Days, Theogony and the Shield of Herakles** (Ann Arbor: The University of Michigan Press, 1965) 15–53.

Invocation of the Muses

Muses, who from Pieria[1] give glory through
   singing,
come to me, tell of Zeus, your own father,
sing his praises, through whose will
mortal men are named in speech or remain un-
   spoken.

Men are renowned or remain unsung
   as great Zeus wills it
For lightly he makes strong,
and lightly brings strength to confusion,
lightly diminishes the great man,
uplifts the obscure one,
lightly the crooked man he straightens,

withers the proud man,
he, Zeus, of the towering thunders,
whose house is highest.

Appeal to Zeus and Perses
Hear me, see me, Zeus: hearken:
direct your decrees in righteousness.
To you, Perses, I would describe the true way
   of existence.

The two Strifes
It was never true that there was only one kind
   of strife. There have always been two on
   earth. There is one
you could like when you understand her.
The other is hateful. The two Strifes have separate natures.
There is one Strife who builds up evil war, and
   slaughter.
She is harsh; no man loves her, but under com-
   pulsion and by will of the immortals men
promote this rough Strife.
But the other one was born
the elder daughter of black Night.
The son of Kronos,[2] who sits on high and
dwells in the bright air,
set her in the roots of the earth and among
   men;
she is far kinder.
She pushes the shiftless man to work,
for all his laziness.
A man looks at his neighbor, who is rich:
then he too
wants work; for the rich man presses on with
his plowing and planting and the ordering of
   his state.
So the neighbor envies the neighbor
who presses on toward wealth. Such Strife is a
   good friend to mortals.
Then the potter is potter's enemy, and
craftsman is craftman's
rival; tramp is jealous of tramp,
and singer of singer.

Exhortation to Perses
So you, Perses, put all this firmly away
in your heart,

nor let that Strife who loves mischief
keep you from working
as you listen at the meeting place
to see what you can make of
the quarrels. The time comes short for litiga-
   tions
and lawsuits,
too short, unless there is a year's living
laid away inside
for you, the stuff that the earth yields,
the pride of Demeter.[3]
When you have got a full burden of that,
you can push your lawsuits,
scheming for other men's goods, yet you
shall not be given another chance
to do so. No, come, let us finally settle our quarrel
with straight decisions, which are from Zeus,
and are the fairest.
Now once before we divided our inheritance,
but you seized
the greater part and made off with it,
gratifying those barons
who eat bribes, who are willing
to give out such a decision.
Fools all! who never learned
how much better than the whole the half is,
nor how much good there is
in living on mallow and asphodel.
For the gods have hidden and keep hidden
   what could be men's livelihood.

The Prometheus story
It could have been that easily
in one day you could work out
enough to keep you for a year,
with no more working.
Soon you could have hung up your steering oar
in the smoke of the fireplace,
and the work the oxen and patient mules do
would be abolished,
but Zeus in the anger of his heart hid it away
because the devious-minded Prometheus[4] had
   cheated him;
and therefore Zeus thought up dismal sorrows
for mankind.

He hid fire; but Prometheus, the powerful son
of Iapetos,
stole it again from Zeus of the counsels,
to give to mortals.
He hid it out of the sight of Zeus
who delights in thunder
in the hollow fennel stalk. In anger the cloud-
gatherer spoke to him:
"Son of Iapetos, deviser of crafts beyond all others,
you are happy that you stole the fire,
and outwitted my thinking;
but it will be a great sorrow to you,
and to men who come after.
As the price of fire I will give them an evil,
and all men shall fondle
this, their evil, close to their hearts,
and take delight in it."
So spoke the father of gods and mortals; and
laughed out loud.
He told glorious Hephaistos[5] to make haste,
and plaster
earth with water, and to infuse it with a human
voice and vigors, and make the face
like the immortal goddesses,
the bewitching features of a young girl;
meanwhile Athene[6]
was to teach her her skills, and how
to do the intricate weaving,
while Aphrodite[7] was to mist her head in
golden endearment
and the cruelty of desire and longings
that wear out the body,
but to Hermes,[8] the guide, the slayer of Argos,[9]
he gave instructions
to put in her the mind of a hussy, and a treacherous nature.
So Zeus spoke. And all obeyed Lord Zeus, the
son of Kronos.
The renowned strong smith modeled her figure
of earth, in the likeness
of a decorous young girl, as the son of Kronos
had wished it.
The goddess gray-eyed Athene dressed and arrayed her;
the Graces,[10]

who are goddesses, and hallowed Persuasion
put necklaces
of gold upon her body, while the Seasons,[11]
with glorious tresses,
put upon her head a coronal of spring flowers,
[and Pallas Athene put all decor upon her
body];
But into her heart Hermes, the guide,
the slayer of Argos,
put lies, and wheedling words
of falsehood, and a treacherous nature,
made her as Zeus of the deep thunder wished,
and he, the gods' herald,
put a voice inside her, and gave her
the name of woman,
Pandora,[12] because all the gods
who have their homes on Olympos
had given her each a gift, to be a sorrow to men
who eat bread. Now when he had done
with this sheer, impossible
deception, the Father sent the gods' fleet messenger, Hermes,
to Epimetheus,[13] bringing her, a gift,
nor did Epimetheus
remember to think how Prometheus had told
him never to accept a gift from Olympian
Zeus,
but always to send it
back, for fear it might prove to be an evil for
mankind.
He took the evil, and only perceived it when he
possessed her.
Since before this time the races of men had
been living on earth
free from all evils, free from laborious work,
and free from
all wearing sicknesses that bring their fates
down on men
[for men grown old suddenly in the midst of
misfortune];
but the woman, with her hands lifting away
the lid from the great jar,
scattered its contents, and her design was sad
troubles for mankind.
Hope was the only spirit that stayed there in
the unbreakable

closure of the jar, under its rim, and could not
  fly forth
abroad, for the lid of the great jar
closed down first and contained her;
this was by the will of cloud-gathering Zeus of
  the aegis;
but there are other troubles by thousands that
  hover about men,
for the earth is full of evil things,
and the sea is full of them;
there are sicknesses that come to men by day,
  while in the night
moving of themselves they haunt us,
bringing sorrow to mortals,
and silently, for Zeus of the counsels took the
  voice out of them.
So there is no way to avoid what Zeus has intended.

The story of the five ages

Or if you will, I will outline it for you in a different story,
well and knowledgeably—store it up in your
  understanding—
the beginnings of things, which were the same
  for gods as for mortals.

The golden age

In the beginning, the immortals
who have their homes on Olympos
created the golden generation of mortal people.
These lived in Kronos'[14] time, when he was the
  king in heaven.
They lived as if they were gods,
their hearts free from all sorrow,
by themselves, and without hard work or pain;
  no miserable
old age came their way; their hands, their feet,
  did not alter.
They took their pleasure in festivals,
and lived without troubles.
When they died, it was as if they fell asleep.
All goods
were theirs. The fruitful grainland
yielded its harvest to them

of its own accord; this was great and abundant,
while they at their pleasure
quietly looked after their works, in the midst
  of good things
[prosperous in flocks, on friendly terms with
  the blessed immortals].
Now that the earth has gathered over this generation,
these are called pure and blessed spirits;
they live upon earth,
and are good, they watch over mortal men and
  defend them from evil;
they keep watch over lawsuits and hard dealings;
they mantle
themselves in dark mist and wander all over
  the country;
they bestow wealth; for this right as of kings
  was given them.

The silver age

Next after these dwellers upon Olympos created
a second generation, of silver, far worse than
  the other.
They were not like the golden ones either in
  shape or spirit.
A child was a child for a hundred years,
looked after and playing
by his gracious mother, kept at home, a complete booby.
But when it came time for them to grow up and
  gain full measure,
they lived for only a poor short time;
by their own foolishness
they had troubles, for they were not able
to keep away from
reckless crime against each other,
nor would they worship
the gods, nor do sacrifice on the sacred altars of
  the blessed ones,
which is the right thing among the customs of
  men,
and therefore
Zeus, son of Kronos, in anger engulfed them,
  for they paid no due

honors to the blessed gods who live on Olympos.

The bronze age

But when the earth had gathered over this generation
also—and they too are called blessed spirits
by men, though under
the ground, and secondary, but still
they have their due worship—
then Zeus the father created the third generation of mortals,
the age of bronze. They were not like the generation of silver.
They came from ash spears. They were terrible
and strong, and the ghastly
action of Ares[15] was theirs, and violence.
They ate no bread,
but maintained an indomitable and adamantine spirit.
None could come near them; their strength was big,
and from their shoulders
the arms grew irresistible on their ponderous bodies.
The weapons of these men were bronze,
of bronze their houses,
and they worked as bronzesmiths. There was not yet
any black iron.
Yet even these, destroyed beneath the hands of each other,
went down into the moldering domain of cold Hades;[16]
nameless; for all they were formidable black death seized them, and they had to forsake the shining sunlight.

The heroic age

Now when the earth had gathered over this generation
also, Zeus, son of Kronos, created yet another
fourth generation on the fertile earth,
and these were better and nobler,
the wonderful generation of hero-men, who are also

called half-gods, the generation before our own on this vast earth.
But of these too, evil war and the terrible carnage
took some; some by seven-gated Thebes[17]
in the land of Kadmos
as they fought together over the flocks of Oidipous;[19]
others
war had taken in ships over the great gulf of the sea,
where they also fought for the sake of lovely-haired Helen.[20]
There, for these, the end of death was misted about them.
But on others Zeus, son of Kronos, settled a living and a country
of their own, apart from human kind, at the end of the world.
And there they have their dwelling place, and hearts free of sorrow
in the islands of the blessed by the deep-swirling stream of the ocean,
prospering heroes, on whom in every year three times over
the fruitful grainland bestows its sweet yield. These live
far from the immortals, and Kronos
is king among them.
For Zeus, father of gods and mortals, set him free from his bondage,
although the position and the glory still belong to the young gods.

The iron age

After this, Zeus of the wide brows
established yet one more generation of men,
the fifth, to be on the fertile earth.
And I wish that I were not any part of the fifth generation
of men, but had died before it came,
or been born afterward.
For here now is the age of iron. Never by daytime
will there be an end to hard work and pain,
nor in the night

to weariness, when the gods will send anxieties
to trouble us.
Yet here also there shall be some good things
mixed with the evils.
But Zeus will destroy this generation of mortals also,
in the time when children, as they are born,
grow gray on the temples,
when the father no longer agrees with the children,
nor children with their father,
when quest is no longer at one with host,
nor companion to companion,
when your brother is no longer your friend,
as he was in the old days.
Men will deprive their parents of all rights,
as they grow old,
and people will mock them too,
babbling bitter words against them,
harshly, and without shame in the sight of the
gods;
not even
to their aging parents will they give back
what once was given.
Strong of hand, one man shall seek
the city of another.
There will be no favor for the man
who keeps his oath, for the righteous
and the good man, rather men shall give their
praise
to violence
and the doer of evil. Right will be in the arm.
Shame will
not be. The vile man will crowd his better out,
and attack him
with twisted accusations and swear an oath
to his story.
The spirit of Envy, with grim face
and screaming voice, who delights
in evil, will be the constant companion
of wretched humanity,
and at last Nemesis[21] and Aidos,[22] Decency and
Respect,
shrouding their bright forms in pale mantles,
shall go

from the wide-wayed earth back on their way
to Olympos,
forsaking the whole race
of mortal men, and all that will be left by them
to mankind
will be wretched pain. And there shall be no defense
against evil.

The fable of the hawk and nightingale
Now I will tell you a fable for the barons;
they understand it.
This is what the hawk said when he had caught
a nightingale with spangled neck in his claws
and carried her
high among the clouds.
She, spitted on the clawhooks, was wailing pi-
tifully,
but the hawk, in his masterful manner,
gave her an answer:
"What is the matter with you? Why scream?
Your master has you.
You shall go wherever I take you,
for all your singing.
If I like, I can let you go. If I like,
I can eat you for dinner.
He is a fool who tries to match his strength
with the stronger.
He will lose his battle, and with the shame
will be hurt also."
So spoke the hawk, the bird who flies so fast
on his long wings.

The blessings and curses offered by Justice
But as for you, Perses, listen to justice;
do not try to practice
violence; violence is bad for a weak man; even
a noble
cannot lightly carry the burden of her,
but she weighs him down
when he loses his way in delusions; that other
road
is better
which leads toward just dealings. For Justice
wins over violence

as they come out in the end. The fool knows
after he's suffered.
The spirit of Oath is one who runs
beside crooked judgments.
There is an outcry when Justice[23] is dragged
    perforce,
when bribe-eating
men pull her about, and judge their cases
with crooked decisions.
She follows perforce, weeping, to the city
and gatherings of people.
She puts a dark mist upon her and brings a
    curse
upon all those
who drive her out, who deal in her
and twist her in dealing.
But when men issue straight decisions
to their own people
and to strangers, and do not step at all
off the road of rightness, their city flourishes,
    and the people
blossom inside it.
Peace, who brings boys to manhood, is in their
    land,
now does Zeus
of the wide brows ever ordain that hard war
shall be with them.
Neither famine nor inward disaster comes the
    way
of those people who are straight and just; they
    do their work
as if work were a holiday;
the earth gives them great livelihood,
on their mountains the oaks
bear acorns for them in their crowns,
and bees in their middles.
Their wool-bearing sheep are weighted down
with fleecy burdens.
Their women bear them children
who resemble their parents.
They prosper in good things throughout.
They need have no traffic
With ships, for their own grain-giving land
yields them its harvest.
But when men like harsh violence

and cruel acts, Zeus
of the wide brows, the son of Kronos,
ordains their punishment.
Often a whole city is paid punishment
for one bad man
who commits crimes and plans reckless action.
On this man's people
the son of Kronos out of the sky
inflicts great suffering,
famine and plague together, and the people die
and diminish.
The women bear children no longer, the houses
    dwindle
by design of Olympian Zeus; or again at other
    times,
he destroys the wide camped army of a people,
or wrecks
their city with its walls, or their ships
on the open water.
(The next section is an exhortation to the barons to pursue a life of justice.)
Justice herself is a young maiden.
She is Zeus's daughter,
and seemly, and respected by all the gods of
    Olympos.
When any man uses force on her by false im-
    peachment
she goes and sits at the feet of Zeus Kronion,
her father,
and cries out on the wicked purpose of men,
so that their people
must pay for the profligacy of their rulers,
who for their own greedy purposes
twist the courses of justice aslant
by false proclamations.
Beware, you barons, of such spirits.
Straighten your decisions
you eaters of bribes. Banish from your minds
the twisting of justice.

Hesiod's belief in Zeus's just rule
The man who does evil to another does evil
to himself,
and the evil counsel is most evil for him who
    counsels it.

The eye of Zeus sees everything. His mind understands all.

He is watching us right now, if he wishes to,
nor does he fail to see what kind of justice this community keeps
inside it.

Now, otherwise I would not myself be righteous among men nor have my son be so; for it is a hard thing
for a man to be righteous, if the unrighteous man
is to have the greater right.

But I believe that Zeus of the counsels
will not let it end thus. . . .

Her is the law, as Zeus established it for human beings;

as for fish, and wild animals, and the flying birds,
they feed on each other, since there is no idea of justice among them;
but to men he gave justice, and she in the end is proved the best thing
they have. If a man sees what is right
and is willing to argue it,
Zeus of the wide brows grants him prosperity.
But when one, knowingly, tells lies and swears an oath on it,
when he is so wild as to do incurable damage
against justice, this man is left a diminished generation hereafter,
but the generation of the true-sworn man
grows stronger.

NOTES

[1]A spring on the slopes of Mount Olympos where the Muses and Apollo were born.

[2]Zeus.

[3]Goddess of agriculture.

[4]The name means "Forethought." In the **Theogony** Prometheus is the son of Iapetus and Klymene and the brother of Atlas, Menoitius and Epimetheus ("Afterthought").

[5]The craftsman god.

[6]Goddess of wisdom.

[7]Goddess of love.

[8]The messenger of the gods.

[9]The hundred-eyed giant who guarded Io, a daughter of Inachus whom Zeus loved and then turned into a heifer to avoid Hera's suspicion. Hera ordered Argos to guard the heifer, but Zeus sent Hermes to kill Argos. Io, tormented by a gadfly, wandered over many parts of the world and finally returned to Egypt, where she was transformed back into a woman and bore Zeus a son named Epaphus.

[10]Daughters of Zeus and Eurynome. Young, beautiful and modest, they were personifications of gracefulness.

[11]Daughters of Zeus and Themis.

[12]Literally "all gifts."

[13]Brother of Prometheus whose name means "Afterthought."

[14]A Titan and the youngest son of Ouranos and Gaia who castrates his father in the **Theogony** but then establishes his own tyrannical rule. He is later defeated by Zeus.

[15]The god of war.

[16]God of the underworld.

[17]Capital of Boeotia.

[18]Founder of Thebes.

[19]One of the kings of Thebes renowned for his misfortune in unknowingly killing his father, Laius, and marrying his mother, Jocasta.

[20]Wife of Menelaus who was taken by Paris and was thus the cause of the Trojan War.
[21]Goddess of vengeance.
[22]Conscience or shame.
[23]Daughter of Zeus and Themis (Law).

THE THEOGONY

Hesiod's **Theogony**, like the Mesopotamian **Enuma Elish**, is a mythic account of the origin of the gods and the process by which the cosmological and human orders have been established. Unlike the Babylonian myth, however, the **Theogony** begins with an invocation of the Muses which indicates that it is the creative achievement of a single poet, rather than the recording of the official version of an annually re-enacted myth in the state temple. Hesiod is an inspired poet and prophet who is actively reinterpreting and reorganizing older Greek myths, some of which undoubtedly did have an origin in cult. In the invocation he recounts an experience comparable to that of the call of the biblical prophets like Amos or Isaiah.

> And it was they (the Muses) who once taught
>   Hesiod his splendid singing
> as he was shepherding his lambs on holy Helikon,
> and these are the first words of all
>   the goddesses spoke to me,
> The Muses of Olympia, daughters of Zeus of the aegis:
>   "You shepherds of the wilderness, poor fools,
>   nothing but bellies,
> we know how to say many false things
>   that seem like true sayings,
> but we know also how to speak
>   the truth when we wish to."

Like the Babylonian myth, the **Theogony** traces through three generations the development of divine rule from gods who represent the forces and processes of nature to the establishment of a cosmos under a single monarchical power. Both myths also have the motif of conflict between the older and younger generations of the gods, although in the Greek tradition the divine mother remains on the side of her children against a tyrannical father. Recall that Tiamat initially opposed Apsu's plans to destroy the younger gods, but after he was slain by Ea, she turned against her children. In the first generational conflict in the **Theogony**, Ouranos, the starry Sky, is pushing his children "back again deep inside Gaia (Mother Earth)." She groans under the pressure and decides to create a flint sickle with which to castrate her husband for his brutal treatment. Only "devious-devising" Kronos is willing to undertake the job, and, with the aid of his mother, he severs the members of his father. Kronos in turn also becomes a tyrannical king. As he produces children through Rheia, he swallows them so that no other children of Ouranos "should ever hold the king's position among immortals." Again the divine mother rebels against her despotic and paranoid husband, Rheia entreats her parents, Gaia and Ouranos, and Gaia aids her in hiding Zeus, the youngest of the children, from Kronos in an inaccessible cave on the island of Crete. She then gives Kronos "a great stone in baby-clothes" to swallow. When he comes of age, Zeus forces Kronos to vomit up his brothers and sisters: Hestia, Demeter, Hera, Hades and Poseidon. He also frees his father's brothers, the Titans, whom Ouranos had chained. In gratitude, they furnish Zeus with thunder and lightning so that he is associated with forces which enable him to command "both mortals and immortals." In an episode not included in this selection, Zeus defeats Kronos and the Titans by blasting them with lightning and imprisons them underground in Tartarus under the guard of the three hundred-armed Giants.

At this point in the Babylonian myth, Marduk establishes the cosmic order from the lifeless corpse of the slain Tiamat and then receives the obeissance of the other gods. In the **Theogony**, however, Zeus does not reconstruct the natural order. The creative and dynamic order of nature has been there from the beginning of the process of procreation of the gods. Zeus' task is to establish a government which is not totally tyrannical and repressive like his predecessors', but allows for the creative and dynamic forces in nature and at the same time brings forth order. This concept reflects the consistent Greek belief in the essential goodness of the natural order, but also the need for order and control.

Zeus establishes his rule through a series of marriages with goddesses who personify rational, ordering, and creative powers. Through these he incorporates into his rule wisdom, justice and creativity, although he still retains elements of tyranny. He first marries Metis (Wisdom) who "knew more than all the gods or mortal people." When she was about to be delivered of her first child, Athene, Zeus, on the advice of Gaia and Ouranos, put her away in his own belly so that he himself would not be succeeded by another wiser god. Athene is eventually born from Zeus' head and "she is the equal of her father in wise counsel and strength." Zeus next takes Themis (Law) as his wife, and they produce Seasons, Lawfulness, Justice and Peacetime who "oversee the actions of mortal people," and the Fates who "distribute to mortal people what they have for good or evil." Zeus' marriage with Eurynome produces the Three Graces. He is associated with the fertility of the crops through his marriage to Demeter, the goddess of grain, and their daughter Persephone whom he allows Hades to kidnap. Zeus' love for Mnemosyne (Memory) produces the Nine Muses "whose pleasure is all delightfulness, and sweetness of singing." Leto bears Apollo for Zeus; he is the patron of music and fine arts and his twin sister, "Artemis of the showering arrows," the moon-goddess and goddess of hunting. Finally, Zeus takes Hera who bears Hebe (the cup-bearer), Ares (War) and Eileithyia (goddess of childbirth). Through these liaisons Zeus has not abolished the polarities with which the cosmos is full; rather, they are absorbed in a sublimated form into a new order that still has an element of repression as expressed in the Athene episode.

In the **Theogony** the greatest gifts that the gods have given humanity are the Muses who can bring them justice through inspiring noble rulers and dreams of a better world through inspired poets.

And when on one of these kingly nobles,
at the time of his birth,
the daughters of great Zeus cast their eyes
and bestow their favors,
upon his speech they make a distillation
of sweetness,
and from his mouth the words run blandishing,
and his people
all look in his direction as he judges
their cases
with straight decisions, and,
by unfaltering declaration
can put a quick and expert end even
to a great quarrel . . .
Such is the holy gift the Muses
give to humanity.
So it is from the Muses, and from Apollo
of the far cast,
that there are men on earth who are poets,
and players on the lyre.
The lords are from Zeus; but blessed
is that one whom the Muses
love, for the voice of his mouth runs
and is sweet, and even
when a man has sorrow fresh
is the troublement of his spirit
and is struck to wonder over the grief
in his heart, the singer,
the servant of the Muses singing
the glories of ancient
men, and the blessed gods
who have their homes on Olympos,
makes him presently forget his cares,
he no longer remembers
sorrow, for the gifts of the goddesses
soon turn his thoughts elsewhere.

The translation is by Richmond Lattimore in **Hesiod**: **The Works and Days, Theogony, The Shield of Herakles** (Ann Arbor: the University of Michigan Press, 1965) 123–186. For further reading see Norman O. Brown, **Theogony: Hesiod** (New York, Indianapolis: Bobbs-Merrill Company, Inc., 1953).
(The text begins with a long invocation of the Helikonian Muses. Our section begins with Hesiod's account of the origin of the first generation of the gods.)

The first generation of gods

Hail, then, children of Zeus:[1] grant me lovely
    singing.
Now sound out the holy stock of the everlasting
    immortals
who came into being out of Gaia[2] and starry
    Ouranos[3]
and gloomy Night, whom Pontos, the salt sea,
brought to maturity;
and tell, how at the first the gods and the earth
    were begotten
and rivers, and the boundless sea,
raging in its swell,
the blazing stars, and the wide sky above all,
tell of
the gods, bestowers of blessings,
who were begotten of all these,
and how they divided their riches
and distributed their privileges,
and how they first took possession
of many-folded Olympos,
tell me all this, you Muses
who have your homes on Olympos,
from the beginning, and tell who was first
to come forth among them.
First of all there came Chaos,[4]
and after him came
Gaia of the broad breast,
to be the unshakable foundation
of all the immortals who keep the crests
of snowy Olympos,
and Tartaros[5] the foggy in the pit
of the wide-wayed earth,
and Eros,[6] who is love, handsomest among all
the immortals,
who breaks the limbs' strength,
who in all gods, in all human beings
overpowers the intelligence in the breast,
and all their shrewd planning.
From Chaos was born Erebos,[7] the dark,
and black Night,
and from Night again Aither and Hemera,
the day, were begotten,
for she lay in love with Erebos
and conceived and bore these two.
But Gaia's first born was one

who matched her every dimension,
Ouranos, the starry sky,
to cover her all over,
to be an unshakable standing-place
for the blessed immortals.
Then she brought forth the tall Hills,
those wild haunts that are beloved
by the goddess Nymphs who live on the hills
and in their forests.
Without any sweet act of love
she produced the barren
sea, Pontos, seething in his fury of waves,
and after this
she lay with Ouranos, and bore him
deep-swirling Okeanos
the ocean-stream; and Koios, Krios,
Hyperion, Iapetos,
and Theia too and Rheia, and Themis,
and Mnemosyne,
Phoibe of the wreath of gold,
and Tethys the lovely.[8]
After these her youngest-born
was devious-devising Kronos,
most terrible of her children;
and he hated his strong father.
She brought forth also the Kyklopes,
whose hearts are proud and powerful,
Brontes and Steropes, and Arges
of the violent spirit,
who made the thunder and gave it to Zeus,
and fashioned the lightning.
These in all the rest of their shape
were made like gods,
but they had only one eye set in the middle
of the foreheads.
Kyklopes, wheel-eyed, was the name given
    them,
by reason
of the single wheel-shaped eye
that was set in their foreheads.
Strength and force, and contriving skills,
were in all their labors.

Kronos castrates Ouranos
And still other children were born
to Gaia and Ouranos,

three sons, big and powerful, so great
they could never be told of,
Kottos, Briareos, and Gyes,
overmastering children.
Each had a hundred intolerably strong arms
bursting
out of his shoulders,
and on the shoulders of each grew fifty
heads, above their massive bodies;
irresistible
and staunch strength matched the appearance
of their big bodies,
and of all children ever born
to Gaia and Ouranos
these were the most terrible,
and they hated their father
from the beginning, and every time each one
was beginning
to come out, he would push them back again,
   deep inside Gaia,
and would not let them into the light,
and Ouranos exulted
in his wicked work; but great Gaia
groaned within for pressure
of pain; and then she thought of an evil,
treacherous attack.
Presently creating the element of gray flint
she made of it a great sickle,
and explained it to her own children,
and spoke, in the disturbance of her heart,
to encourage them:
"My sons, born to me of a criminal father,
if you are willing
to obey me, we can punish your father
for the brutal treatment
he put upon you, for he was first to think
of shameful dealing."
So she spoke, but fear took hold of all,
nor did one of them
speak, but then great devious-devising Kronos
took courage
and spoke in return,
and gave his gracious mother an answer:
"My mother, I will promise to undertake
to accomplish
this act, and for our father,

him of the evil name, I care
nothing, for he was the first
to think of shameful dealing."
So he spoke, and giant Gaia
rejoiced greatly in her heart
and took and hid him in a secret ambush,
and put into his hands
the sickle, edged like teeth, and told him
all her treachery.
And huge Ouranos came on
bringing night with him, and desiring
love he embraced Gaia and lay over her
stretched out
complete, and from his hiding place his son
reached with his left hand
and seized him, and holding in his right
the enormous sickle
with its long blade edged like teeth,
he swung it sharply,
and lopped the members of his own father,
and threw them behind him
to fall where they would,
but they were not lost away when they were
   flung
from his hand, but all the bloody drops
that went splashing from them
were taken in by Gaia, the earth,
and with the turning of the seasons
she brought forth the powerful Furies[9]
and the tall Giants
shining in their armor
and holding long spears in their hands;
and the Nymphs they call, on boundless earth,
the Nymphs of the Ash Trees.
But the members themselves, when Kronos
had lopped them with the flint,
he threw from the mainland
into the great wash of the sea water
and they drifted a great while
on the open sea, and there spread
a circle of white foam
from the immortal flesh, and in it
grew a girl, whose course first took her
to holy Kythera,[10]
and from there she afterward made her way
to sea-washed Cyprus

and stepped ashore, a modest lovely Goddess,
and about her
light and slender feet the grass grew,
and the gods call her
Aphrodite,[11] and men do too,
and the aphro-foam-born
goddess, and garlanded Kythereia,[12]
because from the seafoam
she grew, and Kythereia because she had gone
to Kythera,
and Kyprogeneia,[13] because she came forth
from wave-washed Cyprus,
and Philommedea,[14] because she appeared
from medea, members.
And Eros went with her, and handsome
    Himeros[15]
attended her
when first she was born, and when she joined
the immortal community,
and here is the privilege she was given
and holds from the beginning,
and which is the part she plays among men
and the gods immortal:
the whispering together of girls,
the smiles and deceptions,
the delight, and the sweetnesses of love,
and the flattery.
But their great father Ouranos,
who himself begot them,
bitterly gave to those others, his sons,
the name of Titans,
the Stretchers, for they stretched
their power outrageously and accomplished
a monstrous thing, and they would some day
be punished for it. . . .

Zeus's conflict with Kronos
Rheia, submissive in love to Kronos,
bore glorious children,
Histia[16] and Demeter,[17]
Hera[18] of the golden sandals,
and strong Hades,[19] who under the ground
lives in his palace
and has a heart without pity;

the deep-thunderous Earthshaker,[20]
and Zeus of the counsels,
who is the father of gods and of mortals,
and underneath whose thunder
the whole wide earth shudders;
but, as each of these children
came from the womb of its mother
to her knees, great Kronos swallowed it down,
with the intention
that no other of the proud children
of the line of Ouranos
should ever hold the king's position
among the immortals.
For he had heard, from Gaia
and from starry Ouranos,
that it had been ordained for him,
for all his great strength,
to be beaten by his son,and through the designs
    of great Zeus.
Therefore he kept watch, and did not sleep,
but waited
for his children, and swallowed them,
and Rheia's sorrow was beyond forgetting.
But when she was about to bear Zeus,
the father of mortals
and gods, then Rheia went
and entreated her own dear parents,
and these were Gaia and starry Ouranos,
to think of some plan
by which, when she gave birth to her dear son,
the thing might not
be known, and the fury of revenge
be on devious-devising Kronos
the great, for his father,
and his own children whom he had swallowed.
They listened gladly
to their beloved daughter, and consented,
and explained to her
all that had been appointed to happen
concerning Kronos, who was King, and his son,
of the powerful
spirit, and sent her to Lyltos,
in the fertile countryside of Crete
at that time when she was to bring forth
the youngest of her children,

great Zeus; and the Earth, gigantic Gaia,
took him inside her
in wide Crete, there to keep him alive
and raise him.
There Earth arrived
through the running black night, carrying
him, and came first to Lyktos,
and holding him in her arms, hid him
in a cave in a cliff, deep in
under the secret places
of earth, in Mount Aigaion
which is covered with forest.
She wrapped a great stone in baby-clothes,
and this she presented
to the high lord, son of Ouranos,
who once ruled the immortals,
and he took it then in his hands
and crammed it down in his belly,
hard wretch, nor saw in his own mind
how there had been left him
instead of the stone a son
invincible and unshakable
for the days to come, who soon by force
and his hands defeating him
must drive him from his title,
and then be lord over the immortals.
And presently after this the shining limbs
and the power
of the lord, Zeus, grew great,
and with the years circling on
great Kronos, the devious-devising,
fooled by the resourceful
promptings of Gaia, once again
brought up his progeny.
First he vomited up the stone,
which last he had swallowed,
and this Zeus took and planted in place,
on earth of the wide ways,
at holy Pytho, in the hollow ravines
under Parnassos,
to be a portent and a wonder
to mortal men thereafter.
Then he set free from their dismal bonds
the brothers of his father,
the sons of Ouranos, whom his father

in his wild temper had enchained,
and they remembered, and knew gratitude
for the good he had done them,
and they gave him the thunder,
and the smoky bolt, and the flash
of the lightning, which Gaia the gigantic
had hidden till then.
With these to support him, he is lord
over immortals and mortals.
(At this point Hesiod recounts another version
of the Prometheus story which tells of his attempt to deceive Zeus in a matter of sacrificial
offerings. When Prometheus cut up a great ox
to be divided between him and Zeus, he enclosed the meat and entrails in the stomach,
and the bones in a wrapping of fat. He gave
Zeus his choice of the two portions, and Zeus,
though he saw through the trick, chose the
bones. In punishment for what Prometheus
had done, Zeus deprived humans of fire; but
Prometheus stole it in a hollow fennel-stalk
and gave it to men. Prometheus was bound by
Zeus to a rock, and each day an eagle flew over
and ate his liver, which grew again during the
night. Finally Heracles, by the will of his father Zeus, released Prometheus from his
bonds. In the next section Zeus establishes his
rule by first defeating the Titans and then Tyh-
poeus, the youngest child of Earth and Tartarus, a terrible monster with a hundred snakes'
heads sprouting from his shoulders. We resume the text as Zeus consolidates his rule.)

Zeus' monarchy and offspring
Now when the immortal gods had finished
their work of fighting,
they forced the Titans to share with them
their titles and privilege.
Then, by the advice of Gaia, they promoted
  Zeus, the Olympian
of the wide brows, to be King
and to rule over the immortals
and he distributed among them their titles
and privilege.

Zeus, as King of the gods,
took as his first wife Metis,[21]
and she knew more than all the gods
or mortal people.
But when she was about to be delivered
of the goddess, gray-eyed
Athene, then Zeus, deceiving her perception
by treachery
and by slippery speeches,
put her away inside his own belly.
This was by the advices of Gaia,
and starry Ouranos,
for so they counseled,
in order that no other everlasting
god, beside Zeus, should ever be given
the kingly position.
For it had been arranged that, from her,
children surpassing in wisdom
should be born, first the gray-eyed girl,
the Tritogeneia[22]
Athene; and she is the equal of her father
in wise counsel
and strength; but then a son to be King
over gods and mortals
was to be born of her, and his heart
would be overmastering:
but before this, Zeus put her away
inside his own belly
so that this goddess should think for him,
for good and for evil.
Next Zeus took to himself Themis,[23]
the shining, who bore him the Seasons,
Lawfulness, and Justice,
and prospering Peacetime: these
are concerned to oversee the actions
of mortal people;
and the Fates, to whom Zeus of the counsels
gave the highest position:
they are Klotho, Lachesis, and Atropos:
they distribute
to mortal people what people have,
for good and for evil.
Eurynome,[24] daughter of Okeanos,
lovely in appearance,

bore to Zeus the three Graces
with fair cheeks; these are
Aglaia and Euphrosyne and lovely Thalia,
and from the glancing of their lidded eyes
bewildering
love distills; there is beauty
in their glance, from beneath brows.
Zeus entered also into the bed
of fruitful Demeter,
who bore him Persephone of the white arms,
she that Aidoneua[25]
ravished away from her mother,
and Zeus of the counsels granted it.
Then again, he loved Mnemosyne,[26]
of the splendid tresses,
from whom were born to him the Muses
with veils of gold, the Nine
whose pleasure is all delightfulness,
and the sweetness of singing.
Leto, who had lain in the arms of Zeus
of the aegis,
bore Apollo, and Artemis
of the showering arrows,
children more delightful than all
the other Ouranians.
Last of all, Zeus took Hera
to be his fresh consort,
and she, lying in the arms
of the father of gods and mortals,
conceived and bore Hebe to him, and Ares,
and Eileithyia.[27]
Then from his head, by himself,
he produced Athene of the gray eyes,
great goddess, weariless,
waker of battle noise, leader of armies,
a goddess queen who delights in war cries,
onslaughts, and battles,
while Hera, without any act of love,
brought forth glorious
Hephaistos, for she was angered and quarrel-
     ing with her husband;
and Hephaistos in arts and crafts
surpasses all the Ouranians. . . .

NOTES

[1]The Muses who produce poetry.
[2]Mother Earth.
[3]Father Sky.
[4]The shapeless mass whose appearance could not be described.
[5]The lowest region of the underworld where the rebellious Titans will be confined by Zeus.
[6]Greek god of love.
[7]Darkness.
[8]These Titans are the offspring of Gaia and Ouranos and the first race of gods and goddesses.
[9]The three avenging spirits.
[10]Island in the Ionian Sea.
[11]The goddess of love.
[12]Name for Aphrodite, taken from island Kythera, a center of her worship.
[13]Another title of Aphrodite.
[14]A third title of Aphrodite.
[15]God of desire and longing love.
[16]Goddess of the hearth and symbol of the home.
[17]Goddess of agriculture and productive soil. Guardian of marriage.
[18]Wife and sister of Zeus, queen of the gods.
[19]Ruler of the underworld and brother of Zeus.
[20]Poseidon.
[21]"Thought." An Oceanid, one of the daughters of Okeanos and Thetys.
[22]A title of Athena meaning "thrice born."
[23]"Law."
[24]"Wide-wayed."
[25]Pluto or Hades.
[26]"Memory."
[27]Goddess of childbirth.

THE MYSTERY RELIGIONS

Although Hesiod's conception of Zeus as the guardian of justice was reaffirmed by a number of later poets and dramatists like Solon and Aeschylus, Zeus never seems to have acquired the ethical qualities of the Hebrew God in the popular belief of the Greeks. The social tensions accompanying the rise of the *polis* in the seventh through fourth centuries B.C.E. manifested themselves instead in the growth of the mystical salvation cults which often ran counter to the rationalism and heroic virtue associated with the official worship of the Olympians. These cults often arose out of the fertility cults of the Greeks which resembled the worship of the mother goddess under the names of Ishtar, Anat, Astarte, Isis, or Cybele in the different parts of the Near East. Like the rise of tyranny in the political sphere, these mystery cults reflected the breakdown of the traditional order and reason under the impact of economic change and class conflict. Significantly most of the tyrants patronized the new cults and gave them official status.

THE ELEUSIAN MYSTERIES

Eleusis was the locale of the most famous of the mystery cults, that associated with the Olympian harvest goddess Demeter and her daughter Persephone. In the sixth century B.C.E. Eleusis became part of the city-state of Athens, but before that time it was the site of the local agricultural cult comparable to the fertility cults of the Near East. The mysteries of Eleusis came to be sponsored by the Athenian government and did not involve any repudiation of the traditional gods or the ethos associated with them.

The myth associated with the cult is preserved in the beautiful work entitled **The Homeric Hymn to Demeter** which is dated to the sixth century B.C.E. It accounts for the death and rebirth of nature each year and also for the foundation of the sanctuary at Eleusis. Toward the end of the myth there are references to the secret cult associated with the mystery.

The myth contains the touching story of how Demeter's motherly love and devotion to Persephone her daughter are able to triumph in part over the callous actions of Zeus and Pluto who have agreed without consulting Demeter that Persephone is to be Pluto's wife. Throughout the story feminine figures predominate. They show the virtues of loving devotion and gracious hospitality which eventually lead to the recovery of Persephone and the establishment of Eleusis as Demeter's shrine. The contrast with the male-dominated world of Homer and Hesiod is striking.

The action begins with an event alluded to in Hesiod's **Theogony**: the rape of Persephone (or Kore, "the daughter") by Hades (Aidoneus, "the unseen one," or Pluton, "the wealthy one") and the subsequent search for the girl by her mother Demeter (or Deo). Finally Helios (the sun-god) tells her that Zeus had decided to marry Kore to his brother Pluton. Angry and grief-stricken, Demeter does not return to Olympos. In the guise of an old woman she goes to Eleusis where she is graciously received by the king's daughters and accepts their invitation to nurse the infant son of the queen, Metaneira. At the reception she refuses to drink red wine and demands kykeon, a mixture of barley groats, water and pennyroyal. At this point Demeter seems to try to immortalize Demophoon, the infant son, presumably to replace the lost Persephone and as a reward for her gracious reception at Eleusis. She rubs him with ambrosia and at night hides him "like a firebrand in the might of the flame." However, one night Metaneira observes what is happening to her son and wails, "My child Demophoon, the strange woman is hiding you in blazing fire, and is making grief and bitter sorrow for me." After chiding the mother's foolishness in interrupting the immortalizing process, Demeter reveals herself in all her splendor and demands a great temple and altar be built for her, where she will teach her rites to human beings. When the sanctuary is completed, Demeter retires inside, but then brings on a terrible drought as she wastes away in sorrow for her daughter. Now Zeus is forced to ask Pluto to bring Persephone back, but before she leaves Hades, Pluto succeeds in putting a pomegranate seed in her mouth and making her swallow it. For some unstated reason, this assured Persephone's annual return to her husband for four months. When her daughter returns, Demeter rejoins the gods on Olympos and the earth is miraculously fertile again. However, before returning, the goddess reveals her rites and mysteries to four initiates. These are described as "sacred rites which it is forbidden to transgress, to inquire into, or to speak about, for great reverence of the gods constrains their voice."

The actual contents of the rites remain one of the best kept secrets in all history. According to the blessing recited toward the end of the text, the initiates seem to have witnessed some kind of dramatic spectacle which entitled them to happiness in the next life. This belief in a happy afterlife stands in sharp contrast to the unfulfilling picture of Hades in Homer.

"Blessed of earth-bound men is he who has seen these things, but he who dies without fulfilling the holy things, and he who is without share of them, has no claim ever on such blessings, even when departed down to the moldy darkness."

The translation is from David G. Rice and John E. Stambaugh, **Sources for the Study of Greek Religion** (Missoula: Scholars Press, 1979) 171–183.

THE HOMERIC HYMN TO DEMETER

The rape of Persephone

I begin my song of the holy goddess, fair-haired Demeter, and of her slim-ankled daughter whom Aidoneus snatched away; and Zeus the loud-crashing, the wide-voiced one, granted it. She was playing with the deep-bosomed daughters of Ocean, away from Demeter of the golden weapon and glorious fruit, and she was gathering flowers throughout the luxuriant meadow—roses, saffron, violets, iris, hyacinth, and a narcissus which was a trap planted for the blossoming maiden by Earth in accord with Zeus's plans, a favor to Hades the receiver of many guests; it was radiantly wonderful, inspiring awe in all who saw it, whether immortal god or mortal man; a hundred stems grew from its root; and the whole wide heaven above, the whole earth, and the salt surge of the sea smiled for joy at its fragrance. The girl was charmed by it, and reached out both hands to pluck the pretty plaything—suddenly, the earth split open wide along the plain and from it the lord host of many, Kronos' son of many names,[1] darted out on his immortal horses. He grabbed her, resisting and screaming, and took

her away in his golden chariot. She lifted her voice in a cry, calling upon father Zeus, the almighty and good. But no one, god or mortal, heard her voice, not even the glorious—fruited olive-trees, except the childish daughter of Perses, Hecate of the glistening veil,[2] who—from her cave—heard, and so did Lord Helios the glorious son of Hyperion,[3] as the maiden calling upon father Zeus, though he was sitting, removed from the other gods, in his much-besought temple, receiving fine sacrifices from mortal men.

Her, all unwilling, with the approval of Zeus, he took away on his immortal horses, Kronos' son of many names, brother of her father, designator of many, host of many. As long as the goddess could see the earth and the starry sky, the glowing, fish-filled sea and the rays of the sun, she still had hope that her holy mother and the race of the immortal gods would see her, and there was still much hope in her heart in spite of her distress. . . .

Demeter's search for Persephone

The peaks of the mountains and the depths of the sea echoed back the immortal voice, and her blessed mother heard her. Then sharp grief seized the mother's heart; she tore the headress upon her ambrosial hair, and threw her dark veil down from both her shoulders; and like a bird she darted over land and sea, searching. None of the gods or of mortal men would give her a true report, nor would any of the birds come to her as a true messenger.

For nine days then lady Deo wandered the earth, holding blazing torches in her hands; in her grief she touched neither ambrosia nor the sweetness of nectar, nor did she bathe her body with water. But when the tenth day dawned Hecate, bearing light in her hands, encountered her and spoke to her this message: "Lady Demeter, bringer of seasons and glorious gifts, who of the gods of heaven or of mortal men has taken Persephone and pained your own heart? I heard her voice, but did not see who it was. I am telling you everything promptly, and accurately."

So spoke Hecate. The daughter of fair-haired Rheia did not answer a word, but she immediately darted off with her, holding blazing torches in her hands, and they came to Helios, the viewer of gods and men. They stood before his horses and the divine goddess said, "Helios, as a god, respect me, as a goddess, if ever in word or deed, I have warmed your heart. The maiden whom I bore—sweetest blossom—beautiful—I heard her voice, sobbing, as if she were being raped, but I did not see her. But you survey from the bright heaven all the earth and the sea with your rays; tell me accurately whether you have seen who of gods or mortal men has forced her and taken her away, all unwillingly, in my absence."

So she spoke, and the son of Hyperion answered her: "Lady Demeter, daughter of fair-haired Rheia, you will know all: I have great respect for you and pity you in your grief for your slim-ankled child: none of the immortals is responsible except Zeus the cloud-gatherer, who has granted to Hades his own brother that she be called his tender wife; and he has taken her, screaming a loud cry, away on his horses down into the misty darkness. So, goddess, stop

your loud lament; you should not rashly hold on to this boundless anger; Aidoneus, the designator of many, is after all not an unsuitable son-in-law for you, since you have the same mother and father; and his honor he gained when at the beginning a division into three parts was made;[4] and he dwells with those over whom the lot made him king." When he had said this he called to his horses, and at his command they bore the swift chariot like broad-winged birds.

(At this point the grief-stricken Demeter wanders in disguise until she comes to the house of King Keleos' home in Eleusis where Keleos' wife Metaneira makes her the nurse to her son Demophoon. The boy grew like a god because Demeter anointed him each day with ambrosia, and held him each night in an immortalizing flame until Metaneira kept watch one night and snatched the boy from the fire. We resume the text where Demeter reveals herself and requests a temple and cult at Eleusis.)

Demeter reveals herself and requests a temple and cult at Eleusis

So she spoke, lamenting, and the divine goddess heard her. Demeter of the beautiful crown was amazed at her; with her immortal hands she put from her the dear child whom (Metaneira) had borne, all unexpected, in the palace, and threw him at her feet, drawing him out of the fire, terribly angry at heart, and at the same time she said to fair-belted Metaneira, "Humans are short-sighted, stupid, ignorant of the share of good or evil which is coming to them. You by your foolishness have hurt him beyond curing. Let my witness be the oath of the gods sworn by the intractable water of Styx, that I would have made your son deathless and ageless all his days, and given him imperishable honor. But now it is not possible to ward off death and destruction. Still he will have imperishable honor forever, since he stood on my knees and slept in my arms; in due season, as the years pass around, the children of Eleusinians will conduct in his honor war (games) and the terrible battle-cry with each other for ever and ever. I am Demeter, the Venerable, ready as the greatest boon and joy for immortals and mortals. So now, let the whole people build me a great temple, and an altar beneath it, below the city and the towering wall, above Kallirhoe on the ridge which juts forth. I myself will establish rites so that henceforth you may celebrate them purely and propitiate my mind."

With these words the goddess altered size and form and sloughed off old age; beauty wafted about her. A lovely fresh smell radiated from her lovely gown and the radiance from the skin of the immortal goddess shone afar. Her blonde hair flowed down over her shoulders, and the sturdy house was filled with light like a flash of lightning. She went out through the palace. As for the other, her knees gave way, and for a long time she was speechless. She did not even remember the child, her favorite, to pick him up from the floor. His sisters heard his piteous crying, and they leapt down from their well-covered beds. Then one of them took the child in her hands and put him in her lap, one kindled a fire, and another hurried on gentle feet to rouse her mother out of the fragrant chamber. Crowding around they washed him, covering him with love as he squirmed; his heart was not comforted, however, for less skillful nurses and nurse maids were holding him now.

The construction of Demeter's temple

All night long the women, quaking with fear, propitiated the glorious goddess. As soon as dawn appeared they gave a full report to wide-ruling Keleos, as Demeter of the beautiful garlands commanded. He summoned the people from their many boundaries and ordered them to build an elaborate temple to fair-haired Demeter and an altar on the ridge which juts forth. They obeyed him straightway, and hearkened to him as he spoke, and

started to build as he commanded. And it grew at the dispensation of the divinity. When they had finished and ceased from their toil, each person went back to his home. Blonde Demeter stayed there, seated far from all the blessed gods, wasting with grief for her deep-belted daughter.

Demeter causes a drought upon the land

She made the most terrible, most oppressive year for men upon the nourishing land, and the earth sent up no seed, as fair-garlanded Demeter hid it. Cattle drew the many curved plows in vain over the fields, and much white barley seed fell useless on the earth. By now she would have destroyed the entire race of men by grievous famine, and deprived those who dwell on Olympus of the glorious honor of offerings and sacrifices, if Zeus had not taken notice and taken counsel with his mind. First he roused gold-winged Iris[5] to summon fair-haired Demeter, of the very desirable beauty. So he spoke, and she obeyed Zeus wrapped in clouds, at the citadel of fragrant Eleusis. In the temple she found Demeter dark-clad, and addressed her with winged words. "Demeter, father Zeus who understands imperishable things summons you to come among the race of the immortal gods. So come, and let my message from Zeus not be fruitless."

Demeter demands from Zeus the return of Persephone

So she spoke in supplication, but her heart was not persuaded. Therefore the Father sent out the blessed, everliving gods one after another, and they went in turn and implored her, and offered her many fine gifts and whatever honors she might choose among the immortal gods. None, however, was able to persuade the heart and mind of the angry goddess. She rejected their speeches firmly, and claimed that she would never set foot upon fragrant Olympus, nor allow any fruit to grow on the earth, until she saw with her eyes the beautiful face of her daughter.

The release of Persephone

When Zeus the loud-crashing, the wide-voiced one, heard this he sent Hermes the slayer of Argos[6] with his golden wand to Erebos, to use smooth words on Hades and lead pure Persephone out of the misty darkness into the light to join the deities, in order that her mother might see her with her eyes and turn from her anger. Hermes obeyed, and eagerly rushed down under the recesses of the earth, leaving the seat of Olympus. He found the Lord inside his house, seated on couches with his modest and very unwilling wife, yearning for her mother. . . .

The mighty slayer of Argos came near and said, "Dark-haired Hades, ruler of the departed, Father Zeus has ordered me to lead glorious Persephone out of Erebos to join them, in order that her mother might see her with her eyes and cease from her anger and terrible wrath, since she is contriving a tremendous deed, to destroy the fragile race of earth-born men, hiding the seed under the earth and obliterating the honors of the immortals. Her anger is terrible, she has no contact with the gods, but sits apart inside her fragrant temple, holding the rocky citadel of Eleusis."

So he spoke, and Aidoneus the lord of the under-world smiled with his brows, and did not disobey the injunctions of Zeus the king. Promptly he gave the command to diligent Persephone: "Go, Persephone, to your dark-clad mother, and keep gentle the strength and heart in your breast. Do not be despondent to excess beyond all others. I shall not be an inappropriate husband for you among the immortals; I am a brother of Father Zeus. Being there, you will rule over all that lives and moves, enjoying the greatest honors among the immortals. And there shall be punishment forever on those who act unjustly and who do not propitiate your might with sacrifices, perform-

ing the pious acts and offering appropriate gifts."

So he spoke, and Persephone the discreet was glad, and swiftly leapt up for joy. But he gave her a honey-sweet pomegranate seed to eat, having secretly passed it around (himself?), so that she might not stay forever there by modest dark-clad Demeter. Aidoneus, designator of many, harnessed the immortal horses in front of the golden chariot, and she stepped on the chariot; beside her the mighty slayer of Argos took the reins and a whip in his hands and drove out of the palace. The pair of horses flew willingly. They finished the long journey quickly. Neither sea nor rivers nor grassy glens nor mountain peaks held back the rush of the immortal horses; they went above them, and out through the high air. He drove them where Demeter of the fair crown waited in front of her fragrant temple, and he stopped them there. Seeing them, she darted up like a maenad[7] in the woods on a thick-shaded mountain.

The reunion between Demeter and Persephone

(Demeter asked Persephone if she had eaten anything in the underworld. If not,) "you will come up and dwell with me and Zeus of the dark clouds, and be honored by all the immortals. But if you have tasted anything, then you shall go back down and dwell there for the third part of the season, and for the other two, here with me and the other immortals. Whenever the earth blossoms with all the sweet-smelling flowers of spring, then you will come back up from the misty darkness, a great wonder to gods and to mortal men. But what trick did the powerful host of many use to deceive you?"

(At this point Persephone recounts for her mother how she ate the pomegranate seed and also the circumstances of her rape.)

Then with minds in concord they spent the whole day warming their hearts and minds, showering much love on each other, and her mind found respite from its griefs, and they gave and received joys from each other. And there came near them Hecate of the glistening veil, and she also showered much love on the daughter of holy Demeter, and ever since she has been her attendant and Lady-in-waiting. (Now Zeus sends Rheia to invite Demeter to return to Olympus.)

Demeter restores the fruitfulness of the land and reveals her sacred rites

So she spoke, and Demeter of the fair crown obeyed. Promptly she sent up fruit on the rich-soiled fields, and the whole broad land was loaded with leaves and flowers. She went to the royal stewards of the right and to Triptolemos, Diokles the driver of horses, mighty Eumolpos and Keleos the leader of the people. She showed the tendance of the holy things and explicated the rites to them all, to which it is forbidden to transgress, to inquire into, or to speak about, for great reverence of the gods constrains their voice. Blessed of earth-bound men is he who has seen these things, but he who dies without fulfilling the holy things, and he who is without a share of them, has no claim ever on such blessings, even when departed down to the moldy darkness.

(The text ends with Demeter's return to Olympus and a concluding request for Demeter's blessing.)

NOTES

[1] Hades or Pluto.
[2] Hecate later in the myth becomes Demeter's Lady-in-Waiting.
[3] Son of Hyperion and Thia. Later identified with Apollo.
[4] Zeus ruled the sky, Poseidon the sea, and Hades the underworld.
[5] Goddess of the rainbow and messenger of the gods.
[6] The messenger of the gods.
[7] Female followers and priestesses of Dionysus, the god of wine and revelry.

THE CULT OF DIONYSUS

The cult of Dionysus seems to have originated in Thrace and to have come to Greece as early as the eighth century B.C.E. Dionysus was not originally an Olympian god; he was a male god of fertility and wine, of the sap rising in the trees, of the reproductive seed. A major source for information about his cult is Euripides' play **Bacchae** which was produced in the late fifth century B.C.E. This play portrays the tragedy of King Pentheus who resists the cult of Dionysus only to be destroyed by his own mother in a Bacchic frenzy. The play gives evidence of the power of Dionysus' cult as hordes of worshipers, especially women, assembled at night in forests and on the tops of mountains and worked themselves into a frenzied exaltation by dancing to the sound of flutes, fondling snakes, and devouring the raw flesh of animals in whom their god had become incarnate. At these times the participants believed themselves possessed by a divine spirit, endowed with supernatural powers, and assured of immortality.

Dionysus was incorporated into the Olympian pantheon by means of a later story according to which he was the son of Zeus and a mortal woman, Semele, a princess of the Boeotian city of Thebes. Semele had been blasted by lightning before her son was born, but the infant had been rescued from her womb by Zeus and afterward born out of Zeus' thigh. By the sixth century, Dionysus had become one of the Olympians, with regular festivals, purified of their original hysteria, in the leading cities, and had even become reconciled with the god Apollo, who stood for reason, self-control and aristocratic rule. In Apollo's temple at Delphi, Dionysus' image was carved on the back pediment. In the course of the centuries the two gods seemed to have merged into each other, sharing the same functions and epithets. This union of Apollo and Dionysus, or order and enthusiasm, aristocratic restraint and popular emotionalism, is symbolic of the whole development of Greek culture. Our passage from the **Bacchae** is a hymn of praise sung in honor of Dionysus *Bromios* ("Roarer") by the chorus of Bacchant women, who congregate in a sacred band known as a *thiasos*. The translation is in David G. Rice and John E. Stambaugh, **Sources for the Study of Greek Religion** (Missoula: Scholars Press, 1979) 195–97.

Bacchae

From Asian land, passing by sacred Tmolos,[1] I quickly ply for Bromios[2] my pleasant toil, my easy-labored labor shouting *eua*! to Bacchus.[3]

Who is on the road? Who is on the road? Who is in the palace? Let everyone come away, let every one consecrate his mouth with holy silence. For I shall sing a traditional hymn to Dionysus.

O happy is he who with the god's blessing and knowledge of the rites of the gods leads a pious life and joins his soul to a *thiasos* and Bacchic revels in the mountains with devoted purifications, observing the ceremonies of the Great Mother Kybele,[4] brandishing the *thyrsos*,[5] and crowned with ivy, serves Dionysus.

Go, Bacchants;[6] go, Bacchants, and bring Dionysus Bromios, divine son of God, back out of the Phrygian[7] mountains into the broad streets of Greece. Bromios!

He it is whom his mother[8] carried and bore in compulsive pangs of child-birth, casting him from her womb when the lightning bolt of Zeus came flying at her, and she departed the world at the stroke of the thunder. But then Zeus the son of Kronos immediately received him in his birthing-chamber, and enclosed him in his thigh and fastened it with golden needles, to hide him from Hera.

And he bore, when the Fates brought him to term, the bull-horned god, and he crowned

him with crowns of serpents, which is the reason the maenads festoon their hair with their beast-bred prey.

O Theban nurses of Semele, crown yourselves with ivy! Be laden with green bryony with its beautiful berries. Play the Bacchant with branches of oak or pine, and deck your garments of dappled fawn-skin with fillets of white wool; be reverent in wielding the violent wands. Soon all the earth will dance—he is Bromios, whoever leads the *thiasos* (or "whenever Bromios leads the *thiasos*)—to the mountain, to the mountain, where the crowd of women waits, goaded from their looms and shuttles by Dionysus.

O inner chamber of the Kouretes,[9] O divine haunts of Crete which gave birth to Zeus, where the Korybantes[10] with their triple crowns discovered in the caves this my round drum of stretched hide. And in the tense strained Bacchic dance they mixed it with the sweet-voiced breath of Phrygian flutes, and they put it into Rhea's[11] hand, an accompaniment to the *eua*-song of the Bacchants. The raving Satyrs[12] got it from the goddess mother, and they attached it to the biennial dances in which Dionysus rejoices.

He is pleasant on the mountains, when he falls to the ground out of the swift-running *thiasoi*, wearing his holy fawnskin, tracking down the blood of the slaughtered goat, the joy of flesh eaten raw, yearning for the Phrygian mountains, the Lydian, and Bromios is the leader, *euoi*!

The plain flows with milk, it flows with wine, it flows with the nectar of bees; the Bacchic one holds up the pine torch bright blazing like the smoke of Syrian incense from his staff, and he darts at a run, with dances rousing the stragglers and urging them on with his cries, tossing his delicate locks in the air.

And at the same time he roars out, with shouts of *eua*!, thus: "O Bacchants, go; Bacchants, go! with the glitter of Tmolos flowing with gold sing Dionysus to the sound of deep-roaring drums, glorifying with *eua*! the god of the *eua*-cry, in Phrygian shouts and cries, whenever the sacred melodious flute plays its roaring sacred song, joining the pilgrimage to the mountain, to the mountain. Joyfully, then, like a colt at the manger with its mother, the Bacchant moves her limbs in quick swift leaps."

NOTES

[1]Tmolos was the husband of Omphale, and king of Lydia. He was killed by Artemis for ravishing one of her attendants.

[2]"Roarer."

[3]Bacchus was the Roman name for Dionysys.

[4]Mother Kybele is the Phrygian name for Rhea, the Titan earth goddess.

[5]A staff or spear tipped with a pine cone, and sometimes wreathed with ivy or vine branches, carried by Dionysus and his votaries.

[6]Followers of Dionysus.

[7]A country in Asia Minor whose greatest city was ancient Troy.

[8]Semele.

[9]Priests of Kybele.

[10]Another term for priests of Kybele.

[11]Daughter of Uranus and Gaia.

[12]Sylvan deities that represented the luxuriant forces of nature; attendants of Dionysus. They looked like men, but had the legs and feet of goats, with short horns on their heads, and their entire bodies covered with hair.

SOCRATES AND PLATO

Socrates (469–399 B.C.E.) and Plato (427–347 B.C.E.) are primarily known as philosophers—in fact, some would argue, the greatest philosophers in the history of Western civilization. They are also important for the development of religious thought in the West. Both were crucial transitional figures who marked the end of the age of the ancient Greek *polis* and the beginning of the Hellenistic age of the *cosmopolis*—the world city state. Socrates was the last great religious thinker in classical Athens who lived through the golden age of Periclean Athens and its subsequent collapse in the Peloponnesian War. Plato was the product of that collapse who sought in the moral vision of his mentor for an explanation for the moral and religious deterioration of Athens. Together Socrates and Plato represent the culmination of the Greek religious spirit in the fifth century, and they have an enormous influence on the religious outlook of the Hellenistic age, the philosophers of late antiquity and the early Christian Church fathers.

Socrates and Plato were heirs to an already well-developed Greek philosophical tradition which is one of the unique contributions of the vigorous Greek mind to Western civilization. Unfortunately the works of the early Greek philosophers, or Pre-Socratics, come to us largely as a collection of fragments and scattered observations in later philosophers and the early Christian fathers. A thorough treatment of the religious thought of the early Greek philosophers may be found in Werner Jaeger's **The Theology of the Early Greek Philosophers** (London, Oxford, New York: Oxford University Press, 1968).

Greek thinkers had been critiquing the Homeric and Hesiodic myths since the beginning of the sixth century. The earliest Greek philosophers came from Miletus in Ionia and were concerned with the same question as the cosmological myths—how did the world come to be an ordered place? In contrast to the myths, however, they focused their attention on the physical world and searched for a natural and rational explanation of the ordered world rather than the mythic one provided by Hesiod. In some ways Hesiod was a preparation for their work in that he had already begun to think in abstract terms by the recognition of certain eternal laws that can be found in the diversity of human experience. Hesiod, however, still expressed these laws in mythical and metaphorical terms like Chaos, Eros, Strife, and Justice.

The Ionian philosophers did not completely break from this mythological way of thinking, but they began to postulate some underlying physical element or impersonal concept as the basis for the unity in the diversity of the material world rather than having reference to stories about the gods. They came up with a variety of explanations; Thales (c. 640–546 B.C.E.) suggested that water was the primeval stuff; his student Anaximander (c. 610–545 B.C.E.) believed that the basic principle of reality was the *apeiron*, the "boundless" or "limitless" which is the source and regulator of the coming and going of all that was, is or will be. The third of the Milesians, Anaximenes (fl. 550 B.C.E.), chose air as the principle (*arche*) which governs all existence, divine as well as human, by the principle of condensation and rarefaction. Although their theories may seem rather fanciful to us, the importance of their approach cannot be overestimated. In attempting to explain reality in terms of its own innate laws rather than through reference to myths about the gods, they were beginning the process that would lead to Western science.

The heirs in the fifth century B.C.E. to this tradition of searching for some physical stuff as the basis for the unity and diversity in the world were philosophers like Empedocles and Democritus. Empedocles (c. 490–455) was a poet as well as a philosopher, and his thinking still has mythic and poetic elements. He distinguished four elements: earth, air, fire and water as the "roots of all things." He explained the "coming into being" and "passing away" of combinations of these elements as the result of the cyclic interaction of love and strife. Democritus (c. 460–370) held that reality is made up of a plurality of unchanging particles (atoms) which are indivisible. He accounted for change by the multiple configurations and transformations of these atoms in various shapes and relations. His atomism was a materialism and had subsequent influence on the ethical thought of Epicurus in the Hellenistic Age. The traditional picture of the gods themselves had also been criticized by philosophers like Xenophanes of Colophon in Ionia (c. 570–500 B.C.E.) He noted that sometimes the name of an Olympian deity is simply an explanation for a "natural" phenomenon. In connection with Iris, the goddess of the rainbow, he says:

> She whom men call "Iris," too, is in reality a cloud, purple, red, and green to the sight.[1]

He was also extremely critical of the anthropomorphic picture of the gods in Homer and Hesiod.

> Mortals believe that the gods are begotten, and that they wear clothing like our own, and have a voice and a body. . . .

> And if oxen and horses and lions had hands, and could draw with their hands and do what man can do, horses would draw the gods in the shape of horses, and oxen in the shape of oxen, each giving the gods bodies similar to their own.[2]

The moral behavior of the gods in Homer and Hesiod was a special target of Xenophanes' criticism. He ridiculed their portrayal as being less exemplary than that which we expect of humans.

> Homer and Hesiod have attributed to the gods all those things which in men are a matter for reproach and censure: stealing, adultery, and mutual deception.[3]

This criticism has a direct influence on the thought of Plato.

In place of this anthropomorphic view of the gods Xenophanes substituted a rational monotheism which also had an influence on Socrates and Plato. Xenophanes had a humble recognition of the limits of human language about the gods.

> One god, greatest among gods and men, in no way similar to mortals either in body or mind . . . [4] The being of god is spherical, not like that of man. He sees all over and hears all over, but does not breathe. He is the totality of mind and thought, and is eternal . . . [5]

> No man knows the truth, nor will there be a man who has knowledge about the gods . . . [6]

Xenophanes believed in a progressive growth of human understanding of reality through a search for wisdom as opposed to relying upon myths as the basis for knowledge.

> The gods have not revealed all things from the beginning to mortals; but, by seeking, men find out, in time, what is better.[7]

Socrates will also be committed to a humble recognition of the limits of our human knowledge and to a continous search for fuller human understanding of "what is better."

Another philosophical tradition which had a great influence on Plato was Pythagoreanism. Pythagoras (c. 570–490 B.C.E.) founded a religious and philosophical community in Croton in southern Italy, Magna Graecia. According to tradition he was the first "to call himself a philosopher" (i.e., a "lover of wisdom")[8] and the first "to call what surrounds us a cosmos, because of the order in it."[9] Instead of searching for the unity of the cosmos in some physical stuff, Pythagoras believed that the source of order was number. Mathematics and geometry provide the basis for harmony and order in the universe and in the individual. Plato shares with Pythagoras the belief that mathematics is one of the highest forms of knowledge because it is not of particulars but of universal principles of order.

Pythagoras' philosophy had mystical and religious dimensions which were quite different in spirit from the traditional Homeric religion and were closer to mystery cults like Orphism. In contrast to Homer for whom the soul was like a shadow which at death "flitters out like a dream and flies away," Pythagoras said that the soul is immortal and migrates into other kinds of animals and that therefore all things with souls should be regarded as akin. The soul is the immortal aspect of the human which for the sake of punishment is yoked to a body and buried in it as in a tomb. Pythagoras' belief in the transmigration of souls led to certain ascetic practices which also contrast with the Homeric tradition. He forbade the killing and eating of animals because they share with us the privilege of having a soul. Pythagoras' belief in the immortality and transmigration of the soul also had a major place in Plato's theory of knowledge and in his eschatology.

One of the most influential and intriguing of the so-called Pre-Socratic philosophers was Heraclitus of Ephesus (fl. c. 504–501 B.C.E.) whose enigmatic writings have earned him the title of the "obscure one." For Heraclitus there is *logos,* "word" or "thought" "which steers all things through all things." Wisdom consists in coming to understand this, but unfortunately most people are not attuned to this fact. Heraclitus, like Hesiod, sees a continuous strife and tension between opposites in the universe which is necessary for its unity.

> It is necessary to understand that war is universal and justice is strife, and that all things take place in accordance with strife and necessity.[10]

The symbol for the unity in diversity of the cosmos is fire which is ever moving and changing while somehow remaining one.

> For fire lives the death of earth, and air lives the death of fire; water lives the death of air, and earth that of water.[11]

Heraclitus' thought had a strong influence on the Stoical philosophers in the Hellenistic period and through them on the religious thought of Roman thinkers like Cicero and Virgil and early Christian theologians like Justin Martyr, Clement and Origen.

The philosopher who is usually contrasted with Heraclitus is Parmenidides (c. 500–450 B.C.E.). While Heraclitus emphasized the dynamic, changing, tension-filled nature of reality, Parmenidides' thought affirmed the permanence of being, that which is, and its relation to our thought.

For thought and being are the same. Thinking and the thought that it is are the same; for you will not find thought apart from what is, in relation to which it is uttered.[12]

For Parmenides there are two paths open for thought: the investigation of being which is and is unchanging and the investigation of non-being which is not and is therefore unknowable.

The one is the way of how it is, and how it is not possible for it not to be; this is the way of persuasion, for it attends Truth. The other is the way of how it is not, and how it is necessary for it not to be; this, I tell you, is a way wholly unknowable. For you could not know what is not—that is impossible—nor could you express it.[13]

These two philosophers, Heraclitus and Parmenides, have an important influence on Plato. With Heraclitus, Plato will affirm the changing nature of the physical world around us, but he will also want to agree with Parmenides that there is a permanence to reality which our thought is capable of knowing after a rigorous pursuit of wisdom.

The immediate context for Socrates was the crisis of the fifth century B.C.E. in Athens. After the glory years of the so-called Periclean Golden Age (461–431), the last quarter of the fifth century was marked by the tragic Peloponnesian War (430–404 B.C.E.) so memorably chronicled by Thucydides (c. 460–396 B.C.E.) in his **History of the Peloponnesian War.** As Thycydides tells the story, the war is a tragedy in which the once powerful and proud *polis* of Athens loses its soul in the pursuit of power and glory. The defeat of the Athenian forces at Syracuse in 414 B.C.E. and the eventual defeat of the city itself in 404 B.C.E. are the direct consequence of Athenian *hubris*.

Socrates (469–399) had been born in the early days of peace following the Persian War and lived most of his life in the glory and brilliance of the Periclean Golden Age (461–432). He, like his contemporaries the dramatists Sophocles and Euripides, witnessed the strains of Athenian empire on the moral character of the people of Athens and the city's tragic loss of its ideals in the atrocities and blunders of the Peloponnesian War. Although he himself did not leave any philosophical writings, most scholars agree that the early so-called Socratic dialogues of Plato and Xenophon's dialogues and **Memoirs of Socrates** give us a fairly accurate picture of the historical Socrates. According to these sources, for Socrates much of the blame for the moral corruption of Athens belonged to a new group of philosophers called sophists.

In the fifth century this new type of wise man had become popular in Athens. The sophists were traveling teachers who instructed the wealthy youth of Athens for a fee and were particularly adept at rhetoric, the art of persuasion—an important skill in a democratic city-state. They were not interested in the investigation of nature but instead focused on the study of human nature and particularly morality. Our knowledge of their thought comes primarily from Plato's own dialogues where they are the opponents of his beloved mentor Socrates. As they are portrayed in Plato, the sophists are skeptics in regard to the possibility of absolute human knowledge about nature (*physis*) and relativists in matters of human morality. Morality is simply a matter of custom (*nomos*) and has no foundation in the world of nature which cannot be known with certainty in any case. The best known of the sophists was Protagoras who is said to have taught that "Man is the measure of all things, of the existence of things that are, and of the non-existence of things that are not."[14] Other sophists like Thrasymachus are portrayed by Plato as reducing morality to a matter of power in teaching that "what is 'right' is the same everywhere: the interest of the stronger power."[15]

In the Platonic dialogues Socrates attacks the skepticism and relativism of the sophists by searching through dialectical questioning for universal definitions of such concepts as justice, piety and courage which would serve as the basis for absolute and immutable principles of knowledge and behavior. Often, in the early so-called Socratic dialogues of Plato, Socrates' inquiries are inconclusive; they simply serve to point out the limitations of human pretension to wisdom and the need for true knowledge if one is to find virtue. Socrates did not believe that "man is the measure of all things." He recognized the limits of ordinary human wisdom, but he believed that this wisdom was but a shadow of absolute abiding realities such as justice and goodness. Socrates did not teach in the traditional sophistic sense of imparting preformulated knowledge to his pupils, and he did not charge a fee for his services. Rather, he served as what he called a "midwife" who helped others give birth to knowledge which was already inherent within their souls. He aimed at self-knowledge and the discipline of the soul's faculties. The soul for Socrates represented the person's spiritual capacity for knowledge and virtue which made the human more than simply a body with physical drives and desires.

To outsiders Socrates appeared to be another sophist who was seeking to mislead the youth and undermine the traditional Olympian religion and moral code by his questioning. In the political chaos in the aftermath of the Peloponnesian War Socrates found himself being accused of having taught and been friends with leaders like the infamous Alcibiades, and Critias and Charmides who fell from power when democratic order was restored to Athens. In 400/399 B.C.E. Socrates was brought to trial on the charges of not worshiping the gods whom the state worshiped, introducing new and unfamiliar religious practices and corrupting the youth. Plato's **Apology** is a highly artistic account of Socrates' brilliant defense before the Athenian Council of Five Hundred. The **Apology** is one of Plato's early dialogues and is thought to give us an accurate picture of the historical Socrates. It should be noted, however, that Plato's very favorable picture of his teacher differs markedly from the satirical portrayal of Aristophanes in his comic play **The Clouds.**

In the **Apology** Plato skillfully uses comic and tragic techniques in portraying Socrates' life and mission as a basis for a new understanding of the Greek religious tradition. In his apology Socrates is cleverly and humorously able to turn the tables on his accusers and on the city of Athens itself. Very quickly Socrates, the one who is supposed to be on trial, becomes the one who is doing the questioning and in the dialectical process exposes Meletus' false charges and lack of real concern for the welfare of Athens and its youth. By the end of the dialogue we are ironically convinced that Socrates, who is going to his death, is the more just, happier and freer man and that his accusers and condemners, who will continue to live, have unjustly condemned him and therefore have lost all that can make one truly happy and fulfilled.

Plato is also able to portray Socrates as a new heroic and tragic model for Athens. His quest is not an external one for fame and honor on the battlefield like Achilles, but an internal one for wisdom and virtue which can be found by the disciplined art of dialectic. He fearlessly pursues this quest even at the risk of death.

This quest has religious dimensions in that it is given to Socrates by Apollo's oracle at Delphi which has announced that he is the wisest of all men. Socrates is humbly aware of his own lack of wisdom, and in an effort to prove the oracle wrong he embarks on a search to find someone wiser than himself. This inevitably leads to making many enemies as his questions unmask the pseudo-wisdom of politicians, poets and artisans. Socrates' heroic quest for the truth also leads to enlightenment. He says to the court,

> "The truth is, O men of Athens, that God only is wise; and by his answer he intends to show that the wisdom of men is worth little or nothing; he is not speaking of Socrates, he is only using my name by way of illustration, as if he said, He, O men, is the wisest, who like Socrates, knows that his wisdom is in truth worth nothing."

Socrates' heroic life also leads to the fearless acceptance of death, like the Homeric hero Achilles. However, as Socrates speculates about death and the afterlife, we can see that he is not content with the old Homeric eschatology which pictured the realm of the dead as an abode of unsubstantial shades. Socrates considers two possibilities for the state of humans after death. One is that they will enjoy an endless, untroubled sleep. The other is similar to what is found in Orphism and Pythagorean speculation—that humans will be delivered from the professors of justice in this world and find "true judges who are said to give judgment there, Minos and Rhadamanthus and Aeacus and Triptolemus, and other sons of God who were righteous in their own life . . . " In that state Socrates speculates that he will continue to pursue the type of existence he has in this life.

> Above all, I shall then be able to continue my search into true and false knowledge; as in this world, so also in the next; and I shall find out who is wise, and who pretends to be wise, and is not. . . . In another world they do not put a man to death for asking questions: assuredly not. For besides being happier than we are, they will be immortal, if what is said is true.

Plato seems to be saying that the Socratic mode of existence has already achieved immortality in this life.

THE REPUBLIC

Plato was a follower of Socrates who immortalized his beloved mentor by making him the major character and spokesman in his dialogues and continued his philosophical quest for a permanent basis for wisdom and virtue. He was born to an aristocratic Athenian family in 428/7, shortly after the death of Pericles in the plague which ravaged Athens in the early years of the Peloponnesian War. As a young man Plato witnessed the moral and religious collapse of Athens as it fell victim to democratic demagogues during the course of the war. Although he had planned on a political career, when Plato saw the injustices of the oligarchy in trying to force Socrates to condemn an innocent man and then the trial and execution of the same Socrates by the restored democracy, he became disillusioned with the "whirlpool of public life"[16] and withdrew into a life of philosophy.

Plato was convinced by the events of his early life that all the city-states in the Greek world had bad systems of government and that their respective constitutions were beyond redemption. He sought in philosophy a way of finding a vantage point from which he could discern "what is just for communities and for individuals."[17] His conviction was that "the human race will not see better days until either the stock of those who rightly and genuinely follow philosophy acquire political authority, or else the class who have political control be led by some dispensation of providence to become real philosophers."[18]

In Plato's opinion Athens fell because its leaders were led astray from the traditional religious beliefs of the *polis* into a pursuit of wealth, personal honor, and power. He agreed with Socrates that the relativism of the sophists was responsible for undermining any sense of the common good, service to the community and the gods. However, he was also aware, like Euripides and Socrates, that the traditional mythic religion of Homer and Hesiod and the educational system founded on that tradition was inadequate for the needs of late fifth-century Athens. The gods and heroes of the traditional mythology were simply too immoral and petty in their own behavior to be moral models for this more sophisticated age. His philosophy was an attempt to find a permanent basis for morality in the *polis*.

Plato's **Republic** is his greatest work and is the best place to see him struggling with reconstructing the religious, social, economic and political institutions of the *polis* on a purely philosophical basis. He probably wrote this work after his first trip to Syracuse in 388/87 in which he witnessed the debauched life of the Italian and Sicilian city-states but also had the opportunity to discuss his political ideals with a noble young aristocrat by the name of Dion.

In his **Republic** Plato does not give us a systematic philosophical treatise in the manner of his pupil Aristotle. Rather, Plato's dialogue is an experience of the philosophical quest for the meaning of justice which must form the basis for the life of the individual soul and the state. In form and content the **Republic** is comparable to the Book of Job in the Hebrew tradition. Both works are dialogues which dramatize the search for a new and higher wisdom within their respective traditions. Both are concerned with the question of justice: the capacity of the individual to live a life of justice, even without external reward, and the justice of God's governing of the universe. In the Book of Job, Job must hold on to his own life of justice in the face of incredible suffering and in defiance of the traditional wisdom of his "friends." In the **Republic** Socrates attempts to defend a life of justice based simply on the possession of that virtue and without the appearance of or traditional rewards for the life of justice.

The "resolution" of the two works also reflect their respective cultures. The Book of

Job ends with the awe-inspiring speeches of the Lord from the whirlwind in which Job encounters the mystery and superhuman wisdom of the Creator and does not receive a rational explanation for his innocent suffering. Plato's **Republic** reflects the Greek confidence in the human capacity for wisdom and responsibility for one's actions. It ends with a justification of the life of justice pursued simply for its own sake. In Plato's final explanation God is not blamed for the evil which humans experience. Evil and injustice are blamed on the ignorant choices which humans make in choosing a pattern of life which is not based on the highest good.

The setting for the **Republic** is a discussion in the house of a rich merchant named Cephalus in the Piraeus, the port city of Athens, during the Peace of Nicias, a truce in the Peloponnesian War. The participants have just been spectators at a celebration of a foreign religious festival. The key figures in the dialogue represent in their persons many of the philosophical issues raised in the course of the discussion. The host is Cephalus ("head") who is a retired businessman and head of a business family. He is a man of experience and sound opinion who realizes that a person's character is the determining factor in attaining happiness. However, he departs early because he apparently is not willing to pursue the rigorous discussion of the definition of justice. He is a representative of the artisan class. His son Polemarchus ("war-lord") is a pupil of Lysias, a teacher of rhetoric, and is a representative of the soldier or auxiliary class. Thrasymachus ("rash fighter") is a sophist from Thrace who is a potential tyrant and represents what can become of the guardian class if they are given over to the pursuit of personal power. Adeimantus ("singer of oracles") is an older half-brother of Plato and his medium is poetry. Glaucon ("gleaming eyes" or "owl") is another half-brother of Plato. He represents the idealistic young followers of Socrates. Finally there is Socrates himself who leads the discussion and narrates the incident on the day after it occurs.

In Book I Socrates turns the discussion to the question of a definition of justice and is soon challenged by Thrasymachus who proposes "that justice is nothing else than the interest of the stronger." According to Thrasymachus, might is right. The ruler is always just. When Socrates suggests that the ruler, like a physician, should seek the advantage of his subjects, not himself, Thrasymachus goes off on another tack and argues that injustice is virtuous and justice is vicious. He proposes that justice is always at the mercy of injustice and the only reason injustice is avoided is that people fear to suffer it. At the end of Book I Socrates attempts to establish that justice is wise and virtuous and more profitable than injustice. However, he admits that he is still without a definition of justice.

In Book II Glaucon and Adeimantus develop further objections to Socrates' conclusions. Glaucon uses the graphic story of the ring of Gyges, which can make a person invisible, to propose that men are moral in public only because of the artificial restraints of law and that their private conduct shows that they are motivated simply by the urge to obtain what is pleasant and avoid what is unpleasant. Glaucon insists that we can appreciate the true value of justice in a person's life only if we compare the life of a thoroughly unjust man who has the appearance of justice with that of a just man who does not have the appearance of virtue.

In order to show the inability of the traditional city-state religion and morality to answer this dilemma, Plato at this point puts on the lips of Adeimantus the argument that the great poets from Homer and Hesiod to Musaeus and Pindar do not praise the ideal of justice for its own sake but simply the appearance of justice and only for the sake of the rewards which the gods give the apparently just man. He points out that the poets often make the life of justice seem very difficult and even portray the gods as susceptible to bribes by sacrifices and prayers if one sins. Another alternative is to turn to the mystery cults which promise forgiveness of sin or a pleasure-filled afterlife simply for participation in the mystery. This represents the heart of the problem facing Plato. The traditional morality and religion seem to be founded on enlightened self-interest, and if the atheistic sophists can show that one's self-interest is better served by ignoring the old beliefs as mere superstitions, why not pursue a life of injustice which promises riches and power? Glaucon and Adeimantus sincerely come to Socrates asking him to show them how justice is not just something socially profitable but a good for the soul to possess, a good which leads to ultimate happiness. They want to know the effects of justice and injustice on the core character of the person, the inner life of the soul.

Their question leads Socrates to propose that the nature of justice is best seen in the macrocosm, the *polis,* than in the microcosm, the individual. Although much of the rest of the **Republic** discusses the ideal state and its educational system, Plato never loses sight of the question of justice as a quality of the individual soul, and he returns to this question in the concluding books. Plato believed that both the state and the soul are divided into three basic parts or functions. In the state there are artisans who supply the physical needs on the community (farmers, builders, bakers, tailor, cobblers, etc.), guardians or soldiers who protect the city, and leaders or rulers who come from the guardian class. Likewise the soul has three functions or powers: the appetites (the desires for food, drink, etc.), the spirited part (the capacity for courageous action), and reason (the capacity for wisdom). Justice will represent the orderly and harmonious functioning of all these parts together under the guidance of wisdom.

After discussing the economic origins of the state and the nature of the various classes, Socrates suggests that a society flourishes when it enables each person to dedicate himself to the task for which he is best suited. Plato has the basic aristocratic assumption that some classes are suited to be husbandmen and artisans, others to be soldiers, and only a rare few are qualified by their endowment and character to be rulers. According to Plato, the vast majority of citizens are incapable of the knowledge of good and evil. They can learn important civic virtues if they are brought up right and if they are instructed in "right opinions."

In this context, Socrates discusses the education of the guardians and in the process criticizes the traditional Greek education which was founded on Homer, Hesiod and the other poets. Our first selection from the end of Book II and the beginning of Book III gives Plato's critique of the old poetic tradition as not having a suitable moral and philosophical base.

First of all, he is critical of the way the poets portray the gods, i.e., their theology. The anthropomorphic picture of warring, violent, fickle, changing, and lying gods is completely unacceptable from Plato's philosophical viewpoint. In the ideal state God must be portrayed as the author of good only and not of evil. He is also immutable and incapable of falsehood. This picture of God as all-good, unchanging and truthful becomes an important part of Plato's legacy to Western religious thought. It also causes problems with the question of the origin of evil. Plato does not accept the traditional Homeric notion of Fate. He wants to insist that humans are morally responsible for their own fate and are not the playthings of the gods. His answer to this problem comes in the conclusion of the **Republic** in the myth of Er where each soul makes a choice which will determine its personal lot in the next life.

Plato is also critical of the heroic model found in the Homeric epics. He rejects what he considers the excessive emotionalism of the Homeric heroes, especially their fear of death for themselves or others. According to Plato, this fear is rooted in a defective eschatology. For Plato the soul is immortal and will live an even fuller existence after it has departed from the body. Death is not something to fear but to be embraced as the release of the soul which allows it to return to its true home. Here no doubt Plato has in mind the heroic and fearless death of Socrates as his model.

Our second selection from the **Republic** is Plato's famous allegory of the cave which is found in Book VII. The context for this myth is Socrates' discussion of the philosophical education which the guardians of the republic are to have. The purpose of this education is to provide a new religious foundation for the *polis* which is based on the true nature of reality. In Book VI Socrates says that the highest truth of all which underlies justice and all other virtues is the form of the Good which is the guiding star of the soul and the end of the philosopher's quest. The Good for Plato is his concept of God or the ultimate principle *(arche)* of reality. It is the source of all beauty, right and truth. His favorite metaphor for the Good is the sun; as the sun is to the world of sight, the form of the Good is to the world of mind and to the highest reality.

The Good cannot be known through the senses which simply give us appearances; these can be very deceptive as the arguments of Glaucon and Adeimantus have shown in the case of justice in Book II. For Plato, the ultimate source of everything that exists is not physical. The physical world is like a world of shadows in comparison to the real world of eternal truths like Beauty, Justice and the Good. At the end of Book VI Socrates illustrates his famous theory of the Forms, Ideas or Archetypes by using the image of the divided line. The first and smaller part of the line represents the physical world of the sun, the changing world of the senses and appearances where people may "seem" to be just. It represents the domain of opinion in which most people are content to live. It is divided into two parts. In its lower class are images, such as shadows and reflections, and in its higher class physical objects, such as animals and trees. Corresponding to these two divisions are two types of "knowledge": conjecture and belief. The longer part of the line represents the spiritual world of the Good, the permanent world of the mind. It represents the domain of true knowledge which only the philosopher can attain. It also is divided into two parts. In its lower level are thought-images and ideas such as the ideal circle, and in its higher level are the Ideas or Forms such as perfect Beauty, Justice, and the Good. Corresponding to these two divisions are two higher types of "knowledge": understanding and the exercise of reason.

The allegory of the cave is a mythic or poetic way of representing the same view of reality found in a more discursive form in the divided line. In it Plato uses the journey motif to express what he believes to be the human situation. Humans are like prisoners in a cave who are fettered by the neck and legs so that they can only look forward to a wall in front of them. On the wall are shadows which are projected by the light of a fire behind a parapet on which pass figures. This is an image for the world of opinion in which most humans are content to live. In such a world the appearance of justice would be adequate to convince one's fellow prisoners that one was just. In the allegory one of the prisoners is compelled to leave his chains and make a difficult and painful journey out of the cave to the upper world of the sun. After a period of adjustment to the glaring sunlight, he is able to first look at the objects in the real world and finally at the sun itself. This is an image for the philosopher's movement beyond, or conversion from, the world of opinion to true knowledge of justice, beauty and ultimately the Good. The man then returns to the cave and attempts to instruct his fellow prisoners that they see only shadows and that he brings them knowledge of the real world. He is at first very much out of place in the world of the cave, as he has trouble adjusting to the darkness. The prisoners threaten to kill him if he persists in his attempt to expose their view of the world—an image for the trial and death of Socrates.

Socrates then interprets the allegory for Glaucon in the following passage.

> . . . the prison-house is the world of sight, the light of the fire is the sun, and you will not misapprehend me if you interpret the journey upwards to be the ascent of the soul into the intellectual world according to my poor belief, which, at your desire, I have expressed—whether rightly or wrongly God knows. But, whether true or false, my opinion is that in the world of knowledge the idea of good appears last of all, and is seen only with an effort; and, when seen, is also inferred to be the universal author of all things beautiful and right, parent of light and of the lord of light in this visible world, and the immediate source of reason and truth in the intellectual; and this is the power upon which he who would act rationally either in public or private life must have his eye fixed.

In Books VII, VIII and IX Socrates is finally able to formulate an answer to the questions about justice and injustice raised by Thrasymachus, Glaucon and Adeimantus in Books I and II. He draws parallels between the various forms of government for the *polis* and the various types of individuals and sets up a hierarchy of governments and types of souls. The most just form of government is an aristocracy, government by "the best people," who have been trained in the rigorous educational program which Socrates details at the end of Book VII. In such a state only the wise will govern with the wisdom they have acquired by the pursuit of philosophy. The honor-loving warrior class will defend the state with courage, and the artisans will live in temperance. In the corresponding "kingly" soul reason rules over the spirited and appetitive parts of the soul, and love of goodness, justice and beauty take precedence over honor and the physical appetites.

In a timocratic (honor-loving) government the warrior class prevails over the wisdom-loving class, and pursues a militant policy dictated by ambition and love of fame. Likewise, in the soul of an honor-loving man the spirited element gains precedence over the reason, and the person becomes a brave but contentious and ambitious individual, not unlike Achilles in the **Iliad.**

In an oligarchy love of honor turns to love of money. The city is ruled by a rich few who dominate a large number of poor subjects. In the soul of the oligarchic man, the love of money and pleasure overwhelms the reason and the spirited part of the soul.

In a democracy the poor are in an oligarchic state of revolt, and then all are set free to live an intemperate life. The corresponding democratic man casts off all restraint and gives free rein to his desires.

Tyranny arises when men tire at last of the lawlessness of democracy which has become pure license. They appoint a powerful man to restore order. According to Socrates the tyrannical soul is the worst of all because it is ruled by the worst class of unnecessary desires. The tyrannical soul is driven by a boundless excess of passion which he can never sate. He is literally a slave to fear, want, every sort of misery and wickedness. He is therefore the least happy of individuals, and this is Socrates' first answer to the argument of Thrasymachus in Book I.

Book IX gives a final response to the argument of Thrasymachus. As so often at decisive points, Plato has Socrates use an image to illustrate his concept. He uses an allegory to describe the nature of the soul as a composite of three things: a many-headed monster, a lion, and a man. The monster is man as a creature of desire. The lion is man as an emotional being, feeling anger, shame, courage, excitement. The true man, the "man" or "god" in man is the intellectual part of the soul which is capable of wisdom and virtue. According to this image, anyone who praises injustice is giving free rein to the wild beast with many heads. Only the philosopher, who strengthens the tame part of us and makes it dominant, subordinates everything in us to the divine. It can never be profitable to make the better element in us serve the worse, for that is against nature. Socrates concludes by talking about the order of the "state within" which the philosopher is able to create on the model of the ideal city which he and his interlocuters have been able to construct. The discussion concludes with Socrates recognizing that the realization of the ideal city does not exist on earth and may in fact never exist. In spite of that, the philosopher sets his own house in order after the model of that city. We can already sense here the demise of the ancient city-state and the birth of the individualism that will mark the cosmopolitan Hellenistic age in which the individual will seek refuge against the vagaries of a chaotic world order.

In heaven, I replied, there is laid up a pattern of it (the ideal city), methinks, which he who desires may behold, and beholding, may set his own house in order. But whether such an one exists in fact, is no matter; for he will live after the manner of that city, having nothing to do with any other.

Our final section of the **Republic** is the myth of Er which concludes Plato's great work. In this myth Plato uses the idea of the judgment and transmigration of the soul which is found in Orphism and Pythagorean mysticism. He has Socrates place the fate of the just and the unjust soul in the context of eternity rather than of a single earthly lifetime. Although the myth talks about the reward of the just and the punishment of the unjust, Plato's real interest is in the problem of theodicy which had been raised in Book II. Plato rejects the traditional concept of Fate found in Homer and the fifth century dramatists; humans are not the playthings of the gods. He wants to insist upon the moral responsibility of each individual for their personal fate. The important part of the myth of Er is the choice of lives which the souls make after their thousand years' wandering. There is only a limited number of souls, and after their sojourn beyond they must return to earth and start a new existence. This is a doctrine which Plato borrows from Orphism, and it enables him to give a profound significance to the importance of education and moral responsibility. In the myth of Er a prophet takes lots symbolizing various forms of life from Lachesis' knees but unlike Homer these are not handed out to mortals by Zeus in a random fashion. Each soul must choose a life for itself. Once the soul chooses a life it must keep it. The chooser is responsible and heaven is guiltless. As we watch the scene and hear the prophet's warning, the first soul selects the life of the most powerful tyrant. When it sees the burden of guilt and unhappiness it has taken on itself, the soul complains, but we can see the injustice of the complaint. In the further examples of choices we can also see that for Plato the choice that the soul makes is conditioned by the experiences of its previous life. In light of this, the only knowledge which is important is that which enables us to make the right choice of a pattern of life. For Plato one should spend this life preparing for the great choice one will make in the next life, when, after a thousand years of wandering, the soul will put on a new life for better or worse and return to earth. The soul is not totally free in that it is hampered by past guilt. But the soul will be more perfectly prepared for the choice if it persists in its journey upward toward perfect justice, truth, beauty and goodness.

The translation is by Benjamin Jowett, **The Dialogues of Plato** (London: Oxford University Press, 1871).

THE REPUBLIC BOOK: BOOK II

Socrates' Critique of Homer and Hesiod
(Adeimantus has argued that the great poets from Homer and Hesiod to Musaeus and Pindar do not advocate the ideal of justice for its own sake but the appearance of justice for the sake of the rewards which the gods give the apparently just man. Socrates expresses admiration for Glaucon's and Adeimantus' formulation of the problem and then suggests that the nature of justice is most easily seen in the macrocosm of the state, rather than the microcosm of the individual. Socrates and Glaucon are now discussing the nature of the education of the guardian in the ideal state which they are attempting to construct on the basis of justice.)

Then the first thing will be to establish a censorship of the writers of fiction, and let the censors receive any tale of fiction which is good, and reject the bad; and we will desire mothers and nurses to tell their children the authorised ones only. Let them fashion the mind with such tales, even more fondly than they could the body with their hands; but most of those which are now in use must be discarded.

Of what tales are you speaking? he said.

You may find a model of the lesser in the greater, I said; for they are necessarily of the same type, and there is the same spirit in both of them.

Very likely, he replied; but I do not as yet know what you would term the greater.

Those, I said, which are narrated by Homer and Hesiod, and the rest of the poets, who have ever been the great story-tellers of mankind.

But which stories do you mean, he said; and what fault do you find with them?

A fault which is most serious I said; the fault of telling a lie, and what is more, a bad lie.

But when is this fault committed?

Whenever an erroneous representation is made of the nature of gods and heroes,—as when a painter paints a portrait not having the shadow of a likeness to the original.

Yes, he said, that sort of thing is certainly very blameable; but what are the stories which you mean?

First of all, I said, there was that greatest of all lies, in high places, which the poet told about Uranus, and which was a bad lie too,—I mean what Hesiod says that Uranus did, and how Cronus retaliated on him.[19] The doings of Cronus, and the sufferings which in turn his son inflicted upon him, even if they were true, ought certainly not to be lightly told to young and thoughtless persons; if possible, they had better be buried in silence. . .

Why, yes, said he, those stories are extremely objectionable.

Yes, Adeimantus, they are stories not to be repeated in our State; the young man should not be told that in committing the worst of crimes he is far from doing anything outra-

geous; and that even if he chastises his father when he does wrong, in whatever manner, he will only be following the example of the first and greatest among the gods.

I entirely agree with you, he said; in my opinion those stories are quite unfit to be repeated.

Neither, if we mean our guardians to regard the habit of quarrelling among themselves as of all things the basest, should any word be said to them of the wars in heaven, and of the plots and fightings of the gods against one another, for they are not true. No, we shall never mention the battles of the giants, or let them be embroidered on garments; and we shall be silent about the innumerable other quarrels of gods and heroes with their friends and relatives. If they would only believe us we would tell them that quarrelling is unholy, and that never up to this time has there been any quarrel between citizens; this is what old men and old women should begin by telling children; and when they grow up the poets also should be told to compose for them in a similar spirit. But the narrative of Hephaestus binding Hera his mother or how on another occasion Zeus sent him flying for taking her part when she was being beaten, and all the battles of the gods in Homer—these tales must not be admitted into our State, whether they are supposed to have an allegorical meaning or not. For a young person cannot judge what is allegorical and what is literal; anything that he receives into his mind at that age is likely to become indelible and unalterable; and therefore it is most important that the tales which the young first hear should be models of virtuous thoughts.

There you are right, he replied; but if any one asks where are such models to be found and of what tales are you speaking—how shall we answer him?

I said to him, You and I, Adeimantus, at this moment are not poets, but founders of a State: now the founders of a State ought to

know the general forms in which the poets
should cast their tales and the limits which
must be observed by them, but to make the
tales is not their business.

Very true, he said; but what are these
forms of theology which you mean?

Something of this kind, I replied:—God is
always to be represented as he truly is, whatever be the sort of poetry, epic, lyric or tragic,
in which the representation is given.

Right.

And is he not truly good? and must he not
be represented as such?

Certainly.

And no good thing is hurtful?

No, indeed.

And that which is not hurtful hurts not?

Certainly not.

And that which hurts not does no evil?

No.

And can that which does no evil be a cause
of evil?

Impossible.

And the good is advantageous?

Yes.

It follows therefore that the good is not the
cause of all things, but of the good only?

Assuredly.

Then God, if he be good, is not the author
of all things, as many assert, but he is the cause
of a few things only, and not of most things that
occur to men. For few are the goods of human
life, and many are the evils, and the good is to
be attributed to God alone; of the evils the
causes are to be sought elsewhere, and not in
him.

That appears to me to be most true, he
said.

Then we must not listen to Homer or any
other poet who is guilty of the folly of saying
that two casks

'Lie at the threshold of Zeus, full of lots,
   one of good, and the other of evil lots,'
and that he to whom Zeus gives a mixture of
the two

'Sometimes meets with evil fortune, at
other times with good; but that he to whom
is given the cup of unmingled ill, 'Him wild
hunger drivers o'er the beauteous earth.'

And again—

'Zeus, who is the dispenser of good and evil
to us.'[20]

And if any one asserts that the violation of
oaths and treaties which was really the work
of Pandarus, was brought about by Athene and
Zeus, or that the strife and contention of the
gods was instigated by Themis and Zeus,[21] he
shall not have our approval; neither will we allow our young men to hear the words of Aeschylus, that

'God plants guilt among men when he desires utterly to destroy a house.'

And if a poet writes of the sufferings of
Niobe[22]—the subject of the tragedy in which
these iambic verses occur—or of the house of
Pelops,[22a] or of the Trojan war or on any similar
theme, either we must not permit him to say
that these are the works of God, or if they are
of God, he must devise some explanation of
them such as we are seeking; he must say that
God did what was just and right and they were
the better for being punished; but that those
who are punished are miserable, and that God
is the author of the misery—the poet is not to
be permitted to say; though he may say that
the wicked are miserable because they require
to be punished, and are benefited by receiving
punishment from God; but that God being good
is the author of evil to any one is to be stren-
ously denied, and not to be said or sung or
heard in verse or prose by any one whether old
or young in any well-ordered commonwealth.
Such a fiction is suicidal, ruinous, impious.

I agree with you, he replied, and am ready
to give my assent to the law.

Let this then be one of our rules and principles concerning the gods, to which our poets
and reciters will be expected to conform—that
God is not the author of all things, but of good
only.

BOOK VII

The allegory of the cave
(In Book VI Socrates had insisted that the guardians were to be philosophers in the true sense in that they were to be concerned with true Beauty and Justice and not with the changing world of senses. He recognizes that this is not the ordinary image of the philosopher and that the philosopher will never be a popular hero. At the end of Book VI Socrates illustrates his theory of the philosophical quest with the image of the Divided Line which distinguishes between the physical world and the world of thought and the various levels of knowledge corresponding to each. Book VII opens with Socrates speaking to Glaucon and introducing the figure of the cave to illustrate his theory of the philosophical pursuit of true wisdom and the relation of the philosopher to the rest of the world.)

And now, I said, let me show in a figure how far our nature is enlightened or unenlightened:—Behold! human beings living in an underground den, which has a mouth open towards the light and reaching all along the den; here they have been from their childhood, and have their legs and necks chained so that they cannot move, and can only see before them, being prevented by the chains from turning round their heads. Above and behind them a fire is blazing at a distance, and between the fire and the prisoners there is a raised way; and you will see, if you look, a low wall built along the way, like the screen which marionette players have in front of them, over which they show the puppets.

I see.

And do you see, I said, men passing along the wall carrying all sorts of vessels, and statues and figures of animals made of wood and stone and various materials, which appear over the wall? Some of them are talking, others silent.

You have shown me a strange image, and they are strange prisoners.

Like ourselves, I replied; and they see only their own shadows, or the shadows of one another, which the fire throws on the opposite side of the cave?

True, he said; how could they see anything but the shadows if they were never allowed to move their heads?

And of the objects which are being carried in like manner they would only see the shadows?

Yes, he said.

And if they were able to converse with one another, would they not suppose that they were naming what was actually before them?

Very true.

And suppose further that the prison had an echo which came from the other side, would they not be sure to fancy when one of the passers-by spoke that the voice which they heard came from the passing shadow?

No question, he replied.

To them, I said, the truth would be literally nothing but the shadows of the images.

That is certain.

And now look again, and see what will naturally follow if the prisoners are released and disabused of their error. At first, when any of them is liberated and compelled suddenly to stand up and turn his neck round and walk and look towards the light, he will suffer sharp pains; the glare will distress him, and he will be unable to see the realities of which in his former state he had seen the shadows; and then conceive some one saying to him, that what he saw before was an illusion, but that now, when he is approaching nearer to being and his eye is turned towards more real existence, he has a clearer vision,—what will be his reply? And you may further imagine that his instructor is pointing to the objects as they pass and requiring him to name them,—will he not be perplexed? Will he not fancy that the shadows which he formerly saw are truer than the objects which are now shown to him?

Far truer.

And if he is compelled to look straight at the light, will he not have a pain in his eyes which will make him turn away to take refuge in the objects of vision which he can see, and which he will conceive to be in reality clearer than the things which are now being shown to him?

True, he said.

And suppose once more, that he is reluctantly dragged up a steep and rugged ascent, and held fast until he is forced into the presence of the sun himself, is he not likely to be pained and irritated? When he approaches the light his eyes will be dazzled, and he will not be able to see anything at all of what are now called realities?

Not all in a moment, he said.

He will require to grow accustomed to the sight of the upper world. And first he will see the shadows best, next the reflections of men and other objects in the water, and then the objects themselves; then he will gaze upon the light of the moon and the stars and the spangled heaven; and he will see the sky and the stars by night better than the sun or the light of the sun by day?

Certainly.

Last of all he will be able to see the sun, and not mere reflections of him in the water, but he will see him in his own proper place, and not in another; and he will contemplate him as he is.

Certainly.

He will then proceed to argue that this is he who gives the season and the years, and is the guardian of all that is in the visible world, and in a certain way the cause of all things which he and his fellows have been accustomed to behold?

Clearly, he said, he would first see the sun and then reason about him.

And when he remembered his old habitation, and the wisdom of the den and his fellow-prisoners, do you not suppose that he would felicitate himself on the change, and pity them?

Certainly, he would.

And if they were in the habit of conferring honours among themselves on those who were quickest to observe the passing shadows and to remark which of them went before, and which followed after, and which were together; and who were therefore best able to draw conclusions as to the future, do you think that he would care for such honours and glories, or envy the possessors of them? Would he not say with Homer,

'Better to be the poor servant of a poor master.'

and to endure anything, rather than think as they do and live after their manner?

Yes, he said, I think that he would rather suffer anything than entertain these false notions and live in this miserable manner.

Imagine once more, I said, such a one coming suddenly out of the sun to be replaced in his old situation; would he not be certain to have his eyes full of darkness?

To be sure, he said.

And if there were a contest, and he had to compete in measuring the shadows with the prisoners who had never moved out of the den, while his sight was still weak, and before his eyes had become steady (and the time which would be needed to acquire this new habit of sight might be very considerable), would he not be ridiculous? Men would say of him that up he went and down he came without his eyes; and that it was better not even to think of ascending; and if any one tried to loose another and lead him up to the light, let them only catch the offender, and they would put him to death.

No question, he said.

This entire allegory, I said, you may now append, dear Glaucon, to the previous argument; the prison-house is the world of sight, the light of the fire is the sun, and you will not misapprehend me if you interpret the journey upwards to be the ascent of the soul into the intellectual world according to my poor belief, which at your desire, I have expressed— whether rightly or wrongly God knows. But, whether true or false, my opinion is that in the world of knowledge the idea of good appears last of all, and is seen only with an effort; and, when seen, is also inferred to be the universal author of all things beautiful and right, parent of light and of the lord of light in this visible world, and the immediate source of reason and truth in the intellectual; and that this is the power upon which he who would act rationally either in public or private life must have his eye fixed.

I agree, he said, as far as I am able to understand you.

Moreover, I said, you must not wonder that those who attain to this beatific vision are unwilling to descend to human affairs; for their souls are ever hastening into the upper world where they desire to dwell; which desire of theirs is very natural, if our allegory may be trusted.

Yes, very natural.

And is there anything surprising in one who passes from divine contemplations to the evil state of man, misbehaving himself in a ridiculous manner; if, while his eyes are blinking and before he has become accustomed to the surrounding darkness, he is compelled to fight in courts of law, or in other places, about the images or the shadows of images of justice, and is endeavoring to meet the conceptions of those who have never yet seen absolute justice?

Anything but surprising, he replied.

BOOK X

The Myth of Er
(The last section of Book X follows the fate of the just and the unjust to the afterlife. The argument returns to the beginning of the discussion and the idea that justice of her own nature is best for the soul. Socrates is speaking to Glaucon.)

Well, I said, I will tell you a tale; not one of the tales which Odysseus tells to the hero Alcinous, yet this too is a tale of a hero, Er the son of Armenius, a Pamphylian by birth. He was slain in battle, and ten days afterwards, when the bodies of the dead were taken up already in a state of corruption, his body was found unaffected by decay, and carried away home to be buried. And on the twelfth day, as he was lying on the funeral pile, he returned to life and told them what he had seen in the other world. He said that when his soul left the body he went on a journey with a great company, and that they came to a mysterious place at which there were two openings in the earth; they were near together and over against them were two other openings in the heaven above. In the intermediate space there were judges seated, who commanded the just, after they had given judgment on them and had bound their sentences in front of them, to ascend by the heavenly way on the right hand; and in like manner the unjust were bidden by them to descend by the lower way on the left hand; these also bore the symbols of their deeds, but fastened on their backs. He drew near, and they told him that he was to be the messenger who would carry the report of the other world to men, and they bade him hear and see all that was to be heard and seen in that place. Then he beheld and saw on one side the souls departing at either opening of heaven and earth when sentence had been given on them; and at the two other openings other souls, some ascending out of the earth dusty and worn with travel, some descending out of heaven clean and bright. And arriving ever and anon they seemed to have come from a long journey, and they went forth with gladness into the meadow, where they encamped as at a festival; and those who knew one another embraced and conversed, the souls which came from earth curiously enquiring about the things above, and the souls which came from heaven about the things beneath. And they told one another of what had happened by the way, those from below weeping and sorrowing at the remembrance of things which they had endured and seen in their journey beneath the earth (now the journey lasted a thousand years), while those from above were

describing heavenly delights and visions of inconceivable beauty. The story, Glaucon, would
take too long to tell; but the sum was this:—He
said that for every wrong which they had done
to anyone they suffered tenfold; or once in a
hundred years—such being reckoned to be the
length of man's life, and the penalty being thus
paid ten times a thousand years. If, for example, there were any who had been the cause of
many deaths, or had betrayed or enslaved cities or armies, or been guilty of any other evil
behaviour, for each and all of their offences
they received punishment ten times over, and
the rewards of beneficence and justice and holiness were in the same proportion. I need
hardly repeat what he said concerning young
children dying almost as soon as they were
born. Of piety and impiety to gods and parents,
and of murderers, there were retributions
other and greater far which he described. He
mentioned that he was present when one of the
spirits asked another, 'Where is Ardiaeus the
Great?' (Now this Ardiaeus lived a thousand
years before the time of Er: he had been the tyrant of some city of Pamphylia, and had murdered his aged father and his elder brother, and
was said to have committed many other abom-
inable crimes.) The answer of the other spirit
was: 'He comes not hither and will never come.
And this,' said he, 'was one of the dreadful
sights which we ourselves witnessed. We were
at the mouth of the cavern, and having completed all our experiences, were about to reas-
cend, when of a sudden Ardiaeus appeared and
several others, most of whom were tyrants; and
there were also besides the tyrants private individuals who had been great criminals: they
were just, as they fancied, about to return into
the upper world, but the mouth, instead of admitting them, gave a roar, whenever any of
these incurable sinners or some one who had
not been sufficiently punished tried to ascend;
and then wild men of fiery aspect, who were
standing by and heard the sound, seized and
carried them off; and Ardiaeus and others they
bound head and foot and hand, and threw them

down and flayed them with scourges, and
dragged them along the road at the side, card-
ing them on thorns like wool, and declaring to
the passers-by what were their crimes, and
that they were being taken away to be cast into
hell.' And of all the many terrors which they
had endured, he said that there was none like
the terror which each of them felt at that moment, lest they should hear the voice; and
when there was silence, one by one they ascended with exceeding joy. These, said Er, were
the penalities and retributions, and there were
blessings as great.

Now when the spirits which were in the
meadow had tarried seven days, on the eighth
they were obliged to proceed on their journey,
and on the fourth day after, he said that they
came to a place where they could see from
above a line of light, straight as a column, extending right through the whole heaven and
through the earth, in colour resembling the
rainbow, only brighter and purer; another
day's journey brought them to the place, and
there, in the midst of the light, they saw the
chains of heaven let down from above: for this
light is the belt of heaven, and holds together
the circle of the universe, like the under gir-
ders of a trireme. From these ends is extended
the spindle of Necessity, on which all the revolutions turn. The shaft and hook of this spindle are made of steel, and the whorl is made
partly of steel and also partly of other materials. Now the whorl is in form like the whorl
used on earth; and the description of it implied
that there is one large hollow whorl which is
quite scooped out, and into this is fitted another lesser one, and another, and another, and
four others, making eight in all, like vessels
which fit into one another; the whorls show
their edges on the upper side, and on their
lower side all together form one continous
whorl. This is pierced by the spindle, which is
driven home through the centre of the eighth.
The first and outermost whorl has the rim
broadest, and the seven inner whorls are nar-
rower, in the following proportions—sixth is

next of the first in size, the fourth next to the sixth; then comes the eighth; the seventh is fifth, the fifth is sixth, the third is seventh, last and eighth come the second. The largest (or fixed stars) is spangled, and the seventh (or sun) is brightest; the eighth (or moon) coloured by the reflected light of the seventh; the second and fifth (Saturn and Mercury) are in colour like one another, and yellower than the preceding; the third (Venus) has the whitest light; the fourth (Mars) is reddish; the sixth (Jupiter) is in whiteness second. Now the whole spindle has the same motion; but, as the whole revolves in one direction, the seven inner circles move slowly in the other, and of these the swiftest is the eighth; next in swiftness are the seventh, sixth, and fifth, which move together; third in swiftness appeared to move according to the law of this reversed motion the fourth; the third appeared fourth and the second fifth. The spindle turns on the knees of Necessity; and on the upper surface of each circle is a siren, who goes round with them, hymning a single tone or note. The eight together form one harmony; and round about, at equal intervals, there is another band, three in number, each sitting upon her throne: these are the Fates, daughters of Necessity, who are clothed in white robes and have chaplets upon their heads, Lachesis and Clotho and Atropos, who accompany with their voices the harmony of the sirens—Lachesis singing of the past, Clotho of the present, Atropos of the future; Clotho from time to time assisting with a touch of her right hand the revolution of the outer circle of the whorl or spindle, and Atropos with her left hand touching and guiding the inner ones, and Lachesis laying hold of either in turn, first with one and then with the other.

When Er and the spirits arrived, their duty was to go at once to Lachesis; but first of all there came a prophet who arranged them in order; then he took from the knees of Lachesis lots and samples of lives, and having mounted a high pulpit, spoke as follows: 'Hear the word of Lachesis, the daughter of Necessity. Mortal souls, behold a new cycle of life and mortality. Your genius will not be alloted to you, but you will choose your genius; and let him who draws the first lot have the first choice, and the life which he chooses shall be his destiny. Virtue is free, and as a man honours or dishonours her he will have more or less of her; the responsibility is with the chooser—God is justified.' When the Interpreter had thus spoken he scattered lots indifferently among them all, and each of them took up the lot which fell near him, all but Er himself (he was not allowed), and each as he took his lot perceived the number which he had obtained. Then the Interpreter placed on the ground before them the samples of lives; and there were many more lives than the souls present, and they were of all sorts. There were lives of every animal and of man in every condition. And there were tyrannies among them, some lasting out the tyrant's life, others which broke off in the middle and came to an end in poverty and exile and beggary; and there were lives of famous men, some who were famous for their form and beauty as well as for their strength and success in games, or again, for their birth and the qualities of their ancestors; and some who were the reverse of famous for the opposite qualities. And of women likewise; there was not, however, any definite character in them, because the soul, when choosing a new life, must of necessity become different. But there was every other quality, and they all mingled with one another, and also with elements of wealth and poverty, and disease and health; and there were mean states also. And here, my dear Glaucon is the supreme peril of our human state; and therefore the utmost care should be taken. Let each one of us leave every other kind of knowledge and seek and follow one thing only, if peradventure he may be able to learn and may find some one who will make him able to learn and discern between good and evil, and so to choose always and everywhere the better life as he has the opportunity. He should consider the bearing of all these things which have been mentioned severally and collectively upon virtue; he should know what the effect of beauty is when combined with poverty or wealth in a particular soul, and what are the good and evil consequences of noble and humble birth, of private and public station, of strength and weakness, of cleverness and dullness, and of all the natural and acquired gifts of the soul, and the operation of them when conjoined; he will then look at the nature of the soul, and from the consideration of all these qualities he will be able to determine which is the better and which is the worse; and so he will choose, giving the name of evil to the life which will make his soul more unjust, good to the life which will make his soul more just; all else he will disregard. For we have seen and know that this is the best choice both in life and after death. A man must take with him into the world below an adamantine faith in truth and right, that there too he may be undazzled by the desire of wealth or the other allurements of evil, lest, coming upon tyrannies and similar villainies, he do irremediable wrongs to others and suffer yet worse himself; but let him know how to choose the mean and avoid the extremes on either side, as far as possible, not only in this life but in all that which is to come. For this is the way of happiness.

And according to the report of the messenger from the other world this was what the prophet said at the time: 'Even for the last comer, if he chooses wisely and will live diligently, there is appointed a happy and not undesirable existence. Let not him who chooses first be careless, and let not the last despair.' And when he had spoken, he who had the first choice came forward and in a moment chose the greatest tyranny; his mind having been darkened by folly and sensuality, he had not thought out the whole matter before he chose, and did not at first sight perceive that he was fated, among other evils, to devour his own children. But when he had time to reflect, and saw what was in the lot, he began to beat his breast and lament over his choice, forgetting the proclamation of the prophet; for, instead of throwing the blame of his misfortune on himself, he accused chance and the gods, and everything rather than himself. Now he was one of those who came from heaven, and in a former life had dwelt in a well-ordered State, but his virtue was a matter of habit only, and he had no philosophy. And it was true of others who were similarly overtaken, that the greater number of them came from heaven and therefore they had never been schooled by trial, whereas the pilgrims who came from earth having themselves suffered and seen others suffer were not in a hurry to choose. And owing to this inexperience of theirs, and also because the lot was a chance, many of the souls exchanged a good destiny for an evil or an evil for a good. For if a man had always on his arrival in this world dedicated himself from the first to sound philosophy, and had been moderately fortunate in the number of the lot, he might, as the messenger reported, be happy here, and also his journey to another life and return to this, instead of being rough and underground, would be smooth and heavenly. Most curious he said, was the spectacle—sad and laughable and strange; for the choice of the souls was in most cases based on their experience of a previous life. There he saw the soul which had been Orpheus[23] choosing the life of a swan out of enmity to the race of women, hating to be born of a woman because they had been his murderers; he beheld also the soul of Thamyras[24] choosing the life of a nightingale; birds, on the other hand, like the swan and other musicians, wanting to be men. The soul which obtained the twentieth lot chose the life of a lion, and this was the soul of Ajax the son of Telamon,[25] who would not be a man, remembering the injustice which was done him in the judgment about the arms. The next was Agamemnon,[26] who took the life of an eagle, because, like Ajax, he hated human nature by reason of his sufferings. About the middle came the lot of Atalanta;[27] she, seeing the great fame of an athlete, was unable to resist the temptation: and after her there followed the soul of Epeus the son of Panopeus[28] passing into the nature of a woman cunning in the arts; and far away among the last who chose, the soul of the jester Thersites[29] was putting on the form of a monkey. There came also the soul of Odysseus having yet to make a choice, and his lot happened to be the last of them all. Now the recollection of former toils had disenchanted him of ambition, and he went for a considerable time in search of the life of a private man who had no cares; he had some difficulty in finding this, which was lying about and had been neglected by everybody else; and when he saw it, he said that he would have done the same had his lot been first instead of last, and that he was delighted to have it. And not only did men pass into animals, but I must also mention that there were animals tame and wild who changed into one another and into corresponding human natures—the good into the gentle and the evil into the savage, in all sorts of combinations.

All the souls had now chosen their lives, and they went in order of their choice to Lachesis, who sent with them the genius whom they had severally chosen, to be guardian of their lives and the fulfiller of the choice: this genius led the souls first to Clotho, and drew them within the revolution of the spindle impelled by her hand, thus ratifying the destiny of each; and then, when they were fastened to this, carried them to Atropos, who spun the threads and made them irreversible, whence without turning round they passed beneath the throne of Necessity; and when they had all passed, they marched on in a scorching heat to the plain of forgetfulness, which was a barren waste destitute of trees and verdure; and then towards evening they encamped by the river of Unmindfulness, whose water no vessel can hold; of this they were all obliged to drink a certain quantity, and those who were not saved by wisdom drank more than was necessary; and each one as he drank forgot all things. Now after they had gone to rest, about the middle of the night there was a thunderstorm and earthquake, and then in an instant they were driven upwards in all manner of ways to their birth, like stars shooting. He himself was hindered from drinking the water. But in what manner or by what means he returned to the body he could not say; only, in the morning awaking suddenly, he found himself lying on the pyre.

And thus, Glaucon, the tale has been saved and has not perished, and will save us if we are obedient to the word spoken; and we shall pass safely over the river of Forgetfulness and our soul will not be defiled. Wherefore my counsel is that we hold fast ever to the heavenly way and follow after justice and virtue always, considering that the soul is immortal and able to endure every sort of good and every sort of evil. Thus shall we live dear to one another and to the gods, both while remaining here and when, like conquerors in the games who go round to gather gifts, we receive our reward. And it shall be well with us both in this life and in the pilgrimage of a thousand years which we have been describing.

NOTES

[1]John Mansley Robinson, **An Introduction to Early Greek Philosophy** (Boston: Houghton Mifflin Company, 1968) 52. Henceforth: Robinson.

[2]Robinson, 53.

[3]Robinson, 55.

[4]Robinson, 53.

[5]Robinson, 54.

[6]Robinson, 56.

[7]Robinson, 56.

[8]Robinson, 62.

[9]Robinson, 77.

[10]Robinson, 93.

[11]Robinson, 93.

[12]Robinson, 110.

[13]Robinson, 110.

[14]Plato, **Theatetus,** 151.

[15]Plato, **Republic,** 338.

[16]Plato, **Letter VII,** 326.

[17]Plato, **Letter VII,** 326.

[18]Plato, **Letter VII,** 326.

[19]Hesiod, **Theogony,** 154, 459.

[20]Homer, **Iliad,** xxiv, 527.

[21]Homer, **Iliad,** xx.

[22]The daughter of Tantalus and Dione; sister of Pelops. According to Hesiod, she married Amphion and had ten sons and ten daughters. She taunted Leto for having only two children, and the outraged mother appealed to the gods for revenge. As a result, all Niobe's children were killed except Choloris, and Niobe was turned into stone.

[22a]The house of Pelops was legendary for its violence within the family.

[23]The legendary lyre player who failed to rescue Eurydice his wife from Hades because he turned to look at her. Later he is dismembered and murdered by bacchants in Thrace.

[24]A celebrated musician and minstrel of Thrace, who challenged the Muses to a musical contest, was defeated, blinded, deprived of his melodious voice, and had his lyre destroyed.

[25]He contended with Odysseus for the armor of the dead Achilles and was enraged when Odysseus won.

[26]Killed by his wife Klytaimnestra on his return from Troy.

[27]Daughter of Schoeneus, king of Scyros. She desired perpetual virginity, but her great beauty gained her many admirers; in proposed races she killed those who conquered; she was finally defeated and married by Hippomenes.

[28]The designer and builder of the wooden horse.

[29]A deformed, foul-mouthed trouble-maker among the Greeks at Troy.

4

HELLENISTIC AND ROMAN RELIGIONS

Introduction

In the last three and a half centuries B.C.E. the ancient world went through profound changes. The conquests of the East by Alexander the Great (334–323 B.C.E.) and the subsequent imperial expansion of Rome absorbed the native city-states of Greece and the Near East into vast multinational empires. The individual *polis* was replaced by the *cosmopolis,* the world city. *Koine,* or common, Greek became the *linqua franca* of the Mediterranean and Near Eastern worlds which were interconnected as never before by travel and commerce. Religions and philosophical ideas were no longer limited to their native city-states; they traveled with their adherents from one end of the Mediterranean to the other. The new Hellenistic culture which emerged was highly syncretistic—a blend of Greek culture with the indigenous cultures of the ancient Near East and Rome.

The facade of Greek culture could be found everywhere with its gymnasia, temples, theaters, agora, and statuary, but the Greeks were influenced in turn by the ancient cultures and religions of the East. The old city-state religions continued to exist, but they were increasingly influenced by the spirit of syncretism in which there was almost a scientific search for analogies between various religions and their gods. In Egypt, for example, Isis was identified and worshiped as Demeter and the other mother gods of the East; Horus as Apollo; Thot as Hermes; and Amon-Re as Zeus.

The individual city-states continued to exist as physical entities, and Alexander even constructed new cities, like Alexandria in Egypt, on the Greek model. But these cities were different from the *poleis* of the Classical Age. They had lost control of their own foreign affairs and even internal arrangements were often determined by distant foreign monarchs. The *polis* was no longer the free and independent city-state, but a municipality, a commercial center in a large military empire.

The religious spirit of the Hellenistic Age reflects this loss of independence and responsibility for political destiny. People were obsessed with the idea of Fate (Greek *Moira*), the belief that an irrevocable destiny determined one's life and that the individual was largely powerless to alter this. Therefore, many turned away from communal and political solutions for problems, as in the thought of Aeschylus, Plato and Aristotle, to more personal responses to the hopes and fears of a turbulent age. Some intellectuals even turned from the traditional state religions and sought fulfillment in new individualistic philosophies like Stoicism and Epicureanism which offered their adherents a rational analysis of reality and the promise of some happiness amidst the changing fortunes of life.

In contrast to the adherents of these rational philosophies, others turned away from reason and embraced mystery religions, like the very popular cult of the Egyptian goddess Isis or Mithras the Persian savior god of light. These mystery religions offered a mystical experience of personal salvation which liberated their initiates from the tyranny of fate. The pessimism of the age was also reflected in the widespread popularity of astrology and magic. A fine source book on Hellenistic religions is Frederick C. Grant's **Hellenistic Religions: The Age of Syncretism** (Indianapolis: The Liberal Arts Press, 1953).

CLEANTHES: *THE HYMN TO ZEUS* (STOICAL THEOLOGY)

Although the traditional city-state religions continued to be practiced, many of the educated classes turned to philosophy for a more individualized sense of salvation in an increasingly complex, rapidly changing and chaotic world. One of the most popular Hellenistic philosophies was Stoicism, a deeply religious and highly moral philosophy. The Stoics taught that the universe was not an arbitrary place, governed by chance, *Tyche*. Rather, following Heraclitus, they believed that Reason and Purpose, *logos* ("Word"), guided the whole of the world order. This *logos* was the Divine Reason that ordered the physical world by a natural law, and, if humans were to find happiness, they must conform by living in accord with this Divine Reason. If they failed to conform to Destiny, they would be dragged along with it against their will, like a dog tied to a cart. According to the Stoics, a spark or seed of the universal Reason (*logos spermatikos*) resided within humans, and wisdom consisted in obeying this *logos* at all costs. The ethical ideal for the Stoics was *apatheia,* a state of passionlessness and self-control which enables the person to face any circumstance with equanimity and thus conquer fate.

The Stoics pictured the universe as a vast body in which everything was meant to work with everything else. They spoke of all humans not simply as citizens of this or that city-state but as citizens in the cosmos. They also believed that the cosmos was involved in a cyclical process; when the planets return to the same position they had in the beginning, there will be a conflagration and destruction of everything, and then the cosmos will begin again.

The Stoics made some acknowledgement of the traditional Greek gods, like Zeus, but, as can be seen in the following **Hymn to Zeus** by Cleanthes, the understanding of Zeus is that of the supreme god of the universe who governs all according to Divine Reason, and not the highly anthropomorphic god of the traditional mythology. The hymn also illustrates the highly religious and moral tone of Stoical thought which tends toward a rational and ethical monotheism. Zeus is praised for guiding all things providentially so that "all things are harmonized,/ The evil with the good . . . " Wickedness is to ignore God's universal law and to seek happiness in fame, folly, or the pleasures of the flesh. The hymn ends with the prayful request for "true understanding" of God's universal law.

Cleanthes of Assos (331–233 B.C.E.) was a disciple and successor of Zeno (c. 336–263), the founder of the Stoical school in Athens. Zeno taught in the Painted Porch (*Stoa*) at Athens—whence the name of the school.

The translation is by Frederick C. Grant in **Hellenistic Religions: The Age of Syncretism** (Indianapolis: The Liberal Arts Press, 1953) 152–154.

Cleanthes: Hymn to Zeus

Invocation
Lead me, O Zeus, and thou, O Destiny, to the
end that ye have ordained for me. I will follow
without reluctance. Were I a fool, and refused,
I should nevertheless have to follow!

Hymn
Most glorious of immortals, Zeus
The many-named, almighty evermore,
Nature's great Sovereign, ruling all by law—
Hail to thee! On thee 'tis meet and right
That mortals everywhere should call
From thee was our begetting; ours alone
Of all that live and move upon the earth
The lot to bear God's likeness.
Thee will I ever chant, thy power praise!
For thee this whole vast cosmos, wheeling
　　round
The earth, obeys, and where thou leadest
It follows, ruled willingly by thee.
In thy unconquerable hands thou holdest fast,
Ready prepared, that two-tined flaming blast,
The ever-living thunderbolt:
Nature's own stroke brings all things to their
　　end.
By it thou guidest aright the sense instinct
Which spreads through all things, mingled
　　ever
With stars in heaven, the great and small—
Thou who art King supreme for evermore!
Naught upon earth is wrought in thy despite,
　　O God,
Nor in the ethereal sphere aloft which ever
　　winds

About its pole, nor in the sea—save only what
The Wicked work, in their strange madness.
Yet even so thou knowest to make the crooked
　　straight,
Prune all excess, give order to the orderless;
For unto thee the unloved still is lovely—
And thus in one all things are harmonized,
The evil with the good, that so one Word
Should be in all things everlastingly.
One Word—which evermore the wicked flee!
Ill-fated, hungering to possess the good
They have no vision of God's universal law,
Nor will they hear; though if obedient in mind
They might obtain a noble life, true wealth.
Instead, they rush unthinking after ill:
Some with a shameless zeal for fame,
Others pursuing gain, disorderly;
Still others folly, or pleasures of the flesh.
[But evils are their lot,] and other times
Bring other harvests, all unsought—
For all their great desire, its opposite!
But, Zeus, thou giver of every gift,
Who dwellest within the dark clouds, wielding
　　still
The flashing stroke of lightning, save, we pray,
Thy children from this boundless misery.
Scatter, O Father, the darkness from their
　　souls,
Grant them to find true understanding—
On which relying thou justly rules all—
While we, thus honored, in turn will honor
　　thee,
Hymning thy works forever, as is meet
For mortals, while no greater right
Belongs even to the gods than evermore
Justly to praise the universal law!

EPICURUS: *EPISTLE TO MENOECEUS* (EPICUREANISM)

Another philosophy which attempted to meet the spiritual needs of the Hellenistic Age was Epicureanism. Epicurus (c. 342–270 B.C.E.) was from the island of Samos and founded a philosophical school in Athens toward the end of the fourth century B.C.E. He concurred with Plato and Aristole that the aim of all humans was happiness, but he was influenced by the materialistic atomism of Democritus and therefore understood happiness as the highest form of pleasure. By pleasure Epicurus did not mean an unbridled enjoyment of the things of the flesh as in the phrase, "Eat, drink and be merry, for tomorrow we die." Rather, Epicurus understood pleasure or happiness as a tranquility of soul which comes from a moderate and prudent pursuit of virtue.

According to Epicurus, the greatest obstacle to *ataraxia*, "tranquillity of soul," was irrational fear which he proposed to remove by the study of philosophy understood as a rational analysis of the universe in terms of Democritus' atomism. The three great fears which Epicurus addresses in the following **Epistle to Menoecus** are anxiety over the existence of the gods, dread of death and the threat of sudden misfortune. Epicurus is not an atheist who denies the existence of the gods, but he attacks the common opinion that the gods are the guardians of public morality. He insists that they are incorruptible and immortal beings, but solely concerned with their own happiness and not with human affairs. Therefore, they need not be a source of needless human anxiety. According to Epicurus the fear of death is rooted in humans' irrational desire for immortality. Once they realize that death itself is no more than the separation of the atoms which constitute our bodies, then death loses its terrifying character, because "as long as we exist death is not present with us, and when death comes then we no longer exist." Finally, misfortune is beyond human control, and the only thing the individual can do is to arrange his or her life in accord with virtue, especially prudence, so as to be as tranquil and pleasant as possible.

The translation is by Frederick C. Grant in **Hellenistic Religions: The Age of Syncretism** (Indianapolis: The Liberal Arts Press, 1953) 156–160.

Epicurus: *Epistle to Menoeceus*

Let no one when he is young postpone the study of philosophy; nor let him when he is old grow weary of its study. For neither can one start too early nor continue too late in attending to his soul's health. And anyone who says either that the time for philosophy has not come yet, or has already gone by, is like one who says that the time for happiness has not yet come [for him], or is no longer present. Accordingly, a man ought to study philosophy both when he is young and when he is old, in order that as he grows old he may remain young in [enjoying] good things through his gratitude for what has taken place [in his life], and so that equally in youth and in age he may know no fear of things to come. We ought to take care, then, for those things that make for happiness, seeing that when happiness is present we have everything, but when it is absent we do everything to possess it.

The things I used constantly to urge upon you, these practice and care for, recognizing that they are the first principle of the good life. First of all believe that God is a being incorruptible [i.e., immortal and unchangeable] and blessed, just as in the common idea of God which is engraved on the mind, and do not assign to him anything contrary to his incorruption or unsuited to his blessedness, and believe about him whatever safeguards his blessedness and incorruption. For gods there certainly are, since the knowledge of them is a matter of immediate perception. But they are not what the majority of men believe them to be; in fact, they do not take care to represent them as they really believe them to be. And the irreligious man is not the one who denies the gods of the majority, but the one who applies to the gods the opinions of the majority. For what the majority say about the gods are not conceptions derived from sensation [*prolepsis*], but false suppositions [*hypolepseis*], according to which the greatest injuries overtake the wicked and the greatest blessings come to [the good] from the gods. For since men are always accustomed to their own virtues, they welcome those who are like themselves; but whatever is not of this sort they regard as alien.

Get accustomed to the idea that death means nothing to us. For all good and evil consist in sensation, and death is only the deprivation of sensation. Hence a real understanding that death means nothing to us makes the mortality of [our] life enjoyable, not by adding to it an unlimited length of time, but by taking away the desire for immortality. For there is nothing dreadful in life for the man who has really grasped the idea that there is nothing dreadful in not living. So that anyone is foolish who says that he is afraid of death, not because it will be painful when it comes, but because it is painful in prospect. For what gives [us] no trouble when it comes is only an empty pain as we look forward to it. So death, the most terrifying of evils, is nothing to us; for as long as we exist death is not present with us, and when death comes then we no longer exist. It is no concern, therefore, either of the living or the dead; for the former it does not exist, while the latter themselves no longer exist.

But the majority at one time flee from death as the greatest of all evils, but at another time [they yearn for it] as a rest from the [evils] in life. [But the wise man neither seeks to escape from life] nor fears to cease living; for neither does life annoy him nor does nonliving seem to be anything evil. Just as in the case of food he does not by any means choose the larger share, but rather the most delicious, so he seeks to enjoy [literally, plucks as fruit], not the longest period of time, but the most pleasant.

And whoever counsels the young man to live well but the old man to make a good end is silly, not merely because life is desirable, but also because it is the same discipline which teaches [us] to live well and to die well. Yet far worse is the man [Theognis, it is supposed] who says it is good not to be born, "but once being born, make haste to pass through the gates of death." For if he says this from conviction, why does he not depart out of life? For it is open to him to do so, if he has firmly made up his mind to it. But if he is only jesting, his words sound idle to men who cannot receive them.

We must bear in mind, then that the future is neither ours nor yet altogether not ours, so that we may not look forward to it as absolutely sure to come nor give up hope of it as if it will certainly not come.

[Having dealt with the nature of the gods and the fact of death, Epicurus goes on to the moral principles which he has taught Menoeceus: Some desires are good, others are not; one must choose his course with reference to (a) health of the body and (b) repose of the soul (*ataraxia*); in both, pleasure—or rather happiness—is the standard and test, the beginning and the end of the life of blessedness. Pleasure is always good, but not all pleasures are free from pain; we must judge, and choose the relatively better. We must be content with little; then the luxuries will be sweeter if they come. Health, for example, is fostered by a simple diet. Pleasure is not the enjoyment of the physical sense, but health of body and the occupation of the mind with philosophy. The greatest thing of all is prudence (*pronesis*), which teaches us the other virtues, and the virtues are inseparable from a life of happiness.]

The beginning of all these [achievements of philosophy] and the greatest good [of all] is prudence. Therefore prudence is something even more precious than philosophy itself. From it the other virtues are born, since it teaches [us] that it is impossible to live happily unless we live prudently, honestly, and justly; or to live prudently, honorably, and justly without living happily. For the virtues are one in origin with the life of happiness, and the life of happiness is inseparable from the virtues. For who do you imagine is better than the man who thinks reverently of the gods, and is entirely fearless of death, and has thought through the purpose of nature? He realizes that the limit of [attainable] good things is easy to fulfill and easy to reach, while the limit of [possible] evils is short and slight as regards either their duration in time or the intensity of the suffering involved; and he simply laughs at [Destiny], whom some have introduced as the supreme goddess ruling over all things. . . . [A lacuna in the text occurs here.] [Some things happen by necessity,] others by chance, and some are entirely within our control. Since necessity cannot be called to account and since

chance is obviously inconstant, what is committed to us is free from [external] control, and accordingly praise or blame must be attached to what we do. For it would be much better to follow some myth about the gods than to be a slave to the Destiny pictured by the natural philosophers; for the myth [at least] sketches out a hope of winning over the gods by worship, whereas the latter represents Necessity [*Anagke*] as inexorable. Nor does he suppose Chance [*Tyche*] is to be a god, as the majority assume (for there is nothing disorderly in what a god does), nor that it is the unstable cause [of all things]; for he does not think that good or evil have been given men by chance for [the making of] the blessed life, but that the starting points of great good and great evil are thus provided. He deems it better to be unlucky but reasonable than to be unreasonable but favored by fortune. For it is better in practice to choose the right and fail than to choose the wrong and succeed by luck.

Cherish these things and those like them day and night, by yourself and with someone [a companion] like yourself, and you will never be upset, but will live like a god among men. For the man who lives among the eternal values has lost all likeness to the beasts that perish.

THE PRAISES OF ISIS (THE MYSTERY RELIGIONS)

One of the most popular of the mystery religions which were widespread during the Hellenistic Age was the cult of the Egyptian goddess Isis whose temples and inscriptions have been found as far west as Rome and as far east as Asia Minor. The following aretalogy, or list of praises on behalf of the goddess, was found on a stele in Asia Minor and is dated to the second century C.E. It illustrates the syncretism of the Hellenistic period in that Isis is called "the oldest daughter of Kronos," i.e., Demeter, and is even given functions normally attributed to male Greek gods like Poseidon and Zeus. The hymn is also a brilliant example of the tendency toward monotheistic thinking in the Hellenistic Age. Isis claims to be the creator, the source of cosmic order, natural law, language, culture and beauty. Most importantly, she is superior to Fate because she is the one who established the order of the celestial bodies which were thought to determine Fate in astrology.

The translation is by Frederick C. Grant, **Hellenistic Religions: The Age of Syncretism** (Indianapolis: The Liberal Arts Press, 1953) 131–133.

The Praises of Isis

I am Isis, the mistress of every land, and I was taught by Hermes,[1] and with Hermes I devised letters, both the sacred [hieroglyphs] and the demotic,[2] that all things might not be written with the same [letters].

I gave and ordained laws for men, which no one is able to change.

I am eldest daughter of Kronos.[3]

I am wife and sister of King Osiris.[4]

I am she who findeth fruit for men.

I am mother of King Horus.[5]

I am she that riseth in the Dog Star.

I am she that is called goddesss by women.

For me was the city of Bubastis built.

I divided the earth from the heaven.

I showed the paths of the stars.

I ordered the course of the sun and the moon.

I devised the business in the sea.

I made strong the right.

I brought together woman and man.

I appointed to women to bring their infants to birth in the tenth month.

I ordained that parents should be loved by children.

I laid punishment upon those disposed without natural affection toward their parents.

I made with my brother Osiris an end to the eating of men.

I revealed mysteries unto men.

I taught [men] to honor images of the gods.

I consecrated the precincts of the gods.

I broke down the governments of tyrants.

I made an end to murders.

I compelled women to be loved by men.

I made the right to be stronger than gold and silver.

I ordained that the true should be thought good.

I devised marriage contracts.

I assigned Greeks and barbarians their languages.

I made the beautiful and shameful to be distinguished by nature.

I ordained that nothing should be more feared than an oath.

I have delivered the plotter of evil against other men into the hands of the one he plotted against.

I established penalties for those who practice injustice.

I decreed mercy to suppliants.

I protect [or honor] righteous guards.

With me the right prevails.

I am the Queen of rivers and winds and sea.

No one is held in honor without my knowing it.

I am the Queen of war.

I am the Queen of the thunderbolt.

I stir up the sea and I calm it.

I am in the rays of the sun.

I inspect the courses of the sun.

Whatever I please, this too shall come to an end.

With me everything is reasonable.

I set free those in bonds.

I am the Queen of seamanship.

I make the navigable unnavigable when it pleases me.

I created walls of cities.

I am called the Lawgiver [Thesmorphoros, a classical epithet of Demeter.]

I brought up islands out of the depths into the light.

I am Lord [note masculine form] of rainstorms.

I overcome Fate.

Fate harkens to me.

Hail, O Egypt, that nourished me!

NOTES

[1]The messenger of the gods who had a very complex series of attributes including manual skill, oratory and eloquence.

[2]A later form of hieroglyphs which used Greek characters.

[3]The father of the twelve Olympians in Greek mythology.

[4]The brother and husband of Isis who was murdered by his brother Seth (Greek Typhon) and restored by Isis. Was the Egyptian god of the underworld and judge of the dead.

[5]Son of Osiris who reigns in his stead on earth.

APULEIUS: *METAMORPHOSES* (THE MYSTERIES OF ISIS)

As with the Eleusian mysteries in Greece, we do not have much information about the secret side of most of the mystery cults of the Hellenistic period. However, in the case of the cult of Isis, more information than usual has been preserved in a second century C.E. novel entitled **Metamorphoses** (sometimes referred to as **The Golden Ass**) by Apuleius of Madaura, in North Africa. Apuleius was himself an initiate in the cult of Isis and therefore his information is considered reliable. Our selection is taken from Book XI of the novel, a popular literary form in the Hellenistic Age, in which the hero, Lucius, is initiated into the mysteries of Isis. As the book opens, Lucius has been transformed into an ass because he had accidently drunk the wrong potion in an overly curious experiment with magic. The story goes on to recount how, through the mercy of Isis, he is restored to human form and eventually initiated into her saving mysteries.

The warm appeal of the mystery cults is evident from this selection by Apuleius. Repeatedly we hear how the merciful and provident Isis is able to free her followers from the blind caprice of Fortune where noble birth, high social rank and astute learning may fail. The epiphany of Isis in a dream vision is both awe-inspiring and consoling. The rites themselves are filled with pageantry and rituals deeply rooted in the history of religion and reminiscent of the early celebrations of the Christian mysteries of baptism and Eucharist. Lucius is warmly received by the priest, Mithras, and prepares for his initiation with a ten day fast from meat and wine and a ritual washing before his presentation in the temple. The initiation itself is not divulged fully, but it is clear that Lucius has some experience of death and rebirth like that in the Eleusian mysteries. Afterward he is given special clothing and symbols signifying his new life under the protection of Isis; Lucius receives an embroidered garment called the "twelve gowns," a palm crown and a flaming torch as he stands before the beautiful statue of Isis in the presence of the whole assembly.

There are several significant comparisons and contrasts between the mysteries of Isis as they are described in Apuleius and early Christianity as we find it, for example, in the Acts of the Apostles. In both the deity manifests providential guidance through dream visions (cf. Paul's vision in Acts 9 or Peter's vision about Cornelius in Acts 10). Both works also emphasize the warm fraternity of the community (cf. Luke's numerous idyllic summaries of the community in Jerusalem in Acts). A significant difference is that, although both religions make universal claims for its respective divinity, in the Isis cult there is no official doctrine, like the Christian kerygma, but rather a syncretistic tolerance of other gods and cults.

The translation is by Frederick C. Grant, **Hellenistic Religions: The Age of Syncretism** (Indianapolis: Liberal Arts Press, 1953) 136–145.

Metamorphoses

Introduction

[Book XI opens with an auspicious note of mystery. Lucius is spending the night asleep on the warm sand of the seashore.] About the first watch of the night, I awoke in sudden terror; the full moon had risen and was shining with unusual splendor as it emerged from the waves. All about me lay the mysterious silence of the night. I knew that this was the hour when the goddess [Isis] exercised her greatest power and governed all things by her providence—not only animals, wild and tame, but even inanimate things were renewed by her divine illumination and might; even the heavenly bodies, the whole earth, and the vast sea waxed or waned in accordance with her will.

The Epiphany of Isis

[Lucius decides to make his appeal to Isis for release from his asinine disguise, and the goddess responds. His prayer in section 2 recounts her titles as Queen of heaven, Ceres, Proserpina, celestial Venus.]

(3) So I poured out my prayers and supplications adding to them much pitiful wailing, and once more fell sound asleep on the same bed of sand. Scarcely had I closed my eyes when lo! from the midst of the deep there arose that face divine to which even the gods must do reverence. Then a little at a time, slowly, her whole shining body emerged from the sea and came into full view. I would like to tell you all the wonder of this vision, if the poverty of human speech does not prevent, or if the divine power dwelling within that form supplies a rich enough store of eloquence.

First, the tresses of her hair were long and thick, and streamed down softly, flowing and curling about her divine neck. On her head she wore as a crown many garlands of flowers, and in the middle of her forehead shone white and glowing a round disc like a mirror, or rather like the moon; on its right and left it was bound about with furrowed coils of rising vipers, and above it were stalks of grain. Her tunic was of many colors, woven of the finest linen, now gleaming with snowy whiteness, now yellow like the crocus, now rosy-red like a flame. But what dazzled my eyes more than anything else was her cloak, for it was a deep black, glistening with sable sheen; it was cast about her, passing under her right arm and brought together on her left shoulder. Part of it hung down like a shield and drooped in many a fold, the whole reaching to the lower edge of her garment with tasseled fringe. (4) Here and there along its embroidered border, and also on its surface, were scattered sequins of sparkling stars, and in their midst the full moon of midmonth shone forth like a flame of fire. And all along the border of that gorgeous robe there was an unbroken garland of all kinds of flowers and fruits.

In her hands she held emblems of various kinds. In her right hand she carried a bronze rattle [the sistrum] made of a thin piece of metal curved like a belt, through which were passed a few small rods; this gave out a tingling sound whenever she shook it three times with a quivering pulsation. In her left hand was a golden cup, from the top of whose slender handle rose an asp, towering with head erect and its throat distended on both sides. Her perfumed feet were shod with sandals woven of the palm of victory.

Such was the vision, and of such majesty. Then, breathing forth all the blessed fragrance of happy Arabia, she deigned to address me with voice divine:

(5) "Behold, Lucius, I have come, moved by thy prayers! I, nature's mother, mistress of all the elements, earliest offspring of the ages, mightiest of the divine powers, Queen of the dead, chief of them that dwell in the heavens, in whose features are combined those of all the gods and goddesses. By my nod I rule the shining heights of heaven, the wholesome winds of

the sea, and the mournful silences of the underworld. The whole world honors my sole deity under various forms, with varied rites, and by many names. There the Phyrgians, first-born of men, call me the Mother of the Gods, she who dwells at Pessinus; there the Athenians sprung from their own soil, know me as Cecropian Minerva; there the sea-girt Cyprians call me Paphian Venus; the Cretans, who are archers, call me Diana Dictynna [of the hunter's net]; the Sicilians, with their three languages, call me Stygian Proserpina; the Eleusinians, the ancient goddess Ceres. Others call me Juno, others Bellona, others Hecate, while still others call me the Rhamnusian.[1] But those on whom shine the first rays of the sun-God as daily he springs to new birth, the Arii and the Ethiopians, and the Egyptians mighty in ancient lore, honoring me with my peculiar rites, call me by my true name, **Isis the Queen.**

"I have come in pity for thy woes. I have come propitious and ready to aid. Cease from thy weeping and lamentation, and lay aside thy grief! For thee, by my providence, the day of salvation is dawning! Therefore turn thy afflicted spirit, and give heed to what I command. The day, even the very day that follows this night, is dedicated to me by an everlasting dedication; for on this day, after I have laid to rest the storms of winter and stilled the tempestuous waves of the sea, my priests shall dedicate to the deep, which is now navigable once more, a new boat, and offer it in my honor the first fruits of the year's seafaring. Thou must await this festival with untroubled heart and with no profane thoughts."

[The goddess tells Lucius that he must mingle with the crowd at the Ploiaphesia and edge his way up to the priest, who will be wearing a garland of roses. Having been forewarned by the goddess in a vision, the priest will be prepared for what is to happen, namely, that Lucius (still the ass) will seize the priest's garland and eat it, whereupon he will be restored to human form. And so it takes place. Transformed once more into human shape, Lucius is exhorted by one of the priests, "whose smiling face seemed more that mortal":]

(15) "O Lucius, after enduring so many labors and escaping so many tempests of Fortune, you have now at length reached the port and haven of rest and mercy! Neither your noble lineage nor your high rank nor your great learning did anything for you; but because you turned to servile pleasures, by a little youthful folly you won the grim reward of your hapless curiosity. And yet while Fortune's blindness tormented you with various dangers, by her very malice she has brought you to this present state of religious blessedness. Let Fortune go elsewhere and rage with her wild fury, and find someone else to torment! For Fortune has no power over those who have devoted themselves to serve the majesty of our goddess. For all your afflictions—robbers, wild beasts, slavery, toilsome and futile journeys that ended where they began, and the daily fear of death—all these brought no advantage to wicked Fortune. Now you are safe, under the protection of that Fortune who is not blind but can see, who by her clear light enlightens the other gods. Therefore rejoice and put on a more cheerful countenance, appropriately matching your white robe, and follow with joyful steps the procession of this Savior Goddess. Let all such as are not devout followers of the goddess see and acknowledge their error[, saying]: 'See, here is Lucius, freed from his former miseries by the providence of the great goddess Isis, and rejoicing in triumph over his Fortune!' And in order that you may live even more safely and securely, hand in your name to this sacred militia [i.e., join the isiac order]—for it is only a little while ago that you were asked to take the oath—and dedicate yourself to obey our religion and take upon yourself the voluntary yoke of ministry. For when you have begun to serve the goddess, then will you realize more fully the fruits of your liberty."

The Initiation of Lucius

[And so the priest prophesied and made his appeal to Lucius, and Lucius consented and joined the procession, amid the jeers of the unbelievers. But his conversion, like that of many others, was a slow process, and only gradually did he come to identify himself with the Isiac priests; for, like many another, he believed the strict profession of religion was something too hard for him: "The laws of chastity and abstinence are not easy to obey" (19). And yet he continued to frequent the services of worship (21), and eventually came to desire earnestly to be admitted to the mysteries of Isis. This took place on "the night that is sacred to the goddess."]

(22) The priest finished speaking, and I did not mar my obedience by any impatience, but with a quiet and gentle and edifying silence I rendered attentive service at the daily observance of the sacred rites. Nor did the saving grace of the mighty goddess in any way deceive me or torture me with long delays, but in the dark of night, by commands that were not in the least dark, she clearly signified to me that the day so long desired had come, in which she would grant the fulfillment of my most earnest prayers. She also stated what amount I must provide for the supplications, and she appointed Mithras himself, her high priest, to administer the rites to me; for his destiny, she said, was closely bound up with mine by the divine conjunction of the stars.

These and other gracious admonitions of the supreme goddess refreshed my spirit, so that even before it was clear day I shook off sleep and hastened at once to the priest's lodging. I met him just as he was coming out of his bedchamber, and saluted him. I had decided to request with even more insistence that I should be initiated, now that it was due me. But he at once, as soon as he saw me, anticipated me, saying, "Lucius, you happy, you greatly blessed man, whom the august diety deigns to favor with such good will! But why,"

he asked, "do you stand here idle, yourself delaying? The day you have so long asked for by your unwearied prayers has come, when by the divine commands of the goddess of many names you are to be admitted by my hands into the most holy secrets of the mysteries." Then, taking my right hand in his, the gentle old man led me to the very doors of the huge temple; and after celebrating the morning sacrifice, he brought out from a hidden place in the temple certain books whose titles were written in undecipherable letters. Some of these [letters] were shaped like all kinds of animals and seemed to be brief ways of suggesting words; others had their extremities knotted or curved like wheels, or intertwined like the tendrils of a vine, which was enough to safeguard them from the curiosity of profane readers. At the same time he told me about the various preparations it was necessary to make in view of my initiation.

(23) I lost no time, but promptly and with a liberality even beyond what was required I either bought these things myself or had my friends buy them for me. And now, the time drawing near and requiring it, as he said, the priest conducted me with an escort of the religiously-minded to the nearest baths; and when I entered the bath, where it is customary for the neophytes to bathe, he first prayed to the gods to be gracious to me and then sprinkled me with purest water and cleansed me. He then led me back to the temple, and since the day was now more than half over he placed me at the feet of the goddess herself; then, after confiding certain secret orders to me, those which were too holy to be spoken, he openly, before all who were present, bade me for ten successive days to abstain from all pleasures of the table, to eat no meat and drink no wine. All these requirements I observed with scrupulous care. And at last came the day designated by the divine guarantee. The sun was sloping downward and bringing on the evening when lo! from everywhere came crowds of the initi-

ates, flocking around me, and each of them, following the ancient rite, presented me with various gifts. Finally, all the uninitiated having withdrawn, they put on me a new linen robe, and the priest, seizing me by the hand, led me to the very inmost recesses of the holy place.

It may be, my studious reader, that you would very much like to know what was said there and what was done. I would tell you if it were lawful for me to tell, and you would know all if it were lawful for you to hear. But both tongue and ear would be infected as the consequence of such rash curiosity! Yet it may of course be a pious longing that torments you, and so I will torture you no longer. Hear then and believe, for what I tell you is true. I drew near to the confines of death, treading the very threshold of Proserpine.[2] I was borne through all the elements and returned to earth again. At the dead of night, I saw the sun shining brightly. I approached the gods above and the gods below, and worshiped them face to face. See, I have told you things which, though you have heard them, you still must know nothing about. I will therefore relate only as much as may, without committing a sin, be imparted to the understanding of the uninitiate.

(24) As soon as it was morning and the solemn rites had been completed, I came forth clothed in the twelve gowns that are worn by the initiate, apparel that is really most holy, but about which no sacred ban forbids me to tell, since at that time there were many who saw me wearing it. For in the very midst of the holy shrine, before the image of the goddess, there was a wooden platform on which I was directed to stand, arrayed in a robe which although it was only of linen, was so richly embroidered that I was a sight to behold. The precious cape hung from my shoulders down my back even to the ground, and it was adorned, wherever you looked, with the figures of animals in various colors. Here were Indian dragons, there griffins from the Hyperborean regions, winged like birds, but out of another

world. This cape the initiates call the Olympian. In my right hand I carried a flaming torch, and my head was decorated with a crown made of white palm leaves, spread out to stand up like rays. After I had been thus adorned like the sun and set up like an image of a god, the curtains were suddenly withdrawn, and the people crowded around to gaze at me.

Thereafter I celebrated this most joyful birthday of my initiation, and there were feasts and gay parties. The third day was likewise celebrated with formal ceremonies, with a solemn breaking of my fast, and the due consummation of my initiation. I remained a few days longer, enjoying the ineffable delight of being near the image of the goddess, to whom I was now pledged by blessings which I could never repay. But at length being admonished by the goddess, I offered up my humble thanks—not indeed in the full measure of my debt to her, but to the best of my poor abilities—and made a tardy preparation for my homeward journey; but it was hard to break the bonds of burning desire that held me back. At last I entered into the presence of the goddess and prostrated myself before her; and after I had for a long time wiped her feet with my face, I spoke, though there were tears in my eyes and my voice was so broken with sobs that my words were swallowed up:

(25) "O holy and eternal guardian of the human race, who dost always cherish mortals and bless them, thou carest for the woes of miserable men with a sweet mother's love. Neither day nor night, nor any moment of time, ever passes by without thy blessings, but always on land and sea thou watchest over men; thou drivest away from them the tempests of life and stretchest out over them thy saving right hand, wherewith thou dost unweave even the inextricable skein of the Fates; the tempests of Fortune thou dost assuage and restrainest the baleful motions of the stars. Thee the gods above adore, thee the gods below worship. It is thou that whirlest the sphere of heaven, that givest light to the sun, that governest the uni-

verse and tramplest down Tartarus.[3] To thee the stars respond, for thee the seasons return, in thee the gods rejoice, and the elements serve thee. At thy nod the winds blow, the clouds nourish [the earth], the seeds sprout, and the buds swell. Before thy majesty the birds tremble as they flit to and fro in the sky, and the beasts as they roam the mountains, the serpents hiding in the ground, and the monsters swimming in the deep. But my skill is too slight to tell thy praise, my wealth too slender to make thee due offerings of sacrifice. Nor has my voice that rich eloquence to say what I feel would suffice for thy majesty—no, not even had I a thousand mouths, a thousand tongues, and could continue forever with unwearied speech!

Therefore the only thing one can do, if one is devout but otherwise a pauper, that I will strive to do. Thy face divine and thy most holy deity—these I will hide away deep within my heart; thine image I shall treasure forever!"

Having thus pleaded with the mighty deity, I embraced Mithras the priest, now my spiritual father, and hanging upon his neck with many a kiss I begged his forgiveness, since I could make no proper return for all the great benefits that he had conferred upon me. (26) Then, after many words of thanks, long drawn out, I finally set out for home by the shortest route . . . a few days later, led on by the mighty goddess, I reached Rome on the eve of the ides of December.

NOTES

[1] Isis claims to be the universal mother goddess worshipped in all lands under these various titles and forms.

[2] The daughter of Zeus and Demeter who was abducted by Pluto and taken to Hades where she became queen of the underworld.

[3] The lowest region of Hades.

CICERO: *LAWS* (ANCIENT ROMAN RELIGION)

During the Hellenistic period religious and philosophical ideas traveled widely, and the ancient city-state religions were influenced by the outlook of the various Greek philosophies and the religious traditions of other areas. The development of Roman religion offers a good illustration of the changes an ancient religious tradition underwent in the Hellenistic period. In its most ancient form the old Roman religion was simply a very conservative system of religious observances centered around the family home and farm; it had no myth, theology, statues of the gods or temples. Rather, the Roman religious spirit was based on the experience of the numinous, an impersonal sense of a will or force in the universe which is viewed as alive with the power of the divine. The following excerpt from one of Seneca's (c. 4 B.C.E.-65 C.E.) letters illustrates this sense of the numinous.

When you find yourself within a grove of exceptionally tall, old trees, whose interlocking boughs mysteriously shut out the view of the sky, the great height of the forest and the secrecy of the place together with a sense of awe before the dense impenetrable shades will awaken in you the belief in a god. And when a grotto has been hewn into the hollowed rock of a mountain, not by human hands but by the powers of nature, and to great depth, it pervades your soul with an awesome sense of the religious. We honor the sources of great rivers. Altars are raised where the sudden freshet of a stream breaks from below ground. Hot springs of steaming water inspire veneration. And many a pond has been sanctified because of its hidden situation or immeasurable depth.[1]

In ancient Rome the home was considered sacred because of the presence of numerous *numina*. The father, *pater familias* embodied the *genius* or procreating power of the family and was the celebrant of the rites at the altar in the family home. The conceiving and nurturing power of the mother was her *juno*. The cult in the home honored the ancestors (*manes*) and the general dead (*parentes*) in reverence for the mystery of the family's continuity in time. There were *nunima* for the various parts of the home: the *penates* for the larder, the *lares* for the household effects. Vesta was the goddess who guarded the family hearth; Janus was the god of the doorway; Terminus was the boundary mark for the fields. During this early stage of Roman religion there were also numerous agricultural festivals associated with seedtime and harvest: the Saturnalia, Vinalia, Consualia, and Opiconsivia.

At this early stage certain *numina* had a more substantial character and became gods of the state. They were destined to be identified with the gods of the Greeks when Roman poets borrowed Greek mythology to write Roman epics and myths. These included Jupiter, the god of the heavens and storm who was identified with Zeus; Mars, the war and agricultural god, assimilated to Ares; Neptune, the god of waters, who was associated with Poseidon. Among the female deities, Ceres the goddess of grain was identified with Demeter; Venus with Aphrodite; and Juno with Hera.

During the period from the founding of the Roman Republic (509 B.C.E.) to the establishment of Augustus' principate (27 B.C.E. to 14 C.E.), Roman religion developed into a public state religion and, like most other ancient religions in the Mediterranean world, was subject to syncretism. It was influenced by the Etruscans who built temples and were experts in interpreting natural prodigies, by the mystery religions of the East, and especially by the mythology and philosophy of the Greeks whom the Romans conquered militarily, but who in turn conquered the Romans intellectually with their literature and philosophy. By the time of Cicero (106–43 B.C.E.) and Virgil (70–19 B.C.E.), two of our best sources for Roman religious thought, the old Roman agricultural and family and state religion had been inseparably assimilated with Greek mythology and philosophy. However, with some care we can still discern the spirit of the old Roman religion in their works. A fine source book on ancient Roman religion is Frederick C. Grant's **Ancient Roman Religion** (Indianapolis: The Liberal Arts Press, 1957)

Our first selection is from Cicero's **De Legibus (Laws).** It reflects the religious outlook of a noble Roman in the late Republican period; Cicero began the work in 52 B.C.E., and it was published posthumously in 43 B.C.E. In the following section he is outlining, in a Platonic fashion, a code of religious practices for an ideal state. In this summary we find the characteristic Roman emphases on the gods of the fatherland (*patria*) and on piety (*pietas*), proper devotion to the gods and the rites of the family and the ancestors. Cicero mentions important ancient Roman deities like the *Lares,* the tutelary deities of the household, and Quirinus, the name given Romulus, the son of Mars and the founder of

Rome, who was deified by the Romans. He also includes in his ideal state the elaborate Roman organization of pontiffs and *flamens,* priests, as well as the Vestal Virgins who guarded the eternal fire of the goddess Vesta on the public hearth of the city. The importance of omens and augury and the interpretation of prodigies and portents by the Etruscan soothsayers reflects the early influence of Etruscan customs on Roman religion and the obsession of Cicero's age with the question of fate.

Cicero, who was a conservative Republican Roman, shows a certain openness to outside cults, but, on the whole, reflects the more traditional Roman attitude which looked on these with suspicion. He allows the worship of the Greek hero-gods like Hercules, Aesculapius, Castor and Pollux whose merits admitted them to heaven, but he forbids all initiation into mystery cults with the exception of the Eleusian mysteries, i.e., Greek rites of Ceres, the Roman goddess of grain who was identified with Demeter. He also seems to allow the cult of Cybele, the Phrygian mother goddess whose cult and sacred stone was introduced into Rome in the 204 B.C.E. in an effort to turn the tide of the Second Punic War in Rome's favor.

The selection also illustrates the close tie between traditional Roman morality and religion. Cicero wants shrines to the qualities through which one gains access to heaven: Intellect, Virtue, Piety, Good Faith. He also includes severe punishments for sacrilege, perjury, incest, and the violation of vows.

Although Cicero himself was an eclectic who was heavily influenced by various forms of Greek philosophy, his account of the body of religious laws in **De Legibus** provides a good source for Roman religious thought and practice in the late Republican period.

The translation is by Clinton Walker Keyes, **Cicero: De Re Publica, De Legibus,** Vol XVI in The Loeb Classical Library (Cambridge, Mass., Harvard University Press, 1928) 393–399.

Laws

They shall approach the gods in purity, bringing piety, and leaving riches behind. Whoever shall do otherwise, God Himself will deal out punishment to him.

No one shall have gods to himself, either new gods or alien gods, unless recognized by the State. Privately they shall worship those gods whose worship they have duly received from their ancestors.

In cities they shall have shrines; they shall have groves in the country and homes for the Lares.[2]

They shall preserve the rites of their families and their ancestors.

They shall worship as gods both those who have always been regarded as dwellers in heaven, and also those whose merits have admitted them to heaven; Hercules,[3] Liber,[4] Aesculapius,[5] Castor, Pollux,[6] Quirinus;[7] also those qualities through which an ascent to heaven is granted to mankind: Intellect, Virtue, Piety, Good Faith. To their praise there shall be shrines, but none for the vices.

They shall perform the established rites.

On holidays they shall refrain from lawsuits; these they shall celebrate together with their slaves after their tasks are done. Let holidays be so arranged as to fall at regularly recurring breaks in the year. The priest shall offer on behalf of the State the prescribed grains and the prescribed fruits; this shall be done according to prescribed rites and on prescribed days; likewise for other days they shall reserve the plenteous offerings of the milk and the offspring.[8] And so that no violation of these customs shall take place, the priest shall determine the mode and the annual circuit of such offerings; and they shall prescribe the victims which are proper and pleasing to each of the gods.

The several gods shall have their several priests, the gods all together their pontiffs, and the individual gods their flamens. The Vestal Virgins shall guard the eternal fire on the public hearth of the city.

Those who are ignorant as to the methods and rites suitable to these public and private sacrifices shall seek instruction from the public priests. Of them there shall be three kinds: one to have charge of ceremonies and sacred rites; another to interpret those obscure sayings of soothsayers and prophets which shall be recognized by the Senate and the people; and interpreters of Jupiter the Best and Greatest, namely the public augurs, shall foretell the future from portents and auspices, and maintain their art. And the priests shall observe the omens in regard to vineyards and orchards and the safety of the people; those who carry on war or affairs of State shall be informed by them beforehand of the auspices and shall obey them; the priests shall foresee the wrath of the gods and yield to it; they shall observe flashes of lightning in fixed regions of the sky,[9] and shall keep free and unobstructed the city and fields and their places of observation. Whatever an augur shall declare to be unjust, unholy, pernicious, or ill-omened, shall be null and void; and whosoever yields not obedience shall be put to death.

IX. The fetial priests shall be judges and messengers for treaties, peace and war, truces, and embassies; they shall make the decisions in regard to war.

Prodigies and portents shall be referred to the Etruscan soothsayers, if the Senate so decree; Etruria shall instruct her leading men in this art. They shall make expiatory offerings to whatever gods they decide upon, and shall perform expiations for flashes of lightning and for whatever shall be struck by lightning.

No sacrifies shall be performed by women at night except those offered for the people in proper form;[10] nor shall anyone be initiated except into the Greek rites of Ceres,[11] according to the custom.

Sacrilege which cannot be expiated shall be held to be impiously committed; that which can be expiated shall be atoned for by the public priests.

At the public games which are held without chariot races or the contest of body with body,[12] the public pleasure shall be provided for with moderation by song to the music of harp and lute, and this shall be combined with honour to the gods.

Of the ancestral rites the best shall be preserved.

No one shall ask for contributions except the servants of the Idean Mother,[13] and they only on the appointed days.

Whoever steals or carries off what is sacred or anything entrusted to what is sacred shall be considered as equal in guilt to a parricide.

For the perjurer the punishment from the gods is destruction; the human punishment shall be disgrace.

The pontiffs shall inflict capital punishment on those guilty of incest.

No wicked man shall dare to appease the wrath of the gods with gifts.

Vows shall be scrupulously performed; there shall be a penalty for the violation of the law.

No one shall consecrate a field; the consecration of gold, silver, and ivory shall be confined to reasonable limits.

The sacred rites of families shall remain for ever.

The rights of the gods of the lower world shall be sacred. Kinsfolk who are dead shall be considered gods; the expenditure and mourning for them shall be limited.

NOTES

[1]Seneca, Epistle 41:3.

[2]Minor household deities that presided over household and family.

[3]The son of Zeus and Alcmena who was renowned for feats of strength, particuarly the Twelve Labors.

[4]Another name for Bacchus, the Roman name for Dionysus, the god of wine and the son of Zeus and Semele, the daughter of Cadmus.

[5]The son of Apollo by Coronis. He was the physician to the Argonauts and restored many to life. He became the god of healing and medicine.

[6]Twin brothers, sons of Leda by Zeus. Castor became an excellent horseman; Pollux became an expert boxer. Both brothers joined the Argonauts and were in the Calydonian boar hunt. When they died they were placed in heaven as Gemini (Twins), a constellation which became the third sign of the zodiac.

[7]A name given Romulus when he became a minor god of war.

[8]Milk, wine and honey were offered to Ceres, the Roman goddess of grain and the equivalent of the Greek Demeter. "Offspring" refers to the offspring of the flocks.

[9]The Etruscans divided the sky into sixteen regions for this purpose.

[10]The solemn rites of Bona Dea, from which men were strictly excluded.

[11]Evidently the Eleusian mysteries as practiced at Rome.

[12]Athletic contests.

[13]Cybele, whose worship was introduced during the Punic Wars in 204 B.C.E. The Ludi Megalensis were held in her honor, but Roman citizens were not allowed to enter her priesthood.

CICERO: "THE DREAM OF SCIPIO" IN
ON THE REPUBLIC (THE HELLENIZATION OF ROMAN RELIGION)

An excellent example of how traditional Roman religious views were influenced by the thought of Greek philosophy and science is Cicero's "Dream of Scipio," the concluding vision of his **On the Republic** written in imitation of Plato's **Republic** which also ended with the myth of Er who returned from the dead and described the fate of the souls in the afterlife. In the work as a whole Cicero does not construct an ideal city on the philosophical principles of justice as Plato did. Instead, in characteristic Roman fashion, he describes the birth, growth and development of the Roman Republic. His concluding vision is meant to instill in readers a dedication to the *patria,* the fatherland, as the highest of virtues.

The youth he selected to be the subject of his work was Scipio Africanus the Younger (185–129 B.C.E.) who sees his grandfather, Scipio Africanus the Elder (237–183 B.C.E.), in a vision. The Elder Africanus had immortalized himself for the Roman people by invading Africa and defeating Hannibal in the Second Punic War. Now he reveals to his grandson his own future destiny as a soldier and statesman, and, in the process, he gives a new spiritual view of the universe and humanity's place in it.

Cicero had studied philosophy at Athens, and he makes liberal use of various Greek philosophical and scientific notions in an eclectic fashion. The cosmology he uses is no longer that found in the ancient cosmological myths in which the earth was a flat disk, surrounded by a cosmic sea. His view of the universe is taken from Hellenistic science which pictured the cosmos as a series of concentric spheres. The earth is the ninth, innermost sphere. It is motionless and stationary in the center of the universe. This view will be later systematized by Ptolemy. Cicero was also influenced by the number theory of the Pythagoreans; the other eight spheres move and produce the "music of the spheres" which is imitated by "learned men" in their harmonies on stringed instruments and in song.

Cicero was aware of the physical magnitude of the world with its various temperate zones, opposite poles, and great seas. And, surprisingly for a patriotic Roman, he pictures the smallness of the proud Roman empire of the Republic within the vast reaches of the cosmos. Yet, while affirming this new scientific view of the universe, Cicero can use a combination of Stoical and Platonic philosophical ideas to give continued emphasis to the Roman virtues of dedication to family and fatherland. Cicero borrows the Platonic and Orphic-Pythagorean idea of the soul imprisoned in a body as a tomb, but he does not make it a basis for fleeing from this world and the responsibilities of history. Rather, as a good Stoical Roman, Cicero emphasizes obedient commitment to responsibility for caring for the earth. He has the Younger Scipio ask his father Paulus why he cannot immediately hasten to the heavenly realm. The father answers:

> "Unless that God whose temple is the whole visible universe releases you from the prison of the body, you cannot gain entrance here. For men were given life for the purpose of cultivating that globe, called earth, which you see at the center of this temple. Each has been given a soul, [a spark] from those eternal fires which you call stars and planets, which are globular and rotund and are animated by divine intelligences, and which with marvelous velocity revolve in their established orbits. Like all god-fearing men, therefore, Publius, you must leave the soul in the custody of the body, and must not quit the life on Earth unless you are summoned by the one who gave it to you; otherwise you will be seen to shirk the duty assigned by God to man."

For Cicero, the noblest of pursuits for the immortal soul is service to the country. The Elder Africanus concludes by telling his grandson:

> "Exercise it (the soul), therefore, in the noblest pursuits! The best occupations concern the welfare of your country. A spirit exercised and trained in such patriotic activities will fly the more swiftly to this its true home and habitation . . . "

The translation is by Frederick C. Grant, **Ancient Roman Religion** (Indianapolis: The Liberal Arts Press, 1957) 147–156.

The Dream of Scipio

[Scipio is speaking:] "When I went to Africa on the staff of the consul Manius Manilius with the rank, as you know, of military tribune of the Fourth Legion [i.e., in 149 B.C., at the beginning of the third Punic War], my strongest desire was to meet King Masinissa, who for very good reason was a devoted friend of our family. When I entered the king's presence, that grand old man threw his arms around me and wept freely. After a little time he looked up to heaven and said, 'I give thee thanks, O Sun supreme, and you also, ye other heavenly beings, that before I depart this life I see within my kingdom and under my roof Publius Cornelius Scipio, the very sound of whose name refreshes me—so little can I forget that noble and invincible man!' [I.e., Scipio Africanus the Elder, Scipio's grandfather.]

"I then questioned him about his kingdom, while he in turn inquired about our Republic; thus we spent the whole day in conversation. (10) After we had been entertained with royal hospitality, we continued our conversation until late in the night, the old king talking of nothing but Africanus, and recalling not only his every deed but also all his words. At last we parted for the night, and as I was tired from my journey, and also had sat up late, I fell at once into a much sounder sleep than usual. Then the following dream came to me, suggested no doubt by the subject of our conversation. For it often happens that our thoughts and words affect us during sleep somewhat in the way that Ennius[1] records with reference to [the vision of] Homer, about whom, as you know, he was constantly thinking and speaking during his waking hours. In my case, Africanus appeared to me in the form with which I was familiar from his bust, rather than from my personal recollection. When I recognized him, I trembled with terror, but he said, 'Courage, Scipio; do not be afraid, but remember carefully what I am about to tell you.

(11) " 'Can you see that city yonder, which I forced to obey the Roman people, but which is now renewing its old hostility and cannot be at rest?' (He was pointing to Carthage, from a high starlit place, bathed in light.) 'That city,' he continued, 'you, now scarcely more than a common soldier, have come to lay siege to; but within two years, you, a consul, will lay it level with the ground. The surname [Africanus] to which you are now only an heir will then be your own through personal achievement. After destroying Carthage you will celebrate a triumph; then you will be censor, and will go on embassies to Egypt, Syria, Asia, and Greece. Finally, though absent from Rome, you will be elected consul for a second time and by the destruction of Numantia[2] you will bring a great war to a close. However, after your triumphal entry into the Capitol you will find the Republic disturbed as the result of the schemes of my grandson [Tiberius Gracchus].[3] (12) At that critical moment, Africanus, you must show forth in the service of your fatherland the light of your spirit, your abilities, your wise counsel.

" 'Nevertheless, at that time, I see, two paths of destiny will confront you. For when your age has reached eight times seven solar circuits [i.e., 8×7 years], and when in the course of nature these two numbers—each of which is perfect, though for different reasons—have combined to produce the sum [= 56] so big with fate for you, then the whole State will turn to you and to your name alone. The Senate, all good citizens, the allies, the Latin peoples, will all look to you. You will be the only one who can save the nation. In a word, it will be your duty as dictator to restore order to the commonwealth—provided you escape the wicked hands of your kinsmen [the Gracchi].' "

(At this Laelius cried aloud, and the others uttered deep groans. But Scipio smiled gently and said: "Shhh! I beg you, do not wake me from sleep, but listen for a little while and hear the rest.")

(13) " 'However, Africanus, in order to encourage you in your endeavors to safeguard the State, consider this: all those who have preserved, aided, or extended their fatherland have a special place assigned to them in heaven where they may enjoy an eternal life of happiness. For nothing done on earth more greatly pleases the supreme deity who rules the entire universe than assemblies or communities of men bound together by justice, which are called states. Their rulers and preservers go forth from here, and hither they return.'

(14) "By this time I was thoroughly ter-

rified, not so much fearing death as the treachery of my own kin. Nevertheless, I [went on and] inquired of Africanus whether he himself was still alive, and also whether my father Paulus was, and also the others whom we think of as having ceased to be.

" 'Of course they are alive,' he replied: 'They have taken their flight from the bonds of the body as from a prison. Your so-called life [on earth] is really death. Do you not see your father Paulus coming to meet you?'

"At the sight of my father I broke down and cried. But he embraced me and kissed me and told me not to weep. (15) As soon as I had controlled my grief and could speak, I began: 'Why, O best and saintliest of fathers, since here [only] is life worthy of the name, as I have just heard from Africanus, why must I live a dying life on earth? Why may I not hasten to join you here?'

" 'No indeed,' he replied. 'Unless that God whose temple is the whole visible universe releases you from the prison of the body, you cannot gain entrance here. For men were given life for the purpose of cultivating that globe, called Earth, which you see at the center of this temple. Each has been given a soul, [a spark] from those eternal fires which you call stars and planets, which are globular and rotund and are animated by divine intelligences, and which with marvelous velocity revolved in their established orbits. Like all god-fearing men, therefore, Publius, you must leave the soul in the custody of the body, and must not quit the life on Earth unless you are summoned by the one who gave it to you; otherwise you will be seen to shirk the duty assigned by God to man.

(16) " 'But, Scipio, like your grandfather here, like myself, who was your father, cultivate justice and the sense of duty (*pietas*), which are of great importance in relation to parents and kindred but even more in relation to one's country. Such a life [spent in the service of one's country] is a highway to the skies, to the fellowship of those who have completed their earthly lives and have been released from

the body and now dwell in that place which you see yonder' (it was the circle of dazzling brilliance which blazed among the stars), 'which you, using a term borrowed from the Greeks, call the Milky Way.'

"Looking about from this high vantage point, everything appeared to me to be marvelous and beautiful. There were stars which we never see from the earth, and the dimensions of all of them were greater than we have ever suspected. The smallest among them was one which, being farthest from Heaven and nearest the Earth, shone with a borrowed light [the Moon]. The size of the stars, however, far exceeded that of the Earth. Indeed, the latter seemed so small that I was humiliated with our empire, which is only a point where we touch the surface of the globe.

(17) "As I gazed still more intently at the Earth, Africanus said: 'How long, I wonder, will your mind continue to be fastened to the soil? Do you not see what a temple you have entered? Here are the nine circles, or rather spheres, by which all things are held together. One of these, the outermost, is Heaven, which contains within it all the rest, and is itself the supreme deity, embracing all, enclosing all. Within it are fastened those [spheres] that revolve, the everlasting courses of the stars. Beneath it are seven spheres revolving the other way, in the direction opposite to that of Heaven. One sphere is occupied by that star which on earth they call Saturn. Next comes that of the bright light called Jupiter, bringing prosperity and health to mankind. Then there is one which you call Mars, of reddish hue and horrifying to the lands of men. Farther down, nearly midway between Heaven and Earth, is the region ruled by the Sun, who is the leader, prince, and governor of the other lights, the mind of the universe and its guiding principle, of such magnitude that he illumines and fills all things with his light. He is followed by two companions, so to speak, Venus and Mercury, in their courses. In the lowest sphere revolves the Moon, lighted up by the rays of the Sun.

But below the Moon there is nothing but what is mortal and doomed to decay, except souls which are given by the gods to the human race. Above the Moon all things are eternal. The earth, which is the ninth and central sphere, does not rotate, being at the lowest point of all; toward it all things are drawn by reason of their weight.'

(18) "When I had recovered from my astonishment over this great panorama, and had come to myself, I asked: 'Tell me, what is this loud, sweet harmony that fills my ears?'

"He replied, 'This is the music produced by the impulse and motion of these spheres themselves. The unequal intervals between them are arranged according to a strict proportion, and so the high notes blend agreeably with the low, and thus various sweet harmonies are produced. Such immense revolutions cannot, of course, be so swiftly carried out in silence, and it is only natural that one extreme should produce deep tones and the other high ones. Accordingly, this highest sphere of Heaven, which bears the stars, and whose revolution is swifter, produces a high shrill sound, whereas the lowest sphere, that of the Moon, rotates with the deepest sound. The Earth, of course, the ninth sphere, remains fixed and immovable in the center of the universe. But the other eight spheres, two of which move with the same speed, produce seven different sounds—a number, by the way, which is the key to almost everything. Skillful men reproducing this celestial music on stringed instruments have thus opened the way for their own return to this heavenly region, as other men of outstanding genius have done by spending their lives on Earth in the study of things divine.

(19) " 'Men's ears, being always filled with this music, have grown deaf to it. For it is a fact that none of your senses is so dull as that of hearing. Thus in the neighborhood of Catadupa, where the Nile comes rushing down [in a cataract] from high mountains, the people that live there have lost their sense of hearing as a result of the deafening noise. But this mighty

music of the spheres, produced by the swift speed with which the whole universe spins round, is so overwhelming that no human ear can sense it, any more than you can look straight at the sun, whose rays would overpower the keenness of your sight.'

"While I marveled at this explanation, I still kept turning my eyes back in the direction of the Earth. (20) Then Africanus went on: 'I see that you are still looking in the direction of the home and dwelling place of man! If the Earth appears small to you, as it really is, then keep your gaze fixed upon these heavenly things, and disregard the human and earthly. For how can you achieve fame merely from the lips of men, or how can you gain real glory? You see that the Earth is inhabited only sparsely and in limited areas, and that vast stretches of wilderness lie between these scattered patches, as we may call them, which are inhabited. Moreover, the inhabitants of the Earth are so widely separated that no communication is possible between the different groups. Some live in a different zone [i.e., northern or southern] from you, others live under different meridians, while still others are at your antipodes. Surely, you cannot expect any glory from them!

(21) " 'The Earth, you will further notice, is girdled about with something like belts. Two of these zones, which are in entirely opposite parts of the Earth and which at either end lie directly under the celestial poles, are buried, as you see, under ice and snow; while the middle zone, which is also the widest, scorches under the heat of the sun. There remain only two zones that are habitable; of these the southern, whose inhabitants set their footsteps in an opposite direction to yours, is cut off from all communication with your zone; the other zone, the northern, which you inhabit—see how small a territory belongs to you [i.e., the Romans]. In fact, the whole region inhabited by you is only a small island, narrow from south to north, though wider from west to east, and surrounded by that sea which on Earth you call

the Atlantic, the Great Sea, or ocean—but you can see how small it is in spite of its great name!

(22) " 'Now, do you suppose that from these lands that are known and settled, your name or that of any of us could ever cross over this Caucasus which you see, or swim across yonder Ganges? Who among the dwellers in the rest of the Orient or Occident, or in the farther North or South, will ever hear of your name? Leave these out of account, and you will certainly realize what a limited area it is over which your glory is so eager to spread!

" 'Moreover, those who actually do speak of us—how long will they keep on doing so? (23) And even if the generations to come were willing to transmit to their descendants the fame of each and every one of us as they had received it from their sires, still we can acquire no glory for any length of time much less for ever, because of the floods and conflagrations of the earth, which necessarily recur at state times.

" 'Besides, what does it really matter if you are going to be talked about by generations who are still unborn, when you have not been mentioned by those who lived before you? (24) Yet the men of the past were not fewer in numbers and they were certainly better men. Furthermore, at the very best not one of those who do hear our names can for even the space of a year retain the memory of us.

" 'People ordinarily measure the length of a year by the complete revolution of the sun, that is, of a single star. But when all the stars have returned to their starting points and have restored, after long periods, the original configuration of the entire heavens, then that can truly be called a revolving year [i.e., the "great year" of Plato]. I hardly venture to say how many generations of men are contained within it. As once upon a time the Sun appeared to men to suffer total eclipse when the soul of Romulus entered this region, so, when the Sun undergoes another eclipse in the same part of the heavens and on the same date, then you may assume that all the stars and constella-

tions will have returned to their original positions and that a [great] year has elapsed. But you may be sure that thus far not a twentieth part has yet elapsed.

(25) " 'Consequently, if you despair of ever returning to this place, which is the reward of great and eminent men, how slight, I ask, must be your fame on Earth if it endures for only a fraction of a single year? Therefore, look up on high and contemplate this, your eternal home and dwelling place, and pay no attention to the foolish talk of the vulgar herd nor set your hope on human reward for your great deeds. Virtue herself, by her own charms, ought to lead you on to true glory. What others say of you is their own concern—they will see to it, and whatever it is they will talk anyway. But all their talk is limited to those narrow regions which you now look upon, nor will any man's fame last forever, since what men say dies with them and is extinguished in the silence of posterity.'

(26) "When he had finished speaking, I replied, 'Yes, dear Africanus, though from my boyhood up I have walked in my father's footsteps and in yours, and have never lacked in honor, still if such a pathway to Heaven lies open to those who have served their country faithfully, I am determined to redouble my efforts, spurred by the prospect of so splendid a reward.'

" 'Yes, you must use your best efforts,' he replied, 'and be sure that it is not **you** who are mortal, but only your body; nor is it **you** whom your outward form represents. Your spirit is your true self, not that bodily form which can be pointed to with the finger. Know yourself, therefore, to be a god—if indeed a god is a being that lives, feels, remembers, and foresees, that rules, governs, and moves the body over which it is set, just as the supreme God above us rules this world. And just as that eternal God moves the universe, which is partly mortal, so an eternal spirit moves the fragile body.

(27) " **That which is always in motion is eternal.** But, on the other hand, that which

imparts motion to something else, but is itself set in motion by some external force, must cease to exist when its motion ceases. Consequently, that alone never ceases to move which moves by its own inherent power, since it never abandons itself. Nay, it is itself the source and first cause of motion for all other things that move. But this first cause has no beginning, since all things spring from the first cause, while it itself cannot originate from any other: that would not be a first cause which derived its origin from something else. And since it never has had a beginning, it can never come to an end. For if a first cause were once extinct, it could never begin again from anything else, nor could it bring anything else into existence, since everything has to originate from a first cause. Hence it follows that motion begins with that which is moved by itself. But this can neither be born nor die: otherwise, the whole structure of the heavens would fall and all nature would perish and never revive, since it possesses no power from which to derive the first impulse to motion.

(28) " 'Since it is evident, then, that that is eternal which moves of itself, who can deny that this is the nature of the spirit? For whatever is moved by an external force is lifeless; whereas whatever is animate moves by its own inner power, for that is the proper nature of the soul and its power. And as the spirit is the only force that moves itself, it surely has never had a beginning and is also eternal.

(29) " 'Exercise it, therefore, in the noblest pursuits! The best occupations concern the welfare of your country. A spirit exercised and trained in such patriotic activities will fly the more swiftly to this its true home and habitation. Its flight will be even swifter if, while yet an inmate of the body, it looks without and by contemplation of the world outside frees itself as much as possible from the body. The souls of those who are given to sensual pleasures, and are, so to speak, its slaves, who follow their desire in a life devoted to pleasure, and violate the laws of gods and men—such souls, after leaving their bodies, still fly about close to the earth, and do not return to this place until after many centuries of torment.'

"Africanus departed, and I awoke from sleep."

NOTES

[1]Ennius was a Roman epic poet.

[3]Numantia was a city in northern Spain which the Romans destroyed in 134 B.C.E.

[3]Tiberius Gracchus was a populist Roman leader from a noble family who attempted a land reform without going through the traditional channels of Senate approval. He and three hundred of his followers were assassinated by members of the senatorial class and their clients in 133 B.C.E.

VIRGIL, *THE AENEID*

The poet who gave Rome a national epic of the stature of Homer's **Iliad** and **Odyssey** was Virgil (70–19 B.C.E.). In contrast to Homer's "primary" epics which represent the culmination of a long oral tradition, Virgil's is a "secondary" or literary epic which, like other Hellenistic epics, fuses the Greek epic tradition with elements of romance, tragedy, philosophy, and history.

Unlike Homer who came at the beginning of the Greek literary tradition and stabilized and shaped Greek religion and heroic values well into the classical age, Virgil wrote **The Aeneid** late in Roman history (30–19 B.C.E.), during the Augustan Age, in order to create a Roman epic on the basis of the Greek epic tradition and to inspire Romans with a sense of rededication to traditional Roman religious values and a sense of their national destiny as rulers of the Mediterranean world. When Virgil composed **The Aeneid,** Rome was war weary and burdened with guilt from over a century of civil war and violence which had shaken the constitutional foundations of the old Republic and threatened the old Roman virtues of *pietas,* dedication to the family, the gods, and the state, and *gravitas,* a sense of seriousness of purpose.

As early as the second half of the second century B.C.E., the pressures of a Republic trying to govern an empire had resulted in populist leaders like the Gracchi brothers, Tiberius and Gaius (133–121), violating the Republic's constitution. With their violent deaths at the instigation of the conservative senatorial class, Rome was thrown into a century of civil war and chaos in which ambitious generals like Marius (157–86 B.C.E.) and Sulla (138–78 B.C.E.), and later Pompey (106–48 B.C.E.) and Julius Caesar (100–44 B.C.E.), used their armies to gain personal political power. With Octavian's victory over Marc Antony in the Battle of Actium (31 B.C.E.) and the beginning of his religious and political reforms, Virgil sensed that Rome through Augustus had the opportunity to recover its ancient greatness and govern the world in peace.

Virgil's hopes for Augustus are most clearly expressed in Anchises' words to his son Aeneas in the underworld:

> And this man, the man you've heard promised so often,
> is Caesar Augustus, a God's own son who will settle
> a Golden Age once more on Latium's meadows,
> ruled by Saturn before. He'll open the empire
> to India, Africa, lands lying beyond the ecliptic,
> beyond the sun's annual journey, where Atlas
> turns the sky's wheel on his back as it's burning with inlaid stars.

If Rome and Augustus were to succeed in issuing in a Golden Age, Virgil believed it would be through Rome's greatest "art": governing with magnanimity and firmness. Anchises concludes his words to Aeneas in the underworld:

> "Others may hammer bronze into delicate breathing
> and draw, I'm sure it's true, life-signs from marble;
> some plead causes better or track with a stylus
> paths in the sky to tell us what stars will be rising.
> But Romans, remember to rule people, to govern:
> there's your art: to make peace like a custom,
> to spare dependents and put down those who are pompous."

Virgil's theme, as the opening lines of the poem announce, is the founding of Rome by a Trojan exile who though "tossed on land and sea" and "suffering greatly in war" succeeded in founding a city and bringing to Latium his gods. Although Virgil has Aeneas go through an **Odyssesy** in Books I-VI in which he is "tossed on land and sea" and an **Iliad** in Books VII-XII in which he is "suffering greatly in war," he is not an individualistic hero, like Achilles or even Odysseus, but a communal hero who sacrifices self-fulfillment and suffers greatly for the good of his people and their destiny.

Significantly, Virgil does not mention Aeneas' name in the opening lines. In fact his name does not appear until almost a hundred lines into the poem when, in the midst of a terrifying storm sent by Juno, he prays to the stars and asks why he could not have perished with his fellow Trojans in the Fall of Troy. The chaos which Aeneas finds himself in at the beginning of the poem is reminiscent of the chaos in burning Troy which Aeneas describes so graphically in Book II and the chaos of civil war which Rome had experienced in the century before the Battle of Actium. Aeneas will be a model of how a suffering leader can move beyond individualistic aspirations and bring his people to a land where their future destiny lies. In this respect Aeneas is more like Moses, the Israelite hero in the exodus tradition, who with the Lord's help leads his people out of the slavery of Egypt, gives them the Lord's law to guide their lives, but himself dies outside the land of promise.

Early in the epic Aeneas' heroic struggle is to transcend the instinct for personal glory or fulfillment for the sake of his people's higher destiny to become a part of the Latin race. This is a struggle which is not easily won and it continues throughout the first six books of **The Aeneid,** as Aeneas repeatedly has to triumph in a Stoical fashion over emotional and individualistic instincts which would lead him away from his destiny.

In Aeneas' own account of the Fall of Troy in Book II, Virgil brilliantly illustrates how his hero is transformed from a maddened warrior whose instinct, much like Hector's in **The Iliad,** was to fight for personal glory in defending his doomed city. Despite the fact that the ghost of a mutilated Hector has appeared to Aeneas and told him to escape because Troy is doomed and he is entrusted with Troy's Household Gods and relics to be carried to a new city which he will found, Aeneas' first instinct, when he sees the burning of his beloved Troy, is to fight in defense of the city and for the sake of personal glory.

> "I grabbed madly at weapons—weapons were mindless—
> still my spirits burned for a fight, to gather a cordon
> of friends and rush the palace. Frenzy and anger
> drove me headlong. It seemed splendid to die in my
> armor."

Although he then meets Panthus, a priest of Apollo who has his grandson and household gods and tells him the city is doomed, Aeneas rushes into the fighting. Only after he has witnessed the horrifying death of Priam at the hands of Pyrrhus who slays the old king in his son's blood at the family altar, does Aeneas think of *his* family: his father Anchises, his wife Creusa, and his son Ascanius. Still, when he sees Helen huddled by the altar of Vesta, he is enflamed with the instinct to revenge, and it is only with the appearance of his mother Venus that he begins to accept his destined role by returning home to his family.

Venus' speech is a good illustration of how Virgil is able to adapt the traditional Homeric pantheon in their Roman guise for his purposes of speaking about Aeneas' need to conform himself in Stoical fashion to destiny. Venus herself is no longer the Aphrodite of Greek mythology who is the personification of emotional and erotic love, but is a protective mother who guides her son to accept his destiny. She chides him for his madness in seeking revenge by killing Helen, while forgetful of his family, and then she tells him that the Fall of Troy is not due to Helen or Paris, but is decreed by the gods who have overthrown it. She then removes the cloud from his mind and shows him how all the gods are conspiring in the destruction of Troy. Neptune is overturning the foundations of his own city with his trident; Juno is calling up her Greek troops from their ships; Pallas Athene is planted upon the citadel; and Jupiter is giving courage and strength to the Greeks.

With this new vision and Venus' protection, Aeneas returns to his home and, with the help of miraculous omens from the gods in connection with young Ascanius' destiny, is able to convince his crippled and elderly father Anchises to depart from Troy. The picture of the family's departure from burning Troy for the ancient shrine of Ceres outside the city is a classic illustration of Roman *pietas*: dedication to family, the Household Gods, and the state of Rome. Aeneas bears on his shoulders his crippled father who is carrying the Household Gods. Ascanius twines his fingers in Aeneas' hand, and Creusa follows behind. Aeneas literally bears his family's *genius* and Household Gods with him as he leads his son to his future destiny of founding Rome.

Virgil, ever sensitive to the "tears in things" and the painful cost of founding Rome, does not end the account of the Fall of Troy with the idyllic picture of the family departing from the burning city. Creusa is lost as they make their way out of Troy, and when Aeneas frantically returns to search for her, her ghost appears and chides him for his emotional attachment to her. Creusa's shade speaks of her own death as part of Jupiter's purpose which includes Aeneas' marriage to a royal bride in a "Western Land":

> "Why do you take much pleasure in mourning and madness,
> my sweet husband? Things happen according to
> Gods' wishes. Your taking Creusa from here as your comrade
> is not allowed or decreed by the high King of Olympus.
> A long exile is yours. You'll plow deserts of water.
> You'll come to a Western Land where the Lydian Tiber
> gently meanders through rich fields of Etruscans.
> A time of joy will be there, a realm and a queenly
> wife to be claimed. Resist tears for your darling Creusa."

In Book III Virgil has Aeneas tell the Carthaginians of his wanderings after leaving Troy in a way reminiscent of Odysseus' tale to the Phaeacians in **The Odyssey.** Although Aeneas has encounters that are modeled on those of Odysseus, a major difference in the two tales is that Aeneas is not striving to return to his home as Odysseus was. He is "unsure where the Fates would lead or allow us to settle" and has to learn his ultimate destination through omens and encounters with fellow Trojan exiles. In his agonizing search to discover where he is to found the "new" Troy, Aeneas is the model of a "conscientious" (*pius*) Roman who is obedient to the will of the gods as it is revealed to him. He and his people leave Thrace when he is warned about this "faithless" and "cursed land" by the voice of his murdered relative Polydorus. Aeneas and his people then attempt to settle in Crete because they had been told by the oracle of Apollo at Delos to "seek their ancient mother," but they are attacked by a plague. At this point Aeneas finally learns in a vision from his Household Gods that "Hesperia" or "Italy" is the original home of Dardanus, the ancestor of the Trojans, and is to be his destination. Finally, after being attacked by the Harpies, Aeneas lands on Epirus, where he meets Andromache and Helenus; the latter prophesies that Aeneas must make for Italy where he is to finally conciliate the wrathful Juno and consult the Sibyl at Cumae about the wars he must fight to gain a foreign bride.

The episode which most clearly illustrates Virgil's sensitivity to the cost of the heroism which Aeneas represents is the Dido affair. Virgil has expanded the Homeric epic tradition by making the Dido episode a romance and a tragedy within his epic. When Dido first appears in Book I, Virgil pictures her in a very favorable light. She has survived her own harrowing escape from Tyre and her wicked brother Pygmalion, and is now leading her people in building the city of Carthage. It is the kind of civilized city that the Romans would admire, with great buildings, city gates, walls, a citadel, a theater and the institutions of government—magistrates and a senate. Aeneas is tearfully aware that he is in a civilized place where he may dare to hope for salvation, because he sees in the temple of Juno a series of frescoes depicting the suffering in the Fall of Troy. When Dido herself first appears she is beautiful, but, more importantly, eager to forward the work and growth of her realm. When Aeneas' men first approach her, she is seated on a throne and giving equitable laws and ordinances, and she extends to them the gracious hospitality which Aeneas had been led to expect from seeing the mural of the Trojan War.

Like a tragic heroine, Dido is fated to fall from this position of controlled leadership and civilized hospitality to maddened and destructive self-pity and hatred. The mythological explanation for Dido's destruction is Venus' plan to outwit Juno by capturing Dido in a passionate love which will inevitably lead to her suicide. At the end of Book I Venus sends Cupid to Dido in the form of the young Iulus/Ascanius to make her fall in love with Aeneas. At the banquet which Dido has arranged for her guests, the love-god, disguised as Ascanius, jumps into her lap, "breathes his flame" into her and erases all memory of Sychaeus, her dead husband, to whom she had sworn lasting fidelity. By the time Aeneas has finished the story of his adventures at the beginning of Book IV, Dido is hopelessly stricken with the wound of love.

The consequences of her romance are disastrous for the city, Dido, and Aeneas' destiny. All work on the construction of Carthage stops, as Dido and Aeneas pursue their love affair. When our selection begins in Book IV, Aeneas has been instructed by Jupiter through Mercury that he must be mindful of his destiny and depart from Carthage. Dido's frantic reaction to the planned departure is both pathetic and understandable. She, like Medea in Euripides' play, has sacrificed all for this love affair: alliances with Numidians, Lybians and even with some of her own Tyrians. Her reputation has been ruined, and she does not even have a child, a "young Aeneas" as a memory of their love. In her maddened state, Aeneas' pleas that the decision to depart is not his wish, but the gods' decree, have no effect. Virgil's lengthy and sympathetic description of Dido's suicide, with its elements of black magic and curses forshadowing Aeneas own death and the hostilities between Carthage and Rome, show his sensitivity to the cost of Rome's policy of putting the destiny of the state over personal concerns and sympathy.

> "You Sun-God, whose fire regards and brightens all our labor,
> you, Juno, driving love's pain and remembering,
> Hecate, wailing nightly at the crossroads in cities,
> you vengeful Furies, Gods of dying Elissa:
> hear and accept my prayer, attend with your power—
> my pain has earned it. If sailing and reaching a harbour
> is necessary for this unspeakable person,
> if Jupiter's word demands that goal be accomplished,
> still let war convulse him and swords of presumputous people.
> Let him be torn from his own land and the face of Ascanius.
> Let him beg for help and witness the shameful
> deaths of friends. Let him yield to unfair terms in a peace-pact
> and never enjoy his rule or the sunlight he's longed for,
> but fall before his time on open gravel, unburied.
> There is my plea—the last word to be poured with my life-blood.
> And you Tyrians: pursue that whole tribe in the future
> and hate them. Send word of this favor down to my ashes:
> let there be no love or pact with these people.
> And rise from my bones, whatever revenger
> will follow Trojan settlers with torches and lances,
> now or whatever time gives you strength in the future.
> Let seas be against seas, shoreline at shoreline:
> I call on arms to fight with arms—their own and their children's."

Virgil is also quite aware of the personal cost to Aeneas for his commitment to destiny. In Book VI when Aeneas descends with the Sibyl of Cumae into the underworld to learn from his father Achises of the destiny of his son and the whole of Rome's glorious history, he meets Dido in the Fields of Mourning among those who had died because of the cruelties of love. Now he is the one who weeps and is overwhelmed with regret when he sees the consequences of his departure. He speaks to her "fondly and gently":

> "Unhappy Dido, the story that came was correct then.
> I heard you had died, pursued your death with a sword-thrust.
> And I—my God—I caused your death? I swear by the starlight,
> by Gods in the sky and faith in the earth's depths if there's any:
> I never wished, my queen, to go from your shoreline.
> Gods told me—just as they force me to travel
> now through Night's depths, through briars and shadows.

They drive me by their own rules. And how could I think that
leaving would bring such deep distress to your spirit?
Please don't go—don't walk from where I can see you—
Who do you run from? This is the last that the Fates let me tell you."

Despite Aeneas' pleading, Dido turns from him with her face hardened like "flint" and "hard Marpesian rockstands."

Virgil's capacity to see both sides of the greatness of Rome—its moral vigor and piety as well as the painful cost of total commitment to the state—makes him more than a simple propagandist, and ranks him as what Pierre Boyance has called "Rome's most fervent, but also most faithful interpreter."

The translation, original for this anthology, is by Edward McCrorie.

BOOK I: THE ARRIVAL IN CARTHAGE[1]

My song is of war and the first man from a Trojan
coast to arrive in Italy, forced by Fates[2] to Lavinian[3]
shores: Gods' powers repeatedly tossed him
on land and sea, Juno's[4] fierce and remembering anger
caused him to suffer greatly in war while founding a city,
bringing his Gods to Latium, leading to Latin people,
Alba's fathers, and high Rome's fortifications.[5]

Invocation of the Muse
Muse, tell me the reasons: what slight to her power,
what grief drove the Queen of the Gods to involve him—
a man so known for his reverence—in struggle and hardship
over and over? Can so much spite reside in a Goddess?

The anger of Juno
An old city, held by Tyrian settlers,
Carthage faced the far-off Italian Tiber's[6]
mouth: it was rich, resourceful, intent and fierce in a battle.
Juno they say loved this land more than all others,

preferred it even to Samos; keeping her weapons
and chariot here, the Goddess warmly strove from the outset
to make it a world kingdom—if only the Fates would allow it.
But now she'd heard of a family descended from Trojan
blood who would someday crumble her Tyrian towers;
a widely ruling people, proud of their warfare,
would come to destroy Carthage: the Fates had unrolled it.
Saturn's daughter was anxious. She thought of the former
war she'd waged first at Troy, the Greeks she had cared for;
pretexts for anger and bitter grief had not vanished
yet from her mind: stored deep in her memory
lay Paris'[7] judgment, her beauty scorned and insulted;
Troy was hateful, and kidnapped Ganymede's[8] honors
worse provocation. Trojans were scattered on every
sea—remnants left by the Greeks and ruthless Achilles—[9]
she'd kept them far from Latium. They'd wandered for many
years on all those waters, forced by Fates into circles.

Founding the Roman nation required enormous exertion.

Juno decides on a storm

Glad Trojans had hardly unruffled their canvas,

bronze churning the foam, Sicily's farmland behind them,

when Juno, preserving the old wound in her bosom,

asked herself, "Have I lost? Should I stop what I started,

helpless to keep this Trojan leader from Italy?

Of course the Fates prevent me! But how could Pallas[10] incinerate

Greek ships and push those Greek crews under water

because of one mad crime of Ajax, the son of Oileus?[11]

She hurled Jupiter's lightning herself from a cloudburst,

scattered their hulls and overturned waves with a windstorm.

Ajax was struck, he exhaled fire from a chest-wound,

she seized and thrust him on sharp rock, using a whirlwind.

But I, Queen of the Gods, who walk as the sister

and wife of Jupiter, fight this war with a single people for years. Does anyone reverence Juno's name now or humbly honor my altars?"

The Goddess visits Aeolia

These things fired her heart as she mulled them. The Goddess

came to a land of raincloud, a place where Southwinds were feuding,

called Aeolia. King Aeolus tempered and mastered

wrestling gales and highpitched gusts in a monstrous

cave here: chains and a prison restrained them.

But winds bridled; they rumbled the whole of the mountain,

growling around in their cages. Aeolus sat in a stronghold

above and held a scepter; he soothed and steadied their anger.

The winds—had he not—would have quickly and surely carried the oceans,

lands and depths of the sky away and swept them through heaven.

But fearing as much, a powerful Father[12] removed them

to dark caves and massed high mountains above them;

he gave them a king who knew how to tighten and loosen

their bindings, to follow the rules of a definite compact.

Juno now unassumingly spoke to this ruler.

"Aeolus, the Gods' Father and monarch of mankind

gave you the seas to calm or build with your windstorms.

A people I hate are sailing and crossing the Tyrrhene,

carrying Troy's Household Gods into Italy.

Strike force in your winds: overwhelm those decks and capsize them,

drive them apart—acquaint their bodies with sea-depths.

I have fourteen Nymphs of exceptional beauty;

Deiopea's the one whose form is the finest.

I'll say she's yours: I'll join you in durable marriage.

She'll spend all of her years with you for the service

you do me, and make you the father of beautiful children."

The storm begins

Aeolus answered, "Your task, my Queen, is to study

your own desires; my law is to clasp your commandments.

Whatever I rule, you gave it—Jupiter's friendship,

my scepter—you gave me the Gods' couches to lie on.

You made me ruler of rainclouds and violent
  tempests."
Soon as he finished he turned and struck at the
  mountain's
hollow side with a spear. The winds, like vol-
  leys of soldiers
given an opening, rushed out and blew through
  the countryside, twirling.
They fell on the sea and roiled its bottom completely.
Eastwind joined with Southwind; Southwes-
  terly, crowded
with squalls, dashed out and rolled huge tum-
  blers on beaches.
Men soon cried out. Their cables were creak-
  ing,
clouds had suddenly stolen the sky and daylight
from Trojan eyes: black night sat on the water.
Poles thundered; the air, crowded with lightning, ignited.
Everything threatened instant death for these
  crewmen.

Aeneas wishes he had died at Troy
Chills weakened the legs now of Aeneas.
He sighed and held out both his hands to the
  heavens,
directing his voice there: "You who were three
  and four times as lucky,
falling by chance at the high walls of Troy as
  your fathers
watched—and you, bravest of Greeks,
  Diomedes:[13]
I wish I could have fallen there in some Trojan
field, struck by your hand, pouring my life out
where fierce Hector[14] fell by a spear from
  Achilles,
where big Sarpedon[15] lay, and the Simois River
  collected
so many strong men's shields, and carried off
  bodies and helmets."

The storm intensifies
He threw out the words but a Northwind
  screamed and collided

hard with his sail, and built up seas to the star-
  heights.
Oars were snapped; his ship was turned and
  presented
to waves broadside, and swamped by a torn-off
  seawater mountain.
Men hung on the sea's crest; to others the gaping
wave exposed ground—sand swarmed in the
  water.
A Southwind stole three ships to grind them on
  hidden
rocks (Italians call them 'the Altars'—surrounded by water,
a massive ridge on the deep sea). And an Eastwind
drove three ships from the depths into shal-
  lows—the scene was pathetic—
it slapped them with surf and piled them with
  girdles of pebbles.
One ship carrying Lycians and loyal Orantes
Aeneas could see: a peaked and ponderous
  roller
struck her astern, it ripped out and tumbled
  the helmsman
headlong, the water twirled the ship in the
  same place
three times, she spun around, and a whirlpool
  quickly devoured her.
A few swimmers appeared in that desolate
  swirling,
men's weapons and shields, Troy's wealth in
  the water.
The storm was beating them now. The durable
  galley
of Ilioneus, of steadfast Achates, of Abas
and aging Aletes—all shipped damaging water,
timbers loosened and seams turned into fissures.[16]

*Neptune[17] rebukes the Winds and dispels the
storm*
Meanwhile Neptune sensed this mixed-up and
  far-flung

commotion of seas. A storm was loose: even the bottom's
currents were shifting. The God was seriously troubled.
He gazed at the water, raised his calm face to the wave-tops
and saw Aeneas' fleet completely dispersed on the water,
Trojans crushed by waves and the sky's inundation.
Juno's anger and guile were not concealed from her brother.
He called Eastwind and Westwind and told them in person:
"Since when did such great pride in your birthright possess you?
Without my will you winds now dare to entangle
heaven and earth, to raise great masses of water
which I—! But first I'll calm these turbulent billows.
Later you'll pay with unusual pain for your doings.
Hurry back to your master now and inform him
that rule of the sea, this rugged trident, was given
to me, not him, by lot. He owns that monstrous rockpile—
your home, Eastwind. Let Aeolus busy himself there,
ruling you winds in a locked-up jail for his palace."
He finished and quicker than words he quieted puffed-up
seas and dispersed dense clouds, restoring the sunshine.
Triton helped Cimothoe[18] work at and push from
sharp rocks the ships which Neptune raised with his trident.
He cleared wastes of sandbanks and steadied the sea-swells,
his nimble chariot wheels brushing the wave-tops.

Just as in great nations a riot will often
begin and common crowds will be willfully savage,
rocks and torches are flying (rage provides them with weapons):
by chance if they spot one man of serious merit
and justice their ears perk up, they stand there in silence—
his words guide their minds and calm their emotions.
So all the sea's noise diminished when Neptune
gazed at the water. The sky cleared where he guided
his willing horses, giving them rein, his chariot flying.

Aeneas arrives at a strange shore
Aeneas' men were exhausted. They made for the nearest
shore, changing course for the Libyan coastline.
There in a deep lagoon was a place like a harbor,
formed by an island's barriers. Every roller
broke and divided here into ripples and eddies.
On either side was high rock that menaced the heavens—
a pair of cliffs. The water was quiet and harmless
under their broad crowns. The heights were a picture of trembling
leaves, darkly hanging trees and bristling shadows.
Facing one cliff was a cave with stalactites hanging
inside, freshwater pools, and couches of living
rock where Nymphs made a home. Here was no mooring
to hold tired ships, no biting hook of an anchor.
Aeneas approached with seven ships of the total
number regrouped. With love for the land overwhelming,

Trojans emerged and clutched at sand they had
prayed for.
They lay on the beach while salt dripped from
their shoulders.
First Achates struck sparks with a flint-piece.
He started a fire in leaves and circling wood-
chips.
He fed it fuel and drew out flame from the tin-
der.
Some grain had been spoiled by the sea; the
men, who were weary
of things, brought out Ceres'[19] tools to grind
down the remnant
of flour with stones. A fire was readied for bak-
ing.

The killing of the deer

Aeneas meanwhile climbed a bluff to examine
the whole far sea. He hoped for a glimpse of the
wind-thrown
ship of Antheus there or the Phrygian galleys,
Capys, the arms of Caicus, high on that fan-
tail.[20]
No sign of a ship. He did see deer on the
beaches,
three stray stags; a whole herd was behind
them—
a long line that followed and grazed in the low-
land.
Aeneas paused nearby, holding a bow and
some lively
arrows, weapons Achates had loyally carried.
He struck at the leaders themselves first as
they carried
their tree-like antlers high. Then scattering,
driving
the whole herd into bushes and woods with his
weapons,
he'd only won and rested when seven cumber-
some bodies
lay on the ground—matching his number of
vessels.
Then he made for the harbor to share with all
of his comrades.

Wine was apportioned—a kindly Acestes[21] had
laden
the jars on a Sicily beach—a kingly gift when
they left there.

The Trojans' ultimate goal

Aeneas' words eased the distress they were
feeling.
"My friends, haven't we known disaster before
this?
You've suffered worse. A God will end this agony also.
You've come close to the raucous cliffs of a
rabid
Scylla, and once you even hazarded Cyclops'[22]
boulders. Renew you spirits: abandon this
mourning
and fear. Perhaps remembering all this someday will cheer you.
Through every crux, through every separation
and setback,
we head for Latium's peaceful homes which the
prophecies
aimed at: God's word on Troy's kingdom reviv-
ing.
Be hard. Save yourselves for things that will
follow."
He finished but large concerns made him un-
easy.
He put on hopeful looks, his heart repressing
its sorrow.
His men girded themselves for the prize meat
that was coming:
they tore off hides from ribs, exposing the in-
nards;
men sliced and fixed quivering cutlets
on spits, placed bronze on the beach, and
tended to fires.
Food recalled their strength. They lay on the
dune-grass,
filling with old wine and fat-dripping game-
flesh.
After feasting ended their hunger, removing
the tables,

in long talks they felt the loss of their comrades,
doubting whether to hope or fear—to believe they were living
or suffering the worst, no longer hearing when called to.
Aeneas rightfully mourned the death of that forceful Orontes
especially now, and Amycus, the merciless killing
of Lycus, intrepid Gyas, intrepid Cloanthus.

Venus complains to Jupiter
As all that ended, Jupiter gazed from the highest
heaven down on spread-out lands and the sail-winged
sea, on far-off nations: he paused on a sky-peak
and focused the lights of his eyes on Libya's kingdom.
Concern ruffled his heart. Venus[23] approached him,
speaking sadly, her eyes filled with the shining
tears of a Goddess. "You are the Ruler forever
of Gods' and mens' affairs, and your lightning is frightful:
what crime has my Aeneas committed against you?
What could the Trojans have done to suffer such losses,
cut off from the whole world? Italy caused this?
Romans would surely come—that was your promise.
Leaders would help restore one day the bloodline of Teucer[24]
when years had rolled by: they'd rule the sea and preside in
every land. Father: what feeling has changed you?
That promise consoled me in fact when Troy was forlornly
collapsing, I tried to weigh good luck and bad luck;
now the same mischance follows these men with its many

disasters. Great King, will you end their affliction?
Antenor[25] could slip through throngs of Greeks: he was able
to pass through Illyrian gulfs and penetrate safely
remote Liburnian kingdoms. He reached the Timavus,
its nine springs rumbling a desolate mountain—
the water an uproar that swamped pastures and broke for its delta.
Here Antenor established the city of Padua
and Trojan homes. He gave his name to his people,
retired his Trojan arms and settled for quiet and peacetime.
And we, your family, promised a fortress in heaven,
lose our ships. It's an outrage. The spite and deception
of one person keeps us far from Italy's coastline.
Is this your prize for loyalty? This the scepter you saved us?"

Jupiter describes the Trojans' future in Italy
The Father of Gods and men lavished on Venus
the smile with which he cleared storms from the heavens.
He kissed his daughter's lips and gave her this
. answer:
"Cytherean[26] Lady, don't be alarmed. Your family's future
remains unchanged. You'll see the city I promised,
the walls of Lavinium. You'll bear the great soul of Aeneas
high into starlight. No one's thinking has changed me.
I'll speak right now in fact for anxiety gnaws you—
I'll show you the distant Fates' twists and their secrets.
Aeneas will wage full-scale war in Italy, shattering

fierce tribes. He'll set down customs and walls
for his people.
Three summers will see him reigning in Latium;
three winters will pass once the Rutulians[27]
are conquered.
Then his boy Ascanius, surnamed Iulus
(Ilus at Troy, as long as that kingdom was
standing),[28]
will rule through a full thirty cycles of ample,
revolving years. He'll move his throne from
Lavinium's
base and greatly fortify Alba Longa.
Here Hector's people will rule for a total
of three centuries. Until Ilia, priestess
and queen, is pregnant and bears twins to the
War-God:
Romulus,[29] proud of the tan hide from the wolf
which has nursed him,
now will assume the line: he'll settle a city
for Mars and call it Rome—after his own
name.
I set no limits of time or wealth on these Romans:
I give them endless rule. And what about
Juno?
Harsh and worried, wearing the sea and sky
and the land out?
She'll change for the better. My own counsel
will help her
to cherish Romans as world rulers, these men
in their togas.
That's my pleasure. An age will come, after the
lustral
years have passed, when Assaracus'[30] house
will grind into slavery
Phthia, dazzling Mycenae[31]—even the Greeks
will be conquered.
A Trojan Caesar will spring from this beautiful
bloodline:
only stars will limit his fame, the Ocean his
empire:
Julius[32]—the name comes down from a great
one—Iulus.
Someday you'll welcome the man into heaven
serenely,

loaded with Eastern riches; prayers will also
invoke him.
War will end then—violent times will diminish.
Elderly Faith and Vesta,[33] Remus and Romulus, brothers,
will draft laws. The feared Gates of War, with
their iron
hinges tight, will close. Vicious Rage will be
sitting
inside on cruel weapons, tied behind by a
hundred
bronze knots, its mouth bloody and savagely
howling."
He finished and sent down Maia's son[34] from
the heavens
to open the young fields and fortress of Carthage,
to welcome Trojans and not let Dido, unaware
of her future,
close her boundaries. Quickly plashing the air-
waves—
great wings were his oars—Mercury came to
the Libyan
coastline and followed orders: Phoenicians discarded uncivil
desires, as the God wished; the queen was especially gentle
in spirit, well disposed to receiving the Trojans.

Aeneas encounters Venus in the forest
Aeneas had conscientiously pondered plenty of
matters
that night. As soon as a kindly dawn was given
he settled
on going, exploring the strange place where
the sea-winds had brought him,
searching and finding what men or animals
held it
(he saw it was farmless), and bringing news to
his comrades.
Hiding his fleet in a cove closely surrounded
by trees, hollowed rocks and chilly obscurity,
Aeneas himself set out, joined by only Achates.
Each hand gripped a spear with their broad
spearpoints of iron.

His mother crossed his path. Surrounded by
forest
she'd put on a girl's dress, looks and the weapons
of Spartan girls, or those like Harpalyce's, tir-
ing
horses in Thrace and winning a race with the
fast-flowing Hebrus.
A supple and fashionable bow hung from her
shoulder.
This huntress had let her hair spread in the
breezes.
Her knees were bare and her flowing garments
were gathered
in knots. "Hello, you men," she spoke up first,
"can you tell me
whether you've seen by chance one of my sisters?
She carried a spotted lynx's hide and a quiver.
She trailed a sweaty boar, she was chasing and
shouting."
The son of Venus answered when Venus had
finished.
"I haven't seen or heard one of your sisters,
but you, young lady, what shall I call you?
Your features
and vocal sounds are not just human. Of course
you're a Goddess.
One of the Nymphs' families? A sister of Phoebus?[35]
Be kind, whoever you are, and lighten our bur-
dens:
tell us what sky we're under, what world and
shore we've been thrown on,
please: we wander around, not knowing this
country
and people, forced here by winds and a waste-
land of water.
My hand will bring down plenty of beasts at
your altars."

Dido's marriage and escape from Tyre
But Venus told him, "I hardly deserve such dis-
tinctions!
Tyrian girls customarily carry a quiver

and lace their calves high with violet boot-
straps.
You see a Punic kingdom; our city is Tyrian—
Agenor's.[36]
But Libyans live nearby—intractible fighters.
Dido governs this realm. She left the city of
Tyre
to escape from her brother—a long story of outrage,
with long twists—but I'll trace these matters
in outline.
Her husband Sychaeus was one of the richest
Phoenician
farmers, and loved by this wretched woman
immensely:
her father had given his virgin daughter in
marriage
first to Sychaeus. But Tyre was ruled by her
brother
Pygmalion—a vicious criminal worse than all
others.
Anger came between them. Pygmalion, blind
with desire
for gold, overcame Sychaeus in secret, wielding
his weapon
profanely before the altars—the love of his sister
irrelevant. He hid the fact for days from the
sickened
woman, played with her love, falsely hoped and
deceived her.
But now a vision came in a nightmare to Dido,
her husband himself: unburied, alarmingly
lifting
his drained face, he showed her the cruel altars, the chest-wounds
where metal had pierced—the whole secret
family murder.
Then he urged her to hurry and run from the
country:
to help her travel he showed her underground
treasure,
old and secret silver and gold in abundance.
Dido was shaken. She planned escape with
companions—

those who hated the despot's crimes or intensely
feared him joined her. By chance vessels were ready;
they took them and loaded the gold; and a greedy Pygmalion's
wealth was borne to sea. Commanding this work was a woman.
They arrived here where soon you'll see the enormous
walls of a young Carthage—a citadel rising.
They bought up land and called it Byrsa, 'The Bull's-Hide':
all they could circle with thin strips of the skin.
But tell me, who are you men? What coast have you come from?
What course have you set?"
Aeneas answered her questions—
sighing deep in his chest, dragging the words out—
"Goddess, if I should trace and repeat it right from the outset,
if we had time to hear each annal of struggle,
Evening would sooner close down Day and lock up Olympus.
Old Troy was our home—if Troy's name has happened
to reach your ears. Through different seas we've been driven—
a storm's own caprice forced us to Libya's coastline.
I, who revere the Gods, am Aeneas. I saved from my enemies
House-Gods I carry in ships. My name is known in the heavens.
I look for a home in Italy, high Jupiter's nation.
With twenty ships I scaled the Phrygian sea-peaks.
My Goddess-Mother my guide, I followed Fates I was given.
Hardly seven are left now, convulsed by Eastwind and water.
I am unknown, destitute, wandering Libyan deserts,
thrown out of Asia and Europe."

The omen of the twelve swans
Venus could suffer
no more of his anguished complaint. She now interrupted,
"Whoever you are, I hardly believe you are hateful to heaven:
you breathe, you're alive, and close to a Tyrian city.
Only persist—go on from here to the threshold of Dido.
As for your friends and ships, I tell you they're rescued,
nudged into safe harbor by gathering North-winds—
unless my parents were foolish and taught me of omens for nothing.
Look at those twelve swans in a happy formation:
Jupiter's bird just plunged from the sky's heights and dispersed them
in open air, but now they seem to be gazing
at land in a long line, or landing already.
Just as they're saved, their wings whistling and playing—
just as they circle the sky, regrouping and singing—
your ships and crews I'm sure are either approaching
a harbor in full sail or actually mooring.
Just keep on; walk this path where it leads you."

Venus encloses Aeneas in a mist and leaves
She finished, turned, and her neck was rose-colored, glowing,
her Goddess' hair exhaled the scent of ambrosia,
her clothing loosened and flowed down to her ankles:
her walk revealed she was truly a Goddess.
Aeneas
recognized his mother; he followed and spoke as she left him:
"Even you—cruel to your son! Why do you always

play with tricks and disguises? Why are we stopped from
joining hand to hand, from hearing our actual voices?"
Having accused her he took the path to the city.
But Venus enclosed their walk in an air of obscurity:
the Goddess spread around them a heavy garment of vapor
so no one could see them, no one could touch them
or cause delays, or ask their reasons for coming.
And Venus returned to Paphos: she left for her pleasant
home in those hills where a hundred shrines in her temple
breathed of fresh flowers and smoldering incense from Saba.[37]

The Carthaginians work like bees
The men meanwhile hurried along the path she had shown them.
Already they'd climbed a long ridge overlooking
the city and gazed down at the fortress that faced them.
Aeneas admired these heights, formerly hovels,
admired the gates and noisy paving of roadways.
Tyrians worked hard, some rearing a stronghold
and raising walls, manually rolling the stones up;
others picked out homesites and framed them with trenches.
They chose magistrates, laws, and a venerable senate.
Here they dredged a harbor; there they were laying
a theater's deep foundations and sculpting its massive
columns in rock—high decor for scenes that were coming.
Just as labor tires bees in the sunlight

of young summer on blossoming farms when the elders
lead out the hive's young or pack syrupy honey
in cells and fill the hive with nectar-like sweetness:
they either take on loads from arrivals or form up
ranks to keep some lazy crowds of drones from the storage
as workers press on and the thyme-scented honey is fragrant.
"How lucky you are—your walls are rising already,"
Aeneas told them, watching the skyline of Carthage.
He entered the city. Enclosed in mist—it's amazing to speak of—
he mixed right in, surrounded by men; no one observed him.

Aeneas discovers paintings of Troy
A grove in the central city was pleasantly shady.
When Tyrians first were hurtled here by water and whirlwind,
they broke ground where Queen Juno instructed,
unearthing a wild stallion's head—a sign of the future
greatness in war and lasting natural wealth of this nation.
Here the Sidonian, Dido, designed a magnificent temple
to Juno, lavish with gifts and the Goddess's power:
stairs rose to a bronze threshold and cross-beams
of linked bronze, and bronze portals rang on their hinges.
And here in this grove for the first time an unusual
thing lessened Aeneas' fear. He hoped to be safe here,
despite his losses: he dared to trust in change for the better.

For while he gazed at the huge temple's particulars,
expecting the queen and amazed at the luck of
the city—
at craftsmen's hands competing among themselves in their artworks—
he saw *Troy*. A long sequence of battles—
word had spread that war worldwide already—
Atreus' sons, Priam, and menacing both men,
Achilles.[38]
He paused. Tears came. "What place," he asked
of Achates,
"what part of the world is still not full of our
struggle?
Look at that Priam! Even here honor's rewarded,
things cause tears, and hearts are touched by
the dying.
Dismiss your fear: you're saved by your own
reputation."
He fed his heart, as he spoke, with substance-
less pictures.
He often sighed and big tears wetted his cheekbones
because he saw how Greeks, in a roundabout
skirmish
at Troy, were routed—young Trojans pursued
them.
Or Trojans were chased—by the team of created Achilles.
In tears Aeneas recognized the bivouac of Rhe-
sus
nearby like sails of snow—till Diomedes exposed them
in deep sleep, wrecked their camp, bloodied
and killed them—
and turned his sweated horses back to his
campsite before they
could taste Trojan fodder or drink from the
Xanthus.[39]
Another part had Troilus[40] losing his weapons
and running.
A sorry youngster, he'd faced a full-grown
Achilles
and slipped backwards, still holding his empty

chariot's reins—the horses pulled him, dragging his neckbone
and hair on the ground. His reversed spear
scrawled in the gravel.
Meanwhile Trojan women filed to the temple
of unfair Pallas. Wildhaired, bringing her vestments,
palms beating their breasts, they wailed and
were abject.
The Goddess kept her looks on the ground to
avoid them.
And Hector: Achilles had hauled that spiritless
body
three times around Troy's walls, and he sold it
for gold now.
Truly Aeneas felt this deeply, heavily groaning
to see the spoils and chariot, even his comrade's
corpse—and Priam's hands, weaponless,
reaching.
Aeneas saw himself as well in a tangle with
Grecian
chiefs; brigades from the East; dark Memnon's
equipment;[41]
and crazed Penthesilea, the Amazon leader,
who blazed among crescent shields in the midst
of her thousands—
baring one breast, a gold girdle beneath it,
the war-queen dared to charge among men
though a virgin.

Dido makes her entrance
Now as Aeneas, a Dardan, stared at these wonders
astonished, his gaze fixed in a single direction,
the queen entered the temple—most beautiful
Dido,
thronged by youngsters and large groups of her
people.
Just as Diana[42] works her circles of dancers
across Mount Cynthus' slopes or the banks of
the River Eurotas,
while gathering here and there a thousand Oreads follow:
she shoulders a quiver, strides and outshines
every Goddess,
stunning with joy the quiet heart of Latona:

Dido carried herself just as proudly and gladly,
surrounded and urging forward the work of her
  kingdom.
Soon at the temple's arched center, at portals
  of Juno,
she sat on a raised throne cordoned by weapons.
She spelled out laws and men's rights, distributed labor
in equal parts or drew lots for each duty.

The lost Trojans appear and ask Dido for help
Suddenly a large crowd was approaching.
  Aeneas
made out Antheus, brave Cloanthus, Sergestus
and other Trojans—those who were scattered
  completely
by dark whirlwinds at sea to some other coastline.
Just as Aeneas was struck, so was Achates
stunned by joy and fear. Anxious, eager for
  handshakes,
still they were faced with unknowns; their
  spirits were troubled.
They hid in the mist's cave-like covering,
  watching
these men tell of their luck, what beach their
  ships had been left on
and why they'd come here—a selection of men
  leaving their vessels
to head for this temple's commotion and ask for
  Dido's indulgence.
After they entered, permission was granted to
  speak in her presence.
Ilioneus, the eldest, began with quiet emotion.
"My queen, Jupiter gave you the power to settle
a new city and bridle people's pride with your
  justice.
We are miserable Trojans, driven by every sea-
  wind.
We beg you—stop your men from burning our
  ships—it's unspeakable.
Spare our good people; look on our cause with
  more kindness.

We don't come here with swords to plunder the
  House-Gods
of Libya or drag stolen goods to the beaches.
Such great force and swagger are not for us losers.
There is a place, the Greeks called it Hesperia,
an ancient land with rich soil and powerful armies;
Oenotrians lived there, but now they say that
  a younger
nation has named it after their leader—Italy.
We held that course
when stormy Orion[43] suddenly rose on the water,
heaved us at blind shoals and drove us completely
apart with blustering Southwinds, immense
  waves, and impassible
sea-cliffs. A few of us reached your beaches—
  by swimming.
Who are these men, your people? What barbarous country
allows such customs? We're kept from the wel-
  coming beachsand;
we're goaded to fight; we're stopped from
  standing our ground here.
If human kind and dying weapons are sneered
  at,
remember that Gods remember the law and
  the outlaw.
Our king was Aeneas. No one's justice was
  higher,
no one more conscientious, or stronger with
  weapons in wartime.
If Fates have rescued the man, if he still savors
  this higher
air, not resting yet with harsh Underworld
  shadows,
we fear nothing. And first competing in kindness
won't harm you. There's also Sicily's farmland
  and cities,
the land of a Trojan family—well-known
  Acestes.
Allow us to haul our wind-rattled ships from
  the water,

to shape new oars and refit our hulls with your
timber.
If Gods give back our king, our friends, and a
heading
for Italy, gladly we'll make for Latium's country.
If not—if you're not safe, you best father of Trojans,
if Libyan waters hold you, and hopes of Iulus
have fallen—
we still have Sicily's straits at least. Homes are
prepared there;
that's where we came from. We'll look for that
ruler, Acestes."
When Ileoneus was done, all of the Trojans
voiced approval.

Dido warmly welcomes the strangers
With eyes downcast Dido spoke to them briefly.
"Release fear from your hearts, Trojans. Banish anxiety.
Things are hard here: our kingdom's youth has
compelled me
to mass defenses and post watches at outlying
borders.
The house of Aeneas! Who's not heard of the
city
of Troy, your men's courage, that great war
and its firestorms?
Our own Phoenician hearts have not been so
weakened;
the Sun-God's horse-team is not so far from this
Tyrian city.
Whether you choose your great Hesperia, the
farmlands of Saturn,
or head for the borders of King Acestes and
Eryx,[44]
I'll help. I'll send you in safety. My wealth will
assist you.
And what if you wish to stay as equals with me
in this kingdom?
The city I'm building is yours: draw out your
vessels:
I'll treat Trojan and Tyrian with no discrimi-
nation.

If only Aeneas himself, your leader, were present,
compelled by the same Southwind! In fact I'll
order dependable
parties to search the shore and Libyan outposts
to see if he's thrown by waves into woods or lost
in some village."

Aeneas emerges from the mist and greets Dido
Her words inspirited both steady Achates
and lordly Aeneas, who now for a long time had
been eager
to break from the mist. Achates first encouraged Aeneas:
"You're the son of a Goddess—what thoughts
arise in your mind now?
You see they're all safe: our fleet and friends
have been rescued.
One is missing; we saw him ourselves in the
maelstrom,
sucked down. The rest confirms the words of
your mother."
He'd hardly spoken when suddenly all the surrounding
mist parted itself and cleared away on some
breezes.
Aeneas stood there, a bright glow on his godlike
shoulders and face: his mother herself had exhaled on
her son's hair a splendor, a youthfully ruddy
light on his face, on his eyes a luster and gladness:
just as a craftsman's hands will add splendor to
ivory
or set in yellow gold Parian marble or silver.
He suddenly spoke to the queen and everyone
present,
his voice a surprise: "I'm here, the person
you're seeking,
Aeneas of Troy, snatched from Libyan waters.
And you, the only person to pity the unspeakable
throes of Troy, to share your home and your
city

with remnants exhausted by Greeks on land
    and by every
mischance at sea, utterly beggared: to thank
    you properly,
Dido, is not in our power. Whatever is left of
    the Trojan
people throughout the great world is every-
    where scattered.
Gods will bring the rewards you deserve, if a
    Power
regards reverence, if justice continues to mat-
    ter,
and men's knowledge of right. What glad gen-
    eration
gave you birth? What great parents conceived
    you?
While rivers flow into deltas, while clouds in
    the mountains
move among coombs, and skies nourish the
    starlight,
your name and honor and praise will always
    continue,
whatever land calls me." He finished and
    reached for
his friend Ilioneus' hand; his left, to Serestus;
then to the others—solid Gyan, solid Cloan-
    thus.

Dido invites Aeneas to her palace
Dido of Sidon was struck first by his features,
then by the man's great losses. She answered,
"The Goddess's son—and what great danger
    and losses
pursue you? What power steers you to primi-
    tive shorelines?
Are you the real Aeneas whom kindly Venus
    delivered
to Troy's Anchises[45] close to the flow of the
    Phrygian Simois?
And yes, I recall a Teucer[46] coming to Sidon.
Expelled from the land of his fathers, he looked
    for a younger
kingdom with help from Belus—when Belus,
    my Father,
took Cyprus' wealth and held it under his
    power.

From that time on I knew of the fall of your
    Trojan
city, the names of Pelasgian[47] rulers, and your
    name.
Teucer, your enemy, gave you Trojans excep-
    tional credit:
he claimed he branched himself from an old
    family of Trojans.
Come, then, you young men—enter our house-
    hold.
A similar luck drove me as well through a
    number
of hardships and finally chose this land for my
    settling.
I know of evil—I've learned to alleviate mis-
    ery."
She finished and led Aeneas at once to the
    royal
palace, commanding thanks be to Gods in the
    temples.
Meanwhile she sent no fewer than twenty bulls
    to the seashore,
a hundred huge swine with bristling backs to
    his comrades,
adding a hundred plump ewes with their young
    ones
and glad gifts of the Wine-God.
The palace built up inside to a queenly res-
    plendence
now in the central hall, a banquet was readied
in proud purple, with tapestries' intricate pat-
    terns,
silver massed on tables, and golden engrav-
    ings—
strong ancestors' works, a long sequence of ac-
    tions
traced through many men from the ancient
    birth of this people.

*Aeneas sends for his son and for presents for
the queen*
Aeneas, whose fatherly love truly prevented
his mind from resting, despatched Achates fast
    to the moorage
to bring Ascanius news and guide him back to
    the city:

all his care, his parental concern, stood in Ascanius.

He ordered gifts to be brought as well that were saved from

Troy's wreckage: a cloak stiff with some figures in gold; a veil bordered in saffron acanthus,

worn by the Greek, Helen—brought from Mycenae

to Troy when she sought that perverse marriage with Paris—

Helen's marvellous gift from Leda, her mother;[48]

a scepter, too, which Priam's eldest daughter Ilione once carried; a pearl necklace; a double crown with gold plaiting and jewels. Achates hurried away to do all this at the moorage.

Venus approaches Cupid with a new plan

But Venus mulled some new maneuvers, a novel

scheme in her heart: how Cupid[49] might alter his features

and come as her dear Ascanius, fever and frenzy

the queen with gifts, and wind a fire through her marrow.

The Goddess feared that Tyre's house was evasive and two-tongued,

that Juno was cruel and seething. At night her anxiety rushed back

and so she said these words to the quick-flying Love-God:

"My son, my supreme strength and power—it's only

my son who can shrug off the highest Father's Typhoeus-destroying[50]

bolts—I've fled to you humbly to ask for your power.

Your brother Aeneas is tossed at sea and on every

shore due to the caustic hatred of Juno:

you know all that: you've often shared his grief and your mothers's.

Now this Phoenician, Dido, detains him with lovely

talk. And I'm worried. How will all these welcomes of Juno

turn out? At such a crux she's hardly relaxing.

Therefore I plan to capture Dido beforehand,

to trick her, to ring her with fire which no one can alter:

to keep her by me, through a great love for Aeneas.

Adopt my plan now on how you might do this.

The boy, my prince and greatest worry, is ready

to go to Dido's city. His dear father has called him.

He brings gifts which survived the fires at Troy and the sea-storm.

I'll hide him in dreamy sleep on the heights of Cythera

or lay him down in my sacred shrine at Idalium:

he won't be aware of our tricks so he can't interrupt them.

You might feign the child's appearance for only one night—put on (you're a boy) a boy's familiar expression.

So that when Dido receives you in all joy on her lap there

among the royal tables and wines of Lyaeus,[51]

as soon as she hugs you and kisses you firmly and sweetly,

you'll breathe your flame in, unnerve her with dark aphrodisiac."

The banquet begins and Cupid appears as Ascanius

The Love-God complied with his loving mother's instructions.

He doffed his wings and gladly skipped like Iulus

while Venus diffused a gentle sleep through Ascanius'

body: the Goddess took him, warmed in her lap, to the Cyprus

high country where soft marjoram blossoms

embraced him with fragrance and kept him in amiable shadow.

Cupid was moving now—complying with orders and bearing
princely gifts to the Tyrians—and gladly led by
Achates.
The queen, when he came, had already re-
clined on a golden
sofa placed in the midst of exquisite curtains.
Aeneas, his father, and Trojan youths had already
joined her and lay on spreads emblazoned in
purple.
Servants washed their hands, carrying shaggy
towels, and presented the breads of Ceres in
baskets.
Fifty girls inside were concerned with arranging
long lines of food and with fires that honored
the Hearth-Gods;
two hundred others, girls and boys of the same
age,
helped by loading tables with courses and setting the cups out.
Tyrians too were gathering, crossing the joyful
threshold in groups, and shown to embroidered
couches to lie on.
Admiring Aeneas' gifts, admiring Iulus
(the Love-God's flagrant cheek and play-acting
chatter),
they gazed at the cloak, at the veil in painted
yellow acanthus.
Dido especially (sadly doomed to a future
illness) could not get her fill of feverish gazing:
the queen was moved as much by the gifts as
the boy-God.
And he, after he'd hung on the neck of Aeneas
and satisfied the great love of his make-believe
father,
sought out the queen. Her eyes and bosom completely
cherished him now on her lap—Dido, sadly un-
knowing
how great a God sat there. But Cupid remembered
his Acidalian[52] mother: he slowly started erasing

Sychaeus and tried to distract the queen with
a living
desire—her feelings had long stagnated, un-
used.

Dido offers thanks to the Gods
After the banquet's first lull and the tables' removal
wines were set out in large garlanded wine-
bowls.
They caused an ovation—the shouts rolled
through the building's
ample foyer. Lamps that hung from gold-
paneled ceilings
were lit and their torches' flames mastered the
darkness.
Now the queen called for a vessel of heavy
gold and gems. She filled it with wine which
Belus
and all his descendents were used to; she made
the hallways be silent.
"Jupiter, known to provide justice for
strangers:
let this day be a glad one for Tyrians and Trojan
refugees; let our children remember this moment.
Let Bacchus bring us joy, and kindly Juno be
present.
Celebrate, you Tyrians—cherish this company!"
Finished, she poured wine first on the table
to honor the Gods. She touched her lips with
the vessel
next then daringly gave it to Bitias. He drained
it aggressively,
face deep in the gold splashing in wine-foam.
Other leaders followed.

Iopas sings and Dido asks for Aeneas' story
    Shaghaired Iopas,
taught by Atlas the great, strummed on a
golden
lyre and sang of the moon's wandering, solar
eclipses,

men's and beasts' origins, downpour and lightning,
rains of Arcturus, the twin Bears and the
Hyades.[53]
He told why sunsets dye the Ocean so quickly
in winter
only and what prevents slow nights from moving.
Tyrians doubled their cheers, followed by Trojans.
Yes, and a luckless Dido was drawing the night
out:
changing topics, drinking the depths of desire,
she asked all about Priam, all about Hector;
at times of the arms that came with the son of
Aurora,
at times of Diomedes' horses; how great was
Achilles.
"But no, tell us, my guest, from the very beginning,
of Greek deceit," she said, "the fall of your people,
and all your travels. For seven summers already
have borne you on every land and sea as a wan-
derer."

BOOK II:

AENEAS TELLS OF THE FALL OF TROY

Aeneas complies painfully with Dido's request
They all hushed, their looks fixed and attentive.
High on his couch like a father Aeneas responded,
"The grief you want revived, my queen, is unspeakable.
Greeks uprooted Troy's pitiful kingdom
and wealth, and I myself witnessed that misery—
I shared it in large part. Who could describe
it—
Dolopians, Myrmidons, hard troops of Ulysses—[54]

and hold back tears? And late-night dew has
already
dropped from the sky: declining stars are making us drowsy.
Still if you greatly desire to hear of our downfall,
to learn briefly of Troy's ultimate struggle,
I'll start—though it chills and grieves my heart
to remember.

The appearance of the Trojan horse
"War had broken the Greeks: their Fates had
rejected
their leaders and many years now had slipped
by them.
They built a horse high as a hill with the cunning
of Pallas the Goddess, fitting sections of pine in
its ribcage.
It looked like a prayer for safe return—that
was the rumor—
in fact they'd secretly drawn lots for the bodies
of men and shut them blindly inside, deep in
that cavern.
They'd filled the huge belly with soldiers and
weapons.

*As the Greeks have apparently gone, Troy
rejoices*
"From Troy you can see our well-known Tenedos Island,
resourceful and rich while Priam's kingdom
was standing—
now there's only a bay with dangerous mooring.
Greeks had gone to its empty shores and lay
hidden.
We thought they'd left—followed a wind to Mycenae.
So all of Troy was released from long lamentation.
We opened gates and took delight in visiting
empty
Greek camps. We stared at desolate beaches:

here Dolopians camped, there a savage
   Achilles;
here was a place for ships, there a front they
   had fought for.

What to do with the horse?
"We stared at the deadly gift of husbandless
   Pallas,
amazed at the horse's girth. Thymoetes advised us
first to haul it inside our walls to the fortress.
Was he a traitor? Or Troy's fate was already
leaning . . . but Capys and others whose judgment was better
ordered the Greeks' design to be dumped in the
   water.
'Or burn it,' they said, 'fire the treacherous offering.'
'Or probe those hiding-places, puncture its
   belly.'
The crowd split into groups, opposed or uncertain.

*Laocoon, a priest of Neptune, condemns the
horse*
"But first of all, with a large crowd of attendants,
Laocoon came down hot from the heights of the
   city.
He called from a distance, 'You wretched Trojans, what is this madness?
You think the enemy's gone? You believe that
   a single
Greek gift is guileless? Is that what Ulysses is
   known for?
Either Greeks hide in that wooden interior
or someone's crafted a weapon to spy on our
   city,
to come inside the walls and leer in our houses.
Some trick is here, you Trojans. The horse is
   not to be trusted.
Whatever it is, I fear Greeks even with presents.'
"He finished and threw an immense spear at
   the horse's

flank with all his strength. It struck at the
   rounded
belly: the thing stood there quivering. Noises
came from the cave-like womb that sounded
   like groaning.
If God's words and our minds had not been unlucky
that driving steel would have bloodied Greeks
   in concealment,
Troy would be standing, and Priam's high towers remaining.

The capture of Sinon
"But look: Trojan shepherds meanwhile were
   dragging
a man to the king, hands tied at his back, and
   an uproar
around him. Sinon had known what was coming beforehand:
he'd rigged his capture himself to open a Trojan
gate for Greeks. A brash character, ready
for either twirling lies or falling and dying.
Young Trojans came running from everywhere, wanting
to see him. The crowd jostled and poked fun at
   the captive.
Listen to fraud now and learn from a single
Greek how all of them lie.

Trojans begin to pity Sinon
"Since he stood in our sight, surrounded and
   trembling,
unarmed and rolling his eyes at Trojan formations,
'What world now,' he says, 'what waters are
   able
to take me? What end remains for someone so
   wretched?
My place among Greeks is utterly gone. And
   the Trojans
hate me themselves, demanding punishment,
   bloodshed.'
His groans changed our minds. All of our
   harshness
dwindled. We urged him to say what bloodline
   he came from,

what he could tell us or hope to achieve as a
captive.

An involved story of enmity with Ulysses
"After his fear finally settled he answered,
'Whatever happens, King of Troy, all that I tell
you
is true. First, my people. I cannot deny it:
I'm Greek. If Luck has painted Sinon a
wretched
man she'll never paint me a joker or liar.
Has Palamedes' name come to your hearing
by chance, Nauplius' son? His fine reputation
was widespread. But Greeks charged this innocent person
falsely just for opposing the war: they viciously
framed him
and sent him to die. And as soon as he lost the
daylight they mourned him!
The man was my close blood relation and comrade.
My Father, poor in my early years, had sent me
to soldier
with Palamades; as long as he ruled safely and
prospered
in kings' councils, we shared in some of his
honor
and pride. But after the lies of that vicious
Ulysses—
you know what I'm saying—my friend withdrew from the shoreline
of life. It stunned me. I dragged out sorrow and
darkness,
raging inside at the death of this innocent comrade.
I spoke out madly, swearing vengeance if any
chance came, if I ever re-entered in triumph
my Greek homeland. My words aroused the
bitterest hatred:
that was my first slip and from here it was always Ulysses
threatening new charges, scattering tricky
tales among people and openly looking for conflict.
He hardly rested until the collusion of Calchas
. . .⁵⁵

but why unroll all this? It's thankless and futile.
Why am I stalling? If all Greeks are considered
alike you've heard enough. Impose my overdue
torture.
Atreus' sons would pay you plenty. Ulysses
would love it.'

The need for a sacrificial victim
"We really yearned to hear and study these mo-
tives,
not aware of his great malice and Greek mach-
inations.
He faltered, went on and spoke with spurious
feeling.
'Exhausted Greeks had often desired to abandon
Troy, to quit and run from a war that was endless.
If only they had! But just as often a bitter
sea-storm scared them—Southwinds kept
them from going.
Especially after this maple planking was fitted,
the horse stood there but all the sky was an uproar.
Confused, we sent Eurypylus back to the
shrine of Apollo
to learn more; but he brought us dismal word
from the temple:
"Blood pleased the Winds in the death of a virgin
first when you Greeks came to the beaches of
Trojans;
blood is desired for return now in a single
Greek's death." Soon as those words came to
the people's
ears their minds scrambled, cold tremors were
running
through bones' depths: who'd be claimed by the
Fates and Apollo?
Here Ulysses dragged out Calchas the seer
in our midst with a loud racket and called for
the heavens'
will. Many had warned me already of cruel

plots of this schemer; they quietly watched
what was coming.
For ten long days Calchas lay hidden and
quiet,
refusing to name or expose one man to the
slaughter.
Finally, goaded by fierce yells from Ulysses,
he broke that peace—as agreed—and fixed on
me for the altar.
They all approved. What everyone dreaded beforehand,
turned into one man's miserable death, they
accepted.

Sinon claims to have escaped

" 'Now the unspeakable day arrived. They
were ready
with salt meal for the rite and they wreathed
my temples with fillets.
I fled from that death. I admit it: I broke from
my bindings
and hid in a lake's marshy sedge through the
night hours,
until the Greeks sailed—if only they *would*
sail.
Now I can never hope to gaze on my ancient
homeland, the children I love, the Father I long
for—
Greeks will probably punish my family and
make them
pay for my guilty escape by dying in misery.
And so I beg you, through Powers above who
are conscious
of truth, if anything's left to us humans, some
remnant
of pure trust: have pity on one who has struggled
greatly, pity a soul not deserving such bur-
dens.'

Priam himself pardons Sinon

"We gave him life for his tears—and even compassion.
Priam himself was first to command us to
loosen

the man's tight chains. He spoke as a friend
would:
'Whoever you are, Greeks are gone now and
forgotten.
You'll be ours. And reveal the truth when I ask
you:
why did they set up this massive horse? Who
designed it?
What Gods were they begging? Or is it a battle
contraption?'

Sinon tells of the Greeks' quarrel with Pallas

"He finished and Sinon, trained in the art of deception
by Greeks, raised his chainless hands to the
heavens.
'You Fires that last forever, undamageable
Powers,
I call you to witness,' he said, 'you altar and
horrible weapons
I ran from, you Gods' fillets I wore as a victim:
allow me to end my sacred Greek obligations,
allow me to hate those men and expose all of
their secrets,
whatever concerns me, and not to be bound by
laws of my homeland.
You Trojans, only keep your trust and a promise:
save me if I've saved you: if my truth is great
then reward it.
All the Greeks hopes and trust in the war from
the outset
always rested in Pallas' aid. But after that impious
Diomedes helped the crime-monger, Ulysses,
to raid her hallowed shrine and steal the fateful
Palladium,[56] killing guards on the citadel's
rooftop,
grabbing the sacred statue and daring to
bloody
and manhandle garlands reserved for the vir-
ginal Goddess:
from that time on the Greeks' hopes were a
backward

gliding flow, their strength broken, the Goddess against them.

Pallas gave them signs, nothing was doubtful:
her image was hardly placed in their camp when the upraised
eyes flashed and flamed, the torso exuded
salt sweat and it leaped from the ground—
amazing to say it—
three times by itself, shaking the shield and the javelin!
Calchas immediately chanted, "Try for escape on the water:
your Greek weapons cannot demolish that city
unless you return to your homeland for signs of the Goddess' power,
which carried your rounded keels to sea in the first place."
So now, with a wind, they search for their native Mycenae.
Armed and ready with Gods on their side they will recross
the sea and arrive suddenly—Calchas sorting the omens.
They stood this figure here to atone for the insult
to Pallas' statue and power—a crime they've regretted.
But Calchas commanded this huge mass to be raised up,
oakwood-plaited and drawn right out in the daylight,
to stop your people from guiding it past the gates of the city,
from being helped by our ancient religious protection.
For if your hands profane this present to Pallas
Troy and Priam's rule will meet with total destruction—
I wish the Gods would turn that curse on its speaker!
But if your hands help it to climb to the city
then Asia will march in a great war on Pelopennesian
walls. That fate is waiting for all of our children.'

With just such skillful falsehood and trickery of Sinon
the thing was believed. We were captured by gushes of tears and by lying—
not by Diomedes or Larissaean Achilles—[57]
ten years of war and a thousand ships had not beat us.

The death of Laocoon and his sons
"Here another greater and more frightening omen
crossed our paths, disordered our feelings and shocked us.
The priest of Neptune chosen by lot was Laocoon.
Just as he killed a large bull at a ritual altar,
picture it: two sea-snakes came from Tenedos' quiet
waters—I freeze to recall it—their coils were enormous,
they leaned into waves and made for our beaches together,
breasting seas. Their raised crests were a bloody
red high on the swells and trailing behind them
were long backs and slithering tails in the current.
They made noise in the frothy surf and already
reached land, their eyes burning, bloody and fiery,
their flickering tongues and mouths licking and hissing.
We scattered, pale at the vision. The serpents were aiming
straight at Laocoon. First they entangled in windings
his two small sons' bodies and each snake
bit off pieces of hapless muscle and chewed them.
Laocoon ran to help, carrying weapons.
They seized him, tied him in huge rounds and already
his chest and neck were circled twice by the scaly

tails—their high necks rising above him.
The man gripped their knots and tried to untie
them,
his garlands a darkling slaver of bloodstains
and poison,
his horrible screams raised at once to the heavens—
just as a bull bellows after it's wounded
and runs from the altar, shaking the clumsy ax
from its neck-bone.
The two dragons left for the heights of the temple
slowly, heading for truculent Pallas' fortress.
They hid at her feet by the round shield on the
Goddess.
A new and sinuous terror certainly troubled
all our hearts now. Some men said he deserved
it:
Laocoon paid for the sin of damaging sacred
wood with a spear, the weapon he threw up was
evil.
They shouted: the horse must be led to the Goddess' temple,
her will begged for.

The horse is led into Troy
"We spread our walls; we bared the homes of
our city.
Everyone worked: wheels went under the
horse's
hooves for rolling; we stretched towlines of
oakum
tight at its neck. A death machine rose to our
walltops,
crammed with weapons. Boys went hymning
around it;
unmarried girls kept touching the towlines
and laughing.
The horse moved closer. It menaced the heart
of the city.
Ah, my country! Home of the Gods, famous in
battle,
you walls of Troy . . . The horse got stalled at
the gateway

itself four times, four times weapons clanked in
its belly
and still we pushed, mindless or blind from
some madness.
We brought that beast, our curse, to a stop at
the temple.
Cassandra too opened her mouth about coming
death. But a God had commanded that Trojans
never believe her.
Cursed: we adorned shrines of Gods on that final
day and strung festival greens through the
city.
Meanwhile the sky changed and dusk ran to
the Ocean,
wrapping in deep shadow the earth and the
heavens—
and Greek lies. Trojans were spread through
the city,
silent and weary. Sleep encompassed their bodies.

The attack begins
"And now the Greek fleet was sailing from Tenedos,
ships in line through the quiet moonlight's af-
fable silence.
They headed for well-known shores. The flag-
ship discreetly
signaled by flare and Sinon, saved by some unfair
Gods' Fates, secretly loosened the pinewood
doors for Greeks enclosed in that belly. The
opened
horse returned to the night-air men who were
glad to emerge from
their hardwood cave: Thessandrus and Sthenelus, leaders;
cruel Ulysses slid down a rope; Acamas, Thoas,
and Pyrrhus, Achilles' son; Machaon, a chief-
tain;
Menelaus; Epeus himself, the hoax's designer.[58]
The city was buried in wine and sleep. They attacked it,

cut down guards, opened gates for an army
of welcome friends, and joined and plotted their
    forces.

The vision of Hector
"A time had come when the first relaxation had
    started
to seep through sickly men, thanks to the Sky-
    Gods.
But look: a vision appeared of a sorrowful Hec-
    tor
present before my eyes, heavily weeping,
dirtied by blood and dust, by the chariot's drag-
    ging,
his feet pierced and swollen by thongs at his
    ankles.
My God, what man was this? How changed
    from that Hector
who'd come back to Troy sporting the gear of
    Achilles,
who'd hurled Phrygian fires at the ships of Da-
    naans![59]
His beard was mucked, his hair stiffened with
    bloodshed.
He carried wounds he'd taken so often defend-
    ing
Troy's walls. I soon seemed to be weeping
myself as I called to the man and spoke to him
    sadly.
'Light of Troy, surest hope of our people,
what's kept you away so long? What shore do
    you come from?
How we have looked for you, Hector, after the
    many
deaths of your friends, the different struggles
    of people!
Troy is exhausted. What criminal dirt has dis-
    figured
your clear face? Why do I see lacerations?'
Nothing: he'd waste no time responding to tri-
    fles.
His chest heaved, he moaned deeply and told
    me:
'Ah, retreat, you Goddess' son, escape from this
    firestorm!

Greeks hold the walls: Troy will drop from its
    summit.
Enough's been given to Priam's country. If Tro-
    jan
defenses were possible, *here* was the hand to
    defend them!
Troy will trust you with Household Gods and
    our relics.
Take them as Fates' friends and look for the
    massive
walls you'll finally found when you've wan-
    dered the sealanes.'
He finished and brought in his hands powerful
    Vesta's
fillets and permanent fire from the heart of the
    temple.

Aeneas awakes and is inclined to do battle
"Mingled wails meanwhile came from the city.
More and more, although my Father Anchises'
house was far removed and shrouded by foli-
    age,
noise was clearer and warfare's terror was
    mounting.
Shaken from sleep I climbed upstairs to the
    building's
rooftop and stood there, my ears excited and
    tingling.
It looked like a fire that falls on cornfields
    when Southwinds
rage, or whitewater rushing from hillsides to
    flatten
farmland, flatten the proud crops, the labor of
    oxen,
and drag down trees headlong. The farmer, as-
    tounded,
stands on a tall rock, resigned to the bedlam.
Then indeed the truth was clear, the deception
of Greeks plain. Already the sumptuous house
    of Deiphobus[60]
fell into rubble, the Fire-God above it. His
    neighbor's,
Ucalegon's, burned, and broad Sigean Straits
    were reflecting

its firelight. Mens' cries and the blaring of
trumpets were rising.
I grabbed madly at weapons—weapons were
mindless—
still my spirits burned for a fight, to muster a
column
of friends and rush to the palace. Frenzy and
anger
drove me headlong. It seemed splendid to die in
my armor.
But see—a priest named Panthus eluding the
weapons
of Greeks. Othrys' son, from the temple of
Phoebus,
his own hands carried relics—our conquered
Gods—and a small grandson. He ran to my
doorstep distracted.
'Panthus, how is the palace? What fort do we
seize on?'
I'd hardly spoken when Panthus moaned and
responded,
'The last day's done, the inevitable ending
of Troy. Trojans belong to the past, with the
signal
glory of Troy. Jupiter's wild, everything's
shifting
to Argos: Greeks have burned and mastered
the city.
That high horse we stood in the midst of our
buildings
has poured out troops. Sinon's victoriously
scattering arson,
cavorting. Thousands of others have come
through the open
gates—as they came once from splendid Mycenae—
while others have blocked our winding alleys
with weapons:
you're faced with tight lines of steel, standing
and glinting,
ready to kill. The first guards hardly attempted
to fight at the gates. The War-God's blind. Who
can resist him?'
The words of Othrys' son and the will of some
Sky-God

moved me to arm and burn—some sorrowful
Fury
called me and snarled for the hurling of death-
cries to heaven.
Friends like Ripheus joined me; an excellent
fighter,
Epytus; Dymas and Hypanis appeared in the
moonlight
and swelled our ranks. The young Coroebus
was Mygdon's
son—just that week he'd happened to enter
Troy, fired by a mad love for Cassandra.[61]
He'd brought a son-in-law's aid to the Trojans
and Priam.
Luckless, because he ignored his furious woman's
warnings.
Seeing these men gathered and anxious for
battle
I started to speak. 'Your hearts are strong but
it's futile,
you men. If you really desire to back me by daring
the worst and the last, you'll see what luck's in
the matter:
our shrines and altars are empty, abandoned
by every
God our empire stood on. You're helping a city
in flames. Let's die, then—rush in the middle
of battle!
The only help for losers is hoping for nothing to
help them.'

Aeneas and his friends engage Greek forces
"So frenzy addled the men's minds. Like a
wolfpack
hunting in dark fog when desperate hunger
blindly compels them to leave their pups in the
wolf-den
waiting with dry mouths: we passed by the
weapons
of enemies, hardly in doubt about death. We
made for the center
of Troy. The night was black, hovering, hollow.
Who could reveal that night's death and destruction?

Whose words or tears could ever come up to our
  struggle?
An old city fell, a ruler for decades.
Dozens of listless bodies casually littered
the streets and yards, the Gods' venerable
  doorways.
And Trojans were not alone paying with bloodshed:
strength came back at times to the guts of the
  losers
and Greek conquerors fell. Everywhere mourning
was bitter, everywhere fear, and death with its
  dozens of faces.
The first Greek to confront us, followed by
  numbers
of friends, was Androgeos. Guessing naively
  our soldiers
were comrades, he spoke blithely and harried
  us outright:
'Move it, you men! Why such stalling and dragging?
It's late, and others have burned, looted and
  hauled off
Troy. Did you come just now from the tall-
  masted vessels?'
He stopped and immediately sensed it—no answer we gave him
was true enough—he'd slipped into enemy circles.
Dumbfounded, stepping backwards, he ended
  the parley,
just as a man who's put some weight on a sudden
snake in rough bush: he backs off abruptly,
scared by the angry swell of that purple and
  rising
neck. So Androgeos feared what he saw and retreated.
We rushed in. Keeping our ranks close we out-
  flanked them,
they hardly knew the locale and were seized by
  their terror:
we killed them. Fortune favored the first of our
  efforts.

The use of the Greek disguises

"And here Coroebus—entranced with success
  and with spirit—
urged us, 'My friends, Fortune's pointed the
  way to our safety
first: let's follow the right path she has shown
  us
and swap shields with the Greeks, wear their
  insignia
ourselves. Is courage required to fight them?
  Or cunning?
They'll give us their own arms.' While speaking he put on
Androgeos' crested helmet and shield with its
  graceful
design. He strapped a Greek sword to his hip-
  bone.
Ripheus gladly followed, together with Dymas
and all our group—recent plunder armoring
  each man.
We moved and mixed among Greeks, hardly
  with Powers
of our own in the groping dark, and skirmish-
  ing often—
we grappled and sent down plenty of Greeks to
  the Hell-God.
Some men fled to the ships to look for protect-
  ing
beach while others in shameful fear climbed in
  the monstrous
horse again and hid in that womb that they
  knew of.

Aeneas and his men encounter reversals

"It must be right to believe in nothing if Gods
  will oppose you . . .
Look at the virgin daughter of Priam, Cassandra,
dragged by her strung-out hair from the altar
  and temple of Pallas,
her eyes yearning and reaching in vain to the
  heavens—
her eyes, for her soft hands were manacled
  tightly.
Coroebus could not stand this maddening picture.

He threw himself—a sure death—at the midst
of that column.
We all followed in close ranks and attacked
them.
But first, weapons: from high on the roof of the
temple
our friends overwhelmed us—a pitiful slaughter—
the looks of our Greek armor and helmets had
fooled them.
Then the Greeks howled in rage at our stealing
that virgin:
they gathered, struck us from all sides, and
Ajax was fiercest,
Atreus' sons and a whole army of Dolopians.
Just as a whirlwind bursts at times into warring
gusts, Westwind and Northwind, Eastwind
that glories
in Dawn's horses: trees groan and a foam-
flecked
Nereus rattles his trident, churning the sea-
depths.
And those we'd scattered that blurred night
through the shadows,
men we'd tricked and chased through all of the
city,
showed up now. First they recognized all our
deceitful
swords and shields; they noted the wrong
sound of our voices.
A mob instantly crushed us. Coroebus was toppled
first by Penelus' hand close to the war-strong
Pallas' altar. Ripheus fell—one of the justest
men at Troy who'd preserved the best of the
law-courts.
(Gods may see things otherwise). Hypanis, Dymas—
speared by friends. And none of your reverence, Panthus,
your headbands of Phoebus, could hide you or
keep you from falling.
Cinders of Troy, you last cremations of comrades:
witness how, when you fell, I never avoided

Greek weapons or setbacks. If Fates had been
willing
my hand would have earned death.

Aeneas escapes to the palace
　　But then we were pulled off,
Iphitus, Pelias and I, Iphitus heavier
now with age and Pelias slowed by a wound
from Ulysses.
Outcries called us straight to the palace of
Priam.
And here was a truly enormous battle, as if
there were fighting
nowhere else and no one died in all of the city.
The War-God was wild, Greeks had rushed at
the building,
we saw them ram doors with shielded formations.
Ladders were hooked on walls; close to the portals
themselves men struggled to climb: their left
hands were holding
shields to ward off arrows, their right hands
grasping for ledges.
Trojans faced them, wrenched off the roofing of
towers,
the palace's heights, and prepared, now that
the final
moment of death could be seen, to use them as
weapons.
The oldest gold-leafed oakbeams, our Father's
adornments,
were tumbled down. Others below at the doorway
closed up ranks and blocked it, swords in a
cluster.

Aeneas helps the rooftop defenders
"My spirits revived. I'd run to the roof of the
building,
add my strength to those men's, and help out
the losers.
There was a door in back, an invisible entrance
used among Priam's family, a way through the
building.

As long as our realm lasted Andromache often
used this route. Sad, unattended, she'd visit
her in-laws or lead Astyanax, her boy, to his
　grandfather.
I slipped upstairs and emerged on top of the
　roofwork
where sorry Trojans threw down impotent mis-
　siles.
One tower stood at the edge, raised to the high-
　est
stars from the roof. All of Troy used to be
　sighted
from here, the Greek ships, the camps of Achai-
　ans.
We started chopping around it wherever the
　higher
levels provided weak joints. We ripped out and
　toppled
the tower from its high base—and sudden de-
　struction
fell roaring, it dragged down and it slashed
　through
Greek ranks. But others ran up. None of our
　boulders,
no weapons now could stop them.

*Pyrrhus leads the Greek attack on the palace
doors*
"Right at the threshold itself of the entrance
　was Pyrrhus.
He leaped in the light there, his weapons
　flashy and brazen,
just as a snake in daylight after feeding on bit-
　ter
plants in cold ground when its fatness was cov-
　ered by winter:
now with skin sloughed, new and sleek as an
　infant,
its chest raised, it twirls its unctuous hind-
　parts
and flicks out a three-forked tongue high in the
　sunlight.
A hulking Peripas joined him; Achilles' chariot
　driver
and weapons carrier, Automedon; whole Scy-
　rian cohorts:[62]

they all bore down on the house and flung
　torches at rooftops.
Leading was Pyrrhus: he'd gripped a two-edge
　ax and he broke through
the hard doors. He sheared from their sockets
　the doorrails
of bronze. Already he'd gouged a panel of solid
oak and made a whole as large as a window.
The house's interior showed, long hallways
　were open.
The chambers of ancient kings were revealed,
　and of Priam.
Armed men, the Greeks could see, stood in the
　entry.

Pandemonium inside the palace
"Inside, however, the house was a tangle of tu-
　mult
and misery, women yelled and wailed to the
　concave
ceilings inside and the noise carried to gold
　constellations.
Trembling mothers wandered the expanse of
　their quarters
and clung to doors, embracing and giving them
　kisses.
Pryyhus drove with his father's force: nothing
　could stop him,
no bolts or guards themselves—his battering
　weakened
door-rails, dislodged them from sockets, and
　crumbled them forward.
Force found its way. Greeks broke through the
　entrance,
cut down sentries and filled wide spaces with
　soldiers.
Whitewater is not so wild when it ravages lev-
　ees,
breaches and wrecks barriers with masses of
　water,
rages across meadows and all the fields in a
　body,
and drags off cattle and stalls. I witnessed a
　raging,
killing Pyrrhus myself, and Atreus' sons at the
　threshold.

I saw Hecuba's hundred daughters by marriage, and Priam—
an altar he'd blessed with fire he'd soon smear
with his bloodshed.
Fifty bridal rooms, such great hopes for descendants,
doorframes proud of their Eastern gilding and
prizes,
fell forward. Greeks held them. Our hearth-
fires were failing.

Priam takes refuge by an altar with Hecuba
"Perhaps you'll also ask what happened to
Priam.
Soon as he saw that Troy was taken and falling,
the palace's doors destroyed, Greeks in the
building's interior,
he foolishly cupped his quavering shoulders in
disused
armor. Old as he was he belted a futile
sword on, determined to die surrounded by enemies.
Under the bare axis of sky in the central
court was a large altar next to an aging laurel—
it leaned on the altar and thickly shaded the
House-Gods.
Hecuba huddled around the altar in vain with
her daughters,
like doves in a dark storm darting and diving.
At times they crouched and embraced a Goddess's image.
But Hecuba, seeing Priam himself decked in a
young man's
armor, asked him, 'What madness compels
you, my pitiful husband,
to don those weapons now? Where will you
rush to?
The hour is not desperate for help or defenses
like those—no, not even if Hector were present.
Please come here. Either this altar will guard
us
or we'll all die.' She finished, embraced him,
and sat the aging king on a seat by the altar.

Polites is killed by Pyrrhus
"But look: one of the sons of Priam, Polites,
escaped from Pyrrhus'[63] killing and ran from
the spear-throws
of Greeks through a long arcade. He circled the
empty
courtyard, wounded. Pyrrhus was threatening,
sweating
behind him—now he's grabbed him, *now* he's
pushing the spear in.
Just as the son had escaped in the eyes of his
parents
he fell in all that blood and emptied his life out.
And here Priam, although surrounded now by
the dying,
could not hold back or keep from screaming in
outrage:
'For such a crime, for all your daring,' he
shouted,
'may Gods grant you the prizes and thanks that
you rightly
deserve—if holiness lives and cares in the
heavens!
To make me witness my son's death in my presence,
to smear a father's face with such family killing:
not even Achilles (they say you're his offspring) related
to Priam, an enemy, this way. The rights and
trust of a lowly
petitioner shamed him. He gave me the bloodless body
of Hector to bury and sent me back to my kingdom.'
The old man finished and hurled an impotent
weapon
without much force—it clunked on the shield
and was quickly repelled there,
idly scratching the boss high on the circle.

Pyrrhus kills Priam
" 'Well, then,' Pyrrhus answered, 'carry a message:
go to Achilles, my Father, remember to tell
him

how awful the actions have been of Pyrrhus—
his bastard.
But now you'll die.' While speaking he dragged
the king to the altar
itself as he doddered and slipped in the thick
blood of Polites.
He twisted the king's hair with his left hand
and brandished
a sword with his right, then sank it deep in the
ribcage.
So Priam's luck ended. That was the finish
that took him, by lot—watching Troy in flames
and collapsing,
Troy with its many once-proud peoples and
homelands—
the ruler of Asia! He lay there, a big trunk on
the beachsand,
head swiped from the shoulders. The body was
nameless.

Aeneas is tempted to kill Helen

"Now for the first time a fierce cold was around
me.
Amazed, I saw my dear Father rise in a vision,
he looked like the old king breathing his life
out,
brutally wounded. And lonely Creusa[64] was
rising,
my house wrecked, and the death of little Iulus.
I looked back: I searched for forces around me:
they'd all left—thrown themselves in exhaustion
down to the ground or surrendered themselves
insanely to fires.
So I was alone, still living. I recognized Helen:
keeping quiet, she hid in a dark place by the
doorway
of Vesta the Virgin. Fires gave off glare as I
wandered
past and my sight could carry completely in
places.
She dreaded Troy's wrath since Troy was
demolished;
she dreaded the Greeks' angry reprisals, having deserted

her husband. A curse on both Troy and her
homeland!
She'd hidden herself by sitting unseen at the
altar.
A fire burned in my mind, anger surged, and
revenge for
the fall of my country—to make her pay for the
outrage.
'Will this one actually gaze on her native Mycenae
and Sparta safely, go as a queen to deliver some
triumph,
look on her husband, parents, her home and
her children,
with Trojan women and Trojan slaves in attendance?
And Priam's put to the sword? Troy's an in-
ferno?
And all that Trojan shoreline sweated with
bloodshed?
It won't be so. For while no name is remembered
for punishing women—the victory merits no
honor—
I'll still be praised for quashing a sacrilege,
causing
deserved pain. I'll fill my heart with the pleasure
of burning revenge and appease my relatives'
ashes.'

*Venus reveals the Gods' destruction of Troy to
Aeneas*

"I threw out the words, my mind borne off by
some madness,
when there before my eyes, and never so brilliant,
my caring Mother appeared, a clear radiance
glowing
through all that darkness. She showed her godhead, a vision
accustomed to dazzling Sky-Gods. Her right
hand restrained me.
She paused and her rose-colored mouth added
this warning:

'My son, what unbridled anger and great sorrow has stirred you?

Why are you furious? Where's your concern for your mother?

Shouldn't you look first where you left your father Anchises,

tired with age? Is your wife Creusa surviving? Your boy Ascanius? Greeks were around them completely

in close ranks: unless my love had withstood them,

flames would have taken your family and Greek swords would have drained them.

It's not for you to condemn the face of Tyndareus'[65] daughter

or Paris' guilt: Gods and Goddesses' rancor

uproots your Trojan wealth and levels your city.

See it: I'll remove the entire cloud which is blurring

your human vision now, that mist which is dulling

your eyesight: so you won't fear the commands of your mother

at all and you won't neglect to follow my orders.

Here in this mass of rubble where stones have been broken

from stones and you see dust and smoke mixing and curling,

Neptune heaves with his huge trident and rumbles

walls and foundations—he tears the city completely

loose from its base. And there Juno is first at the Scaean

gates: she holds them fiercely and furiously summons

weapons and men from the ships.

Look behind you: Tritonian Pallas has settled

high on that fortress, a stormcloud flashing, fierce as a Gorgon.[66]

Jupiter strengthens Greek spirit himself and encourages

force on his own, abetting the Gods' war with the Trojans.

Escape, my son—put an end to your struggle.

I'll never leave you: I'll bring you safe to the house of your father.'

Aeneas returns home

"She finished and disappeared in the dense, shadowy midnight.

Terrifying faces appeared, hostile to Trojans— the great Gods and their wills.

Then I saw the whole city actually settle

in cinders, Neptune's Troy pried from its bases:

just like an old ash-tree high in the mountains,

struck by two-edged axes of farmers repeatedly

trying to fell it. It keeps threatening to topple

as each blow rustles its hair, its forehead is jolted,

and slowly the wounds win: finally sighing,

torn from its ridge, it drags down clutter behind it.

Down from the roof, led by the Goddess, I managed among them—

Greeks and fire gave way and weapons retreated.

Anchises refuses to leave his ancestral home

"Now as I reached our threshold, the house of my Father,

our ancient home, I wanted to carry my Father

first into high mountains, I looked for him first, but

the man refused, with Troy cut down, to continue

living or suffer exile. 'You, with your youthful

blood intact,' he said, 'your strength solid as standing

hardwood—you should escape.

Had Gods of the sky wanted my life to continue,

they'd save my house. I've seen more than enough of

disaster—I lived through Troy's earlier capture.

So my body's laid out: greet it and leave it.

This hand will find some death. Or Greeks will have mercy,

taking my wealth. A toss in the grave will be easy.

I've stalled death for years now, useless and hated

by Gods from the time when mankind's king
and the Father
of Gods exhaled the wind of his lightning and
scorched me with fire.'
So he went on, fixed on his memories, rigid.
We were in tears—my wife Creusa was crying,
Ascanius, all our household—afraid my Father
would topple
us all with him, just pile one death on another.
Still he refused: he clung to the same purpose
and sat there.
Again I was moved to fight. I longed for some
wretched
death—what else had luck or discussion provided?
'You actually hoped I could run off and leave
you,
Father? Such sacrilege fell from the lips of my
Father?
If Gods are pleased that nothing is left of our
city's
greatness, if adding to Troy's death your own
and your children's
death is your pleasure, the door to such killing
is open.
Pyrrhus will stand here shortly, blood-spat-
tered from Priam,
a butcher of sons while fathers watch, and of
fathers on altars.
Dear Mother,' I shouted, 'is this the reason you
saved me
from spears and flames? To see Greeks right
here in my household,
Ascanius next to my Father and close to
Creusa,
each in each other's blood like beasts at a
slaughter?
Bring some weapons, you men, weapons! Back
at the enemy:
a last light calls to us losers. Let me re-enter
and see some *fighting*. We won't go down today
completely revengeless.'

An omen of fire appears over Ascanius
"Again I was belted in armor, passing my left
arm

fast through a shield and turning myself to an
exit
when look—my wife clasped my knees at the
doorway.
She held our little Iulus up to his father.
'You're going to die? We're yours in everything: take us.
Still, if you place your trust in the armor you're
wearing,
guard this house first. To whom will little Iulus
be left, and your father and I—they called me
your wife once.'
Her cries and moans were filling each room of
the building
when suddenly a sign arose—it's amazing to
speak of—
for there between the hands and tearful looks
of his parents
we saw a gentle flame at the top of Iulus'
head that lit and licked at the soft hair with a
harmless
tongue and seemed to feed on his forehead and
temples.
We trembled in fear. We tried to shake out his
burning
hair and extinguish the sacred fire with water.
My Father Anchises however gazed at the
heavens
in joy, extending his hands to the sky and im-
ploring,
'All-powerful Jupiter, watch us if any
prayer inclines you: if faith deserves it I only
ask that you give your sign: confirm everything, Father.'

Jupiter answers the prayer of Anchises
"The older man had hardly spoken when thunder
suddenly cracked on our left and a star plum-
meted downwards,
leading a brilliant trail of fire through the
darkness.
We watched it fall past the building's rooftops
and bury itself with a flash in forested Ida,
marking trails. For a while the luminous fur-
row

gave off light and sulfurous fumes covered the region.
Now my Father was truly convinced. Rising to heaven
he spoke to the Gods and called that meteor sacred:
'Now no delays—now I'll be there where you lead me,
Gods of my Fathers! Save us, save my house and my grandson.
The omen was yours: Troy lies in your power.
My son, I yield truly. I want to go as your comrade.'

Aeneas leads his family out of the city
"He finished—and fires could be heard already more clearly
through walls—waves of seething heat had come nearer.
'Come then, kindly Father, climb on my shoulders.
My own back will support you. The task is no trouble.
Whatever happens we'll face each danger together
and find safety together. Let little Iulus
walk as my friend. My wife should follow our steps at a distance.
You servants: give my instructions all your attention.
Leaving the city you see a hill and an aging
temple of lonely Ceres. An old cypress is near it,
saved for many years by the faith of our Fathers.
From different routes we'll come to that one destination.
Father, hold the sacred Household Gods of our Fathers:
for me it's sinful to touch them—I've come from such bloody
recent fighting—not till I've washed in a living river.'
After speaking I lowered my neck and I covered
my shoulders' breadth with a hide—the tan skin of a lion.

I carried my burden. Little Ascanius threaded
his fingers in mine and followed, walking and skipping.
My wife followed behind. We moved through shadowy places
and I, not bothered before by any projectiles,
not even by lines of Greeks in massed opposition,
trembled now at every nightwind, and every
sound tensed me: I feared for both my son and my Father.

The loss of Creusa
"In time we approached gates. I seemed to have traveled
the whole way when suddenly footsteps were thudding
close by—a crowd in my ears—and my Father peered through the shadows
and told me, 'My son, hurry! Son, they are closing—
I see their burning shields and shimmering breast-plates.'
I still don't know what hostile Power alarmed me
there and stole my focus. For while I was quickly
running away and leaving the byways I knew of,
some Fate seized Creusa, my wife. How wretched it made me!
Where did she lose her way? Or stop in exhaustion?
No one knows. She was never returned to my vision.
I gave no thought nor searched for anyone missing,
not till we came to an ancient hill and the sacred
temple of Ceres. We all assembled finally—and only
one was missing. Slipped from her friends, her son and her husband.
What Gods or men did I blame now in my madness?

What crueler thing did I witness in Troy's devastation?
I placed our Trojan House-Gods, my son and my Father Anchises
in fiends' hands; I hid them in thicketed hollows.

Aeneas returns to Troy alone
"I made for the city again. Belted in glittering armor,
bent on renewing every risk in returning,
through all of Troy I'd offer my neck again to the danger.
First I looked for the entrance, the gate I escaped through,
along the dark wall. I followed my footsteps'
trail back through the blackness, my eyes probing and circling.
Cold and even quiet everywhere scared me.
I went to my house—by chance she had walked there, if only
by chance—but Greeks had rushed through the whole building and held it.
Now a starving fire rolled to the rooftops,
wind-blown flame and heat surged, rampaging skyward.
I went on. I saw Priam's palace again, that fortress.
Picked guards were already in Juno's deserted
shrine, by the columns. Phoenix and vengeful Ulysses[67]
watched some booty. Treasure from all through the city—
pulled from burning altars, crater-like drinking
bowls of gold, tables of Gods and stolen vestments—
piled high. Boys in long lines with their mothers
were standing around, shivering.

The form of Creusa appears
"I even dared at times to hurl shouts at the shadows.

I filled streets with sad calls for Creusa.
I sighed and called again and again. It was futile.
I kept on searching angrily past homes in the city.
A somber image appeared: a shade of Creusa
herself before my eyes, a form familiar but taller.
My hair stood up, my tongue stuck in my throat and I stood there,
senseless. She spoke these words and eased my anxiety:
'Why do you take such pleasure in mourning and madness,
my sweet husband? Things happen according
to Gods' wishes. Your taking Creusa from here as your comrade
is not allowed or decreed by the high King of Olympus.
A long exile is yours. You'll plow deserts of water.
You'll come to a Western Land where the Lydian Tiber
gently meanders through rich fields of Etruscans.
A time of joy will be there, a realm and a queenly
wife to be claimed. Resist tears for your darling Creusa.
I won't look on the insolent thrones of Dolopians
or Myrmidons: I won't slave for Greeks and their mothers.
I am Trojan—Venus' daughter in marriage!
I'm kept on this coast by the great Mother of Sky-Gods.[68]
For now good-by. Love your son and mine—and protect him.'
She finished speaking and left me weeping and wanting
to say so much. She vanished as thinly as night-air.
Three times my arms reached for her neck to embrace her;
three times the image escaped my grasp. My reaching was futile.

She moved like a dream with wings or a stirring of breezes.

Aeneas finally leaves Troy with his friends
"At last I returned to my friends. Nighttime
was ending.
And there I found a huge number had joined us.
I marveled at new groups of soldiers and mothers
and young ones gathered for exile. A sorry as-
sortment—
they'd come from everywhere, ready with sav-
ings and spirit
for sea or land, wherever I wanted to lead them.
The morning star was rising over the ridges of
Ida,
signaling dawn. And Greeks held and block-
aded
Troy's gates: no hope for help was allowed
there.
Resigned, I raised my Father and made for the
mountains."

FROM BOOK III:
AENEAS TELLS OF HIS JOURNEY
WESTWARD

"After the Gods had seen to the wrecking of
Priam's
nation, the undeserved fall of his Asian
city, with all of Neptune's proud Troy in a
smoke-cloud,
the Gods drove us far and wide into exile,
their signs pointing to empty lands. In the
Phrygian
mountains near Ida we built a fleet, close to
Antandros,[69]
unsure where the Fates would lead or allow us
to settle.
We gathered men, and the first summer had
hardly
begun when my Father Anchises ordered our
sails to be trusted
to Fates. In tears I left the shores of my native

land, the harbor and fields where Troy had
been. As an exile
I went to sea with my friends, my son, our
Household Gods and the Nation's.

The voice of the plants at Thrace
"Far to the north were large fields of the War-
God
(Thracians planted and tilled them): ruled by a
bitter Lycurgus
once, an old friend of Troy, with sociable
House-Gods,
when Luck was ours. Borne to that sinuous
coastline
I founded my first city—led on by some hostile
Fate—and I named it Aenos, after my own
name.
I carried sacred gifts to my Mother, Dione's
daughter,
and all the Gods who'd helped us make this beginning.
I killed a glistening bull for the Sky-Gods' King
on the beachsand.
By chance a nearby hilltop was covered with
copses,
cornel trees, and myrtles bristling densely
with spikes. I approached and tried to pull up
some saplings,
to cover the altar with green branches and leaflets.
I saw an omen—I marvel and shudder to tell
you—
the first sapling's roots that I tore from the hu-
mus
began to bleed: black-red drops of blood were
flowing,
staining and clotting the soil. Terror was freez-
ing
and shaking my body—my own blood was congealing.
Yet I tried once more. I tore up a second
tough shoot, probing deep for the cause of the
omen.
And black-red blood flowed from the bark of
the second.

So much occurred to my mind—I called on
Nymphs of that woodland,
on Lord Grandivus, presiding in Thracian
farmland,
to make this omen auspicious, to lighten the vision.
But after I came to a third shoot and engaged
it
with greater effort, my knees in soil that resisted—
how can I say this? or keep it quiet?—I heard a
pathetic
moan deep in the ground, a voice restored to my
hearing:
'Why do you tear my wretched body, Aeneas?
Spare my burial! Keep your sacred hands from
pollution.
Troy bore me: no stranger's blood runs from
these saplings.
But leave this cruel shore and run from the
greed of this country!
I'm Polydorus[70]: metal pierced me here and a
harvest
of weapons covered me; now they sprout into
thornpoints.'

The Trojans leave that land
"My mind teetered. Awe completely possessed
me.
My hair stood up, my tongue stuck in my
throat, I was senseless.
A luckless Priam once had secretly trusted
Polydorus with huge weights of gold to be kept
by
the king of Thrace, who soon lost faith in the
Trojan
army, knowing Troy was besieged and surrounded.
When Luck left us and Trojan resources were
shattered
the king joined Agamemnon's cause, a conquering army;
he broke all faith and law, he killed Polydorus,
and took the gold by force. That cursed hunger
for money—

where will it drive men's minds? After the
trembling
left my bones I brought these signs of the Gods
to my Father
first and the people's chosen leaders. I asked
their opinion.
All agreed: we'd leave a cursed land which had
dirtied
hospitality; we'd trust our fleet to the Southwind.
Once more we began rites and mourned Polydorus.
A large earth-mound rose and altars stood for
the Manes[71]
in sad sky-blue fillets and darkling cypress.
Trojan women, their hair loosened, moved in a
circle.
We brought out warmed milk, frothing its vessels,
and dishes of ritual blood. We lowered the
spirit
in burial, loudly calling his name for the last
time.
As soon as the sea was trustworthy and breezes
provided
gentle swells—the Southwind's rustling call on
the water—
my friends were crowding the shore and dragging the ships down.
We left that port. Land and buildings receded.

Apollo's oracle: does it point to Crete?
"Sacred ground is tilled in the central Aegean,
dear to the Nereids' mother and Neptune.[72]
The island had wandered from shore to shore
till Apollo
moored it to hilly Gyaros again, and to Myconos,[73]
making its farms stable; now it shrugs at the
windstorms.
I sailed in here. Safe, quiet anchorage welcomed
our tired people. We emerged and reverenced
the town of Apollo.

Anius, both king of his people and priest of
Apollo,
his temples wreathed by holy fillets of laurel,
met us. He recognized an old friend in Anchises.
Host and guests joined hands and entered his
household.
I prayed to the God in an old temple constructed of granite.
'Lord of Thymbra, grant us a permanent city,
our own home, the walls of a second Troy for
exhausted
Trojans left by the Greeks and ruthless
Achilles.
Command us: whom do we follow? Where do we
sail and settle?
Send a sign, Father—descend on our spirits.'
I'd scarcely spoken when all the doors of the
temple
suddenly opened and shuddered, the God's laurels, the hillside
moved around me, the Delphic cauldron droned
on its tripod.
We fell to the ground, prostrate. A voice was
borne to my hearing:
'You durable Trojans! The same earth which
delivered
your parents first will take you back to her joyful
breast. Return: find your primordial Mother.
The sons of Aeneas will dominate everyone's
country—
the sons of his sons and the men born of those
children.'
What great surges of joy at the words of the
Sun-God—
everyone shouted! But where is that city, they
wondered,
calling to wanderers? Where had Phoebus told
to return to?
Then my Father remembered stories of elders.
'Listen, you leaders,' he said, 'learn and be
hopeful.
Crete, great Jupiter's island, lies in the middle
sea, and Mount Ida: there's the crib of our people.

A hundred great cities to live in, bountiful
kingdoms!
And Teucer, our grandest Father, was borne
from there to Rhoetean
shores first—if memory serves me correctly—
he chose that land for his realm. Troy and the
Trojans'
towers were not yet standing. They lived in the
lowlands.
Our Mother Cybele cares for Crete, for the Corybants' cymbals
and groves on Ida—that silent faith in her mysteries.
Lions yield and are yoked to the Goddess's
chariot.
Placate the Winds, make for the kingdom of
Cnossus.[74]
It's not a long run. If only Jupiter joins us
the third dawn will rest our fleet on the coastline
of Crete.' Finished, he honored shrines with appropriate victims:
a bull for Neptune, a bull for you, brilliant
Apollo,
a dark ram for the Storm-God, a light one for
following Westwinds.
Rumors flitted: King Idomeneus was driven
from Crete, he'd left his fathers' land, the shore
was deserted,
houses cleared of our enemies, homes standing
abandoned.
We left the Ortygian harbor and flew on the
sea-swells,
past the Wine-God's heights at Naxos, verdant
Donysa,
Olearos, snow-peaked Paros, and Cyclades
scattered
at sea. We sighted crowds of islands and straits
that were bubbling.
Sailors mingled their shouts, loudly competing,
encouraging friends, 'Head for Crete! The land
of our Fathers!'
The wind came up astern and held our momentum.
We finally glided ashore at ancient Curetes.

Plague strikes

"I anxiously chose a site and raised the walls of
a city.
I gladly called it Pergamea, after my people.
I urged them to love their hearths, and to raise
the citadel's roofbeams.
Now as the fleet lay high and dry on the beachsand,
the young were involved with new farmland
and marriage
and I was proposing laws and homesites, when
sudden
disease from a tainted tract of sky wasted our
bodies,
a wretched blight on our crops and trees—a
death-burdened season.
People dropped their precious lives or they
dragged on
sick; fields were sterile, burned by the Dogstar;[75]
plants dried up and pale shoots refused to be
nourished.
My Father urged us back to the Ortygian oracle,
back to sea, to ask for help from Apollo:
the God would end our weariness, show us
who'd help with
our labor and tell us what course we should follow.

The vision of the Household Gods

"Then it was night. Land and livestock were
sleeping.
I saw the sacred forms of the Phrygian House-
Gods,
figures I'd brought from Troy when the heart
of the city
burned: standing close to my eyes as I lay there
sleeping, they shone with a clear glow like the
moonlight
that pours through windows placed in its way
at the full moon.
Then they said these words and eased my anxiety:
'The things Apollo would say when you sail to
Ortygia

he sings here. He freely sends us, look! to your
threshold.
Since Troy's burning we have followed your
army.
With you commanding the fleet we've measured the sea-swells.
We'll also raise your future descendants to
starlight
and give your city an empire. And you? Prepare for construction,
great for the great! But accept a long labor of
travel.
You home must change. Apollo advised you at
Delos:
he never ordered Crete's shores to be settled.
There is a place, the Greeks called it Hesperia,
an ancient land with rich soil and powerful armies.
Oenotrians lived there; but now they say that
a younger
nation has named it after their leader, Italy.
There's our proper home. Dardanus grew up
there, and Iasius—the leader who first fa-
thered our nation.
Rise quickly and bring to your long-lived father these joyful
words. They are not to be doubted: look for
Etruscan
land in Italy: Crete's fields are forbidden by Jupiter.'

Departure from Crete

"They stunned me. The vision and voice of
these Gods were like thunder.
And that was no dream: I seemed to recognize
faces
in person, mouths up close, the wreaths on
their foreheads.
Cool sweat soon flowed the length of my body.
I leaped from the bed and prayed, directing my
upturned
hands to the sky. Then I offered inviolate
gifts on the hearth. The ritual finished I gladly
informed Anchises and told of the whole situation.

He admitted the double parentage of Troy was confusing.
A new mistake about old places had tricked him.
He said, 'My son—how Troy's fate has fatigued you!—
only Cassandra spoke of this chance in our future:
now I recall she often prophesied Western
Land owed to our people, and sang of kingdoms in Italy.
But who'd believe Trojans would venture to Western
shores? And who was moved by Cassandra's predictions in those days?
We'll yield to Apollo and follow his warnings—it's better.'
He finished speaking and all concurred and applauded.
We left that home as well. A few would remain there;
the rest set sail to run through deserts of sea in our galleys.

A storm at sea

"After our ships had reached deep water, and nothing
of shoreline was visible—sky everywhere, everywhere water—
a blue-black stormcloud stood there upright before us,
bringer of noise and night. Waves shivered in darkness,
the wind quickly raised up and tumbled enormous
seas—in the monstrous troughs we were jumbled and scattered.
Cloud concealed daylight, the sky was removed by a squally
blackness. At breaks in the clouds lightning redoubled.
Pushed off course by the seas, wandering blindly,
Palinurus himself, our helmsman, could not distinguish

day from night, nor retrace his path through the water.
For three whole days of dark mist and obscurity
we wandered at sea—for three whole nights without starlight.
Land was finally sighted at dawn of the fourth day.
Mountains appeared to rise, and smoke curled in the distance.
We dropped sail immediately, rose to the rowing,
our sailors worked up curling foam as they swept through the water.

The island of the Harpies

"The shore of the first Strophades Island received us
and saved us from seas. Greeks had called them the Strophades
Islands—they stood in the wide Ionian, home for Celaeno
and other fearsome Harpies. After Phineius[76]
closed his former house they left his table in terror.
Monsters grimmer than any, the worst epidemic
brought up by angry Gods from Stygian waters,
these birds have girls' faces but guts with the vilest
droppings, hands with claws, and permanently whitened
mouths from hunger.
Borne here, we entered the harbor. We spotted
fat herds in fields, picture it—cattle were scattered
across the grass, and goats—with no herdsman.
We rushed in, called on the Gods, especially Jupiter,
to share our prize, and we speared them. Soon on the winding
shore we built up couches and feasted—an excellent banquet.

Celaeno attacks and curses the Trojans

"But suddenly there, in a fearsome dive from the mountains,

were Harpies, their wings a loud clatter and flapping.

They ripped at the meat with grimy talons and dirtied

it all while smelling foul and frightfully screeching.

We moved to a deep hollow, and under a concave

cliff densely circled by trees and bristling shadow

we set out tables again and restored fires on altars.

Again that noise pealed from the sky, from a hidden

and different quarter, those talons circled our prizes,

their mouths defiled our food. But now I told my companions

to take up arms and wage war with this horrible species.

They did just as I ordered: they covered their weapons

with grass and shrubs, kept their shields in concealment;

so now when the Harpies made that racket and dove on the winding

shore Misenus gave a signal up high as a lookout,

using a horn; my friends attacked. The fight was a strange one—

our swords trying to bloody disgusting seabirds.

They took no wounds on their backs or swipes at their feathers

however but glided swiftly back to the sky when their eating

was half done, their rancid claw-marks behind them.

Celaeno's curse

"One bird perched on a tall boulder—Celaeno.

A voice broke from her chest predicting disaster:

'War as well, you sons of Laomedon?[77] Ready

to make war for the bulls you killed and the heifers you slaughtered?

And drive guiltless Harpies away from the realm of their fathers?

Well, then. Take my words to heart and remember:

what all-powerful Jupiter told to Phoebus, and Phoebus

to me, I'll show you—for I'm the greatest of Furies.[78]

You've set your course for Italy: Winds have been summoned;

you'll reach an Italian port with permission to enter.

But no walls will surround the town you were promised

before your desperate hunger and criminal killing

compel you to gnaw your own tables and eat them.'

She finished and fled, on the lift of her wings, into forest.

Anchises orders the Trojans to leave at once

"Sudden fear chilled and slowed my companions'

blood. Their spirits dropped. They told me to battle

no more but to seek peace through prayer and promise,

whether the birds were divine or vile and disgusting.

My Father Anchises, his hands stretched out on that shoreline,

called on the great Powers and named gifts that were due them:

'Gods, void that curse: you Gods, avert the disaster,

be pleased and save your holy people.' He ordered the cables

cut at the beach, our sails loosened and shaken.

Southwinds tensed the canvas, we fled on the foaming

water, our course directed by wind and by helmsman.

Already the woods of Zachynthos appeared on
the water,
Dulichium, steep cliffs of Neritos, Samos.
We ran on past Laertes' kingdom, Ithaca's
boulders—
and cursed the land that nursed that savage,
Ulysses.[79]
Mount Leucata soon appeared with its misty
ridgeline—Apollo's coast, dreaded by seamen.
We put in here, exhausted. We entered the little
city—our anchors thrown from the bows, our
ships on the shoreline.
We'd finally taken land which no one had
hoped for.
Our altars blazed with Jupiter's gifts: we were
purified.
Trojans gathered for games on Actium's
beaches.[80]
Bare, in slippery oil, my friends were engaging
in wrestling bouts, glad to have skirted so
many
Greek cities and held their speed past enemy
centers.

Aeneas' boast
"The great wheel of the sun meanwhile was
turning.
Frozen winter chafed the water with North-
winds.
I fastened a curved shield of bronze—it was
carried
by Abas, a great one—to fronting pillars, and
wrote an inscription:
AENEAS DEPRIVED CONQUERING GREEKS OF
THESE WEAPONS.
I ordered men to their thwarts then to depart
from that harbor.
Their strokes competing, my friends were
sweeping the water.
In time we were hidden from airy Phaeacian
towers.
We followed Epirus' coast; we entered Chaonia's

port and climbed to the high town of Buthro-
tum.[81]

Andromache and Helenus are alive
"Here unbelievable words command our attention:
a son of Priam, Helenus, rules Greeks in the
city!
Through marriage he's gained the scepter of
Pyrrhus, son of Achilles;
Andromache's passed once more to a man of
her homeland!
Stunned and moved, I burned with wonder and
longing
to face this man, to learn of these great transformations.
Leaving the ships and shore I marched from
the harbor.
By chance Andromache now was offering
mourning
gifts of meal in a grove by a would-be Simois
River
before the city. She called on Manes, the ashes
of Hector—the cause of her tears—at a grassy
but empty
tomb, a mound she'd sanctified along with two
altars.
Soon as she saw me coming, with Trojan weapons around me,
she lost her senses—afraid we were terrible
omens,
she stiffened, lost in her vision—the warmth of
her marrow
left her: she fainted. In time she spoke to us
weakly:
'Your form is real? You bring me news? Is it
truthful?
The Goddess' son—you're alive? Or if nourishing light has been taken,
where is my Hector?' Tears flowed when she
finished.
Her cries filled the entire locale. Alarmed by
her raving
I offered some few words, I muttered some
phrases.

'Yes, I'm alive—and alive through every ex-
tremity.
Don't doubt it: you see what is real.
And you, thrown down from your great marriage, my God, what misfortune
takes you now? What luck deserves you
enough, and revisits
Hector's Andromache? You survive as the wife
of Pyrrhus?'
She lowered her glance and voice as she answered.
'The luckiest one of all was a virgin daughter
of Priam,
ordered to die at the high walls of Troy, at her
enemy's
death-mound! No casting of Greek lots would
oppress her:
she'd never touch some lord-and-master's bed
as a slave-girl.
But we, forced to diverse seas when our homeland was burning,
have borne that proud son of Achilles—an insolent offspring—
I bore him slaves. In time he went chasing Hermione,
Leda's grandchild, he wanted a wedding in
Sparta.
He turned me over to Helenus, slave to be had
by
slave. But Orestes, fired by intense love for his
stolen
bride and driven by Furies for old crimes, overtaking
Pyrrhus he hacked him down from behind at
the shrine of his fathers.[82]
And Pyrrhus' death restored and yielded part
of this kingdom
to Helenus now. He's called these meadows
Chaonian,
he called it all Chaonia, after Chaon, the Trojan.
But you—what winds and course and Fates
were you given?
What God landed you here, unaware, on our
coastline?

And what of your boy Ascanius? Enjoying
these airs and surviving?
In Troy already . . .
still does the boy love and feel the loss of his
mother?
And some of the old male spirit and courage
aroused by his father Aeneas and Hector, his
uncle?"

A new and lesser Troy
"She poured out tears while speaking, use-
lessly crying,
mourning and mourning. Then Helenus came
from the city
walls, Priam's son, a leader with many companions.
He recognized his own people and gladly conducted
us back to his home, often speaking and weeping together.
I went along and saw a little Troy that resembled
the great one, a near-dry brook they'd labeled
the Xanthus,
the threshold and frame of a Scaean gate—I
embraced it.[83]
My Trojan friends were also enjoying the city.
The king welcomed us all on his portico
broadly;
we raised cups in the central hall to the Wine-
God.
A feast was served on gold. We held up the vessels.

Aeneas asks Helenus for a prophecy
"And now a day passed, and another, and
breezes
called to our sails, Southwinds filling the canvas.
I sought out Helenus, asking king to be
prophet:
'Son of Troy, you've read the Gods' wishes,
Apollo's
tripods and laurels at Claros, you've sensed the
stars' intimations,

birds' language, the fleeting omens of feathers:
speak to me now. For everything holy has told
    me
of fine travel, all the Gods' powers have urged
    me
to seek out Italy, to aim for that faraway coun-
    try.
Only a Harpy, Celaeno, sang of a startling
portent, revolting to speak of, and blamed our
    lamentable anger
and sinful hunger. What risks can I avoid at
    the outset?
To get by great hardship what course can I fol-
    low?'

Apollo speaks through Helenus
"Now Helenus killed some steers according to
    custom.
He prayed for the Gods' peace and loosened the
    garlands
around his priestly head. He took my hand in
    his own hand
and led me, awed by a powerful will, to your
    threshold, Apollo.
He sang these words as priest and voice of the
    Sun-God:
'Son the Goddess! Your sea journey is clearly
affirmed by great omens: the Gods' King has
    allotted
your Fates and rolled your wheel: that cycle is
    turning.
I'll show you some few things among many to
    help you
watch and wander alien sealanes in safety
and rest at Ausonian moorage. Fates prevent
    me from knowing
the rest: Juno, Saturn's daughter, stops me
    from speaking.

The Trojans still have far to go
" 'But first the Italian soil you think you are
    close to—
you're ready to enter a nearby port in your ig-
    norance—

it's far. Uncharted ways keep you far from that
    country.
Your oars must bend in Trinacrian waters be-
    forehand,
your ships must wander the salt swells of Au-
    sonia,
Underworld lakes, and the island of Circe,
    Aeaea,
before you can reach safe land and establish
    your city.[84]
I'll tell you the signs. Keep them stored in your
    memory.
You'll find a huge sow by the flow of a secret
river will ease your concern. Near oaks at the
    sea-shore
her womb will bear thirty strenuous young
    ones:
she'll lie on the ground, as white as the young
    at her nipples.
There's the place for your city, and sure rest
    from your labors.
Don't be scared by a distant prospect of eating
    your tables:
Fates will find an escape: Apollo will come
    when you call him.
But run from the land this side of the Italian
    coastline,
the near shore bathed by our own sea's fluctua-
    tions:
vicious Greeks have settled all of those cities.
It's here the Locrians massed the walls of Na-
    rycium;
Idomeneus of Crete filled Salentinian clear-
    ings
with Greek soldiers. Here is that little Petelia,
trusting the walls of its Meliboean prince, Phil-
    octetes.
Indeed when your ships have crossed the sea
    and stood on those beaches,
set down altars directly and offer your pledges,
wearing a purple robe. Your hair should be cov-
    ered,
to stop hostile forms from opposing your holy
fires in the Gods' honor or troubling your
    omens.

Your friends and you yourself should keep to
this custom—
your rites and faith should stay pure in your
children.

Avoiding Scylla and Charybdis
" 'But then, when winds move you away to Sicily's coastline,
and close headlands appear to diverge at Pe-
lorus,
hold to port! The waters and lands on the port
side
are long and roundabout; still, run from the
seas on the starboard.
Those land masses once tore from each other—
aeons of time can cause change that's enormous—
a vast rupture, they say, where both had been
parts of
the same stretch. Violent seas entered between
them
and cut the Sicilian side from Hesperia, leaving
fields and towns divided by beach and turbulent narrows.
Scylla blocks the right side and hungry Char-
ybdis
blocks the left—three times each day she sucks
a tremendous
wave down to her Underworld depths and
uplifts it
again to the sky, lashing the stars with her water!
But Scylla stays in a blind cave, unobtrusive—
only thrusting her mouth out to drag ships into
boulders.
Her form is human down to the waist with a
virgin's
lovely breasts; below her body is gross as a sea-
beast's—
dolphins' tails are entwined with wolves in her
belly.
Better to wander, slowly, Sicily's shore-points
and gaze at Pachynus—a long, circuitous journey—

than see just once the immense cave of that
hideous
Scylla, her sea-blue dogs and re-echoing rock-
piles.[85]

Honoring Juno first
" 'Besides, if Helenus knows these things, if he
merits
your faith as a seer and Apollo has filled his
mind with reality,
more than all else, son of the Goddess, I'll warn
you
of one thing, I'll tell you this one thing over and
over:
pray and honor the will first of powerful Juno.
Intone your vows gladly to Juno and conquer
that great Lady with humble gifts: you'll finally win her.

The importance of the Sibyl at Cumae
" 'Sent from Sicily next, you'll leave for Italy's
coastline.
And borne there you'll reach the city of Cumae,
lakes of the Gods, and the rustling woods of Avernus.
You'll see a Sibyl who sings of the future in
trances,
committing her names and knowledge to
leaves in the depths of a cavern.
Whatever songs this virgin inscribes on leaves
she arranges
in sequence and sets them back in the cavern.
They stay right there in place, remaining in order.
But when a door swings open, even a slender
breeze can move them, ruffling the delicate foliage.
She never cares to catch them in flight through
the rocky
cave or link and recall the oracles later.
Unhelped, people leave with disdain for the
cave and the Sibyl.
You should stay. Don't think so much of loss
and delay here,

though friends chide and the sea's powerful currents
call to your sails and following winds billow your canvas.
No: linger and pray for the Sibyl's predictions.
Ask her to open her mouth herself and will-ingly speak out.
She'll tell you of coming wars and people in It-aly,
how to escape from someone or carry your bur-dens.
Revere this woman: she'll give you a course to rely on.
These are all the warnings our voice may de-liver.
Go and act. Carry Troy's greatness to heaven.

(In the remainder of Book III Aeneas, after de-parting from Andromache and Helenus, sights Italy finally after a short sea journey. He man-ages to avoid the straits of Scylla and Char-ybdis as well a confrontation with the Cyclops. At the nearby port of Drepanum however his father Anchises dies. Shortly afterward the Trojans are forced to the shores of North Africa by a storm which was described at the outset of Book I. Aeneas has now finished the story of his travels for Dido.

At the start of Book IV Dido already feels an intense passion for Aeneas. Aeneas lingers at Carthage, he helps Dido with various ad-ministrative duties and, during a violent storm when they are driven to a cave together, he makes love to her. Jupiter must now send Mer-cury down from Mount Olympus with a warn-ing that Aeneas should get on with the task of fulfilling his and Rome's destiny.)

FROM BOOK IV:
DIDO AND AENEAS AT CARTHAGE

Mercury stopped Aeneas: "You're laying foun-dations
for high Carthage now? Building a beautiful city—

a woman's—and sadly forgetting your own realm and resources?
The Gods' ruler himself has dispatched me from brilliant
Olympus—his will revolves the land and the heavens—
he told me himself to carry commands on the fast-moving air-waves.
What do you plan or hope for, idling in Libyan country?
If taking glory in great affairs will not move you,
if honor itself won't make you carry your bur-dens,
look to Ascanius—growing, in hope of inherit-ing
Roman land—an Italian kingdom is owed to Iulus." Cyllenius[86] finished speaking and left him
there in the midst of his speech: he vanished from human
sight in the distance while riding some tenuous breezes.

Aeneas' confusion; his decision to leave
Aeneas was truly struck senseless and dumb by the vision.
His voice had stuck in his throat; his hair had risen in terror.
He yearned to escape, to leave this pleasurable country,
stunned as he was by the Gods' momentous power and warning.
But how should he act? Now the queen would be outraged.
How could he dare approach and start to ad-dress her?
He thought rapidly now, distinguishing this way and that way,
taking different sides, considering everything.
One option seemed worthwhile as he looked at alternatives:
he told Sergestus, Mnestheus and daring Ser-estus
to ready the fleet quietly, gather companions

and break out arms on the beach—and improvise reasons
for all the strange moves. Meanwhile his wonderful Dido
would not know or expect that her great love could be injured:
Aeneas would try at the gentlest time to approach her
and speak: he'd look for the right way. Everyone quickly
and gladly accepted the orders. Each one left to enact them.

Dido's violent reaction

Ah, but the queen suspected deceit—can a lover
be fooled by anyone? First she heard of those movements;
afraid of it all, though safe, she fumed; Rumor maliciously
told her the fleet was armed and ready to travel.
She felt helpless, enraged: she dashed through the city
feverish, the way Bacchae react to their brandished
icons when shouts to the Wine-God startle and call them
at night to Mount Cithaeron's biennial revels.[87]
At length she confronted Aeneas and willfully told him,
"You actually hoped to hide the extent of your evil?
To break faith and sneak from my country in silence?
Our love won't keep you? The hand that you gave me
once? Or the hard death that's coming to Dido?
No: you even load your ships under this winter
sky, you rush off to sea surrounded by Northwind.
Ruthless man . . . what if the fields and homes you are seeking
were known and friendly—if ancient Troy were surviving—

would ships go looking for Troy in seas this heavy?
It's *me* you run from? But let my tears and the hand that you gave me
implore you—I left myself with nothing else in my misery—
our marriage rite, the wedding we started together,
if I've deserved well of you, think of the pleasure
I gave you, if any, and pity a house that's collapsing.
Change your mind. If prayer has its place, then I pray you.
You're the reason Numidian chiefs and Libyan people
hate me, Tyrians hate me—*you* are the reason
my shame's extinguished, my former name—and my only
approach to the stars. My guest, what death do you leave me?
Is 'guest' all that's left? Once you were 'husband'. . . .
But why live longer? Either my brother Pygmalion
wrecks these walls or Iarbas, the African, makes me his captive.
At least if I'd borne your child before you had left me,
if only an infant were here, a little Aeneas
to play in these halls, to go on recalling your features,
I shouldn't seem so utterly seized and discarded."

Aeneas reluctantly pleads his divine mission

She stopped there. Aeneas, warned by Jupiter, struggled
to keep his vision steady and deeply contain his emotion.
Then he answered briefly. 'My queen, I'll never deny them—
all these claims you have power to list, and deserve to.
Nor will I ever feel shame to remember Elissa,[88]

as long as spirit and memory itself preside in this body.

I'll speak of my cause in brief. My hope was not to dissemble

and run off—don't think that. And I never extended

the husband's torch or entered a marital contract.

If God's word had allowed me to live out my life there—

freely arranging my own concerns and my omens—

I'd live in the city of Troy first and care for my precious

remnant of people. Priam's high roof would remain there;

or I could revive Troy myself for us losers.

But now Grynaean Apollo commands me to Italy.

Wrest Italy's greatness, the lots of Lycia tell me:[89]

there's my love, my homeland. If Carthage's towers,

the views of an African city, engage you Phoenicians,

why then hate us Trojans for settling Ausonian

land? For us as well seeking a kingdom is lawful.

My Father Anchises warns me, as often as midnight

covers the land with damp shadow: as often as burning

stars rise, that troubled form frightens my dreaming.

My boy Ascanius, too—should I injure this person

I love, defraud him of Western fields he's predestined to govern?

And now even the Gods' herald—Jupiter sent him

himself, I swear on our heads—carries my orders

down on a speeding wind. I saw him myself in the clearest

daylight: he walked through walls, I heard his voice and absorbed it.

Stop, then. Don't burn yourself and me with resentment.

I don't pursue Italy freely."

Dido curses Aeneas
She eyed him askance all the time he was speaking,

turning her glance this way and that, silently taking

him all in. Now seared by anger she told him,

"No God was your parent, no Dardanus founded your people,

traitor: hard rock and frost of the Caucasus

gave you birth and the teats of Hyrcanian tigresses nursed you.[90]

Why should I hold back? To save myself for a greater

pain? Has he sighed at my tears, lowered his glances,

shed tears himself, felt lost, or pitied his lover?

What shall I say first? Neither powerful Juno

now nor fatherly Jupiter sees all this with some fairness.

Trust is safe nowhere. Thrown on the beach he came begging,

I took him and madly offered him part of my kingdom,

I saved his lost fleet and friends from disaster.

This pain, these Furies that move me and scald me . . . Apollo's your prophet

now, some Lycian oracle. Heaven's messenger even

sent by Jupiter now through the air with your dreadful instructions.

Hard work for your Gods—I'm sure anxiety troubles

their rest! I won't detain you or counter your speeches.

Go and chase your Italian winds and waves. Look for your kingdom.

If honest Gods can arrange it I hope you will drink in

pain—surrounded by rock and calling on Dido's

name often—I'll follow. A black fire, though I'm absent:

when death's cold severs the flesh from the
spirit
I'll be shadow everywhere. Crime will be punished, criminal.
I'll hear in the Manes' depths. Your story will
reach me."

The Trojans prepare to leave

Halfway done she broke off and ran as if sickened,
she turned from his looks, the air he breathed,
and she left him
deeply worried and hesitant, ready to tell her
more. Servants helped her. They carried her
slumping
body back to her marble bedroom and laid her
on couches.
Aeneas had done his duty, although he was
longing
to soothe and soften her pain, to speak and
avert her anxiety.
He sighed deeply, unnerved by great love for
this woman.
Still he complied with the Gods' commands and
returned to his vessels.
Now on the whole shore Trojans fell to their labor,
hauling tall ships down, caulking the bottoms,
launching, carrying shoots and untrimmed
boughs from the forest—
they really longed to escape.
Look at them rushing, quitting the city completely,
just like ants when they plunder enormous
caches
of corn and haul it back to their hill to anticipate winter:
the black column moves through fields on a
narrow
track in the grass, transporting prizes, some of
them pushing
huge grains with their struggling backs, while
others are driving
and snapping at stragglers—the whole path
seething with labor.

Dido asks her sister for help with Aeneas

What did you feel then, Dido, observing that
struggle?
How did you sigh watching the whole feverish
coastline
from high in your tower, seeing the breadth of
that water
aswirl before your eyes with full-scale working
and shouting?
Extreme passion—what end will you pressure
a human
heart to? Again she was driven to tears, again
to the effort
of begging humbly. Her spirit gave in to her
passion:
she'd leave nothing untried—nor die for no reason.
"Scurrying around the whole beach—look at
them, Anna.
They're massed everywhere. Winds are calling
their canvas
already and sailors are gladly sporting their
garlands.
If I've been able myself to see such agony coming,
I'm able to bear it, sister. I'm wretched—but do
me
a single favor, Anna. That liar made you his
only
friend at times; he even told you some innermost feelings.
You alone may know the gentlest time to approach him.
Go to him, sister. Humbly remind our imperi-
ous
guest I never swore with Greeks at Aulis[91] to
wipe out
Troy's people. I sent no fleet to his city
or pulled up his father Anchises' ashes or
Manes'.
Why is he hard to my words, refusing to hear
me?
Why run off? Ask him to do me a last turn, for
a wretched
lover: wait for following winds and for easier
sailing.

I ask for no marriage now. He's disavowed it.
It's over.
He shouldn't lose or neglect Latium's beautiful
kingdom.
I ask for empty time, a space to rest from this
madness,
while Luck teaches me how to lose and be
sorry.
I pray for this last favor, sister. Have pity.
I'll pay him back, if he grants this, in full when
I'm dying."

Aeneas remains resolved
Such were the pleas and tears which her miserable sister
brought and re-brought to Aeneas. But nothing
could move him.
He heard no words, no tears: the man was intractable.
Fates blocked him—a God stilled and closed up
his hearing.
Just as an old, strong oaktree is buffeted
this way and that by Alpine Northwinds that
struggle
among themselves to uproot it: it creaks and its
highest
leaves cover the ground when the treetrunk is
jostled,
yet it holds to its cliff—as high as it reaches
for air and sky, its roots extend into Tartarus—[92]
so with this leader. Words struck him continually
here, now there, he felt anxiety deeply,
still he remained unmoved. Tears went rolling
for nothing.

Dido sees new visions
Dido then truly feared for her future.
Cursed, weary of seeing the arched sky, she
was begging
for death. To help her leave the light, to end
what she started
sooner, she saw while placing incense and gifts
on an altar

the ritual water (to tell it is frightening)
blacken.
Wine she poured turned into blood which was
loathsome.
She told this vision to no one, not even her sister.
Besides, a marble shrine stood in the palace,
tended by Dido with great devotion to honor
her former
husband—white wool and sacred foliage
clasped it.
There she seemed to hear this man as he called
her:
his voice was clear when nighttime held the
land in obscurity.
A lonely owl often complained from a rooftop
in drawn-out hoots—sad, funereal bird-calls.
Many predictions, too, of older prophets
terrified and warned her. A savage Aeneas
himself drove her mad in her dreams—always
abandoned
and left to herself, always friendless, she
seemed to be walking
a long road through bare country, looking for
Trojans.
Just as a crazed Pentheus saw those cordons of
Furies,
paired suns, and Thebes revealed as if doubled;[93]
or Agamemnon's son Orestes, when driven
across the stage, fled from his mother, armed
with her torches
and black snakes, while Furies lingered in
doorways.

The Massylian priestess
Therefore, wrecked by grief and caught in her
madness,
she fixed on death. She picked her moment and
method
herself and approached her distraught sister to
tell her—
a hopeful face and calm brow concealed her decision—
"I've found a way, Anna—be glad for your sister—

I'll bring him back or free myself from this passion.
Close to the setting sun, bordering the ocean,
is Ethiopia's far-off land where powerful
Atlas[94]
turns the world on his back as it's burning with
inlaid
stars. From there I've met a Massylian priestess
who's watched at the temple of Evening's
daughters and offered her serpent
its meals: she's guarded the sacred boughs of
its tree there,
sprinkling honey and poppy seeds for its sleeping.
This woman claims to liberate minds that she
wants to
through song, and to burden others with bitter
anxieties.
She stops the flow of rivers, changes directions
of stars and moves Manes at night. Ground
that you stand on
will low, you'll see, and ash-trees come down
from the mountains.
Dear sister, I swear by the Gods and your precious
life, I don these arts of magic unwillingly.
Raise a pyre under the open sky of the courtyard
quietly. Heap it with all the remnants and
weapons
that vicious man left or attached to my room—
and the marriage
bed that destroyed me. Erasing every remembrance
of the odious person will give me joy; and the
priestess demands it."

Dark Gods are invoked
She stopped and was quiet. Pallor covered her
features.
But Anna did not believe her sister was hiding
death in these odd rites. She could not conceive
of such monstrous
rage or suppose all this was worse than the
death of Sychaeus.

Therefore she followed orders.
Soon as the pyre rose in the central palace's
open
air—a huge mound of pine branches and oak-
logs—
the queen went stringing garlands and crown-
ing the structure
with death-leaves. She placed on a couch on top
the sword he had left her,
a picture, some clothes. Now she was surely
aware of her future.
Altars rose in a circle. Her hair streaming, the
priestess
pealed her three hundred Gods—Erebus,
Chaos,
three-formed Hecate, three-faced Diana, the
virgin.
She sprinkled water supposed to have sprung
from Avernus;[95]
she'd looked for mature plants and cut them
with copper
knives by moonlight—their milk was poison-
ous, blackish;
she looked for a love-charm too—the mem-
brane torn from a newborn
foal's brow, yanked by its mare.
Dido, close to the altar, was dutifully holding
grain, one foot unstrapped. Her robe was un-
belted;
soon to die she called on the Gods and on starlight
conscious of destiny; she prayed to any just and
remembering
Power that cared for lovers contracted un-
fairly.

The queen's resentment and sleeplessness
Now it was night. Weary bodies were grasping
for sleep and rest throughout the earth, forests
and savage
seas had quieted, stars had rolled halfway
through heaven
and every field was still. Cattle and painted
birds near wide ponds, roosting in brambles
and rough woods, were settled in sleep in the
silent

dark, less anxious—their hearts were unconscious of labor.
But not the wretched Phoenician's heart—it
was never
relaxed for sleep. Her eyes and breast never accepted
night, her concerns multiplied, passion and anger
surged again in a long, moiling surf of resentment.
She said to herself, her heart tumbling inside
her,
"But look—what do I do? Try some earlier
suitor
again and be laughed at? Humbly beg for some
Nomad in marriage?
By now I've scoffed too often myself at such
husbands.
What, then? Follow the Trojan ships and the
Trojans'
commands to the end? Because they're pleased
that I helped them?
And thanks for my former acts will stay in
their memories?
But even suppose I want that, what proud ship
will accommodate
someone they hate? Lost, ignorant Dido—
still not seeing the lies of Laomedon's people.
What then? Run off alone with a party of clam-
oring sailors?
Crowd my own Tyrians around me and set
out—
with people I pulled just now from Sidonian cities?
Drive them again into sea-winds, tell them to
spread out their canvas?
No. Die. You deserve to. A sword gets rid of
your sadness.
My tears prevailed on Anna first, on my sister.
She piled me with evil, she made me mad, exposed to a stranger.
I wasn't allowed to pass through life as a
widow,
free from fault, untouched by care, like some
animal.

I failed my trust, my pledge to the dust of Sychaeus."
Breaking her own heart, she went on with bitter complaining.

Mercury warns Aeneas again

Aeneas, high on a stern now and decided on
leaving,
was catching some sleep—things were prepared and in order.
A God's form returned: similar features
confronted the man while dreaming. They
seemed to admonish—
in every respect like Mercury's voice and com-
plexion,
the hair like gold, the torso youthful and graceful—
"Son of the Goddess! You linger and sleep in
such danger?
You cannot see the threats now that surround
you?
Insane or deaf to the favoring breath of the
Westwind?
The queen's breast is a swirl of deceit and desperate evil:
she's fixed on death: she's a moiling surf of resentment.
Will you fly headlong from here while flight's
in your power?
You'll soon see this water a jumble of timber,
torches glaring fiercely, the shore glowing with
firelight,
unless you break from this land. Stop waiting
for daybreak—
wake up—no more delays! A woman is always
a mixed-up, changeable thing." He melded in
dark night when he finished.

Aeneas orders immediate departure

Really alarmed now by the abrupt apparition
Aeneas pulled his body from sleep. He scolded
companions,
"Quickly, you men. Take to your thwarts and
your watches,
loosen the sails fast. A God's been sent from the
highest

air to rush our escape, look!—he impels us again to
cut those twisted cables. Holy Lord, we will follow,
whoever you are: we accept your rule again—we applaud it!
Be near us, help us calmly and bring from the heavens
the right stars." He finished and yanked a sword from its scabbard
and slashed a cable—the sharp blade was like lightning.
The same heat possessed them all. They were seizing and running,
deserting the whole beach. Ships now covered the roadstead;
they strained, churned up blue-grey foam, and swept through the water.

Dido's rage intensifies
Dawn was leaving the saffron bed of Tithonus[96]
now and scattering first light on the country.
The queen, soon as she saw from her tower the whitening
day and moving ships and sails in formation,
struck her lovely breast with a fist three times and four times
and tore out her blond hair. "Jupiter, look at
the upstart go," she said, "making fun of our power!
Won't all of Carthage take out weapons and chase them?
Won't men wreck their ships and moorings? Hurry and bring me
torches, go! Drive at the oars, hand out the weapons!
What did I say? Where am I? What madness muddles my thinking?
Wretched Dido: what godless actions impress you?
They suited you *then*—when you gave him your scepter. Look at the faithful
hand of a man who carried his fatherland's House-Gods,
they say, and shouldered his aging, weakening father.

Couldn't I clutch him, dismember and scatter his body
at sea? Put to the sword his friends and Ascanius
himself? And set that feast on a board for his father?
Yes, a battle's outcome is doubtful. What of it?
Whom do I fear?—I am dying. If only I'd fired
his camp and filled his gangways with flame, killing the father,
son, and the lot—and tossed myself on the ash-heap.

Carthage's curse on the Rome of the future
"You Sun-God, whose fire regards and brightens all of our labor,
you, Juno, divining love's pain and remembering,
Hecate, wailing nightly at crossroads in cities,
you vengeful Furies, Gods of a dying Elissa:
hear and accept my prayer, attend with your power—
my pain has earned it. If sailing and reaching a harbor
is necessary now for this unspeakable person,
if Jupiter's word demands that goal be accomplished,
still let war convulse him and swords of presumptuous people.
Let him be torn from his own land and the face of Ascanius.
Let him beg for help and witness the shameful
deaths of friends. Let him yield to unfair terms in a peace-pact
and never enjoy his rule or the sunlight he's longed for,
but fall before his time on open gravel, unburied.
There is my plea—the last word to be poured with my life-blood.
And you, Tyrians: pursue that whole tribe in the future
and hate them. Send word of this favor down to my ashes:
let there be no love or pact with these people.
And rise from my bones, whatever revenger

will follow Trojan settlers with torches and
lances,
now or whatever time gives you strength in the
future.
Let seas be against seas, shoreline at shoreline:
I call on arms to fight with arms—their own
and their children's."

Dido's end draws near

Her mind as she spoke was turning in every direction,
longing to break soon from the daylight she
hated.
She spoke briefly to Barce, the nurse of Sychaeus
(the old country held her nurse's ashes and
shadow):
"Nurse dear to me, go bring Anna, my sister.
Tell her to hurry, to wash her body in river
water and lead out calves, the atonements prescribed us.
Both of you come, your temples covered with
ritual garlands.
My thought is to finish the rites I prepared and
properly started
for the Underworld's Jupiter—put an end to
my troubles,
send off in flames from the pyre that Dardan
commander."
She stopped and the old one bustled away with
intentness.
But Dido trembled wildly now that the dreadful
thing had begun, her eyes bloody and rolling,
her nervous
cheeks flecked with red. Pale at the death
which approached her
she dashed in the house's inner court and dis-
tractedly
climbed the tall pyre, disclosing the Dardan
sword—a present she hadn't desired for this
purpose.
Here when she saw her familiar bed and the
Trojan's
clothes, she was moved to tears a little and
brooding.

She lay on the bed and spoke—the words were
her last ones:
"My sweet spoils—while God and the Fates
were permitting.
Take my spirit. Free my heart from its caring.
I lived—I finished the course which Fortune
provided.
Now my exalted form goes down to the Underworld.
I've seen my walls: I've built an illustrious city.
I made a hostile brother pay, in revenge for my
husband.
Happy—alas, too happy—if only those Trojan
keels had never touched the beaches of Carthage."
She stopped and pressed her face on the bed.
"We'll die unavenged here—
but die," she said. "So. It helps to go down into
darkness.
The cruel Trojan's eyes may absorb this cremation
at sea and carry an evil sign from my dying."

A city in consternation

The words broke off—and servants could see
she had fallen,
the sword was a froth of blood, the forearms of
Dido
all stained. Shouts went up to the courtyard
roof and stories dashed through the city and
stunned it.
Buildings echoed the sighs and wailing of
women
in grief, the immense sky re-echoed the outcry—
just as though the whole of Carthage were falling
to enemy charges, or ancient Tyre in a frenzy
of rolling flames from people's and Goddesses'
rooftops.

Anna rebukes her sister

Anna rushed back terrified, breathless and
trembling.
She beat her breast, her nails disfigured her
cheekbones,

she ran through the crowd and called on the dying
woman by name. "It's this, my sister? You wanted to trick me?
For *this* we prepared that pyre, the altars and firelight?
I'm lost. How shall I scold you first? For scorning your sister's
friendship in dying? The same death should have called me:
the same sword's pain could have taken us both in this hour.
My own voice called on our Fathers' Gods, and my fingers
worked to place you cruelly here—and I'm absent.
You kill yourself and me, sister, your people,
your city, Sidonian fathers. Give me some water—
I'll wash these wounds. Is a last wandering breath there?
My mouth will catch it." She'd climbed the steep ladder while speaking,
she held her near-dead sister, embraced her and warmed her.
She cried and sopped up dark blood with her clothing.

Iris helps Dido to die

The queen tried once more to lift up her heavy
eyes but failed. Her chest, deeply wounded, was gasping.
She struggled three times to raise herself on an elbow;
she rolled back on the bed three times. Her wandering vision
searched the sky's depth for sunlight. She sighed when she found it.
Powerful Juno now pitied her sorrow
and long hard death. Iris was sent from Olympus[97]
to free the wrestling spirit from knots of the body.
For Dido was neither deserving of death nor predestined,

but sudden grief and madness before her time had consumed her.
Proserpine[98] still had not taken a golden
curl from her head and sent her soul to the Styx and to Orcus.
So Iris flew down through the sky, trailing a thousand
moist colors reflecting the sun, using her saffron
wings and pausing above that life: "I'm taking an offering
now at the Death-God's command: I release your life from its body."
Her hands clipped hair as she spoke. Quickly and wholly
the warmth diminished and life went out into breezes.

(In Book V the Trojans hold funeral games in honor of Anchises, Aeneas' dead father. The site is the kingdom of the Trojan Acestes in Sicily. There is a ship race, a foot race, a boxing match, an archery contest, and a boys' parade. After a brief panic caused by a fire on the Trojan ships [extinguished by a downpour from Jupiter], Aeneas departs on the final leg of his journey to Italy. A valuable helmsman, Palinurus, is lost overboard at night before the Trojans arrive at Cumae, not far from modern Naples.)

BOOK VI:
THE DESCENT INTO THE UNDERWORLD

The Trojans' arrival at Cumae

Aeneas wept as he spoke, then slackened the reins on his vessels.
At length he glided ashore at Cumae, a port of Euboeans.[99]
Prows were turned seaward and anchors were holding
ships fast with their bites; the shoreline was bordered
with rounded hulls. Young men who burned for Italian

soil leaped out—one group searching for seed-ings

of fire in a flint's veins while others were snatching

wood near animals dens or finding and point-ing to rivers.

Aeneas, recalling his duty, made for the lofty

heights where Apollo presided, close to the monstrous and private

cave of a fearsome Sybil on whom the Delian Prophet

exhaled his great mind and will, exposing the future.

The story of Daedalus

Trojans went under the golden roof and grove of Diana.

Daedalus fled, as the story goes, from Minos' kingdom,

daring to trust himself to the sky and his rapid

wingbeats, making his cold unlikely way to the Arctic,

and finally touching down on this hilltop at Cu-mae.[100]

On first returning to land, Apollo, he offered

you his wings' oars and built an enormous tem-ple.

Androgeos' death was carved on the doors, and the wretched

Athenians, forced to pay by surrendering seven

sons each year—the urn stands there, the lots to be drawn out.

Raised from the sea, Crete's land responds from the portal

facing, and here is brutal love for a bull—Pa-siphae

furtively mounted, a hybrid being inside her,

the Minotaur, man and beast—a reminder of sexual outrage.

Daedalus built its house himself, inextricable mazes,

but pitied the intense love of a queen, Ariadne,

and loosened the knots and tricks of the build-ing for Theseus,[101]

guiding his blind steps with string. Icarus[102] also

would take a major part in this great work—if his father's

grief had allowed him: twice he tried to capture that downfall

in gold and twice his hands failed him. The Trojans were reading

all this closely just as Achates (sent on before them)

arrived with Diana's priestess, the Sybil of Phoebus

named Deiphobe—Glaucus' daughter. She spoke to their leader:

"Those are not the pictures required at present.

Now it's best to sacrifice—seven bullocks that never

were yoked and seven chosen ewes. It's the cus-tom."

Aeneas' men, when she finished, immediately followed her ritual

orders. The priestess called them on high to her temple.

The transformation of the Sybil

A cave had been cut from a huge breadth of Cu-maean

rock where a hundred broad paths converged on a hundred

mouths where voices could rush out—the Sy-bils' responses.

Trojans came to an entrance. The virgin com-manded,

"It's time to demand the God's word—look! my Apollo—"

her face and color at once changed as she spoke at the entrance,

her breast heaved, her hair lost its arrange-ment,

a wild fury filled her heart, she seemed to be taller

now that the God's will gave her more than a human

voice and breathed close. "You're slow in your prayer?

Aeneas of Troy," she said, "you're slow with vows? But before then
the great mouth of this sky-struck house will not open."

Aeneas insists on peace with the Gods

She stopped and was quiet. Cold tremors ran through the Trojans'
strong bones. From deep in his chest their leader poured out his prayer.
"Phoebus: you always pitied the hard labor of Trojans.
You guided the hand and Trojan arrow of Paris[103]
into Achilles' body. With you as my leader
I entered seas that bordered great countries, Massylian
people's far interiors, fields stretched out at the Syrtes.[104]
At last we cling to a fleeting Italian beachhead.
Let Troy's bad luck follow this far and no farther!
All you Gods and Goddesses thwarted by Trojan
glory and greatness: now it's right that you pity
Troy's people. And you, most holy of seers
who know the future: I claim the kingdom that's owed me
by Fates: give us Latium, rest for us Trojans
and Troy's wandering Gods, our disquieted Powers.
I'll start on a temple of solid marble for Phoebus,
Diana as well; I'll name festal days for the Sun-God.
And priestess, majestic shrines wait in our kingdom
for you: I'll place the oracles told to my people
and all your mysteries there; I'll dedicate hand-picked
men to your service. But don't be trusting your verses
to leaves where a flighty and quick breeze might disturb them:

sing them yourself, please." His prayer was ended.

Apollo masters the Sybil and speaks through her

But now the seer, not yet submitting to Phoebus,
dashed through the huge cave as if able to shake off
the great God from her breast. But all the more he oppressed her,
mastered her wild heart and mouth, gripped and subdued her.
The hundred large doors of her house had swung open
now by themselves and winds carried the Sybil's responses:
"At last you're done with extreme danger on water;
worse remains on land. Trojans will enter
Lavinium's realm—drop that one heartfelt anxiety—
then wish they hadn't arrived. War's in my vision,
war's horror—all that foaming blood in the Tiber.
You won't be lacking a Simois River, a Xanthus,
or Greek camps: a new Achilles emerging in Latium,
born himself of a Goddess. And add Juno, who'll never
be far from you Trojans. How you'll grovel for things like a pauper
and plead with every city and people in Italy!
A strange wife again will cause much trouble for Trojans—
a marriage again to a foreigner.
Don't concede to this trouble. Fight it more boldly
wherever Luck permits. The pathway to safety
will first be cleared by a Greek city—you'd hardly expect it."
So the Cumaean Sibyl chanted ambiguous,

frightening words in her shrine, wrapping the truth in her darkness,

and doubling the cave's moans. Apollo had shaken

his reins and twisted spurs in her breast to incite her.

Aeneas longs to see his father in the Underworld

Soon as her frenzied and wild cries had diminished

Aeneas, the leader, began. "None of this hardship,

virgin, is new in form or appears unexpected.

I've known it all; I've pondered or lived it beforehand.

I ask one thing. It's said the gates of the Ruler of Darkness

are near, and the murky swamp from the Acheron River's[105]

overflow. Let me go down to see the face of the Father

I love: teach me the way: open the sacred portals.

I saved him myself from fire and a thousand pursuing

weapons—my shoulders took him from crowds of our enemies.

He was my partner at sea; in all of our travels

he bore each threat from water and sky and exceeded

the strength and duties of age even when sickly.

The man prayed, in fact he gave commands that I humbly

seek and approach your entrance. Your power is total:

Hecate[106] gave you control of these woods of Avernus

to *use* it. If Orpheus could summon Eurydice's shadow,

trusting his Thracian lyre and strumming melodiously,

if Pollux could save his brother by dying another

way, by going and coming so often: why should I mention

Hercules, Theseus? And *I'm* of high Jupiter's blood-line."[107]

The Sybil tells of a golden bough

He spoke these words while firmly grasping an altar.

So the seer began, "You *are* of the bloodline of heaven.

Son of Anchises at Troy, the descent to the Underworld's easy:

the Hell-God's dark door is open morning and evening.

But climbing back to the air above, retracing those footsteps—

there's the work, there's your struggle. A few have been able:

loved by a helpful Jupiter, raised by a fire-like courage

to heaven, or sons of Gods. Woods are all intervening;

a stream, the Cocytus, glides and surrounds it with pitchy meanderings.

But if you love so much, if you greatly desire

to enter the Styx's waters twice and to witness

Tartarus' darkness twice—if mad labor enthralls you—

listen and do this first. The leaves and the supple

bend of a golden bough hide in a shady

tree said to be sacred to the Underworld's Juno.[108]

A grove completely obscures the bough in a shadowy valley.

But no one's allowed to enter the underground's coverts

before he pulls that goldhaired child from its tree-trunk:

Proserpine's ordered the fine gift to be carried

down to herself. Once you've broken the first off

a second bough of gold will sprout similar leaflets.

Look up high therefore; soon as you find it

pull with your hands; the bough is easy and willing to follow

if God's word has called you—otherwise nothing

can wrench it free, no hardest muscle or iron.

Besides . . . your friend has died. His corpse is unburied.

You could not know, sadly. The body dishonors your every

ship as you seek guidance and ponder things at our doorway.

Carry this man to his tomb first. Bury him duly.

Lead black rams and make them your first expiation.

Only then will you see the Styx River and forest—

realms uncrossed by the living." Her mouth closed. She was quiet.

The brashness of Misenus

Aeneas left the cave with a mournful expression,

eyes downcast, his mind puzzling over

this blind turn of events. The friend he trusted, Achates,

walked with him side by side and shared the anxiety.

Between themselves they linked a number of different questions:

what friend had the seer told of? Whose dead body demanded

burial? Soon as they came there, they looked at Misenus

on dry beachsand, cut off by death undeservingly.

A son of the Wind-God, a standout at stirring his comrades

and rousing the War-God with calls on his trumpet, Misenus

had joined with strong Hector and gone into combat

with Hector's group, excelling with spear as with bugle.

But after Achilles had stripped Hector of life and had triumphed,

Misenus gave his leadership, courage and friendship

to Troy's Aeneas—following no one inferior.

Now by chance with a hollow conch he had rumbled the seacoast,

madly challenging Gods with his calling and blaring.

And Triton[109] was envious. Grasping the man (if the story

deserved belief) on a rock, he plunged him in sea-froth.

So everyone circled now, mourning him loudly—

Aeneas with special devotion. They followed the Sibyl's

commands promptly—still in tears—and erected

an altar and tomb with timber. They worked to raise it to heaven,

going to old pine-stands close to the deepest burrows of mammals. They felled pitch-pines and ash-trees;

oaks grunted at axe-blows, wedges split up the oak-logs

and huge cords of rowan tumbled down from the mountains.

The two doves and the golden bough

First indeed in all this work was Aeneas,

encouraging friends and using the tools that his men used.

By chance he offered a prayer himself as he sadly

and deeply pondered things and gazed at the forest's immensity:

"If only that tree and its golden bough could be shown us

now in this vast forest! Because the seer was truthful,

sadly: she spoke too well of your dying, Misenus."

By chance a pair of doves appeared when Aeneas

had hardly finished—they veered from the sky
and under his very
eyes they landed on green moss. This greatest
of leaders
recognized his Mother's birds: he prayed to
them gladly,
"Be my guides! Set a course through the air-
waves
and find some way if you can to the grove
where that priceless
bough is shade for the rich soil. My Goddess
and Mother,
don't leave at a doubtful time." He stopped,
paused in his walking
and noted the signs they made, the course that
they stayed on.
The doves kept feeding, only flying before him
as far as his eyes could follow. He kept them in
focus;
then they reached the malodorous throat of Avernus,
climbed quickly and glided down through the
air-waves,
both perching high in the tree they'd looked
for. A second
color, a gold brilliance, shone through the
branches.
Just as mistletoe tends to blossom in woods in
the winter
cold and its fresh leaves circle a slender
tree (not its parent) with berries of yellow:
so these golden leaves appeared in the oaktree's
shadows and metal tinkled softly in breezes.
Aeneas gripped it at once and eagerly pulled it.
It gave slowly. He brought it back to the house
of the Sybil.

The funeral pyre for Misenus
Nonetheless Trojans mourned on the shore for
Misenus
meanwhile; they went through the last rites
for ungrateful ashes.
First they built a huge pyre out of chopped-up
oak and tacky pine. They plaited the sides with
a darker

wood, leaning the death-tree against them—
the cypress.
Weapons gleamed on top of the pyre as adornment.
Some men heated cauldrons; fires bubbled the
water;
others washed the cold body and oiled it.
Moaning, drained of tears, they settled the
body
back on its couch and draped it with garments
of purple—
his well-known clothes. The large bier was
then carried
(a somber task) and a torch applied in the way
of their fathers,
with eyes averted. Piled-up presents of incense,
oil poured in bowls, and meal were cremated.
After the ashes fell and the fire diminished,
wine moistened the thirsty dust and the remnants.
Corynaeus gathered the bones. A bronze jar
would enclose them.
Three times with clean water he circled the
company,
sprinkling them lightly with flowering
branches of olive—
a ritual cleansing. He offered some final
verses.
Aeneas conscientiously raised an enormous
monument here with the man's oars, weapons
and trumpet.
A windy hill now known as Misenus
would keep his friend's name alive through the
ages.

Preparations for entry into the Underworld
With all that done they quickly followed the Sibyl's
commands near a deep cave with enormous
and jagged
mouth, guarded by oil-black pools and a nighttime of forest.
Hardly a single bird could navigate safely
or wing overhead—such was the vapor that
seeped from

those dark jaws and rose to the dome of the
heavens
(Greeks called the place Aornos, 'The Bird-
less').
First the priestess stationed four of her black-
backed
heifers here and poured wine on their foreheads.
Clasping hair near the horns she snipped off
the topmost
and placed them on ritual fires—the first of her
offerings.
She called loudly, "Hecate! In heaven and hell
you have power."
Others cut the throats and caught the arterial
gush in bowls. Aeneas slaughtered a black-
wooled
lamb himself for Night, the mother of Furies,
and Earth, her great sister; a calfless cow for
Proserpine;
then, for the Styx's King, he started an altar
service at night: thick beef was piled on the
fires
and fatty oil poured on the sizzling entrails.
And look: under the first glare of the rising
sun the ground lowed underfoot, forested
ridges
began to move, and dogs peered and whined at
the shadows.
"The Goddess is coming," the seer yelled, "you
must leave us,
all you men not purified, go from this forest
completely.
Aeneas, take to the path, rip your sword from
its scabbard!
You'll need spirit now and steady emotion."
She broke off and wildly flung herself in the
open
cave. Without timid steps he followed his
leader.

Invocation of the Underworld's Powers
Lords of the spiritual empire: shadow and silence,
Chaos, Phlegethon, mute stretches of midnight,[110]

make it right to say what I've heard. Give me
your power
to bare things deep in the earth, covered in vapor.

Strange phantasms near the entrance
They moved through obscure darkness, desolate shadow,
past empty houses of Dis, unoccupied throne-
rooms,
just as a path goes through woods when moonlight is doubtful
or sparse, when Jupiter's hidden the sky or ob-
scured it,
and black Night has drained things of their
color.
Before the entrance Grief and vindictive Anxiety
smoothed their beds in the gullet itself of the
Hell-God.
Wan Diseases lived with comfortless Aging
and Fear. Crime-encouraging Hunger and
grimy
Poverty—forms frightful to witness. Death and
the throes of
Death. Lethargy, Death's brother. And sickly
minds' Giddiness. War, the bringer of Death,
on the threshold
opposite. Furies on iron couches. Mad Revolution,
its hair a tangle of blood-soaked fillets and serpents.
A huge elm in the center extended shadowy
branches
like old arms. They say dozens of idle
dreams are at home in all that foliage, cling-
ing.
More prodigies lay beyond it, a melange:
Centaurs at doors of stalls, Scyllas doubly con-
torted,
the hundred-handed Briareus, the Hydra from
Lyrna,
fiercely hissing. Chimaera, armed with its
flame-spears.
Gorgons, Harpies, and Geryon's three-bodied
shadow.[111]

Here Aeneas gripped his sword, suddenly
trembling
in fear, and presented the sharp blade to those
coming—
unless his well-taught friend had told him
these bodies
were hollow forms of reality, tenuous flittings,
the man would have charged with a sword in
vain and severed the shadows.

Charon and the Styx River
The road led down from there to Tartarus—
Acheron's waters.
A whirlpool churned and seethed with mud in
a monstrous
swirling that dumped tons of sand in Cocytus.
A boatman guarded the water's flow: Charon
was frightful,
in dire filth, the beard on his chin like a jumble
of grey briars, his eyes steady as firelight;
a soiled, knotted coat hung from his shoulders.
He punted the skiff himself, took care of its
canvas,
and carried bodies across in his rust-colored
ferry.
Now he was old, yet raw and green—old as a
God is.
And crowds ran and thronged the banks of this
river:
men and mothers, the bodies of great-hearted
heroes
relieved of life, boys, unmarried daughters,
children set on pyres before the eyes of their
parents—
dense as leaves falling and drifting in forests
in autumn at first frost, or birds flocking to sea-
shores
from whirlpools at sea when the cold season
pursues them
over the waves and sends them to sun-loving
countries.
They stood there and begged to be first crossing
that current.
Their hands reached out and longed for the opposite shoreline.

The dour boatman picked out this one and that
one
now but kept the others far back on the gravel.
Aeneas was deeply moved, alarmed by the uproar,
and said, "Tell me, virgin, why is that crowd at
the river?
What do the spirits want? What decides that
they keep from
this bank while others pull on oars through the
indigo water?"
The aging priestess briefly answered Aeneas:
"Son of Anchises, and surely the son of a Goddess,
the deep marsh you see is a pond of the Styx
and Cocytus.
Even Gods fear to swear and renege by its
power.
One whole crowd you see is helpless—unburied.
Charon's the boatman. He carries those who
are buried.
They're not allowed to cross that grumbling
stream from this fearsome
bank before their bones find rest in some
death-house.
They wander and flit about this bank for a
hundred
years. Accepted at last they come back to the
pond they had longed for."

The meeting with Palinurus
Anchises' son paused and stopped in his walking.
He pondered all the unfair luck and pitied it
deeply.
He saw in the crowd that sadly lacked burial
honors
Leucaspis, Orontes—the Lycian squadron
commander—
both borne from Troy on windy seas, till a
Southwind
tumbled their ships and crews in the water and
swamped them.

And look: Palinurus, the helmsman—guiding himself now.

Checking the stars on the recent voyage from Libya

he'd dropped astern, was thrown and surrounded by water.

Aeneas could just make out the somber man in that heavy

gloom. He spoke up first: "Which of the Gods, Palinurus,

tore you from friends and plunged you deep in that water?

Tell me—we hardly found Phoebus deceptive

before that time when he mocked my heart with his answer,

saying you'd reach the coast of Italy safely,

unharmed at sea. Is that how his promise was faithful?"

But he: "Phoebus' oracle never deceived you,

son of Anchises, my leader—no God plunged me in water.

A sharp and random violence broke off the tiller.

Charged with holding our course, I clung to the steering

and flew off, dragging it with me. I swear by the bitter

sea that I feared not so much for my body

as yours: with steerage stripped and an overboard helmsman

your ship could capsize in deep, gathering white-caps.

For three wintry nights a vehement Southwind

rushed me along on immense seas. From high on a roller's

crest on the fourth dawn I recognized Italy.

I swam gradually ashore. Then, as I reached out for safety,

my fingers hooked on jagged ledge of a sea-cliff,

clothes heavy and drenched, some barbarous people

struck me with daggers, foolishly thinking of booty.

Wind and wave toss and possess me now on that shoreline.

I beg you—by all the breath and light of delectable

skies, by your father, the hopes that rise with Iulus—

save me from wrong like this! You can, you're unconquered:

look for Velia harbor and throw some soil on my body!

Or if a way exists, some way for the Goddess, your Mother,

to show you—I'm sure you're ready to enter the Styx's

pond and broad current with power from heaven—

give your hand to a wretch on that water, carry me with you.

Help me rest in peace at least as a dead man."

The Sybil answers for Aeneas

He'd said these words when the seer started to answer,

"Why this cruel desire, Palinurus, this longing

to see the grim flow of the Styx? You are unburied:

how can you go to the Furies' banks before you are told to?

Stop hoping to bend the Gods' laws with your begging.

Your fall was hard; take these words to console you, be grateful:

people far and wide in neighboring cities,

urged by heavenly signs, will atone for your death by erecting

a tomb and presenting annual gifts at the death-mound.

The place will have a permanent name: Palinurus."

Her words removed his concern; for the moment some sadness

was forced from his heart. He was pleased to hear of the place-name.

Charon's challenge

The others, completing a course they'd started, came to the river.

Soon as the ferryman saw them now from the Styx's
water, passing mute scrub as they turned to the shoreline,
first he shouted, his words challenging quickly:
"Whoever you are, armed and approaching our river,
stop walking there! Tell me why you have come here—
a land of Shadows, languid Midnight and Nightmare.
To transport living flesh in the Styx's ferry is sinful.
I hardly enjoyed taking Hercules over
this pond, or Theseus, no, or Pirithous—[112]
although Gods bore them and men could not beat them.
One wanted to chain Tartarus' watchdog,
and dragged him trembling away from the very throne of our Ruler;
the others tried to escort our Queen from the bed of her husband!"

The showing of the golden bough
Apollo's priestess answered him shortly.
"Don't be troubled. No one here is deceitful.
Our weapons have no force. That monster, your watchdog,
may bark in his cave forever and terrify bloodless
ghosts; let Proserpine stay chaste at the door of her uncle.
Aeneas of Troy, known for his filial love and his armor,
goes down to Erebus' depths, to the shade of his father.
If no one sign of his great devotion will move you,
here's a bough you'll know." She opened her vestments,
revealing the bough. The puffed-up anger of Charon subsided.
No more words. Amazed at that venerable offering,
the ominous branch he'd seen far back in his past life,

he swung the coal-blue ferry around to the bank and approached them.
Next he dislodged from the long benches the other
souls who'd sat there. He cleared the boat's gang-planks and took on
the bulk of Aeneas. The ferry groaned under the living
weight; swampwater spurted through stitches and fissures.
At length the man and priestess were transported safely.
They landed in grey sedge and featureless mudflat.

The Sibyl subdues Cerberus
Cerberus shook this realm with his three-throated barking,
a huge beast crouched in the cavern that faced them.
The Sibyl, seeing his necks bristling already with serpents,
threw him scraps of fruit, drugged and honeyed to make him
sleep. Savagely hungry he gaped and snapped at the pieces
with all three mouths. The large hindquarters buckled;
he sprawled on the gound, hugely and wholly stretched through the cavern.
Aeneas passed the entrance, the watchdog unconscious,
and quickly left the riverbank no one recrosses.

Pain and judgment in the Underworld
Immediately voices were heard—the noise was enormous
of spirits weeping, children deprived of joy on the very
threshold of life by Luck, removed by a darkling
day from their mothers' breasts and plunged in some bitter
death. Nearby were spirits condemned to die through a perjuror's

charges—given their true places by lot or by judgment

now as Minos[113] presided, shook the urn, and assembled

a silent court; he studied their lives and the charges.

The next places were held by innocent, downcast

spirits who'd caused their own deaths—despising the sunlight

and ditching their lives. How they were willing to labor

hard now in the air above and suffer as paupers!

But Gods' laws blocked them: dreary, unloveable waters

constrained them: the nine-coiled Styx intervened and enclosed them.

Aeneas encounters Dido once more

Not far from there, spread out in every direction,

appeared Fields of Mourning (the name they were known by),

where those consumed by a hard love's ruthless infection

kept to themselves on footpaths covered by myrtle

woods—in death too their anxiety lingered.

Here were seen Phaedra, Procris, and wretched Eriphyle,

showing the wound her son cruelly inflicted.

Evadne and Pasiphae walked with a friend, Laodamia.

The Nymph Caeneus, once a boy, now was a woman

again, changed by Fates back to her earlier figure.[114]

Among them, roaming the far-flung woodland, was Dido,

the Phoenician. Her wound was fresh. As soon as the Trojan

leader stood up close and saw through the shadows

her dusky form—as a man, when the month is beginning,

sees or thinks he has seen the moon rising through cloud-trails—

he shed tears. He spoke fondly and gently:

"Unhappy Dido, the story that came was correct then:

I heard you had died, pursued your death with a sword-thrust.

And I—my God—I caused your death? I swear by the starlight,

by Gods in the sky and faith in the earth's depths if there's any:

I never wished, my queen, to go from your shoreline.

Gods told me—just as they force me to travel

now through Night's depths, through briars and shadows.

They drive by their own rules. And how could I think that

my leaving would bring such deep distress to your spirit?

Please don't go—don't walk from where I can see you—

who do you run from? This is the last that the Fates let me tell you."

Still in tears, Aeneas had spoken to calm her.

But she looked grim; the woman's spirit was burning,

she turned and kept her looks fixed on the stubble.

Her face had changed once he began to address her

no more than flint would or hard Marpesian rock-stands.

She finally tore herself away like an enemy,

running for shadowy woods. Sychaeus, her former

husband, equaled her love and requited her caring.

Aeneas was no less stunned by her death's unfairness. He followed

a long ways pitying, weeping. She moved off.

The warriors' fields

He trudged back to the way provided. Now he was reaching

the farthest fields, set off for crowds famous in
battle.
He met Tydaeus here, Parthenopaeus
(his arms well known), and the pale form of Adrastus.[115]
Trojans were here, killed in war and deeply la-
mented
above on earth. Aeneas watched them all in
their drawn-out
lines and sighed: Thersilochus, Medon and
Glaucus
(Antenor's three sons); Ceres' priest, Poly-
boetes;
Idaeus—still tending his weapons and chariot.[116]
They stood around, left and right, spirits in
clusters.
Unsatisfied now with merely a glimpse of
Aeneas
they gladly walked a ways and detained him to
ask why he'd come here.
But Greek princes and cordons of King Agamemnon,
seeing the man's weapons gleam through the
shadows,
trembled, acutely afraid. Some turned away—
as they'd headed
once for their ships—while others were raising
their voices
but feebly—the shouts they started belied by
their gaping.

The fate of Deiphobus
Aeneas could see a son of Priam, Deiphobus,
totally mangled here. His lips were viciously
cut off,
lips and both his hands. The ears ripped from
their temples,
torn off, and the nose cropped—a scandalous
maiming.
Aeneas could hardly recognize the man as he
shivered
and covered the ghastly wounds. He spoke up
first as a friend would:

"Deiphobus—strong in war, from the high
bloodline of Teucer—
what man chose to inflict such barbarous torture?
Who could allow it—on *you*? They told me a rumor
that last night: worn out in the slaughter from
killing Pelasgians
you fell on top of a mixed-up litter of corpses.
Later I built an empty tomb on Rhoeteum's[117]
coastline myself; I called loudly three times to
your spirit.
Your name and weapons guard the place. But
I could not discover
your body, my friend, and give you rest in the
land I was leaving."
And Priam's son: "My friend, nothing's remaining:
you settled it all for the dead shade of Deiphobus.
My own bad luck and the lethal crimes of a
Spartan
woman plunged me in pain: Helen left these
mementoes.
Recall, we wasted ourselves in trivial pleasures
that last night—we're forced too much to recall
it.
After that deadly horse came running and
leaping
on Troy's heights, its belly loaded with weapons
and soldiers, that female pretended to dance.
Leading some Trojan
women and shouting, "Euhoe," holding the
largest
torch in their midst, she actually signaled
Greeks from a rooftop.
Just then, exhausted from worry, heavy and
drowsy,
I lay on a wretched bed. Deep and pleasurable
stillness
covered my body—so like the stillness of dead
men.
My prize wife in the meantime cleared all arms
from the building,

even pulling a sword I trusted from under my
pillow.

She opened the house's doors and hailed Menelaus,

hoping of course that here was a fine gift for
her lover,

and talk of the old mistakes now would be
smothered.

Why delay it? They rushed in the bedroom,
adding a single

crime-mongering friend—Ulysses. Gods, if you
let me

demand rightful vengeance, start on Greeks
with this torture!

But now it's your turn. Tell me what happen-
ings brought you

alive here. Did seas confuse and compel you?

You've come with a God's warning? What luck
has fatigued you?

Why visit a place of disquiet, so dismal and
sunless?"

Now as they talked Aurora had driven already

across the zenith and coursed through the sky
in her rose-colored chariot.

All the allotted time perhaps could be lost in
this manner

and so the Sibyl spoke up briefly—her warning
was friendly:

"Night runs on, Aeneas. We lose these hours to
your sorrow.

Here's the place where the road divides into
two paths:

the right one leads to the walls of powerful
Pluto—

our path to Elysium; the left one leads to a
ruthless

Tartarus' depths—where criminals' pains are
exacted."

Deiphobus told her, "Don't be harsh, powerful
priestess.

I'll leave and complete the number of those
back in the darkness.

Go and enjoy better luck, you pride of the Trojans!"

He said that much, turned while speaking, and
left him.

The punishments of Tartarus

Aeneas abruptly noticed a cliff on the left
side.

He saw wide walls, three belts of fortification,

ringed by a river whose rapids were burning
and boiling—

the Underworld's Phlegethon, rolling its clatter of boulders.

Huge gates were in front, and solid columns of
iron.

No human force, no Sky-Gods themselves in a
battle

could wreck them. Against the sky stood a
tower of iron:

the Fury Tisiphone sat on top, wrapped in a
bloody

coat, a guard day and night on the courtyard.

Groans were audible here and cracks of relent-
less

whips, dragged chains and the grating of
metal.

Aeneas paused in terror, held by the uproar.

"Tell me what forms of evil, virgin priestess,
are driven

to punishment here. What loud noises are rising?"

The seer began to speak: "Well-known leader
of Trojans,

by Law no pure spirit may cross that criminals'
threshold.

When Hecate made me rule the groves of Avernus

she taught me the Gods' vengeance herself—
she led me through everything.

Rhadamanthus[118] of Crete holds this kingdom
of iron.

He listens to tricksters, checks them, and
forces confessions.

Each one sinned in the world above with a fur-
tive and empty

pleasure, and delayed expiation too late—till
the death-hour.

Instantly straddling the guilty spirit is vengeful

Tisiphone, armed with her stinging whip: as
her left hand

brandishes fierce snakes she calls for hordes of
her sisters.

At length the awesome gates are opened on
screeching

hinges and sockets. And see what sort of a
watchman

sits at the entrance, the form that's guarding
the threshold:

the fifty black and monstrous mouths of the
Hydra.

It holds a place fiercer inside. Then Tartarus
opens

itself—a headlong plunge that reaches far into
darkness—

twice as far as your view to the sky or the air
of Olympus.

The Titan people are there, Earth's primordial
children,

downed by thunderbolts, rolling around in the
deepest

holes. I saw those twin giants, the sons of Al-
oeus,[119]

who strove to destroy the breadth of Jupiter's
heaven

by hand and thrust him down from the heights
of his kingdom.

I saw Salmoneus[120] too paying a brutal

price for copying Jupiter's fire and the noise of
Olympus:

drawn in a four-horse chariot, shaking his
torches,

he'd gone in triumph through Greek crowds
and the city

at Elis' center and claimed for himself Olympian worship.

Madman: to mimic a stormcloud's inimitable
lightning

with brass wheels and the stamp of horn-footed
horses!

But the all-powerful Father hurtled a fire-
spear

from massed clouds—not some torch or a smoldering pine-wood's

glow—and its violent whirlwind twisted him
headlong.

I saw Tityus[121] also, foster child of everyone's
Mother,

the Earth. He lay outstretched, his body extended

nine full acres. A vulture, monstrous and hook-
beaked,

skimmed his ageless liver, whose tissue was
ripe for the torture

continually: the bird grubbed deep in his ribcage

for meat and gave no rest to that flesh which
always recovered.

Why mention the Lapithae? Pirithous,
Ixion,[122]

threatened by black granite that's tilting already

and falling apparently *now*. High festival
couches

shine on their golden legs and dishes arranged
for a monarch's

delight are before their eyes. But an elderly
Fury

lounges next to them, stops their hands from
touching the table—

she leaps up, cocking a torch, and her voice is
like thunder.

Here are those who despised their brothers
while living,

struck their fathers, or tangled dependents in
hoaxes.

Or those—the largest crowd—who came upon
riches

and lived alone, sharing no wealth with their
children.

Some were killed for adultery. Others had followed

traitors' ranks and dared to break faith with
their masters.

Now they're jailed, waiting punishment. Don't
be too curious

how they're punished, what form or fate overwhelms them.

They roll huge boulders; others hang from the
turning

spokes of wheels. Theseus miserably sits there—

he'll sit forever. And no one's sadder than Phle-
gyas.[123]

He warns them all, his voice loud through the
shadows:

'Be warned! Learn justice and stop scorning the
Sky-Gods.'

One man sold his country for gold and inflicted
despotic rule. Another rigged laws for a price
or unrigged them.

This one forced forbidden sex on his daughter.

They all dared to offend grossly—and did as
they dared to.

If I had a hundred mouths and tongues and a
hundred

iron voices I could not number all of those evil

forms or run through the names of every sentence."

The presentation of the golden bough

Having said all this the aging priestess of
Phoebus

added, "But come now. Take to the road. Finish
the labor

you started. Hurry—I see walls raised by the
Cyclops'[124]

forges ahead where arched portals confront us.

There we'll place the gift we were told to beforehand."

She ended. They walked the dim roadway together.

They covered the ground intervening and came
to the portals.

Aeneas reached the entrance and sprinkled his
body

with fresh water. He set the bough in the doorway that faced him.

*Aeneas and the Sibyl arrive at the Elysian
Fields*

Done, finally, the office performed for the Goddess,

they came to a joyful place, the green and delightful

groves of happy people, the homes of Elysium.

Headier air was here; lilac color was clothing

fields that recognized their own starlight and
sunlight.

Men on the grass were training their bodies for
wrestling,

or grappling on tawny sand, competing in
matches.

Others were singing songs, tapping their feet
to a dance-time.

A Thracian priest[125] in long vestments was
keeping

time as well on the seven clear strings of his
lyre,

playing now with his fingers, now with an
ivory plectrum.

Teucer's old nation was here, a beautiful people:

the great spirits of leaders born in a better

age like Ilus, Assaracus; Troy's patriarch, Dardanus.[126]

Aeneas admired from a distance the weapons
and empty

chariots, upright spears in the ground, and the
scattered

and loose-reined horses cropping fieldgrass.
The credit

they'd taken in horse-teams and weapons
while living, in careful

feeding and shining of mounts, had followed
them down into earth-depths.

In fact he saw on the grass, to his left and his
right side,

men feasting while singing, enjoying their
paeans in chorus

under scented laurels, from where the
Eridanus[127]

River's fullness above them rolled through the
forest.

The poet Musaeus helps the Sibyl

These had suffered wounds in a fight for their
country;

those were devoted priests during their lifetime.

These were sacred prophets who sang things
worthy of Phoebus,

and those had discovered new ways of enhanc-
ing
others' lives—they made them remember their
service.
All had white headbands circling their temples.
The Sibyl spoke up now as they crowded
around her,
Musaeus[128] above them all—he stood in the
center,
the large crowd regarding his out-standing
shoulders.
"Tell us, you glad spirits, and you, exceptional
seer:
What part of this world holds Anchises? We
came here
for his sake, crossing wide Underworld waters."
That leader made a brief response to the Sibyl:
"No one's home is fixed here. We live in the
shaded
groves, on couches of stream-banks; we occupy
meadows
freshened by brooks. But you, if your will and
heart will support you,
climb this hill and I'll find you an easier foot-
path."
He finished and walked before them. Higher,
he showed them
fields of light. They left the hilltop behind
them.

Aeneas and Anchises are reunited
Anchises now like a father was earnestly gazing
at spirits confined in a deep green valley and
destined
for higher light. By chance he reviewed and
considered
this whole line of his dear people, his offspring—
men's good luck and bad luck, their customs
and artworks—
just as he saw Aeneas approaching directly
there on the grass. He raised both hands in excitement,

words fell out, tears dropped from his cheekbones—
"You finally came? The love your father expected
has conquered that hard road? I'm favored to
witness
my son's face and hear and return familiar language?
I really suspected—my heart knew of this future.
I marked our time—my own concern has not
failed me.
From which immensely driving seas do I take
you,
my son? What land, what extreme danger has
thrown you?
How worried I was that Libya's kingdom might
harm you."
Aeneas answered, "Father, your sad apparition,
meeting me often, compelled me to strive for
these dwellings.
The fleet stands in the Etruscan Sea. But give
me your right hand,
Father, please—don't withdraw—let me embrace you."
Big tears had wetted his face as he begged him.
Three times his arms reached for that neck to
embrace him;
three times the image escaped his grasp—the
reaching was futile—
it moved like a dream with wings or a stirring
of breezes.

The gathering at the Lethe River
But now Aeneas could see in a separate valley
a grove apart where forest and copses were rustling.
The Lethe River flowed by peaceable homes
there;
huge crowds of people were dashing and circling
just as bees in clear summer might settle
on various flowers in meadows or swarm in a
circle

by white lilies and make the whole countryside
murmur.
Not knowing the cause Aeneas was chilled by
the sudden
vision and asked what waters were those in the
distance,
who those men were, filling the banks like an
army.
His father Anchises: "Spirits destined for other
bodies by Law—they've come to this river, the
Lethe,
for carefree water, a long drink of oblivion.
In fact I've wanted to tell you, to show you in
person
now for a long time this line of descendants,
the more to celebrate together your sighting of
Italy."
"But Father, must we think some spirits go
soaring
skyward from here, again reverting to heavy
flesh? Why such mad desire for daylight and
sadness?"
"I'll tell you, my son. I'd hardly leave you uncertain."

The great wheel of life and death
Anchises began to reveal each phase of a cycle.
"First a Spirit inside them nourishes heaven
and earth's marshy plains, the luminous orbits
of moon, stars and sun: Mind streams through
their members
completely, stirs their mass, and unites with
voluminous Body.
Then come species of birds, animals, people,
and prodigies borne by the marbled surface of
ocean.
That Force is fire-like. The source of that seed
is celestial
until some weight of bodily sickness retards it
or earth-bound joints and death-bound members may dull it.
So people fear and crave, they relish and whim-
per—
they see no air, confined in dark prisons of
blindness.
Even when life's last glimmer has left them

still some harm remains: not all the body's diseases
entirely go from their wretched selves: things
which have deeply
grown together for years must become mysteriously grafted.
Therefore they work off old wrongs. They are
punished
and pay their debts, some by hanging exposed
in the empty
wind while others are washed in a violent
whirlpool
or fire burns away the last of their malice.
We all endure our own spirit's correction.
Then they're sent through wide Elysium—
some of them staying
glad in these fields till days pass and they finish a cycle
of time that frees them from hard flaws, leaving awareness
pure as the highest air and simple as firelight.
All the others roll the wheel of a thousand
years, when a God calls them in long lines to
the Lethe,
clearly to help them start forgetting, desire returning
again to the arched sky and turn back to the
body."

Future kings of Rome
Anchises finished and drew his son and the Sibyl
together right through the crowd's boisterous
center.
He climbed a mound from where he could scan
all of the spirits'
long lines and study the faces of those who approached him.
"Look, now: honor at last will follow the children
of Troy and descendants go on from the people
of Italy:
brilliant spirits to come with our own reputation!
Let my words present them. I'll teach you your
future.

See that youth who leans on the spear with no
  spearpoint?
He holds by lot the place closest to daylight and
  rises
to higher air first from our mix with Italian
  bloodlines.
Silvius, surname of Alban kings, and the last-
  born
son your wife Lavinia rears in the forest
when you are old—but a ruler and father of rulers:
he'll make our people masters of Alba
  Longa.[129]
Next is Procas, a pride of the Trojan people;
Capys, Numitor; Silvius Aeneas will bring
  back
your own name—and just as outstanding in
  honor
or battle—if Alba will ever yield to his power.
Look at those men, what great strength they're
  displaying!
Their shaded temples carry the citizens' oak-
  leaves.
These will build Nomentum, Gabii, the town of
  Fidenae;
those, the fortresses high on the hills of Collatia,
Pometia, Camp Inuus, Bola and Cora.[130]
Names will appear where land is nameless at
  present.

The glory of Rome itself
"Even Mars' child will join his grandfather-
  comrade:
Romulus,[131] Ilia's boy, born of Assaracus'
blood. See that double crest rise from his helmet?
The Gods' Father himself marks him now with
  that honor.
Look, my son, Rome's glory comes from his
  omens:
a match for the world in rule, for Olympus in
  spirit,
Rome will enclose her seven hills with a single
wall and rejoice in her children, her men—just
  as our Mother
Cybele rides her chariot, crowned with her tur-
  ret, through Phrygian
towns and exults in her son-Gods, embracing
  her hundred grandsons,
all Sky-Gods and all holding heights of Olympus.[132]
Look there, focus your eyes now on these people,
your own Romans: Caesar and all of Iulus'
lineage under the great axle-tree of the heavens.

The vision of Augustus
"And this man, the man you've heard promised
  so often,
is Caesar Augustus,[133] a God's own son who
  will settle
a Golden Age once more on Latium's meadows'
ruled by Saturn before. He'll open the empire
to India, Africa, lands lying beyond the eclip-
  tic,
beyond the sun's annual journey, where Atlas
turns the sky's wheel on his back as it's burning with inlaid
stars. Already Caspian kingdoms dread his arrival,
Scythian land shudders at answers from
  heaven
and seven mouths of the Nile are anxiously
  foaming.
Even Hercules never covered such country
tranfixing the bronze-hoofed deer or quieting
  forests
of Mount Erymanthus and scaring the Hydra
  with arrows,
nor Bacchus in triumph, vine-shoots for reins
  on his chariot,
driving his tigresses down from the highest
  ridges of Nysa.[134]
And still we're slow extending our power
  through action?
Fear prevents us from settling land in Ausonia?

Other rulers of Rome

"But who's in the distance, crowned with tendrils of olive
and carrying relics? The grey beard and hair of
a Roman
king, I'm sure. With laws he'll strengthen the infant
city after he's sent from the poor district of little
Cures to rule an empire.[135] Next in succession,
disrupting his country's leisure by goading inactive
men to war, is Tullus—now his troops are not used to
victory. Ancus, a braggart, follows behind him—
too pleased already with breezes of popular feeling.
Want to see the Tarquin kings?[136] And the vengeful,
proud spirit of Brutus? The man who recovers the fasces[137]
and first to receive Consular power and Lictors'
brutal axes? His sons will make war on their father.
Wretched, he'll call for their punishment—all for the beauty
of freedom. Whatever the future makes of his action,
love of the land prevails and intense desire for honor.

Future conflict between Julius Caesar and Pompey

"There are the Decius and Drusus families. Look at Torquatus'
brutal axe. And Camillus, recovering standards.[138]
But those two men you see matched in glittering armor,
of one mind now while darkness surrounds them,
my God, what war between themselves when they make it

to life's light, what slaughter of ranks they will foster!
The father comes down from Alpine redoubts, his fort at Monoecus;
the son-in-law builds Eastern forces against him.[139]
No, my children—don't get used to such warfare—
don't turn such fighting force on your fatherland's entrails.
You stop first—you come from a race of Olympus—
throw down your spear, my grandchild.

Rome's destiny is to govern strongly

"That man, known for killing Greeks, will be Corinth's
conqueror, driving his winner's chariot high up the Capitoline.[140]
There's the wrecker of Argos and Agamemnon's Mycenae,
who'll kill the sons themselves of war-strong Achilles,
avenging our Fathers at Troy and the outraged shrine of Minerva.[141]
Who'd leave your greatness, Cato, or Cossus, in silence?
Or Gracchus' family? Or twin Scipios, lightnings
of war that destroy Libya? And little Fabricius
but strong! Serranus, planting seeds in his furrows.
And where do you take my tired spirit, you Fabians? Maximus,
you'll save our state alone by stalling invaders.[142]
Others may hammer bronze into delicate breathing
and draw, I'm sure it's true, life-signs from marble.
Some plead causes better or track with a stylus
paths in the sky to tell us what stars will be rising.
But Romans, remember to rule people, to govern:

there's your art: to make peace like a custom,
to spare dependents and put down those who
are pompous."

Loss of the young Marcellus

Aeneas' father went on, his listeners awes-
truck:
"Watch Marcellus, known for the wealth of his
prizes,
march in triumph, a man taller than all
men.[143]
He'll shore up Rome at a time of noise and confusion.
His horsemen will trample Carthage and
Gauls in rebellion.
He'll hang captured weapons three times for
his father Quirinus."
Aeneas now caught sight of a beautiful youngster
in brilliant armor, walking along with Marcellus.
His face lacked joy, however—his looks were
dejected.
"Father, who's that person attending Marcellus?
A son? Some other eminent family member?
What loud friends around him! His form itself
like a painting!
But night-like sadness circles and shadows his
features."
His father Anchises began to weep as he answered.
"My son, don't press me for deep family sorrow.
The Fates will merely show this boy to our
country: beyond that
they'll let him be nothing. You Gods, Roman
expansion
must seem too strong if our own gift like this
one had lasted.
What loud people's mourning will move from
the Campus
of Mars through the whole city—what funeral
sorrow
the Tiber will witness gliding past a death-
mound so recent!

No one child from a Trojan clan will have
raised up
so much hope in his Latin grandfathers, and
Romulus' country
will never pride itself in such a descendent.
Ah, for the old trust and goodness, the hands
undefeated
in battle! No one man could have met him in
armor
safely, whether he'd go to his enemy walking
or dig spurs in the sweated flanks of a stallion.
Sad, pitiful boy—if hard Fates can be shattered,
you'll be Marcellus. Fill my hands with some
lilies,
I'll scatter violet blossoms at least for my
grandson,
heaping gifts for his spirit, providing an empty
service." And so they roamed through all of the
aery
and wide fields of that region and gazed at each
subject.

Aeneas' coming struggle

Anchises led his son through all the particulars,
firing his heart with love for the name that was
coming.
Next he informed the man of conflict soon to be
managed,
described Laurentian people, the town of Latinus,[144]
and how to escape or endure each of his hardships.

The gates of ivory

Two gates of Sleep are there: according to legend,
one is of horn and offers an easy exit to actual
spirits; the other, of ivory, polished and shining,
sends to the sky elusive Underworld fantasies.
When done speaking Anchises walked his son
and the Sibyl
together and saw them out through the portals
of ivory.

Aeneas is reunited with his friends

Aeneas cut a path to the ships and rejoined his
  companions.
Soon he sailed straight up the coast to the port
  of Caieta.[145]
Anchors thrown from prows, the ships stood on
  the beachsand.

(In Books VII through XII Virgil describes the
Trojans' arrival in the area of Rome and their
struggle with various forces which oppose
them there. King Latinus rules this area,
called Latium; his daughter Lavinia is courted
by Turnus, king of the nearby Rutulians. According to a prophecy however the hand of Lavinia must go to a foreigner. Latinus is thus well
disposed toward Aeneas. But Juno dispatches
Allecto, a Fury, to stir up enmity between the
different factions. Turnus works especially
hard to align other neighboring peoples in opposition to Aeneas. Initial skirmishes eventually lead to major battles. Many warriors are
killed on both sides until Latinus confronts
Turnus, at the start of Book XII, with strong
arguments for seeking peace.

But Turnus remains intractable. One way
or another, though Aeneas also seeks peace,
Juno arouses Turnus to continue hostilities. At
one point single combat between Turnus and
Aeneas appears to settle all the issues; but an
arrow is directed awry, other warriors become
incensed, and a new battle begins. Aeneas is
actually wounded and helped from the field.
But he returns before long and the battle intensifies.

Jupiter finally holds up the scales of destiny and finds Turnus wanting. Jupiter then
urges Juno to put an end to her vengeance.)

FROM BOOK XII:
THE END OF THE WAR IN ITALY

Jupiter orders an end to Juno's spite
Meanwhile the all-powerful King of Olympus
spoke to Juno who gazed on the fight from a
  golden

cloud. "My wife: what end now is remaining?
Aeneas is lord of this land—you know it yourself and admit it.
He's owed to the stars; Fates will raise him to
  heaven.
What hopes or plots do you cling to there in
  your chilly
cloud? Was it right for Gods to be hurt, dishonored by humans?
For Turnus to get a lost sword back (and
  Juturna[146]
could do nothing without you), to strengthen
  the losers?
No: stop now. Yield at last to our prayers.
Don't let such grief consume you in silence or
  gloomy
concerns recur so often—from lips of such
  sweetness!
The end has come. On sea and land you've been
  able
to vex Trojans, to fire this blasphemous fighting,
disgrace a king's house and tangle a marriage
  in mourning.
I'll block further attempts." As Jupiter finished, the Goddess—
Saturn's daughter—lowered her eyes and responded,
"Because I've known that will of yours and
  your power,
Jupiter, I've left the land of Turnus. Unwillingly.
You would not see me now alone on this cloud-
  bank
enduring dishonor and honor: I'd rather be
  standing
surrounded by war and flame, dragging Troy to
  its enemies.
Admittedly I urged Juturna to run to her
  wretched
brother and take some great risks for his life—
  I approved it.
But not to bend her bow and fight with her arrows:
I swear by the Styx's springs and implacable
  head-waters—

the only name and oath which are binding on
Sky-Gods.
I do concede now. I'm done with this war; I de-
test it.
I ask one favor—no Fate or law is against it.
For Latium now and your own family honor,
when peace is confirmed by a happy marriage—so be it!—
when both sides link their laws and their treaties,
don't let Latins change the old name of their
country.
Don't let them be called Trojans, turn into Trojans,
change their people's language, or alter their
clothing.
Let Alban kings and Latium stay through the
ages:
a Roman people, strengthened by Italy's courage.
Troy and its name fell—let them always be
fallen."

In the future Trojans will be Romans

Man's and the world's Maker smiled as he answered.
"You *are* Jupiter's sister, and second daughter
to Saturn—
such waves of intense rage rush through your
body!
But come. Subdue this wrath—it was vain
from the outset.
I'll grant your wish. I yield, I'm willingly conquered!
Ausonians will keep the ways and speech of
their fathers.
Their name will stay as it is. In a body the Trojans will merely
mix and subside. I'll add their rites and their
customs
to Latins'; I'll make one tongue for all of these
people.
A nation will rise from this mingled Ausonian
bloodline
above all men, above the Gods in devotion:

you'll see no other people match them in honoring Juno."
The Goddess was pleased and nodded. She altered her purpose:
she soon withdrew from the heavenly cloud she
had stayed on.

Jupiter sends a dire warning to Juturna

That done the Father himself considered another
task: sending Juturna away from the army of
Turnus.
They say two plagues (people call them the Furies)
were born from Night's sickly womb in a single
birth with hell's Megaera. Tangles of serpents
knotted them all and wind-quick wings were
allowed them.
They loom by King Jupiter's threshold or
throne when he's angry,
ready to point fear and sickness in humans
whenever the Gods' Ruler amasses revolting
disease and death or alarms with war those
towns that deserve it.
Jupiter quickly sent one down from the sky-top
with orders to meet Juturna and act as an
omen.
Riding a turbulent wind she flew to that country
just like an arrow that's twanged through mist
from a bowstring,
tipped by a Parthian archer with virulent poison—
Cretans' and Parthians' arrow wounds are incurable—
hissing and fast it passes unseen through the
shadows.
This daughter of Night bore down on the earth
in the same way.
After she saw the Trojan forces and army of
Turnus
she suddenly shrank down to the form of a little
owl that squats at times on graves or abandoned

rooftops late at night and rudely drones through the shadows.

So transformed the Fury flapped and re-flapped by

Turnus' face—she squawked and struck his shield with her wingbeats.

A strange fear numbed and softened his muscles.

His scalp chilled and tingled. Words stuck in his gullet.

Juturna's final lament

But soon as Juturna knew the noise of that Fury's

wings in the distance, she mussed and tore her hair in her misery.

She scratched her cheeks and beat her breasts with a sister's

grief: "Turnus—how can your sister protect you?

What's left of my harshness now? What art will continue

your life's light? Can I myself block such an omen?

Yes, I'm leaving. No need to ruffle or scare me, filthy bird. I know your wings and their whiplash,

your death's rattle. Great-souled Jupiter's lordly

commands don't miss. And these are his thanks for a virgin?

Why give me an endless life, why is my human condition lost? I'd end my anguish now and for certain,

be able to go as my wretched brother's friend through the shadows—

but no, I'm deathless. And which of my joys will be joyful

without you, brother? For me, where is the deepest

earth gaping and sending me down to the deepest

Dead?" She said that much, covered her head in a blue-grey

shawl, sighed deeply, and hid in the depths of the river.

Turnus tries to defend himself alone

Aeneas closed in. Flashing a weapon against him—

big as a tree—he called with the heart of a savage,

"What stalls you now, Turnus? Why so reluctant?

Don't run off! We must fight fiercely, with weapons.

Change yourself into any form, gather whatever

spirits or tricks you can, follow the highest

stars if you like, or block and conceal yourself in some hollow."

Turnus shook his head. "None of your fiery orations

can scare me, wildman. The Gods—Jupiter's enmity scares me."

He said no more but looked around for a ponderous boulder.

A huge old stone happened to lie on the field-grass,

used as a landmark to settle disputes among farmers.

The backs of twelve hand-picked men could barely support it—

bodies of men the land might yield in our own age.

This leader restlessly grasped it, hefted it higher,

ran with it swiftly and hurled the stone at his enemy.

Yet he could not recognize himself as this runner,

his hands raised and the huge boulder above him.

His knees quavered; his blood was chilled and congealing.

Then the boulder itself rolled through some open

space and stopped short: the blow did not carry.

As though in a dream when languid quiet has
covered
our eyes at night we seem full of desire and we
struggle
to run, eager but helpless, weak in the midst of
our efforts:
we slump, speech unavailing, the usual body
strength fails, and words we form do not follow:
so with Turnus. However he strove to demonstrate courage
a stern Fury denied the advance. His heart was
a welter
of mixed feelings: he looked at the town, his
Rutulians;
slowed by fear (that spear was closer) he trembled.
He saw no escape, no way to charge at his enemy.
He saw no chariot now or the driver, his sister.

Aeneas hurls his weapon
And while he delayed, Aeneas kept flashing
the deadly
spear and looked for his chance. He threw from
a distance
with all his force. Stones from siege-slings
have never
roared or smashed into walls nor has lightning
and thunder
cracked so hard. Appearing dark as a whirlwind,
bearing its bitter conclusion, the spear went
flying and broke through
the corselet's edge, the seven-fold shield at the
bottom,
grinding, and tore through thigh. Turnus was
buckled.
His massive knee dropped to the ground from
the impact.
Rutulians moaned and leaped up—all the
mountains around them
echoed their moans—deep woods answered
their voices.
The man was humbled. He raised his eyes and
extended

a hand: "I did deserve this. I won't be a beggar,"
he said, "use your chance. If any concern for a
wretched
Father can touch you—you had such a Father,
Anchises—
I ask that you pity Daunus. My Father is
aging.
Return me alive, or my corpse despoiled of this
daylight,
if that's your choice. You've won. The loser's
hands are extended:
Ausonians can see it. She's yours—marry Lavinia—[147]
but don't stretch hatred further." Armored and
trenchant,
Aeneas stood there. He looked around and held
back his sword-hand.

The sword-belt of Pallas
More and more these words had begun to deter
him
now when there, high on the shoulder of Turnus,
appeared a sad sword-belt, its studs familiar
and shiny—
young Pallas' belt. Having wounded and
sprawled him,
Turnus had killed him and sported the enemy's
prize on his shoulder.
After Aeneas gazed at the prize and absorbed
this reminder
of bitter grief, a crazed and frightening anger
burned him. "You—wearing that prize from
my comrade—
you want to escape? Pallas wounds you, it's
Pallas
who takes your blood as the price for the crime
you committed."
He finished and buried the sword in his enemy's ribcage
avidly. Turnus collapsed. His muscles were
cooling.
His life, protesting and sighing, ran off to the
shadows.

NOTES

Not every allusion or proper name in Virgil's poem is noted here. Very minor characters have not been noted, nor have place-names or characters for which no information outside of **The Aeneid** is available.

Book I

[1]Carthage was a city on the western Mediterranean coast of North Africa, settled by Phoenicians (whom Virgil also calls Tyrians or Sidonians), and a serious rival with Rome in later times.

[2]The Fates—Clotho, Lachesis and Atropos—were associated with personal and national destiny and were pictured as spinning a web of time and events. They are of central importance in providing a sense of direction and momentum in *The Aeneid*. The Latin word *fatum* also means "something spoken," by a God such as Jupiter, and hence has the connotation of "Law."

[3]Lavinian, that is, named after Lavinia, the princess and daughter of Latinus whose hand in marriage Aeneas will win at the end of the poem.

[4]Juno, sister and wife of Jupiter (Hera and Zeus were their Greek names), was queen of the gods and long opposed to Aeneas and the Trojan cause.

[5]Latium, Latin, Alba, Rome: place-names along the central western shore of Italy, where the Trojans will eventually conquer and settle.

[6]The Tiber remains the principal river flowing through Rome.

[7]Paris, a Trojan prince, judged Venus to be more beautiful than Juno; hence the anger of Juno at Trojans in general.

[8]Ganymede, another Trojan prince, was carried off to heaven by Jupiter for his beauty. He was made cupbearer to the gods.

[9]Achilles was the principal warrior among Greek forces at Troy and the central figure of Homer's *Iliad*.

[10]Pallas, the Greek name of Minerva, was the goddess of wisdom.

[11]Ajax, king of the Locrians, was another warrior on the Greek side at Troy.

[12]A reference to Jupiter, king and father of gods and men, the most powerful deity in the Roman pantheon, residing on his throne on Mount Olympus.

[13]Diomedes, a son of Tydeus, survived the Trojan War and eventually settled in Italy. He appears later in *The Aeneid* where he declines to engage in further hostilities with the Trojans.

[14]Hector, greatest of the Trojan princes, was killed by Achilles.

[15]Sarpedon was a son of Jupiter who fought for the Trojans and was killed by Patroclus, a close friend of Achilles.

[16]Aletes, Abas, Ilioneus and Orantes were all warriors at Troy who managed to survive and escape westward led by Aeneas. Achates was an especially close comrade-in-arms of Aeneas.

[17]Neptune—the Roman name for Poseidon—was a brother of Jupiter. He ruled the seas and was generally well disposed towards the Trojans.

[18]Triton and Cimothoe were Neptune's assistants; the former was also a son of the sea-god and a deity himself.

[19]Ceres was the Roman goddess of grain, bread and the harvest.

[20]Capys, Caicus and Antheus were also Trojan warriors and followers of Aeneas.

[21]Acestes was a Trojan leader who settled in Sicily after the war.

[22]Scylla and Charybdis were two monstrous forms presiding over the Sicilian Straits, the former

associated with a cliff and the latter with a whirlpool. The Cyclops were a race of one-eyed giants inhabiting the southern coast of Sicily.

[23]Venus—the Roman name for Aphrodite—was the goddess of love. As the mother of Aeneas she also advances the Trojan cause strongly.

[24]Teucer was the first king of Troy; hence the Trojans were sometimes called the Teucrians.

[25]Antenor was another Trojan warrior who, like Aeneas, eventually settled in Italy.

[26]Venus is called "Cytherean" because of her fondness for the island of Cythera, off the southwestern coast of Greece.

[27]The Rutulians, led by Turnus, were a tribe hostile to the Trojans after Aeneas' arrival in Italy.

[28]Ascanius, Iulus, and Ilus were all names of Aeneas' son. His mother Creusa, a daughter of King Priam at Troy, had not survived the war.

[29]Romulus and Remus were the twin sons of Mars, the god of war, and the priestess Ilia, or Rhea Silva. The boys were raised, according to a popular Roman legend, by a she-wolf.

[30]Assaracus was a king of Phrygia, grandfather of Anchises, the father of Aeneas, and another revered ancestor of Troy.

[31]Phthia and Mycenae were Greek cities strongly associated with the invasion of Troy since the former was Achilles' birthplace in Thessaly and the latter was ruled by Agamemnon in southern Greece.

[32]The name of Julius Caesar, Rome's great general and first dictator (killed in 44 B. C. E.), is connected by Jupiter here with the name of Aeneas' son, Iulus or (more commonly) Ascanius.

[33]Vesta was the Roman goddess of the hearth and domestic life.

[34]Maia's son is Mercury, the gods' messenger (the Greek Hermes).

[35]Phoebus—the Roman name for Apollo—was the god of the sun and leader of the nine Muses associated with various arts.

[36]Agenor was an ancestor of the Tyrians, an early king of Phoenicia. Though Virgil sometimes calls the Carthaginians "Libyans" later in the poem, here the Libyans are hostile neighbors.

[37]Paphos was a town on the island of Cyprus sacred to Venus. Saba was a district in Arabia well known for its scented products.

[38]Priam was king of Troy and Aeneas' father-in-law. The Greek sons of Atreus—Agamemnon and Menelaus—were principal enemies of Priam in the Trojan War.

[39]Rhesus was a king of Thrace who came to the aid of Priam. The Xanthus, like the Simois, was a river at Troy.

[40]Troilus was another son of Priam.

[41]Memnon, a son of Aurora (goddess of the dawn) and the king of Ethiopia, fought on the Trojan side and was killed by Achilles. Penthesilea was also slain eventually by Achilles.

[42]Diana, the daughter of Jupiter and Latona, was the goddess of the moon and of the hunt. She was called three-formed and three-faced: Luna in heaven, Diana on earth, and Hecate in the lower world. The Oreads were mountain nymphs. Mt. Cynthus was in Delos in Greece and the Eurotas was a river in Sparta.

[43]Orion was a winter constellation in the figure of a hunter with bow and arrow. He was often associated with stormy weather.

[44]Eryx was a mountain and city on the Sicilian coast. Saturn (in the preceding line) was an old Latin god, later identified with the Greek Kronos, and the father of Juno.

[45]Anchises, son of Capys, a Trojan patriarch, was Aeneas' father. His role as guide and counselor is very important in Books II, III and VI.

⁴⁶Not the ancient king of Troy, this Teucer had been a king of Salamis, a Greek, and the brother of Ajax.

⁴⁷The Pelasgians were the oldest inhabitants of Greece. Like Homer Virgil uses words like "Pelasgians" and "Achaians" to refer to the Greeks in general.

⁴⁸When Paris judged Venus to be more beautiful than Juno, he was rewarded by Venus with Helen, the beautiful wife of Menelaus, who lived in Sparta. When Menelaus and other Greeks pursued Helen to Troy, the great war began.

⁴⁹Cupid, Venus's son, was the Roman god of love.

⁵⁰Typhoeus was a giant who tried to force Jupiter from Mt. Olympus and was repulsed by a thunderbolt and buried beneath Mt. Etna.

⁵¹Lyaeus, literally, "the releaser from care," was another name for Bacchus, the Roman god of wine.

⁵²Acidalia was the name of a fountain in the Boeotian region of Greece where the Graces, Venus' daughters, were said to be fond of bathing.

⁵³Arcturus, the bright star in the constellation Bootes, was associated with damp weather, as were Ursa Major and Minor—"the twin Bears"—and the Hyades, a star cluster in Taurus.

Book II

⁵⁴Dolopians and Myrmidons were both peoples of Thessaly. The latter were followers of Achilles in the Trojan War; the former followed Pyrrhus, his son.

⁵⁵Calchas, a son of Thestor, acted as prophet or soothsayer for the Greeks at Troy.

⁵⁶The Palladium was an ancient image of Pallas, the Goddess of wisdom, which according to legend had fallen from heaven. Ironically, though Pallas was often ill-disposed to the Trojans, her image rested in their city and Troy's safety was believed to rest in the Palladium's remaining there. There were also legends that the image eventually found its way to a temple in Rome.

⁵⁷Larissaean, that is, Thessalian, the region in Greece where Achilles came from, the greatest of the Greek warriors.

⁵⁸Among the Greek warriors listed here Sthenelus was a son of Capaneus and a leader of the Argives (from Argos in southern Greece); Acamas was a son of Theseus and Phaedra; Thoas was a king of Lemnos, a Greek island in the Aegean Sea; and Machaon was a Greek army surgeon, brother of Podalirius the physician.

⁵⁹Phrygian, that is, Trojan. Danaans—from the Greek city of Argos—could also refer to the Greeks in general. See Note 47.

⁶⁰Deiphobus was a son of King Priam and the husband of Helen after Paris' death. His mutilation at the hands of the Greeks is vividly described in Book VI.

⁶¹Among these comrades-in-arms Coroebus was from Phrygia, a region friendly to Troy; Rhipeus, Hypanis, Dymas and Panthus are destined to die shortly in battle; Epytus is not named after this point.

⁶²Scyria was an island in the Aegean Sea near Euboea whose warriors had allied themselves with the Greek cause.

⁶³Pyrrhus, also called Neoptolemus, led Andromache, the wife of Hector, into slavery after the war. His death at the hands of Orestes is described below in Book III.

⁶⁴Creusa was a daughter of Priam and the wife of Aeneas at Troy.

⁶⁵Tyndareus, husband of Leda, was supposed in some accounts to be the father of Helen. In other accounts Jupiter, in the form of a swan, was her father.

[66]The Gorgons were female monsters with snakes for hair. Pallas is called 'Tritonian' because she was born near Lake Triton in Africa.

[67]Phoenix was a companion of Achilles in the Trojan War.

[68]The 'Mother of Sky-Gods' was Cybele, an ancient Phrygian Goddess, later worshipped at Rome as Rhea, Magna Mater, and under other names.

Book III

[69]Ida was a mountain not far from Troy.

[70]Polydorus was another prince and son of Priam at Troy.

[71]Manes were the spirits of the dead in the lower world.

[72]The Nereids were sea-goddesses, daughters of Nereus and Doris. Neptune of course was the Roman god of the sea.

[73]Gyaros and Myconos were islands in the Cyclades group in the Aegean Sea, adjacent to Delos.

[74]Cnossus or Gnossus was an ancient city on the island of Crete, said to be Jupiter's birth-place. The Corybants were priests of Cybele, the great mother-goddess.

[75]Sirius was the 'dogstar,' in the constellation *Canis Major,* often associated with dry weather.

[76]Phineius was a king of Thrace who was blinded and tormented by the Harpies for having put his sons to death wrongly. The Harpies were monsters, half bird and half woman.

[77]Laomedon was the father of Priam, King of Troy.

[78]The Furies were avenging goddesses who worked for Jupiter to punish criminal acts.

[79]The Trojans were sailing generally north along the western coast of Greece. Zachynthos and Dulichium were islands in the area, as was Samos. Neritos was a mountain on Ithaca, the island home of Ulysses, whose father was Laertes. Mount Leucata, on a promontory, lay a short distance to the north.

[80]Actium was a promontory in Arcanania on the northwest coast of Greece where a temple of Phoebus-Apollo stood. The area became famous after 31 B. C. E. because of a naval battle between Octavian (later Caesar Augustus) and Antony.

[81]Buthrotum was a town on the coast of Epirus, a region of northwestern Greece.

[82]Orestes, son of Agamemnon and Clytemnestra, had married Hermione earlier. An 'old crime' referred to was the murder of his mother after she murdered his father.

[83]The Scaean Gate had been the west gate of Troy. The Xanthus, like the Simois mentioned earlier, were rivers at Troy.

[84]Phoebus refers to bodies of water around Italy. Trinacria was an ancient name for Sicily; Ausonia, a name for south central Italy. The 'Underworld Lakes' were near Cumae, not far from modern Naples. Circe was an enchantress who turned Ulysses' men into swine in *The Odyssey.*

[85]Phoebus is thus urging Aeneas not to sail through the straits that separate Sicily from Italy. Pachynus was a promontory on the southeast shore of Sicily.

Book IV

[86]Cyllenius was another name for Mercury because the Gods' messenger was born and raised on Mt. Cellene in Arcadia in Greece.

[87]Mt. Cithaeron was on the southwest side of Boeotia, northwest of Athens. It was well known for the rituals of the Bacchae, devotees of Bacchus, the wine god.

[88]Elissa was another name for Dido.

[89]Lycia was a country in Asia Minor associated with Phoebus/Apollo. Gyrnia was a town in Aeolis, also in Asia Minor, where a temple of Apollo stood.

[90]Hyrcania was a distant land between Parthia and the Caspian Sea. The Caucasus Mountains, associated by Dido here with barbaric customs, separated Europe from Asia.

[91]Aulis was the port city on Boeotia where the Greeks assembled before invading Troy.

[92]Tartarus was a name for the underworld.

[93]Pentheus, a king of Thebes, treated the worship of Bacchus with scorn and was torn to pieces by Bacchae in a frenzy—Pentheus' mother was among them. Orestes was pursued by the Furies after killing Clytemnestra, his mother.

[94]Atlas was a giant changed into a mountain on which the sky rested.

[95]Avernus was a lake close to the underworld's entrance. Chaos, a name for the lower world, was the father of Erebus and Night, gods of the lower world. On Diana see Note 42.

[96]Tithonus, husband of Aurora, goddess of the dawn, achieved immortality but not immortal youth.

[97]Iris was another messenger of the gods and also the goddess of the rainbow.

[98]Proserpine, daughter of Jupiter and Ceres, was taken to the underworld by Pluto (also called Dis), where the two ruled as king and queen together. Orcus was both a name for Pluto and for the underworld. The Styx was one of the principal rivers of the lower world.

Book VI

[99]Cumae was an ancient city of Campania on the west coast of Italy and was widely known as the residence of the Cumaean Sibyl, a priestess and seer of Phoebus/Apollo. The Euboeans, from the Greek island in the Aegean Sea, were supposed to have settled this area.

[100]Daedalus was a renowned Athenian craftsman. Minos was a king of Crete. His son Androgeos was killed by the Athenians, for which crime Minos attacked Athens and forced the Athenians to sacrifice sons and daughters annually to the Minotaur, a half-man, half-bull creature inhabiting the Labyrinth on Crete—a dark and intricate series of caves designed to house the creature by Daedalus. Pasiphae, Minos' wife and queen, had been assaulted and mounted earlier by a bull, the Minotaur resulting. A sister of Circe, Pasiphae was also the mother of Ariadne and Phaedra.

[101]Theseus was a renowned king of Athens who with the help of Ariadne succeeded in killing the Minotaur.

[102]Icarus was the son of Daedalus. He drowned in the Aegean while trying to fly from Crete on wings designed by his father.

[103]Paris, a Trojan prince, succeeded in killing the otherwise invincible Achilles by shooting an arrow—guided by Phoebus/Apollo—into Achilles' heel, the only vulnerable spot on his body.

[104]The Syrtes were vast sandbanks on the North African coast. The Massylians were a people of Numidia.

[105]The Acheron was another principal river of the lower world.

[106]Hecate was one of Diana's names. See Note 42.

[107]Aeneas claims, as a descendant of Jupiter through Venus, the right to enter the lower world enjoyed earlier by Orpheus, whose beautiful music charmed Pluto, King of the underworld, to release Eurydice, Orpheus' beloved; and by Pollux, who had redeemed his brother Castor by living on earth and in the underworld on alternate days. Theseus and Hercules (a son of Jupiter and a great Boeotian hero) had also descended into the lower world.

[108]The 'Underworld Juno' would be Proserpine.

[109]Triton, son of Neptune, was a sea-god.

[110]The Phlegethon was another major river of the lower world.

[111]Geryon was the three-bodied ruler of Erythia Island. The Gorgons were three daughters of

Phorcus, monsters with snakes for hair. Chimaera was a fire-breathing monster, part lion, goat and dragon. The Hydra was a many-headed water snake of the Lernaean Lake. Briareus was a giant son of Uranus with a hundred arms and fifty heads. Centaurs were beasts with bodies of horses and upper torsoes of men.

[112]Pirithous, king of the Lapithae, joined his friend Theseus when the latter ventured into the underworld to carry off Proserpine.

[113]Minos, king of Crete (described in Note 100), was also well known as a lawgiver.

[114]Caeneus, originally the daughter of Elatus, was changed by Neptune into a boy. Laodamia killed herself on the death of Protesilaus, her husband. Evadne threw herself onto the funeral pyre of Capaneus, her husband. Pasiphae (see Note 100), was mounted by a bull and bore the Minotaur. Eriphyle betrayed her husband, Amphiaraus, and was slain by her son Alcmaeon. Procris, mistaken in a forest for an animal, was killed by her husband, Cephalus. Phaedra, another daughter of Minos, fell in love with Hippolytus, her stepson, and eventually caused his death.

[115]Adrastus was a king of Argos who fought against Thebes, as did Parthenopaeus and Tydeus, the latter a son-in-law of Adrastus.

[116]Ideaus was a herald and the charioteer of Priam at Troy. See Note 25 on Antenor.

[117]Rhoeteum was a promontory not far from Troy.

[118]Rhadamanthus was a brother of Minos, king of Crete, and a son of Jupiter. He served as a judge in the lower world.

[119]Aloeus was the father of Otus and Ephialtes, Titans or giants who tried to storm Jupiter's heights.

[120]Salmoneus, a son of Aeolus, the god of the wind, was a king of Elis, a territory of western Peloponnessus, in southern Greece.

[121]Tityus, a son of Jupiter, was punished for insulting Latona, the mother of Diana.

[122]The Lapithae were a savage mountain race living near Olympus. Pirithous was their king (as Ixion, his father, had been); he was punished for insulting Juno.

[123]Phlegyas was another king of the Lapithae and the father of Ixion. Theseus was punished (in this version of his story) for attempting to carry off Proserpine, the queen of the lower world.

[124]The Cyclops were a race of one-eyed giants living in Sicily.

[125]The 'Thracian priest' is Orpheus, renowned for his playing of the lyre.

[126]Teucer, Ilus, Assaracus and Dardanus were all figures associated with Troy's early development.

[127]The Eridanus was the mythical name of the Padus, or modern Po, Italy's largest river. This passage is somewhat obscure in the Latin text.

[128]Musaeus was a legendary Greek poet.

[129]Alba Longa was the oldest Latin town said to have been built by Ascanius, the son of Aeneas, on the ridge of Mount Albanus, not far from Rome. Anchises is naming some of its future kings: Silvius, Procas, Capys, Numitor, and Silvius Aeneas.

[130]Cora, Bola and Pometia were all towns in Latium in central Italy. Inuus was probably near Ardea, another town in Latium. Collatia was a town of the ancient Sabines near Rome. Fidenae and Gabii were other towns in Latium and Nomentum was a town about fourteen miles from Rome.

[131]Romulus, the son of Mars and Rhea Silvia, the priestess, was the founder and first king of Rome; the city bears his name.

[132]Cybele was the mother of the sky-gods. See Note 68.

[133]Augustus was the surname of Octavian after he became the first emperor of Rome in Virgil's time.

[134]Nysa is a reference to a city in India where Bacchus, the wine god, was said to have been reared. Mt. Erymanthus was near the area of Elis in Greece.

[135]The reference is to Numa Pompilius, a king distinguished for the religious foundations which he set down. Cures was an ancient Sabine town.

[136]The Tarquin kings, associated with Tarquinii, an old town in Etruria, were Tarquinius Priscus and Tarquinius Superbus.

[137]The fasces were bundles of sticks with an ax projecting, carried by Lictors—assistants to Roman administrators—in state processions. Lictors could also carry out punishments. The reference here could be to the Brutus who assassinated Julius Caesar or to Junius Brutus, a relative of Tarquinius Superbus, who freed Rome from kingly power about 500 B. C. E.

[138]Camillus was a Roman leader who according to legend won back gold from the Gauls about 300 B. C. E.

[139]Anchises is anticipating the civil strife between Julius Caesar and Pompey. When he says, 'You stop first,' he is addressing Julius, whose name recalls Iulus, Aeneas' son, of divine descent.

[140]Corinth's conqueror was L. Mummius, who sacked the city in 146 B. C. E.

[141]The destroyer of Argos and Mycenae was L. Aemilius Paullus (168 B. C. E.).

[142]Fabius Maximus Cunctator, Hannibal's opponent in the Second Punic War, won his fame by delaying tactics. The Gracchi, Scipios and Fabricii were notable Roman families. 'Serranus' may be a reference to C. Atilius Regulus, said to be planting seeds when called to the consulship.

[143]M. Claudius Marcellus was Consul in 222 B. C. E. The other Marcellus in the passage, a youth who died in 23 B. C. E., was Octavia's son, the nephew and son-in-law of Augustus Caesar. Quirinus could be a reference to an old Sabine god; the name was also used to refer to Romulus, Rome's founder.

[144]Latimus was king of the Laurentians, a people inhabiting central Italy, at the time of Aeneas' arrival.

[145]Cajeta (or Caieta) was a town on the Latium sea-coast.

Book XII

[146]Juturna was a nymph and goddess associated with a spring in Latium. Turnus, her brother, was a king of the Rutulians and Aeneas' principal enemy in Italy.

[147]Lavinia, the daughter of King Latinus, had been promised in marriage earlier to Turnus.

JOSEPHUS: "THE JEWISH SECTS"
FROM *ANTIQUITIES OF THE JEWS*
(PALESTINEAN JUDAISM DURING THE HELLENISTIC PERIOD)

During the Hellenistic period Judaism was subjected to the same forces of syncretism as the other ancient religions of the Near East. The effect of Hellenism in the native country of Judea was to splinter Judaism into a number of sects which were divided over the question of how far Judaism could be accommodated to the spirit of Greek culture and philosophy. We have already seen this issue in the persecutions of the Seleucid emperor Antiochus IV (175 B.C.E.-164 B.C.E.) who attempted to force Hellenism on his Jewish subjects. The Maccabean revolt liberated the Jews from this threat, and the apocalyptic Book of Daniel (c. 160 B.C.E.) reflects the tensions and aspirations of the Pious or *Hasidim* during this crisis. Once the Maccabees or Hasmoneans, as they were called, established independent rule of Palestine, they illegitimately proclaimed themselves high priests, governors and commanders of Israel (cf. 1 Mac 14:41–47), and in turn became a wealthy and Hellenized aristocracy. Although they succeeded in gaining control of much of the territory once ruled by David centuries before, they had little popular support. After the crisis of the second century B.C.E. the issue of the accommodation of Judaism with Hellenism continued to divide Judean Judaism until the destruction of the second temple by the Roman armies under Titus in 70 C.E.

One of our best sources of information for this period is the Jewish historian Josephus, a member of a priestly family, who fought in the Roman-Jewish war of 66–70 C.E. In the course of the war he surrendered to the Roman general and future emperor Vespasian. Because of his conduct during the war, he was accused of treason by his fellow Jews, and he composed his **The Jewish War** as a detailed account of the war for his co-religionist in Babylonia. In addition, he wrote in Greek **The Antiquities of the Jews,** a history in twenty volumes of the Jewish people from the beginning to his own time. Both works have an apologetic purpose; they attempt to defend the Jewish people and their religion to a learned, but often hostile, Graeco-Roman audience.

Our selection is Josephus' description of the three sects of the Jewish religion in the first century of the common era. His descriptions are designed to be understandable to someone familiar with Graeco-Roman philosophy and they therefore are expressed in Greek philosophical terms. The Sadducees were the temple and priestly aristocratic party who were extremely conservative in religious ideas. They held that the Torah alone constituted the canonical scriptures and rejected any further interpretation by oral law. The Pharisees, on the other hand, advocated the oral interpretation of the Torah and were open to the prophetic books and belief in the more recent doctrine of the resurrection of the just. This group was destined to become the preserver of the Jewish religion after the destruction of the temple in 70 C.E. The Pharisees were the spiritual ancestors of the rabbinical Judaism of the Mishnah and Talmud. The third group which Josephus mentions is the Essenes who withdrew from contact with the pollutions of everyday life into monastic communities, where they emphasized meticulous ritual purity. They are also probably the authors of the famous Dead Sea Scrolls which can be found in a fine translation by Geza Vermes, **The Dead Sea Scrolls in English** (Baltimore: Penguin books, 1962).

The translation is by William Whiston, **The Works of Flavius Josephus** (London: George Routledge and Sons, n.d.).

Antiquities of the Jews

BOOK XVIII: THE JEWISH SECTS

The Jews had, for a great while, three sects of philosophy peculiar to themselves; the sect of Essenes, and the sect of the Sadducees, and the third sort of opinions was that of those called Pharisees, of which sects, although I

have already spoken in the second book of the Jewish War, yet will I a little touch on them now.

Now for the Pharisees, they live meanly and despise delicacies in diet, and they follow the conduct of reason; and what that prescribes to them as good for them they do, and they think they ought earnestly to strive to observe reason's dictates for practice. They also pay a respect to such as are in years, nor are they so bold as to contradict them in anything which they have introduced; and when they determine that all things are done by fate they do not take away the freedom from men of acting as they think fit, since their notion is that it hath pleased God to make a temperament whereby what he wills is done, but so that the will of man can act virtuously or viciously. They also believe that souls have an immortal vigor in them, and that under the earth there will be rewards and punishments, according as they have lived virtuously or viciously in this life; and the latter are to be detained in an everlasting prison, but that the former shall have power to revive and live again; on account of which doctrines they are able greatly to persuade the body of the people; and whatsoever they do about divine worship, prayers, and sacrifices, they perform them according to their direction, insomuch that the cities gave great attestation to them on account of their entire virtuous conduct, both in the actions of their lives and their discourses also.

But the doctrine of the Sadducees is this: that souls die with the bodies; nor do they regard the observation of anything besides what the law enjoins them, for they think it an instance of virtue to dispute with those teachers of philosophy whom they frequent; but this doctrine is received by but a few, yet by those still of the greatest dignity. But they are able almost to do nothing themselves; for when they become magistrates, as they are unwillingly and by force sometimes obliged to be, they addict themselves to the notions of the Pharisees, because the multitude would not otherwise bear them.

The doctrine of the Essenes is this: that all things are best ascribed to God. They teach the immortality of souls and esteem that the rewards of righteousness are to be earnestly striven for; and when they send what they have dedicated to God into the Temple, they do not offer sacrifices, because they have more pure lustrations of their own, on which account they are excluded from the common court of the Temple but offer their sacrifices themselves; yet is their course of life better than that of other men, and they entirely addict themselves to husbandry. It also deserves our admiration how much they exceed all other men that addict themselves to virtue, and this in righteousness; and indeed to such a degree that, as it hath never appeared among any other men, neither Greeks nor barbarians—no, not for a little time—so hath it endured a long while among them. This is demonstrated by that institution of theirs which will not suffer anything to hinder them from having all things in common, so that a rich man enjoys no more of his own wealth than he who hath nothing at all. There are about four thousand men that live in this way, and neither marry wives nor are desirous to keep servants, as thinking the latter tempt men to be unjust and the former give the handle to domestic quarrels; but as they live by themselves, they minister to one another. They also appoint certain stewards to receive the incomes of their revenues and of the fruits of the ground, such as are good men and priests, who are to get their corn and their food ready for them. They none of them differ from others of the Essenes in their way of living, but do the most resemble those Dacae who are called Polistae ("dwellers in cities").

PHILO: *THE CREATION OF THE WORLD* (HELLENISTIC JUDAISM)

In the diaspora Judaism was affected more positively by the process of Hellenization. In Alexandria in Egypt, which was the literary, scientific and cultural center of the Hellenistic world, the Jews had a large and vibrant community which attempted to adapt in a positive way to Hellenistic culture. The Hebrew Scriptures were translated into Greek in the important Septuagint version. Jewish works written in Greek like *The Wisdom of Solomon* emphasized the superiority of Jewish religious "wisdom" over the various forms of atheistic and idolatrous pagan wisdom. Other works like the *Fourth Book of Maccabees* used the heroism of the Maccabean martyrs as an occasion for discourses on reason and the passions—a favorite Stoical theme.

The most significant effort at using the forms and thought of Greek culture to give a reasoned defense of Judaism in the sophisticated environment of Hellenistic culture was the work of Philo of Alexandria (c. 20 B.C.E.–50 C.E.). His work is highly significant for the development of Western religious thought because in it the Jewish belief in a single moral God who guides history and has revealed himself to his chosen people meets with the Greek tradition of pursuing universal truth and a life of virtue through the use of reason. The guiding motive of Philo's writings was to show that Judaism was a respectable philosophical religion in the Platonic and Stoical traditions. He did this by interpreting the Jewish Torah in an allegorical fashion which explained the offensive anthropomorphisms as figurative language for universal religious truth. The Homeric and Hesiodic myths were also being subjected to the same type of interpretation by philosophically minded religious thinkers. Philo also attempted to prove that Jewish ethical and cosmological thought was in accord with the best of Greek philosophy. Despite his strong attraction to Greek philosophy, Philo remained a believing Jew and never doubted that the Jewish Torah was the absolute revealed truth.

Our selection is taken from **The Creation of the World,** Philo's commentary on the first creation account in Genesis 1. It is designed to show an interested Gentile, or nonbeliever, that the biblical account of creation is compatible with the best of Greek philosophy. Philo, like all the Jews of his day, accepted the Mosaic authorship of the Torah and he portrays Moses as one who had "reached the very summits of philosophy." In this work Philo's philosophical eclecticism is quite evident. He accepts Plato's doctrine of the Divine Ideas as well as the Stoical concepts of a natural law and man as a citizen of the cosmos. His reflections on the appropriateness of God's creating in six days shows the influence of the Pythagorean mystical understanding of number. Despite his indebtedness to Greek philosophy, Philo's views remain biblical and Jewish. He rejects the idea that the world is governed by fate and insists that God guides history by his providence. God, whose essence is beyond human reason, is more than Plato's "Idea of the Good;" he is also "the father and creator" who "has care for that which has been created."

Philo's immediate impact was greater on early Christian thought than on Judaism. The Christian Fathers used Philo's methods and insights in adapting the Christian message to the Hellenistic thought world. But within Judaism the Rabbinic literature in the Talmuds shows little influence from Philo.

The translation is by C.D. Yonge, **The Works of Philo Judaeus,** 4 vols (London, 1854).

The Creation of the World

I. Of other lawgivers, some have set forth what they considered to be just and reasonable, in a naked and unadorned manner, while others, investing their idea with an abundance of amplification have sought to bewilder the people, by burying the truth under a heap of fabulous inventions. But Moses, rejecting both of these methods, the one as inconsiderate, careless, and unphilosophical, and the other as mendacious and full of trickery, made the beginning of his laws entirely beautiful, and in all respects admirable, neither at once declaring what ought to be done or the contrary, nor (since it was necessary to mould beforehand the disposition of those who were to use his laws) inventing fables himself or adopting those which had been invented by others.

And his exordium, as I have already said, is most admirable; embracing the creation of the world, under the idea that the law corresponds to the world and the world to the law, and that a man who is obedient to the law, being, by so doing, a citizen of the world, arranges his actions with reference to the intention of nature, in harmony with which the whole universal world is regulated. Accordingly no one, whether poet or historian, could ever give expression in an adequate manner to the beauty of his ideas respecting the creation of the world; for they surpass all the power of language, and amaze our hearing, being too great and venerable to be adapted to the sense of any created being. . . .

II. For some men, admiring the world itself rather than the Creator of the world, have represented it as existing without any maker, and eternal; and as impiously as falsely have represented God as existing in a state of complete inactivity, while it would have been right on the other hand to marvel at the might of God as the creator and father of all and to admire the world in a degree not exceeding the bounds of moderation.

But Moses, who had early reached the very summits of philosophy, and who had learnt from the oracles of God the most numerous and important principles of nature, was well aware that it is indispensable that in all existing things there must be an active cause, and a passive subject; and that the active cause is the intellect of the universe, thoroughly unadulterated and thoroughly unmixed, superior to virtue and superior to science, superior even to abstract good or abstract beauty; while the passive subject is something inanimate and incapable of motion by any intrinsic power of its own, but having been set in motion, and fashioned, and endowed with life by the intellect, became transformed into that most perfect work, this world. And those who describe it as being uncreated, do, without being aware of it, cut off the most useful and necessary of all the qualities which tend to produce piety, namely, providence: for reason proves that the father and creator has a care for that which has been created; for a father is anxious for the life of his children, and a workman aims at the duration of his works, and employs every device imaginable to ward off everything that is pernicious or injurious, and is desirous by every means in his power to provide everything which is useful or profitable for them. But with regard to that which has not been created, there is no feeling of interest as if it were his own in the breast of him who has not created it.

It is then a pernicious doctrine, and one for which no one should contend, to establish a system in this world, such as anarchy is in a city, so that it should have no superintendant, or regulator, or judge, by whom everything must be managed and governed.

But the great Moses, thinking that a thing which has not been uncreated is as alien as possible from that which is visible before our eyes (for everything which is the subject of our senses exists in birth and in changes, and is not always in the same condition), has attributed eternity to that which is invisible and discerned only by our intellect as a kinsman and a brother, while of that which is the object of our external senses he had predicated generation as an appropriate description. Since, then, this world is visible and the object of our external senses, it follows of necessity that it must have been created; on which account it was not without a wise purpose that he recorded its creation, giving a very venerable account of God. III.   And he says that the world was made in six days, not because the Creator stood in need of a length of time (for it is natural that God should do everything at once, not merely by uttering a command, but by even thinking of it); but because the things created required arrangement; and number is akin to arrangement; and, of all numbers, six is, by the laws of nature, the most productive: for of all the numbers, from the unit upwards, it is the first perfect one, being made equal to its parts, and being made complete by them; the number three being half of it, and the number two a third of it, and the unit a sixth of it, and, so to say, it is formed so as to be both male and female, and is made up of the power of both natures; for in existing things the odd number is the male's, and the even number is the female's; accordingly, of odd numbers the first is the number three, and of even numbers the first is two, and the two numbers multiplied together make six. It was fitting therefore, that the world, being the most perfect of created things, should be made according to the perfect number, namely, six: and, as it was to have in it the causes of both, which arise from combination, that it should be formed according to a mixed number, the first combination of odd and even numbers, since it was to embrace the character both of the male who sows the seed, and of the female who receives it. And he allotted each of the six days to one of the portions of the whole, taking out the first day, which he does not even call the first day, that it may not be numbered with the others, but entitling it one, he names it rightly, perceiving in it, and ascribing to it the nature and appellation of the limit.

IV.   We must mention as much as we can of the matters contained in his account, since to enumerate them all is impossible; for he embraces that beautiful world which is perceptible only by the intellect, as the account of the first day will show: for God, as apprehending beforehand, as a God must do, that there could not exist a good imitation without a good model, and that of the things perceptible to the external senses nothing could be faultless which was not fashioned with reference to some archetypal idea conceived by the intellect, when he had determined to create this visible world, previously formed that one which is perceptible only by the intellect, in order that so using an incorporeal model formed as far as possible on the image of God, he might then make this corporeal world, a younger likeness of the elder creation, which should embrace as many different genera perceptible to the external senses, as the other world contains of those which are visible only to the intellect.

But that world which consists of ideas, it were impious in any degree to attempt to describe or even to imagine: but how it was created, we shall know if we take for our guide a certain image of the things which exist among us.

When any city is founded through the exceeding ambition of some king or leader who lays claim to absolute authority, and is at the same time a man of brilliant imagination, eager to display his good fortune, then it happens at times that some man coming up who, from his education, is skillful in architecture, and he, seeing the advantageous character and beauty of the situation, first of all sketches out in his own mind nearly all the parts of the city which is about to be completed—the temples, the gymnasia, the prytanea, the markets, the harbour, the docks, the streets, the arrangement of the walls, the situations of the dwelling houses, and of the public and other buildings. Then, having received in his own mind, as on a waxen tablet, the form of each building, he carries in his heart the image of a city, perceptible as yet only by the intellect, the images of which he stirs up in memory which is innate in him, and, still further, engraving them in his mind like a good workman, keeping his eyes fixed on his model, he begins to raise the city of stones and wood, making the corporeal substance to resemble each of the incorporeal ideas. Now we must form a somewhat similar opinion of God, who, having determined to found a mighty state, first of all conceived its form in his mind, according to which form he made a world perceptible only by the intellect, and then completed one visible to the external senses, using the first one as a model. . . .

VII. Moses says also; "In the beginning God created the heaven and the earth:" taking the beginning to be, not as some men think, that which is according to time; for before the world time had no existence, but was created either simultaneously with it, or after it; for since time is the interval of the motion of the heavens, there could not have been any such thing as motion before there was anything which could be moved; but it follows of necessity that it received existence subsequently or simultaneously. It therefore follows also of necessity, that time was created either at the same moment as the world, or later than it—and to venture to assert that it is older than the world is absolutely inconsistent with philosophy. But if the beginning spoken of by Moses is not to be looked upon as spoken of according to time, then it may be natural to suppose that it is the beginning according to number that is indi-

cated; so that, "In the beginning he created," is equivalent to "first of all he created the heaven;" for it is natural in reality that that should have been the first object created, being both the best of all created things, and being also made of the purest substance, because it was destined to be the most holy abode of the visible Gods who are perceptible by the external senses; for if the Creator had made everything at the same moment, still those things which were created in beauty would no less have had a regular arrangement, for there is no such thing as beauty in disorder. But order is a due consequence and connection of things precedent and subsequent, if not in the completion of a work, at all events in the intention of the maker; for it is owing to order that they become accurately defined and stationary, and free from confusion.

In the first place therefore, from the model of the world, perceptible only by intellect, the Creator made an incorporeal heaven, and an invisible earth, and the form of air and of empty space: the former of which he called darkness, because the air is black by nature; and the other he called the abyss, for empty space is very deep and yawning with immense width. Then he created the incorporeal substance of water and of air, and above he spread light, being the seventh thing made; and this again was incorporeal, and a model of the sun, perceptible only to intellect, and of all light-giving stars, which are destined to stand together in heaven. . . .

PLOTINUS: *THE ENNEADS* (NEO-PLATONISM)

The last great non-Christian philosopher and religious thinker of the Hellenistic period was Plotinus (c. 204–270 C.E.) who came from Alexandria in Egypt and eventually established a philosophical school in Rome. By the third century the Roman empire was in the midst of serious military, economic and political difficulties which resulted in widespread social and spiritual unrest. During Plotinus' lifetime the empire was attacked on three fronts: the Sassanids in the east, the Goths along the Danube frontier and the Franks and Allemani further to the west. The Roman army was now composed primarily of barbarian mercenaries who demanded high pay and were less than effective fighters.

Taxes were high; agricultural production was low; piracy and neglect of the Roman road system reduced trade. Finally the office of emperor itself was in complete disarray. After the death of Alexander Severus in 235 C.E., eighteen emperors ruled along with eight designated colleagues and a host of pretenders in the period leading up to Diocletian (284–305 C.E.). Only one of the twenty-six recognized rulers died a natural death. In the midst of this chaos the empire was flooded with a great variety of religious cults and philosophical schools which attest to the desperate attempt to find some explanation for life and destiny. The religion which was destined to survive this period was Christianity. Plotinus' Platonic philosophy was another important effort to find spiritual peace in the turbulence of the third century, and his religious vision was to have an enormous impact on the thinking of St. Augustine (354–430 C.E.), the greatest of the Christian theologians of the Early Church, and, through him, on the thinking of the Christian Middle Ages.

Plotinus was a pupil of Ammonius Saccas, an influential Platonic philosopher in Alexandria, who also taught Origen (185–254 C.E.), the great Christian Alexandrian theologian. Alexandria was an intellectual and spiritual crossroads of the Hellenistic world. All of the Hellenistic philosophical schools were represented there as well as the religious traditions of the East. Plotinus' own spiritual vision was a unique combination of Greek intellectualism with Eastern mysticism. He developed a highly speculative view of reality which was influenced by Plato and synthesized it with a religious doctrine of salvation through mystical union with the soruce of all reality which he called The One.

It is significant that both Plato and Plotinus develop their highly idealistic and mystical philosophies in times of political and social chaos. Plato developed his philosophy in the early fourth century B.C.E. after the collapse of Athens at the end of the fifth century B.C.E. Plotinus produced his even more idealistic and mystical philosophy during the chaotic third century C.E. when the Roman empire was tottering on the brink of collapse.

The One of Plotinus is the absolutely transcendent source of reality or Being. It is totally ineffable and cannot be described positively by our conceptual language; yet it is the very center and source of our being. The primary attribute which can be applied to the One, but only with great qualification, is absolute simplicity or unity. Although the One is even beyond Plato's Form of the Good, it is diffusive of itself and produces all reality by a process of emanation like rays from the sun or water from a spring. However in this process the One is neither diminished nor changed.

Plotinus postulated intermediate principles between the One and the material world. He speaks of The Good which is not the highest principle as in Plato, but derived from The One. There is also the *Nous,* or "Intelligence" which was the divine mind that gave intelligibility to the world by containing the Platonic forms of knowledge. He also speaks of "The Soul" or "World-Soul" which mediated between the eternal realm of the forms and the material and temporal realm of matter which was the principle of disorder and change.

For Plotinus, like Plato, the individual soul was trapped in the prison of a material body, and therefore the goal of human existence was to attain union with the One (God) who was beyond the cycle of change. The way of escape for Plotinus is through a process of contemplation which begins with rigorous pursuit of knowledge in the Platonic fashion of finding universal Truth, Justice, Beauty, but ends in a union with the One which goes beyond knowledge to a mystical resting with the center and source of our being.

Plotinus' search for wisdom took him to the East and involved him with the highest political powers of his day. In c. 243 he became involved with an expeditionary army of Emperor Gordianus in Persia, and, when the expedition failed, he returned to Rome and opened his own philosophical school which attracted the intellectual elite, including Emperor Galienus and his wife. He even attempted to form a city to be called Platonopolis which was to be based on the teachings of Plato's **Republic,** but the project never materialized.

The writings of Plotinus come to us through his disciple Porphyry (c. 232–305 C.E.) who edited and preserved them in six books of nine treatises from which comes the name **Enneads.** Porphyry also wrote a **Life of Plotinus** in which he states that four times in his life he achieved the mystical union with The One (God) which he speaks about in the following selection. Our selection is taken from a description of the One and the soul's union with the One as the center of its being.

It is noteworthy that The One of Plotinus is different from the God of Judaeo-Christian Platonists like Philo, Origen and Augustine. The essential difference is that Plotinus never describes The One in personal terms. The One is not a caring creator who enters history to redeem his fallen creation. Rather, The One is the absolute center and foundation of reality which can be glimpsed only in moments of highest contemplation and repose.

The translation is by Elmer O'Brien S.J., **The Essential Plotinus** (Indianapolis: Hackett Publishing Com., 1975) 81–88.

THE ENNEADS

(VI, 9 {9})

In what sense, then, do we call the supreme The One? How can we conceive of it?

We shall have to insist that its unity is much more perfect than that of the numerical unit or the geometrical point. For with regard to these, the soul, abstracting from magnitude and numerical plurality, stops indeed at that which is smallest and comes to rest in something indivisible. This kind of unity is found in something that is divisible and exists in a subject other than itself. But "what is not in another than itself" is not in the divisible. Nor is it indivisible in the same sense in which the smallest is indivisible. On the contrary, The One is the greatest, not physically but dynam-

ically. Hence it is indivisible, not physically but dynamically. So also the beings that proceed from it; they are, not in mass but in might, indivisible and partless. Also, The One is infinite not as extension or numerical series is infinite, but in its limitless power. Conceive it as intelligence or divinity; it is more than that. Compress unity within your mind, it is still more than that. Here is unity superior to any your thought lays hold of, unity that exists by itself and in itself and is without attributes.

Something of its unity can be understood from its self-sufficiency. It is necessarily the most powerful, the most self-sufficient, the most independent of all. Whatever is not one, but multiple, needs something else. Its being needs unification. But The One is already one. It does not even need itself. A being that is multiple, in order to be what it is needs the multiplicity of things it contains. And each of the things contained is what it is by its union with the others and not by itself, and so it needs the others. Accordingly, such a being is deficient both with regard to its parts and as a whole. There must be something that is fully self-sufficient. That is The One; it alone, within and without, is without need. It needs nothing outside itself either to exist, to achieve well-being, or to be sustained in existence. As it is the cause of other things, how could it owe its existence to them? And how could it derive its well-being from outside itself since its well-being is not something contingent but is its very nature? And, since it does not occupy space, how can it need support or foundation? What needs foundation is the material mass which, unfounded, falls. The One is the foundation of all other things and gives them, at one and the same time, existence and location; what needs locating is not self-sufficing.

Again, no principle needs others after it. The principle of all has no need of anything at all. Deficient being is deficient because it aspires to its principle. But if The One were to aspire to anything, it would evidently seek not to be The One, that is, it would aspire to that which destroys it. Everything in need needs well-being and preservation. Hence The One cannot aim at any good or desire anything: it is superior to the Good; it is the Good, not for itself, but for other things to the extent to which they can share in it.

The One is not an intellective existence. If it were, it would constitute a duality. It is motionless because it is prior to motion quite as it is prior to thinking. Anyhow, what would it think? Would it think itself? If it did, it would be in a state of ignorance before thinking, and the self-sufficient would be in need of thought. Neither should one suppose it to be in a state of ignorance on the ground that it does not know itself and does not think itself. Ignorance presupposes a dual relationship: one does not know another. But the One, in its aloneness, can neither know nor be ignorant of anything.

Being with itself, it does not need to know itself. Still, we should not even attribute to it this presence with itself if we are to preserve its unity.

Excluded from it are both thinking of itself and thinking of others. It is not like that which thinks but, rather, like the activity of thinking. The activity of thinking does not itself think; it is the cause that has some other being think and cause cannot be identical with effect. This cause, therefore, of all existing things cannot be any one of them. Because it is the cause of good it cannot, then, be called the Good; yet in another sense it is the Good above all.

If the mind reels at this, The One being none of the things we mentioned, a start yet can be made from them to contemplate it.

Do not let yourself be distracted by anything exterior, for The One is not in some one place, depriving all the rest of its presence. It is present to all those who can touch it and absent only to those who cannot. No man can concentrate on one thing by thinking of some other thing; so he should not connect something else with the object he is thinking of if he wishes really to grasp it. Similarly, it is impossible for a soul, impressed with something else, to conceive of The One so long as such an impression occupies its attention, just as it is impossible that a soul, at the moment when it is attentive to other things, should receive the form of what is their contrary. It is said that matter must be void of all qualities in order to be capable of receiving all forms. So must the soul, and for a stronger reason, be stripped of all forms if it would be filled and fired by the supreme without any hindrance from within itself.

Having thus freed itself of all externals, the soul must turn totally inward; not allowing itself to be wrested back towards the outer, it must forget everything, the subjective first and, finally, the objective. It must not even know that it is itself that is applying itself to contemplation of The One.

After having dwelled with it sufficiently,

the soul should, if it can, reveal to others this transcendent communion. (Doubtless it was enjoyment of this communion that was the basis of calling Minos[1] "the confidant of Zeus"; remembering, he made laws that are the image of the One, inspired to legislate by his contact with the divine.) If a man looks down on the life of the city as unworthy of him, he should, if he so wishes, remain in this world above. This does indeed happen to those who have contemplated much.

This divinity, it is said, is not outside any being but, on the contrary, is present to all beings though they may not know it. They are fugitives from the divine, or rather from themselves. What they turn from they cannot reach. Themselves lost, they can find no other. A son distraught and beside himself is not likely to recognize his father. But the man who has learned to know himself will at the same time discover whence he comes.

Self-knowledge reveals to the soul that its natural motion is not, if uninterrupted, in a straight line, but circular, as around some inner object, about a center, the point to which it owes its origin. If the soul knows this, it will move around this center from which it came, will cling to it and commune with it as indeed all souls should but only divine souls do. That is the secret of their divinity, for divinity consists in being attached to the center. One who withdraws far from it becomes an ordinary man or an animal.

Is this "center" of our souls, then, the principle we are seeking? No, we must look for some other principle upon which all centers converge and to which, only by analogy to the visible circle, the word "center" is applied. The soul is not a circle as, say, a geometrical figure. Our meaning is that in the soul and around about it exists the "primordial nature," that it derives its existence from the first existence especially when entirely separate from the body. Now, however, as we have a part of our being contained in the body, we are like a man whose feet are immersed in water while the rest of his body remains above it. Raising ourselves above the body by the part of us that is not submerged, we are, by our own center, attaching ourselves to the center of all. And so we remain, just as the centers of the great circles coincide with that of the sphere that surrounds them. If these circles were material and not spiritual, center and circumference would have to occupy definite places. But since the souls are of the intelligible realm and The One is still above The Intelligence, we are forced to say that the union of the intellective thinking being with its object proceeds by different means. The intellective thinking being is in the presence of its object by virtue of its similarity and identity, and it is united with its kindred with nothing to separate it from them. Bodies are by their bodies kept from union, but the bodiless are not held by this bodily limitation. What separates bodiless beings from one another is not spatial distance but their own difference and diversities: when there is not difference between them, they are mutually present.

As the One does not contain any difference, it is always present and we are present to it when we no longer contain difference. The One does not aspire to us, to move around us; we aspire to it, to move around it. Actually, we always move around it; but we do not always look. We are like a chorus grouped about a conductor who allow their attention to be distracted by the audience. If, however, they were to turn towards their conductor, they would sing as they should and would really be with him. We are always around The One. If we were not, we would dissolve and cease to exist. Yet our gaze does not remain fixed upon The One. When we look at it, we then attain the end of our desires and find rest. Then it is that, all discord past, we dance an inspired dance around it.

In this dance the soul looks upon the source of life, the source of The Intelligence, the origin of Being, the cause of the Good, the root of The Soul.

All these entities emanate from The One without any lessening for it is not a material mass. If it were, the emanants would be perishable. But they are eternal because their originating principle always stays the same; not fragmenting itself in producing them, it remains entire. So they persist as well, just as light persists as long as sun shines.

We are not separated from The One, not distant from it, even though bodily nature has closed about us and drawn us to itself. It is because of The One that we breathe and have our being: it does not bestow its gift at one moment only to leave us again; its giving is without cessation so long as it remains what it is. As we turn towards The One, we exist to a higher degree, while to withdraw from it is to fall. Our soul is delivered from evil by rising to that place which is free of all evils. There it knows. There it is immune. There it truly lives. Life not united with the divinity is shadow and mimicry of authentic life. Life there is the native act of The Intelligence, which, motionless in its contact with The One, gives birth to gods, beauty, justice, and virtue.

With all of these The Soul, filled with divinity, is pregnant; this is its starting point and its goal. It is its starting point because it is from the world above that it proceeds. It is its goal because in the world above is the Good to which it aspires and by returning to it there its proper nature is regained. Life here below in the midst of sense objects is for the soul a degradation, an exile, a loss of wings.

Further proof that our good is in the realm above is the love innate in our souls; hence the coupling in picture and story of Eros with Psyche.[2] The soul, different from the divinity but sprung from it, must needs love. When it is in the realm above, its love is heavenly; here below, only commonplace. The heavenly Aphrodite[3] dwells in the realm above; here below, the vulgar, harlot Aphrodite.

Every soul is an Aphrodite, as is suggested in the myth of Aphrodite's birth at the same time as that of Eros. As long as soul stays true to itself, it loves the divinity and desires to be at one with it, as a daughter loves with a noble love a noble father. When, however, the soul has come down here to human birth, it exchanges (as if deceived by the false promises of an adulterous love) its divine love for one that is mortal. And then, far from its begetter, the soul yields to all manner of excess.

But, when the soul begins to hate its shame and puts away evil and makes its return, it finds its peace.

How great, then, is its bliss can be conceived by those who have not tasted it if they but think of earthly unions in love, marking well the joy felt by the lover who succeeds in obtaining his desires. But this is love directed to the mortal and harmful—to shadows—and soon disappears because such is not the authentic object of our love not the good we really seek. Only in the world beyond does the real object of our love exist, the only one with which we can unite ourselves, of which we can have a part and which we can intimately possess without being separated by the barriers of flesh.

Anyone who has had this experience will know what I am talking about. He will know that the soul lives another life as it advances towards The One, reaches it and shares in it. Thus restored, the soul recognizes the presence of the dispenser of the true life. It needs nothing more. On the contrary, it must renounce everything else and rest in it alone, become it alone, all earthiness gone, eager to be free, impatient of every fetter that binds below in order so to embrace the real object of its love with its entire being that no part of it does not touch The One.

Then of it and of itself the soul has all the vision that may be—of itself luminous now, filled with intellectual light, become pure light, subtle and weightless. It has become divine, is part of the eternal that is beyond becoming. It is like a flame. If later it is weighted down again by the realm of sense, it is like a flame extinguished.

Why does a soul that has risen to the realm

above not stay there? Because it has not yet entirely detached itself from things here below. Yet a time will come when it will uninterruptedly have vision, when it will no longer be bothered by body. The part of us that sees is not troubled. It is the other part which, even when we cease from our vision, does not cease from its activity of demonstration, proof and dialectic. But the act and faculty of vision is not reason but something greater than, prior and superior to, reason. So also is the object of the vision. When the contemplative looks upon himself in the act of contemplation, he will see himself to be like its object. He feels himself to be united to himself in the way that the object is united to itself; that is to say, he will experience himself as simple, just as it is simple.

Actually, we should not say, "He will see." What he sees (in case it is still possible to distinguish here the seer and the seen, to assert that the two are one would be indeed rash) is not seen, not distinguished, not represented as a thing apart. The man who obtains the vision becomes, as it were, another being. He ceases to be himself, retains nothing of himself. Absorbed in the beyond he is one with it, like a center coincident with another center. While the centers coincide, they are one. They become two only when they separate. It is in this sense that we can speak of The One as something separate.

Therefore is it so very difficult to describe this vision, for how can we represent as different from us what seemed, while we were contemplating it, not other than ourselves but perfect at-oneness with us?

This, doubtless, is what is back of the injunction of the mystery religions which prohibit revelation to the uninitiated. The divine is not expressible, so the initiate is forbidden to speak of it to anyone who has not been fortunate enough to have beheld it himself.

The vision, in any case, did not imply duality; the man who saw was identical with what he saw. Hence he did not "see" it but rather was "oned" with it. If only he could preserve the memory of what he was while thus absorbed into The One, he would possess within himself an image of what it was.

In that state he had attained unity, nothing within him or without him effecting diversity. When he had made his ascent, there was within him no disturbance, no anger, emotion, desire, reason, or thought. Actually, he was no longer himself; but, swept away and filled with the divine, he was still, solitary, and at rest, not turning to this side or that or even towards himself. He was in utter rest, having, so to say, become rest itself. In this state he busied himself no longer even with the beautiful. He had risen above beauty, had passed beyond even the choir of virtues.

He was like one who, penetrating the innermost sanctuary of a temple, leaves temple images behind. They will be the first objects to strike his view upon coming out of the sanctuary, after his contemplation and communion there not with an image or statue but with what they represent. They are but lesser objects of contemplation.

Such experience is hardly a vision. It is a seeing of a quite different kind, a self-transcendence, a simplification, self-abandonment, a striving for union and a repose, an intentness upon conformation. This is the way one sees in the sanctuary. Anyone who tries to see in any other way will see nothing.

By the use of these images, the wise among the soothsayers expressed in riddles how the divinity is seen. A wise priest, reading the riddle, will, once arrived in the realm beyond, achieve the true vision of the sanctuary. One who has not yet arrived there and knows the sanctuary is invisible, is the source and principle of everything, will also know that by hypostasis[4] seen, and that like alone joins like. He will leave aside nothing of the divine the soul is capable of acquiring. If his vision is not yet complete, he will attend to its completion, which, for him who has risen above all, is The One that is above all. It is not the soul's nature to attain to utter nothingness. Falling into evil it falls, in this sense, into nothingness, but still not complete nothingness. And when it reverses direction, it arrives not at something different but at itself. Thus, when it is not in anything else, it is in nothing but itself. Yet, when it is in itself alone and not in being, it is in the supreme.

We as well transcend Being by virtue of The Soul with which we are untied.

Now if you look upon yourself in this state, you find yourself an image of The One.

If you rise beyond yourself, an image rising to its model, you have reached the goal of your journey.

When you fall from this vision, you will, by arousing the virtue that is within yourself and by remembering the perfection that you possess, regain your likeness and through virtue rise to The Intelligence and through wisdom to The One.

Such is the life of the divinity and of divine and blessed men: detachment from all things here below, scorn of all earthly pleasures, the flight of the alone to the Alone.

NOTES

[1]Minos was a famous lawgiver who became one of the judges of the dead in Hades.

[2]Psyche was the personification of the human soul. She married Cupid (Eros), the god of love, and was made immortal by Zeus.

[3]Aphrodite was the goddess of love.

[4]Literally, "substance."

5

THE NEW TESTAMENT

The most significant religious figure in Western civilization history is Jesus of Nazareth. Although he lived a relatively short life of slightly more than thirty years and died the ignominious death of a criminal executed by Roman crucifixion (c. 30 C.E.), the life, teaching, death, and resurrection of this Jewish prophet became the basis of Christianity, a new Western religion which was destined to break from Judaism and become the major religious tradition in the West. Jesus' vision of the Fatherhood of God and his providential love for all humanity has been the source of spiritual inspiration throughout Western history. His command of love for all, even the enemy, has remained as a statement of the highest ethical aspirations of the Western tradition. In his death on the cross Christian believers have found a symbol of self-sacrificing love and a sign of the divine forgiveness of their sins. His resurrection from the dead has formed the basis for the Christian belief in the triumph, at the end of history, of God's love over the power of sin and death and the hope for personal resurrection. Finally, New Testament affirmations of the identity of Jesus as the unique Son of God, even the pre-existent Word of God, who will return triumphantly at the end of history as the glorious Son of Man to complete God's kingdom became the basis from which the Christian Church began to develop, in the course of the first five centuries C.E., its unique faith in the full divinity and humanity of Jesus.

Within the context of the first centuries C.E., Christianity combined the features of Jewish monotheism and ethical teaching with belief in a savior figure, comparable to the Hellenistic mystery religions. However, unlike the mystery religions, in Christianity the savior who had died and rose was an historical personage who had lived and taught a message about God and his kingdom which was adaptable to the highest ethical aspirations of the Hellenistic age.

From a purely historical perspective Jesus and Christianity represent an intersection of the three major cultural traditions of the ancient world which were to form the foundations of subsequent Western civilization: the Hebrew, Greek and Roman. Jesus was the product of the Hebrew tradition. Most of his ethical teachings can be paralleled in the teachings of Jewish rabbis of the same period. For example, the great Hillel, a rabbi of the first century C.E. taught,

"Be disciples of Aaron, loving peace and pursuing peace, loving mankind and bringing them nigh to the Law." (Aboth I. 12)

283

But, according to the gospel tradition, Jesus was understood by his Jewish contemporaries as more than a teacher. They saw him as a prophet who announced the arrival of the awaited kingdom of God in a poetic and apocalyptic manner.

After his death at the hands of Pontius Pilate, the Roman procurator of Palestine (c. 26–36 C.E.), the teachings of Jesus and the message of belief in him rapidly moved beyond the confines of Judaism and into the Graeco-Roman world. In the first two centuries C.E. the story of Jesus' life, teachings, death and resurrection was spread by Christian missionaries throughout the Mediterranean world which had been united by the relative peace of the Roman empire. By the middle of the second century C.E. the books which were to comprise the New Testament had been written in the Greek language which could be understood throughout the Mediterranean world. And, after a period of official persecution by Roman authorities, Christianity became, by the end of the fourth century C.E., the official religion of a dying Roman empire. Its spiritual vigor enabled it to survive the collapse of Rome and become the dominant cultural institution in the Middle Ages.

Jesus, like Socrates, left no personal literary legacy. And, although he is mentioned in passing by Josephus and in Roman sources, our primary sources of information about him are the books of the New Testament, the twenty-seven early Christian writings in Greek which were selected by the Church from among the large body of early Christian literature as the basis for its faith and worship. The title New Testament or "covenant" comes from the Christian belief that in the events attested to in these books, i.e., the life, teachings, death and resurrection of Jesus of Nazareth, the God of Israel has established the "new covenant" which the prophet Jeremiah had spoken of over five hundred years previously (Jer 31:31–34; 2 Cor 3:6–15; Heb 9:15–20; Matt 26:28; Mk 14:24; 1 Cor 11:25).

The Christian Scriptures, in contrast to the Hebrew Scriptures, were written over a relatively short period of time. The earliest writings are the letters of Paul which were composed in the period between c. 50–65 C.E., and the latest writings, 2 Peter and 1, 2, and 3 John, probably are to be dated to c. 110 C.E. The New Testament also has a more limited variety of literary genres than the Hebrew Bible and reflects the literary conventions of the Graeco-Roman world of the first and second centuries C.E. Twenty-one of the books are in the form of letters, a popular Hellenistic genre, written by leaders to either Christian communities in the various cities or provinces of the Eastern Roman empire or to other individuals. Four of the works (Matthew, Mark, Luke and John) are biographies of Jesus, another well-attested Hellenistic form, called "gospels," accounts of the "good tidings" of Jesus' life. The Acts of the Apostles, a second volume by the author of Luke's Gospel, is an idealized history, comparable to the Roman histories of the period, which recounts the spread of the Church from Jerusalem to Rome in the period between c. 30–60 C.E. Finally, the last book in the New Testament is an apocalypse, The Revelation to John, which has similarities to the apocalypses in the Jewish literature of the same period.

The books of the New Testament do not represent the only Christian writings from the early years of Christianity. The process of selecting these books and rejecting others for inclusion in the canon, or list of sacred books, was a long and complicated one, lasting more than two centuries. During the second half of the second century, most of the Christian churches acknowledged a canon which included the present four gospels, Acts, thirteen letters attributed to Paul, 1 Peter and 1 John. Seven books still lacked general recognition: Hebrews, James, 2 Peter, 2 and 3 John, Jude, and Revelation. Other books, not now included in the New Testament, like the Letter of Barnabas and the Shepherd of Hermas, were accepted by some Church writers, but not by the majority. During this period and the third century, the Church fathers, in connection with the struggle with gnosticism which appealed to a secret or esoteric understanding of the Christian revelation, began to develop certain criteria for acceptance or rejection of books in the Christian canon. These were: conformity with the rule of faith, or the simple creed taught to converts at baptism, apostolic authorship or connection with the preaching of an apostle, and wide usage in most of the churches. The fourth century was marked by authoritative pronouncements, first by bishops in provincial churches, and later by synods and councils, on the list of books in the Christian canon. St. Athanasius in his Festal Letter of 367 C.E. was the first to name the twenty-seven books of the New Testament as exclusively canonical. This remains the canon for both Roman Catholic and Protestant traditions to this day, although the various traditions put special emphasis on certain books within this collection.

The quotations from the New Testament in the introductory essay are taken from **The Revised Standard Version Bible** copyrighted 1946, 1952 © 1971, 1973 by the Division of Christian Education of the National Council of the Churches of Christ in the U.S.A., and used by permission. For a fine introduction to the entire New Testament see Pheme Perkins, **Reading the New Testament: An Introduction** (New York, N.Y./Ramsey, N.J.: Paulist Press, 1978).

THE LETTERS OF PAUL

The earliest documents in the New Testament are the letters of Paul which were written in the period between 50–65 C.E. Significantly, the earliest literary expression of the Christian faith reflects its missionary character; Paul's writings were, for the most part, letters addressed to the fledgling Christian communities which he had founded in the cities and provinces of Asia Minor and Greece.

Paul, more than anyone else in the early Christian Church, is responsible for insuring that Christianity moved from a sect within Judaism to a world religion which proselytized Gentiles (the nations or non-Jews). This development was not at all self-evident to the early Christian community. Jesus himself was a Jew who had confined his preaching to "the lost sheep of Israel" (Matt 10:5–6), and the first Christian community in Jerusalem was content to continue as an observant group within Judaism (cf. Galatians 2; Acts 15). Paul seems to have been the first Christian missionary to insist that the gospel message be preached to the Gentiles without demanding that they first become circumcised Jews. In the process of fighting for this viewpoint, Paul became the first Christian theologian, i.e., someone who thinks reflectively about the implications of Christian belief. And, in many respects, Paul put his indelible stamp on Christian theology in the same way Plato did on Western philosophy.

Paul's background ideally suited him for the task of being the first Christian theologian. He was a zealous Hellenistic Jew from the important city of Tarsus in the province of Cilicia in southern Asia Minor. According to his own testimony, Paul was always proud of his Jewish background; he "boasts" of being from the tribe of Benjamin and a member of the Pharisee sect (Gal 1:13–14; Phil 3:4–6). According to Acts, he studied at the feet of the great rabbi Gamaliel in Jerusalem (Acts 22:3), and there is some evidence that he may even have worked as a Jewish missionary among the Gentiles (Gal 5:11). His letters reflect this Jewish background in that he worked out his theology using Jewish apocalyptic categories and rabbinical techniques for argumentation.

But Paul was also a learned citizen of the Hellenistic and Roman world. He spoke and wrote *koine* Greek and was familiar with the various Hellenistic philosophies and mystery religions whose influence can also be seen in his letters. He even had the privilege of Roman citizenship which, according to the account in Acts, he was able to use to his advantage in demanding a trial from the Roman emperor (Acts 22–28) after his arrest in the temple area in Jerusalem. The symbol of Paul's membership in both the Jewish and Hellenistic worlds is the fact that he had two names: Saul, the name of the first Israelite king also from the tribe of Benjamin, and Paulus, a Graeco-Roman name.

The most important event in the life of Paul was undoubtedly his conversion/call on the road to Damascus (Acts 9; 22; 26; Gal 1:10–17; 1 Cor 15:8–11). Paul had not known Jesus during his public ministry, and his zeal for the traditions of his Jewish ancestors led him to be a violent persecutor of the nascent Christian sect—a fact which he does not attempt to hide even from his enemies (Gal 1:13–14; Phil 3:5–6). But, in one dramatic encounter with the risen Jesus, Paul was changed forever from a persecutor to an active apostle for the Christian faith. The more familiar versions of this incident are Luke's varying accounts in Acts of Paul's being blinded while on the way to Damascus to arrest Christians and bring them to Jerusalem (Acts 9; 22; 26). But Paul's own more circumspect description in his letters is more reliable for giving the import of his initial encounter with the risen Christ. In Galatians, where Paul is defending his gospel and apostolic credentials against opponents, he gives the following account of his call:

> For I would have you know, brethren, that the gospel which was preached by me is not man's gospel. For I did not receive it from man, nor was I taught it, but it came through a revelation of Jesus Christ. For you have heard of my former life in Judaism, how I persecuted the church of God violently and tried to destroy it; and I advanced in Judaism beyond many of my own age among my people, so extremely zealous was I for the traditions of my fathers. But when he who had set me apart before I was born, and had called me through his grace, was pleased to reveal his Son to me, in order that I might preach him among the Gentiles, I did not confer with flesh and blood, nor did I go up to Jerusalem to those who were apostles before me, but I went away into Arabia; and again I returned to Damascus (Gal 1:11–17).

From this account it is evident that Paul saw the Damascus experience as a call, like that of the prophets of old (cf. Jer 1:4–10; Is 49:1–6), to announce the gospel message about Jesus the risen Son of God to the Gentiles (the non-Jewish nations). This mission was the driving force of Paul's missionary career. He preached in the Nabatean kingdom of Arabia, in Damascus in Syria, in his native Tarsus, in Antioch, and then engaged in missions to Asia Minor, Greece, and finally Rome itself. According to his letter to the Romans, he also planned to move from Rome and expand his missionary work to Spain, the westernmost area of the Roman Empire.

GALATIANS

For the sake of this Gentile mission Paul was forced to fight vehemently, especially with elements in the Christian community who wanted to limit Christian missionary efforts to Jews or converts who were willing to embrace Judaism. The Letter to the Galatians, a community in Asia Minor, is concerned with precisely this issue.

Paul had founded this Gentile community sometime previously when he had preached the gospel to them from a sickbed (Gal 4:13–16). Paul's gospel had asked them to turn from their nature religion in which they worshiped what he called "the weak and beggarly elemental spirits" and introduced them to the one true God (Gal 4:8–11). The content of Paul's gospel message was couched in highly Jewish apocalyptic language, but had made no mention of the Galatians' need to be circumcised and become observant Jews. He believed that the death and resurrection of Jesus, the Messiah or Christ (the Greek term for Messiah or "anointed one") had broken through the power of sin and death, established the justice of God's kingdom, and inaugurated the final messianic age which would be soon completed with the triumphal return of Christ in glory. In this final age salvation was now available to Jews and Gentiles alike if they would believe that through Jesus the Lord and Messiah "who gave himself for our sins to deliver us from the present evil age . . . " (Gal 1:3–4) the salvation that God had promised to the Jews was now available to all those who turned from their former idolatry and sin.

Subsequently Paul's version of the gospel had come under attack by other Christian missionaries who were preaching another gospel which insisted that the Galatians must become circumcised and become observant Jews in order to be members of the Christian or messianic community (cf. Gal 1:7–9; 5:2–11). Their preaching also seems to have been accompanied by an attack on Paul and his apostolic credentials. Paul writes the letter to defend himself and his version of the gospel in order to win the Galatians back to what he considers the true saving message about Jesus.

In his salutation (1:1–5) Paul is already defending himself as "an apostle—not from men nor through man, but through Jesus Christ and God the Father . . . " and he omits the customary thanksgiving section of the letter and replaces it with a curse on anyone who would preach a gospel contrary to the one which they originally received (1:6–9).

Galatians 1:10–2:21 is a long apologetic defense of Paul's apostleship. In this section he wants to insist that his version of the gospel comes directly through a revelation of

Jesus the Christ and not through human agency (1:10–24). However, at the same time, Paul shows that his circumcision-free gospel does have the approval of the authorities in Jerusalem by giving a detailed account of his meeting with "the pillars" in the Jerusalem community in which they approved of the version of the gospel he was preaching among the Gentiles (2:1–10). Paul's version of this so-called "council of Jerusalem" differs substantially from Luke's more idealized account in Acts 15. Paul concludes his defense with an account of an unpleasant incident in Antioch in which he chided Cephas (Peter) for being two-faced about the obligatory character of the Jewish dietary laws (2:11–14). The section ends with a statement of Paul's gospel. Salvation, even for Jews like Paul and Cephas, does not come through the observance of the Mosaic law but through belief in Jesus Christ and his death on the cross through which, Paul says, "he loved me and gave himself for me." This event has "justified," or set right with God, all humanity—Jews by birth as well as Gentiles who had not previously known the one true God.

In 3:1–5 Paul gives a proof of his gospel from the experience of the Galatians. He begins by recalling their experience when they first heard and received in faith his gospel about Jesus Christ crucified without any mention of an obligation to observe the law of Moses. Apparently their initial conversion was accompanied by many experiences which Paul attributed to the Spirit of God which was to be poured out in the messianic age (cf. Jl 2:28–32). Paul contrasts this with their foolish acceptance of his opponents' gospel which demands the works of the law, a gospel which Paul antithetically labels as belonging to the flesh.

In 3:6–29 Paul develops a complicated scriptural argument to prove that the justification of the Gentiles is by faith in the promise made to the Jewish forefather Abraham through whom all the nations were to be blessed (Gen 12:1–3; etc.), and not through the observance of the law of Moses. The key texts for Paul are: Gen 15:6—he (Abraham) "believed and it was reckoned to him as righteousness"—and Gen 12:3—the promise to Abraham which said, "In you shall all the nations be blessed." In contrast to these Abraham traditions which are based on faith in a promise, the terms of the law are based on a curse for those who do not obey its precepts (3:10–11). According to Paul, Christ, the "offspring" referred to in the promises to Abraham, has by his death on the cross liberated humanity from the curse due to the law and made it heir to the promises made to Abraham which could not be annulled by a law that came four hundred and thirty years later (3:12–18). The role of the law was simply to be a temporary custodian for the Jews to restrain sin until the Messiah came (3:19–24). But now that the Messiah has come the distinctions between Jew and Greek, slave and free, male and female have been obliterated for those who have been baptized and entered the messianic community as heirs to the promise made to Abraham (3:26–29).

The consequences of belief in Christ are then described in terms of a contrast between the state of Jews and Gentiles before and after the coming of the Messiah (4:1–31). Until the coming of the Messiah, both groups were in a state of slavery or children under a guardian, but now through the Messiah they have become "free" and fully adopted heirs of God's kingdom. Jews, who, like Paul, were living under the law, were comparable to slaves or children who had not yet come of age so that they could take their inheritance. But now, in the fullness of time, God had "sent forth his Son, born of woman, born under the law, to redeem those who were under the law, so that we might receive adoption as sons" (4:4–5). Likewise, the Gentile Galatians had been in their idolatry in "bondage to beings that by nature are no gods," but now they have been liberated from that slavery, and Paul does not want them to return to that state by reintroducing their old religious observances (4:8–10). He uses the allegory of Hagar, Abraham's slave, and Sarah, Abraham's wife, to exhort the Galatians to remain as free children of the promise and not return to their former slavery (4:21–31).

The freedom of the Christian is further clarified in chapter 5 where Paul contrasts the life of "the flesh" with the life of "the Spirit." Christian freedom is not a life under the law of Moses, but it is also not license which gives free rein to "the desires of the flesh," i.e. "fornication, impurity, licentiousness, idolatry, sorcery, enmity, strife, jealousy, anger, selfishness, dissension, party spirit, envy, drunkenness, carousing, and the like" (5:19–21). Rather, Christian freedom is for Paul life in "the Spirit" whose fruits he describes as "love, joy, peace, patience, kindness, goodness, faithfulness, gentleness, self-control" (5:22–23). Christians are able to live such a life because they "have crucified the flesh with its passions and desires" (5:24).

1 CORINTHIANS

In his correspondence with the Christian community which he had founded in the lively port city of Corinth in the region of Achaia in Greece, Paul faces a completely different set of problems which arose from distortion of the Christian message through understanding it as a Hellenistic philosophy or mystery religion. Paul had founded the church there during an eighteen-month stay in 50–52 C.E., but, judging from 1 Corinthians, this gifted but chaotic community was subsequently racked by factionalism, distortions of Paul's original teaching in ethical matters, and even denial of bodily resurrection which was for Paul the very foundation of Christian faith. Most of the problems were rooted in an attempt to make Christianity into an esoteric mystery religion on the Hellenistic model.

After the customary salutation and thanksgiving (1:1–9), Paul begins 1 Corinthians by addressing the problem of factionalism (1:10–4:21). The community has apparently been divided into groups claiming allegiance to Paul, Apollos (another apostle from Alexandria in Egypt), Cephas (Peter), and Christ. For Paul such division is rooted in a misunderstanding of the Christian gospel and the subordinate role of apostles in the spreading of the gospel message. The Christian gospel is not the "wisdom" of a particular Christian preacher. In fact, by the standards of philosophical wisdom, the gospel is folly, because its focal point is the cross, i.e., the message about Jesus, a crucified Messiah. Paul reminds the Corinthians who apparently had allegiance to the apostle who had baptized them that

> Christ did not send me to baptize but to preach the gospel, and not with eloquent wisdom, lest the cross of Christ be emptied of its power. For the word of the cross is folly to those who are perishing, but to us who are being saved it is the power of God (1:17–18).

The apostles are simply servants through whom the Corinthians came to belief.

> I planted, Apollos watered, but God gave the growth. So neither he who plants nor he who waters is anything, but only God who gives the growth (3:6–7).

Finally, Paul sarcastically chides the Corinthians for claiming to be somehow already "filled" and "rich" from the gospel message as if it were some mystery religion which granted its initiates deliverance from the sufferings and obligations of earthly reality. He contrasts their boasts with the present condition of the apostles who suffer in order to spread the gospel of the crucified Christ.

> We are fools for Christ's sake, but you are wise in Christ. We are weak, but you are strong. You are held in honor, but we in disrepute. To the present hour we hunger and thirst, we are ill-clad and buffeted and homeless, and we labor, working with your own hands. When reviled, we bless; when persecuted, we endure; when slandered, we try to conciliate; we have become, and are now as the refuse of the world, the offscouring of all things (4:10–13).

In 1 Corinthians 5–6 Paul treats some problems related to ethical behavior which have divided the Corinthian community. Many of these problems stem from misinterpretations of Paul's earlier preaching that have led to irresponsible and immoral behavior detrimental to the unity of the community. Some members were evidently justifying their behavior by saying "All things are lawful for me . . . " (6:12). This slogan may have been based on Paul's preaching that Christian faith had superseded the Mosaic law and its demands. Paul responds by insisting that "not all things are helpful" and that "I will not be enslaved by anything" (6:12–13). On this basis, he tells them to expel from the community the man who was cohabiting with his father's wife (5:1–13). Paul's hope is that by such drastic action "his spirit may be saved in the day of the Lord Jesus" (5:3–5). Paul is also extremely critical of Christians bringing litigation against one another before pagan law courts, and he suggests that they settle these matters among themselves even if it means suffering a wrong (6:1–8). Finally, Paul confronts the problem of sexual license which was notoriously rampant in the city of Corinth (6:12–20). He rejects the analogy that satisfying the sexual appetite is no different from taking food to satisfy hunger. The sexual act involves the whole body which for the Christian has become a member of Christ, a temple of God's spirit.

Shun immorality. Every other sin which a man commits is outside the body; but the immoral man sins against his own body. Do you not know that your body is a temple of the Holy Spirit within you, which you have from God? You are not your own; your were bought with a price. So glorify God in your body (6:18–20).

In chapter 7 Paul addresses a series of questions about marriage and sexuality which the Corinthians themselves have raised in a letter. In interpreting this section, it is important to realize that Paul is an apocalyptic thinker who believed that the Christian community was living at the end of the present evil age and on the brink of the end of the old world order.

I mean, brethren, the appointed time has grown very short; from now on, let those who have wives live as though they had none, and those who mourn as though they were not mourning, and those who rejoice as though they were not rejoicing, and those who buy as though they had no goods, and those who deal with the world as though they had no dealings with it. For the form of this world is passing away (7:29–31).

Because of this, Paul's basic advice is: "Everyone should remain in the state in which he was called" (7:20).

However, he does urge the Corinthians not to attempt ascetic behavior beyond their human capacity. Married couples should be sensitive to each other's conjugal needs (7:2–7). If they are not exercising self-control, unmarried people and widows should marry (7:8–9). In general, married couples should not divorce even if one of the parties is an unbeliever. Paul does, however, allow an exception if the unbelieving partner desires to separate (7:12–16). In the case of the unmarried, Paul would prefer, in light of the apocalyptic times, that they remain celibate as he is, but prudently allows them to marry if they wish (7:32–40).

In 8:1–11:1 Paul treats two difficult questions about Christians' relationship to the pagan cults: the problem of food offered to idols which was sold in the marketplace and the matter of participation in banquets held in honor of pagan gods. Paul's treatment of these issues is a good illustration of how his ethical teaching is based on the Christian command to love rather than on "knowledge" as in a philosophical ethics or a "mystery religion." For Paul, love "builds up" the community by being concerned with the physical and spiritual welfare of others. "Knowledge" puffs up the individual with no regard for the needs of others. Paul sarcastically agrees with the knowledgable that the idols have no real existence, but he asks that out of consideration for the weaker brethren who are recent converts they not eat the food that has been offered to idols in their presence (10:23–28). In the matter of the pagan banquets, Paul forbids participation because the Christian eucharistic meal is a participation in the body and blood of Christ and this precludes participation in the pagan sacrifices (10:14–22). In the midst of this section, Paul offers his own behavior as an example to the Corinthians (9:1–27). As an apostle he has certain rights, like the right to support from his communities and to be accompanied by a wife.

However, he has freely given up those rights in order to be of service to those to whom he preaches the gospel. In the same manner he asks the Corinthians to be willing to give up their liberties and privileges for the sake of one another's spiritual needs.

In chapter 11 Paul gives advice to correct abuses which had arisen in the conduct of Christian worship services, particularly the celebration of the Eucharist which Paul calls "the Lord's supper." In the course of exhorting the Corinthians to avoid factionalism and drunken and inconsiderate behavior in the conduct of the Lord's supper, Paul gives us the earliest record of Jesus' actions and words at his final meal with his disciples the night before he died. It is clear from Paul's account that the meal was celebrated as a proclamation of Jesus' saving death and in anticipation of his coming again in glory.

> For I received from the Lord what I also delivered to you, that the Lord Jesus on the night when he was betrayed took bread, and when he had given thanks, he broke it, and said, "This is my body which is for you. Do this in remembrance of me." In the same way also the cup, after supper, saying, "This cup is the new covenant in my blood. Do this, as often as you drink it, in remembrance of me." For as often as you eat this bread and drink the cup, you proclaim the Lord's death until he comes (11:23–26).

Paul now turns to the troublesome problem of the spiritual gifts which were also dividing the Corinthian community (12:1–14:40). Apparently some were using the possession of these gifts as a basis for claiming superiority within the community. Paul approaches the problem from several angles—all of them designed to exhort the church to unity through a considerate love that aims at building up the community. He reminds the Corinthians that for the common good one and the same Spirit gives a variety of gifts: the utterance of wisdom, the utterance of knowledge, faith, healing, working of miracles, prophecy, speaking in tongues, and interpreting tongues (12:4–11). Then Paul returns to the body of Christ metaphor which he now uses to express the interdependence of each member of the community—Jews or Greeks, slave or free—upon one another (12:12–26). In the conclusion of this section Paul provides a ranking of the gifts (apostles, prophets, teachers, miracle workers, healers, helpers, administrators, speakers in tongues), but he ends by noting that no one possesses all of these.

In a memorable and lyrical passage, Paul goes on to describe love (*agape*) as the most necessary, greatest and lasting gift.

> If I speak in the tongues of men and of angels, but have not love, I am a noisy gong or a clanging cymbal. And if I have prophetic powers and understand all mysteries and all knowledge, and if I have all faith, so as to remove mountains, but have not love, I am nothing. If I give away all I have, and if I deliver my body to be burned, but have not love, I gain nothing. Love is patient and kind; love is not jealous or boastful; it is not arrogant or rude. Love does not insist on its own way; it is not irritable or resentful; it does not rejoice at wrong, but rejoices in the right. Love bears all things, believes all things, hopes all things, endures all things. Love never ends; as for prophecies, they will pass away; as for tongues they will cease; as for knowledge, it will pass away. For our knowledge is imperfect and our prophecy is imperfect; but when the perfect comes, the imperfect will pass

away. . . . For now we see in a mirror dimly, but then face to face. Now I know in part; then I shall understand fully, even as I have been fully understood. So faith, hope, and love abide, these three; but the greatest of these is love (13:1–13).

Paul's concept of *agape* is quite distinct from the traditional Greek notion of love, *eros*. *Eros* is the dynamic within the person which aims at self-fulfillment through union with the beloved. *Agape* as Paul describes it is unselfish love which is concerned with the welfare of others to the point of giving up self-fulfillment. *Eros* is rooted in a philosophical and psychological analysis of the human soul. *Agape* is a divine gift which enables the person to live for the needs of others.

Chapter 14 contains a more detailed discussion of the gifts of prophecy and tongues which were of special concern to the Corinthian church. Paul finds prophecy much more valuable because it builds up, encourages and consoles the members of the community. Tongues, a gift which was highly prized by some, is not essential in Paul's estimation because it cannot be understood by others and therefore does nothing to build up the community.

In chapter 15 Paul turns his attention to the most important problem of all: the fact that some were denying the resurrection of the dead. To Greeks, who were accustomed to the Platonic belief in an immortal soul, talk of a resurrected body after death must have seemed ridiculous. The body was a prison for the immortal soul; it was the source of the passions and appetites which kept the soul/mind from attaining the truth.

Paul's response to this challenge is a firm reaffirmation of his teaching that belief in the resurrection of the crucified Christ and the future resurrection of the dead at the apocalyptic return of Christ is central to the Christian faith. He begins by reminding the Corinthians of the basic gospel message which he first preached to them in which he lists the various appearances of the risen Jesus that he is aware of, including his own:

For I delivered to you as of first importance what I also received, that Christ died for our sins in accordance with the scriptures, that he was buried, that he was raised on the third day in accordance with the scriptures, and that he appeared to Cephas, then to the twelve. Then he appeared to more than five hundred brethren at one time, most of whom are still alive, though some have fallen asleep. Then he appeared to James, then to all the apostles. Last of all, as to one untimely born, he appeared also to me . . . so we preach and so you believed (15:3–11).

Paul then goes on to suppose that there is no resurrection of the dead and examines what happens to the gospel message in such a case (15:12–19). If there is no resurrection from the dead, then Christ has not been raised. This means that Paul's initial preaching was a misrepresentation of God whom Paul testified had raised Christ from the dead. If Paul's preaching was in vain, then the Corinthians' faith is futile and they are still in their sins. Paul concludes:

If for this life only we have hoped in Christ, we are of all men most to be pitied (15:19).

But the fact is, insists Paul, that Christ has been raised from the dead, and he is like the first fruits of a harvest which will affect the whole of humanity. Paul uses the Adam/ Christ typology to express his belief that Christ's resurrection is the first event in an apocalyptic transformation in which the dead will be raised and God's kingdom will be definitively established.

> For as by a man came death, by a man has come also the resurrection of the dead. For as in Adam all die, so also in Christ shall all be made alive. But each in his own order: Christ the first fruits, then at his coming those who belong to Christ. Then comes the end, when he delivers the kingdom to God the Father after destroying every rule and every authority and power . . . (15:21–24).

To those who question the manner of the resurrection of the dead and the nature of their bodies Paul replies with a metaphor drawn from the planting of seeds.

> What you sow does not come to life unless it dies. And what you sow is not the body which is to be, but a bare kernel, perhaps of wheat or of some other grain. . . . So is it with the resurrection of the dead. What is sown is perishable, what is raised is imperishable. It is sown in dishonor, it is raised in glory. It is sown in weakness, it is raised in power. It is sown a physical body, it is raised a spiritual body. If there is a physical body, there is also a spiritual body . . . (15:36–45).

ROMANS

The longest and most significant of Paul's epistles is his Letter to the Romans. It is written to introduce Paul and his gospel to an important Christian community which he had not founded or visited but whose support he needs to further his missionary work (1:8–14; 15:22–33); therefore, it contains the fullest statement of his gospel.

At the time of writing, Paul is very concerned with the question of the unity between the Jewish mother church in Jerusalem and the Gentile churches which he has founded in Asia Minor and Greece, and the question of the unity between Jews and Gentiles in a single Christian or messianic community will dominate the letter. This question was also of great interest to the Roman Christian community which was made up of Jewish and Gentile Christians.

When Paul writes Romans, he has completed his missionary work in the eastern part of the Mediterranean and is on his way to Jerusalem with aid for the Christian community there which he has collected, with some difficulty, from the churches in Macedonia and Achaia (15:25–26). For Paul, this collection had important symbolic significance. The Gentile churches are in debt to the Jewish mother church in Jerusalem because they "have come to share in their (the Jews') spiritual blessings," i.e., membership in the messianic community. Now the Greek churches are in a position to help the "saints at Jerusalem" with material aid. After delivering the collection to Jerusalem, Paul is planning a missionary journey to Spain and expects to stop in Rome on the way to gain their support for his missionary work in the West. In the meantime, he asks for the prayers of the Christian community in Rome for the success of his journey to Jerusalem, as he fears he may be delivered to "the unbelievers" there (15:30–33)—a fear that was justified. According to Acts, Paul was arrested in Jerusalem for causing a riot in the temple area and came to Rome as a prisoner demanding his right, as a Roman citizen, to trial by the emperor (Acts 22–28).

In the salutation (1:1–7) Paul, in identifying himself, already makes a preliminary statement of his gospel and credentials as an apostle. The heart of the gospel is the message about Jesus' death and resurrection which Paul describes in two stages using the categories of flesh and Spirit. Jesus is the Christ or Messiah. He was "descended from David according to the flesh," but now is "designated Son of God in power according to the Spirit of holiness by his resurrection from the dead." Paul is also very careful to emphasize both the continuity of the gospel with the Jewish Scriptures but also the inclusion of the nations or Gentiles in God's plan through faith in that message.

> Paul, a servant of Jesus Christ, called to be an apostle, set apart for the gospel of God which he promised beforehand through his prophets in the holy scriptures, the gospel concerning his Son, who was descended from David according to the flesh and designated Son of God in power according to the Spirit of holiness by his resurrection from the dead, Jesus Christ our Lord, through whom we have received grace and apostleship to bring about the obedience of faith for the sake of his name among all the nations, including yourselves who are called to belong to Jesus Christ . . . (1:1–6).

> For I am not ashamed of the gospel: it is the power of God for salvation to every one who has faith, to the Jew first and also to the Greek. For in it the righteousness of God is revealed through faith for faith; as it is written, "He who through faith is righteous shall live" (1:16–17).

Paul's statement of the gospel is expressed in apocalyptic terms because he believes that the death and resurrection of Jesus has inaugurated the final age. In the gospel "the righteousness of God is revealed," i.e., the establishment of God's justice which was expected, in Jewish apocalyptic works, with the full coming of God's kingdom. The mode of entry into the community of salvation is through faith in the act of God through Jesus the Christ—a way that is open first to the Jews but also to the Greeks (Gentiles). What is not said here, but is implied, is that salvation is not, as the Jews might have expected, through obedience to the Torah, the law of Moses (cf. 3:21ff.).

In 1:18–3:31 Paul sets out to show how both Gentiles and Jews were in need of this saving gospel because both groups were under the judgment of God's just wrath for their failure to live up to the demands of his justice. Again Paul expresses himself in highly apocalyptic terms. He announces that "the wrath of God is revealed" against the "ungodliness and wickedness" of the Gentile world which should have found God through their reason and the law of their conscience but instead turned to idolatry in worshiping images rather than the Creator (1:18–23) and therefore God has punished them by giving them

over to a life of moral corruption (1:24–32). This section reads like a standard Jewish indictment of Gentile idolatry and immorality (cf. Wisdom of Solomon 13–15). But then
Paul also points out that, although the Jews have been favored with the law, they too have
fallen short of God's demands (2:1–20).

> But if you call yourself a Jew and rely upon the law and boast of your relation to God and
> know his will and approve what is excellent, because you are instructed in the law, and if
> you are sure that you are a guide to the blind, a light to those who are in darkness, a
> corrector of the foolish, a teacher of children, having in the law the embodiment of knowl-
> edge and truth—you then who teach others, will you not teach yourself? While you preach
> against stealing, do you steal? You who say that one must not commit adultery, do you
> commit adultery? You who abhor idols, do you rob temples? You who boast in the law, do
> you dishonor God by breaking the law? For, it is written, "The name of God is blasphemed
> among the Gentiles because of you" (2:17–24).

For Paul, the failure of both Gentiles and Jews, as a whole, to live up to the demands
of the law indicates that God's justice had to be established in some other way; the law
had only established a "knowledge of sin" (3:19–20). But God has now gratuituously justified both groups by accepting the death of the righteous Jesus as "an expiation by his
blood" for their sin; they may both receive this salvation through faith in the power of
God's forgiving action.

> But now the righteousness of God has been manifested apart from the law, although the
> law and the prophets bear witness to it, the righteousness of God through faith in Jesus
> Christ for all who believe. For there is no distinction; since all have sinned and fall short
> of the glory of God, they are justified by his grace as a gift, through the redemption which
> is in Christ Jesus, whom God put forward as an expiation by his blood, to be received by
> faith. This was to show God's righteousness, because in his divine forbearance he had
> passed over former sins; it was to prove at the present time that he himself is righteous
> and that he justifies him who has faith in Jesus (3:21–26).

Paul now goes on to state that his gospel of justification through faith and apart from
the works of the law excludes any human boasting and is necessary if God is the God of
both Gentiles as well as the Jews. In fact, Paul insists that his gospel does not overthrow
the law, in the sense of the five books of the Torah, but upholds it (3:27–31). Paul's proof
for this is his interpretation of the Abraham tradition (4:1–25). Again his key text is Genesis 15:6: "Abraham believed God, and it was reckoned to him as righteousness." Paul
interprets this text as proving that Abraham, the forefather of the Jews and the one
through whom the nations were to be blessed, received God's justification, not through the
"works" of the law, but through trust in God's promises. Abraham's justification occurred
before he was circumcised (Genesis 17), and therefore he is the forefather of all who believe: the uncircumcised Gentiles as well as the circumcised Jews who believe.

The purpose was to make him the father of all who believe without being circumcised and thus have righteousness reckoned to them, and likewise the father of the circumcised who are not merely circumcised but also follow the example of the faith which our father Abraham had before he was circumcised (4:11–12).

Abraham's faith in the promise that he would become "the father of many nations" (Gen 17:5), even when his hundred year old body "was as good as dead" and Sarah's womb was barren, is understood by Paul as being written not for Abraham's sake alone, but also for the Christians of his own day "who believe in him that raised from the dead Jesus our Lord, who was put to death for our trespasses and raised for our justification" (4:23–24).

Romans 5:1–11 examines the consequences of the death and resurrection of Christ for humanity. Paul expresses the salvation available in Christ through several metaphors: "justified by faith," "peace with God," "access to . . . grace" (5:1–2). However, although in one sense salvation has been achieved, Paul is also aware that it is not complete; the kingdom of God has not yet been fully established. Christ's death has made salvation accessible, but the Christian community must endure in faith and hope until Christ's return. The source of Christian hope in this time of suffering is what God has already done for humanity through the death of Christ.

> While we were still weak, at the right time Christ died for the ungodly. Why, one will hardly die for a righteous man—though perhaps for a good man one will dare even to die. But God shows his love for us in that while we were yet sinners Christ died for us. Since, therefore, we are now justified by his blood, much more shall we be saved by him from the wrath of God. For if while we were enemies we were reconciled to God by the death of his Son, much more, now that we are reconciled, shall we be saved by his life (5:6–10).

In Romans 5:12–21 Paul explains how the death and resurrection of Jesus Christ could effect the salvation of all humanity. He uses, as he had in 1 Corinthians 15, the Adam-Christ typology. Just as the disobedient act of the one man unleashed sin and death, like two demonic characters, into the world and brought condemnation in that all fell into sin, so the obedient act of Christ, the new man, has brought the gift of righteousness and grace. This Adam-Christ typology, first introduced here by Paul, becomes a standard part of Christian theology, and we will see it in the work of the Church fathers, like Irenaeus and Augustine, in their discussion of the effects of sin and redemption from sin through the death and resurrection of Christ.

In chapter 6 Paul, in diatribe fashion, raises and answers a possible objection to his gospel of salvation through faith in Christ. The question is: Does Paul's gospel encourage continuation in sin "that grace may abound" (6:1)? Paul's answer is a definitive "No!" He substantiates this by a reflection on the effects of the baptism which Christian converts received. Paul interprets Christian baptism, somewhat like the Hellenistic mystery cults, as an entrance into the death and resurrection of Christ which leads to walking in a newness of life (6:1–4). However, Christian baptism involves an ethical conversion: a "death" to enslavement to sin and a "resurrection" into a life in which Christians "have become slaves of righteousness" (6:18).

In chapter 7 Paul turns to a question which was particularly sensitive to the Jewish-Christians in his audience: Was the Mosaic law or Torah, which Paul says is no longer operative even for Jews (7:1–6), the same as "sin" (7:7)? For Jews the Torah was God's gift of revelation which saved them from the idolatry and sin of the pagan Gentile world. Paul's answer is that the law is by no means the same as sin; in fact it is "holy, just and good." However, according to him, the law only had a temporary role in salvation history: to reveal to the Jew living under the law the power of sin. Paul's description, in the first person singular, of the Jew vainly struggling to live up to the demands of the law is one of the most memorable passages in all of his letters. In it he personifies sin as a demonic agent which enslaves the person trying to live up to the law and thus makes it powerless to bring its intended blessings.

> Yet, if it had not been for the law, I should not have known sin. I should not have known what it is to covet if the law had not said, "You shall not covet." But sin, finding opportunity in the commandment, wrought in me all kinds of covetousness. Apart from the law sin lies dead. I was once alive apart from the law, but when the commandment came, sin revived and I died; the very commandment which promised life proved to be death to me. For sin, finding opportunity in the commandment, deceived me and by it killed me. So the law is holy, and the commandment is holy and just and good. Did that which is good, then, bring death to me? By no means! It was sin, working death in me through what is good, in order that sin might be shown to be sin, and through the commandment might become sinful beyond measure. We know that the law is spiritual; but I am carnal, sold under sin. I do not understand my own actions. For I do not do what I want, but I do the very thing I hate. Now if I do what I do not want, I agree that the law is good. So then it is no longer I that do it, but sin which dwells within me. For I know that nothing good dwells within me, that is, in my flesh. I can will what is right, but I cannot do it. For I do not do the good I want, but the evil I do not want is what I do. Now if I do what I do not want, it is no longer I that do it, but sin which dwells within me. So I find it to be a law that when I want to do right, evil lies close at hand. For I delight in the law of God, in my inmost self, but I see in my members another law at war with the law of my mind and making me captive to the law of sin which dwells in my members. Wretched man that I am! Who will deliver me from this body of death? (7:7–25).

The painful dualism which Paul describes here is not the same as the body-soul dualism of Plato. For Paul the whole human person is "sold under sin" without the help of God's Spirit which has been poured out with the coming of Christ in the final age. Paul's description of the inability to live up to the law of God makes a striking contrast with Plato's thought that "knowledge is virtue." For Plato, with his Greek emphasis on "mind" and "knowledge," if one truly knows the good, then one will pursue it. Paul, with his Jewish sense of the power of sin, is equally convinced that one can "know" and even "will" what God wants and still be incapable of doing it because of the enslaving power of sin.

For Paul, the Jew who has come to believe in Christ has been freed from the dilemma described so poignantly in Romans 7. Chapter 8 is a lyrical description of the liberating effects of the death and resurrection of Christ for the Jew who had formerly been under the law. Paul uses his favorite antithetical categories of flesh and Spirit to categorize the "before" and "after" of being under the law and being "in Christ":

> For God has done what the law, weakened by the flesh, could not do: sending his own Son in the likeness of sinful flesh and for sin, he condemned sin in the flesh, in order that the just requirement of the law might be fulfilled in us, who walk not according to the flesh but according to the Spirit (8:3–5).

Romans 8:18–39 returns to the themes of 5:1–11: a moving and lyrical apocalyptic description of the present state of the Christian community, having received the Spirit through the saving act of God in Jesus' death and resurrection and awaiting in confident hope with the rest of creation the completion of God's kingdom.

Chapters 9–11 complete Paul's treatment of the question of the relationship between Israel and the Gentiles with the coming of Christ. The fact that most of the Jews, Paul's "kinsmen by race," had not accepted the gospel message about Jesus was deeply troubling to him because they are the chosen people of God (9:1–5). However, Paul points out, through the stories about the patriarchs, Abraham and Isaac, and other scriptural texts, that in God's providential plan the true Israel has always been the children of faith and the promise, and not simply the physical descendants of Abraham, and that the salvation of the Gentiles had been envisioned from the beginning (9:7–33). Paul also insists that God will never abandon his promises to Israel; the Jews will be saved when the "full number of Gentiles comes in" (11:25ff.). At the present time their failure to accept the gospel has had the fortuitous result of the Gentiles as "wild olive shoots" becoming "grafted in" to the "natural olive tree" of Israel, but the Gentile Christians are warned not to become proud; they are totally dependent upon God's ancient relationship with Israel. He reminds them: "Remember, it is not you that support the root, but the root that supports you" (11:17–24).

Paul concludes Romans with a long exhortation section (12:1–15:12) which has some similarities to the ethical instruction in 1 Corinthians. Of particular interest is Paul's advice in 13:1–7 that the Roman Christians be law-abiding, tax-paying citizens. He is convinced that if they do so, they will have no trouble from the Roman authorities whom Paul calls "God's servant for your good." This advice which Paul meant for the fledgling Christian community in the middle of the first century C.E. was not intended as a universal statement of church-state relations. Paul was not confronted with the problem which was soon to face the Christian church: the choice of loyalty to the Christian faith or allegiance to the state religion of Rome.

THE GOSPELS

Although Jesus is mentioned obliquely by the Roman historians Tacitus and Suetonius and in Josephus' **Antiquities,** our primary sources of information about the historical

Jesus are the four gospels of the New Testament. These works are not eyewitness reports of the teachings and life of Jesus, but faith-inspired proclamations of the *evangelion*, "good news," that the crucified and resurrected Jesus is the long-awaited Messiah and Savior. The gospels bear some similarities to other biographies of the period like Philo's **Life of Moses** or Philostratus' **Life of Apollonius,** a famous philosopher of the second century, in that they are highly rhetorical narratives which aim to praise or idealize the hero by emphasizing his wisdom, heroic virtue, or unusual power. They also tend to put the opponents of the hero—in the case of the gospels, the Jewish leaders and sages—in the worst possible light. However, the New Testament gospels also differ markedly from the spirit of the other biographies of the time in that all four emphasize Jesus' failure to win over the leaders of official Judaism and his subsequent death by crucifixion at the hands of Pontius Pilate.

Most scholars agree that the gospels were probably composed in the period between 70 and 100 C.E. as the need arose in the various churches for written records of the significance of Jesus' teachings and life because of the deaths of the original eye-witnesses and the delay of the expected triumphant return of Jesus as the glorious Son of Man. Prior to that time, the traditions about Jesus seem to have been preserved primarily in the oral preaching and instruction of the apostles and early Christian missionaries. Although the four gospels have certain basic similarities, they present four quite distinct portraits of Jesus and unique insights into the significance of his teaching, deeds, passion and resurrection. Because of this diversity in the gospel accounts, it is very difficult to arrive at a confident reconstruction of the "historical" Jesus. The situation is analogous to the problem of discovering the "historical" Socrates behind the diverse pictures created by Plato, Aristophanes and Zenophon.

The gospels of Matthew, Mark and Luke have enough similarity in the sequence of their narratives and even the wording of their texts to prompt scholars to postulate a common literary source and designate them as the "synoptic" gospels, meaning that they see the story of Jesus "with one eye." The usual solution proposed for this so-called "synoptic problem" is that Mark was the earliest gospel and that Matthew and Luke used some form of Mark as a source. Some of the reasons for this assumption are: Mark is the shortest of the gospels (only 661 verses); most of Mark is included in the other two gospels which seem to follow his sequence of events; the other two supplement Mark's narrative, which contains relatively little of the teaching of Jesus, with either collections of teaching material drawn from a common source (usually designated as Q for the German word *Quelle,* "source") or with their own sources. For this reason I will begin with a discussion of Mark's gospel.

MARK'S GOSPEL

The superscription, "The Gospel according to Mark," is a later second century addition to the gospel which is anonymous. According to the fourth-century Christian historian Eusebius, who cites Papias, a second-century bishop of Hierapolis, Mark's account goes back to Peter's preaching of the gospel in Rome, and Irenaeus (c. 130–200 C.E.), an early Christian apologist, states that the gospel was composed in Rome after the martyrdom of Peter and Paul in 64 C.E. In the following essay I will use Mark to designate the author of the gospel.

The prologue (1:1–13) begins with the announcement of Mark's theme—"the gospel of Jesus Christ, the Son of God" (1:1). Two major concerns throughout Mark's narrative will be the nature of "the good news" and identity of Jesus implied in these titles. He will present Jesus inaugurating the kingdom of God by announcing "the good news" of its arrival and by attacking, in apocalyptic fashion, the dominion of Satan through numerous miracles and authoritative teaching about God's will. However, the gospel will end, not with the final triumph of God's kingdom as in traditional apocalyptic visions, but with Jesus' death by crucifixion and his awaited return as the triumphant, resurrected Messiah (Mark 15–16). Mark's Gospel is an attempt to comprehend this full picture of Jesus as both the powerful Messiah and Son of God who inaugurated the kingdom of God with powerful deeds and words, but also the suffering Son of Man who died on the cross and will complete his work with a triumphant return as Son of Man only after the nations have heard his gospel (Mark 13).

The story begins abruptly with the penitential preaching in the wilderness by John the Baptizer, who, as the awaited prophetic precursor of the Messiah, announces the coming of "he who is mightier than I" (1:2–8). The baptism by John in the Jordan is the occasion for Jesus' learning his own identity. In a dramatic but private moment he sees the heavens open and the Spirit of God descend upon him, and he hears a heavenly voice announcing, "Thou art my beloved Son; with thee I am well pleased" (1:9–11). Immediately, Jesus is driven by the Spirit into the wilderness for forty days where he undergoes a temptation from Satan, but is ministered to by God's angels as he lives with the wild beasts.

After John's arrest, Mark begins the Galilean ministry (1:14–9:50) with Jesus' announcement of the arrival of the kingdom of God (1:14–15). Jesus then demonstrates its presence by authoritative teaching and powerful miracles. By the Sea of Galilee, he calls Simon and Andrew, James and John to join him as "fishers of men" simply by the command "Follow me" (1:16–20). In Capernaum and the surrounding region, Jesus impresses the crowds as a superior teacher to the scribes by his power to command the unclean spirits to leave those possessed of leprosy, fever and other diseases (1:21–45). However, at the same time, Jesus does not want his full identity as "the Holy One of God" to be known. He commands the demons who recognize him to "be silent" (1:25; 1:34) and tells a leper who has been cleansed: "See that you say nothing to anyone . . . " (1:43). For Mark, the proper time for the full revelation of Jesus' identity to the world will not come until he has suffered, died and been raised up in Jerusalem. Only then can the full significance of Jesus be appreciated (9:9). Despite Jesus' efforts at secrecy at this stage of his ministry, people flock to him to be cured and he is forced to withdraw to a lonely place for prayer (1:35ff.).

In 2:1–3:6 Jesus' activity already begins to meet opposition from the scribes and Pharisees who object to his violations of traditional Jewish piety by forgiving sins (2:1–12), associating with tax collectors and sinners (2:13–17), failing to fast (2:18–22), and violating the sabbath (2:23–28; 3:1–6). Throughout Mark's gospel, the Jewish teachers and leaders are portrayed as legalistic hypocrites which should in no way be understood as giving an accurate historical picture. Mark uses the scribes and Pharisees in a highly rhetorical way as a foil to Jesus who defends his behavior by authoritative claims to be the Son of Man who has authority on earth to forgive sin and be lord over the sabbath (2:10; 2:28), and also by parabolic sayings which point to the nature of his mission as a physician for sinners and the uniqueness of this time as one of rejoicing and newness. Even at this early stage Mark allows the shadow of the cross to fall over the narrative by noting at the end of the section that the Pharisees and Herodians began to plan "how to destroy him" (3:6).

Having met opposition from official Judaism, Jesus withdraws with his disciples (3:7–12) to the Sea of Galilee and then calls to himself on a mountain twelve of his choice (symbolic of a renewal of the twelve tribes of Israel) and sends them out to share in his work of preaching and casting out demons (3:7–19).

Jesus himself continues to manifest his power through numerous miracles, but also to command secrecy about his full identity. He heals many of unclean spirits, but does not allow them to confess him as "Son of God" (3:7–12). In calming the stormy waters of the Sea of Galilee by the simple command, "Peace! Be Still!" he demonstrates to his disciples that even "wind and sea obey him"; but he does not answer their question about his identity (4:35–41). In the longest and most dramatic miracle story in the gospel, Jesus releases a legion of demons who recognize him as "the Son of God Most High" from the Gerasene demoniac into a herd of swine (5:1–20), but then he refuses to remain in that region. Even after he has raised Jairus' daughter from the dead (5:21–43), Jesus insists that "no one should know this" (5:43).

Despite these impressive demonstrations of Jesus' power to make the kingdom of God present, the hostile response to him intensifies. The disciples and crowds marvel at Jesus' miracles, but many reject him. The scribes from Jerusalem accuse him of being possessed by Beelzebul, the prince of demons (3:22–30). Jesus' own family thinks that he is "beside himself" (3:21), and when he returns to his own country from the region of the Decapolis across the Jordan, his fellow countrymen wonder where this mere carpenter got this wisdom and power (6:1–6).

Jesus continues to defend himself by insisting that he is indeed attacking the dominion of Satan (3:23–27), and he calls upon those who witness his deeds to believe in the power of God and to do his will (3:31–35; 5:36ff.). In the case of the woman who had a "flow of blood for twelve years," her faith that the mere touch of Jesus' garments would bring healing effects a cure for her (5:24–34). On the other hand, lack of belief limits Jesus' power in his home town where he could "do no mighty work" (6:5–6).

The various responses to Jesus in this section are exemplified in his parable of the sower (4:1–9) and its allegorical interpretation (4:14–20). Like the sower in the parable, Jesus has sowed his seed widely, but he has not met with a totally favorable response. The twelve have been privileged to "receive the secret of the kingdom of God," but, for those who have refused to respond in faith to Jesus' actions, the kingdom has remained a "riddle" which they cannot comprehend (4:10–12). Despite the lack of immediate success, Jesus expresses his confidence in the ultimate triumph of the kingdom of God in the highly apocalyptic parables of the lamp (4:21–25), the seed growing secretly (4:26–29), and the mustard seed (4:30–32).

In 6:7–12 Jesus sends the twelve out "two by two" with authority over "unclean spirits." They do essentially what Jesus has done: preach repentance, cast out demons, and heal the sick. However, before they have returned (6:30–31), Mark has inserted King Herod Antipas' reaction to Jesus (6:14–16) and, in a flashback, the story of his beheading of John the Baptizer (6:17–29). This keeps the question of Jesus' identity before the reader and prepares for the violent death of Jesus and the persecution which his disciples will experience once he has gone, both of which will be stressed with increasing frequency as Jesus moves toward Jerusalem (8:31–10:52).

In 6:30–8:21 Mark has two parallel cycles of stories involving Jesus' miraculous feeding of a crowd (6:30–44; 8:1–10), a lake crossing (6:45–56; 8:10), a dispute with the Pharisees (7:1–13; 8:11–13) and a discourse about food and defilement (7:14–23; 8:14–21). He continues to present Jesus as the powerful and compassionate (6:34) Son of God who "has done all things well" (7:37), but still commands secrecy about his deeds (7:36). Jesus' opposition to the legalistic hypocrisy of the Pharisees' comes to a head when he attacks their insistence upon the externals of the elders' human traditions to the point of abrogating God's law as given in the commandments of Moses (7:1–13). In contrast to this external piety which overturns the law, Jesus teaches his disciples an internal spirituality which fulfills the law. He explains to them in private that "what comes out of a man is what defiles a man," i.e., "evil thoughts, fornication, theft, murder, adultery, coveting, wickedness, deceit, licentiousness, envy, slander, pride, foolishness" (7:14–23). Mark follows this section on the Pharisees' hypocrisy with a touching picture of the receptiveness of the Gentile world to Jesus, symbolized by the Syro-Phoenician woman who cleverly begs for the healing of her daughter (7:24–30).

Another major theme in this section is the twelve's inability to fully comprehend the significance of Jesus and his actions. After they have seen Jesus feed the five thousand and walk toward them on the sea in the midst of a storm, "they were utterly astounded, for they did not understand about the loaves, but their hearts were hardened" (6:51–52). Later when Jesus warns them about the "leaven" (i.e., the hypocrisy and legalism) of the Pharisees, they are more concerned with their lack of bread (8:14–16), and Jesus has to remind them of the Messianic significance of his two feeding miracles.

> "Why do you discuss the fact that you have no bread? Do you not yet perceive or understand? Are your hearts hardened? Having eyes do you not see, and having ears do you not hear? And do you not remember? When I broke the five loaves for the five thousand, how many baskets full of broken pieces did you take up? . . . Do you not yet understand?" (8:17–21).

Their need to overcome being deaf and blind to the significance of Jesus is symbolized by the placement of the cures of a deaf man and a blind man around this section (7:31–37; 8:22–26).

As he moves toward Jerusalem (8:27–10:54), Jesus reveals to his disciples his full identity as the Son of Man who will suffer rejection and death at the hands of the Jewish leaders and the Gentiles in Jerusalem, but will also be raised up and return as the glorious Son of Man. The twelve's inability to comprehend the full significance of Jesus and the demands of being his disciples becomes the dominant theme.

At Caesarea Philippi Peter, on the basis of what he has witnessed, is prepared to confess that Jesus is more than a prophet and is indeed "the Christ" or "Messiah" (8:27–29). However, Jesus still charges him "to tell no one about him" (8:30); now he begins to teach "that the Son of Man must suffer many things, and be rejected by the elders and the chief priests and scribes, and be killed, and after three days rise again" (8:31). Peter refuses to accept such a destiny and has to be rebuked, in the most shocking of terms, as a "Satan" who is judging by human standards rather than those of God (8:32–33). Jesus follows this rebuke by a teaching on discipleship which insists that willingness to follow Jesus to the point of self-denial and even loss of life will be determinative of the disciples' judgment when the Son of Man comes "in the glory of his Father with his holy angels," an event which, Jesus announces, will take place before the death of some of those who "are standing here" (8:34–9:1).

This first of three passion predictions is followed immediately by the transfiguration scene on a high mountain where Jesus' full identity is revealed to Peter, James and John by a heavenly voice which announces: "This is my beloved Son; listen to him" (9:2–8). However, even this revelation does not remove the darkness that clouds the disciples' understanding of Jesus' destiny. As they descend from the mountain, they are told not to reveal what they have seen until after Jesus as Son of Man has risen from the dead, but they do not understand what "the rising from the dead meant," and they have to question Jesus about the tradition that Elijah must precede the Messiah. Jesus' answer identifies the Elijah figure with John the Baptizer whom Herod had beheaded and again reiterates that the Son of Man, like the suffering servant spoken of in Isaiah 53, will be treated with contempt (9:9–13).

As Jesus moves through Galilee, to Judea, and eventually toward Jerusalem (9:30; 10:1; 10:32), he continues to teach his disciples in increasingly explicit terms about his destiny as the Son of Man who will be delivered to the chief priests and scribes, condemned to death, delivered to the Gentiles, mocked, and killed, only to rise after three days (9:31; 10:33–34). After each of these passion predictions, Mark notes the disciples' failure to understand the nature of Jesus' suffering mission and instead has them arguing among themselves about "who was the greatest" or who will sit at Jesus' right hand when he enters into his glory (9:32–34; 10:35–37). In both cases Jesus follows the disciples' misunderstanding of his destiny with an instruction on the type of discipleship he demands (9:35–37; 10:38–45). Since Jesus is like the servant in Isaiah 53 who gives his life for a ransom for many (10:45), following him involves being a child-like servant who is willing to be the slave of all (9:35–37; 10:38–45).

Within this section Mark has included a good deal of instructional material on the nature of Christian discipleship. The model for discipleship throughout this section is childlike reception of the kingdom of God (9:36–37; 9:42; 10:13–16). And the demands are given a sense of apocalyptic urgency by being linked with the fate of the disciples at judgment (9:41; 9:43–50; 10:29–31). When the disciples are not able to cure a man with a dumb spirit, Jesus expresses exasperation at their lack of faith and proclaims to them the importance of prayer (9:14–29). The disciples' jealousy over seeing a man casting out a demon in Jesus' name becomes the occasion for Jesus' chiding them not to forbid him and a long instruction on caring for the childlike "little ones" who believe in Jesus (9:38–50). A confrontation with the Pharisees over the question of divorce presents Jesus with the opportunity to teach his disciples privately that "whoever divorces his wife and marries another commits adultery against her . . ." (10:2–12). Finally, the meeting with the rich man is the occasion for Jesus' reiterating the validity of the commands of God given in the law of Moses but also the danger of attachment to riches (10:17–31). The curing of the blind Bartimaeus at Jericho immediately before Jesus enters Jerusalem dramatically symbolizes the need for faith on the part of the disciples if they are to "follow" Jesus on his way (10:46–52).

Jesus' actions upon his long-awaited arrival in Jerusalem immediately precipitate the final conflict with the Jewish leaders. His entrance into the city has messianic overtones (11:1–10). He rides in on a colt as had been predicted of the messianic king in the book of the prophet Zechariah (11:1–8; Zech 9:9) and is greeted by the crowds as the long-awaited Messiah in the line of David (11:9–10). When Jesus drives out the moneychangers in the temple and declares, like the prophets of old, that they have turned God's house into a "den of robbers" instead of "a house of prayer for all nations" (11:15–17; Jer 7:11; Is 56:7), the chief priests and scribes seek a way to destroy him out of fear for the multitude who are astonished at his teaching. The bankruptcy of the temple and its institutions seems to be symbolized by the story of Jesus' cursing of the fig tree which envelops the cleansing of the temple (11:12–14; 11:20–25).

A series of hostile confrontation scenes follows in which Jesus cleverly avoids his opponents' attempts to entrap him and, at the same time, attacks their hypocrisy and intentions to destroy him (11:27–12:44). When questioned by the chief priests, scribes and elders about the source of his authority, Jesus responds with his own question about whether the baptism of John was "from heaven" or "from men" (11:27–33). They cannot answer, because if they say "from heaven," then Jesus will confront them with their rejection of John, and if they say "from men," they will lose the people who did accept John as a prophet. Jesus follows up his advantage with the parable of the wicked tenants (12:1–11) which is an allegory for the leaders' rejection of the prophets and John, and their intention to kill him, the "beloved son" in the parable. The parable ends with prediction of the destruction of the wicked tenants and the giving of the vineyard to others. This is an allusion to the eventual destruction of Jerusalem and the Christian mission to the Gentiles—both of which were probably realities when Mark was writing. Having failed to entrap Jesus on the question of his authority, the leaders attempt to trip Jesus up on the question of paying taxes to Caesar and his teaching on the resurrection, but in each case Jesus is again able to cleverly outwit them (12:13–27).

In the midst of these hostile encounters, Mark has placed two positive examples of a proper response to the kingdom of God. First of all, a scribe comes to Jesus and sincerely asks him which is the greatest of the commandments (12:28–34). When Jesus answers by quoting the commands to love God and neighbor (Deut 6:4; Lev 19:18), the scribe joyously approves of his answer, and Jesus in turn says, "You are not far from the kingdom of God." Secondly, a poor widow's donation of two copper coins into the temple treasury is contrasted with the hypocrisy of the leaders with their "long robes" and "places of honor" (12:38–44).

The disciples' admiration for the wonderful temple complex becomes the occasion for Jesus giving an apocalyptic discourse on the destruction of the temple, the trials and tribulations of his disciples ("the elect") in the final age, and the final arrival of the kingdom with the Son of Man's coming in the clouds with great power and glory (13:1–37). Apocalyptic visions can usually be dated by the most recent specific event referred to in the vision. In this case the Roman destruction of Jerusalem is referred to in 13:2 and then seems to be alluded to in 13:14–16. This has led scholars to date Mark to the period of the Roman-Jewish War in 66–70 C.E. This sermon probably represents the author's understanding of his own time. He sees "the elect," the Christian community, living in the first stage of tribulations which are to precede the final age (13:4–23), but still awaiting the completion of the time when the gospel will be preached to all nations (13:10). The community has not yet entered the final time when the cosmos will be shaken and the Son of Man will come to gather "the elect" (13:24–27). The parables of the fig tree (13:28–31) and the man going on a journey (13:32–37) emphasize the nearness of these events and the need for watchfulness.

Mark's gospel narrative reaches its frequently announced climax in the passion, death and resurrection of Jesus (14:1–16:8). At the outset Mark skillfully portrays Jesus as the Messiah or "anointed one" who is also destined to be executed. He does this by inserting the story of Jesus' anointing at Bethany by a woman (14:3–9) into the account of the plots of the authorities for Jesus' arrest and Judas' betrayal (14:1–2, 10–11).

In Mark's account of Jesus' Last Supper (14:12–31), he carefully links Jesus' words and actions to his earlier passion predictions and presents him as in total control of events. Jesus informs his disciples that the room for the celebration of the passover has already been arranged ahead of time (14:12–16). He begins the meal by announcing that one of the twelve will "betray" (literally "hand over") him (14:17–21) which is the same verb that was used in earlier predictions (9:31; 10:33). Jesus' words in connection with the bread and the wine use allusions to the suffering servant in Isaiah 53 and make reference to his sacrificial death which will seal a covenant for "the many"—something he had earlier alluded to in teaching his disciples (10:45).

In the Mount of Olives and Gethsemane scenes (14:26–50), Mark continues to present Jesus as painfully submissive to his preordained destiny and the disciples' inability to comprehend and follow their master. As they go out to the Mount of Olives, Jesus predicts to his disciples that "you will all fall away," but goes on to announce that this failure will be overcome when he is raised up and goes before them to Galilee (14:26–28). After further predicting to a boastful Peter that he will deny him three times (14:29–31), Jesus, in a most human fashion, prays that "the hour might pass from him," but then ends by accepting his Father's will (14:36). The disciples, on the other hand, although they have been warned of the upcoming crisis, are not able to watch with him in his hour of agony, and when he is seized by the crowd brought by Judas from the Jewish leaders, they forsake him and flee (14:37–50).

The trial before the Jewish leaders (14:53–65) brings to a conclusion the themes of their rejection of Jesus and his public revelation of his full identity. After their false witnesses have not been able to agree on testimony brought against Jesus, the high priest asks him: "Are you the Christ, the Son of the Blessed?" Jesus responds by saying, "I am; and you will see the Son of Man seated at the right hand of Power, and coming with the clouds of heaven." This announcement leads to the council's decision that Jesus is deserving of death. Mark has placed in this scene the whole scope of Jesus' identity. He is the Christ or Messiah, the beloved Son of God, who is about to die as the rejected and betrayed one, but will return as the triumphant Son of Man in power to complete his kingdom. As Jesus reaches his destiny, the whole so-called "messianic secret" can be revealed. Ironically, just as Jesus is announcing his full identity before the hostile Jewish high priest, Peter, the leader of the disciples, is in the courtyard vehemently denying that he knows Jesus (14:66–72).

The trial before Pilate (15:1–15) continues to emphasize the active role of the Jewish leaders in securing Jesus' death and the Roman official's unwilling complicity in their action. After holding a consultation, the Jewish council sends him to the Roman procurator where Jesus refuses to defend himself against their accusations. When Pilate, aware that the chief priests have delivered him up out of jealousy, tries to release the murderer Barabbas, they stir up the crowd to demand Jesus' crucifixion. Finally, Pilate, "wishing to satisfy the crowd," releases Barabbas and, after scourging Jesus, gives him up to be crucified.

The actual crucifixion scene (15:16–41) is filled with bitter and painful irony. Using frequent references to Psalms 69 and 22 which were laments of righteous sufferers, Mark has the Roman soldiers, the crowds, and the chief priests and scribes engaging in taunts and mockery which point to Jesus' true identity and the salvific effects of his death. The Roman soldiers ridicule him as a would-be king (15:16–20), place on the cross an inscription which reads "The King of the Jews" (15:26) and, like the mockers in Psalm 22:18, cast lots for his garments (15:24). The crowd "wags their heads" like the taunters in Psalm 22:7 and challenges Jesus to "save" himself by coming down from the cross (15:29–30). Finally the chief priests and scribes, consistent with their portrait throughout Mark, mock him by saying, "He saved others; he cannot save himself. Let the Christ, the King of Israel, come down now from the cross, that we may see and believe" (15:31–32).

In contrast to the taunts and disbelief of the above, the Roman centurion, when he sees ominous darkness and Jesus' death with the rending of the temple curtain (15:33–38), confesses Jesus' full identity: "Truly this man was the Son of God!" (15:39). This confession is extremely significant for Mark's Christology. Only after Jesus has endured

his destiny to suffer as Son of Man and put an end to the need for the temple and its sacrifices is it possible to confess Jesus as Son of God with full understanding.

Mark ends his gospel with the discovery of the empty tomb by the women who had
followed him from Galilee and had the courage to observe, from afar, the crucifixion and
burial by Joseph of Arimathea, a respected member of the Jewish council who was also
"looking for the kingdom of God" (15:40–16:9). When they come on the first day of the week
to anoint the body, the women discover that the stone has been rolled away, and when
they enter the tomb, a young man dressed in a white robe announces to them:

> "Do not be amazed; you seek Jesus of Nazareth, who was crucified. He has risen, he is not
> here; see the place where they laid him. But go, tell his disciples and Peter that he is going
> before you to Galilee; there you will see him, as he told you" (16:6–7).

This announcement confirms that Jesus' repeated predictions of his passion and resurrection have come true (8:31; 9:31; 10:33–34). The only prediction that awaits fulfillment
is his appearance to the disciples in Galilee (14:28).

Surprisingly, the earliest manuscripts of Mark's gospel do not contain an account of
Jesus appearing to his disciples in Galilee as he had announced. Instead, they end with
the notice that the women, in trembling and atonishment, fled from the tomb and were
too afraid to say anything about what they had seen. The reader has been prepared, however, for such a response. Repeatedly in the gospel Jesus' authoritative teachings have
met with astonishment and lack of understanding; yet each time, despite these responses,
his miracles have made present the kingdom of God to believers and his predictions about
his destiny have come to pass. The reader is challenged to go beyond the women's fear and
astonishment and believe that Jesus indeed will return in glory as Son of Man to complete
the kingdom as he has promised (13:24–27; 14:62).

THE GOSPEL OF MATTHEW

The text of Matthew's gospel, like that of the other canonical gospels, is anonymous.
Early church tradition assigned the gospel to Matthew, a disciple of Jesus (cf. Matt 9:9)
who is called Levi in Mark 2:14. According to Eusebius (c. 260–340 C.E.), again following
Papias (died c. 140), Matthew first compiled his gospel of "sayings" in Aramaic. However,
this alleged Aramaic text is no longer extant, and our present Greek gospel of Matthew
is believed by most scholars to be dependent upon Mark's gospel and written c. 80–90 C.E.
Matthew appears to follow Mark's sequence of events and preserves, in a somewhat altered form, ninety percent of Mark.

Although the gospel of Matthew uses most of Mark, it goes well beyond Mark in its
presentation of Jesus. Matthew portrays Jesus as the descendant of David and Son of God
who fulfilled the messianic expectations of the Hebrew Scriptures; he makes frequent allusions to the biblical texts and, at least a dozen times, he puts special emphasis on the
fulfillment of prophecy by stating, "All this took place to fulfill what the Lord had spoken

by the prophet," or its equivalent. Matthew also presents Jesus as the final revealer of God's will who taught the definitive and fulfilling interpretation of the Mosaic law. According to Matthew, Jesus was sent to Israel alone (15:4), but after his resurrection he manifested himself in Galilee to his apostles in his messianic glory and sent them with his teaching to the entire world (28:16–20).

In order to fulfill this purpose Matthew supplements Mark's narrative with a whole variety of material drawn from his own sources and from the sayings collection which he shares with Luke. In the beginning of the gospel he adds a genealogy which links Jesus to Abraham and David and a nativity story which announces Jesus' messianic and divine identity and prepares for his ultimate destiny of being rejected by Judaism and accepted by the Gentiles (Matthew 1–2). Throughout the account of Jesus' public ministry Matthew adds a large amount of teaching material which is organized into five long discourses addressed primarily to his disciples to prepare them for their worldwide mission (5:1–7:29; 10:5–11:1; 13:10–53; 18:1–19:1; 24:3–26:1). Finally at the end of the gospel Matthew has an appearance of the risen Jesus on a mountain in Galilee in which he commissions his disciples to go with his authority to make disciples of all nations (28:16–20).

Matthew's genealogy (1:1–17) establishes Jesus' identity as a messianic descendant of David and Abraham who is born in the fullness of time. Three sets of fourteen generations link Jesus, who is called Christ (i.e., Messiah), to Abraham the forefather of Israel and David, the king to whom the prophet Nathan had promised a lasting dynasty (2 Samuel 7). By placing Jesus' birth at the beginning of the seventh set of seven generations, Matthew indicates that Jesus' birth is in the fullness of time because in the biblical tradition the number seven indicates fullness or completion.

The birth announcement to the just Joseph (1:18–25) goes beyond the genealogy by further indicating Jesus' status as Son of God and announcing his destiny to "save his people from their sins." Joseph learns that Jesus has been conceived by the Holy Spirit of God, and the narrator links this to the fulfillment of Isaiah 7:14 in the Greek Septuagint Version which reads, "Behold, a virgin shall conceive and bear a son, and his name shall be called Emmanuel" (which means God with us). This theme of Jesus as the special and enduring presence of God will be maintained to the very end of the gospel (cf. 28:20).

Matthew's infancy narrative (2:1–23) is totally unique to his gospel and is quite different from Luke's. It illustrates the well-known theme of the escape of the hero from near death as a helpless child and bears a resemblance to the birth of Moses during the time of the Exodus, especially in Philo's **Life of Moses.** Matthew presents the child Jesus as recapitulating his people's experience and fulfilling prophecies concerning the Messiah (2:6,15,18,23). The story also foreshadows his destiny to be rejected by the Jewish leaders and Jerusalem and to be ultimately accepted by the Gentile world. Gentile wise men from the East, who have been following a mysterious star, come with gifts of gold, frankincense and myrrh (cf. Isaiah 60) to joyfully worship the child king. In contrast, the Jewish king Herod the Great and all Jerusalem with him are troubled by the news of the birth of the Messiah/Savior, and Herod, like the Pharaoh of the exodus, attempts to slaughter the child by killing all the two-year-old males in the city of Bethlehem, the place of the Messiah's birth (cf. Mic 5:2). Jesus himself re-experiences his people's descent into Egypt when he is providentially spared the wrath of the "troubled" king by God's intervention through an angel who tells Joseph in a dream to flee to Egypt. When Herod has died, the family returns to the land of Israel where they settle in Nazareth in Galilee to avoid Archelaus the wicked son of Herod the Great.

Beginning with the ministry of John the Baptist (3:1–12) Matthew starts to follow Mark's narrative, but he makes significant alterations and additions to it which emphasize that John begins the announcement of the arrival of the kingdom of heaven which Jesus brings to fulfillment. John's initial preaching is the same as that of Jesus: "Repent, for the kingdom of heaven is at hand" (3:2; 4:17), and he, like Jesus, challenges the Sadducees and Pharisees to "bear fruit" befitting repentance in light of the imminent arrival of the kingdom of heaven (3:7–12; 7:15–20). For Matthew, John will later be identified by Jesus himself as Elijah, the prophet who was to return before the coming of the Messiah (11:7–15), but he clearly belongs to the time of the law and the prophets, the time of preparation (3:11–12; 11:7–15) for the fulfillment.

Jesus' obedient fulfillment of God's will is particularly emphasized in the baptism and temptation scenes which immediately follow. When John wants to be baptized by Jesus, he insists, with his first spoken words in the gospel, "Let it be so now; for thus it is fitting for us to fulfill all righteousness" (3:15). Matthew also expands Mark's brief temptation scene to emphasize that Jesus is the obedient Son of God who rejects the devil's temptation to false messianic programs for the sake of doing the will of God (4:1–11). To each of the temptations Jesus responds with quotations from Deuteronomy which indicate his willingness to fulfill God's will (cf. 4:4,7,10).

Matthew' major addition to the early part of Mark's Galilean ministry is his majestic Sermon on the Mount (5:1–7:29). Jesus in solemn apocalyptic fashion announces the blessings of the kingdom to his disciples who aspire to live under God's rule and be "the light of the world" (5:1–16) and then gives an authoritative reinterpretation of the law and the prophets which is "not to abolish them but to fulfill them" (5:17–7:29). The tone of the whole discourse is supremely apocalyptic. It begins with the proclamation of heavenly reward for those who are sincerely longing for the arrival of God's kingdom (5:1–12) and ends with the solemn warning that only those who hear and do "these words of mine" will survive the judgment (7:1–27).

Matthew's presentation of Jesus' authoritative interpretation of the law (5:21–48) is not meant to be complete but illustrative. Jesus takes six examples of the commands of the "old" law and brings them to their fulfillment by either interiorizing their demands or actually overturning them. Each instance is introduced by slight variants of the same formula: "You have heard that it was said . . . But I say to you . . . " (5:21–22,27–28,31–32,33–34,38–39,43–44). Included in these teachings are some of the most memorable of Christian ethical ideals: avoiding anger, lustful desire, divorce, turning the other cheek and praying for the enemy. Jesus concludes by challenging his disciples to "be perfect, as your heavenly Father is perfect" (5:48).

In 6:1–18 Jesus takes three examples of Jewish piety—almsgiving, prayer, and fasting—and warns against hypocritically practicing them "before men in order to be seen by them" (6:1). Rather, these actions are to be done only for "your Father who is in heaven" and "who sees in secret." In the section concerned with prayer, Matthew has Jesus illustrating for his disciples the way they are to pray by the "Our Father" which is a highly apocalyptic request for the arrival of God's kingdom (6:7–15).

In 6:19–34 Jesus further warns his disciples that they must choose which kingdom they will serve: the perishable kingdom "on earth" or the lasting kingdom "in heaven." The choice of God over "mammon" should be a liberating one which frees them from anxiety over life, food, drink and clothing (6:24–34). The basis for confidence in making the choice for the kingdom of God and his righteousness (6:33) is the beautiful image of God's care for the "birds of the air" and "the lilies of the field." Jesus reminds his disciples that they are of much more value in their Father's eyes than these.

In 8:1–9:38 Matthew uses some of the miracles and controversy stories from Mark's Galilean ministry, but adds special emphases of his own. Jesus' miracles are related to the fulfillment of prophecies from the Hebrew Scriptures, specifically the figure of the suffering servant in the Book of Isaiah (8:17; cf. Is 53:4). Matthew also prepares for the acceptance of Jesus in the Gentile world and the rejection by Israel by adding the story of the cure of the centurion's servant (8:5–13). Jesus praises the centurion's faith by saying:

> "Truly, I say to you, not even in Israel have I found such faith. I tell you, many will come from east and west and sit at table with Abraham, Isaac, and Jacob in the kingdom of heaven, while the sons of the kingdom will be thrown into the outer darkness; there men will weep and gnash their teeth" (8:10–11).

Matthew sets the stage for Jesus' second major discourse by using prophetic images of the Messianic ingathering of God's people (9:35–38). He notes Jesus' compassion for the harassed and helpless crowds that have followed him. They are "like sheep without a shepherd," and therefore Jesus sends out his disciples like laborers going into a plentiful harvest. Jesus then calls the twelve to himself and gives them authority to make the kingdom of God present by casting out unclean spirits and healing (10:1); they do not yet share in Jesus' teaching mission because they have not yet been fully formed by Jesus' own teaching. They are also sent only "to the lost sheep of the house of Israel" (10:5–15). Matthew carefully saves the teaching mission of the disciples to the Gentiles until the end of the gospel when the risen Jesus commissions them "to make disciples of all nations, baptizing them in the name of the Father and of the Son and of the Holy Spirit, teaching them to observe all that I have commanded you . . . " (28:19–20).

The second part of the commissioning discourse (10:16–42) already envisions this worldwide mission which would have been a reality in Matthew's day. The disciples are warned that they are sent out "as sheep in the midst of wolves" and will face persecution in bearing testimony before the Jews in their synagogues and "the Gentiles." Despite the danger and division that will be caused by their mission (10:16–18, 21–23, 34–36), Jesus exhorts his disciples not to fear. He assures them that the Spirit of their Father will speak through them (10:20), that he, their master and teacher, has also been attacked (10:24–25), and that he will acknowledge his faithful disciples before his "Father who is in heaven." The discourse ends with Jesus solemnly announcing to his disciples that those who receive them receive Jesus who has sent them, and in turn receive the Father who has sent Jesus (10:40–42; cf. 25:31–46; 28:20).

In 11:2–12:50 Matthew presents Jesus as making increasingly greater claims about his identity as the revelation of God, and the Jewish leaders as responding with ever growing hostility. When the imprisoned John sends his disciples to inquire whether Jesus is "he who is to come," Jesus answers affirmatively by pointing to the prophetic signs which he has fulfilled (11:2–6; cf. Is 29:18–19; 35:5–6; 61:1), but then he goes on to decry "this generation" for rejecting John as an ascetic and "the Son of Man" as a "glutton and drunkard, a friend of tax collectors and sinners" (11:7–24). In a series of sabbath controversies (12:1–14) Jesus claims to be "greater than the temple" and "the Son of Man" who "is lord of the sabbath," but the Pharisees respond by taking "counsel against him, how to destroy him." The hostilities continue when the Pharisees accuse Jesus of performing his exorcisms by the power of Beelzebul, the prince of demons (12:24). Jesus answers with the clever parables of the kingdom/house divided and the strong man's house (12:25–29) and then announces that the one unforgivable sin is the Pharisees' rejection of God's Holy Spirit which is present in Jesus' miracle working (12:30–32). Finally, when the scribes and Pharisees demand a sign from Jesus, he answers that the only sign that will be given them is the sign of the prophet Jonah, i.e., his death and resurrection on the third day (12:38–40). Jesus concludes the hostilities by announcing that the pagan Ninevites and the queen of Sheba will arise on judgment day against this generation, for they responded to the preaching of Jonah and the wisdom of Solomon, and one greater than these is present to this generation.

Throughout this same section (11:2–12:50) Matthew draws a sharp contrast between Jesus' disciples who are open to the presence of God's kingdom and "this generation" who refuse to accept it. In 11:25–27 Jesus thanks his Father that the kingdom has been hidden from "the wise and understanding" and revealed to "babes." He, like Lady Wisdom in Proverbs, invites these "babes" who "labor and are heavily laden" to come to him to "find rest for their souls" (11:28–30). For the disciples Jesus is revealed as the gentle suffering servant spoken of in Isaiah (11:15–21; cf. Is 42:1–4). The section ends with a startling contrast between "this evil generation" and the disciples (12:43–50). The generation which rejects Jesus is compared to a man/house which had a demon driven out only to have it return with "seven other spirits more evil than the first." Jesus identifies his disciples, on the other hand, as his true family because they do "the will of my Father in heaven."

This contrast continues into the parable discourse in chapter 13. After Jesus has spoken the parable of the sower to the crowds (13:1–9), Jesus' disciples ask him, "Why do you speak to them in parables?" (13:10). Jesus answers that the reason the kingdom of God is hidden from his opponents and that he speaks to them in parables (i.e., riddles) is their own hardness of heart (13:11–13)—"seeing they do not see, and hearing they do not hear, nor do they understand." In them the terrifying prophecy of Isaiah 6:9–10 has been fulfilled (13:14–15). In contrast, the disciples are the "blessed" who are witnessing and hearing what "many prophets and righteous men longed to see" (13:16–17).

In 13:18–33 Jesus' teaching emphasizes the eventual triumph of God's kingdom despite opposition. In the allegorical interpretation of the parable of the sower (13:18–23), Jesus announces that, despite the wasted seed which is identified with those who for various reasons reject the kingdom, the seed on good soil (those who hear and understand the word) will produce abundant fruit. Jesus then addresses the crowd with three more parables which emphasize the ultimate triumph of God's kingdom despite opposition or the smallness of beginnings: the parable of the weeds in the wheat (13:24–30), the mustard seed (13:31–32), and the leaven (13:33). The section ends with a summary statement which reiterates that Jesus' teaching only spoke to the crowds in parables (13:34–35).

At this point Jesus withdraws from the crowds, goes into the house and addresses his disciples with teaching which announces the ultimate outcome of the kingdom and again highlights their privileged position (13:36–50). The interpretation of the parable of the weeds in the wheat (13:36–43) and the parable of the dragnet (13:47–50) are apocalyptic revelations that the evil and the righteous will co-exist until the coming of God's judgment. The parables of the treasure in the field and the pearl of great price (13:44–46) are images of the kingdom of heaven as a great gift which leads those who find it to "sell all they have and buy it." In striking contrast to Mark's portrayal of the disciples, the discourse concludes with the disciples' understanding Jesus' teaching and his comparing them to scribes "trained for the kingdom of heaven" who can bring out of their treasures "what is new and what is old" (13:51–52).

In 13:53–18:35 Matthew is following Mark's narrative of the latter part of Jesus' Galilean ministry and his preparation of the disciples for his rejection, crucifixion and resurrection in Jerusalem. However, again Matthew reshapes the material and adds his own characteristic emphases. He stresses the important role of Peter as the willing, but still only partially believing, spokesman for the disciples (14:28–33; 15:15–20; 16:13–20; 18:21–22). Matthew also pictures the disciples as having a fuller understanding of Jesus and his teaching because they will, in Matthew's scheme, replace the Pharisees and scribes and eventually succeed their master as the "church" or "assembly" which will continue his work until the triumph of the kingdom of heaven (14:33; 16:12; 17:13; 18:1–35).

Peter's bold, but still immature, faith is evident in two memorable incidents. First of all, when Jesus comes walking toward the disciples in the storm at sea (14:22–27), Peter attempts to walk on the water and come to Jesus, only to lose faith and to cry out "Lord, save me," for which Jesus chides him as a "man of little faith" (14:28–33). Second, at Caesarea Phillipi Peter confesses his faith that Jesus is "the Christ, the Son of the living God," and he is blessed by Jesus as having received this knowledge by revelation from "my Father who is in heaven" and given authority in the "church" which Jesus is founding

(16:13–20). However, this same Peter is still not ready to accept Jesus' teaching "that he must go to Jerusalem to suffer many things from the elders and chief priests and scribes, and be killed, and on the third day be raised" (16:21–23).

Matthew's fourth discourse (18:1–35) is like a community rule for the disciples, comparable to **The Community Rule** from Qumran. The discourse sets ideals for the disciples' behavior and gives instructions for caring for the "little ones" in the community and for resolving disputes. It begins with Jesus responding to the disciples' question about who is the greatest in the kingdom of heaven by calling a child and pronouncing that "unless you turn and become like children, you will never enter the kingdom of heaven" (18:1–4). This is followed by severe warnings to those who are a source of sin or temptation for the innocent ones in the community (18:5–9). Jesus then instructs his followers to seek after the lost "little ones" like the shepherd who leaves the ninety-nine sheep on the mountains in order to search for the one that went astray (18:10–14). When a brother has been sinned against, he is first to take the matter up with his brother. If this fails, he is to try with one or two others or the whole church, and, if that fails, the person is to be treated "as a Gentile or tax collector." The community is assured that its decisions "on earth," like Peter's in 16:18–20, are binding "in heaven" (18:18–20). Peter's question about how frequently he must forgive the brother, leads to Jesus' pronouncement that forgiveness is to be "seventy times seven," i.e., unlimited (18:21–23). Finally, the absolute seriousness of failure to forgive the brother is brilliantly illustrated in the parable of the unforgiving servant (18:23–35).

In Jesus' journey from Galilee to Jerusalem (19:1–20:34) Matthew uses the encounters along the journey to have Jesus continue to instruct the disciples in the demands and the privileges of their discipleship. The question of the Pharisees about divorce is the occasion for Jesus' teaching that "whoever divorces his wife, except for unchastity, and marries another, commits adultery" (19:3–9). In this context Jesus also tells his disciples that for some it is possible to become a "eunuch for the sake of the kingdom of heaven" (19:10–12). The contrast between the children who are brought to Jesus and the young man who refused to follow Jesus because "he had great possessions" brilliantly illustrates the need to be detached from riches for entrance into the kingdom of God (19:13–24). To those disciples who have followed him and "left everything," Jesus assures a role in "judging the twelve tribes of Israel" and "everlasting life." This privilege does not mean, however, that his disciples will be "first" in this world. In fact, as followers of Jesus who is on his way to death in Jerusalem (20:17–19), they will drink of the same cup as Jesus and must be servants of the others (20:20–28). They, like the laborers hired at the last hour in the parable of the laborers in the vineyard, will become "first" only at the time of the payment when the generous vineyard owner rewards them (20:1–16).

Matthew's account of Jesus' Jerusalem ministry (21:1–23:39) is based on Mark's, but he makes several additions which highlight even more the Jewish leaders' rejection of Jesus and the harsh consequences of that. The parable of the two sons (21:28–32) and the allegory of the marriage feast (22:1–10) stress that this generation has rejected God's invitation through John and Jesus and that this will result in the destruction of their city and an invitation to others (i.e., the Gentiles; see 28:16–20). In 23:1–36 Jesus addresses a tirade to the crowds and his disciples against the hypocrisy of the Pharisees who "sit on Moses' seat." Although this chapter no doubt reflects the controversies between Christian church and synagogue in the first century C.E., by addressing it to his disciples, Matthew shows that he is aware of the dangers of hypocrisy in the church (cf. 16:5–12). The chapter ends with Jesus' moving lament over the city of Jerusalem which he already sees as forsaken and desolate because of its rejection of the prophets and him (23:37–39).

In Jesus' final long discourse (24:1–26:1) Matthew uses Mark's apocalyptic sermon (Mk 13:1–37), but adds material which prepares Jesus' disciples for the delay of his expected return as Son of Man and for the need to be watchful and responsible as they await the completion of the kingdom. To illustrate the need for readiness in light of the unknown time and suddenness of the return of the Son of Man, Matthew has a saying comparing it to the generation of Noah and the flood and the parable of the householder and thief (24:36–44). The parables of the ten maidens (25:1–13) and the talents (25:14–30) both emphasize the delay of the bridegroom/master's return and the need to be prepared and responsible in the interim.

Matthew's concluding great judgment scene (25:31–46) is related to early sayings of Jesus in which he insisted that acceptance of his "childlike" disciples was acceptance of him and of his Father who sent him (cf. 10:40–42; 18:5). The scene is not concerned with the judgment of Israel or Jesus' disciples. Matthew's criteria for the judgment of these groups are given elsewhere (cf. 5:1–7:27; 11:20–24; etc.). Rather, this vision is concerned with the judgment of the nations to whom Jesus' disciples are sent at the end of the gospel (25:32; cf. 28:16–20). At the coming of the Son of Man in his glory the nations will be judged on the basis of their acceptance or rejection of Jesus' disciples who have come to them as "the least": hungry, thirsty, strangers, naked, sick and imprisoned.

Matthew's passion narrative follows Mark's quite closely, but he does make some additions which reflect his themes of Jesus' messianic fulfillment of the Scriptures (26:54–56; 27:7–10) and the Jewish rejection of Jesus who was recognized as innocent by Pilate and his wife (27:11–26). The actual death of Jesus in Matthew is followed by several apocalyptic signs which confirm for "the centurion and those who were with him" that Jesus was truly "the Son of God."

Matthew has expanded Mark's burial and resurrection accounts by noting the effort on the part of the Pharisees to spread the rumor that Jesus' disciples stole his body (27:62–66; 28:11–15) and adding an account of the appearance of the risen Jesus, as he had announced (26:32), to his disciples in Galilee (28:16–20). The commissioning of the disciples is the climax of the entire gospel. The disciples have been prepared for this moment by the instruction of Jesus from the opening Sermon on the Mount, and especially since 13:36 when Jesus left the crowds and began to focus entirely on the preparation of his disciples. Jesus now appears to them as the Son of Man who has been given "all authority in heaven and on earth." And after they have worshiped him he sends them with the assurance of his continual presence, to make disciples of all nations by baptizing and "teaching them to observe all that I have commanded you" (28:20).

LUKE-ACTS

The Gospel of Luke and the Acts of the Apostles are two volumes of one history by a single author which traces the beginnings of Christianity as a world religion from its obscure origins in the birth of Jesus in a manger in the little Judean town of Bethlehem (Luke 1–2) to the preaching of the apostle Paul in Rome (Acts 28). Both volumes begin with formal introductions in the style of Hellenistic histories and are addressed to a certain Theophilus ("lover of God"), perhaps a Roman official or simply any Greek reader who loves God (Luke 1:1–4; Acts 1:1–5). The stated purpose of the work is to give "an orderly account" of the events that have been handed on by "eye witnesses and ministers of the word" so that Theophilus may "know the truth" about "the things which have been accomplished among us."

Luke-Acts is a highly polished apologetic history which effectively uses references to "secular" Roman and Jewish history, geography and journey accounts in portraying Christianity as a universal and highly ethical religion. Luke traces for the learned Hellenistic reader the origins of Christianity in the time of recognizable Roman and Jewish historical figures like Herod the Great, king of Judea (1:5), Caesar Augustus (2:1–2), Tiberius Caesar, Pontius Pilate, the Roman governor of Judea, and Herod, the tetrach of Galilee (3:1–2). He carefully locates the foundational events of Christianity in Jerusalem, the holy city of Jews (Luke 19:41–24:53) to which Jesus came on a long and divinely predestined journey (9:51–19:40). Acts chronicles how Christianity was forced by Jewish persecution to spread from Jerusalem (1:6–5:41) to all Judea and Samaria (6:1–9:30), into the Gentile world (9:32–12:23), and through the three missionary journeys of Paul to Asia Minor, Europe, and finally to Rome, the capital of the Empire (12:25–28:31). A second century tradition attributes both works to Luke the "beloved physician" who was a traveling companion of Paul mentioned in Colossians 4:14. In any case, the author uses as sources for his gospel volume Mark's gospel, the so-called Q tradition of sayings of Jesus, and a large body of material that is unique to him which includes some of the most touching material in the New Testament tradition: the nativity story, the parables of the good Samaritan, the prodigal son, the rich man and Lazarus, the rich young man, and the Pharisee and publican. In Acts Luke primarily uses traditions about the Jerusalem church and the preaching and activity of Peter (chapters 1:6–11:18) and the missionary journeys of Paul (11:19–28:31). Included in these are certain sections in the first person plural which have led some to postulate that Luke was using a travelogue for part of his narrative.

Luke begins his narrative with an aura of solemn wonder and joy as God's Holy Spirit begins the fulfillment of the long-awaited time of salvation in the parallel stories of the miraculous births of John the Baptist and Jesus. In the style of the birth stories in Genesis and Samuel, the births and destinies of both are announced by the angel Gabriel (1:8–23; 1:26–38). While fulfilling his priestly duties in the temple in Jerusalem, the elderly and incredulous Zechariah learns that, despite their old age, he and his barren wife Elizabeth will have a son John who will be an ascetic, filled with the Holy Spirit, and like Elijah will "make ready for the Lord a people prepared" (1:15–17). Likewise Mary, a lowly virgin from Nazareth in Galilee, who is betrothed to Joseph of the house of David, obediently accepts the news that by the power of God's Holy Spirit she will conceive and bear a son to be called Jesus who will be "the Son of the Most High" and will reign from the throne of his father David in an everlasting kingdom" (1:32–38).

The births themselves are also accompanied with great wonders. At John's birth (1:57–66), Zechariah's temporary muteness for his unbelief is removed so that he can announce that the child's name is to be "John." This causes all those who heard of these things to say, "What then will this child be?" Jesus' birth in a manger in Bethlehem (2:1–20) is announced by angels to shepherds who learn the "good news of a great joy" that in the city of David a universal Savior has been born. When the shepherds witness "this thing that has happened," they make it known, and all who heard it "wonder at what the shepherds told them." And Luke notes that Mary "kept all these things, pondering them in her heart."

With an eye to his Graeco-Roman audience, Luke carefully dates these events of salvation by reference to the Jewish and Roman secular rulers of the time so that they are understood as taking place within world history. The announcement of John's birth is set "in the days of Herod, king of Judea" (1:5). Jesus' birth takes place when Caesar Augustus ordered a census during the time "when Quirinus was governor of Syria" (2:1–2). These notices, as well as the one at the beginning of John's preaching (3:1), make it clear to the learned Hellenistic reader that the events being narrated are not a mythic account from the hazy past, but the narrative of saving events "which have been accomplished among us" (1:1–5).

In order to dispel the idea that Christianity might be a subversive religious movement, the characters from the very beginning of the narrative are portrayed as very pious and observant Jews. Zechariah and Elizabeth, the parents of John, are described as "righteous before God, walking in all the commandments and ordinances of Lord blameless" (1:6). Both boys are circumcised and named on the eighth day according to Jewish custom (1:59–66; 2:21), and Jesus is brought to Jerusalem for the purification rites "according to the law of Moses" (2:22–38). This emphasis on traditional piety will continue throughout the two volumes.

The joyful significance of the events of these opening chapters is most evident in the beautiful canticles which are sung by Mary (1:46–55), Zechariah (1:67–79), and the "righteous and devout" Simeon who recognizes the child Jesus when he is brought to the temple (2:29–35). Mary's famous "Magnificat," like Hannah's song (1 Sam 2:1–10), praises God who "has put down the mighty from their thrones, and exalted those of low degree; filled the hungry with good things, and the rich sent empty away" (1:51–53). The "scattering of the proud" and raising up of the lowly will be a prominent theme throughout the gospel. Zechariah's canticle blesses God for fulfilling his promises of deliverance made through the prophets and sworn on oath to Abraham (1:67–79). The universal significance of these saving events is evident in Simeon's song when he says:

"Lord, now lettest thou thy servant depart in peace,
according to thy word;
for mine eyes have seen thy salvation
which thou has prepared in the presence of all peoples,
a light for revelation to the Gentiles,
and the glory of thy people Israel" (2:29–32).

Despite the lyrical joy of these chapters, they end on a note that points to Jesus' ultimate destiny to suffer and eventually return to the temple, his Father's house in Jerusalem. Simeon tells Mary his mother that "this child is set for the fall and rising of many in Israel and for a sign that is spoken against . . . " (2:33–35). In the only incident from his boyhood recorded in the gospel tradition (2:41–52), Jesus at age twelve, without his parents' knowledge, remains behind in the temple after the feast of Passover is ended and amazes all with his questions and answers to the teachers. When questioned by his mother, Jesus abruptly announces to his parents, "Did you not know that I must be in my Father's house?" At this stage his parents are not able to understand the full significance of this statement, and his mother continues to keep "all these things in her heart."

The prominence of women, especially Mary, Jesus' mother, is a unique feature of Luke's gospel. In his infancy narrative Luke gives women key roles in the unfolding drama of God's saving action. Mary, in contrast to Zechariah, obediently accepts Gabriel's announcement with the words, "Behold, I am the handmaid of the Lord; let it be to me according to your word" (1:38). Her response is essentially the same as Jesus' at the Mount of Olives when he faces his passion (22:42), and she becomes the model for the disciples in hearing and accepting the word of God (8:19–21). For Luke Mary is the exemplar of the poor who are blessed by God, but will also experience persecution (cf. 1:45; 1:48; 2:35; cf. 6:20–23). Elizabeth, the mother of John, also has an important function in Luke's infancy narrative. She is the first to recognize the Messiah. When Mary visits her, the babe in her womb leaps and she is inspired by the Holy Spirit to exclaim: "Blessed are you among women, and blessed is the fruit of your womb! And why is granted to me, that the mother of my Lord should come to me?" (1:42–45). Likewise, the elderly widow and prophetess Anna is in the temple when Jesus is brought there for the purification rites and she speaks of him to "all who were looking for the redemption of Jerusalem" (2:36–38).

In his account of the preparations for Jesus' public ministry (3:1–4:13), Luke's narrative is close to Matthew's with some significant differences which emphasize the universality of his message for a Gentile audience. For example, John's preaching contains practical advice for repentance which would be applicable to Gentile readers (3:10–14). Those with two coats are told to "share with him who has none." Tax collectors are admonished to "collect no more than what is appointed you," and soldiers are told to "rob no one by violence or false accusation." Likewise, Luke's genealogy, which comes immediately after Jesus' baptism, traces Jesus' ancestry beyond Abraham to Adam, and therefore stresses that Jesus is both Son of God and son of Adam and, as such, a Savior for the whole human family (4:23–38).

Luke provides a solemn programmatic introduction to Jesus Galilean ministry (4:14–9:50) which highlights Jesus' Jewish piety and announces the theme of his preaching. After briefly noting that Jesus returned in the power of the Spirit into Galilee (4:14–15), Luke, in contrast to Mark and Matthew, has Jesus begin his preaching in Nazareth in the synagogue on sabbath when he reads from the prophet Isaiah:

> "The Spirit of the Lord is upon me,
> because he has anointed me
> to preach good news to the poor.
> He has sent me to proclaim release of the captives
> and recovering of sight to the blind,
> to set at liberty those who are oppressed,
> to proclaim the acceptable year of the Lord" (4:18–19; Is 61:1–2).

When Jesus finishes, he announces solemnly, "Today this scripture has been fulfilled in your hearing" (4:21).

The response to this announcement foreshadows the ultimate outcome of the gospel message in Luke-Acts. Jesus' home town rejects him as the mere son of Joseph (4:22–24), and Jesus in turn notes that in the days of Elijah and Elisha those prophets were sent to Gentiles like the widow of Zarephath in the land of Sidon and Naaman the Syrian (4:25–27). When "all in the synagogue" rise up against him and attempt to throw him from a hill, Jesus passes through their midst (4:28–30). This pattern will be repeated in Jesus' Jerusalem ministry where he will be rejected for his preaching in the temple and crucified only to arise and ascend into his glory (19:45–24:53). In his parting words Jesus commissions his disciples to wait in Jerusalem until they "are clothed with power from on high" to be witnesses who will preach repentance and forgiveness of sins in his name to all nations (24:44–49). The same pattern will occur repeatedly in Acts where the apostles Peter and Paul will first preach the gospel message in the temple or synagogue to the Jews, who will reject them, and then they will take the message to the Gentiles (Acts 2:5–28:31).

In 4:31–6:11 Luke follows Mark 1:21–3:19, but he subtly reshapes the material around his theme of Jesus as God's Spirit-led agent who fulfills the Isaian prophecies. Jesus gathers disciples as witnesses of his ministry to the outcast and experiences opposition from the Pharisees and teachers of the law. Luke's version of the call of the first disciples (5:1–11) has them "seeing" a miraculous catch of fishes and then being reassured by Jesus with the words "Do not be afraid; henceforth you will be catching men." These disciples then witness Jesus' controversies with the Pharisees and teachers of the law over forgiveness of sins (5:17–26), eating and drinking with sinners (5:29–32), fasting (5:33–39), and sabbath observance (6:1–11).

Luke's great discourse "in the plain" (6:17–49) is comparable to Matthew's Sermon on the Mount, but it lacks the references to the Mosaic law or the practices of Judaism which characterize Matthew's discourse. Rather, in Luke's sermon, which is aimed at a Gentile audience, Jesus begins with a contrast between the blessings promised to the poor, hungry, mourning, and persecuted disciples and the woes awaiting the rich, full, laughing, and revered (6:20–26). He goes on to authoritatively teach a universalistic ethic of love which extends even to the enemy on the model of the mercy of God himself (6:27–49).

In the remainder of his account of Jesus' Galilean ministry (7:1–9:50), Luke follows Mark 4:1–9:41 with notable additions in 7:1–8:3 which emphasize key Lukan themes. First of all Jesus is portrayed as fulfilling the Isaian prophecies of 4:18–19 (cf. 7:11–23), but he, like John, is rejected by the Pharisees and teachers of the law (7:24–50) and received only by a believing Gentile centurion (7:1–10) and a penitent woman sinner (7:36–50). The contrast between the Pharisaic resistance to Jesus' call to sinners and the openness of the penitent is dramatically illustrated in the story of Simon the Pharisee and the penitent woman (7:36–50). Simon invites Jesus to eat with him, but he is offended when Jesus allows a sinful woman to touch him with extravagant gestures of gratitude (7:36–39). Jesus answers Simon by asking him to judge the parable of the two debtors (7:40–43) which forces Simon to admit that the one who is forgiven more will show greater love. Jesus then goes on to contrast Simon's failure to show the normal courtesies to him as a guest with the woman's tender acts of gratitude (7:44–47). The scene ends with the woman being sent on her way with the assurance, "Your sins are forgiven. . . . Your faith has saved you; go in peace" (7:48–50).

This is immediately followed by the notice that several women "who had been healed of evil spirits and infirmities accompanied Jesus on his journey through Galilee." These women are said to have provided for Jesus and his disciples "out of their means" (8:3) which may indicate that Luke's audience included well-to-do Hellenistic women who would be in a position to control the disposition of the family's wealth (cf. Acts 5:1–11).

The most unique feature of Luke's gospel is Jesus' long journey to Jerusalem (9:51–19:27). Luke begins the journey in a solemn way by noting, "When the days drew near for him to be received up, he (Jesus) set his face to go to Jerusalem" (9:51). Using the biblical and classical motif of the journey as a time of testing and learning, Luke presents Jesus as resolutely proceeding to the divinely prescribed fate which awaits him in Jerusalem where he will not only suffer but also enter his glory through his ascension (9:31; 9:51; 10:1; 13:22–35; 17:11; 18:31–34; 19:28; 19:41–44). Luke also uses the journey narrative to have Jesus teach his would-be disciples the requirements of their journey in "following" Jesus. In this section Luke has some material from Q but also a large number of traditions from his own special material.

The outcome of Jesus' journey and the radical demands of following him are foreshadowed in the opening incidents (9:51–62). Jesus is not received by a Samaritan village because "his face was set toward Jerusalem," where ironically he will also be rejected (9:51–53). This rejection becomes the occasion to teach his disciples not to take vengeful action against the village (9:54–56). Two subsequent encounters with would-be followers provide Jesus with the opportunity to teach them that following him means being willing to abandon home and family ties (9:57–62).

At this point Luke has Jesus sending seventy disciples on a second missionary journey parallel to the one the twelve went on in the Galilean ministry in 9:1–6,10. Luke may be foreshadowing the church's mission to the Gentiles because according to Jewish tradition the number of Gentile nations was seventy. When the disciples return, they are joyful because "the demons are subject to us in your name" (10:17). Jesus, however, does not let them lose sight of the ultimate destiny of their journeys when he tells them, "Do not rejoice in this, that the spirits are subject to you; but rejoice that your names are written in heaven" (10:20).

The meeting between Jesus and a lawyer (10:25–37) provides a brilliant illustration of Jesus' saying that the kingdom is hidden from "the wise and understanding" (10:21–22). The lawyer, like Simon the Pharisee (7:36–50), wants to test Jesus on questions, for example, "What shall I do to inherit eternal life?" or "Who is my neighbor?" Jesus, on the other hand, uses the story of the man who fell among robbers (10:30–37) to challenge the lawyer to lay aside divisive religious distinctions and do mercy to the neighbor as does the Samaritan in the parable.

Luke's use of women to illustrate important aspects of discipleship is again evident in the Martha and Mary episode (10:38–42). The disciples are taught that listening to the words of the master like Mary, who seats herself at the Lord's feet, is more important than the anxious service of her sister Martha.

The importance of prayer for the disciples is a theme that occurs repeatedly in Luke. He, more than any other evangelist, presents Jesus himself as an example of prayer by presenting him as praying before important events in the gospel (cf. 3:21; 5:16; 6:12; 9:18, 28–29; 22:32,44; 23:34,46), and Jesus' prayer in 11:1 is the occasion for the disciples' request, "Lord, teach us to pray, as John taught his disciples." Jesus goes on to teach them the "Our Father" in a more shortened form than that in Matthew (11:2–4) and teaches them to be confident in their prayer through the parable of the friend at midnight and the image of the father who gives good gifts to his children (11:5–13). Later Jesus uses the parable of the importuning widow and the unjust judge as an illustration of persistence in prayer (18:1–8) and follows it with the parable of the Pharisee and the publican as a warning against hypocrisy in prayer to those "who trusted in themselves that they were righteous and despised others" (18:9–14).

Another frequent concern in Luke's journey narrative is the danger of riches for the disciples. This theme is first introduced in 12:13–21 when one of the crowd asks Jesus to arbitrate an inheritance dispute. Jesus rejects the role of judge in such matters and goes on to warn, "Take heed, and beware of covetousness; for a man's life does not consist in the abundance of his possessions" (12:15). This is followed by the parable of the rich fool who told himself, "Soul, you have ample goods laid up for many years; take your ease, eat, drink, be merry," only to hear from God, "Fool! this night your soul is required of you . . ." (12:16–21). Luke returns to this theme in 16:1–31 where he illustrates the fate that awaits the rich who neglect the poor at their gate with the parable of Lazarus and the rich man (16:19–31). Finally, Luke, like Mark and Matthew, has the story of the rich young ruler who refuses Jesus' invitation to "sell all that you have and distribute to the poor, and you will have treasure in heaven; and come, follow me" (18:18–30). A positive example of a rich man who makes proper use of his wealth and thereby finds salvation is provided by Zacchaeus the tax collector who gives half of his goods to the poor and does not defraud any one of anything (19:1–10; see Acts 4:36–37).

In the midst of the journey narrative Luke returns to the theme of Jesus as the agent of God's mercy who reaches out to sinners (15:1–32). The setting is the complaint of the Pharisees and scribes over Jesus' reception of tax collectors and sinners (15:1–2). Jesus proceeds to defend his behavior with three parables which give vivid pictures of joy over finding the lost: the lost sheep (15:3–7), the lost coin (15:8–10), and the lost or prodigal son (15:11–32). The first two end with comparing the human joy over finding a lost sheep or coin to the joy in heaven over the repentance of a sinner. The prodigal son parable includes the character of the elder son who personifies the anger of the Pharisees and scribes (15:25–32; cf. 15:1–2), and is challenged to "make merry and be glad, for this your brother was dead, and is alive; he was lost, and is found" (15:32). No doubt Luke is addressing this challenge to those in his audience who are not prepared to accept God's mercy to outcast and repentant apostates.

Luke's account of Jesus' ministry in Jerusalem (19:28–21:38) follows Mark 11:1–13:37 with some characteristic adaptations. Luke is clearly writing after the destruction of Jerusalem and he stresses that this catastrophe was due to the city's rejection of God's visitation through Jesus (19:41–44; cf. 13:34–35). In Jesus' apocalyptic discourse (21:1–38) Luke removes the note of imminence found in Mark 13 by having Jesus warn his disciples not to follow the "many who will come in my name, saying, 'I am he!' and, 'The time is at hand!' " (21:8). Jesus goes on to tell them that "the end will not be at once" (21:9). For Luke the parousia, or Jesus' coming in glory, has been indefinitely delayed, and the Church is in the era of salvation history when the kingdom of God is to be proclaimed from Jerusalem to the ends of the earth (Luke 24:44–49; Acts 1:8).

Luke's passion narrative follows the general outline of those in Mark and Matthew, but it interprets the death of Jesus in a significantly different manner. In Luke's theology the mercy of God to the repentant sinner has been available from the beginning of Jesus' preaching (cf., for example, 7:36–52 or 15:1–32), and Jesus' disciples will continue to preach repentance for the forgiveness of sins in Jesus' name after his departure (cf. 24:44–49). Therefore, Luke does not understand the death of Jesus as a saving act which atones for the sins of humanity.

Jesus' death in the gospel of Luke is treated as the execution of a prophet who bore witness about God's plans like the prophets before him. His death is part of his predetermined destiny as a prophetic spokesman for God. When, during the course of his journey to Jerusalem, Jesus learns that Herod wants to kill him (13:31), he responds by explicitly linking his death to that of the prophetic martyrs who preceded him.

> "Go and tell that fox, 'Behold, I cast out demons and perform cures today and tomorrow, and the third day I finish my course. Nevertheless I must go on my way today and tomorrow and the day following; for it cannot be that a prophet should perish away from Jerusalem.' O Jerusalem, Jerusalem, killing the prophets and stoning those who are sent to you! How often would I have gathered your children together as a hen gathers her brood

under her wings, and you would not! Behold, your house is forsaken. And I tell you, you will not see me until you say, 'Blessed is he who comes in the name of the Lord!' " (13:32–35).

In the passion and resurrection narratives (22:1–24:52), Luke stresses that Jesus is innocent and that his death was a stage which he had to pass through as he entered his glory in fulfillment of his destiny which had been foretold in Moses and the prophets (24:19–27,44–49). Luke's account of the Last Supper puts emphasis on the future celebration in the kingdom of God (22:14–18), and does not have Jesus interpreting the bread and the cup in terms of an atoning death which forgives sin (22:19–23). In his accounts of the Jewish and Roman trials (22:66–23:25), Luke goes to great lengths to stress Jesus' innocence of false charges brought by the Jewish leaders before the Roman procurator Pilate. The charge that Jesus forbade tribute to Caesar (23:2) is contradicted by an earlier incident in Jesus' Jerusalem ministry (cf. 21:19–26), and three times Pilate says that he finds Jesus guilty of no crime (22:4,14,22). Luke alone has a hearing before Herod (23:6–12), who also finds Jesus innocent of the charges brought against him (23:15). Finally, at the death of Jesus, the Roman centurion does not make an act of faith in Jesus' identity as "Son of God," as in Mark and Matthew, but rather he exclaims, "Certainly this man was innocent!" (23:47)

Luke's handling of the events at the cross makes of Jesus a model of a martyr's death which will subsequently be followed by Stephen who also fearlessly challenges the Jewish leaders in Jerusalem (see Acts 7, especially 7:54–60). As he carries his cross, Jesus continues his prophetic ministry by warning the lamenting women of Jerusalem, "Do not weep for me, but weep for yourselves and for your children . . . " (23:26–31). As he is crucified he prays to his Father for the forgiveness of his persecutors as he had taught during his ministry (23:34; cf. 6:27–36; 11:4), and he offers to the penitent criminal who was crucified with him the assuring promise of God's salvation (23:39–43) as he had done repeatedly in the course of his ministry (cf. 7:36–52). At his death, Jesus prays the confident words of Psalm 31:5: "Father, into thy hands I commit my spirit." A mission thus is accomplished which first began with the descent of God's Spirit upon him at his baptism (3:21–22).

Luke's account of Jesus' resurrection and ascension into heaven is a transitional preparation for his second volume, the Acts of the Apostles, where Jesus' followers will take up his work and extend the message of repentance for forgiveness of sins from Jerusalem, to all Judea and Samaria, and eventually to the ends of the earth (24:44–49; Acts 1:8). Luke, in contrast with Matthew, has located the resurrection appearances in and around Jerusalem, which has a central place in his theology. He began his gospel account there with the priestly ministry of Zechariah (1:5–23), and Jesus' long journey to his divine destiny in Jerusalem is a major feature of the gospel (9:50–19:27; cf. 2:22–52). Now the resurrection appearances in this city will interpret the significance of Jesus' death for the disciples and prepare them for their ministry in continuing Jesus' work (24:13–53; Acts 1:1–5).

In his appearance to the two disciples on the road to Emmaus (24:13–35) Jesus teaches these two disappointed and confused followers that his death and resurrection were part of the divine plan for his entrance into his glory that had been foretold in the Scriptures, and then he reveals himself to them "in the breaking of the bread."

In his second appearance to the eleven in Jerusalem (24:36–52) Jesus again explains how his death and resurrection were part of the divine plan which he had told them about and had been announced in Moses, the prophets and the psalms; then he commissions them to be witnesses who are to preach repentance and forgiveness of sins in his name "to all the nations beginning in Jerusalem" (24:47–48). They are to stay in the city of Jerusalem until they are "clothed with power from on high" (24:49; cf. Acts 2). The gospel ends with Jesus' being carried into heaven and the disciples' returning with great joy to Jerusalem where they are continually blessing God in the temple (24:50–53).

The Acts of the Apostles traces the movement of the gospel message under the guidance of the Holy Spirit from Jerusalem (3:1–5:41) to Judea and Samaria (6:1–9:30), into the Gentile world (9:32–12:23), and to the very "end of the earth" (12:25–28:31): Asia Minor (12:25–15:33), Europe (15:36–19:19), and Rome itself (19:21–28:31). The leading heroes of the narrative are Peter and Paul. Peter, the spokesman of the twelve in the gospel, is the leading character in the first part of Acts (1:1–12:23). He courageously begins witnessing to the "good news" about Jesus' death and resurrection in Jerusalem, and succeeds, despite the opposition of official Judaism, in getting large numbers of Jews to repent of their sins and be baptized in the name of Jesus Christ for the forgiveness of their sins (2:14–5:42). Peter also initiates the mission into the Gentile world when he baptizes the Roman centurion Cornelius and all of his household (10:1–48). Paul, a one-time persecutor of the Christian sect (8:1–3; 9:1–30), is the dominant figure in the second part of Acts. On three missionary journeys he carries the gospel message about Jesus through the Hellenistic cities of Asia Minor (13:1–14:28), Greece (16:6–19:19), and eventually to Rome (19:21–28:31), despite opposition from Jewish leadership in synagogues of the empire and the temple in Jerusalem (21:27–22:29). The tone of the entire work is one of joyful triumph: God's plan for the gospel is reaching the end of the earth despite Jewish opposition.

After his introduction to the second volume (1:1–5), Luke sets the stage for the ministry of the Spirit through the witnessing of the apostles (1:6–2:42). He begins by recounting the appearances of the risen Jesus to his disciples (1:2–11) in which he told them to wait in Jerusalem for the coming of the Holy Spirit which would empower them to be his "witnesses in Jerusalem and in all Judea and Samaria and to the end of the earth" (1:8). The descent of the Spirit on the disciples (1:12–2:42) is a highly symbolic event which foreshadows the eventual spread of the gospel message to the whole Roman world and is meant to be a parallel to Jesus' baptism and the beginnings of his preaching in Galilee (Lk 3:21–4:30). Luke has the community of would-be witnesses gathered together in prayer, as Jesus was at his baptism (Acts 1:12–14; Lk 3:21–22). The group includes the twelve (with Judas' place being taken by Matthias), the women and Mary the mother of Jesus, and his brothers (1:12–26). On the Jewish pilgrimage feast of Pentecost the Holy

Spirit descends upon them with a rush of wind, and tongues of fire appear over each of them. In a symbolic reversal of the confusion of tongues in the tower of Babel incident in Genesis (Gen 11:1–9), Luke presents the disciples preaching in an understandable tongue of "the mighty works of God" to pilgrims from the entire Roman empire (2:1–13).

At this point Peter gives the first of several sermons in which he summarizes Luke's version of the basic gospel message about Jesus (2:14–36; 3:11–26; 4:8–12; 5:29–32; 10:34–43). These sermons, as well as those of Stephen and Paul (cf. 7:2–53; 13:16–41; 17:22–31; 22:3–21; 26:9–43), are Luke's compositions, similar to the speeches composed by Graeco-Roman historians like Thucydides or Livy. They represent Luke's theology and his understanding of the kind of sermon which would be appropriate in addressing various audiences.

In his Pentecost sermon Peter announces the gospel message to the Jewish pilgrims in a way that relates the events to the fulfillment of Jewish messianic expectations. He begins by saying that these unusual events represent the outpouring of God's Spirit which the prophet Joel had said would occur in the final days (2:14–21; see Jl 2:28–32). He goes on to summarize the message about Jesus, "a man attested to by God with mighty works, wonders and signs," who according to God's plan was crucified, but now has been raised up by God (2:22–24). Jesus' heavenly exaltation is the fulfillment of Psalm 16 in which David prophetically spoke of God's not letting his "Holy One see corruption" (2:25–31). Now God has exalted Jesus to his right hand and made him the Lord and Messiah spoken of in Psalm 110:1 (2:32–36); this is the same destiny that had been promised in Gabriel's announcement to Mary in Luke 1:32–33. On the basis of Peter's testimony, three thousand in the crowd are moved to repent of their sins and be baptized "in the name of Jesus Christ for the forgiveness of sins" (2:37–42).

In the remainder of his account of the church in Jerusalem (2:43–5:41) Luke describes the successful growth of the Christian movement despite persecution by the Jewish authorities. Peter and John perform healing miracles like those of Jesus which give them the opportunity to give heroic testimony before the crowds and the Jewish leaders (3:1–4:22; 5:17–42). This moves Gamaliel, the highly respected Pharisaic teacher of the law, to advise the Jewish council to "keep away from these men and let them alone; for if this plan or this undertaking is of men, it will fail, but if it is of God, you will not be able to overthrow them. You might even be found opposing God" (5:33–39). The account is also punctuated with idyllic summaries of the life of the ever-growing Christian community in Jerusalem. They are devoted to prayer, the breaking of bread, a community of property, and the apostles' instruction (2:43–47; 4:32–35); and the "wonders done among the people by the hands of the apostles" lead to believers being steadily added to their number (5:12–16).

Acts 6:1–9:30 traces the spread of the Christian gospel from Jerusalem into Judea and Samaria (cf. 1:8). The catalyst for this movement is the fearless preaching of Stephen, a Hellenistic Jew, who testifies in a long speech before the Jewish council that the temple is not a permanent institution and that the murder of Jesus is simply the culmination of their repeated rejection of the prophets that God's Holy Spirit has sent to them (7:2–53;

cf. Luke 13:34–35; 19:41–44; 21:5–6). Stephen's ringing castigation results in his martyr-dom by stoning which is modeled on Jesus' death, even to the point of his forgiving the sin of those who kill him (7:54–60). Despite the persecution which now arises against the church in Jerusalem, the gospel is now spread through the ministry of Philip and Peter to Samaria, Judea and Galilee (8:1–40; 9:31–43). In the midst of this persecution Luke has the first of three accounts of the all-important call of Saul/Paul who is turned from a per-secutor of "the Way" to the "chosen instrument" who will carry Jesus' name before the Gentiles (9:1–30).

Acts 10:1–12:23 recounts how the persecution that arose over Stephen resulted in the spread of the gospel message into the Gentile world "as far as Phoenicia and Cyprus and Antioch" (11:19). The crucial step of announcing the gospel message in the Gentile world is made by Peter in the conversion and baptism of Cornelius, a devout Roman centurion who was already praying to the God of the Jews and giving alms to them (10:1–48). As always in Luke-Acts, the initiative for this important decision comes from God who tells Peter through a vision that all foods are clean (10:9–16) and sends his Holy Spirit upon Cornelius' household (10:44–48). Peter's sermon on this occasion (10:34–43), like the one at Pentecost (2:14–36), summarizes the gospel message in favorite Lukan terms and serves to inaugurate the Gentile mission which Peter subsequently defends before the community in Jerusalem (11:1–18).

The movement of the gospel to "the end of the earth" (1:8) is achieved by the mis-sionary journeys of Paul and his fellow workers (12:25–28:31). In his first journey from Syrian Antioch to Cyprus and the Hellenistic cities in southern Asia Minor (13:1–14:28), Paul works miracles like Jesus and Peter before him and successfully preaches the gospel to God-fearing Gentiles, who are associated with the synagogues in these areas.

Paul's initial sermon at the synagogue in Pisidian Antioch (13:16–41) is meant to par-allel the first proclamations of the good news by Jesus in the synagogue at Nazareth (Lk 4:16–21) and Peter in Jerusalem at Pentecost (Acts 2:14–36). All three are proclamations of the fulfillment of God's promises in the Hebrew Scriptures of salvation through the for-giveness of sin. Paul addresses both Jews and "God-fearers," and he begins his sermon by recounting the actions of the God of Israel for his chosen people, particularly the raising up of David as the king after his heart (13:16–22). He then announces that God has brought to Israel a Savior from this man's posterity (13:23–25; cf. Lk 1:26–37). Although he was killed by those who live in Jerusalem and their rulers (13:26–29), God has raised him from the dead, and he has appeared to his disciples who are witnessing to the people (13:30–31). Paul now brings them "the good news" that the promises made about the Mes-siah's heavenly exaltation in the psalms (Pss 2:7; 16:10) and the prophets (Is 55:7) have been fulfilled in Jesus (13:32–37). He ends by proclaiming the forgiveness of sins to them in the name of Jesus the Savior (13:38–41).

The response to Paul's preaching throughout this journey is also comparable to that experienced by Jesus and Peter. Many Jews, devout Gentile converts to Judaism, and Greeks believe Paul's message (13:43; 14:1–2; 14:21), but "unbelieving Jews" oppose them, stir up opposition, and even persecute them (13:44–47; 14:2–7; 14:19). As always,

Luke ends the journey on a joyful and triumphant note with the return of Paul and his companions to Antioch and the report of how God "had opened a door of faith to the Gentiles" (14:24–28).

At this point Luke recounts his version of the important council in Jerusalem (15:1–35) which differs substantially from Paul's version (Gal 2:1–10). Luke shapes his account around the theological themes of his entire narrative. For Luke, the city of Jerusalem and the Jerusalem church have crucial importance in the scheme of his two volumes. The apostles in Jerusalem are the original witnesses to all that Jesus did in Galilee from the baptism of John to his resurrection (Lk 24:44–53; Acts 1:1–15). In the plan of Acts, each major step in the progression of the spread of the gospel is approved by the church in Jerusalem: the advance into Samaria (8:14–17), Paul's call (9:26–30), the baptism of the Gentile Cornelius (11:1–18), and the preaching to Greeks in Antioch (11:20–26). Now Luke recounts how the Jerusalem church came to approve Paul's preaching a circumcision-free gospel among the Gentiles. He recognizes that there was some opposition (15:1–2,5), but his emphasis is on the unity of the church and the important role of Peter (15:6–11) and James (15:12–21), members of the Jerusalem community, in approving the work of Paul and Barnabas (15:12). The addition of stipulations about abstention from the pollutions of idols and from unchastity and from blood (15:20–21, 28–29) is not mentioned by Paul and seems to contradict what he says in Galatians 2:11–12 and 1 Corinthians 10:27–29. Luke has probably conflated two separate incidents in his idyllic account of the meeting in Jerusalem.

The highlights of Paul's second missionary journey (15:36–19:19) are the divinely inspired decision to take the gospel message into Macedonia (16:6–10), and his sermon at the Areopagus in Athens, the city of Greek philosophers (17:16–33). Paul's positive approach to Greek philosophy and religiosity in this sermon (17:22–29) is quite different from what is found in his letters (cf. Rom 1:18–32). This sermon, like the others in Acts, is primarily Luke's own composition and probably represents the type of preaching that would be used in the mission to the would-be Hellenistic convert of Luke's own day. There is no mention of the Hebrew Scriptures; instead God is portrayed in universal terms as the Creator of heaven and earth who made every nation. Paul even quotes Greek poets who speak about the universal presence of God and the fact that all humans are God's offspring (17:28). Jesus is portrayed as a man raised by God who will return to judge the world in righteousness (17:31).

The last segment of Acts is Paul's long and much delayed journey to Rome via Jerusalem (19:21–28:31). The journey is reminiscent of Jesus' journey to Jerusalem and his reception there in the gospel (Lk 9:51–23:56). In both cases Luke mentions a conscious decision and repeated resolve to undertake a "necessary" journey which is fraught with danger (Lk 9:51; 13:22; 13:33; 19:11,28; Acts 19:21; 20:22; 21:15,17). The treatment of Paul in Jerusalem is also similar to that which Jesus received. He has an initially enthusiastic reception but is eventually seized by the mob (Acts 21:17–30; Lk 19:37; 22:54). Paul's speech at the temple (22:1–21) is similar to Jesus' Jerusalem ministry (Lk 19:45–21:38) and to Stephen's sermon in Acts 7 in that all three are concerned with the temple, the rejection of Jesus by Jerusalem and the movement of the message into the Gentile world. Finally, Paul's trials before the Sanhedrin, the Roman officials Felix and Festus, and Herod Agrippa emphasize, like those of Jesus, the hostility of the Jewish leaders and his innocence in the eyes of the Roman leaders (cf. Lk 22:66–23:25).

Luke ends his second volume with Paul's journey to Rome (27:1–28:31). The fact that Paul is a Roman citizen gives him the right to a trial by the Roman emperor (25:1–21). Rather than ending with an account of Paul's trial or his eventual martyrdom, Luke concludes with Paul in Rome, under house arrest, but "preaching the kingdom of God and teaching about the Lord Jesus Christ quite openly and unhindered" (28:31). This conclusion satisfies his stated purpose of tracing how the gospel has been carried from Jerusalem "to the end of the earth" (Acts 1:8).

THE GOSPEL OF JOHN

Even to the casual reader, the Gospel of John has a strikingly different character from the other three canonical gospels. Instead of synoptics' apocalyptic picture of Jesus as the Son of God who makes the kingdom of God present through his miracles and authoritative prophetic teaching, John's gospel presents Jesus as the pre-existent divine Word of God whose miracles are symbolic "signs" which reveal his glory and who teaches in long symbolic dialogues and monologues about his divine identity and his eventual return to his heavenly Father. The apocalyptic theme of judgment is also handled differently in John. Rather than having Jesus give an apocalyptic discourse in which the judgment is delayed until the second coming of Jesus as Son of Man in glory (Mk 13:1–37; Matt 24:1–36; Lk 21:8–36), John has the judgment taking place within Jesus' ministry on the basis of belief or disbelief in Jesus' divine identity (cf. Jn 1:10–13).

The organization of Jesus' ministry is also quite different from that of the synoptics. Instead of a Galilean ministry followed by a single journey to Jersualem, John has a three-year ministry and has Jesus moving constantly back and forth between Galilee and Jerusalem (Jn 2–12). Familiar events are placed in new settings; for example, Jesus' cleansing of the temple occurs in the beginning of the ministry in 2:13–25. Other events have surprising omissions; the Last Supper does not contain an account of the institution of the Eucharist, but instead has Jesus' washing the feet of his disciples (13:1–11). Although the gospel of John has some basic similarities to the synoptics in the events it recounts, scholars agree that it comes from a gospel tradition that was shaped by a different environment and set of theological concerns.

According to John 21:20–24, the source of the testimony in this gospel is the unnamed "disciple whom Jesus loved who had lain close to his breast at the supper" (cf. 13:23; 19:26,35–37; 20:1–10). By the end of the second century C.E. the Church attributed the gospel to John, one of the sons of Zebedee, mentioned in the synoptic gospels as one of the twelve (see Mk 1:19–20; 3:13–19; and its parallels), but not named in John's gospel (cf. 21:2). According to this tradition John escaped the early martyrdom experienced by his brother James under Herod Agrippa between 41–44 C.E. (Acts 12:1–2) and lived to an old age in Ephesus where he wrote the gospel, the three letters which bear his name, and the Book of Revelation. Most recent scholars disagree with this picture. They think that John probably suffered the same fate as his brother (cf. Mk 10:39 and parallels) and that he could not have written the gospel which is thought to have been composed about 90–100 C.E. because it presupposes the expulsion of Christians from the synagogue (cf. John 9), a situation which developed in the period between 80–100 C.E. This of course does not exclude the possibility that the gospel tradition goes back to the testimony of John the son of Zebedee.

The text of the gospel also shows signs of a complicated process of composition. The beautiful episode of the woman caught in adultery (7:53–8:11) is not in the oldest and best manuscripts of the gospel. Chapter 21 is clearly an addition to the gospel after the formal conclusion in 20:30–31, as are 12:44–50 and 6:55b–59. Finally, there are apparent dislocations in the gospel; chapters 5 and 6, for example, seem to be in the wrong order.

The gospel of John was influenced by the traumatic expulsion of Christians from the Jewish synagogue in the period between 80–100 C.E. (cf. 9:22; 12:42; 16:2) and clearly comes from a Jewish environment which uses the images of the Hebrew Scriptures in a highly symbolic and dualistic way. It also shows the influence of the language and style of revelation discourses which were extremely popular in the Hellenistic world (cf. **The Praises of Isis** and Apuleius' **Metamorphoses**). In dialogues and monologues Jesus uses the solemn "I am" formula to proclaim his identity as "the bread of life" (6:35), "the light of the world" (8:12), "the one who was before Abraham" (8:58), "the door of the sheep" (10:7), "the good shepherd" (10:11), "the Son of God" and "one with the Father" (10:31–38), "the resurrection and the life" (11:25) and "the true vine" (15:1). This use of the language of revelatory discourses made the gospel of John especially popular among Christian gnostic sects which made Jesus simply a heavenly revealer, although the gospel itself takes great pains to insist upon Jesus' full humanity (1:14; 11:33–37).

The prologue to John's gospel (1:1–18) is absolutely unique in the gospel tradition and immediately sets the narrative in a cosmic and divine perspective. It is a hymn, like that in Philippians 2:6–11, which praises the pre-existent Christ as the divine creative Word of God (1:1–5) who took flesh, dwelt with humanity and revealed his glory as the only Son from the Father (1:14). The hymn introduces dualistic themes which will be operative throughout the gospel: light versus darkness/the world, "children of God" versus "his own" who did not receive him and remained children of mere flesh, grace and truth through Christ versus the law through Moses. Interspersed in the hymn are bits of narrative which speak of John the Baptizer as one who came to bear testimony/witness to the light, but was not himself the light (1:6–8; 1:15).

The background for the hymn is extremely complex, but it was clearly influenced by the creation account in Genesis 1 and the Jewish wisdom tradition of pre-existent Lady Wisdom as the agent of creation (Prov 8:27–30; Sir 24:1–7) who made her tent/dwelling place in Zion/Jerusalem in the form of the law of Moses (Sir 24:8–34). John uses these Jewish traditions to describe the fullness of God's revelation which has come in Jesus. He also uses the Hellenistic philosophical term *Logos,* "Word," in a way reminiscent of Philo who made an effort to find a common ground between Jewish revelation and Greek wisdom. The dualism was a common feature of Jewish thought in the Hellenistic period as is evidenced by the language of the sectarian writings of the Qumran monks (cf. **The Community Rule**).

John's treatment of the ministry of John the Baptist (1:19–36; 3:22–30) is quite different from that found in the synoptics, because John makes the Baptist a witness who bears public testimony before the Jewish leaders and his own disciples to Jesus as the light (cf. 1:6–7,15). There is no messianic secret in John; from the beginning of the gospel Jesus' full identity is proclaimed to all those who would receive him and believe in his name (1:10–13). When the priests and Levites come from Jerusalem and ask John if he is the Messiah, Elijah or a prophet, he rejects these titles and testifies, "I am the voice of one crying in the wilderness, 'Make straight the way of the Lord,' as the prophet Isaiah said" (1:19–23). When the Pharisees ask why he baptizes with water, John answers, ". . . among you stands one whom you do not know, even he who comes after me, the thong of whose sandal I am not worthy to untie" (1:24–27). When Jesus arrives, John bears witness to him as "the Lamb of God" and "Son of God," because he has seen the Spirit descend upon him (1:29–34), and he releases his discples to follow Jesus (1:35–37; 3:22–30).

John's version of the call of the disciples (1:38–51) continues this theme of the testimony of others to Jesus' identity. Andrew becomes a follower of Jesus on the basis of John's testimony that Jesus is "the Lamb of God" (1:35–40). He in turn testifies to his brother Simon Peter, "We have found the Messiah" (1:41). Philip, a disciple called by Jesus (1:43), bears witness to Nathanael: "We have found him of whom Moses in the law and also the prophets wrote" (1:45).

The goal of the testimony of others is to lead the would-be believer to Jesus who then addresses them personally and invites them to full belief in him (1:37–39; 1:42; 1:47–51). This theme comes to its culmination in the dialogue with Nathanael who was prepared to confess Jesus as "Son of God" and "King of Israel," but is told, "Truly, truly, I say to you, you will see heaven opened, and the angels of God ascending and descending upon the Son of man" (1:51).

Chapters 2:1–12:50 are often designated as "The Book of Signs" because they are structured around signs which Jesus performs as symbolic revelations of his glory which replace Jewish institutions like the purification laws (2:1–11), the temple (2:13–25), sabbath (5:1–46), Passover (6:1–70), Tabernacles (7:14–10:21), and the feast of the Dedication of the temple (10:22–39). These signs lead some, like his disciples, to belief (cf. 2:11; 2:22–23; 4:53–54; 9:38; 11:45), but others, especially the leaders in Jerusalem, refuse to believe and violently reject Jesus' revelation (5:10–47; 6:60–71; 8:31–51; 9:40–41; 11:46–53). Included in the signs are seven miracles: the changing of water into wine at Cana in Galilee (2:1–11), the curing of an official's son at Capernaum in Galilee (4:46–54), the curing of a paralytic at Bethzatha (5:1–15), the miraculous feeding in Galilee (6:1–15), the walking on the water (6:16–21), the curing of the blind man in Jerusalem (9:1–7), the raising of Lazarus (11:1–44), and other actions like the cleansing of the temple (2:13–25).

The signs which Jesus performs are usually followed by dialogues in which would-be believers are challenged to move from "an earthly" understanding to a "heavenly" or divine understanding which is belief in Jesus' heavenly identity. These dialogues are filled with misunderstanding and irony because the persons involved are challenged to understand the symbolic language of Christian faith. Nicodemus, for example, is asked to believe that one must be "born anew," a reference to Christian baptism in which "one is born of water and the Spirit" (3:1–15). The Samaritan woman is asked to believe that Jesus can give her "living water," "welling up to eternal life," i.e., the eternal life which comes through belief in Jesus (4:1–15; 7:37–38; 19:34). The crowds in Galilee, who have witnessed Jesus' multiplication of the loaves and fishes (6:1–14), are asked to believe that Jesus is "the bread of life" who will give his flesh for the life of the world (6:25–59). Martha, who has just lost her brother Lazarus, is asked to believe that Jesus is "the resurrection and the life" (11:21–27).

The most arresting of the symbolic and ironical dialogues in the gospel is that following Jesus' cure of the man born blind in John 9:1–41. The episode is related to the favorite Johannine themes of Jesus as the light of the world and the division between believer and unbeliever caused by his entrance into the world (cf. 1:9–13). At the feast of Tabernacles Jesus has just solemnly proclaimed, "I am the light of the world; he who follows me will not walk in darkness, but will have the light of life" (8:12), only to become involved in an extremely hostile debate with the unbelieving Pharisees over his origins and destiny (8:13–59). Now, before he cures the blind man, Jesus announces to his disciples that the man's blindness is not due to sin, but that the works of God done through him as "the light of the world" might be manifest (9:1–5). For John, the only sin/blindness is the unbelief of the Pharisees which they demonstrated in the previous debate (8:14–59), i.e., to refuse to believe in Jesus as "the light of the world" (9:40).

In the dialogue which follows, the blind man becomes a symbol for one who comes to gradual belief in Jesus despite the opposition of official Judaism, a situation which seems to reflect the period between c. 80–100 C.E. when Christians were expelled from the Jewish synagogue as heretics (cf. 9:18–23). During the course of interrogation by his neighbors, the man admits that he was the one cured by "the man called Jesus." When questioned by the Pharisees who will not accept Jesus as a man from God because he has cured on the sabbath, the man confesses that Jesus is a "prophet." His parents, however, are afraid to make such a confession, "because they feared the Jews, for the Jews had already agreed that if any one should confess him to be Christ, he was to be put out of the synagogue." In a second highly ironic dialogue with the Pharisees, the cured blind man insists that Jesus must be from God if God has listened to him in opening the eyes of a man born blind. At the same time the Pharisees ironically say that both Jesus and the former blind man are "sinners," while they are "disciples of Moses". Finally, after the Pharisees have "cast him out," the man comes to Jesus and to full belief in him as "Son of Man."

The incident ends with a final dialogue between Jesus and the Pharisees which ties together the themes of seeing/belief and blindness/sin (9:39–41). After the cured blind man has worshiped him (9:38), Jesus solemnly announces, "For judgment I came into this world, that those who do not see may see, and that those who see may become blind" (9:39). The Pharisees then ask, "Are we blind also?" (9:40). Jesus' response returns to the issue at the beginning of the incident in which the disciples asked if the man's physical blindness was due to sin (9:3): "If you were blind, you would have no guilt; but now that you say, 'We see,' your guilt remains" (9:41). In John's theology sin and judgment are related to belief in or rejection of Jesus.

John 11:1–12:50 is the conclusion of the "Book of Signs" in which Jesus moves to the "hour" of his glorification when he will be lifted up on the cross and draw all men to himself (12:27–36; cf. 2:4; 7:6,30; 8:20; 13:1; 17:1). The last of Jesus' signs is the magnificent raising of Lazarus (11:1–44) which results in the belief of many (11:45), but also sets in motion the plot of the Sanhedrin to have Jesus "die for the nation" (11:46–53).

John 12 is the conclusion of the book of signs and the transition to "the hour of glory" when Jesus as the "light of the world" will judge the world and triumph over the ruler of the world as he is "lifted up from the earth" and draws all men to himself (12:30–36). In this section John has his version of the anointing at Bethany (12:1–7), the messianic entrance into Jerusalem (12:12–19), Jesus' passion predictions, and his teaching on the need for the disciples to follow Jesus in losing their lives in order to save them (12:20–36). Then 12:37–50 concludes the book of signs and summarizes John's themes of Jesus as the light of the world who came to save the world from darkness. The judgment of the world consists in its response in either belief or disbelief to Jesus who has been sent by the Father and has spoken as the Father has commanded him. John notes that on the whole "they (the Jews) did not believe in him" (12:37) a failure which is a fulfillment of Isaiah 53:1 and Isaiah 6:9–10. However, he also adds an observation which reflects the situation at the time of his writing: "Nevertheless many even of the authorities believed in him, but for fear of the Pharisees they did not confess it, lest they would be put out of the synagogue: for they loved the praise of men more than the praise of God" (12:42–43).

Jn 13:1–17:26 is John's version of the Last Supper. Although he has certain incidents in common with the synoptics like the prediction of Judas' betrayal (13:21–30), the character of the Last Supper scene is quite different in John. Instead of the institution of the Eucharist, John has Jesus solemnly wash the feet of his disciples as a sign of the kind of service they are to give to one another (13:1–20) and Jesus' long farewell discourse (13:31–14:31; 15:1–17:26) which prepares his disciples for his imminent departure to the Father.

Essentially 13:31–14:31 is a farewell dialogue in which Jesus announces to his disciples that his hour of glory has come and he is about to depart from them to his Father. He assures them that they will eventually follow him, but in the interim they are to follow his command to "love one another, even as I have loved you" and that this will mark them as his disciples (13:34–35). They know "the way" to the Father and the Father himself because they have "seen" Jesus who "is in the Father" and has done the works of the Father (14:1–11). Although they will be left in a hostile "world," John's term for those who do not believe in Jesus, the disciples are assured of the aid of "the Counselor, the Holy Spirit" who will teach them to keep the command of love and bring to remembrance all that Jesus has taught (14:15–17; 14:25–26). John's word for the Holy Spirit is *parakletos,*

"Paraclete," "the one called beside." For John, the Paraclete is sent from the Father in Jesus' name to be with the believer in his/her struggle to remain a faithful believer and witness in a hostile world (14:16–17,25–26; 15:26–27; 16:7–11). This is not quite the same as Luke's concept of the Holy Spirit of God who overshadows Mary and enables her to conceive Jesus (Lk 1:35) and then descends upon Jesus at his baptism (3:22) and the apostolic community at Pentecost (Acts 2:1–4) to guide them in their ministries of proclaiming the gospel.

The conclusion of 14:31 looks like the original ending of the farewell discourse, but in the present form of the gospel Jesus' last words to his disciples are continued through 17:26. John 15:1–16:33 repeats many of the same themes of 13:31–14:31 but with more emphasis on the hostility that the disciples will experience from the disbelieving world. In 15:1–11 Jesus uses the beautiful image of the vine and the branches to speak of his unity with his disciples and the need for them to abide in him and bear fruit by fulfilling his command to love one another. In 16:16–24 we have John's version of the beatitudes in the synoptic tradition (Matt 5:3–11; Lk 6:20–26) in which Jesus speaks of the sorrow which the disciples will experience while the world is rejoicing, but the eternal joy which they will experience when he will see them again. John concludes Jesus' farewell discourse with a moving prayer in which Jesus, having completed the work his Father had given him, asks him to glorify "thy Son" (17:1–5) and to protect his disciples whom he is leaving behind in the world (17:6–26).

Although John's passion account contains many incidents familiar from the synoptic tradition, they are handled in a way consistent with John's theology. In the arrest in the garden (18:1–14) there is no hint of agony; Jesus has come to the hour of his glory (12:27–32) and he is in complete control as he begins to "lay down" his life only to take it up again (18:4; cf. 10:17–18). When the band of soldiers approaches, Jesus asks them "Whom do you seek?" to which they respond, "Jesus of Nazareth" (18:4–5). When Jesus answers with the solemn "I am he," they draw back and fall to the ground before Jesus' divine presence. He then gives them permission to take him and tells them to let his disciples go. When Peter tries to fight to prevent them, Jesus says, "Put your sword into its sheath; shall I not drink the cup which the Father has given me?" (18:11).

The trials before the high priest and Pilate are also treated in a way that reflects John's unique theology. Using dramatic irony in a way reminiscent of Plato's handling of Socrates' trial in **The Apology,** John makes the trials into scenes of dialogue in which Jesus turns the tables on his accusers and convicts them for failing to believe in him. When the high priest questions Jesus "about his disciples and his teaching," Jesus takes the offensive by challenging him to question his believing disciples:

> "I have spoken openly to the world; I have always taught in synagogues and in the temple, where all Jews come together; I have said nothing secretly. Why do you ask me? Ask those who have heard me, what I said to them; they know what I said" (18:20–21).

The trial before Pilate revolves around the issue of Jesus' kingship and whether it is of this world or not. In the end, both the Jews and Pilate will by their words and actions affirm that they are subjects of Caesar, a king of this world, rather than of Jesus, and will thus condemn themselves. When Jesus is questioned by Pilate about the nature of his kingship (18:33–36), Jesus challenges him to believe in the truth of his divine kingship which he has borne witness to (18:37–38), and later he assures Pilate that he would have no power over him "unless it had been given you from above" (19:11). The Jews, on the other hand, threaten Pilate by saying, "If you release this man, you are not Caesar's friend; every one who makes himself a king sets himself against Caesar" (19:12). The trial scene ends with both the Jews and Pilate judging themselves by their actions. When Pilate presents Jesus to the crowd with the words, "Behold your King!" they ask for his crucifixion and say, "We have no king but Caesar" (19:14–15). At this point Pilate capitulates to their earlier threat and hands Jesus over to be crucified (19:16). In the end, however, Pilate becomes an unbelieving witness to the truth of Jesus' identity. He places a title on the cross in Hebrew, Latin, and Greek which reads, "Jesus of Nazareth, the King of the Jews" (19:19–20). When the chief priests try to get him to change it to read "This man said, I am King of the Jews," Pilate refuses by saying, "What I have written I have written" (19:21–22).

John's portrayal of the crucifixion is consistent with his understanding of Jesus throughout the gospel. Jesus does not really suffer on the cross in John; he reigns as he enters his glory with the completion of the task given him by his Father. Jesus is "the Good Shepherd" who lays down his life to take it up again (10:17–18), "the Lamb of God who takes away the sins of the world" (1:29,36), and the source of living waters (4:13–15; 7:38). Rather than having to be assisted by Simon of Cyrene (Mk 15:21; Matt 27:32; Lk 23:26), Jesus carries his own cross to Golgotha (19:17), and dies with the words "It is finished" (19:30). The time of his death is a day earlier than in the synoptics so that Jesus, as the Lamb of God, dies on the day of Preparation for the Passover, just as the lambs would be slain in the temple (19:31). Like the lambs used for Passover who were not to have a bone broken (19:36; cf. Ex 12:46), Jesus' legs are not broken when the soldiers discover that he is already dead (19:33–37). Instead his side is pierced and blood and water flow out—the fulfillment of the prophecy in Zechariah 12:10, "They shall look on him whom they have pierced" (19:37).

In contrast to the picture in the synoptics where Jesus is deserted by his disciples and where the women look on from a distance (Mk 15:40–41), in John there are believers standing by the cross (19:21), and Jesus speaks with them and commends his mother and the beloved disciple to one another's care—a symbol of the love the community he is leaving behind is to have (19:26–27; cf. 13:34–35; 14:18–21; 15:10–17).

John's resurrection stories in 20:1–31 are again handled quite differently from those in the synoptics, but in ways consistent with Johannine themes. In 20:1–10 Mary Magdelene discovers the empty tomb but meets no angels/men to interpret its significance as in the synoptics. Instead, she thinks the body has been stolen and runs to tell Simon Peter and the disciple "whom Jesus loved" (20:1–2). When they reach the empty tomb, the beloved disciple sees and believes although the disciples have not yet understood that Jesus must rise from the dead. Apparently, then, he believes that Jesus has returned to the Father as he had announced in the farewell discourse (13:31–17:26). This is followed by an appearance of Jesus to Mary Magdalene in which she is told to tell Jesus' brethren that he has arisen and is about to ascend to his Father (20:11–28).

In 20:19–31 Jesus, who has now ascended to the Father, comes to his gathered disciples as he had promised in the farewell discourse (14:18) and greets them by saying "Peace be with you" (20:19,21; cf. 14:27). He then sends them into the world as he had been sent by the Father (20:21; cf. 17:18) and gives them the Holy Spirit, the Paraclete, as he had promised (20:22; cf. 14:16–17,26) who will given them the power to forgive or retain sins (20:23; cf. 15:22–24; 16:8–9).

The appearance to Thomas in 20:24–29 addresses the reader who has not had the privilege of having seen the glorified Jesus. Thomas is transformed from an unbeliever who must see physical signs (20:25) to a believer who confesses Jesus as "My Lord and my God" (20:26–28) when he sees the glorified Jesus. But Jesus' last words praise those who have believed on the testimony of others without having seen (20:29). This leads directly to the conclusion which states the purpose of the gospel:

> Now Jesus did many other signs in the presence of the disciples, which are not written in this book; but these are written that you may believe that Jesus is the Christ, the Son of God, and that believing you may have life in his name (20:3–31).

John 21 is an appendix to the gospel which contains a third resurrection appearance to the disciples at the Sea of Tiberias in Galilee. The concerns in this appendix seem to be primarily ecclesiastical. The meal which Jesus eats with his disciples on the seashore is evocative of the Eucharist (21:9–14). Peter, the acknowledged leader of the apostles who by the time of the composition of this gospel has been martyred (21:18–19), is exonerated for his triple denial of Jesus by three times professing his love for Jesus and his willingness to "feed" the sheep (21:15–17).

REVELATION (THE CHRISTIAN APOCALYPSE)

The only fully apocalyptic book in the canonical New Testament is the Book of Revelation. The author identifies himself as "John," who had been exiled to the island of Patmos because of the testimony he had given to the "word of God" and "Jesus" (1:1,4,9; 22:8). Although there are some similarities in vocabulary and themes between Revelation and the Johannine literature (the gospel of John and the three letters of John), most scholars agree that the author of Revelation is not to be identified with the author of John, nor with John the son of Zebedee.

Revelation was written to Christian communities in Asia Minor (Rev 2–3) who were in the midst of trials to their faith and persecutions from the Roman government for their failure to either recognize the Roman state-gods or to participate in the emperor cult. The probable date for the book is sometime late in the reign of Domitian (81–96 C.E.), an emperor who persecuted Christians and, according to Suetonius, preferred to be addressed as "Our Master and our God."

Revelation uses the popular early Christian letter form with an introductory salutation (1:2–8), letters addressed to seven churches in Asia Minor (2:1–3:22), and a concluding benediction (22:21), but within this framework presents a series of highly symbolic visions assuring faithful Christians, who are being persecuted even to the point of martyrdom, that the risen Christ who is enthroned in heaven and God's kingdom will soon triumph over the bestial forces of evil, particularly the Roman empire. The imagery used in these visions is drawn from Jewish apocalyptic and prophetic books (see Dan 7–12, Zech 7–14, Ez 1–9, 26–27, 39–48) and mythic and holy war traditions (see Ex 7–15).

The prologue (1:1–3) establishes that the "revelation" which John is handing on is a prophecy of the imminent coming end which is meant for God's servants. It comes from God who revealed it to Jesus Christ who in turn made it known to John by sending his angel to him. The introductory salutation (1:4–8) identifies God's servants as the seven churches in Asia who are greeted with grace and peace from the seven protective spirits before God's throne and the triumphant Jesus who was himself a faithful witness ("martyr") and is now "the firstborn from the dead and ruler of the kings on earth." The salutation continues with two doxologies which console the churches with their status as a kingdom of priests, freed from their sins and awaiting the coming of Christ with the clouds, and ends with Christ identifying himself as "the Alpha and the Omega," the beginning and end of all things (1:8).

Revelation 1:9–20 is John's commissioning vision, modeled on that given the prophets (cf. Is 6; Ez 1–3); it is meant to assure John and his readers of Christ's personal triumph over death and his power over the dominion of Death and Hades (1:17–18). In it Christ appears in a glorified human form in the midst of seven golden lampstands, holding seven stars in his right hand, and with a sharp two-edged sword issuing from his mouth. John is commissioned to write "what you see, what is and and what is to take place hereafter," and then he is told that the seven stars are the seven angels of the seven churches and the lampstands are the churches.

The letters to the seven churches in Asia Minor (Ephesus, Smyrna, Pergamum, Thyatira, Sardis, Philadelphia, and Laodicea) are structured as the message of the triumphant Christ to each community. They either praise the community for fidelity to the Christian faith, or blame it for compromise with various heresies or idolatry or encourage it to be faithful in time of persecution. They are all cast in a similar form: an introduction of the words of Christ using titles or descriptions from the commissioning vision, a statement that Christ knows the situation for good or evil in the church and words of encouragement, a promise of heavenly reward for those who remain faithful in the time of trial.

The author prefaces the major revelations (6:1–21:8) with a vision of God within his heavenly throne room (4:1–11) holding a written scroll sealed by seven seals (5:1) that only Christ, "the Lamb who was slain," is worthy to open (5:2–14). This is followed by a series of overlapping apocalyptic visions which use the number seven, symbolizing divine completeness: seven seals (6:1–8:6), seven trumpets (8:2–11:19), seven visions of the Dragon's (Satan's) worldly rule (12:1–13:18), seven visions of those who worship the Lamb and those who honor the Beast (Rome) (14:1–20), seven bowls of the wrath of God (15:1–16:21), seven visions of Babylon's fall (17:1–19:10), seven visions of the victory of Christ and his heavenly armies over Satan and the creation of a "new heaven and a new earth" (19:11–21:8). These visions are not meant to be allegories of successive events in the coming of God's kingdom, but are rather increasingly intensive statements of the same basic vision of destruction of the forces opposed to God and salvation for his faithful ones.

The visions repeat in varying imagery the same basic themes: the persecution of sufferings being endured by the faithful ones, the judgment or destruction to come upon the forces of evil, and the heavenly salvation that awaits the faithful who have endured in the crisis. This last feature is usually depicted in a heavenly scene in which the reader is given a vision of the faithful martyrs who have been saved and are participating in the heavenly liturgy as they await the completion of the persecution.

This pattern can be illustrated by a closer look at the vision of the seven seals (6:1–8:6). The breaking of the first four seals releases four horseman symbolizing conquering power, war and bloodshed, famine, pestilence and death (6:1–8). Opening the fifth seal discloses the martyrs "who had been slain for the word of God and for the witness they had borne" (6:9). They are praying to the Sovereign Lord for vengeance for their innocent blood (6:10). Their prayer is answered when they are each given a white robe and told to rest "a little longer" until "the number of their fellow servants and brethren should be complete . . . " (6:11). This is followed by the opening of the sixth seal which unleashes a great earthquake and cosmic catastrophes which are the wrath of Lamb upon "the kings of the earth and the great men and the generals and the rich and the strong . . . " (6:12–17). In an interlude between the sixth and seventh seals, John has two visions which give assurance that the faithful are protected from God's judgment (7:1–17). A symbolic one hundred and fourty-four thousand Israelites and a great multitude without number, clothed in white robes with palm branches in their hands, are before God's throne and the Lamb singing, "Salvation belongs to our God who sits upon the throne, and to the Lamb" (7:10). The breaking of the seventh seal then leads into the vision of the seven trumpets which repeats the same pattern (8:1–11:19).

The visions in 12:1–17 and 13:1–18 use ancient mythological motifs to speak about the persecution which the churches in Asia Minor are experiencing. The seven-headed red dragon which persecutes a pregnant woman clothed with the sun, moon and a crown of twelve stars has elements of the old creation myth like the Mesopotamian **Enuma Elish** in which the monster of chaos is defeated in battle by a creator-god who brings order to the universe. In this case the dragon is identified as "the Devil and Satan" (12:9). The woman's child, who is destined "to rule all the nations," seems to be the Messiah who in this vision is "caught up to God and to his throne." The woman apparently symbolizes the heavenly representation of God's people—first as Israel (12:1–6) and then as the persecuted Church (12:13–17). In a heavenly battle the dragon is defeated by Michael and his angels and thrown down from heaven to earth (12:7–12), but then he pursues the woman's offspring "who keep the commandments of God and bear testimony to Jesus" (12:17).

The persecution is continued in 13:1–18 where the dragon gives power to a beast with ten horns and seven heads who arises out of the sea (13:1–4). This beast symbolizes the

Roman empire (13:5–8); it blasphemes against God who allows it "to make war on the saints and conquer them" and to have authority "over every tribe and people and tongue and nation" and to be worshiped by all who dwell upon the earth except the faithful who must endure in this time of persecution (13:7–10). A second beast with two horns (the Roman priesthood?) enforces the emperor worship (13:11–17). The vision ends with an enigmatic reference to "the number of the beast" as six hundred and sixty-six. Both Hebrew and Greek letters have numerical values, and on this basis many scholars have suggested that the reference is to Neron Caesar in Hebrew letters. There was a popular first-century legend that Nero had not been killed but would return and lead a conquering army from the East.

This mythological depiction of the persecution of the faithful is then followed in 14:1–20 by seven visions which are meant to give assurance to the churches amid their trials and persecutions. John sees and hears the heavenly liturgy of the symbolic one hundred and forty-four thousand who are worshiping the Lamb and hears the assuring words, "Fear God and give him glory, for the hour of his judgment has come; and worship him who made heaven and earth, the sea and the fountains of water" (14:7). This is followed by the announcement that Babylon (Rome) has fallen and that those who worship the beast will be subject to the judgment of God's wrath (14:8–11). After hearing a voice proclaiming blessing for those who endure to the point of death (14:12–13), John sees a vision in which "one like a son of man" descends on the cloud with a sickle in his hand and begins God's wrathful harvest (14:14–20).

Revelation 15:1–16:21 uses imagery from the traditions in the Book of Exodus about the plagues (Ex 7–11) and the victory of the Lord over Pharaoh and his armies at the Sea (Ex 14–15) to lead up to the defeat of Babylon (Rome) in the battle of Armageddon (cf. Jgs 5:19; 2 Kgs 9:27; 2 Chr 35:22). This is followed by seven visions depicting the fall of Babylon, the great harlot who symbolizes Rome (17:1–19:10). These visions culminate with the praises in heaven for the destruction of Rome (19:1–5) and the rejoicing of a great multitude for the marriage of the Lamb to his Bride, the saints who have been faithful (19:6–10).

The last series of visions (19:11–21:8) leads to the climactic establishment of a new cosmic order in which God's kingdom is finally established. The visions use traditional Jewish images of the battle between God's forces and those of evil (cf. Ez 38–39) and the picture of God's kingdom being established in Jerusalem as a city of peace, joy and paradise (Ez 40–48). It begins with a series of battles: the victory of Christ and his armies over the beast (19:11–21), the temporary binding of Satan and the thousand year reign of the martyrs (20:1–6), the loosing of Satan for the final conflict (20:7–10). These are followed by a vision of the resurrection of the dead (20:11–15) and the creation of a new cosmic order, "a new heaven and a new earth" with the heavenly Jerusalem as the dwelling of God with men in which death, pain and sorrow are excluded (21:1–27).

The concluding vision depicts a return to Paradise as pictured in the Garden of Eden (Genesis 2). John is shown a river which flows from the throne of God and of the Lamb in the middle of the city and along its banks the tree of life bearing twelve kinds of fruit and leaves "for the healing of the nations" (22:1–2). The vision ends with the following assuring promise:

> There shall no more be anything accursed, but the throne of God and of the Lamb shall be in it, and his servants shall worship him; they shall see his face, and his name shall be on their foreheads. And night shall be no more; they need no light of lamp or sun, for the Lord God will be their light, and they shall reign for ever and ever (22:3–5).

The epilogue (22:6–21) is a series of warnings and exhortations in which John is told not to seal up the book, "for the time is near" for the coming of the Lord Jesus and the fulfillment of this prophecy.

6

THE CHRISTIAN FATHERS AND
EARLY CHRISTOLOGICAL COUNCILS
(c. 100–450 C.E.)

INTRODUCTION

The readings in this section illustrate the development of Christian thought from the end of the New Testament era (c. 100 C.E.) to the collapse of ancient Rome (c. 450 C.E.). In the early second century C.E. Christianity was a new, and relatively small, persecuted sect in the urban centers of the eastern half of the Roman empire which ruled the whole Mediterranean world in relative peace and prosperity. By 450 C.E., Christianity had become the official religion of both halves of a divided empire. In the Byzantine East the empire was destined to continue for another thousand years and its form of Christianity survives in the various Eastern Orthodox Churches to this day. In the West by the middle of the fifth century, the empire was dying, but the Roman Christian Church not only would survive the chaos of the barbarian invasions of the fifth century, but would become the dominant cultural institution in the succeeding Middle Ages. Paralleling this institutional development, Christian thinkers moved from a defensive posture toward a hostile Roman government and a pagan Hellenistic-Roman culture to a creative accommodation of certain aspects of the world-view of the late classical world. As a consequence the Christian Church became the vehicle for the transmission of both Christian and classical values to the Middle Ages.

The second-century C.E. was a "golden age" for the Roman empire. The five so-called "good emperors" ruled a vast territory in peace and economic prosperity. For the early Christian communities this was primarily a time of preservation and defensiveness, rather than creative theological development. Under the twin threats of official Roman persecution from without and various heretical doctrines from within their own ranks, the fledgling Christian communities struggled to remain faithful to the gospel message of the inauguration of the age of salvation through the death and resurrection of Jesus, to the spirit of his ethical teachings, and to established teaching authority within their communities. The heroes of the early Christian community were the martyrs, who were

340

willing to witness to their faith even to the point of dying for it in the face of persecution. As might be expected, the bishops, *episcopoi* (literally "overseers"), in the major Christian centers emerged as the leaders and theologians of the period. The so-called Apostolic Fathers, like Clement bishop of Rome and Ignatius bishop of Antioch, continued the New Testament tradition of writing letters to various communities to exhort them to fidelity to the Christian faith and discipline and to ensure orderly structure within communities faced with heresy or rebellion. They began the process of establishing an authority structure for the early communities which can also be seen in the pastoral epistles—Titus and 1 and 2 Timothy. The doctrinal authority was a somewhat fluid creed which summarized the truths of the faith drawn from the writings of Paul and the gospels. It insisted on the historical reality of Christ's birth, life, death, and resurrection and continued in a less urgent form the apocalyptic expectation of his awaited return. The living voice of authority was the presbyter-bishop, the leader of worship and the overseer of discipline in the major urban churches, who was understood as the successor to the apostles. The primary rituals, or sacraments, of the early communities were baptism after public instruction in the faith and the Eucharist which was celebrated on the Lord's day, the first day of the week—in memory of Jesus' resurrection.

In the mid and late second-century C.E., learned apologists, like Justin Martyr, began the important creative work of defending and explaining the Christian faith and practice to Roman authorities and educated outsiders. In the process, they explored similarities between Christian teaching and the philosophical and religious heritage of the classical Greek and Roman world. This effort at accommodation with classical culture was concomitant with the struggle to safeguard the Christian tradition against distortions by various forms of gnosticism which would have turned Christianity into an elitist mystery religion and would have made salvation a matter of secret *gnosis* ("knowledge"), rather than an ethical reformation of life. The most important of the anti-gnostic writers was Irenaeus, bishop of Lyons, who was able to mount a learned defense against the secret traditions of the gnostics by an appeal to the developing canonical list of New Testament books and the plain sense of their message as interpreted by the public tradition of the Christian bishops throughout the Roman world.

In the third century C.E. the Christian churches were still periodically persecuted, but were now well-established throughout the urban centers of an already economically and socially troubled empire. During this period, Christian thinkers struggled with the question of how far the Christian message could be accommodated to the categories of Hellenistic philosophy. In the words of Tertullian, "What has Jerusalem to do with Athens, the Church with the Academy . . . ?" There were certain similarities between the teachings of Christianity and the doctrines of the Neo-Platonic and Stoical philosophies of the third century C.E. These philosophical movements tended toward a form of monotheism which spoke of an absolutely transcendent and impersonal source of all reality. This concept bore an attractive resemblance to the Christian doctrine of monotheism and the concept of God as Creator. However, the historical character of Christianity with its emphasis on creation by a free act of God's love and his revelation of himself in history through the experience of Israel and most fully in Jesus the Christ was not easily expressed in the language of Hellenistic philosophy which arose out of a rational and mystical search for an explanation of reality. At the risk of oversimplification, our selections sample two extreme answers to the question of the accommodation of Christian faith and Hellenistic philosophy. Tertullian (c. 160–240 C.E.), a Latin apologist from Carthage in North Africa, takes a completely negative stance toward philosophy as the source of all heresy in the Church. On the other hand, Origen (c. 185–253 C.E.), a Greek theologian from the influential catechetical school of Alexandria in Egypt, takes a more positive, but not uncritical, approach to Hellenistic philosophy and uses it to explore speculative questions about the traditional Christian teachings in connection with creation, the fall, history, judgment, heaven, hell, and the final end.

The question of accommodation of Christianity with Hellenistic philosophy and the world of the late Roman empire reached a climax in the Christological controversies of the fourth and fifth centuries C.E. and the beginnings of Christian monasticism. The Christian churches showed their institutional strength and spiritual and intellectual vigor when their bishops were able, in the heat of theological controversy, to meet in councils called by the emperors and come to an ecumenical expression of the paradoxical Christian faith in language drawn from both the Christian Scriptures and Hellenistic philosophy. The doctrinal statements of the councils of Nicaea (325 C.E.) and Chalcedon (451 C.E.) on the Christian belief in monotheism, the full divinity and humanity of Christ, and the Trinity are still accepted today as the orthodox statements of the mysteries of the Christian understanding of God in all the major branches of Christianity. At the same time as the Christian persecutions and martyrdom ended with the formal recognition of Christianity as a legitimate and eventually the favored religion of the empire, Christianity found a new form of heroism in the movement of monasticism in which Christian ascetics, like Antony of Egypt, withdrew from the increasingly decadent and chaotic cities of the late empire to find God and live a heroic form of the gospel life in the deserts of Egypt and the Near East.

Our final selections come from the **Confessions** of the great Augustine of Hippo (c. 354–430 C.E.). This enormously influential theologian and bishop literally experienced in his own personal spiritual pilgrimage the death of the ancient world and its value system and the birth of the Christian world which would shape Western culture in the Middle Ages. In his writings he was able to synthesize biblical faith and Hellenistic philosophy in a vision of God, humanity, and history which shaped the thought and life of the Christian West throughout the Middle Ages and even into the Renaissance and Reformation.

For an excellent discussion of this whole period see Henry Chadwick, **The Early Church**, Vol. 1 in **The Pelican History of the Church** (Baltimore, Md.: Penguin Books Inc., 1975).

JUSTIN MARTYR: *THE FIRST APOLOGY (A DEFENSE OF CHRISTIANITY)*

The apologists were Christian writers in the second and third centuries who attempted to make a reasoned defense and recommendation of the Christian faith to outsiders. Our selection is taken from Justin Martyr (c. 110–165 C.E.), the most famous of the early Christian apologists. Justin was a convert to Christianity after a long search for wisdom in Hellenistic philosophy. Even after his conversion, he still considered himself a philosopher and understood Christianity as the only true philosophy. For a time Justin taught as a Christian philosopher in Ephesus and later moved to Rome where he formed a Christian school. He and some of his disciples were denounced as Christians c. 165 C.E., and, when they refused to sacrifice to the state gods and the imperial image, were scourged and beheaded.

The **First Apology** (c. 155 C.E.) is addressed to the emperor Antonious Pius, his family and the senate. Justin appeals to the Roman tradition of *pietas* and to the emperor as a philosopher, a lover of truth and wisdom. He asks the emperor to take a rational approach to handling charges against Christians. They should be condemned only if they have committed crimes against the state and not simply for having the name Christians. In responding to the charge that Christians are atheists because they do not recognize the traditional state gods, Justin compares their situation to that of Socrates, who is obviously a hero for Justin the philosopher. Socrates had endeavored by reason to deliver his contemporaries from the worship of demons only to be condemned to death for introducing new divinities. Justin goes on to point out that Christians like Socrates do not worship the old deities, but they do worship "the most true God, the Father of righteousness and temperance and the other virtues, who is free from all impurity," as well as the Son and the Spirit.

In the course of his defense of Christianity, Justin is one of the first Christian thinkers to attempt to reconcile the claims of Christian faith and philosophical reason. He thinks that traces of the truth are to be found in pagan thinkers since all share in the "generative" word (*logos spermatikos*)—a concept which he borrows from Stoical philosophy. According to Justin, the truth in philosophers like Plato, who taught the immortality of the soul and reward and punishment in the afterlife on the basis of merit and choice, comes from Moses who is of greater antiquity and was borrowed by Plato. Christianity has the fullness of truth because Christ is the Word (*Logos*) incarnate. The reason the Word became incarnate was to teach the truth and to redeem humankind from the power of demons.

The later chapters of the **First Apology** are of great interest because of their account of second-century Christian baptismal ceremonies and Eucharistic beliefs and practices. Justin describes these because of the charges that Christians practiced such things as cannibalism in eating the body and drinking the blood of their God.

The translation is by A. Cleveland Coxe, D.D. in **The Apostolic Fathers with Justin Martyr and Irenaeus** in Vol. 1 of **The Ante-Nicene Fathers** (New York: Charles Scribner's Sons, 1903) 159–187.

The First Apology of Justin

CHAPTER 1:
ADDRESS

To the Emperor Titus Aelius Adrianus Antoninus Pius Augustus Caesar, and to his son Verissimus the Philosopher, and to Lucius the Philosopher, the natural son of Caesar, and the adopted son of Pius, a lover of learning, and to the sacred Senate, with the whole People of the Romans, I, Justin, the son of Priscus and grandson of Bacchius, natives of Flavia Neapolis in Palestine, present this address and petition in behalf of those of all nations who are unjustly hated and wantonly abused, myself being one of them.

CHAPTER 2:
A RATIONAL APPROACH DEMANDED

Reason directs those who are truly pious and philosophical to honour and love only what is true, declining to follow traditional opinions, if these be worthless. For not only does sound reason direct us to refuse the guidance of those who did or taught anything wrong, but it is incumbent on the lover of truth, by all means, and if death be threatened, even before his own life, to choose to do and say what is right. Do you, then, since ye are called pious and philosophers, guardians of justice and lovers of learning, give good heed, and hearken to my address; and if ye are indeed such, it will be manifested. For we have come, not to flatter you by this writing, nor please you by our address, but to beg that you pass judgment, after an accurate and searching investigation, not flattered by prejudice or by a desire of pleasing superstitious men, nor induced by irrational impulse or evil rumours which have long been prevalent, to give a decision which will prove to be against yourselves. For as for us, we reckon that no evil can be done us, unless we be convicted as evil-doers, or be proved to be wicked men; and you, you can kill, but not hurt us.

(In chapters 3–4 Justin demands a judicial investigation of charges against Christians and insists that Christians are being unjustly condemned simply for bearing the name "Christian".)

CHAPTER 5:
CHRISTIANS CHARGED WITH ATHEISM

Why, then, should this be? In our case, who pledge ourselves to do no wickedness, nor to hold these atheistic opinions, you do not examine the charges made against us; but, yielding to unreasoning passion, and to the instigation of evil demons, you punish us without consideration or judgment. For the truth shall be spoken; since of old these evil demons, effecting apparitions of themselves, both defiled women and corrupted boys, and showed such fearful sights to men, that those who did not use their reason in judging of the actions that were done, were struck with terror; and being carried away by fear, and not knowing that these were demons, they called them gods, and gave to each the name which each of the demons chose for himself. And when Socrates endeavoured, by true reason and examination, to bring these things to light, and deliver men from the demons, then the demons themselves, by means of men who rejoiced in iniquity, compassed his death, as an atheist and profane person, on the charge that "he was introducing new divinities;" and in our case they display a similar activity. For not only among the Greeks did reason (Logos) prevail to condemn these things through Socrates, but also among the Barbarians were they condemned by Reason (or the Word, the Logos) Himself, who took shape, and became man, and was called Jesus Christ; and in obedience to Him, we not only deny that they who did such things as these are gods, but assert that they are wicked and impious demons, whose actions will not bear comparison with those even of men desirous of virtue.

CHAPTER 6:
THE CHARGE OF ATHEISM REFUTED

Hence are we called atheists. And we confess that we are atheists, so far as the gods of this sort are concerned, but not with respect to the most true God, the Father or righteousness and temperance and the other virtues, who is free from all impurity. But both Him, and the Son (who came forth from Him and taught us these things, and the host of the other good angels who follow and are made like to Him), and the prophetic Spirit, we worship and adore, knowing them in reason and truth, and declaring without grudging to every one who wishes to learn, as we have been taught.

CHAPTER 8:
SIMILARITIES BETWEEN CHRISTIAN
AND PLATONIC VIEWS
OF THE AFTERLIFE

And reckon ye that it is for your sakes we have been saying these things; for it is in our power, when we are examined, to deny that we are Christians; but we would not live by telling a lie. For, impelled by the desire of the eternal and pure life, we seek the abode that is with God, the Father and Creator of all, and hasten to confess our faith, persuaded and convinced as we are that they who have proved to God by their works that they followed Him, and loved to abide with Him where there is no sin to cause disturbance, can obtain these things. This, then, to speak shortly, is what we expect and have learned from Christ, and teach. And Plato, in like manner, used to say that Rhadamantus and Minos[1] whould punish the wicked who came before them; and we say that the same thing will be done, but at the hand of Christ, and upon the wicked in the same bodies united again to their spirits which are now to undergo everlasting punishment; and not only, as Plato said, for a period of a thousand years. And if any one say that this is incredible or impossible, this error of ours is one which concerns ourselves only, and no other person, so long as you cannot convict us of doing any harm.

(In chapters 9–10 Justin denounces the folly of idol worship and expounds the Christian belief that God is best served by leading a virtuous life.)

CHAPTER 11:
THE KINGDOM CHRISTIANS LOOK FOR

And when you hear that we look for a kingdom, you suppose, without making any inquiry, that we speak of a human kingdom; whereas we speak of that which is with God, as appears also from the confession of their faith made by those who are charged with being Christians, though they know that death is the punishment awarded to him who so confesses. For if we looked for a human kingdom, we should also deny our Christ, that we might not be slain; and we should strive to escape detection, that we might obtain what we expect. But since our thoughts are not fixed on the present, we are not concerned when men cut us off; since also death is a debt which must at all events be paid.

CHAPTER 12:
CHRISTIANS LIVE AS UNDER GOD'S EYE

And more than all other men are we your helpers and allies in promoting peace, seeing that we hold this view, that it is alike impossible for the wicked, the covetous, the conspirator, and for the virtuous, to escape the notice of God, and that each man goes to everlasting punishment or salvation according to the value of his actions. For if all men knew this, no one would choose wickedness even for a little, knowing that he goes to the everlasting punishment of fire; but would by all means restrain himself, and adorn himself with virtue, that he might obtain the good gifts of God, and escape the punishments. For those who, on account of the laws and punishments you impose, endeavour to escape detection when they offend (and they offend, too, under the impression that it is quite possible to escape your detection, since you are but men), those persons, if they learned and were convinced that nothing, whether actually done or only intended, can escape the knowledge of God, would by all means live decently on account of the penalties threatened, as even you yourselves will admit. But you seem to fear lest all men become righteous, and you no longer have any to punish. Such would be the concern of public executioners, but not of good princes.

CHAPTER 13:
CHRISTIANS SERVE GOD RATIONALLY

What sober-minded man, then, will not acknowledge that we are not atheists, worshiping as we do the Maker of this universe, and declaring, as we have been taught, that He has no need of streams of blood and libations and incense; whom we praise to the utmost of our power by the exercise of prayer and thanksgiving for all things wherewith we are supplied, as we have been taught that the only honour that is worthy of Him is not to consume by fire what He has brought into being for our sustenance, but to use it for ourselves and those who need, and with gratitude to Him to offer thanks by invocations and hymns for our creation, and for all the means of health, and for the various qualities of different kinds of things, and for changes of the seasons; and to present before Him petitions for our existing again in incorruption through faith in Him. Our teacher of these things is Jesus Christ, who also was born for this purpose, and was crucified under Pontius Pilate, procurator of Judaea, in the times of Tiberius Caesar; and that we reasonably worship Him, having learned that He is the Son of the true God Himself, and holding Him in the second place, and the prophetic Spirit in the third, we will prove. For they proclaim our madness to consist in this, that we give to a crucified man a place second to the unchange-

able and eternal God, the Creator of all; for they do not discern the mystery that is herein, to which as we make it plain to you, we pray you to give heed.

(In chapters 21–22 Justin points out analogies to the history of Christ from Greek and Roman mythology, and in chapters 23–42 he argues that Christian doctrines alone are true and are to be believed on their own account, not merely because of any resemblance they bear to the sentiments of the poets and philosophers. He asserts the divinity of Christ, arguing from the prophecies about divine incarnation in the Old Testament.)

CHAPTER 43:
CHRISTIAN VIEW OF
FATE AND HUMAN FREEDOM

But lest some suppose, from what has been said, by us, that we say that whatever happens, happens by a fatal necessity, because it is foretold as known beforehand, this too we explain. We have learned from the prophets, and we hold it to be true, that punishments, and chastisements, and good rewards, are rendered according to the merit of each man's actions. Since if it be not so, but all things happen by fate, neither is anything at all in our own power. For if it be fated that this man, e.g., be good, and this other evil, neither is the former meritorious nor the latter to be blamed. And again, unless the human race have the power of avoiding evil and choosing good by free choice, they are not accountable for their actions, of whatever kind they be. But that it is by free choice they both walk uprightly and stumble, we thus demonstrate. We see the same man making a transition to opposite things. Now, if it had been fated that he were to be either good or bad, he could never have been capable of both the opposites, nor of so many transitions. But not even would some be good and others bad, since we thus make fate the cause of evil, and exhibit her as acting in opposition to herself; or that which has been already stated would seem to be true, that neither virtue nor vice is anything, but that things are only reckoned good or evil by opinion; which, as the true word shows, is the greatest impiety and wickedness. But this we assert is inevitable fate, that they who choose the good have worthy rewards, and they who choose the opposite have their merited awards. For not like other things, as trees and quadrupeds, which cannot act by choice, did God make man; for neither would he be worthy of reward or praise did he not of himself choose the good, but were created for this end; nor, if he were evil, would be worthy of punishment, nor being evil of himself, but being able to be nothing else than what he was made.

CHAPTER 44:
FREEDOM OF CHOICE IN
THE OLD TESTAMENT AND PLATO

And the holy Spirit of prophecy taught us this, telling us that God spoke thus to the man first created: "Behold, before thy face are good and evil: choose the good."[2] And again, by the other prophet Isaiah, that the following utterance was made as if from God the Father and Lord of all: "Wash you, make you clean; put away evils from your souls; learn to do well; judge the orphan, and plead for the widow; and come let us reason together, saith the Lord: And if your sins be as scarlet, I will make them white as wool; and if they be red like as crimson, I will make them white as snow. And if ye be willing and obey Me, ye shall eat the good of the land; but if ye do not obey Me, the sword shall devour you: for the mouth of the Lord hath spoken it."[3] And so, too, Plato, when he says, "The blame is his who chooses, and God is blameless,"[4] took this from the prophet Moses and uttered it. For Moses is more ancient than all the Greek writers. And whatever both philosophers and poets have said concerning the immortality of the soul, or punishments after death, or contemplation of things heavenly, or doctrines of the like kind, they have received such suggestions from the prophets as have enabled them to understand and interpret these things. And hence there seem to be seeds of truth among all men; but they are charged with not accurately understanding the truth when they assert contradictories. So that what we say about future events being foretold, we do not say it as if they came about by a fatal necessity; but God foreknowing all that shall be done by all men, and it being His decree that the future actions of men shall all be recompensed according to their several value. He foretells by the Spirit of prophecy that He will bestow meet rewards according to the merit of the actions done, always urging the human race to effort and recollection, showing that He cares and provides for men. But by the agency of the devils death has been decreed against those who read the books of Hystaspes, or by the Sibyl,[5] or of the prophets, that through fear they may prevent men who read them from receiving the knowledge of the good, and may retain them in slavery to themselves; which, however, they could not always effect. For not only do we fearlessly read them, but as you see, bring them for your inspection, knowing that their contents will be pleasing to all. And if we persuade even a few, our gain will be very great, for, good husbandmen, we shall receive the reward from the Master.

CHAPTER 46:
THE WORD IN THE WORLD
BEFORE CHRIST

But lest some should, without reason, and for the perversion of what we teach, maintain that we say that Christ was born one hundred and fifty years ago under Cyreius, and subsequently, in the time of Pontius Pilate, taught what we say He taught; and should cry out against us as though all men who were born before Him were irresponsible—let us anticipate and solve the difficulty. We have been taught that Christ is the first-born of God, and we have declared above that He is the Word of whom every race of men were partakers; and those who lived reasonably are Christians, even though they have been thought atheists, as, among the Greeks, Socrates and Heraclitus, and men like them; and among the barbarians, Abraham, and Ananias, and Azarias, and Misael, and Elias, and many others whose actions and names we now decline to recount, because we know it would be tedious. So that even they who lived before Christ, and lived without reason, were wicked and hostile to Christ, and slew those who lived reasonably. But who, through the power of the Word, according to the will of God the Father and Lord of all, He was born of a virgin as a man, and was named Jesus, and was crucified and died, and rose again, and ascended into heaven, an intelligent man will be able to comprehend from what has been already so largely said.

CHAPTER 59:
PLATO'S OBLIGATION TO MOSES

And that you may learn that it was from our teachers—we mean the account given through the prophets—that Plato borrowed his statement that God, having altered matter which was shapeless, made the world, hear the very words spoken through Moses, who, as above shown, was the first prophet, and of greater antiquity than the Greek writers; and through whom the spirit of prophecy, signifying how and from what materials God at first formed the world, spake thus: "In the beginning God created the heaven and the earth. And the earth was invisible and unfurnished, and darkness was upon the face of the deep; and the Spirit of God moved over the waters. And God said, Let there be light; and it was so." So that both Plato and they who agree with him, and we ourselves, have learned, and you also can be convinced, that by the word of God the whole world was made out of the substance spoken of before by Moses. And that which the

poets call Erebus,[6] we know was spoken of formerly by Moses.

CHAPTER 65:
ADMINISTRATION OF THE SACRAMENTS

But we, after we have thus washed him who has been convinced and has assented to our teaching, bring him to the place where those who are called brethren are assembled, in order that we may offer hearty prayers in common for ourselves and for the baptized [illuminated] person, and for all others in every place, that we may be counted worthy, now that we have learned the truth, by our works also to be found good citizens and keepers of the commandments, so that we may be saved with an everlasting salvation. Having ended the prayers, we salute one another with a kiss. There is then brought to the president of the brethren bread and a cup of wine mixed with water; and he taking them, gives praise and glory to the Father of the universe, through the name of the Son and of the Holy Ghost, and offers thanks at considerable length for our being counted worthy to receive these things at His hands. And when he has concluded the prayers and thanksgivings, all the people present express their assent by saying Amen. This word Amen answers in the Hebrew language to *genoito* [so be it]. And when the president has given thanks, and all the people have expressed their assent, those who are called by us deacons give to each of those present to partake of the bread and wine mixed with water over which the thanksgiving was pronounced, and to those who are absent they carry away a portion.

CHAPTER 66:
OF THE EUCHARIST

And this food is called among us *Eucharistia* [the Eucharist], of which no one is allowed to partake but the man who believes that the things which we teach are true, and who has been washed with the washing that is for the remission of sins, and unto regeneration, and who is so living as Christ has enjoined. For not as common bread and common drink do we receive these; but in like manner as Jesus Christ our Saviour, having been made flesh by the Word of God, had both flesh and blood for our salvation, so likewise have we been taught that the food which is blessed by the prayer of His word, and from which our blood and flesh by transmutation are nourished, is the flesh and blood of that Jesus who was made flesh. For the apostles, in the memoirs composed by them, which are called Gospels, have thus delivered unto us what was enjoined upon them; that Jesus took bread, and when He have given thanks, He said, "This is My blood;" and gave it to them alone. Which the wicked devils have imitated in the mysteries of Mithras, commanding the same thing to be done. For, that bread and a cup of water are placed with certain incantations in the mystic rites of one who is being initiated, you either know or can learn.

CHAPTER 67:
WEEKLY WORSHIP OF THE CHRISTIANS

And we afterwards continually remind each other of these things. And the wealthy among us help the needy; and we always keep together; and for all things wherewith we are supplied, we bless the Maker of all through His Son Jesus Christ, and through the Holy Ghost. And on the day called Sunday, all who live in cities or in the country gather together to one place, and the memoirs of the apostles or the writings of the prophets are read, as long as time permits; then, when the reader has ceased, the president verbally instructs, and exhorts to the imitation of these good things. Then we all rise together and pray, and, as we before said, when our prayer is ended, bread and wine and water are brought, and the president in like manner offers prayers and thanksgivings, according to his ability, and the people assent, saying Amen; and there is a distribution to each, and a participation of that over which thanks have been given, and to those who are absent a portion is sent by the deacons. And they who are well to do, and willing, give what each thinks fit; and what is collected is deposited with the president, who succours the orphans and widows, and those who, through sickness or any other cause, are in want, and those who are in bonds, and the strangers sojourning among us, and in a word takes care of all who are in need. But Sunday is the day on which we all hold our common assembly, because it is the first day on which God, having wrought a change in the darkness and matter, made the world; and Jesus Christ our Saviour on the same day rose from the dead. For He was crucified on the day before that of Saturn (Saturday); and on the day after that of Saturn, which is the day of the Sun, having appeared to His apostles and disciples, He taught them these things, which we have submitted to you also for your consideration.

NOTES

[1]Rhadamanthus and Minos were two of the three judges in Hades.
[2]Deut 30:15,19
[3]Isaiah 1:16ff.
[4]**Republic, X**.
[5]The **Sibylline Oracles** were a collection of oracles imitating the pagan "Sibylline Books". Their genuineness was accepted by many of the Fathers, who drew from them arguments in defense of Christianity. Modern critics assign them to Jewish and Christian authors.
[6]Erebus was the son of Chaos and Darkness, who married Nyx.

IRENAEUS: *AGAINST HERESIES* (THE STRUGGLE WITH GNOSTICISM)

One of the most serious challenges faced by the Christian churches in the second century was the internal threat posed by the widespread and complex religious movement known as Gnosticism. The name is derived from the Greek word *gnosis* ("knowledge"), and indicates the central importance attached to "knowledge" in the process of salvation. Gnosticism shares features with intellectual trends already prominent in Hellenistic mythology and Platonic mystical philosophy, but in its Christian form it appeared as schools of thought commonly associated with particular teachers, for example, Valentinus and Basilides.

Although there was wide variety among the various Gnostic thinkers, certain features characterized the movement as a whole. *Gnosis* in the sense of revealed knowledge of God and of the origin and destiny of humankind, was the means by which the spiritual element in the individual received redemption. The source of this special "gnosis" was not, as in the canonical gospels, the earthly Jesus, but the risen Christ or the apostles, from whom it was derived by a secret tradition. Gnosticism was highly dualistic and distinguished, like Persian Zoroastrianism, between spiritual and material as good and evil. Gnostic teachers, therefore, rejected as evil and inferior the "Creator God" of the Hebrew scriptures. This being, who is portrayed in a human fashion in the Hebrew Scriptures as being petty and jealous, is not, according to the Gnostics, the supreme, remote, unknowable and purely spiritual Divine Being. In Gnostic thought the supreme Perfect One often is described as generating a Divine Triad which is constituted of Father, Mother and Son in contrast to the orthodox Trinitarian theology which describes the Spirit (*pneuma*) in neuter terms. From the latter, the creator and the material world is derived by a series of emanations or "aeons." Often, the material creation is depicted as resulting from some mischance or fall from the higher aeons and is therefore imperfect and antagonistic to the truly spiritual world.

The Gnostic outlook is not totally pessimistic, however. Into the constitution of some humans, a seed or spark of the Divine spiritual substance has entered, and, through *gnosis*—in the form of a revelation of the origin of the world, evil, the fall of the soul, etc.— the spiritual element might be rescued from its evil material environment and returned to its home in the Divine Being. The function of Christ in the Gnostic theology was to come as the emissary of the Supreme God, bringing *gnosis*. In Gnostic thought Christ was often portrayed as a purely divine being who neither assumed a properly human body nor died, but either temporarily inhabited a human being, Jesus, or assumed a merely phantasmal human appearance.

Until the late 1940's C.E., our knowledge of Gnosticism was primarily dependent upon the polemical works written against the gnostics by orthodox Church fathers. However, with the discovery of a Coptic library of Gnostic writings at Nag Hammadi in Egypt, our knowledge of the movement has been immeasurably enriched. Scholars now have at their disposal over fifty Gnostic documents, many of which have been published in English translation in **The Nag Hammadi Library in English** edited by James M. Robinson. The interested student may consult this volume for examples of this complex religious movement. For a fine treatment of Gnosticism the reader may see Pheme Perkin's **The Gnostic Dialogue: The Early Church and the Crisis of Gnosticism** (New York: Paulist Press, 1980).

The most important of the anti-Gnostic writers was Irenaeus (c. 140–202 C.E.), a native of Smyrna in Asia Minor, but the bishop of Lyons in southern Gaul. His chief work, written in Greek, is **Adversus Omnes Haereses,** a detailed attack on Gnosticism, especially the system of Valentinus. Irenaeus criticizes the pagan features of Gnosticism and opposes them to the plain sense of the Scriptures as interpreted by the tradition of the Christian churches throughout the Roman world. In contrast to the secret tradition of the Gnostics, Irenaeus appeals to the public tradition of the Church handed down by a chain of teachers reaching back from the bishops in the large metropolitan cities to the apostles. In opposition to the dualism of the Gnostics, Irenaeus insists on the identity of the Creator and the supreme God, on the goodness of material creation, and on the reality of the earthly life of Jesus, especially his birth, crucifixion and resurrection. In contrast to the Gnostic emphasis on salvation through knowledge of one's spiritual origins and fall into a material environment, Irenaeus insists that the human race needs redemption from an evil will and sin. His doctrine of redemption is called "recapitulation," or summary of human evolution in the humanity of the Incarnate Christ. He uses Paul's doctrine of Christ as the New Adam who by his obedience undoes the sin of Adam and renews the entire race.

The translation is by A. Cleveland Coxe in **The Writings of Irenaeus** (Edinburgh: The T. and T. Clark Company, 1880) I, 42–43; 259–261; 359–360.

AGAINST HERESIES

The universal Christian creed

I, 10. The Church, though dispersed throughout the whole world, even to the ends of the earth, has received from the apostles and their disciples this faith: She believes in one God, the Father Almighty, Maker of heaven and earth, and the sea, and all things that are in them; and in one Christ Jesus, the Son of God, who became incarnate for our salvation; and in the Holy Spirit, who proclaimed through the prophets the dispensations of God, and advents, and the birth from a virgin, and the passion and the resurrection from the dead, and the ascension into heaven in the flesh of the beloved Christ Jesus, our Lord, and His future manifestation from heaven in the glory of the Father "to gather all things in one," and to raise up anew all flesh of the whole human race, in order that to Christ Jesus, our Lord, and God, and Savior, and King, according to the will of the invisible Father, "every knee should bow, of things in heaven and things on earth, and things under the earth, and that every tongue should confess"[1] to Him, and that He should execute just judgment towards all; that He may send "spiritual wickedness," and the angels who transgressed and became apostates, together with the ungodly, and unrighteous, and wicked, and profane among men, into everlasting fire; but may, in the exercise of His grace, confer immortality on the righteous, and holy, and those who have kept His commandments, and have persevered in His love, some from the beginning of their Christian course, and others from the date of their repentance, and may surround them with everlasting glory.

As I have already observed, the church, having received this preaching and this faith, although scattered throughout the whole world, yet, as if occupying but one house, carefully preserves it. She also believes these points of doctrine just as if she had but one soul, and one and the same heart, and she proclaims them, and teaches them, and hands them down, with perfect harmony, as if she possessed only one mouth. For, although the languages of the world are dissimilar, yet the import of the tradition is one and the same. For the churches which have been planted in Germany do not believe or hand down anything different, nor do those in Spain, nor do those in Gaul, nor those in the East, nor those in Egypt, nor those in Libya, nor those which have been established in the central regions of the world. But as the sun, that creature of God, is one and the same throughout the whole world, so also the preaching of the truth shines everywhere, and enlightens all men that are willing to come to the knowledge of the truth. Nor will any one of the rulers in the churches, however highly gifted he may be in point of eloquence, teach doctrines different from these (for no one is greater than the Master); nor, on the other hand, will he who is deficient in power of expression inflict on the tradition. For the faith being ever one and the same, neither does one who is able at great length to discourse regarding it make any addition to it, nor does one who can say but little diminish it.

The gnostic appeal to secret wisdom
III, 2. When, however, they are confuted from the Scriptures, they turn round and accuse these same Scriptures, as if they were not correct, nor of authority, and assert that they are ambiguous, and that the truth cannot be ex-

tracted from them by those who are ignorant of tradition. For they allege that the truth was not delivered by means of written documents, but *viva voce:* wherefore also Paul declared, "But we speak wisdom among those that are perfect, but not the wisdom of this world." And this wisdom each one of them alleges to be the fiction of his own inventing, forsooth, so that, according to their idea, the truth properly resides at one time in Valentinus,[2] at another in Marcion,[3] at another in Cerinthus,[4] than afterwards in Basilides,[5] or has even been indifferently in any other opponent, who could speak nothing pertaining to salvation. For every one of these men, being altogether of a perverse disposition, depraving the system of truth, is not ashamed to preach himself.

But, again, when we refer them to that tradition which originates from the apostles, and which is preserved by means of the successions of presbyters in the churches, they object to tradition, saying that they themselves are wiser not merely than the presbyters, but even than the apostles, because they have discovered the unadulterated truth. For they maintain that the apostles intermingled the things of the law with the words of the Savior, and that not the apostles alone, but even the Lord Himself, spoke at one time from Demiurge, at another from the intermediate place, and yet again from the Pleroma,[6] but that they themselves, indubitably, unsulliedly, and purely, have knowledge of the hidden mystery; that is indeed, to blaspheme their Creator after a most impudent manner! It comes to this, therefore, that these men do now consent neither to Scripture nor to tradition.

Such are the adversaries with whom we have to deal, my very dear friend, endeavoring like slippery serpents to escape at all points. Wherefore they must be opposed at all points, if perchance, by cutting off their retreat, we may succeed in turning them back to the truth. For, though it is not an easy thing for a soul under the influence of error to repent, yet, on the other hand, it is not altogether impossible to escape from error when the truth is brought alongside it.

The apostolic tradition given to the bishops and the importance of the Roman church founded by Peter and Paul

III, 3. It is within the power of all, therefore, in every church, who may wish to see the truth, to contemplate clearly the tradition of the apostles manifested throughout the whole world; and we are in a position to reckon up those who were by the apostles instituted bishops in the churches, and to demonstrate the successions of these men to our own times; those who neither taught nor knew of anything like what these heretics rave about. For if the apostles had known hidden mysteries, which they were in the habit of imparting to "the perfect" apart and privily from the rest, they would have delivered them especially to those to whom they were also committing the churches themselves. For they were desirous that these men should be very perfect and blameless in all things, whom also they were leaving behind as their successors, delivering up their own place of government to these men; which men, if they discharged their functions honestly, would be a great boon to the church, but if they should fall away, the direst calamity.

Since, however, it would be very tedious, in such a volume as this, to reckon up the successions of all the churches, we do put to confusion all those who, in whatever manner, whether by an evil self-pleasing, by vainglory, or by blindness and perverse opinion, assemble in unauthorized meetings; we do this, I say, by indicating that tradition derived from the apostles, of the very great, the very ancient, and universally known church found and organized at Rome by the two most glorious apostles, Peter and Paul; as also by pointing out the faith preached to men, which comes down to our time by means of the succession of bishops. For it is a matter of neccessity that every

church agree with this church, on account of its pre-eminent authority, that is, the faithful everywhere, inasmuch as the apostolical tradition has been preserved continuously by those faithful men who exist everywhere.

The true humanity of Christ and his recapitulating of humanity

III, 22. Those, therefore, who allege that He (Christ) took nothing from the Virgin, do greatly err, since, in order that they may cast away the inheritance of the flesh, they also reject the analogy between Him and Adam. For if the one who sprang from the earth had indeed formation and substance from both the hand and workmanship of God, but the other not from the hand and workmanship of God, then He who was made after the image and likeness of the former did not, in that case, preserve the analogy of man, and He must seem an inconsistent piece of work, not having wherewith He may show His wisdom. But this is to say, that He also appeared putatively as man when He was not man, and that He was made man while taking nothing from man. For if He did not receive the substance of flesh from a human being, He neither was made man nor the son of man; and if He was not made what we were, He did no great thing in what He suffered and endured. But every one will allow that we are composed of a body taken from the earth, and a soul receiving spirit from God. This, therefore, the Word of God was made, recapitulating in Himself his own handiwork; and on this account, does He confess Himself to the Son of man, and blesses "The meek, because they shall inherit the earth."[7] The Apostle Paul, moreover, in the Epistle to the Galatians, declares plainly, "God sent His Son, made of a woman."[8] And again, in that of the Romans, he says, "Concerning His Son, who was made of the seed of David according to the flesh, who was predestinated as the Son of God with power, according to the spirit of holiness, by the resurrection from the dead, Jesus Christ our Lord."[9]

Superfluous, too, in that case is His descent into Mary; for why did He come down into her if He were to take nothing of her? Still further, if He had taken nothing of Mary, He would never have availed Himself of those kinds of food which are derived from the earth, by which that body which has been taken from the earth is nourished; nor would He have hungered, fasting those forty days, like Moses and Elias, unless He was craving after its own proper nourishment, nor again, would John,

His disciple, have said when writing of Him, "But Jesus, being wearied with the journey, was sitting to rest"[10] nor would David have proclaimed of Him beforehand, "They have added to the grief of my wounds";[11] nor would He have wept over Lazarus,[12] nor sweated great drops of blood;[13] nor declared, "My soul is exceeding sorrowful";[14] nor, when His side was pierced, would there have come forth blood and water.[15] For all these are tokens of the flesh which had been derived from the earth, which He had recapitulated in Himself, bearing salvation to His own handiwork.

NOTES

[1]Phil 2:10–11.

[2]An influential Gnostic theologian and founder of the sect called Valentinians.

[3]A heretic whose central doctrine was that the Christian Gospel was wholly a message of Love to the exclusion of the Law. He therefore rejected the Old Testament and held that the Creator God depicted therein had nothing in common with the God of Love revealed by Jesus. He taught that only Paul understood the constrast between law and gospel and proposed a New Testament canon of ten Pauline epistles and an edited form of Luke's gospel.

[4]A gnostic who taught that the world was not created by the supreme God, but by a Demiurge. Jesus began His earthly life as a mere man, but at his baptism "the Christ", a higher Divine power, descended upon him, to depart before the crucifixion. Irenaeus asserts that John wrote his Gospel to refute Cerinthus.

[5]A gnostic who taught at Alexandria in the second quarter of the second century C.E.

[6]Literally "Fullness" of divine being.

[7]Matt 5:5

[8]Gal 4:4

[9]Rom 1:3–4

[10]John 4:6

[11]Ps 69:27

[12]John 11:35

[13]Lk 22:44

[14]Mk 14:34

[15]John 19:34

TERTULLIAN: *THE PRESCRIPTION AGAINST HERETICS* (A CHRISTIAN OPPOSITION TO PHILOSOPHY)

The threat of Gnosticism raised for the Church the serious question of the relation of Christian belief and doctrine to the teachings of Hellenistic philosophy. Apologists like

Justin Martyr were interested in exploring and emphasizing the similarities between Christian belief and Graeco-Roman philosophy and even mythology. However, the development of the various Gnostic sects posed the threat of a distortion of the truly unique and historical character of Christian faith.

In the third century C.E. Christian theologians struggled with the question of how far the Christian message could be accommodated to the thought world and ethical beliefs of Hellenistic philosophy. Although there were certain superficial similarities between these two world views, there were also sharp contrasts. The basic view of reality incorporated in the Christian message was the historical outlook of the Hebrew Scriptures and the Christian New Testament. History was seen as beginning with a material creation by an act of a loving God. The created order was good and humans were the highest creatures in the material order. The disordering of creation was the result of sin—a deliberate choice to disobey the revealed will of God. For creation and humanity to be restored to an orderly state, God had intervened in history by revealing his will to Israel in the law and the prophets, and definitively in the life, teaching, death and resurrection of Jesus, his eternal Son who would return again as judge to complete the process of restoration begun in his earthly life.

This historical outlook is quite different from the world view of Hellenistic philosophy in which reality is seen as an hierarchy of being which necessarily emanates from and eventually returns to The One or the fullness of being. In the view of Hellenistic philosophy, especially Neo-Platonism, the material order is inferior; it is at the farthest remove from the purely spiritual fullness of being. The One or the God of Hellenistic philosophy is not involved in history like the God of the Hebrew and Christian Scriptures, nor is it described by personal terms like "Father" which imply a capacity for love and a propensity to change and novelty in relationship to the human and created order. The god of the philosophers is described in largely negative terms as immutable, incomprehensible, one and simple (i.e., having no parts). The god of the philosophers is removed from matter and direct involvement in the chaos and changes of history.

The concept of the human person in the two world-views is also very distinct. For the Hellenistic philosopher the human person is a soul imprisoned in the matter of a human body and the goal of philosophy is to liberate the soul from the passions and weaknesses of the body. The Christian concept of the human person is that of a free bodily individual who is capable of being addressed and loved by God. The dualism is not between body and soul, but between doing the will of God and not doing the will of God. In Paul's terms it is the conflict between spirit and flesh. The ultimate destiny of the human person is bodily resurrection, not release of the soul from the body.

In the course of the third century C.E. Christian theologians struggled with the difficult problem of accommodating these two world views. The question could not be avoided. Gnostic Christian thinkers were already busily integrating and, in the eyes of the orthodox leaders of the Church, distorting the nature of Christian faith. The Gnostics had to be answered and often they chose the ground of the debate simply because they had already formulated positions on many of the issues. At the risk of a great oversimplification our readings will explore two approaches to the problem. In the work of the great Latin theologian Tertullian of Carthage we will see a Christian apologist who rejects all philosophy as "mere human wisdom" and the source of all heresy. He does this in the name of a preservation of the plain sense of the basic Christian creed with its emphasis on creation and the historicity of Christ and his expected return in judgment. On the other hand, we will also sample the writings of Origen from the catechetical school of Alexandria who will attempt to think through the basic Christian creed using the categories of Neo-Platonic philosophy.

Tertullian (c. 160–240 C.E.) was the first great Christian theologian who wrote in Latin. He was raised in Carthage as a pagan, received a good education in literature and rhetoric and may have practiced as a lawyer. He became a Christian at age forty, but in later years he fell into the rigorist Montanist heresy which expected a speedy outpouring of the Holy Spirit and emphasized severe ascetic practices like excessive fasting, disallowing second marriages, and the prohibition of flight during times of persecution.

Despite his later heresy, Tertullian deserves to be ranked with the greatest of the Latin Church Fathers. He wrote a large number of apologetic, ascetic and theological works in a highly rhetorical and powerful prose and in the process became the father of Latin theology. Our seclection is taken from **The Prescription Against Heretics.** In this work he both encourages Christians to endure in the face of heresy and disposes of all heresy in principle as arising from philosophy. In his own famous phrase, "What indeed has Athens to do with Jerusalem? What concord is there between the Academy and the Church? what between heretics and Christians?" Tertullian's argument against the heretics is similar to Irenaeus' appeal to apostolic succession and the public rule of faith, but with a characteristic Roman legal twist. The bishops' churches include those founded by the apostles, and these apostolic churches are unanimously against the heretics in their interpretation of the Scriptures. The direct historical connection of the Church of the bishops with the apostles, whom Christ taught, plus its unanimity in interpreting the Scriptures, demands a verdict against the heretics, according to the principle of Roman law that prior and uninterrupted possession of goods constitutes just possession of these goods. Therefore, Tertullian concludes, let the heretics abandon their claims to read the Bible more accurately than the bishops.

In the final paragraphs we can see Tertullian's apparently legalistic conception of God as legislator and judge. God lays down a law and judges transgressors. Faith can be judged by behavior. A legalistic approach to broad areas of theology has remained characteristic of the Christian West since Tertullian and stands in sharp contrast to the more mystical tradition of the East.

The translation is by the Rev. Peter Holmes, D.D. in **Latin Christianity: Its Founder, Tertullian,** "The Prescription Against Heretics," Vol 3 in the **Ante-Nicene Fathers,** 243–265.

THE PRESCRIPTION AGAINST HERETICS

Chapter 7: Pagan philosophy the parent of heresies

These are "the doctrines" of men and "of demons" produced for itching ears of the spirit of this world's wisdom: this the Lord called "foolishness,"[1] and "chose the foolish things of the world" to confound even philosophy itself. For (philosophy) it is which is the material of the world's wisdom, the rash interpreter of the nature and dispensation of God. Indeed heresies are themselves instigated by philosophy. From this source came the Aeons, and I know not what infinite forms, and the trinity of man in the system of Valentinus, who was of Plato's school. From the same source came Marcion's better god, with all his tranquillity; he came of the Stoics. Then, again, the opinion that the soul dies is held by the Epicureans; while the denial of the restoration of the body is taken from the aggregate school of all the philosophers; also, when matter is made equal to God, then you have the teaching of Zeno; and when any doctrine is alleged touching a god of fire, then Heraclitus comes in. The same subject-matter is discussed over and over again by the heretics and the philosophers; the same arguments are involved. Whence comes evil? Why is it permitted? What is the origin of man? and in what way does he come? Besides the question which Valentinus has very lately proposed—Whence comes God? Which he settles with the answer: From *enthymesis* and *ectroma.*[2] Unhappy Aristotle! who invented for these men dialectics, the art of building up and pulling down; an art so evasive in its propositions, so far-fetched in its conjectures, so harsh, in its arguments, so productive of contentions—embarrassing even to itself, retracting everything, and really treating of nothing! Whence spring those "fables and endless genealogies,"[3] and "unprofitable questions,"[4] and "words which spread like a cancer?"[5] From all

these, when the apostle would restrain us, he expressly names philosophy as that which he would have us be on our guard against. Writing to the Colossians, he says, "See that no one beguile you through philosophy and vain deceit, after the tradition of men, and contrary to the wisdom of the Holy Ghost."[6] He had been at Athens, and had in his interviews (with its philosophers) become acquainted with that human wisdom which pretends to know the truth, whilest it only corrupts it, and is itself divided into its own manifold heresies, by the variety of its mutually repugnant sects. What indeed has Athens to do with Jerusalem? What concord is there between the Academy and the Church? what between heretics and Christians? Our instruction comes from "the porch of Solomon," who had himself taught that "the Lord should be sought in simplicity of heart."[7] Away with all attempts to produced a mottled Christianity of Stoic, Platonic and dialectic composition! We want no curious disputation after possessing Christ Jesus, no inquisition after enjoying the gospel! With our faith, we desire no further belief.

Chapter 37: Heretics as perverters of Christ's teaching may not claim the Christian Scriptures. These are a deposit, committed to and carefully kept by the church.

Since this is the case, in order that the truth may be adjudged to belong to us, "as many as walk according to the rule," which the church has handed down from the apostles, the apostles from Christ, and Christ from God, the reason of our position is clear, when it determines that heretics ought not to be allowed to challenge an appeal to the Scriptures, since we, without the Scriptures, prove that they have nothing to do with the Scriptures. For as they are heretics, they cannot be true Christians, because it is not from Christ that they get that which they pursue of their own mere choice, and from the pursuit incur and admit the name of heretics.[8] Thus, not being Christians, they have acquired no right to the Christian Scriptures; and it may be very fairly said to them, "Who are you? When and whence did you come? As you are none of mine, what have you to do with that which is mine? Indeed, Marcion, by what right do you hew my wood? By whose permission, Valentinus, are you diverting the streams of my fountain? By what power, Apelles, are you removing my landmarks? This is my property. Why are you, the rest, sowing and feeding here at your own pleasure? This (I say) is my property. I have long possessed it; I possessed it before you. I hold sure title-deeds from the original owners themselves, to whom the estate belonged. I am the heir of the apostles. Just as they carefully prepared their will and testament, and committed it to a trust, and adjured (the trustees to be faithful to their charge), even so do I hold it. As for you, they have, it is certain, always held you as disinherited, and rejected you as strangers—as enemies. But on what ground are heretics strangers and enemies to the apostles, if it be not from the difference of their teaching, which each individual of his own mere will has either advanced or received in opposition to the apostles?"

Chapter 43: The effect of the heretics' teaching is ungodliness

It has also been a subject of remark, how extremely frequent is the intercourse which heretics hold with magicians, with mountebanks, with astrologers, with philosophers; and the reason is, that they are men who devote themselves to curious questions. "Seek, and ye shall find," is everywhere in their minds. Thus, from the very nature of their conduct, may be estimated the quality of their faith. In their discipline we have an index of their doctrine. They say that God is not to be feared; therefore all things are in their view free and unchecked. Where, however is God not feared, except where He is not? Where God is not, there truth also is not. Where there is no truth, then, naturally enough, there is also

such a discipline as theirs. But where God is, there exists "the fear of God, which is the beginning of wisdom."[9] Where the fear of God is, there is seriousness, an honourable and yet thoughtful diligence, as well as an anxious carefulness and a well-considered admission (to the sacred ministry) and a safely-guarded communion, and promotion after good service, and a scrupulous submission (to authority), and a devout attendance, and a modest gait, and a united church, and God in all things.

Chapter 44: Heresy lowers all respect for Christ and destroys all fear of His great judgment.

These evidences, then, of a stricter discipline existing among us, are an additional proof of truth, from which no man can safely turn aside, who bears in mind that future judgment, when "we must all stand before the judgment-seat of Christ,"[10] to render an account of our faith itself before all things. What, then, will they say who shall have defiled it, even the virgin which Christ committed to them with the adultery of heretics? I suppose they will allege that no injunction was ever addressed to them by Him or by His apostles concerning depraved and perverse doctrines assailing them, or about their avoiding and abhorring the same. (He and His apostles, perhaps,) will acknowledge that the blame rather lies with themselves and their disciples, in not having given us previous warning and instruction! They will, besides, add a good deal respecting the high authority of each doctor of heresy,—how that these mightily strengthened belief in their own doctrine; how that they raised the dead, restored the sick, foretold the future, that so they might deservedly be regarded as apostles. As if this caution were not also written record: that many should come who were to work even the greatest miracles, in defence of the deceit of their corrupt preaching. So, forsooth, they will deserve to be forgiven! If, however, any, being mindful of the writings and the denunciations of the Lord and the apostles, shall have stood firm in the integrity of the faith, I suppose they will run great risk missing pardon, when the Lord answers: I plainly forewarned you that there should be teachers of false doctrine in my name, as well as that of prophets and apostles also; and to my own disciples did I give a charge, that they should preach the same things to you. But as for you, it was not, of course, to be supposed that you would believe me! I once gave the gospel and the doctrine of the said rule (of life and faith) to my apostles; but afterwards it was my pleasure to make considerable changes in it! I had promised a resurrection, even of the flesh; but on second thoughts, it struck me that I might not be able to keep my promise! I have shown myself to have been born of a virgin; but this seemed to me afterwards to be a discreditable thing. I had said that He was my Father, who is the Maker of the sun and the showers; but another and better father has adopted me! I had forbidden you to lend an ear to heretics; but in this I erred! Such (blasphemies), it is possible, do enter the minds of those who go out of the right path, and who do not defend the true faith from the danger which besets it. On the present occasion, indeed, our treatise has rather taken up a general position against heresies, (showing that they must) all be refuted on definite, equitable, and necessary rules, without any comparison with the Scriptures. For the rest, if God in His grace permit, we shall prepare answers to certain of these heresies in separate treatises. To those who may devote their leisure in reading through these (pages), in the belief of the truth, be peace, and the grace of our God Jesus Christ for ever.

NOTES

[1] 1 Cor 3:18,25
[2] *Enthymesis* seems to mean "the mind in operation" and *ectroma* is "abortion," "fall."
[3] 1 Tim 1:4
[4] Tit 3:9
[5] 2 Tim 2:17
[6] Col 2:8
[7] Wisdom of Sol. 1:1
[8] "Heretic" comes from the Greek verb meaning "to choose."
[9] Prov 1:7
[10] 2 Cor 5:10

ORIGEN: *ON FIRST PRINCIPLES* (A CHRISTIAN NEO-PLATONIC THEOLOGY)

The third-century Christian theologian who made the most thorough and significant effort at intergrating the Christian faith with Hellenistic philosophy was Origen of Alexandria (d. 254 C.E.) He was the first Christian to create a full system of Christian theology using the categories of Greek (especially Platonic) thought. And, because of his prolific output and the breadth of his treatment of key theological questions, Origen had a lasting influence on Christian theology.

Origen was the son of a father who was a Christian martyr and came from the important city of Alexandria in Egypt which was the second city of the Roman empire in the third century C.E. Through its famous museum it was a center of Hellenistic culture and a place where the Judaeo-Christian and Greek thought worlds had been interacting for several centuries. Alexandria had been an important center for Judaism since its founding by Alexander in the late fourth century B.C.E., and it had the largest community of Jews in any single city in the Roman world. In the second century B.C.E., Alexandria was the place where the Hebrew Scriptures had been translated into Greek in the famous and influential Septuagint version. In the first century C.E. the Alexandrian Jewish philosopher and exegete Philo used an allegorical interpretation of the Jewish Scriptures in an attempt at reconciling Greek philosophy, especially Stoicism and Platonism, with biblical revelation. By the late second and early third centuries C.E., Alexandria had become a center of Christian thought through its celebrated catechetical school which was under the direction of Clement and Origen. The theology of the school was heavily influenced by the Platonic tradition of philosophy which found its pagan expression in the Neo-Platonism of Ammonius Saccas and Plotinus.

Clement (c. 150–215 C.E.) was head of the catechetical school from c. 190–202 C.E., when he was forced to flee because of persecution. In an age of Gnosticism, Clement, under the influence of Platonic philosophy, responded quite differently than did Irenaeus and Tertullian in the West. Clement agreed with the Gnostics that "gnosis" or religious knowledge and illumination was the chief element in Christian perfection. But for him the only true "gnosis" presupposed the Christian faith, which came from the apostles and possessed Divine revelation. While being thoroughly loyal to the Christian faith, Clement, unlike Tertullian, explained and supplemented it with ideas from philosophy, which he regarded as a tutor leading the Greeks to Christ, and therefore a divine gift to mankind as the law was to the Jews. Clement's Christology reflected his emphasis on "gnosis" and Greek wisdom. Christ, the divine Logos, the second Person of the Trinity, is our Pedagogue and Doctor, the source of all human reason, the healer of souls and the interpreter of God to mankind. Christ became man in order to give the supreme revelation and that, through him, we might partake of immortality.

Origen was Clement's successor to head the catechetical school at the tender age of eighteen. He became the greatest of the Alexandrian theologians, and his subsequent influence on Christian theology was enormous. Although he was a prolific writer, many of his works have perished and most of the others survive only in Latin translation. His main work of biblical criticism was his famous **Hexapla,** in which the Hebrew text of the Old Testament, the Hebrew text transliterated into Greek, and four Greek versions of the Old Testament were arranged in parallel columns for the sake of comparison. Our selections are taken from his chief theological work, **On First Principles,** which attempts a total system of theology and treats of God and heavenly beings, creation, man and the material world, free will, sin and its consequences, eschatology (the final outcome of history), and of the interpretation of Holy Scripture.

As a biblical scholar, Origen, like most of the early Christian Fathers, followed Philo in recognizing a triple sense in the meaning of Scripture: the literal, moral and allegorical or spiritual levels. He also distinguished two classes of Christians: the simple who had to be satisfied with the literal or moral level of truth and faith in Christ crucified, and the perfect, who were capable of understanding the spiritual and mystical sense of Scripture and who could ascend to mystical contemplation of the Word dwelling in the Father.

Our selection begins with the preface of **On First Principles** where Origen sets out the literal meaning of the basic Christian doctrines on God the Father, Christ Jesus, the Holy Spirit, heaven and hell, free will, the soul, the Devil, creation, Scripture, etc. Origen carefully distinguishes what is clearly known and accepted on these questions from the apostolic tradition and the teaching of the Church and what areas are open for speculation. In his preface Origen firmly grounds his theology in a literal and historical understanding of the Christian faith.

His speculations in the later sections of **On First Principles** were heavily influenced by Platonic mysticism. His vision of God the Father is one of absolute unity and immutability which is totally beyond human comprehension. Although he believes in the Trinity and the divine nature of Christ the Word and the Holy Spirit, these two persons of the Trinity appear to be subordinate to the Father in Origen's theology. His favorite metaphor for God is also drawn from the Platonic tradition. He compares God, whose nature cannot be grasped or seen by the power of human understanding which is limited by a material body, to the brightness and splendor of the sun which cannot be seen by the naked eye.

Platonic ideas also influenced Origen's understanding of creation, the human soul, and eschatology and led him to theories which were subsequently rejected by the Church. He thought that from the beginning God created a purely spiritual creation which is eternal, because, without an existing world, God would have been inactive and not omnipotent. According to Origen, all spiritual souls were created equal, but through the exercise of their free will, they developed into a hierarchical order. He, like Plato, places the responsibility for evil in the world on the choices made by the created souls and not on God who is all good and perfection. Because of their choices to either conform to God's goodness and perfection or not, some souls became angels, others became demons, and some were imprisoned in bodies. Like Plato, he speculated that death does not finally decide the fate of the soul, which may turn into an angel or a demon. Origen also believed that the ascent and descent of souls goes on uninterruptedly until all free moral creatures—angels, humans, and demons—will be saved by returning to the unity with God that they had in the beginning of creation.

The translation is by Rev. Frederick Crombie in **Fathers of the Third Century,** Vol 4 in **Ante-Nicene Fathers,** (New York: Charles Scribner's Sons, 1905) 239–382.

ON FIRST PRINCIPLES

PREFACE

The Word of God active in history
1. All who believe and are assured that grace and truth were obtained through Jesus Christ, and who know Christ to be the truth, agreeably to His own delcaration, "I am the truth,"[1] derive the knowledge which incites men to a good and happy life from no other source than from the very words and teaching of Christ. And by the words of Christ we do not mean those only which He spake when He became man and tabernacled in the flesh; for before that time, Christ, the Word of God, was in Moses and the

prophets. For without the word of God, how could they have been able to prophesy of Christ? And were it not our purpose to confine the present treatise within the limits of all attainable brevity, it would not be difficult to show, in proof of this statement, out of the Holy Scriptures, how Moses or the prophets both spake and performed all they did through being filled with the Spirit of Christ. And therefore I think it sufficient to quote this one testimony of Paul from the Epistles to the Hebrews, in which he says: "By faith Moses, when he was come to years, refused to be called the son of Pharaoh's daughter; choosing rather to suffer affliction with the people of God, than to enjoy the pleasures of sin for a season; esteeming the reproach of Christ greater riches than the treasures of the Egyptians."² Moreover, that after His ascension into heaven He spake in His apostles, is shown by Paul in these words: "Or do you seek a proof of Christ, who speaketh in me?"³

The apostolic tradition
2. Since many, however, of those who profess to believe in Christ differ from each other, not only in small and trifling matters, but also on subjects of the highest importance, as, e.g., regarding God, or the Lord Jesus Christ, or the Holy Spirit; and not only regarding these, but also regarding others which are created existences, viz., the powers and the holy virtues; it seems on that account necessary first of all to fix a definite limit and to lay down an unmistakeable rule regarding each one of these, and then to pass to the investigation of other points. For as we ceased to seek for truth (notwithstanding the professions of many among Greek and Barbarians to make it known) among all who claimed it for erroneous opinions, after we had come to believe that Christ was the Son of God, and were persuaded that we must learn it from Himself; so, seeing there are many who think they hold the opinions of Christ, and yet some of these think differently from their predecessors, yet as the teaching of

the Church, transmitted in orderly succession from the apostles, and remaining in the Churches to the present day, is still preserved, that alone is to be accepted as truth which differs in no respect from ecclesiastical and apostolical tradition.

The two types of Christians
3. Now it ought to be known that the holy apostles, in preaching the faith of Christ, delivered themselves with the utmost clearness on certain points which they believed to be necessary to every one, even to those who seemed somewhat dull in the investigation of divine knowledge; leaving, however, the grounds of their statements to be examined into by those who would deserve the excellent gifts of the Spirit, and who, especially by means of the Holy Spirit Himself, should obtain the gift of language, of wisdom, and of knowledge: while on other subjects they merely stated the fact that things were so, keeping silence as to the manner or origin of their existence; clearly in order that the more zealous of their successors, who should be lovers of wisdom, might have a subject of exercise on which to display the fruit of their talents,—those persons, I mean, who should prepare themselves to be fit and worthy receivers of wisdom.

The content of the apostolic teaching
4. The particular points clearly delivered in the teaching of the apostles are as follow:—

First, That there is one God, who created and arranged all things, and who, when nothing existed, called all things into being—God from the first creation and foundation of the world—the God of all just men, of Adam, Abel, Seth, Enos, Enoch, Noe, Sem, Abraham, Isaac, Jacob, the twelve patriarchs, Moses, and the prophets; and that this God in the last days, as He had announced beforehand by His prophets, sent our Lord Jesus Christ to call in the first place Israel to Himself, and in the second place the Gentiles, after the unfaithfulness of the people of Israel. This just and good God, the Father of our Lord Jesus Christ, Himself gave the law, and the prophets, and the Gospels, being also the God of the apostles and of the Old and New Testaments.

Secondly, That Jesus Christ Himself, who came (into the world), was born of the Father before all creatures; that, after He had been the servant of the Father in the creation of all things—; "For by Him were all things made"[4]—He in the last times, divesting Himself (of His glory), became a man, and was incarnate although God, and while made a man remained the God which He was; that He assumed a body like our own, differing in this respect only, that it was born of a virgin and of the Holy Spirit: that this Jesus Christ was truly born, and did truly suffer, and did not endure this death common (to man) in appearance only, but did truly die; that He did truly rise from the dead; and that after His resurrection He conversed with His disciples, and was taken up (into heaven).

Then, thirdly, the apostles related that the Holy Spirit was associated in honour and dignity with the Father and the Son. But in His case it is not clearly distinguished whether He is to be regarded as born or innate, or also as a Son of God or not: for these are points which have to be inquired into out of sacred Scripture according to the best of our ability, and which demand careful investigation. And that this Spirit inspired each one of the saints, whether prophets or apostles; and that there was not one Spirit in the men of the old dispensation, and another in those who were inspired at the advent of Christ, is most clearly taught throughout the Churches.

The soul, judgment: heaven and hell
5. After these points, also, the apostolic teaching is that the soul, having a substance and life of its own, shall, after its departure from the world, be rewarded according to its deserts, being destined to obtain either an inheritance of eternal life and blessedness, if its actions shall have procured this for it, or to be deliv-

ered up to eternal fire and punishments, if the guilt of its crimes shall have brought it down to this: and also, that there is to be a time of resurrection from the dead, when this body, which now "is sown in corruption, shall rise in incorruption," and that which "is sown in dishonour will rise in glory."[5] This also is clearly defined in the teaching of the Church, that every rational soul is possessed of free-will and volition; that it has a struggle to maintain with the devil and his angels, and opposing influences, because they strive to burden it with sins; but if we live rightly and wisely, we should endeavour to shake ourselves free of a burden of that kind. From which it follows, also, that we understand ourselves not to be subject to necessity, so as to be compelled by all means, even against our will, to do either good or evil. For if we are our own masters, some influences perhaps may impel us to sin, and others help us to salvation; we are not forced, however, by any necessity either to act rightly or wrongly, which those persons think is the case who say that the courses and movements of the stars are the cause of human actions, not only of those which take place beyond the influence of the freedom of the will, but also of those which are placed within our own power. But with respect to the soul, whether it is derived from the seed by a process of traducianism, so that the reason or substance of it may be considered as placed in the seminal particles of the body themselves, or whether it has any other beginning; and this beginning itself, whether it be by birth or not, or whether bestowed upon the body from without or not, is not distinguished with sufficient clearness in the teaching of the Church.

The devil and his angels
6. Regarding the devil and his angels, and the opposing influences, the teaching of the Church has laid down that these beings exist indeed; but what they are, or how they exist, it has not explained with sufficient clearness. This opinion, however, is held by most, that the

devil was an angel, and that, having become an apostate, he induced as many of the angels as possible to fall away with himself, and these up to the present are called his angels.

Creation

7. This also is a part of the Church's teaching, that the world was made and took its beginning at a certain time, and is to be destroyed on account of its wickedness. But what existed before this world, or what will exist after it, has not become certainly known to the many, for there is no clear statement regarding it in the teaching of the Church.

The Scriptures and its levels of meaning

8. Then, finally, that the Scriptures were written by the Spirit of God, and have a meaning, not such only as is apparent at first sight, but also another, which escapes the notice of most. For those (words) which are written are the forms of certain mysteries, and the images of divine things. Respecting which there is one opinion throughout the whole Church, that the whole law is indeed spiritual; but that the spiritual meaning which the law conveys is not known to all, but to those only on whom the grace of the Holy Spirit is bestowed in the word of wisdom and knowledge. . . .

Items for inquiry

9. We shall inquire, however, whether the thing which Greek philosophers call *asomaton,* or "incorporeal," is found in holy Scripture under another name. For it is also to be a subject of investigation how God himself is to be understood,—whether as corporeal, and formed according to some shape, or of a different nature from bodies,—a point which is not clearly indicated in our teaching. And the same inquires have to be made regarding Christ and the Holy Spirit, as well as respecting every soul, and everything possessed of a rational nature.

Angels

10. This also is a part of the teaching of the Church, that there are certain angels of God, and certain good influences, which are His servants in accomplishing the salvation of men. When these, however, were created, or what nature they are, or how they exist, is not clearly stated. Regarding the sun, moon, and stars, whether they are living beings or without life there is no distinct deliverance.

The project for theology

Every one, therefore, must make use of elements and foundations of this sort, according to the precept, "Enlighten yourselves with the light of knowledge,"[6] if he would desire to form a connected series and body of truths agreeably to the reason of all these things, that by clear and necessary statements he may ascertain the truth regarding each individual topic, and form, as we have said, one body of doctrine, by means of illustrations and arguments,—either those which he has discovered in holy Scripture, or which he has deduced by closely tracing out the consequences and following a correct method. . . .

BOOK I

CHAPTER 1

On God

5. Having refuted, then, as well as we could, every notion which might suggest that we were to think of God as in any degree corporeal, we go on to say that, according to strict truth, God is incomprehensible, and incapable of being measured. For whatever be the knowledge which we are able to obtain of God, either by perception or reflection, we must of necessity believe that He is by many degrees far better than what we perceive Him to be. For, as if we were to see any one unable to bear a spark of light, or the flame of a very small lamp, and were desirous to acquaint such a one, whose vision could not admit a greater degree of light

than what we have stated, with the brightness and splendour of the sun, would it not be necessary to tell him that the splendour of the sun was unspeakably and incalculably better and more glorious than all this light which he saw? So our understanding, when shut in by the fetters of flesh and blood, and rendered, on account of its participation in such material substance, duller and more obtuse, although, in comparison with our bodily nature, it is esteemed to be far superior, yet, in its efforts to examine and behold incorporeal things, scarcely holds the place of a spark or lamp. But among all intelligent, that is, incorporeal beings, what is so superior to all others—so unspeakably and incalculably superior—as God, whose nature cannot be grasped or seen by the power of any human understanding, even the purest and brightest?

6. But it will not appear absurd if we employ another similitude to make the matter clearer. Our eyes frequently cannot look upon the nature of the light itself—that is, upon the substance of the sun; but when we behold his splendour or his rays pouring in, perhaps, through windows or some small openings to admit the light, we can reflect how great is the supply and source of the light of the body. So, in like manner, the works of Divine Providence and the plan of this whole world are a sort of rays, as it were, of the nature of God, in comparison with His real substance and being. As, therefore, our understanding is unable of itself to behold God Himself as he is, it knows the Father of the world from the beauty of His works and the comeliness of His creatures. God, therefore, is not to be thought of as being either a body or as existing in a body, but as an uncompounded intellectual nature, admitting within Himself no addition of any kind; so that He cannot be believed to have within him a greater and a less, but is such that He is in all parts *Monas* ("one"), and, so to speak, *henas*, and is the mind and source from which all intellectual nature or mind takes its beginning.

CHAPTER 6: ON THE END OR
CONSUMMATION

1. An end or consummation would seem to be an indication of the perfection and completion of things. And this reminds us here, that if there be any one imbued with a desire of reading and understanding subjects of such difficulty and importance, he ought to bring to the effort a perfect and instructed understanding, lest perhaps, if he has had no experience in questions of this kind, they may appear to him as vain and superfluous; or if his mind be full of preconceptions and prejudices on other points, he may judge these to be heretical and opposed to the faith of the Church, yielding in so doing not so much to the convictions of reason as to the dogmatism of prejudice. These subjects, indeed, are treated by us with great solicitude and caution, in the manner rather of an investigation and discussion, than in that of fixed and certain decision. For we have pointed out in the preceding pages those questions which must be set forth in clear dogmatic propositions, as I think has been done to the best of my ability when speaking of the Trinity. But on the present occasion our exercise is to be conducted, as we best may, in the style of a disputation rather than of strict definition.

The end of the world, then, and the final consummation, will take place when every one shall be subjected to punishment for his sins; a time which God alone knows, when He will bestow on each one what he deserves. We think, indeed that the goodness of God, through His Christ, may recall all His creatures to one end, even His enemies being conquered and subdued. For thus say holy Scripture, "The Lord said to My Lord, Sit Thou at My right hand, until I make Thine enemies Thy footstool."[7] And if the meaning of the prophet's language here be less clear, we may ascertain it from the Apostle Paul, who speaks more openly, thus: "For Christ must reign until He has put all enemies under His feet."[8] But if even that un-

reserved declaration of the apostle does not sufficiently inform us what is meant by "enemies
being placed under His feet," listen to what he
says in the following words, "For all things
must be put under Him" What, then, is this
"putting under" by which all things must be
made subject to Christ? I am of opinion that it
is this very subjection by which we also wish to
be subject to Him, by which the apostles also
were subject, and all the saints who have been
followers of Christ. For the name "subjection,"
by which we are subject to Christ, indicates
that the salvation which proceeds from Him
belongs to His subjects, agreeably to the declaration of David, "Shall not my soul be subject
unto God? From Him cometh my salvation."[9]

The beginning and the fall of creatures
2. Seeing, then, that such is the end, when all
enemies will be subdued to Christ, when
death—the last enemy—shall be destroyed,
and when the kingdom shall be delivered up by
Christ (to whom all things are subject) to God
the Father; let us, I say, from such an end as
this, contemplate the beginnings of things. For
the end is always like the beginning: and,
therefore, as there is one end to all things, so
ought we to understand that there was one beginning; and as there is one end to many
things, so there spring from one beginning
many differences and varieties, which again,
through the goodness of God, and by subjection
to Christ, and through the unity of the Holy
Spirit, are recalled to one end, which is like
unto the beginning: all those, viz., who, bend-
ing the knee at the name of Jesus, make known
by so doing their subjection to Him: and these
are they who are in heaven, on earth, and under the earth: by which three classes the whole
universe of things is pointed out, those, viz.,
who from that one beginning were arranged,
each according to the diversity of his conduct,
among the different orders, in accordance with
their desert; for there was no goodness in them
by essential being, as in God and His Christ,
and in the Holy Spirit. For in the Trinity alone,

which is the author of all things, does goodness
exist in virtue of essential being; while others
possess it as an accidental and perishable quality, and only then enjoy blessedness, when they
participate in holiness and wisdom, and in divinity itself. But if they neglect and despise
such participation, then is each one, by fault of
his own slothfulness, made, one more rapidly,
another more slowly, one in a greater, another
in a less degree, the cause of his own downfall.
And since, as we have remarked, the lapse by
which an individual falls away from his position is characterized by great diversity, according to the movements of the mind and will, one
man falling with greater ease, another with
more difficulty, into a lower condition; in this
is to be seen the just judgment of the providence of God, that it should happen to every
one according to the diversity of his conduct, in
proportion to the desert of his declension and
defection. Certain of those, indeed, who remained in that beginning which we have described as resembling the end which is to come,
obtained, in the ordering and arrangement of
the world, the rank of angels; others that of influences, others of principalities, others of powers, that they may exercise power over those
who need to have power upon their head. Others, again, received the rank of thrones, having
the office of judging or ruling those who require
this; others dominion, doubtless, over slaves;
all of which are conferred by Divine Providence
in just and impartial judgment according to
their merits, and to the progress which they
had made in the participation and imitation of
God. But those who have been removed from
their primal state of blessedness have not been
removed irrecoverably, but have been placed
under the rule of those holy and blessed orders
which we have described; and by availing
themselves of the aid of these, and being re-
moulded by salutary principles and discipline,
they may recover themselves, and be restored
to their condition of happiness. From all which
I am of opinion, so far as I can see, that this order of the human race has been appointed in or-

der that in the future world, or in ages to come, when there shall be the new heavens and new earth, spoken of by Isaiah, it may be restored to that unity promised by the Lord Jesus in His prayer to God the Father on behalf of His disciples: "I do not pray for these alone, but for all who shall believe on Me through their word: that they all may be one, as Thou, Father, art in Me, and I in Thee, that they also may be one in Us;"[10] and again, when He says: "That they may be one, even as We are one; I in them, and Thou in Me, that they may be made perfect in one."[11] And this is further confirmed by the language of the Apostle Paul: "Until we all come in the unity of the faith to a perfect man, to the measure of the stature of the fulness of Christ."[12] And in keeping with this is the declaration of the same apostle, when he exhorts us, who even in the present life are placed in the Church, in which is the form of that kingdom which is to come, to this same similitude of unity: "That ye all speak the same thing, and that there be no divisions among you; but that ye be perfectly joined together in the same mind and in the same judgment."[13]

The devil and his angels and their possible progressive salvation
3. It is to be borne in mind, however, that certain beings who fell away from that one beginning of which we have spoken, have sunk to such a depth of unworthiness and wickedness as to be deemed altogether undeserving of that training and instruction by which the human race, while in the flesh, are trained and instructed with the assistance of the heavenly powers; and continue, on the contrary, in a state of enmity and opposition to those who are receiving this instruction and teaching. And hence it is that the whole of this mortal life is full of struggles and trials, caused by the opposition and enmity of those who fell from a better condition without at all looking back, and who are called the devil and his angels, and the other orders of evil, which the apostle classed among the opposing powers. But whether any of these orders who act under the government of the devil, and obey his wicked commands, will in a future world be converted to righteousness because of their possessing the faculty of freedom of will, or whether persistent and inveterate wickedness may be changed by the power of habit into nature, is a result which you yourself, reader, may approve of, if neither in these present worlds which are seen and temporal, nor in those which are unseen and are eternal, that portion is to differ wholly from the final unity and fitness of things. But in the meantime, both in those temporal worlds which are seen, as well as in those eternal worlds which are invisible, all those beings are arranged, according to a regular plan, in the order and degree of their merits; so that some of them in the first, others in the second, some even in the last times, after having undergone heavier and severer punishments, endured for a lengthened period, and for many ages, so to speak, improved by this stern method of training, and restored at first by the instruction of the angels, and subsequently by the powers of a higher grade, and thus advancing through each stage to a better condition, reach even to that which is invisible and eternal, having travelled through, by a kind of training, every single office of the heavenly powers. From which, I think, this will appear to follow as an inference, that every rational nature may, in passing from one order to another, go through each to all, and advance from all to each, while made the subject of various degrees of proficiency and failure according to its own actions and endeavours, put forth in the enjoyment of its power of freedom of will.

The transformation of the physical world
4. But since Paul says that certain things are visible and temporal, and others besides these invisible and eternal, we proceed to inquire how those things which are seen are temporal—whether because there will be nothing at all after them in all those periods of the coming world, in which that dispersion and sepa-

ration from the one beginning is undergoing a process of restoration to one and the same end and likeness; or because, while the form of those things which are seen passes away, their essential nature is subject to no corruption. And Paul seems to confirm the latter view, when he says, "For the fashion of this world passeth away."[14] David also appears to assert the same in the words, "The heavens shall perish, but Thou shalt endure; and they all shall wax old as a garment, and Thou shalt change them like a vesture, and like a vestment they shall be changed."[15] For if the heavens are to be changed, assuredly that which is changed does not perish, and if the fashion of the world passes away, it is by no means an annihilation or destruction of their material substance that is shown to take place, but a kind of change of quality and transformation of appearance. Isaiah also, in declaring prophetically that there will be a new heaven and a new earth, undoubtedly suggests a similar view. For this renewal of heaven and earth, and this transmutation of the form of the present world, and this changing of the heavens, will undoubtedly be prepared for those who are walking along that way which we have pointed out above, and are tending to that goal of happiness to which, it is said, even enemies themselves are to be subjected, and in which God is said to be "all in all." And if any one imagine that at the end material, i.e., bodily, nature will be entirely destroyed, he cannot in any respect meet my view, how beings so numerous and powerful are able to live and to exist without bodies, since it is an attribute of the divine nature alone—i.e., of the Father, Son, and Holy Spirit—to exist without any material substance, and without partaking in any degree of a bodily adjunct. Another, perhaps, may say that in the end every bodily substance will be so pure and refined as to be like the aether, and of a celestial purity and clearness. How things will be, however, is known with certainty to God alone, and to those who are His friends through Christ and the Holy Spirit.

BOOK IV

CHAPTER I

The three levels of meaning in Scripture
11. The way, then, as it appears to us, in which we ought to deal with the Scriptures, and extract from them their meaning, is the following, which has been ascertained from the Scriptures themselves. By Solomon in the Proverbs we find some such rule as this enjoined respecting the divine doctrines of Scriptures: "And do thou portray them in a threefold manner, in counsel and knowledge, to answer words of truth to them who propose them to thee."[16] The individual ought, then, to portray the ideas of holy Scripture in a threefold manner upon his own soul; in order that the simple man may be edified by the "flesh," as it were, of the Scripture, for so we name the obvious sense; while he who has ascended a certain way (may be edified) by the "soul," as it were. The perfect man, again, and he who resembles those spoken of by the apostle, when he says, "We speak wisdom among them that are perfect, but not the wisdom of the world, nor of the rulers of this world, who come to nought; but we speak the wisdom of God in a mystery, the hidden wisdom, which God hath ordained before the ages, unto our glory,"[17] (may receive edification) from the spiritual law, which has a shadow of good things to come. For as man consists of body, and soul, and spirit, so in the same way does Scripture, which has been arranged to be given by God for the salvation of men.

NOTES

[1]John 14:6
[2]Heb 11:24-25

³2 Cor 13:3
⁴John 1:3
⁵1Cor 15:42–43
⁶Hos 10:12
⁷Ps 110:1
⁸1 Cor 15:25
⁹Ps 62:1
¹⁰John 17:20–21
¹¹John 17:22-23
¹²Eph 4:13
¹³1 Cor 1:10
¹⁴1 Cor 7:31
¹⁵Ps 102:26
¹⁶Prov 22:20-21
¹⁷1 Cor 2:6-7

ATHANASIUS: *THE INCARNATION OF THE WORD OF GOD* (THE ARIAN CONTROVERSY)

The question of accommodation of Christianity with the world view of Hellenistic philosophy came to a climax in Christological and Trinitarian controversies of the fourth and fifth centuries C.E. The Christian faith as expressed in the New Testament had affirmed that in Christ God had acted to save humanity from sin. This faith was expressed primarily in language drawn from the categories of first-century Jewish thinking which used apocalyptic and traditional Israelite terminology to refer to Jesus and the salvation achieved by his death and resurrection. As Christian faith developed in the second, third and fourth centuries, the challenge that faced Christian theologians was how to be faithful to the expression of faith in salvation through Christ found in the New Testament and at the same time to speak in language that answered the philosophical questions raised by Christian believers who were educated in the Hellenistic philosophy of the day.

In an effort to maintain the Jewish doctrine of monotheism and at the same time be faithful to the New Testament expressions of faith which spoke of Christ as Son of God and of the Holy Spirit of God which was given to the Church in the last days, Christian theologians and Church councils eventually formulated the distinctive Christian paradoxical beliefs in the full divinity and humanity of Christ and the Trinity: the belief in one God who is at the same time eternally Father, Son, and Spirit. In developing these dogmatic formulations of Christian faith, the early Christian churches were frequently and bitterly divided between East and West, between various sees like Antioch and Alexandria, and even within local congregations. It is a tribute to the institutional strength and intellectual and spiritual vigor of the Church that it was eventually able, through a series of ecumenical councils, to come to statements of its beliefs in these difficult areas.

In retrospect we can discover certain principles that seem to have been operative in solving these disputes. First of all, proposed doctrines were not to contradict the Scriptures: both the faith in the one Creator God who revealed himself in the Old Testament and the saving action of Christ spoken of in the books of the New Testament. A second principle was that any doctrine which seemed to endanger the Christian belief in salvation for humanity through Christ's death and resurrection was to be rejected. Finally, the expressions of Christian faith which had developed in the liturgy, like the creeds affirmed by the faithful in baptism or the prayers used in the Eucharist, were not to be contradicted.

By the third century C.E. Christian theologians had already begun to employ Greek philosophical concepts in discussing the faith. We have seen how Justin Martyr made the all-important step of identifying the Logos concept of the Stoics with the Logos of John's Gospel. For the Stoics the Logos was the divine reason or mind which organizes, creates and directs all things. It was clearly subordinate to the highest divine principle. And in Justin's summary of Christian doctrine about God in his **First Apology,** Christ and the Spirit do appear to be subordinate in divinity to the Father. Irenaeus also called Christ the Logos, the complete revelation of the Father's love, but in opposition to the Gnostic notion of emanation he affirmed the eternal co-existence of the Logos with the Father. Concerning the production or "begetting" of the Son from the Father, Irenaeus believed it was indescribable.

> If any one, therefore, says to us, "How then was the Son produced by the Father?" we reply to him, that no man understands that production, or generation, or calling, or revelation, or by whatever name one may describe His generation, which is in fact altogether indescribable . . . " (**Against Heresies**, II. ch. 28. 6)

In Rome in the early third century C.E. three theologians (Noetus, Praxeas, and Sabellius) attempted what proved to be a simplistic solution to the problem of reconciling the notion of monotheism with Christian Trinitarian beliefs. Their theory is called modalism or Sabellianism. They denied the permanence in the distinctions between Father, Son, and Holy Spirit. According to them, the one God had manifested himself in three successive modes in history: as Father, then as Son, and finally as Holy Spirit. Such a solution did not do justice to the evidence of the New Testament where there is a clear distinction between the Father and the Son in a number of texts where, for example, the Father says of Jesus, "This is my beloved Son" (Mk 9:7) or Jesus says of his Father, "The Father is greater than I" (Jn 14:28). In his tract, **Against Praxeas** Tertullian tried to maintain the unity of one God and at the same time a belief in the divinity of the Son and Holy Spirit by using a series of metaphors drawn from nature to give some indication of how the Father produces the Son and Spirit. He refers to the root producing a shoot, the spring producing a river, or the sun producing a ray of light in the following section.

> For God produced the Word, as the Paraclete also teaches, as a root produces the shoot, a spring the river, the sun a ray: for these manifestations are 'projections' of those substances from which they proceed. I would not hesitate to call a shoot 'the son of a root', a river 'the son of a spring', a ray 'a son of the Sun'. For every original source is a parent, and what is produced is its offspring. Much more is this true of the Word of God, who re-

ceived the name of Son as his proper designation. . . . Thus in accordance with those analogies I confess that I speak of two, God and his Word, the Father and his Son. For root and shoot are two, but conjoined. . . . Everything that proceeds from anything must needs be another thing, but it is not therefore separate. When there is one other, there are two; where there is a third, there are three. The Spirit makes the third from God and the Son, as the fruit from the shoot is the third from the tree, the canal from the river the third from the source, the point of focus of a ray third from the sun. But none of those is divorced from the origin from which it derives its own qualities. Thus the Trinity derives from the Father by continuous and connected steps; and it in no way impugns the monarchy while it preserves the reality of the (economy). (**Against Praxeas,** 8)

As is evident from the above, Tertullian's metaphor succeeds in preserving the idea of monotheism, but at the expense of subordinating the Word or Son and Spirit to the Father. Does this mean that they are lesser divinities than God the Father?

The question of the divinity of Christ came to a head in the Arian controversy of the fourth century C.E. which broke out in the Church of Alexandria and rapidly polarized the Churches in the eastern part of the empire. The controversy began as dispute between a local presbyter, Arius, and his elderly and saintly bishop Alexander. At issue was the nature of the Word or Logos; Arius, heavily influenced by the Christology of Origen, tended to subordinate the Logos to the Father. He began with two basic premises which are rooted in Neo-Platonic philosophy rather than in the Scriptures: (1) that God the Father is absolutely unique and (2) that he is totally other than the rest of reality. As such the Father was more like the One of Plotinus than the Father whom Jesus had called "Abba." He was the unoriginate source of all reality, but he never acted in history as the biblical God had. His being or essence, because other and unique, could not be shared by anyone else. The Father, in this view, was completely aloof from the world of becoming. Everything else came into being as an act of creation. God did not share anything of his being with anyone else because of his transcendence and uniqueness.

Beginning with these premises, Arius concluded that the Word, through whom the world was made and who became incarnate in Jesus, was a creature. He was begotten and therefore, said Arius, created. The Father alone was unoriginate and unbegotten and therefore uncreated. The Word had a beginning. There was "then when he was not." Arius avoided speaking of a time when he was not in order to distinguish the Logos from other creatures, a device that was quickly called into question by those who opposed his teaching. Arius wanted to situate the Word above other creatures and yet on the side of creatures vis-à-vis the Father. If the Word had no beginning there would have been two self-existent principles, and this would have contradicted the Christian belief in monotheism.

Arius also concluded that the Son had no strict communion with and no direct knowledge of the Father. He was God's Word and Wisdom, but he was distinct from the Father's very essence. He was, Arius insisted, "alien from and utterly dissimilar to the Father's essence and individual being." Evidence of the essential difference between the Father and Son was the fact that the Son was liable to change, to sin and imperfection, and God himself was immutable and impassible (incapable of suffering).

Arius drew upon the Scriptures, interpreted in a literal sense, to support his position. He saw support for his position in the Old Testament text in Proverbs 8:22–31 in which Wisdom, which was traditionally identified with the Logos, spoke in the following manner:

> The Lord created me at the beginning of his
> work,
> the first of his acts of old.
> Ages ago I was set up,
> at the first, before the beginning of the earth.
> When there were no depths I was brought
> forth . . .

Arius also pointed to New Testament texts which subordinate Christ to God the Father by referring to him as "first-born among many" (Rom 8:29), "the first-born of all creation" (Col 1:15), and Jesus' statement that "the Father is greater than I" (Jn 14:28).

The point at issue in Arius' position was not just the status of the Word, but the nature of the Christian God himself. Arius never speaks of the love of God. In the Neo-Platonic philosophy which had influenced Arius there was no way in which the One could share its nature with anything else, and it was precisely at this point that Neo-Platonism could not do justice to the Christian conception of God. For Arius God was remote, inaccessible, incapable of directly approaching the created world. And thus it was not the eternal God himself who had revealed himself to Moses, who had spoken through the prophets, and who had finally come in Christ for human salvation. For Arius, the Word was an intermediate being, a kind of demi-god, distinct from God, and God himself was not involved in creation or redemption. He was left out, uncondescending, and uncaring.

The key figure in upholding the orthodox position against Arius was Athanasius (c. 293-373 C.E.) who began as a young deacon and assistant to Bishop Alexander and eventually succeeded him as bishop of Alexandria. Our selections are taken from Athanasius **The Incarnation of the Word of God.** According to Athanasius, Arius' Christology was inadequate for explaining the biblical belief in the goodness of God and the salvation of humanity through the death and resurrection of Jesus. For Athanasius, who also thought in Greek categories, salvation involved the change of sinful mortality into divine immortality though the gift of eternal life. Only if Jesus was both fully man and also fully God could the transformation of humanity to divinity have taken place in him. As he says in our selection from **The Incarnation of the Word of God,** "Christ was made man that we might be made divine." The union of the Divine Word with humanity restored the image of God lost in the Fall, and the resurrection wiped out death, the consequence of sin. Athanasius thought that Arius' creature Christ led to a fatalism, the same fatalism found in the decadent Roman culture of the day. Without the divinity and humanity of Christ, apart from the incarnation and the resurrection, humanity is still trapped in the cyclic determinism of Hellenistic philosophy.

The translation is by Archibald Robertson in **Select Writings and Letters of Athanasius, Bishop of Alexandria**, Vol. 4 in **The Nicene and Post-Nicene Fathers** (New York: Charles Scribner's Sons, 1903) 39-41.

THE INCARNATION OF THE WORD

The situation of humanity before the coming of Christ

6. For this cause, then, death having gained upon men, and corruption abiding upon them, the race of man was perishing; the rational man made in God's image was disappearing, and the handiwork of God was in process of dissolution. For death, as I said above, gained from that time forth a legal hold over us, and it was impossible to evade the law, since it had been laid down by God because of the transgression, and the result was in truth at once monstrous and unseemly. For it were monstrous, firstly, that God having spoken, should prove false—that, when once He had ordained that man, if he transgressed the commandment, should die the death, after the transgression man should not die, but God's word should be broken. For God would not be true, if, when He had said we should die, man died not. Again, it were unseemly that creatures once made rational, and having partaken of the Word, should go to ruin, and turn again toward non-existence by the way of corruption. For it were not worthy of God's goodness that the things He had made should waste away, because of the deceit practised on men by the devil. Especially it was unseemly to the last degree that God's handicraft among men should be done away, either because of their own carelessness, or because of the deceitfulness of evil spirits. So, as the rational creatures were wasting and such works in course of ruin what was God in His goodness to do? Suffer corruption to prevail against them and death to hold them fast? And where was the profit of their having been made, to begin with? For better were they not made, than once made, left to neglect and ruin. For neglect reveals weakness, and not goodness on God's part—if, that is, He allows His own work to be ruined when once He had made it—more so than if He have never made man at all. For if He had not made them, none could impute weakness; but once He had made them, and created them out of nothing, it were most monstrous for the work to be ruined, and that before the eyes of the Maker. It was, then, out of the question to leave men to the current of corruption; because this would be unseemly, and unworthy of God's goodness.

Only God's Word could renew His creation

7. But just as this consequence must needs hold, so, too, on the other side the just claims of God lie against it: that God should appear true to the law He had laid down concerning death. For it were monstrous for God, the Father of truth, to appear a liar for our profit and preservation. So here, once more, what possible course was God to take? To demand repentance of men for their transgression? For this one might pronounce worthy of God; as though, just as from transgression men have become set towards corruption, so from repentance they may once more be set in the way of incorruption. But repentance would, firstly, fail to guard the just claim of God. For He would still be none the more true, if men did not remain in the grasp of death; nor, secondly, does repentance call men back from what is their nature—it merely stays them from acts of sin. Now, if there were merely a misdemeanour in question, and not a consequent corruption, repentance were well enough. But if, when transgression had once gained a start, men became involved in that corruption which was their nature, and were deprived of the grace which they had, being in the image of God,

what further step was needed? or what was required for such grace and such recall, but the
Word of God, which had also at the beginning
made everything out of nought? For His it was
once more both to bring the corruptible to incorruption, and to maintain intact the just
claim of the Father upon all. For being Word of
the Father, and above all, He alone of natural
fitness was both able to recreate everything,
and worthy to suffer on behalf of all and to be
ambassador for all with the Father.

The purpose of the Incarnation
8. For this purpose, then, the incorporeal and
incorruptible and immaterial Word of God
comes to our realm, howbeit he was not far
from us before. For no part of Creation is left
void of Him: He has filled all things everywhere, remaining present with His own Father. But he comes in condescension to show
loving-kindness upon us, and to visit us. And
seeing the race of rational creatures in the way
to perish, and death reigning over them by corruption; seeing, too, that the threat against
transgression gave a firm hold to the corruption which was upon us, and that it was monstrous that before the law was fulfilled it
should fall through: seeing, once more, the un-
seemliness of what was come to pass: that the
things whereof He Himself was Artificer were
passing away: seeing, further, the exceeding
wickedness of men, and how by little and little
they had increased it to an intolerable pitch
against themselves: and seeing, lastly, how all
men were under penalty of death: He took pity
on our race, and had mercy on our infirmity,
and condescended to our corruption, and unable to bear that death should have the mas-
tery—lest the creature should perish, and His
Father's handiwork in men be spent for
nought—He takes unto Himself a body, and
that of no different sort from ours. For He did
not simply will to become embodied, or will
merely to appear. For if He willed merely to appear, he was able to effect His divine appearance by some other and higher means as well.

But He takes a body of our kind, and not
merely so, but from a spotless and stainless virgin, knowing not a man, a body clean and in
very truth pure from intercourse of men. For
being Himself mighty and Artificer of everything, He prepares the body in the Virgin as a
temple unto Himself, and makes it His very
own as an instrument, in it manifested and in
it dwelling. And thus taking from our bodies
one of like nature, because all were under penalty of the corruption of death He gave it over
to death in the stead of all, and offered it to the
Father—doing this, moreover, of His loving-
kindness, to the end that, firstly, all being held
to have died in Him, the law involving the ruin
of men might be undone (inasmuch as its power
was fully spent in the Lord's body, and had no
longer holding-ground against men, his peers),
and that, secondly, whereas men had turned
toward corruption, He might turn them again
toward incorruption, and quicken them from
death by the appropriation of His body and by
the grace of the Resurrection, banishing death
from them like straw from the fire.

*The Word by His death has gained for
humanity immortality*
9. For the Word, perceiving that no otherwise
could the corruption of men be undone save by
death as a necessary condition, while it was impossible for the Word to suffer death, being immortal, and Son of the Father; to this end He
takes to Himself a body capable of death, that
it, by partaking of the Word Who is above all,
might be worthy to die in the stead of all, and
might, because of the Word which was come to
dwell in it, remain incorruptible, and that
thenceforth corruption might be stayed from
all by the Grace of the Resurrection. Whence,
by offering unto death the body He Himself had
taken, as an offering and sacrifice free from
any stain, straightway He put away death
from all His peers by the offering of an equivalent. For being over all, the Word of God naturally by offering His own temple and
corporeal instrument for the life of all satisfied

the debt by His death. And thus He, the incorruptible Son of God, being conjoined with all by a like nature, naturally clothed all with incorruption, by the promise of the resurrection. For the actual corruption in death has no longer holding-ground against men, by reason of the Word, which by His one body has come to dwell among them. And like as when a great king has entered into some large city and taken up his abode in one of the houses there, such city is at all events held worthy of high honour, nor does any enemy or bandit any longer descend upon it and subject it; but, on the contrary, it is thought entitled to all care, because of the king's having taken up his residence in a single house there: so, too, has it been with the Monarch of all. For now that He has come to our realm, and taken up his abode in one body among His peers, henceforth the whole conspiracy of the enemy against mankind is checked, and the corruption of death which before was prevailing against them is done away. For the race of men had gone to ruin, had not the Lord and Saviour of all, the Son of God, come among us to meet the end of death.

THE COUNCIL OF NICAEA (THE REJECTION OF ARIANISM)

The Arian controversy over the nature of Christ rapidly polarized the Church in the eastern part of the Empire. The division was so great that the emperor Constantine intervened by calling a council of bishops at Nicaea in Asia Minor near the city of Constantinople. When Constantine had legalized Christianity in 313 C.E., he fully expected this relatively new and vibrant religion to unify the empire that badly needed a new start. He seems to have envisioned Christianity as a new state religion, something that was antithetical to its very nature. In the third century C.E. in the seventy years prior to the reign of Diocletian there had been twenty-three emperors, and twenty of them had been assassinated. The empire was not politically stable, and Constantine hoped that the new religion would contribute to its stability. As sincere as his conversion may or may not have been, Constantine was willing to use force both within and outside the Christian Church to achieve peace and unity. He had already taken up the sword in the name of the cross in the Donatist controversy in North Africa, and now again in 325 C.E. he intervened in what was an internal Church affair. His purpose was to promote unity and peace in the empire, but his behavior after the council indicates that he did not grasp the theological issues that were involved.

The council of Nicaea was attended by over two hundred bishops, most of them from the East. Nicaea would later be judged to be the first of seven ecumenical (or universal) councils of the Church, and it was thought to be a notable event for the Church at the time. Bishops and churchmen who had been persecuted under Diocletian were now received with honor by the emperor. Silvester the bishop of Rome did not attend but sent two Roman presbyters as his representatives. At the solemn opening ceremonies Constantine exhorted the bishops to strive for unity and peace.

After each of the bishops expressed his views on the incarnation, Arius was allowed to explain his own teachings. The creed which the council fathers agreed upon condemned the position of Arius as not adequately expressing the New Testament belief that "God was in Christ reconciling the world unto himself" (2 Cor 5:19), and sided with the position of Athanasius that the Divine Word became man in order that humans might become divine. In order to express the divinity of the Word as truly divine in the same sense as the Father, the council fathers used the Greek term *homoousios,* "the same substance," or the same nature. This was not a scriptural term, but one drawn from the language of Greek philosophy to answer the difficult philosophical question raised by Arius which could not be answered simply by a repetition of creedal language drawn from the New Testament. The creed describes Christ, the Son of God, as begotten of the Father, but clearly excludes the idea that this implies that Christ is a creature like us. The creed, in conformity with the New Testament *kerygma,* also insists on the salvific work achieved by the Divine Son, and his expected return to judge the living and the dead. In a surprising show of unity two hundred and eighteen of the bishops present signed the creed.

The translation is by Henry R. Percival in **The Seven Ecumenical Councils**, Vol. 14 in **Nicene and Post-Nicene Fathers** (New York: Charles Scribner's Sons, 1900) 3.

The Nicene Creed

> We believe in one God, the Father Almighty, Maker of all things visible and invisible; and in one Lord Jesus Christ, the Son of God, the only-begotten of his Father, of the substance of the Father, God of God, Light of Light, very God of very God, begotten, not made, being of one substance (*homoousion*) with the Father. By whom all things were made, both which be in heaven and in earth. Who for us men and for our salvation came down [from heaven] and was incarnate and was made man. He suffered and the third day he rose again, and ascended into heaven. And he shall come again to judge both the quick and the dead.
>
> And [we believe] in the Holy Ghost.
>
> And whosoever shall say that there was a time when the Son of God was not, or that before he was begotten he was not, or that he was made of things that were not, or that he is of a different substance or essence [from the Father] or that he is a creature, or subject to change or conversion—all that so say, the Catholic and Apostolic Church anathematizes them.

THE COUNCIL OF CHALCEDON (LATER CHRISTOLOGICAL CONTROVERSY)

After the council of Nicaea the orthodox position was not universally accepted. Part of the problem was due to the lack of unanimity in understanding the key term *homoousios.* To some it meant a personal or specific identity, but to others simply a much broader, generic identity. Arianism persisted and spread through the fourth century C.E., and Constantine himself was baptized by an Arian bishop. Some of the later emperors were either Arians or sympathetic to that view, and Athanasius was frequently exiled from his position as bishop of Alexandria for steadfastly maintaining the Nicene position. During this period some of the most successful missionaries to the barbarian tribes in the north were Arians, with the result that many of the tribes who entered the empire in the fifth century came in as Arian Christians. Within the empire Arianism was not ended as a serious threat until Emperor Theodosius called the council of Constantinople in 381 which reiterated the Nicene position.

In the fifth century Christological controversies in the East centered on the problem of how the human and divine natures could be united in the one *hypostasis* (person) of Christ. There were two basic schools of theological thought in the East: Antioch in Syria and Alexandria in Egypt. Each shared certain theological convictions, but also had distinctive approaches to Christology. Both, influenced by the Neo-Platonic philosophy of the day, understood the divine nature as absolute and impassible as opposed to the finite and changing character of human nature. Both also believed that the incarnate Christ had brought salvation for fallen humanity. Despite these similarities, their respective understandings of the incarnation and the process of salvation differed. Alexandria was heavily influenced by Platonism and had what has been called a "Word-flesh" or descending Christology; the divine Logos took to himself human flesh in order to deify humanity which had lost the gift of immortality. Antioch was more influenced by Aristotelian philosophy and had what has been called a "Word-man" or ascending Christology; the divine Logos indwelt in a full human person, Christ, in order to renew or restore a fallen humanity.

Each of these Christologies had their dangers and led to exaggerated positions which were condemned by Church councils. Alexandrian Christology stressed the unity of Christ as a single *hypostasis* or person. Its tendency was to lessen the reality and completeness of Christ's humanity. This happened in the theology of Apollonarius (died 390 C.E.). He insisted on the divinity of the Son and his full equality with the Father, but he so explained the unity of the divine and the human in Christ that he denied the rational human soul in Jesus. Christ had a human body, but the divine mind of the Logos. His position was challenged by theologians from Antioch, especially Theodore of Mopsuestia, who pointed out that Apollinarius' Christology contradicted the passages in the gospels in which, for example, Jesus is said to have "grown in wisdom" (cf. Lk 2:52). Apollinarius' position was rejected at the council of Constantinople in 381 C.E.

The school of Antioch, on the other hand, stressed the reality and distinctness of both natures in Christ. The tendency of its approach was to so emphasize the distinction between the human and divine natures in Christ as to make him virtually two beings. This actually happened in the teaching of Nestorius, patriarch of Constantinople, who objected to calling Jesus' mother Mary "the Mother of God" (*theotokos*). For Nestorius Mary was only the mother of Christ, that is, of the human nature in Christ. Nestorius' position went against the faith of Eastern Christians who had been referring to Mary as *theotokos* in their prayer for over a century. His Christology was condemned at the council of Ephesus in 431 C.E. which anathematized anyone who did not confess that "the Holy Virgin is the Mother of God (*theotokos*), in as much as in the flesh she bore the Word of God made flesh . . ."

In the years after the council of Ephesus Eutyches, an aged abbot who lived and taught near Constantinople, under the influence of Alexandrian Christology, began to teach the doctrine called Monophysitism (one nature in Christ). Eutyches said that there were two natures before the incarnation but only one nature after the union, that is, one concrete existence. This was his attempt to explain the unity of Christ and yet to preserve the divinity and humanity. Unfortunately Eutyches' position was approved in a council at Ephesus in 449 which was presided over by Dioscurus, the bishop of Alexandria. This so-called "Robber Council" was opposed by, among others, Pope Leo I in the West who wrote to Flavian, the patriarch of Constantinople, that the teaching of Eutyches was unacceptable. Leo insisted that the person of the God-Man was identical with the person of the Word. He also insisted, like the theologians of Antioch, that in Jesus there were two natures, neither mixed nor confused. Each nature retained its own properties. By nature Leo meant principle of operation. Leo did not explain how these two natures are one in Christ, but simply insisted that both are fully present. The Council of Chalcedon met in 451 C.E. and adopted, among other documents, Leo's letter to Flavian to express its faith in the mystery of Christ. It asserted that Christ was both God and man, that is, he had both a divine and a human nature. He is one in substance with the Father as to his divinity and one substance with man as to his humanity. Both natures are united in one *hypostasis* or "person." This paradoxical solution to the Christological problem does not state how the two natures are united in Christ; it simply outlines the limits of any orthodox Christology. Although the Christological debates in the fourth and fifth centuries may seem excessively abstract to a twentieth-century student, it is important not to lose sight of the fact that in these disputes the councils were trying to clarify the belief that in Jesus Christ God really entered into human history and achieved human salvation.

The translation is from **The Seven Ecumenical Councils**, Vol. 14 in **The Nicene and Post-Nicene Fathers,** 262–265.

The Definition of Faith of the Council of Chalcedon

Following the holy Fathers we teach with one voice that the Son [of God] and our Lord Jesus Christ is to be confessed as one and the same [Person], that he is perfect in Godhead and perfect in manhood, very God and very man, of a reasonable soul and [human] body consisting, consubstantial with the Father as touching his Godhead, and consubstantial with us as touching his manhood; made in all things like unto us, sin only excepted; begotten of his Father before the worlds according to his Godhead; but in these last days for us men and for our salvation born [into the world] of the Virgin Mary, the Mother of God according to his manhood. This one and the same Jesus Christ, the only-begotten Son [of God] must be confessed to be in two natures, unconfusedly, immutably, indivisibly, inseparably [united], and that without the distinction of natures being taken away by such union, but rather the peculiar property of each nature being preserved and being united in one Person and subsistence, not separated or divided into two persons, but one and the same Son and only-begotten, God the Word, our Lord Jesus Christ, as the Prophets of old time have spoken concerning him, and as the Lord Jesus Christ hath taught us, and as the Creed of the Fathers hath delivered to us.

These things, therefore, having been expressed by us with the greatest accuracy and attention, the holy Ecumenical Synod defines that no one shall be suffered to bring forward a different faith, nor to write, nor to put together, nor to excogitate, nor to teach to others. But such as dare either to put together another faith, or to bring forward or to teach or to de-liver a different Creed to such as wish to be converted to the knowledge of the truth from the Gentiles or Jews or any heresy whatever, if they be Bishops or clerics let them be deposed, the Bishops from the Episcopate, and the clerics from the clergy; but if they be monks or laics: let them be anathematized.

ATHANASIUS: *THE LIFE OF ANTONY* (THE BEGINNINGS OF CHRISTIAN MONASTICISM)

With the cessation of the persecutions and the recognition of Christianity as an official religion by Constantine in the early fourth century C.E., Christians found a new form of spiritual martyrdom and heroism in the movement of monasticism. Heroic detachment from "this world" had been a characteristic of Paul's apocalyptic theology in the middle of the first century C.E., because he lived in expectation of the imminent coming of Jesus in glory to complete the kingdom of God (cf. 1 Corinthians 7). The persecutions of the second and third centuries kept alive a martyr's sense of moving through this world as a pilgrim on the way to union with God. As early as the second century, individual Christians were also living as celibates and with a minimum of possessions, but there were no organized monastic movements like the Essenes from Qumran or the Jewish sect of the Therapeutae in Egypt whom Philo describes with admiration.

By the middle of the third century C.E. the deserts of Egypt and Syria were already inhabited by Christian hermits. The reasons for their reversing, as it were, the movement of civilization by withdrawal from the cities and returning to the desert/wilderness were extremely varied. Some sought to continue the martyr-like way of life by seeking new forms of heroic self-denial. Others were influenced by the philosophical thought of late antiquity like Neo-Platonism which emphasized the need to turn away from the physical world in order to purify the soul. Economic and social conditions like high taxation and disillusionment with the social chaos in the cities of the third and fourth centuries also contributed.

One of the earliest and most influential of the early Christian hermits was Antony of Egypt (c. 251–356 C.E.) who was greatly revered in his own lifetime and had a lasting impact upon Christian monasticism through his biography, the **Life of Antony,** which was written by St. Athanasius who met him late in his life and wrote the work c. 356–362 as a guide for monks who wished to imitate Antony. In the work Athanasius is consciously trying to portray Antony as a heroic model of individual asceticism who was at the same time an orthodox member of the Church. One of the consistent dangers of early monasticism was that its adherents might separate themselves wholly from the local community under the bishop and from the sacramental life of the Church, and easily lapse into one of the various forms of heresy. Athanasius' **Life of Antony** was destined to have a lasting impact on Western monasticism. It was translated into Latin by Evagrius (c. 364–373

C.E.) and in Rome and all over the West it inspired many with the desire to become monks; it awoke in Augustine the resolution to renounce the world and give himself wholly to God (cf. **Confessions Book VIII**).

Athanasius begins his narrative with the youth of Antony who was born to an Egyptian family of substantial means. He emphasizes Antony's orthodox piety, obedience to his parents and the fact that, although attentive to what was read, he was illiterate.

Athanasius' account of Antony's call has become a classic model for monastic and religious vocations in the Western Christian tradition. It came from hearing Jesus' gospel injunction addressed to the rich young man: "If thou wouldest be perfect, go and sell that thou hast and give to the poor; and come follow me and thou shalt have treasure in heaven" (Mt 18:21). Because his parents had died a short time before, Antony was in a position to fulfill this command literally. He gave his father's lands to the villagers, sold his movable goods and distributed the money to the poor. After placing his sister in the care of virgins in a local convent, he began to live a life of solitude within his village.

Athanasius' portrayal of the early monastic life of Antony stresses his heroic pursuit of discipline (*askesis*) and his battle with the devil to overcome the allurements of life in the civilized world. There is almost an ancient Greek sense of competition and individual *arete* in the way that Antony observes the practices of other hermits and strives to incorporate them into his own discipline. The frequent conflicts with the devil are reminiscent of Jesus' temptations in the desert in the gospel tradition, and Athanasius stresses that the power to reject the temptations to wealth, family, glory, and the pleasures of life came from Christ.

Gradually Antony withdrew further and further from civilized society in his pursuit of a life of gospel discipline until he was living in inaccessible tombs in the desert. After twenty years as a solitary, Antony reappeared and organized the monks who were attracted to him into a loose community of hermits living under a rule. Our selection includes the first part of his address to the monks in Coptic. The selection emphasizes that the Scriptures form the basis of the monastic life. Antony encourages the monks to be steadfast in their commitment to their life in light of the shortness of life on earth in comparison with eternity.

Our final selection is Athanasius' account of Antony's rejection of various schisms and heresies and his refutation of the Arians. His speech to the Arians reflects Athanasius' own theological reasoning, although there is no reason to doubt that Antony did oppose Arianism.

The translation is by Rev. H. Ellershaw, **Life of Antony** in **Select Writings and Letters of Athanasius, Bishop of Alexandria, Vol. IV** in **Nicene and Post-Nicene Fathers of the Christian Church,** 188–221.

Prologue

The life and conversation of our holy Father, Antony: written and sent to the monks in foreign parts by our Father among the Saints, Athanasius, Bishop of Alexandria.

You have entered upon a noble rivalry with the monks of Egypt by your determination either to equal or surpass them in your training in the way of virtue. For by this time there are monasteries among you, and the name of monk receives public recognition. With reason, therefore, all men will approve this determination, and in answer to your prayers God will give its fulfilment. Now since you asked me to give you an account of the blessed Antony's way of life, and are wishful to learn how he began the discipline, who and what manner of man he was previous to this, how he closed his life, and whether the things told of him are true, that you also may bring yourselves to imitate him, I very readily accepted your behest, for to me also the bare recollection of Antony is a great accession of help. And I know that you, when you have heard, apart from your admiration of the man, will be wishful to emulate his determination; seeing that for monks the life of Antony is sufficient pattern of discipline.

Antony's birth and beginnings

1. Anthony you must know was by descent an Egyptian: his parents were of good family and possessed considerable wealth, and as they were Christians he also was reared in the same Faith. In infancy he was brought up with his parents, knowing nought else but them and his home. But when he was grown and arrived at boyhood, and was advancing in years, he could not endure to learn letters, not caring to associate with other boys; but all his desire was, as it is written of Jacob, to live a plain man at home. With his parents he used to attend the Lord's House, and neither as a child was he idle nor when older did he despise them; but was both obedient to his father and mother and attentive to what was read, keeping in his heart what was profitable in what he heard. And though as a child brought up in moderate affluence, he did not trouble his parents for varied or luxurious fare, nor was this a source of pleasure to him; but was content simply with what he found nor sought anything further.

The call

2. After the death of his father and mother he was left alone with one little sister: his age was about eighteen or twenty, and on him the care both of home and sister rested. Now it was not six months after the death of his parents, and going according to custom into the Lord's House, he communed with himself and reflected as he walked how the Apostles left all and followed the Saviour;[1] and how they in Acts[2] sold their possessions and bought and laid them at the Apostles' feet for distribution to the needy, and what and how great a hope was laid up for them in heaven. Pondering over these things he entered the church, and it happened the Gospel was being read, and he heard the Lord saying to the rich man,[3] 'If thou wouldest be perfect, to and sell that thou hast and give to the poor; and come follow Me and thou shalt have treasure in heaven.' Antony, as though God had put him in mind of the Saints, and the passage had been read on his account, went out immediately from the church, and gave the possessions of his forefathers to the villagers—they were three hundred acres, productive and very fair—that they should be no more a clog upon himself and his sister. And all the rest that was movable he sold, and having got together much money he gave it to the poor, reserving a little however for his sister's sake.

3. And again as he went into the church, hearing the Lord say in the Gospel,[4] 'be not anxious for the morrow,' he could stay no longer, but went out and gave those things also to the poor. Having committed his sister to known and faithful virgins, and put her into a convent to be brought up, he henceforth devoted himself outside his house to discipline, taking heed to himself and training himself with patience. For there were not yet so many monasteries in Egypt, and no monk at all knew of the distant desert; but all who wished to give heed to themselves practised the discipline in solitude near their own village. Now there was then in the next village an old man who had lived the life of a hermit from his youth up. Antony, after he had seen this man, imitated him in piety. And at first he began to abide in places

outside the village: then if he heard of a good man anywhere, like the prudent bee, he went forth and sought him, nor turned back to his own place until he had seen him; and he returned, having got from the good man as it were supplies for his journey in the way of virtue. So dwelling there at first, he confirmed his purpose not to return to the abode of his fathers nor to the remembrance of his kinsfolk; but to keep all his desire and energy for perfecting his discipline. He worked, however, with his hands, having heard, 'he who is idle let him not eat,'[5] and part he spent on bread and part he gave to the needy. And he was constant in prayer, knowing that a man ought to pray in secret unceasingly.[6] For he had given such heed to what was read that none of the things that were written fell from him to the ground, but he remembered all, and afterwards his memory served him for books.

His heroic pursuit of an ascetic life and Christian virtue

4. Thus conducting himself, Antony was beloved by all. He subjected himself in sincerity to the good men whom he visited, and learned thoroughly where each surpassed him in zeal and discipline. He observed the graciousness of one; the unceasing prayer of another; he took knowledge of another's freedom from anger and another's loving-kindness; he gave heed to one as he watched, to another as he studied; one he admired for his endurance, another for his fasting and sleeping on the ground; the meekness of one and the long-suffering of another he watched with care, while he took note of the piety towards Christ and the mutual love which animated all. Thus filled, he returned to his own place of discipline, and henceforth would strive to unite the qualities of each, and was eager to show in himself the virtues of all. With others of the same age he had no rivalry; save this only, that he should not be second to them in higher things. And this he did so as to hurt the feelings of nobody, but made them rejoice over him. So all they of

that village and the good men in whose intimacy he was, when they saw that he was a man of this sort, used to call him God-beloved. And some welcomed him as a son; others as a brother.

The battles with Satan

5. But the devil, who hates and envies what is good, could not endure to see such a resolution in a youth, but endeavoured to carry out against him what he had been wont to effect against others. First of all he tried to lead him away from the discipline, whispering to him the remembrance of his wealth, care for his sister, claims of kindred, love of money, love of glory, the various pleasures of the table and the other relaxations of life, and at last the difficulty of virtue and the labour of it; he suggested also the infirmity of the body and the length of the time. In a word he raised in his mind a great dust of debate, wishing to debar him from his settled purpose. But when the enemy was himself to be too weak for Antony's determination, and that he rather was conquered by the other's firmness, overthrown by his great faith and falling through his constant prayers, then at length putting his trust in the weapons which are[7] 'in the navel of the belly' and boasting in them—for they are his first snare for the young—he attacked the young man, disturbing him by night and harassing him by day, so that even the onlookers saw the struggle which was going on between them. The one would suggest foul thoughts and the other counter them with prayers: the one fire him with lust, the other, as one who seemed to blush, fortify his body with faith, prayers, and fasting. And the devil, unhappy wight, one night even took upon him the shape of a woman and imitated all her acts simply to beguile Antony. But he, his mind filled with Christ and the nobility inspired by Him, and considering the spirituality of the soul, quenched the coal of the other's deceit. Again the enemy suggested the ease of pleasure. But he like a man filled with rage and grief turned his thoughts

to the threatened fire and the gnawing worm, and setting these in array against his adversary, passed through the temptation unscathed. All this was a source of shame to his foe. For he, deeming himself like God, was now mocked by a young man; and he who boasted himself against flesh and blood was being put to flight by a man in the flesh. For the Lord was working with Antony—the Lord who for our sake took flesh and gave the body victory over the devil, so that all who truly fight can say, 'not I but the grace of God which was with me.'[8] (Chapters 6–15 narrate how Antony withdrew further and further from civilized society in his pursuit of an ascetical life in conformity with the Gospel. He first lives in the tombs outside his village, and then he goes to the desert where he lives in a ruined fort for twenty years. When he left the fort, other monks were attracted to him and began to live in cells in the desert and mountains near him. Antony soon became the leader of a monastic movement in Egypt. Our selection resumes with his address to the monks, rendered from Coptic, exhorting them to perseverance, and encouraging them against the wiles of Satan.)

The address to the monks

16. One day when he had gone forth because all the monks had assembled to him and asked to hear words from him, he spoke to them in the Egyptian tongue as follows: 'The Scriptures are enough for instruction, but it is a good thing to encourage one another in the faith, and to stir up with words. Wherefore you, as children, carry that which you know to your father; and I as the elder share my knowledge and what experience has taught me with you. Let this especially be the common aim of all, neither to give way having once begun, nor to faint in trouble, nor to say: We have lived in the discipline a long time: but rather as though making a beginning daily let us increase our earnestness. For the whole life of man is very short, measured by the ages to come, wherefore all our time is nothing compare with eternal life. And in the world everything is sold at its price, and a man exchanges one equivalent for another; but the promise of eternal life is bought for a trifle. For it is written, "The days of our life in them are threescore years and ten, but if they are in strength, fourscore years, and what is more than these is labour and sorrow."[9] Whenever, therefore, we live full fourscore years, or even a hundred in the discipline, nor for a hundred years only shall we reign, but instead of a hundred we shall reign for ever and ever. And though we fought on earth, we shall not receive our inheritance on earth, but we have the promises in heaven; and having put off the body which is corrupt, we shall receive it incorrupt.

17. 'Wherefore, children, let us not faint nor deem that the time is long, or that we are doing something great, "for the sufferings of this present time are not worthy to be compared with the glory which shall be revealed to us afterward."[10] Nor let us think, as we look at the world, that we have renounced anything of much consequence, for the whole earth is very small compared with all the heaven. Wherefore if it even chanced that we were lords of all the earth and gave it all up, it would be nought worthy of comparison with the kingdom of heaven. For as if a man should despise a copper drachma to gain a hundred drachmas of gold; so if a man were lord of all the earth and were to renounce it, that which he gives up is little, and he receives a hundredfold. But if not even the whole earth is equal in value to the heavens, then he who has given up a few acres leaves as if it were nothing; and even if he have given up a house or much gold he ought not to boast nor be low-spirited. Further, we should consider than even if we do not relinquish them for virtue's sake, still afterwards when we die we shall leave them behind—very often, as the Preacher saith,[11] to those to whom we do not wish. Why then should we not give them up for virtue's sake, that we may inherit even a kingdom? Therefore let the desire of possession take hold of no one, for what gain is it to ac-

quire these things we cannot take with us? Why not rather get those things which we can take away with us—to wit, prudence, justice, temperance, courage, understanding, love, kindness to the poor, faith in Christ, freedom from wrath, hospitality? If we possess these, we shall find them of themselves preparing for us a welcome there in the land of the meek-hearted. . . .

Antony's orthodoxy and refutation of the Arians

67. Added to this he was tolerant in disposition and humble in spirit. For though he was such a man, he observed the rule of the Church most rigidly, and was willing that all the clergy should be honored above himself. For he was not ashamed to bow his head to bishops and presbyters, and if ever a deacon came to him for help he discoursed with him on what was profitable, but gave place to him in prayer, not being ashamed to learn himself. For often he would ask questions, and desired to listen to those who were present, and if any one said anything that was useful he confessed that he was profited. . . .

68. And he was altogether wonderful in faith and religious, for he never held communion with the Meletian schismatics,[12] knowing their wickedness and apostasy from the beginning; nor had he friendly dealings with the Manichaeans[13] or any other heretics; or, if he had, only as far as advice that they should change to piety. For he thought and asserted that intercourse with these was harmful and destructive to the soul. In the same manner also he loathed the heresy of the Arians, and exhorted all neither to approach them nor to hold their erroneous belief. And once when certain Arian madmen came to him, when he had questioned them and learned their impiety, he drove them from the mountain, saying that their words were worse than the poison of serpents.

69. And once also the Arians having ly-ingly asserted that Antony's opinions were the same as theirs, he was displeased and wroth against them. Then being summoned by the bishops and all the brethren, he descended from the mountain, and having entered Alexandria, he denounced the Arians, saying that their heresy was the last of all and a forerunner of Antichrist. And he taught the people that the Son of God was not a created being, neither had He come into being from non-existence, but that He was the Eternal Word and Wisdom of the Essence of the Father. And therefore it was impious to say, 'there was a time when He was not,' for the Word was always co-existent with the Father. Wherefore have no fellowship with the most impious Arians. For there is no communion between light and darkness.[14] For you are good Christians, but they, when they say that the Son of the Father, the Word of God, is a created being, differ in nought from the heathen, since they worship that which is created, rather than God the creator. But believe ye that the Creation itself is angry with them because they number the Creator, the Lord of all, by whom all things came into being, with those things which were originated.

70. All the people, therefore, rejoiced when they heard the anti-Christian heresy anathematised by such a man. And all the people in the city ran together to see Antony; and the Greeks and those who are called their Priests, came into the church, saying, 'We ask to see the man of God' for so they all called him. For in that place also the Lord cleansed many of demons, and healed those who were mad. And many Greeks asked that they might even but touch the old man, believing that they should be profited. Assuredly as many became Christians in those few days as one would have seen made in a year. Then when some thought that he was troubled by the crowds, and on this account turned them all away from him, he said, undisturbedly, that there were not more of them than of the demons with whom he wrestled in the mountain.

NOTES

¹Matt 4:20.
²Acts 4:35.
³Matt 19:21.
⁴Matt 6:34.
⁵2 Thes 3:10.
⁶Matt 6:7; 1 Thes 5:17.
⁷Job 40:16. Athanasius uses the description of behemoth and leviathan as allegories for Satan.
⁸1 Cor 15:10.
⁹Ps 90:10 in LXX.
¹⁰Rom 8:18.
¹¹Eccl 4:8; 6:2.
¹²A schismatic group in Egypt.
¹³A dualistic heresy founded by Manes or Mani, a Persian. Augustine belonged to this sect for several years in his youth.
¹⁴2 Cor 6:14.

AUGUSTINE: *THE CONFESSIONS*
(A CHRISTIAN SPIRITUAL AUTOBIOGRAPHY)

St. Augustine (354–430 C.E.), bishop of Hippo in North Africa and the greatest of the early theologians of the Western Church, was like Plato an important transitional figure in the history of Western religious thought. He literally lived through the demise of the Graeco-Roman culture and the fall of the Roman empire. When he was born, Rome still held sway in the West, but by 410 C.E. Alaric the Visigoth had sacked Rome, and in 430 C.E., as Augustine lay dying of a fever in Hippo, the Vandals were at the gates of his city. In his own personal life Augustine experienced a spiritual and intellectual odyssey which led him through the literature, values and philosophies of the dying Graeco-Roman world to the Christian faith which would shape the outlook of Western civilization for over a thousand years following his death. As a theologian and philosopher who incorporated aspects of the dying classical culture with his Christian faith, Augustine, more than any other single individual, formulated a view of God, humanity and history which guided the peoples of the Christian West in the Middle Ages, and even in the Renaissance and Reformation.

Our selection is from Augustine's great spiritual autobiography, **The Confessions.** He wrote the work in 397–98 C.E., approximately ten years after his conversion to Catholic Christianity. In it he looks back on his earlier life from the perspective of a committed believer who now sees the pattern of God's providential love guiding each stage of his life from infancy through youth, adolescence, and adulthood. Although Augustine did not appreciate at the time the significance of personal tragedies like the death of a young friend or the painful separation from his overly protective, but saintly mother, Monica, he now understands how God was gradually leading his "restless heart" to the point where it would find its rest in him.

As Augustine explains in Book X, his "confessions" have more than one audience, and the term itself is used in a variety of senses. **The Confessions** are first of all addressed to God as "confessions" of thanks and praise for his loving and providential guidance and intervention at every stage of Augustine's life. As the opening words indicate, **The Confessions** are a series of prayers and questions addressed to God in the second person in which Augustine, using his memory, retrieves and relives his personal pilgrimage to faith in God.

> Great art Thou, O Lord, and greatly to be praised; great is Thy power, and of Thy wisdom there is no end . . . O Lord, my faith calls on Thee,—that faith which Thou hast imparted to me, which Thou hast breathed into me through the incarnation of Thy Son, through the ministry of thy preacher (Ambrose, Bishop of Milan).

Augustine's "confessions" are also addressed to himself as "confessions" of a past life of sin and weakness. They are a personal reminder of his tortured struggle to find happiness in a pursuit of sensual pleasure, especially lust, and in adulation and honor as a famous rhetoric teacher. They also recall for Augustine his agonizing search for truth in the religious and philosophical options of the late Roman world. He is ever aware that his continued ability to master temptations of the body is only due to God's grace which is given through Christ the true Mediator (cf. last sections of Book X).

The Confessions are also addressed to those who will read Augustine's testimony to God's action in his life. As he says in Book X, if readers approach these "confessions" in faith and charity for Augustine the sinner who has found peace and happiness in God, they too may come to embrace him and find salvation. Augustine's account of his own spiritual journey makes of his own life a paradigm for the Christian view of the human person as created good by God and meant for union with him, but wounded by sin and therefore disordered in the search for happiness and truth.

The literary form of **The Confessions** is a spiritual autobiography which is absolutely unique in the ancient world. The ancients, like Plutarch, wrote biographies of great historical and philosophical figures, but Augustine's is the first ancient autobiography. The contrast with classical values can be seen in the way Augustine portrays himself in **The Confessions.** Unlike the classical heroes, like the largely fictional Roman hero, Aeneas, with whom Augustine seems to deliberately compare and contrast himself, Augustine is not a great warrior who performs noble deeds in the service of his people and their destiny. In fact, Augustine the character is not really the center of **The Confessions.** Although he was a person of considerable importance as a teacher of rhetoric in Rome and Milan and later as a bishop of Hippo, Augustine's account does not emphasize these public aspects of his life. Instead he portrays himself as helpless, worthless, incapable of achieving anything of real significance. God is the center of Augustine's universe. Yet Augustine, and other humans, are the glory of the universe, not because of self-sufficient deeds of public heroism, but because they are infinitely loved by God. Augustine describes for us how the Creator of the universe has followed him, and by analogy all humans, in every step of his life.

As readers enter the world of **The Confessions,** they are ushered into the inner life of the author. Although Augustine's account follows the events of his public life from infancy through childhood, adolescence, and adulthood at age thirty-three, his real concern is with his inner life of the soul, with his spiritual relationship to God.

In unfolding his personal spiritual pilgrimage, Augustine uses the classical theme of the voyage or journey. On the literal level, Augustine, like Aeneas, goes from Carthage to Italy. But Augustine is really using the journey motif on several deeper symbolic levels. His journey is, like Plato's myth of the cave, a painful ascent from the shadowy world of nature to the spiritual realm of Beauty and Truth which for Augustine is God himself. As he says in Book I, "Our hearts are restless till they find rest in Thee." **The Confessions** are the account of Augustine's search for God whom, paradoxically, he does not find in the external world of pleasure, wealth and fame, but within himself. Finally **The Confessions** is a journey into the past. Augustine writes from the perspective of ten years after his conversion, and using his memory he is now able to find a pattern which reveals to him what God had been doing in his life.

In his account of his early life, Augustine uses several biblical images to portray his lost state before his conversion. One is the story of the sin of Adam in the Garden of Eden. For Augustine this story is extremely significant because it locates the cause of evil in the free will which chooses to disobey God, and not in some evil power outside God as the Manicheans taught. In his famous account of the pear tree incident, in which Augustine and his friends steal a neighbor's pears, not out of any need, but simply out of a love for doing with impunity something that was forbidden, he sees himself living out the Garden story. He becomes his own Adam by striving to be like God.

> What, then, was it that I loved in that theft? And wherein did I, ever corruptedly and pervertedly, imitate my Lord? Did I wish, if only by artifice, to act contrary to Thy law, because by power I could not, so that, being captive, I might imitate an imperfect liberty by doing with impunity things which I was not allowed to do, in obscured likeness of Thy omnipotency? Behold this servant of Thine, fleeing from his Lord, and following a shadow! O monstrosity of life and profundity of death! Could I like that which was unlawful only because it was unlawful? (Book II. 6)

Another biblical story which Augustine frequently alludes to in the account of his early life is Jesus' parable of the prodigal son (Lk 15:11–32). He, like the prodigal, left a loving Father, whom he did not fully understand and appreciate, to wander in a foreign land in which he had to come to the point of eating the husks used to feed the swine before he could return. As he was living through this journey, Augustine felt as if he were groping in the darkness, but now as he reflects back upon it, he can see that God was guiding him every step of the way to a deeper knowledge of himself as a fallen sinner who needed God's grace if he was to find the peace, truth and happiness which he desperately sought.

Augustine's journey is like a pilgrimage through the values of the dying ancient world. As a young man he studied and loved classical, especially his native Roman, literature. He was capable of being moved to tears at the death of Dido or at the sight of a dramatic tragedy, and he became a professor of rhetoric, i.e., literature, first at Carthage, then at Rome and finally at Milan, the Western imperial capital. In light of his later conversion, Augustine rejects his early love of "pagan" literature and his sensitive responses to the sufferings of others as being misguided. How could he weep for the fate of fictional characters, when he himself was lost in sin? Only from the perspective of his later conversion, however, can we agree with Augustine in this harsh evaluation of his literary sensibilities. Surely the sensitivity that moved him to empathize with the character of Dido was also important in bringing Augustine to his conversion experience.

From the age of nineteen when he read Cicero's **Hortensius,** Augustine was also an avid student of philosophy and gave himself to the love of wisdom. At this stage he found the Christian Scriptures stylistically and intellectually inferior to Cicero. His search for the truth led him first to the Manicheans who were a popular Gnostic Christian sect founded by Mani (c. 216–276) a Persian religious figure who regarded himself as the Paraclete. By Augustine's time they were numerous in North Africa and Rome. Manicheism was a syncretistic blend of religion and philosophy which had elements of Christianity and dualistic Eastern mythology from Persia. Mani taught that there were two principles operative in the world: Good and Evil or Light and Darkness. God is the good principle, but he is finite, material and limited by the power of Evil. In fact material creation resulted from the primeval invasion of the realm of the Good by Evil. Jesus, Buddha, the prophets, and Mani were sent to the world to release the particles of light which the Evil One had stolen from the world of Light and imprisoned in material creation. Release was to be effected by ascetic practices like vegetarianism. The Manicheans were divided into two groups: the perfect, who stood on the threshold of liberation and took vows of total asceticism including abstinence from sexual intercourse, and the hearers, like Augustine, who lived less strenuously in the hope of being reincarnated and achieving liberation in a future life.

Augustine belonged to this sect for nine years, apparently because it provided some answer to the problem of evil which continuously perplexed him and also because it appealed to reason as opposed to the faith asked of Catholic Christians. Eventually he abandoned this elitist and pessimistic sect when one of its most learned teachers, Faustus, was unable to explain to Augustine's satisfaction superstitious elements in the Manichean doctrines.

His intellectual pilgrimage then took him to the academic philosophers, or skeptics, who suspended belief in any ultimate truth. During this stage Augustine also came to Milan where he met Ambrose and for the first time heard Christian preaching which used an allegorical interpretation of the Scriptures that removed some of his doubts about the obvious contradictions which come from a literal reading of them. It was also at this time that Augustine read the work of Platonic philosophers in whom he found an understanding of the Good, or God, as a purely spiritual and infinite substance, not the crude manlike and finite God of the Manichees, and a satisfactory explanation of evil, not as a force, but as a lack of perfection, an incompleteness resulting from the material creature's separation from God.

Augustine was able to combine these insights from Platonism with the Christian doctrines of a personal God who was Creator and active in the history of humanity and of each individual. A key text for him in this regard is Exodus 3:14 where God identifies himself to Moses as "I am who am," which Augustine inteprets in Neo-Platonic terms as meaning that God is a self-sufficient being in a metaphysical sense.

By this time Augustine had come to the point where he was intellectually ready to embrace Christianity. However, his personal struggle had never been a purely intellectual one. He was also engaged in a moral battle to overcome his enslavement to the powers of lust. For years he had had a mistress whom he apparently loved deeply and who had given him a son, Adeodatus ("gift from God"). When his mother insisted that he be married to a young Roman girl who was two years below marriagable age, he regretfully sent his mistress back to Carthage, but was driven by his enslavement to lust to take another mistress. In this state Augustine realized and struggled with the fact that he still lacked the will to accept the Catholic faith. His conversion was not merely an intellectual decision about truth, but a choice to embrace a new way of life which would demand chastity of him.

In this condition Augustine and his friends withdrew to a villa outside Milan, and he turned his attention to the letters of Paul. In Paul's theology, especially in his description of the struggle to do the demands of God's law in Romans 7, Augustine found a replica of his own experience. He became agonizingly aware of his own inability to break from his life of sexual promiscuity. While at the villa Augustine heard the stories of other conversion experiences, like that of Antony of Egypt, the first of the Christian monks, who, upon hearing the story of the rich young man in the gospels, sold all that he had and began to follow Christ. Finally, in a state of extreme emotional agitation he withdraws with his friend Alypius into a garden where he struggles to choose to break from his life of sin. In the midst of the struggle he prays fervently for God's help.

> I flung myself down, how, I know not, under a certain fig-tree, giving free course to my tears, and the streams of mine eyes gushed out, an acceptable sacrifice unto Thee. And, not in these words, yet to this effect, spake I much unto Thee,—"But Thou, O Lord, how long? . . . Why not now? Why is there not this hour an end to my uncleaness?"

At this moment he hears a child's voice saying "Take up and read; take up and read." Understanding this as a command from heaven, he opens the book of Paul's epistles and reads: "Not in rioting and drunkenness, not in chambering and wantonness, not in strife and envying; but put ye on the Lord Jesus Christ, and make not provisions for the flesh, to fulfill the lusts thereof." (Rom 13:13–14) In this moment of grace all doubt was removed. Augustine describes it as "a light . . . of security infused into my heart . . ."

It is this enlightening experience of God's grace that Augustine asks his readers to share. They are his fellow pilgrims on their way to the heavenly city under the protection of God's providential love. By sharing his conversion experience with them, Augustine is, in Plato's imagery, returning from the world of the forms to the cave to invite the prisoners there to leave the world of shadows. For Augustine, of course, the ascent or pilgrimage cannot take place without the aid of God's grace. He sees his "confessions" as an act of service to his fellow citizens in the kingdom of God. A measure of the impact of Augustine's work is that his vision of the human family as fellow pilgrims on their way to a heavenly destiny shaped the outlook of Western civilization throughout the succeeding Middle Ages.

Because of space limitations I am only able to include Augustine's account of the pear tree incident from Book II and his conversion in Book VIII. The translation is by J. G. Pilkington, **The Confessions and Letters of St. Augustine** in **The Nicene and Post-Nicene Fathers,** Vol. 1 (New York: Charles Scribner's Sons, 1902) 45–145.

BOOK II: AUGUSTINE'S ADOLESCENCE: THE PEAR TREE

(In Book II Augustine describes his adolescence in which he indulged in lustful pleasures, and with his companions committed theft.)

Theft is punished by Thy law, O Lord, and by the law written in men's hearts, which iniquity itself cannot blot out. For what thief will suffer a thief? Even a rich thief will not suffer him who is driven to it by want. Yet had I a desire to commit robbery, and did so, compelled neither by hunger, nor poverty, but through a distaste for well-doing, and a lustiness of iniquity. For I pilfered that of which I had already sufficient, and much better. Nor did I desire to enjoy what I pilfered, but the theft and sin itself. There was a pear-tree close to our vineyard, heavily laden with fruit, which was tempting neither for its colour nor its flavour. To shake and rob this some of us wanton young fellows went, late one night (having, according to our disgraceful habit, prolonged our games in the streets until then), and carried away great loads, not to eat ourselves, but to fling to the very swine, having only eaten some of them; and to do this pleased us all the more because it was not permitted. Behold my heart, o my God; behold my heart, which Thou hadst pity upon when in the bottomless pit. Behold,

now let my heart tell Thee what it was seeking there, that I should be gratuitously wanton, having no inducement to evil but the evil itself. It was foul, and I loved it. I loved to perish. I loved my own error—not that for which I erred, but the error itself. Base soul, falling from Thy firmament to utter destruction—not seeking aught through the shame but shame itself!

BOOK VIII: AUGUSTINE'S CONVERSION IN HIS THIRTY-SECOND YEAR

(In Book VIII Augustine describes his conversion to God. In the early chapters he recounts how he was instructed about the conversion of others including Pontitianus' account of Antony, the founder of Christian monasticism.)

CHAPTER 7: AUGUSTINE DEPLORES HIS OWN WRETCHEDNESS

Such was the story of Pontitianus. But Thou, O Lord, whilst he was speaking, didst turn me towards myself, taking me from behind my back, where I had placed myself while unwilling to exercise self-scrutiny; and Thou didst set me face to face with myself, that I might behold how foul I was, and how crooked and sordid, bespotted and ulcerous. And I beheld and loathed myself; and whither to fly from myself I discovered not. And if I sought to turn my gaze away from myself, he continued his narrative, and Thou again opposedst me unto myself, and thrustedst me before my own eyes, that I might discover my iniquity, and hate it. I had known it, but acted as though I knew it not,—winked at it, and forgot it.

But now, the more ardently I loved those healthful affections I heard tell of, that they had given up themselves wholly to Thee to be cured, the more did I abhor myself when compared with them. For many of my years (perhaps twelve) had passed away since my nineteenth, when, on the reading of Cicero's **Hortensius,** I was roused to a desire for wisdom; and still I was delaying to reject mere worldly happiness, and to devote myself to search out that whereof not the finding alone, but the bare search, ought to have been preferred before the treasures and kingdoms of this world, though already found, and before the pleasures of the body, though encompassing me at my will. But I, miserable young man, supremely miserable even in the very outset of my youth, had entreated chastity of Thee, and said, "Grant me chastity and continency, but not yet." For I was afraid lest Thou shouldest hear me soon, and soon deliver me from the disease of concupiscence, which I desired to have satisfied rather than extinguished. And I had wandered through perverse ways in a sacrilegious superstition; not indeed assured thereof, but preferring that to the others, which I did not seek religiously, but opposed maliciously.

And I had thought that I delayed from day to day to reject worldly hopes and follow Thee only, because there did not appear anything certain whereunto to direct my course. And now had the day arrived in which I was to be laid bare to myself, and my conscience was to chide me. "Where are thou, O my tongue? Thou saidst, verily, that for an uncertain truth thou were not willing to cast off the baggage of vanity. Behold, now it is certain, and yet doth that burden still oppress thee; whereas they who neither have so worn themselves out with searching after it, nor yet have spent ten years

and more in thinking thereon, have had their shoulders unburdened, and gotten wings to fly away." Thus was I inwardly consumed and mightily confounded with an horrible shame, while Pontitianus was relating these things. And he, having finished his story, and the business he came for, went his way. And unto myself, what said I not within myself? With what scourges of rebuke lashed I not my soul to make it follow me, struggling to go after Thee! Yet it drew back; it refused, and exercised not itself. All its arguments were exhausted and confuted. There remained a silent trembling; and it feared, as it would death, to be restrained from the flow of that custom whereby it was wasting away even to death.

CHAPTER 8–9:
AUGUSTINE ENTERS THE GARDEN

In the midst, then, of this great strife of my inner dwelling, which I had strongly raised up against my soul in the chamber of my heart, troubled both in mind and countenance, I seized upon Alypius, and exclaimed: "What is wrong with us? What is this? What heardest thou? The unlearned start up and 'take' heaven, and we, with our learning, but wanting heart, see where we wallow in flesh and blood! Because others have preceded us, we ashamed to follow, and not rather ashamed at not following?" Some such words I gave utterance to, and in my excitement flung myself from him, while he gazed upon me in silent astonishment. For I spoke not in my wonted tone, and my brow, cheeks, eyes, colour, tone of voice, all expressed my emotion more than the words. There was a little garden belonging to our lodging, of which we had the use, as of the whole house; for the master, our landlord, did not live there. Thither had the tempest within my breast hurried me, where no one might impede the fiery struggle in which I was engaged with myself, until it came to the issue that Thou knewest, though I did not. But I was made that I might be whole, and dying that I might have life, knowing what evil thing I was, but not knowing what good thing I was shortly to become. Into the garden, then, I retired, Alypius following my steps. For his presence was no bar to my solitude; or how could he desert me so troubled? We sat down at as great a distance from the house as we could. I was disquieted in spirit, being most impatient with myself that I entered not into Thy will and covenant, O my God, which all my bones cried out unto me to enter, extolling it to the skies. And we enter not therein by ships, or chariots, or feet, no, nor by going so far as I had come from the house to that place where we were sitting. For not to go only, but to enter there, was naught else but to will to go, but to will it resolutely and thoroughly; not to stagger and sway about this way and that, a changeable and half-wounded will, wrestling, with one part falling as another rose.

Finally, in the very fervor of my irresolution, I made many of those motions with my body which men sometimes desire to do, but cannot, if either they have not the limbs, or if their limbs be bound with fetters, weakened by disease, or hindered in any other way. Thus, if I tore my heart, struck my forehead, or if, entwining my fingers, I clasped my knee, this I did because I willed it. But I might have willed and not done it, if the power of motion in my limbs had not responded. So many things, then, I did, when to have the will was not to have the power, and I did not that which both with an unequalled desire I longed more to do, and which shortly when I should will I should have the power to do; because shortly when I should will, I should will thoroughly. For in such things the power was one with the will, and to will was to do, and yet was it not done; and more readily did the body obey the slightest wish of the soul in the moving its limbs at the order of the mind, than the soul obeyed itself to accomplish in the will alone this its great will. . . . Whence this monstrous thing? and why is it? I repeat, it commands itself to will, and would not give the command unless it

willed; yet is not that done which it commandeth. But it willeth not entirely; therefore it commandeth not entirely. For so far forth it commandeth, as it willeth; and so far forth is the thing commanded not done, as it willeth not. For the will commandeth that there be a will;—not another, but itself. But it doth not command entirely, therefore that is not which it commandeth. For were it entire, it would not even command it to be, because it would already be. It is, therefore, no monstrous thing partly to will, partly to be unwilling, but an infirmity of the mind, that it doth not wholly rise, sustained by truth, pressed down by custom. And so there are two wills, because one of them is not entire; and the one is supplied with what the other needs.

CHAPTER 10: AUGUSTINE REFUTES THE MANICHEAN VIEW THAT THERE ARE TWO KINDS OF MINDS,—ONE GOOD AND THE OTHER EVIL

Let them perish from Thy presence, O God as "vain talkers and deceivers"[1] of the soul do perish, who, observing that there were two wills in deliberating, affirm that there are two kinds of minds in us,—one good, the other evil. They themselves verily are evil when they hold these evil opinions; and they shall become good when they hold the truth, and shall consent unto the truth, that Thy apostle may say unto them, "Ye were sometimes darkness, but now are ye light in the Lord."[2] But they, desiring to be light, not "in the Lord," but in themselves, conceiving the nature of the soul to be the same as that which God is, are made more gross darkness; for that through a shocking arrogancy they went farther from Thee, "the true Light, which lighteth every man that cometh into the world."[3] Take heed what you say, and blush for shame; draw near unto Him and be "lightened," and "your faces shall not be ashamed."[4] I, when I was deliberating upon serving the Lord my God now, as I had long purposed,—I it was who willed, I who was unwilling. It was I, even I myself. I neither willed entirely, nor was entirely unwilling. Therefore was I at war with myself, and destroyed myself. And this destruction overtook me against my will, and yet showed not the presence of another mind, but the punishment of mine own. "Now, then, it is no more I that do it, but sin that dwelleth in me,"[5]—the punishment of a more unconfined sin, in that I was a son of Adam. . . .

CHAPTER 11: AUGUSTINE'S STRUGGLE BETWEEN FLESH AND SPIRIT

Thus was I sick and tormented, accusing myself far more severely than was my wont, tossing and turning me in my chain till that was utterly broken, whereby I now was but slightly, but still was held. And Thou, O Lord, pressedst upon me in my inward parts by a severe mercy, redoubling the lashes of fear and shame, lest I should again give way, and that same slender remaining tie not being broken off, it should recover strength, and enchain me the faster. For I said mentally, "Lo, let it be done now, let it be done now." And as I spoke, I all but came to a resolve. I all but did it, yet I did it not. Yet fell I not back to my old condition, but took up my position hard by, and drew breath. And I tried again, and wanted but very little of reaching it, and somewhat less, and then all but touched and grasped it; and yet came not at it, nor touched, nor grasped it, hesitating to die unto death, and to live unto life; and the worse, whereto I had been habituated, prevailed more with me than the better, which I had not tried. And the very moment in which I was to become another man, the nearer it approached me, the greater horror did it strike into me; but it did not strike me back, nor turn me aside, but kept me in suspense.

The very toys of toys, and vainities of vanities, my old mistresses, still enthralled me; they shook my fleshly garment, and whispered softly, "Dost thou part with us? And from that moment shall we no more be with thee for ever? And from that moment shall not this or that be lawful for thee for ever?" And what did they suggest to me in the words "this or that?" What is it that they suggested, O my God? Let Thy mercy avert it from the soul of Thy servant. What impurities did they suggest! What shame! And now I far less than half heard them, not openly showing themselves and contradicting me, but muttering, as it were, behind my back, and furtively plucking me as I was departing, to make me look back upon them. Yet they did delay me, so that I hesitated to burst and shake myself free from them, and to leap over whither I was called,—and unruly habit saying to me, "Dost thou think thou canst live without them."

But now it said this very faintly; for on that side towards which I had set my face, and whither I trembled to go, did the chaste dignity of Continence appear unto me, cheerful, but not dissolutely gay, honestly alluring me to come and doubt nothing, and extending her holy hands, full of a multiplicity of good examples, to receive and embrace me. There were there so many young men and maidens, a multitude of youth and every age, grave widows and ancient virgins, and Continence herself in all, not barren, but a fruitful mother of children of joys, by Thee, O Lord, her Husband. And she smiled on me with an encouraging mockery, as if to say, "Canst not thou do what these youths and maidens can? Or can one or other do it of themselves, and not rather in the Lord their God? The Lord their God gave me unto them. Why standest thou in thine own strength, and so standest not? Cast thyself upon Him; fear not, He will not withdraw that thou shouldest fall; cast thyself upon Him without fear, he will receive thee, and heal thee." And I blushed beyond measure, for I still hear the muttering of those toys, and hung in suspense. And she again seemed to say, "Shut up thine ears against those unclean members of thine upon the earth, that they may be mortified. They tell thee of delights, but not as doth the law of the Lord thy God." This controversy in my heart was naught but self against self. But Alypius, sitting close by my side, awaited in silence the result of my unwonted emotion.

CHAPTER 12: THE ACTUAL
CONVERSION EXPERIENCE

But when a profound reflection had, from the secret depths of my soul, drawn together and heaped up all my misery before the sight of my heart, there arose a mighty storm, accompanied by as mighty a shower of tears. Which, that I might pour forth fully, with its natural expressions, I stole away from Alypius; for it suggested itself to me that solitude was fitter for the business of weeping. So I retired to such a distance that even his presence could not be oppressive to me. Thus was it with me at that time, and he perceived it; for something, I believe, I had spoken, wherein the sound of my voice appeared choked with weeping, and in that state had I risen up. He then remained where we had been sitting, most completely astonished. I flung myself down, how, I know not, under a certain fig-tree, giving free course to my tears, and the streams of mine eyes gushed out, an acceptable sacrifice unto Thee.[6] And, not indeed in these words, yet to this effect, spake I much unto Thee,—"But Thou, O Lord, how long?"[7] "How long, Lord? Wilt Thou be angry for ever? Oh, remember not against us former iniquities;"[8] for I felt that I was enthralled by them. I sent up these sorrowful cries,—How long, how long? Tomorrow, and tomorrow? Why not now? Why is there not this hour an end to my uncleanness?"

I was saying these things and weeping in the most bitter contrition of my heart, when, lo, I heard the voice as of a boy or girl, I know not which, coming from a neighbouring house, chanting, and oft repeating, "Take up and read; take up and read." Immediately my countenance was changed, and I began most earnestly to consider whether it was usual for children in any kind of game to sing such

words; nor could I remember ever to have heard the like. So, restraining the torrent of my tears, I rose up, interpreting it no other way than as a command to me from Heaven to open the book, and to read the first chapter I should light upon. For I had heard of Antony,[9] that, accidentally coming in whilst the gospel was being read, he received the admonition as if what was read were addressed to him "Go and sell that thou hast, and give to the poor, and thou shalt have treasure in heaven; and come and follow me."[10] And by such oracle was he forthwith converted unto Thee. So quickly I returned to the place where Alypius was sitting; for there had I put down the volume of the apostles, when I rose thence. I grasped, opened, and in silence read that paragraph on which my eyes first fell,—"Not in rioting and drunkenness, not in chambering and wantonness, not in strife and envying; but put ye on the Lord Jesus Christ, and make not provision for the flesh, to fulfil the lusts thereof."[11] No further would I read, nor did I need; for instantly, as the sentence ended,—by a light, as it were of security infused into my heart,—all the gloom of doubt vanished away.

Closing the book, then, and putting either my finger between, or some other mark, I now with a tranquil countenance made it known to Alypius. And he thus disclosed to me what was wrought in him, which I knew not. He asked to look at what I had read. I showed him; and he looked even further than I had read, and I knew not what followed. This it was, verily, "Him that is weak in the faith, receive ye;"[12] which he applied to himself, and discovered to me. By this admonition was he strengthened; and by a good resolution and purpose, very much in accord with his character (wherein, for the better, he was always far different from me), without any restless delay he joined me. Thence we go in to my mother. We make it known to her,—she rejoiceth. We relate how it came to pass,—she leapeth for joy, and triumpheth, and blesseth Thee, who are "able to do exceeding abundantly above all that we ask or think;"[13] for she perceived Thee to have given her more for me than she used to ask by her pitiful and most doleful groanings. For Thou didst so convert me unto Thyself, that I sought neither a wife, nor any other of this world's hopes,—standing in that rule of faith in which Thou, so many years before, had showed me unto her in a vision. And thou didst turn her grief into a gladness, much more plentiful than she had desired, and much dearer and chaster than she used to crave, by having grandchildren of my body.

NOTES

[1]Tit 1:10
[2]Eph 5:8
[3]John 1:9
[4]Ps 34:5
[5]Rom 7:17
[6]1 Pet 2:5
[7]Ps 6:3
[8]Ps 79:5,8
[9]See his **Life** by St. Athanasius, secs. 2–3.
[10]Matt 19:21
[11]Rom 13:13–14
[12]Rom 14:1
[13]Eph 3:20